A Variorum Edition of

The Works of Geoffrey Chaucer

Volume VII   The Romaunt of the Rose

Paul G. Ruggiers and Daniel J. Ransom

General Editors

The Variorum Edition

The Romaunt of the Rose

And it was peynted wel and thwrthen
And overal diapred and writen
With ladyes and with Bacheleris
ffull lyghtsom and glad of cheris
These bowes two helde swete lokyng
That semede lyk no gylesyng
And ten brode arowhis hilde he there
Of whych v in his righthoud were
But they were shauen wel and dight
Nokked and fethered right
And all they were with gold bygoon
And strouge peynted euerychoon
And sharp forto keruen well
But iren was ther noon ne stell
ffor al was golde men myght it see
Outake the fetheres and the tree
The swiftest of these arowhis fyue
Out of a bolke forto dryue
And best fethered for to flee
And finest eke was clepid Beaute
That other arowhe that hurteth lasse
Was clepid as y trowe symplesse
The thridde cleped was ffraunchise
That fethred was in noble wyse

Glasgow University Library Manuscript, Hunter 409, folio 18v (lines 933–56).

Reproduced by kind permission of the Librarian, Glasgow University Library.

A Variorum Edition of The Works of Geoffrey Chaucer

Volume VII

The Romaunt of the Rose

Edited by Charles Dahlberg

University of Oklahoma Press : Norman

Library of Congress Cataloging-in-Publication Data

Chaucer, Geoffrey, d. 1400.
    The romaunt of the rose / edited by Charles Dahlberg.
    p. cm. — (A variorum edition of the works of Geoffrey
  Chaucer ; v. 7)
    Includes bibliographical references and index.
    ISBN 0-8061-3147-0 (cloth : alk. paper)
    1. Courtly love—Poetry.   2. Manuscripts, English (Middle).
  3. Romances—Translations into English (Middle).   I. Dahlberg,
  Charles, 1919–   II. Title.   III. Series: Chaucer, Geoffrey, d.
  1400. Works. 1979 ; v. 7.
    PR1888 .D34 1999
    821′.1—dc21   98-37724
                              CIP

The paper in this book meets the guidelines for permanence and durability of the Committee on Production Guidelines for Book Longevity of the Council on Library Resources, Inc. ∞

"Though thou bithenke the never so well,
Thou shalt foryete yit somdell."
(2535–36)

Contents

Illustrations

General Editors' Preface

A Variorum Edition of the Works of Geoffrey Chaucer is a collaborative effort of forty-two medievalists whose chief interest is the work of Geoffrey Chaucer and his time. Originally projected exclusively as a commentary upon the entire canon of Chaucer's poetry and prose, the *Variorum Chaucer* was expanded in 1979 to include a series of facsimiles representing the tradition upon which subsequent editors of the printed editions of his work have based their text and commentary.

I

The facsimile series, the prime support for the various texts provided by the *Variorum Chaucer*, was inaugurated in 1979 with the publication of the facsimile of the Hengwrt manuscript (Peniarth 392D) of *The Canterbury Tales*. The series was begun with this particular manuscript on the obvious ground that it was our base manuscript for *The Canterbury Tales* and that the treatment of *The Canterbury Tales* was the part of the project that initially commanded our greatest attention. An explanation of the reasons for the choice of the Hengwrt manuscript as base text is given in the introductions to the facsimile (see further *The Chaucer Newsletter* 8.ii [1986], 1–2). Other parts of the facsimile series include Tanner 346 (*The Legend of Good Women, The Book of the Duchess, The Parliament of Fowls, Anelida and Arcite*); Bodley 638 (*The Legend of Good Women, The Book of the Duchess, The Parliament of Fowls, The House of Fame, Anelida and Arcite*); Pepys Library 2006 (*The Legend of Good Women, The Parliament of Fowls, The House of Fame, Anelida and Arcite, The Tale of Melibee, The Parson's Tale, Chaucer's Retraction*); Trinity R.3.19 (*The Legend of Good Women, The Parliament of Fowls, The Monk's Tale*); St. John's College L.1 Cambridge (*Troilus and Criseyde*); and Morgan 817, *olim* Campsall (*Troilus and Criseyde*).

II

The commentary series is built upon a model evolved over many years: critical and textual introductions, newly established texts for the poems, collations providing evidence both of the manuscripts and of the printed editions, textual and explanatory notes, and bibliography. It is our conviction that so full an apparatus will constitute a summary of the commentary, both textual and evaluative, that has accumulated over the past six hundred years, as well as afford a starting point for future scholarship.

It should be noted that the textual apparatus, melding evidence from both manuscripts and printed editions, will enable the user of the *Variorum Chaucer* to see at a glance the changes through which the various Chaucer texts have passed over the course of six centuries.

III

The *Variorum Chaucer*, when complete, will follow the plan here offered provisionally:

Volume   I: *The Canterbury Tales: A Facsimile and Transcription of the Hengwrt Manuscript* (and the facsimiles listed above, seven parts)
Volume   II: *The Canterbury Tales* (twenty-five parts)
Volume   III: *Troilus and Criseyde* (three parts)

IV

Because *The Romaunt of the Rose* has only one manuscript witness, and because descendants of this text show relatively few variants, the collations made for the present edition are displayed in a more compact form than that used in fascicles of *The Canterbury Tales*. These collations in their simplicity illustrate a fundamental principle of the Variorum Chaucer project that may usefully be stated here: the edition seeks to offer not a critical text but a record of the points (and times) at which texts were altered or consulted. This record is a natural concomitant of the history of interpretation. Ideally one would like to have an authoritative text as the base of comparison, but even with an imperfect foundation the exercise has utility and practical results. Of course, the closer the base text is to authority, the better the results; so an editor should repair evident flaws in the base. But there is no need, no urgency, to presume that the repaired text is authentic. The making of a critical edition is a different sort of task. In the case of the *Romaunt*, one can see how a flawed text gave rise to copies that both improved and corrupted their source(s), and one can chart the direction taken in each attempt to present the poem. That, in brief, is what the textual component of the Variorum edition seeks to achieve.

The achievement of each Variorum fascicle, indeed its very existence, owes a great deal to the founder and presiding genius of the project, Paul G. Ruggiers, who laid down this burden on 8 April 1998, three weeks shy of his eightieth birthday. With uncommon courage, resourcefulness, and energy he compelled the creation of a collaborative project the scope of which still inspires amazement. He was in the best sense a facilitator, always looking for ways to enhance the life of scholarship—by founding the New Chaucer Society, *Studies in the Age of Chaucer, The Chaucer Newsletter*, and by starting a publishing firm, Pilgrim Books, to make available facsimiles of six Chaucer manuscripts. His love of Chaucer and of book-making, his sense of the scholar's mission, his instinct for what was useful—this part of his spirit lives on in the Variorum. The present volume is a fitting tribute to his industry and his commitment to imagining the past as fully and clearly as possible.

DANIEL J. RANSOM
†PAUL G. RUGGIERS
General Editors

LYNNE HUNT LEVY
Associate Editor

Norman, Oklahoma, 1999

Preface

One of the more pleasant tasks in preparing this edition is the allocation of thanks. The editorial staff of the Variorum Chaucer—Paul Ruggiers, Daniel Ransom, and Lynne Hunt Levy—provided encouragement at every stage and substantial assistance particularly in the Textual Commentary. Grants from the Research Foundation of the City University of New York, the American Council of Learned Societies, and Queens College supported the early stages of the project; Steven Kapnik, Theresa Karcich, Gary Kuris, Frank Rella, Mary Turner, and Steven Williams all helped. Library staffs have been uncommonly active on my behalf: in particular, those of the Queens College Library, the New York Public Library, and the Glasgow University Library. The Interlibrary Loan Service of the Queens College Library has been superb. When I made an early trip to work with the manuscript at the Glasgow University Library, Mr. J. Baldwin, then Keeper of the Special Collections, most courteously provided every possible facility. More recently, my Queens colleague Gordon Whatley and Dr. Nigel Thorp of the Glasgow University Library's Special Collections both checked a set of manuscript readings for me. Dr. Jeremy Smith of the Department of English Language, Glasgow University, has most kindly read the commentary on the manuscript and made helpful suggestions. Special thanks are due to the Librarian of Glasgow University Library, Mr. H. J. Heaney, for permission to reproduce the frontispiece.

The introduction and notes aim to cover scholarship only through 1990, although a few more recent items appear. To the giants of the past—Tyrwhitt, Skeat, Kaluza, to name only three—I owe a debt of wonder at the scope of their accomplishment. My wife has shown patience and support through the whole of this long process; to her (and to our household tutelary spirits) my loving thanks. Finally, I dedicate this volume to the memory of D. W. Robertson, Jr.

Hastings-on-Hudson, New York   CHARLES DAHLBERG

A Brief Guide to the Use of This Edition

This edition provides an introduction to and a text of the Chaucerian *Romaunt of the Rose*, as well as a list of Abbreviations and Sigils, a Bibliography, and a General Index. The Introduction is in two parts, Critical Commentary and Textual Commentary. The first part surveys the criticism of the poem, under the principal headings of authorship, date of composition, nature of the translation, and relationship to the French original. The Textual Commentary discusses the textual tradition in the unique manuscript and the nineteen printed versions that are collated for this edition; and it describes the organization of text, collations, and annotations in the present edition.

The Text is based on the Glasgow manuscript, with modern punctuation and capitalization; emendations are in square brackets. It uses modern equivalents for *u/v*, *i/j*, ð (eth), þ (thorn), and ȝ (yogh), but not for *i/y*; and it expands abbreviations silently. The Collations and Annotations occupy separate sections on each page of text. For a fuller account, see "The Present Edition" in the Textual Commentary (pp. 69–70).

Abbreviations and Sigils

ABBREVIATIONS OF CHAUCER'S WORKS

Note: Following Manly's lead, to permit the scholar the widest latitude of reference, abbreviations are provided suited to specific reference needs; for example, *Monk-Nun's Priest Link* as well as *The Nun's Priest's Prologue*; *Second Nun-Canon's Yeoman Link* as well as *The Canon's Yeoman's Prologue*; and *Knight-Miller Link* as well as *The Miller's Prologue*.

ABC	*An ABC*
Adam	*Adam Scriveyn*
Anel	*Anelida and Arcite*
Astr	*A Treatise on the Astrolabe*
Bal Compl	*A Balade of Complaint*
BD	*The Book of the Duchess*
Bo	*Boece*
Buk	*The Envoy to Bukton*
CkT, CkP, Rv-CkL	*The Cook's Tale, The Cook's Prologue, Reeve-Cook Link*
ClT, ClP, Cl-MerL	*The Clerk's Tale, The Clerk's Prologue, Clerk-Merchant Link*
Compl d'Am	*Complaynt d'Amours*
CT	*The Canterbury Tales*
CYT, CYP	*The Canon's Yeoman's Tale, The Canon's Yeoman's Prologue*
Equat	*The Equatorie of the Planets*
For	*Fortune*
Form Age	*The Former Age*
FranT, FranP	*The Franklin's Tale, The Franklin's Prologue*
FrT, FrP, Fr-SumL	*The Friar's Tale, The Friar's Prologue, Friar-Summoner Link*
Gent	*Gentilesse*
GP	*The General Prologue*
HF	*The House of Fame*
KnT, Kn-MilL	*The Knight's Tale, Knight-Miller Link*
Lady	*A Complaint to His Lady*
LGW, LGWP	*The Legend of Good Women, The Legend of Good Women Prologue*
ManT, ManP	*The Manciple's Tale, The Manciple's Prologue*
Mars	*The Complaint of Mars*
Mel, Mel-MkL	*The Tale of Melibee, Melibee-Monk Link*
MercB	*Merciles Beaute*
MerT, MerE-SqH	*The Merchant's Tale, Merchant Endlink-Squire Headlink*
MilT, MilP, Mil-RvL	*The Miller's Tale, The Miller's Prologue, Miller-Reeve Link*
MkT, MkP, Mk-NPL	*The Monk's Tale, The Monk's Prologue, Monk-Nun's Priest Link*
MLT, MLH, MLP, MLE	*The Man of Law's Tale, Man of Law Headlink, The Man of Law's Prologue, Man of Law Endlink*
NPT, NPP, NPE	*The Nun's Priest's Tale, The Nun's Priest's Prologue, Nun's Priest Endlink*
PardT, PardP	*The Pardoner's Tale, The Pardoner's Prologue*
ParsT, ParsP	*The Parson's Tale, The Parson's Prologue*
PF	*The Parliament of Fowls*

PhyT, Phy-PardL	The Physician's Tale, Physician-Pardoner Link
Pity	The Complaint unto Pity
Prov	Proverbs
PrT, PrP, Pr-ThL	The Prioress's Tale, The Prioress's Prologue, Prioress-Thopas Link
Purse	The Complaint of Chaucer to His Purse
Ret	Chaucer's Retraction [Retractation]
Rom	The Romaunt of the Rose
Ros	To Rosemounde
RvT, RvP	The Reeve's Tale, The Reeve's Prologue
Scog	The Envoy to Scogan
ShT, Sh-PrL	The Shipman's Tale, Shipman-Prioress Link
SNT, SNP, SN-CYL	The Second Nun's Tale, The Second Nun's Prologue, Second Nun-Canon's Yeoman Link
SqT, SqH, Sq-FranL	The Squire's Tale, Squire Headlink, Squire-Franklin Link
Sted	Lak of Stedfastnesse
SumT, SumP	The Summoner's Tale, The Summoner's Prologue
TC	Troilus and Criseyde
Th, Th-MelL	The Tale of Sir Thopas, Sir Thopas-Melibee Link
Ven	The Complaint of Venus
WBT, WBP, WB-FrL	The Wife of Bath's Tale, The Wife of Bath's Prologue, Wife of Bath-Friar Link
Wom Nob	Womanly Noblesse
Wom Unc	Against Women Unconstant

COLLATED TEXTS OF *THE ROMAUNT OF THE ROSE*

In chronological order; for complete citations see the Bibliographical Index. Where necessary or desirable, added lower-case letters distinguish textual notes (t), footnotes (f), and glossary (g) from text or explanatory notes: e.g., URg, SKt, RIf.

MS   Manuscript. Glasgow, University Library, Hunter 409 (formerly Hunterian Museum V.3.7).

TH[1]   William Thynne, *The workes of Geffray Chaucer newly printed / with dyuers workes whiche were neuer in print before*, 1532. *STC* 5068. Collated from the facsimile of 1969, intro. Derek Brewer.

TH[2]   William Thynne, *The workes of Geffray Chaucer newlye printed, wyth dyuers workes whych were neuer in print before*, 1542. *STC* 5069. University Microfilms xerograph.

TH[3]   William Thynne, *The workes of Geffray Chaucer newly printed, with dyuers workes whiche were neuer in print before*, 1550?. *STC* 5073. University Microfilms xerograph.

ST   John Stow, *The workes of Geffrey Chaucer, newlie printed, with diuers addicions, whiche were neuer in print before*, 1561. *STC* 5075. University Microfilms xerograph.

SP[1]   Thomas Speght, *The Workes of our Antient and Learned English Poet, Geffrey Chaucer, newly Printed*, 1598. *STC* 5078. University Microfilms xerograph.

SP[2]   Thomas Speght, *The Workes of Ovr Ancient and learned English Poet, Geffrey Chaucer, newly Printed*, 1602. *STC* 5080. New York Public Library copy *KC+1602.

SP[3]   Thomas Speght, *The Works of our Ancient, Learned, & Excellent English Poet, Jeffrey Chaucer*, 1687. Wing C3736. University Microfilms xerograph.

UR   John Urry, *The Works of Geoffrey Chaucer*, 1721.

TR   Thomas Tyrwhitt, *The Canterbury Tales of Chaucer*, 1775. 4 vols. Does not contain *Rom*; cited for notes and glossary. The glossary (TRg) is in vol. 5, publ. 1778.

BE   Robert Bell, *Poetical Works of Geoffrey Chaucer*, 8 vols., in *The Annotated Edition of the English Poets*, 1854-56. The *Romaunt* occupies vol. 7, published 1855; John M. Jephson wrote the notes; the glossary is in vol. 8.

MO   Richard Morris, *The Poetical Works of Geoffrey Chaucer*, 1866/70. The *Romaunt* is in vol. 6, the glossary in vol. 1.

KA   Max Kaluza, *The Romaunt of the Rose, from the unique Glasgow MS, Parallel with its Original, Le Roman de la Rose*, 1891.

SK   Walter W. Skeat, *The Complete Works of Geoffrey Chaucer*, 6 vols., 1894; second ed., 1899. The *Romaunt* is in vol. 1, the glossary in vol. 6, with a separate glossary (Skg$_2$) for Fragments B and C. SKt = textual notes to the *Romaunt* in this edition.

GL   Alfred W. Pollard, *The Works of Geoffrey Chaucer*, ed. Alfred W. Pollard and others, 1898; rpt. 1965. The Globe Edition. Mark H. Liddell is the editor of the *Romaunt*.

FU   Frederick J. Furnivall, *The Romaunt of the Rose. A Reprint of the First Printed Edition by William Thynne, A. D. 1532*, 1911.

RB^1 F. N. Robinson, *The Complete Works of Geoffrey Chaucer*, 1933.

RB^2 F. N. Robinson, *The Works of Geoffrey Chaucer*, second ed., 1957. RBt = textual notes in this edition.

SU   Ronald Sutherland, The Romaunt of the Rose *and* Le Roman de la Rose: *A Parallel-Text Edition*, 1968.

FI   John H. Fisher, *The Complete Poetry and Prose of Geoffrey Chaucer*, 1977.

RI   Larry D. Benson, *The Riverside Chaucer*, 1987. Third ed. of RB; Alfred David is the editor of the *Romaunt*. RIf = footnotes, RIt = textual notes to this edition.

MANUSCRIPTS OF THE FRENCH *ROMAN DE LA ROSE*

The listing follows Langlois's classification of 1910. Double classifications are for the first part/second part of *RR*; a single classification holds for both parts. In each classification the first letter indicates the manuscript family. Entries in parentheses are the designations of Kaluza, Lecoy, and Sutherland; they appear as cross-references to the Langlois classification.

(A)	Kaluza; see Jb.
Ab	See Ha/Ab.
Ac	See ϕє/Ac.
(B)	Kaluza; see Fo.
Ba	Paris. B. N. fr. 1571
Bâ	Paris. B. N. fr. 1576
Be	Turin. Bibl. del. Univers. L. III. 22
Bê	See Ra/Bê.
Bu	See Go/Bu.
Bû	See Mon/Bû.
(C)	Lecoy; see Ca.
Ca	Dijon. Bibl. mun. 526 (Lecoy's control MS C)
Ce	Amiens. Bibl. mun. 437
(D)	Kaluza; see λο.
(D)	Lecoy; see Da.
Da	Paris. B. N. fr. 12786 (Lecoy's control MS D)
De	Oxford. Bodleian Library, Rawlinson A.446
(E)	Kaluza; see κω.
Eb	See γο/Eḅ.
(Eg)	Sutherland; see κω.

ϕє/Ac	Chantilly. Musée Condé 686
Fo	Berlin. Royal Library 80 in-quarto (Kaluza's B)
Ga	Ghent. University Library 548
Go/Bu	Bruxelles. Bibl. royale 11019
γo/Eb	Paris. B. N. J. de Rothschild 2800
Ha/Ab	Paris. B. N. fr. 1573 (Lecoy's base MS)
He	Copenhagen. Royal Library Fr. LV
Jb	London. British Library. Additional 31840 (Kaluza's A)
Jo	Paris. B. N. fr. 1569
Ke	Paris. B. N. fr. 24390
κω	London. British Library. Egerton 881 (Sutherland's Eg, Kaluza's E)
(L)	Lecoy; see La.
La	Paris. B. N. fr. 1559 (Lecoy's control MS L)
Lb	Paris. B. N. fr. 1561
Li	Paris. B. N. fr. 2196
λo	London. British Library. Royal 20 A XVII (Kaluza's D)
Ly	London. British Library. Royal 19 B XIII (Kaluza's R)
Me	Paris. B. N. fr. 1560
Mon/Bû	Montpellier. Ecole de Médicine H438
(P)	Kaluza; see Bibliography, s.v. Du Pré, ed. 1493/1878
(R)	Kaluza; see Ly.
Ra/Bê	Arras. Bibl. mun. 897
Ri	Florence. Bibl. Riccardi 2775
Tou	Tournai. Musée
(Z)	Lecoy; see Za.
Za	Paris. B. N. fr. 25523 (Lecoy's control MS Z)

OTHER ABBREVIATIONS

Books

For complete citations see the Bibliographical Index.

Bosworth-Toller	Joseph Bosworth and T. Northcote Toller, *An Anglo-Saxon Dictionary and Supplement*, 1882–98, 1921.
Concordance	J. S. P. Tatlock and Arthur G. Kennedy, *A Concordance to the Complete Works of Chaucer and to the Romaunt of the Rose*, 1927.
DNB	*Dictionary of National Biography*, edited by Sir Leslie Stephen and Sir Sidney Lee. London: Oxford University Press, 1917–.
Lc	Félix Lecoy, ed., *Guillaume de Lorris et Jean de Meun, Le Roman de la Rose*, 1965–70. Lcg = glossary in this edition.
Ln	Ernest Langlois, ed., *Le Roman de la Rose par Guillaume de Lorris et Jean de Meun*, 1914–24. Lng = glossary, Lnt = collations in Ln.
LALME	Angus McIntosh, M. L. Samuels, and Michael Benskin, *A Linguistic Atlas of Late Mediaeval English*, 1986.
MED	*Middle English Dictionary*, ed. Hans Kurath et al., Ann Arbor. University of Michigan Press, 1952–.
OED	*Oxford English Dictionary*, ed. James A. H. Murray et al. Oxford: Clarendon Press, 1884-1928. Rev. ed. 12 vols., 1933. *A Supplement to the Oxford English Dictionary*, edited by R. W. Burchfield. 4 vols. Oxford: Clarendon Press, 1972–86.

PL	*Patrologiae cursus completus. Series Latina*, edited by J.-P. Migne. 221 vols. Paris, 1844–65.
STC	*A Short-Title Catalogue of Books Printed in England, Scotland, and Ireland, . . . 1475–1640*, first compiled by A. W. Pollard and G. R. Redgrave [1926]; 2d ed. revised and enlarged by W. A. Jackson, F. S. Ferguson, and Katharine F. Pantzer. 2 vols. London: Bibliographical Society, 1976–86.
Wing	*A Short-Title Catalogue of Books Printed in England, Scotland, Ireland, Wales, and British America . . . 1641–1700*, compiled by Donald Goddard Wing. 3 vols. New York: Columbia University Press, 1945–51. 2d ed. New York: Modern Language Association, 1972–.

Journals

Archiv	*Archiv für das Studium der neueren Sprachen und Literaturen*
ChauR	*Chaucer Review*
ELH	*ELH, A Journal of English Literary History*
ES	*English Studies*
EStn	*Englische Studien*
JEGP	*Journal of English and Germanic Philology*
MLN	*Modern Language Notes*
MLR	*Modern Language Review*
MP	*Modern Philology*
MS	*Mediaeval Studies*
N&Q	*Notes and Queries*
NM	*Neuphilologische Mitteilungen*
PBA	*Publications of the British Academy*
PMLA	*Publications of the Modern Language Association of America*
PQ	*Philological Quarterly*
RPh	*Romance Philology*
RR	*Romanic Review*
SAC	*Studies in the Age of Chaucer*
SP	*Studies in Philology*
YFS	*Yale French Studies*
ZRPh	*Zeitschrift für romanische Philologie*

Other Abbreviations

AF	Anglo-French
AL	Anglo-Latin
B.N.	Bibliothèque Nationale
CF	Central French
De Cons. Phil.	(Boethius) *De Consolatione Philosophiae*
EETS	Early English Text Society
EM	East Midland
e.s.	extra series
f	(with sigil) footnote
Fr.	French
g	(with sigil) glossary
LOE	Late Old English

ME	Middle English
Met.	(Ovid) *Metamorphoses*
n.	note; (in *MED* citations) noun
n.s.	new series
OE	Old English
OF	Old French
om.	omitted
ON	Old Norse
o.s.	original series
RR	*Le Roman de la Rose* (French original); (as title of periodical) *Romanic Review*
SATF	Société des anciens textes français
sb.	somebody; (in *OED* citations) substantive
sg.	singular
sth.	something
str.	strong
s.v.	sub verbo
SW	Southwest
SWM	Southwest Midland
t	(with sigil) textual note
trans.	transitive; (in citations) translated by; (in collations) transposed
[ ]	emendation of the base text; editorial change in quotation
<	is from, is derived from
>	develops to

The Romaunt of the Rose

Introduction

CRITICAL COMMENTARY

The *Romaunt of the Rose* (*Rom*) is a Middle English translation of parts of the French *Roman de la Rose* of Guillaume de Lorris and Jean de Meun (*RR*). It exists in a single manuscript, Hunter 409 of the Glasgow University Library (formerly Hunterian Museum V. 3. 7), and first appears in print in William Thynne's 1532 edition of Chaucer's works. We assume from certain lines of *LGWP* that Chaucer probably translated *RR*, but we are not certain that all parts of *Rom* are his.

In fact, the major question in discussions of *Rom* is "Who wrote it?" or "Is Chaucer the author?" Answers to this question determine scholars' decisions about the date or dates of composition; their opinions of its nature; their analyses of the relationship of the translation to the French original; and, particularly, their attitudes toward the textual tradition. The bulk of the scholarship centers on this question, and our critical commentary begins, appropriately, with the topic of authorship. For summaries of this material, see, among others, Kaluza (1893*a*:1–13), Schoch (1906), Hammond (1908:451–53), Root (1922:51–55), Brusendorff (1925:383–87), French (1947:75–81), Sutherland, ed. (1968:ix–xv), Peck (1988:1–10), and the introductions in the modern editions of Skeat (SK 1.1–11), Robinson (RB², pp. 564, 872), and David (in RI, p. 1103).

Authorship

We can distinguish three periods in the discussion of the authorship of the *Romaunt*. From 1532 until about 1860, there was general acceptance of Chaucer as author. From around 1860 to 1890, there was growing skepticism, mainly on the basis of rhymes. And since Kaluza (1890, 1893*a*), most scholars have accepted Chaucer as author of part; some deny that he wrote any of it, and a few maintain that he wrote all of it. Associated with this chronology is a growing awareness of the state of the *Rom* text, from the recognition that the translation is incomplete (F. Thynne 1599) to the recognition of a major gap that divides the poem into two fragments, A and B (Tyrwhitt 1775) to the discovery that the first of these fragments can probably be further divided into two, A¹ and A², or A and B with the other fragment as C (Kaluza 1890).

The question of authorship involves two separate questions: "Did Chaucer translate *RR*?" and "Did Chaucer write part or all of *Rom*?" It is hard to give an unqualified "yes" in either case. For the first question we have Chaucer's own testimony in *LGWP* (F 322–31, 440–41, 469–71). There, in the context of a dream, the God of Love accuses the first-person dreamer of being his "foe," of slandering his servants and of hindering them with his "translacioun"; "For in pleyn text," he says:

> withouten nede of glose,
> Thou hast translated the Romaunce of the Rose,
> That is an heresye ayeins my lawe,
> And makest wise folk fro me withdrawe.
>
> (F 328–31)

Later, in her plea for the dreamer, Alceste grants that he "mysseyde" the God of Love "in the Rose or elles in Creseyde"; but in the G version she pleads that he did so "Of innocence, and nyste what he seyde" (G 345). The dreamer, in his own defense, argues that true lovers should side with him in his account "of Creseyde . . . or of the Rose," since, whatever his "auctor" meant, his own intent was to promote "trouthe in love" (F 469–72). Since the context is that of a dream vision, the evidence does not actually prove that Chaucer translated *RR*. But the ambiguities of *LGWP* do not seriously alter the probability that Chaucer "translated the Romaunce of the Rose." When the God of Love utters these words to the dreamer, we have as good reason to believe him as we do when in *RR* the God of Love says that Guillaume de Lorris began the poem and that Jean Chopinel will finish it (Lc 10496–10624). Chaucer's other direct allusions to *RR* (*MerT E* 2032, *BD* 334)—as well as the numerous reflections throughout his work—lend further weight to this probability.

External evidence supports the same conclusion. In Eustace Deschamps's "Autre balade," addressed to Chaucer (Spurgeon 1925:3.v.16–17; cf. Sandras 1859:28, 261–62), the refrains refer to Chaucer as "Grant translateur noble geffroy chaucier" (lines 10, 20, 30, 36). "You are," he writes, "the god of worldly love in Albion and of the rose in the angelic land [Angleterre]. . . . You translated the book into good English" (lines 11–12, 16 "Tu es damours mondains dieux en albie / Et de la rose en laterre angelique. . . . En bon angles le livre translatas"). Spurgeon dates this *balade* as "1386?." Nearly 50 years later, Lydgate's *Fall of Princes* (1430) contains a catalogue of Chaucer's works (Spurgeon 1925:1.36–43), one which states that Chaucer "did his besynesse / By greet auys his wittës to dyspose / To translate the Romaunce of the Rose" (p. 38).

Traditional Acceptance of Chaucer's Authorship

Later evidence derives largely from the appearance of *Rom* in the Thynne edition of 1532 and in later editions of Chaucer's works. An allusion in *The Pilgrim's Tale* (dated 1536–40? by Spurgeon 1925:1.82; cf. Blodgett 1984:38) refers to a passage in a printed edition of *Rom* and attributes six quoted lines (*Rom* 7165–70) to Chaucer. John Leland uses Thynne's table of contents to present a catalogue of Chaucer's works in his *Commentarii de Scriptoribus Britannicis* (ca. 1540–1545), where he lists a "De Arte amandi, alias *Romaunce of the Rose*" (text in: Hammond 1908:4–5; Spurgeon 1925:3.iv.17; trans. Lounsbury 1892:1.139). John Bale expands this notice in his *Scriptorum Illustrium Maioris Britanniae . . . Catalogus*: "De arte amandi, Romane, Lib. 1. Plerique fatentur

in somnijs meras" (1557; text in Spurgeon 1925:3.iv.22); and John Pits copies Bale's ascription in his *De rebus anglicis* (1619; text in Hammond 1908:15). In the second volume of Bale's work (*STC* 1296a; 1559:58) the entry "Ioannes Mone. XXXVII." specifies that Chaucer translated John Mone's French original into English meter and added the title "The Romaunt of thæ rose." Bale claims to get this information from Chaucer ("Ex Chavorro"; corrected in the errata to read "Ex Chaucero"). Presumably he refers to the "Letter of Cupid," included as Chaucer's in Thynne's three editions; line 281 names "Iohan de Moone" as the author of *RR*. But the poem does not otherwise support Bale's assertions, which are repeated by Pits (text in Hammond 1908:17).

Other references, along with ascriptions in the biographical material from SP[1] 1598 to Todd 1810 (Hammond 1908:29–39), clearly derive from the tradition established by the inclusion of *Rom* in Thynne's 1532 edition and by Leland's catalogue (ca. 1540–45). In 1569, one "G. B." alludes to Chaucer's "Romance of his Roses" (*A newe Booke called the Shippe of safegarde*, text in Spurgeon 1925:1.103). The French scholar André Thévet, while chastising Bale for portraying Jean de Meun as an Englishman who emigrated to France, counts Chaucer among those who wished "to imitate" Jean's poem (1584:499; text of 1735 in Spurgeon 1925:3.v.22). George (Richard?) Puttenham writes that Chaucer "translated but one halfe" of the "deuice" of "*John de Mehunes*, a French poet" (*Arte of English Poesie*, 1589; text in Brewer, ed. 1978:1.127); and Henry Peacham adapts this statement of Puttenham when he says that Chaucer's *Romaunt* translates "but onely the one halfe" of "the inuention of *Jehan de Mehunes*, a French poet" (*The Compleat Gentleman*, 1622; text in Spurgeon 1925: 1:197). In accepting Chaucer's authorship of *Rom*, the "Arguments" in SP[1] (sig. c5r) similarly ascribe *RR* only to "John Clopinell, *alias* John Moone"; but Francis Thynne points out in his *Animadversions* that *RR* "was begonne by Guilliame de Loris, and fynished . . . by Johne de Meune" (1599;1875:27–28);

Francis's correction appears as part of the argument—transferred to a headnote—in SP[2,3]. Bishop Richard Corbet's reference to Chaucer's *Romant* (*Certain Elegant Poems*, before 1635; text in Spurgeon 1925:1.206) also derives from the tradition that began with William Thynne and Leland.

While some of the earlier evidence may support the probability that Chaucer translated *RR*, neither it nor the later evidence proves that the surviving Middle English translation, *Rom*, is by Chaucer. The Glasgow manuscript has lost eleven leaves including the first text-leaf, and Chaucer's name does not appear anywhere in it (see the description of MS in the Textual Commentary below). Furthermore, since TH[1] and later editions contain works now considered spurious or doubtful, the inclusion of *Rom* is no guarantee of authenticity. Nevertheless, a long-standing tradition ascribes it to Chaucer, and we find this assumption, for example, in both Thomas Warton and Thomas Tyrwhitt at the end of the eighteenth century (Warton 1774–81:1.369; Tyrwhitt 1775:4.80–82, 1778: 5.vii). Tyrwhitt, however, is the first to express a doubt, not so much about Chaucer's responsibility for *Rom* as about the underlying claim that he translated *RR*, for although Tyrwhitt regards it "most probable" that Chaucer did so, he finds it "unaccountable" that there is no mention of his translation in the *Retraction* at the end of the *Canterbury Tales* (1775:3.314).

Growing Skepticism about Chaucer's Authorship

Up to the middle of the nineteenth century the question of Chaucer's authorship of *Rom* was a matter of tradition. About that time, attention turned to the internal evidence of the translation itself, although earlier observations had anticipated some of the later questions. In 1599, Francis Thynne had noted that Chaucer did not translate as much as half of the original (1599;1875:28; cf. Puttenham 1589 and Peacham 1622, cited above). Others are similarly vague in speaking of "several omissions in John of Meun's part" (Warton

1774–81:1.369), of "the great compression and curtailment of Jean de Meun's part" (Craik 1844–45:2.56), or of the "omissions considérables" in Jean de Meun's part (Sandras 1859: 39; cf. Ebert 1862:88). But as early as 1775, Tyrwhitt (3.314) had pointed out that, aside from the fact that the translation is incomplete, these omissions consisted principally of a single large gap, between *Rom* 5810 and 5811 (see note), where over 5500 lines of the French are omitted (Lc 5125–10648).

Bernhard ten Brink still speaks of "gaps" in the plural (1867:307) but admits later (1870:19–20) that two of his three gaps are passages that appear only in certain MSS and in the eighteenth-century edition that he had used earlier, probably that of Lenglet du Fresnoy. Later editions, from Méon through Lecoy, regard these passages as interpolations (after Lc 4370, 10800; see Langlois 1910:425, Ln 10830–31n.); and Brink, in effect, grants that there is only the one major gap that Tyrwhitt had identified. Thus the scholarship of the 1870s and 1880s comes to refer to two fragments, the one before the large gap, the other after, and this recognition raised the possibility that the separate fragments were .by separate authors.

F. J. Child (1870) suggests this possibility. In referring to "the break" that precedes line 5814 (= 5811), he connects two developments, the use of rhyme tests for authorship and the recognition of separate fragments. He doubts that *Rom* is Chaucer's because "the rhymes are not his, and the style is not his"; but he thinks that the part after the break is "better done than the middle" and that "as the Bialacoil of the earlier portion is here called Fair-welcomyng, *perhaps* this part belongs to a different version" (cf. 5856n.).

Earlier, in the 1860s, Henry Bradshaw was the first to use rhyme-tests (Prothero 1888: 352). According to Furnivall (1868:107–11), Bradshaw used them to question the authenticity of several works that had been included in earlier editions of Chaucer, and A. J. Ellis supported this kind of test (Furnivall 1868:108 n.2; cf. Ellis 1869–89:1.251–52). Furnivall reports Bradshaw's analysis of false rhymes, particularly stressed -*y* : -*ye* (cf. 1849–50n.), but he is "not prepared to give up the *Romaunt* as Chaucer's, without a fight," and he raises the possibility that at least some of the false rhymes may be due to scribal alteration in the unique fifteenth-century MS (p. 110).

Brink's studies (1870) of the development and chronology of Chaucer's works, however, raise further doubts for Furnivall. Brink starts from a comparison of the forest-description in *BD* 416–33 with its original in the French *RR* (Lc 1363–80) and with the parallel English translation (*Rom* 1391–1408). On the basis of this comparison he reasons that *Rom* precedes *BD* (1870:14–16), and he cites as a principal proof the existence of defective rhymes, including assonances and, particularly, those that show confusion among the stressed endings *-ie*, *-y*, and *-e*, confusions which rarely appear in the later works (pp. 22–25). Furnivall (1871:7) writes of his hope that he "had strengthened Prof. Ten Brink's position that the Romaunt's rhyming of *-ye -y* might be due to its being the first work of Chaucer," but after reading Brink he backs away from this hope when he writes that:

after-consideration inclined me to think that the best early parts of the *Romaunt* were perhaps too good to be Chaucer's earliest work, and if so, this rendered it almost impossible that he should not have allowed the *-ye -y* ryme in his earliest works, then have allowed it in one of his later books, and again disallowed it in all his most important poems.

Furnivall reports also that F. J. Child (1870) is "against its genuineness" and that "Prof. Ten Brink is now inclined to give . . . up" on Chaucer's authorship.

In fact, Brink does so. In his 1884 book on Chaucer's language and meter, he excludes *Rom* from consideration as not authentic (1884:6), and in 1878 he refers to the spuriousness of the Glasgow fragment of *Rom* (1878:533). His change of mind arose from a growing conviction that *Chaucer's* translation was later, about the time of *TC*, and thus that the Glasgow *Rom* could not be Chaucer's (1883–96:2.77; 1892:8–9).

W. W. Skeat, the most prolific scholar in extending Bradshaw's rhyme-tests during the 1870s and 1880s, proposed in 1874 a new kind of test, rhyme-linked paragraphs in octosyllabic couplets, a nexus in which one verse paragraph ends with the first line of a couplet and the next begins with the second line; he finds that such a link occurs frequently in *BD* and *HF*, but rarely in *Rom*, and he suggests that this result argues against Chaucer's authorship of the latter.

In the "Preliminary Essay" that he wrote for the 1878 revision of Robert Bell's edition of Chaucer's *Poetical Works* (Bell, ed. 1878: 1.1–12), Skeat suggests that the defective and particularly the Northern rhymes of *Rom* argue that the version in the Glasgow MS is not Chaucer's (pp. 8–9). Furnivall's approving review of this essay (1878) shows that he no longer leans toward what he now calls "the superstition that has hitherto defended" the authenticity of *Rom*.

Furnivall's review also gives rise to an exchange of views between T. Arnold (1878*a–b*) and Skeat (1878*a–b*). Arnold (1878*b*) rehearses the evidence for Chaucer's authorship (*LGWP*, Lydgate, Thynne's 1532 ed.), and he replies to Skeat's counter-arguments. To account for the Northern dialect, he suggests "an East-Anglian transcriber"; on the *-y* : *-ye* rhymes, he suggests "Chaucer's own varying practice at different periods"; and on the unusual rhyme *thore : more* (cf. note to lines 1853–54) he "can at present suggest no solution." Skeat (1878*b*) rejoins by multiplying the examples of unusual rhymes, by showing that the Northern forms occur in rhyme and thus cannot be the work of a transcriber, and by introducing a "new" test, that of assonances, one that Brink (1870:22) had already used as evidence for early Chaucerian composition.

The full development of Skeat's argument appears in 1880 (reprinted in Skeat 1884 and, with revision of the final paragraph, in Skeat 1888*c*.) He suggests that other translations of *RR* may have existed and that the Glasgow *Rom* is not Chaucer's. For proof, Skeat presents seven tests to show that the translator of the Glasgow MS was not Chaucer: the rhyming of *-y* with *-yë*; assonant rhymes; the rhyming of *here* with *there*; the existence of strange rhymes; the ungrammatical use of final -*e*; the appearance of Northern dialect forms; and the appearance of un-Chaucerian vocabulary items.

Without having seen this essay, W. Fick (1886*a*) argues for Chaucer's authorship—against Skeat 1878*a* and Brink 1878, 1884, but *for* Brink's earlier view of 1867, 1870—by accepting *Rom* as early, by explaining the Northern forms as the result of early Northern influences on Chaucer, by objecting that Skeat applies rhyme-tests too mechanically and rigorously, and by adducing a body of parallels between *Rom* and Chaucer's genuine works (cf. Kölbing 1888:501). Skeat (1886*a*) writes that Fick "cannot have seen my Essay [1880, 1884] which has been pronounced conclusive by many whose judgment I much value." Fick (1886*b*) admits that he did not know about the essay, which was not available, but after reading it he considers his view completely vindicated.

F. Lindner (1887)—responding to Fick and Skeat—puts forward a new suggestion. On the basis of the large gap at *Rom* 5810–11 he argues that there may have been two translators, one for each of the two fragments, and that the Glasgow MS was made up from these two fragments (pp. 163, 165–67). Relying on Bell's edition (pp. 163–65), he finds comparatively fewer scribal errors and much less use of rich rhymes ("rührende [touching] reime") in the first than in the second part (pp. 167–69); in comparing the treatment of proper names, he notes the switch from *Bialacoil* in the first part to *Fair-Welcomyng* in the second (p. 170; cf. 5856n.); and he finds mistranslations in the second part, but not in the first (pp. 170–71). He concludes (pp. 172–73) that there were two authors, and, while he suspends judgment on their identity, he hints at Chaucer for the first part and the author of the *Testament of Love* (Usk; see Skeat, ed. 1897:xix–xx) for the second; against Chaucerian authorship of the second, he cites the differing translations of the French line "Divers diverses choses distrent" (Lc 10654) in *SqT* F 202 ("Diverse folk diversely they demed") and *Rom* 5814 ("And dyversely they seide hir wille [MS tille]").

Another response to Skeat comes from A. S. Cook (1887), who deals only with Skeat's vocabulary test, the appearance of words that are unusual in Chaucer's other works. Cook's principal argument is that many of Skeat's examples from *Rom* are borrowed directly or indirectly from the original and are thus hardly evidence against Chaucer's authorship (pp. 143–45). He also points out that "some of these words are to be found in one of Chaucer's undoubted poems" (p. 143), specifically *TC* (p. 146). Finally, he reasons that it is unsafe to argue against authenticity by comparing the *peculiar* words of a work with the vocabulary of the genuine works (pp. 143, 146); he makes this last point by quoting a list of over forty words that appear only in *LGW* but that do not therefore disprove Chaucer's authorship of that poem.

In the following year Skeat takes note of Lindner's work in three publications (1888*a*–*c*). While he accepts the idea that the two fragments are by different hands (1888*a*; 1888*b*:xxiv; 1888*c*:xciv), he opposes Lindner's hint that Chaucer might have written Fragment A but not Fragment B (1888*a*); "if any part of the English translation of this poem is by Chaucer," he writes, "it is fragment B; and even against this I believe that something (yet much less) can be urged" (1888*b*:xxv). The principal point of interest, however, lies in Skeat's *Academy* article (1888*a*), where he proposes another test for authenticity, the comparison of borrowings from *RR* in Chaucer's genuine works and in *Rom*. Although Skeat calls this "an entirely new point" (p. 154), Lindner had used the same kind of evidence (1887:172) when he cited the French line "Divers diverses choses distrent" and compared the versions in *SqT* and *Rom* (see above). Skeat's formulation of this test is rather categorical (p. 153): "if in Chaucer's works we find quotations from the *Roman de la Rose*, they will be mere repetitions from his own translation. They will, therefore, agree *word for word* with the existing English translation, *if that be his*. And if not, not. Well, they do *not*." Skeat's examples show borrowings from *RR* in *BD* and the corresponding translations in *Rom*.

Whatever one may think of the validity of this test, the significant fact is that six of Skeat's seven examples, which he uses to prove that Chaucer did *not* write Fragment A (1–5810), come from its early part (1–1705), the new Fragment A[1] that Skeat himself later accepts as Chaucer's. It was Max Kaluza who discovered this new fragment.

Partial Acceptance of Chaucer's Authorship

1890–1892. Up to 1890, the principal tendencies had been either to accept Chaucer's authorship uncritically, largely on the basis of tradition, or to reject *Rom* from the canon entirely. Kaluza's work gave a new basis for seeing Chaucer as author of part of *Rom*. His discovery of the new fragment, A[1], arose as a by-product of his parallel-text edition, for the Chaucer Society, of *Rom* and the corresponding parts of the French *RR.* This edition was announced (Kaluza 1888) just a week before Skeat's article appeared; in 1890 Kaluza published a brief letter that he had sent to Furnivall, in which he takes up the authorship question. This letter deserves full quotation (the line numbering is Morris's; lines 5813–14 = 5810–11, 7694 = 7692, 7526 = 7522):

(1) The fragments of the *Romaunt of the Rose* in the Glasgow MS. are by two different men; lines 1–1704 (or 1768?) and lines 5814–7694 are fragments of Chaucer's translation, but the middle part (lines 1705–5813) is another man's.

(2) Chaucer's translation (1–1704 and 5814 to end) follows the original (as his *Boece* does) almost word for word and line for line, while the other man paraphrases rather than translates, omits long passages, and inserts others. The difference between the two translations in this respect is at once evident, if you cast a glance at the Parallel Text.

(3) In lines 1–1704, and 5814–7694, all the phrases and rimes, all the metrical and dialectal peculiarities, are quite the same as in Chaucer's genuine works; while, with a few exceptions, all the non-Chaucerian rimes and forms pointed out by Prof. Skeat in his Essay I.–VI. occur only in the middle part, lines 1705–5813. There is, moreover, the difference between Chaucer's English name *Faire-welcomyng* (l. 7526 [*sic* for 7524], ed. Morris), and the other man's French-following *Bialacoil* (3573, &c., &c.,) for the same woman.

(4) So, also, the French *bouton*, the object of the lover's ardent desire, is called *knop* by Chaucer in line 1702—*knoppes*, lines 1675, 1683, 1685, 1691—but always *botheum, bothon,* by the other man, in the middle part. (See lines 1721, 1761, 1770, 1786, 1790, &c.)

I shall discuss this question at large as soon as I am at leisure.

Kaluza takes up the question in two subsequent publications. One (1893*a*) will be examined in the present discussion of authorship, the other (1893*b*) in the Textual Commentary ("The Glasgow Manuscript and the Thynne Print").

There were many responses to this finding. W. W. Skeat's were the earliest and most urgent, for he was preparing his edition of the Oxford Chaucer (1894–97); indeed, he probably had to revise the copy for his first volume, which contains *Rom* and the Minor Poems and, in the Introduction, a discussion of their genuineness. It is clear that Skeat and Kaluza were in close touch during the early 1890s, since many of Skeat's suggestions for emendation of *Rom* for the 1894 publication appear in Kaluza's edition of 1891; and Kaluza twice acknowledges this cooperation (1893*a*:vi; 1893*b*:108–09).

Skeat's first reaction (1890), published two weeks after Kaluza's letter, is both congratulatory and understandably defensive. He calls Kaluza's "chief point"—the identification of Fragment A[1]—"a really important discovery," and sees in this fragment "a very marked superiority to the rest. I never noticed it before." Skeat does not consider the question of authenticity as "quite settled," but he admits that it has entered upon a new and more satisfactory phase (1890:51–52). Skeat does contest as "quite untenable" Kaluza's claim that Chaucer wrote all of *Rom* except Fragment A[2] (1705–5811), arguing that while "Fragment B [5811–7692] is nearer to Chaucer than Fragment A[2]. . . , it cannot be his" (1890:51).

The positions developed by Skeat and Kaluza have, to a large degree, dominated subsequent discussion of the authorship question. Their impact begins with Skeat's "Postscript on 'The Romaunt of the Rose'" (1887) appended to his Introduction to Marshall and Porter's *Ryme-Index to . . . Chaucer's Minor Poems*; although the book is dated 1887, Skeat's "Postscript" was written no earlier than 1890, since it refers to Kaluza's letter of that year. In the "Postscript," Skeat calls his earlier position (1884), that *Rom* is not Chaucer's, "fairly justified; for it is true as regards ll. 1705–7698 (5993 lines out of 7698, or considerably *more than three-fourths* of the whole)" (1887:vii). But the main object of the postscript is to examine the doubtful rhymes of Fragment A[1] to show that most were originally Chaucerian, and he thus supports Kaluza's position for that part of *Rom*.

John Koch (1890) agrees that only the "first portion" (*Rom* 1–1704) might possibly be Chaucer's, but after a further examination of doubtful rhymes and meter in this portion (pp. 10–12), he rejects that possibility. The youthful Chaucer's translation of *RR*, Koch concludes (pp. 12–13), is now lost (see further "Date of Composition," below). In 1891, Skeat makes "a small correction" to Kaluza's claim regarding lines 1–1704, adding line 1705 on the basis of the anomalous syntax and rhyme (see 1705n.). Skeat also introduces the designations A, B, and C for the three fragments (previously A[1], A[2], B) and develops a theory about the make-up of the ancestor of the Glasgow MS (see "Description of the Manuscript" below).

Kaluza's brief notice was easy to overlook. Thomas R. Lounsbury's argument for Chaucer's authorship of the entire *Rom* (1892:2.3–166) clearly had been written for the most part before 1890, and there is only a brief allusion in the Introduction (1.xx) to what he calls the "untenable" views that concede only "the genuineness of certain portions" or of "a certain portion." No names appear, but the reference is clearly to Kaluza and Skeat. Lounsbury's argument that the entire *Rom* is genuine has two parts; the first (2.17–77) attacks Skeat's seven tests against Chaucer's authorship of *Rom* (see Skeat 1880, 1884, 1888c), and the second (2.77–160) advances a battery of "literary tests" to argue for Chaucer's authorship.

Of Skeat's seven tests, Lounsbury dismisses the rhyming of *here* and *there*, pointing out (2.17–19) that this rhyme also appears in *BD*. He devotes much more space to the vocabulary test (2.19–34, 537–38); he examines *Th* and *GP* to show that they have greater proportions of peculiar words than does *Rom*. To counter Skeat's objection to *Rom*'s Northernisms, including Northern rhymes, Lounsbury (2.34–35) argues that Chaucer, a Londoner, became familiar with the Northern dialect through his supposed three-year residence at Hatfield in Yorkshire in the service of Elizabeth Countess of Ulster (2.47; cf. Crow and Olson, eds. 1966:13–18, and Pollard 1892:173). He notes also that this familiarity appears not only in *RvT*, where one expects it in the speech of the Northern students, but occasionally elsewhere in Chaucer's genuine works (2.48–51).

Lounsbury gives somewhat briefer treatment to Skeat's other four tests. He posits that Chaucer's "established usage" of not rhyming *-y* with *-ye* had not yet been established at the time that the translation was made (2.58; cf. 1.388–94). He argues that there are a few assonant rhymes in poetry undoubtedly written by Chaucer (2.58–59, 1.394–98), and strange rhymes as well (2.59–65); the latter Lounsbury dismisses as "the liberties" of a youthful writer (2.65). And on the (un)grammatical use of final *-e* (2.65–72; cf. 1.399–406), he argues that "Chaucer does occasionally tolerate rhymes" that violate the expected grammatical forms (2.67), although he grants that *Rom* "furnishes rather more examples proportionately . . . than can be found in the admittedly genuine works" (2.68).

To Skeat's tests Lounsbury adds another, one that favors Skeat's position: the use of *do* or *did*, with infinitive, as the modern emphatic auxiliary rather than as the causative (2.72–75). To Lounsbury this usage presents "the strongest evidence against the genuineness" of *Rom* "that can be adduced" (2.75).

Finally Lounsbury employs "literary tests" to support his case for Chaucer's authorship (2.77–160); these tests, he believes, are as important as, and perhaps superior to, any others (2.78). In general he argues that the fidelity and felicity of the translation raise it above the level of other contemporary translations (2.78–81). His argument may seem a little circular—the "strongest . . . evidence for [*Rom*'s] genuineness is the Chaucerian character of the translation" (2.81)—but the rest of his development tries to lay out reasons for this "impression" (2.82).

These reasons rest mainly on the occurrence, in the genuine works of Chaucer and in *Rom*, of 1) words and phrases, familiar and special (2.86–117); 2) peculiarities of inflection (2.117–18); 3) phrases not suggested by the original (2.118–21); 4) a set of parallels to *RR* (2.121–53); 5) the practice of using two synonymous words for the same idea (2.153–58).

1. Lounsbury divides the first category into "familiar" (2.86–113) and "special" (2.113–17) words and phrases. "Familiar" ones include: a) single words like *iwis* and *certes* (2.90–91); b) the adverbial phrase *withoute(n)* (or *out of*) plus noun, e.g. *withouten doute* (2.91–94); c) phrases consisting of noun or adverb plus the infinitive phrase *to tell* or *to say*, e.g. *(soth, shortly) to telle* (2.94–98); d) modifying clauses or phrases like *I undertake, I gesse, trust(eth) well, God wot* (2.98–100); and e) invocatory phrases like *so mote I go, God you see* (2.101–02). Unexceptional in themselves, these phrases are, Lounsbury maintains, significant in their totality, for contemporaries like Gower (2.105–11) and Barbour (2.112–13) use them in significantly smaller proportions than do Chaucer and the translator of *Rom*. The second division (2.113–17), "special phrases" common to Chaucer and *Rom*, includes those like *To quite one's while, for (pure) wood*, and such a relatively rare phrase as *farewell fieldfare* (cf. 5510n.).

2–3. Two other tests rest on the appearance in both Chaucer and *Rom* of a) "peculiarities of inflection," like the use of both weak and strong preterites, *stikede* and *stak* (2.117–18); and b) phrases not suggested by the original, like *intyl Inde* (2.118–21).

4–5. The major contribution of this portion of Lounsbury's argument consists in a list of parallels to *RR* that appear in both Chaucer and *Rom* (2.121–53); he separates these parallels into those characterized by remote resemblance (2.121–35) and by close resemblance (2.135–53). The first group includes nine transitional expressions (2.121–22), 49 parallels where the French is not the source of the wording (2.122–34), and six where the parallels follow the French. The second group has the longest list, of 77 parallels where Chaucer and *Rom* bear close similarity to *RR*. This work continues what W. Fick had begun (1886*a*) and what Kaluza was to develop much more fully (1893*a*:141–241; see below). The last of Lounsbury's literary tests shows the presence in Chaucer and *Rom* of synonymous words for the same idea, e.g. *compass and caste* (2.153–58).

Lounsbury's closing argument (2.160–63) appeals to tradition when he points out that the genuineness of *Rom* was not questioned by the earlier printers, editors, and readers.

Responses to Lounsbury's study appeared quickly. A. W. Pollard (1892) commends Lounsbury's arguments as fair-minded but also criticizes them as long-winded, diffuse, and, in some cases, "of no great force"; and he particularly regrets Lounsbury's dismissal of Kaluza 1890 (cf. Unidentified reviewer 1892*a*:215–16). Skeat's initial reaction (1892*a*) avoids direct discussion of the genuineness of the entire *Rom* but reaffirms his belief that Fragment A is genuine and announces that Kaluza agrees with him that Fragment A ends with line 1705. Indirectly he challenges Lounsbury's case for the genuineness of Fragments B and C when he reveals weaknesses in Lounsbury's analysis of rhymes in Chaucer and Gower (1892*a*–*b*). It is interesting that, in arguing against assonant rhymes in Chaucer, Skeat (1892*a*:206) undermines his own argument against Chaucer's authorship of Fragment B: he suggests that an assonant rhyme in *TC* (2.884), *sike* ("sigh"), be emended to *site* ("be sorrowful, mourn"), a word attested only in the *Cursor Mundi*, a Northern text; Skeat thus implies a Northern influence on Chaucer in *TC* and indirectly raises the possibility of such influence in *Rom*.

The fullest response is by G. L. Kittredge (1892), who first examines Lounsbury's attacks on Skeat's seven tests (pp. 1–12); then considers his affirmative arguments, those that "are based on similarity or identity of style" (p. 12); and closes (pp. 63–65) with a refutation of Lounsbury's "appeal to the authority of the sixteenth-century editors" (p. 63). In general, where Lounsbury finds the translation faithful but not servile, Kittredge thinks that it "is at best respectable; it is servile and loose by turns, and by no means free from blunders" (p. 1).

Kittredge agrees with Lounsbury (and with Cook 1887) that Skeat's vocabulary test is a "dubious criterion" (p. 1), but he challenges Lounsbury's attack on the validity of the other tests. He finds some circularity in Lounsbury's argument that Northernisms in Chaucer's work help to place Chaucer in Prince Lionel's Yorkshire household, and that his presence there would explain the Northernisms. Similarly Kittredge attacks Lounsbury's hypothesis concerning Chaucer's avoidance of rhymes in *-y -ye*: for Lounsbury to claim "that Chaucer did not conform to this rule in his youth," Kittredge writes, "is to beg the question, for we have no proof that he disregarded it, unless we assume that this translation is from his pen" (p. 4). Also, Kittredge dismisses Lounsbury's assertion that assonance is unusual in ME poetry and therefore is an idiosyncracy that links Chaucer and *Rom*. He finds only one instance of assonance in works undoubtedly by Chaucer (*TC* 2.884) and observes that one can find assonances in Layamon, the metrical romances, and the popular ballads (pp. 4–5). At any rate, neither this nor Lounsbury's "sounder" criticism of the "strange rhyme" test (p. 5) "is of the very first importance" (p. 6).

He gives that position to the *-e* test, "the translator's disregard of Chaucerian final *e* in rhyme," a test that involves meter, grammar, and dialect (p. 6). Like Lounsbury, Kittredge lists four categories of the test: the rhyming of a) weak preterite with weak past participle; b) infinitive with strong preterite; c) infinitive with weak past participle; d) strong preterite with weak preterite. In the first category, he says, Lounsbury fails to recognize the fact that monosyllabic weak past participles are sometimes inflected in Chaucer (p. 7; cf. Skeat 1892*a*:206). While Kittredge finds other errors

and questions in the evidence that Lounsbury presents, he faults him particularly for "arbitrarily" restricting the application of the *-e* test and for neglecting "to consider *between one and two hundred instances* in which the rhymes of the *Romaunt* run counter to Chaucer's practice with regard to this sound"; accordingly, Kittredge provides a list of nearly forty such examples (p. 10).

Kittredge also points out (p. 11) that Lounsbury has failed to recognize Kaluza's discovery (1890) that the first 1704 lines of *Rom* do not violate Skeat's tests (cf. Lounsbury 1892:1.xx). Further, he says (p. 11), "the argument from the inconsistency of calling an important character *Bial-Acoil* in one part of the poem, *Fair-Welcoming* in another is . . . by no means answered by Mr. Lounsbury's summoning the three gray horses from the *Canterbury Tales*" (*GP* 616 "pomely grey"; *CYP* G 559 "pomely grys"; *Th* B² 2074 "dappull gray"; see 5856n., Lounsbury 1892:2.13, and Unidentified reviewer 1892*b*:556).

Kittredge next considers Lounsbury's affirmative arguments, which he divides into five classes: (i) the argument from the usage in common of "certain individual words and brief phrases," (ii) the argument from "certain matters found in this translation which do not appear in the original but do appear in Chaucer," (iii) the argument from mannerisms in transition; (iv) the argument from parallel passages, and (v) the argument from synonyms (p. 12). Kittredge (pp. 13–63) rebuts these arguments by showing that the features identified by Lounsbury are common in other Middle English works and not specific to Chaucer, and in some cases have their immediate source in *RR*. In applying this strategy (pp. 25–60) to the fourth argument, he reduces Lounsbury's list of 126 parallel passages to 12, which may be "more reasonably explained on the theory of imitation . . . than on the theory of identity of authorship" (p. 55).

Finally, after this detailed refutation of Lounsbury's affirmative arguments (the "literary tests"), Kittredge closes by noting that Lounsbury's "appeal to the authority of the sixteenth-century editors . . . can have no weight, even as *a priori* reasoning." Lounsbury's reasoning that Thynne chose Chaucer's out of a group of translations, says Kittredge, is fallacious, since "there is no evidence that any manuscripts of Chaucer's version of the *Roman* were in existence in 1532 unless, begging the question, we assume that the translation now extant is Chaucer's" (p. 63). Kittredge concludes that *Rom* "is not Chaucer's, with the possible exception of the first seventeen hundred lines" (p. 65).

A further development of 1892 is an article by Brink on the chronology of Chaucer's writings. In it he alludes to his dating of *Rom* and his denial of Chaucer's authorship, a position that he had adumbrated earlier (1878, 1884:6). In his *Geschichte der englischen Literatur* (trans. 1883–96:2.76–77) he had proposed that John of Gaunt instigated Chaucer's version of *RR*; that it belongs to the period around 1380; that it is lost to us; and that it is *not* the version of the Glasgow MS. In the 1892 article (pp. 9–10) Brink develops his evidence from *LGWP*, particularly G 344–48. There he takes the phrase "som persone" (G 346, F 367) to refer to John of Gaunt, the line "For he hath write many a bok er this" (G 348) to preclude an early date of composition, and the conjunction of "the Rose and ek Crisseyde" (G 344) to indicate consecutive dates of composition for the two; by implication, the Glasgow fragments are not good enough to qualify as Chaucer's work during this period. Kaluza says (1893*a*:6) that in this article Brink does not discuss the authenticity of the Glasgow fragment. In fact Brink's main concern is with dating; but in a note (1892: 10–11) he writes that those scholars who consider only one part of the fragments as Chaucerian will have to take account of the arguments above. (For a reply to the questions of chronology raised in this article, see the "Appendix" [added 1892] in Koch 1890:81–87.)

Kaluza 1893a. Kaluza takes Brink's argument into account at the beginning of his book, *Chaucer und der Rosenroman*, where he accepts the later date (see below, "Date"), without, however, denying Chaucer's authorship of a good deal of *Rom*. He provides in his Introduction a brief account of the Glasgow MS and a survey of previous scholarship in

which he prepares for the presentation of his thesis by showing that parts of it had been anticipated (pp. 5–13). He writes that Brink (1870:177 n. 14) saw the first 1800 lines (roughly, our Fragment A) as sharply distinct in the treatment of rhyme; that Child (1870:721) thought the part after the break (our Fragment C) better than the middle; that Skeat's evidence against Chaucer's authorship (1884, 1888*c*), rarely comes from our Fragments A and C; and that Lindner's argument (1887) suggests that the part after the gap (our Fragment C) was by a different author.

Kaluza's thesis, much like his 1890 formulation, appears in his table of contents (1893*a*: 255; quotations are my translations of Kaluza's German). Part I (pp. 15–52) argues that Fragments A (lines 1–1705) and C (lines 5811–7692) of *Rom* were done by a single translator who did not write Fragment B (lines 1706–5810); and Part II (pp. 53–248) argues that Chaucer is the author of Fragments A and C.

The evidence for the first proposition comes from three areas: the "relationship to the French original in A, C, and B" (pp. 15–41); dialect (pp. 41–44); and meter (pp. 44–52). With respect to the French source, Kaluza shows that "while A and C . . . follow the original almost line for line . . . Fragment B is more a paraphrase than a translation" (1893*a*: 15). A statistical comparison (pp. 17–18) reveals that "to the 1705 lines of A correspond 1660 lines of the original or 97.4%," that the percentage for C is almost identical, 97.3%, but that the percentage for B is lower, 84.7% (p. 17). Another such comparison studies the rate of retention of French rhyme-words in the translation: 17.7% in A, 12% in B, and 20.4% in C (pp. 19–20). Kaluza provides specimen parallel passages in the original and the translation (pp. 20–33) to illustrate a more detailed comparison of the differences between A and C on the one hand, B on the other (pp. 34–36). He notes differences in phraseology (pp. 36–38), like those between *Bialacoil* in B and *Fair-Welcoming* in C (see 5856n.) or *knoppe* in A and *bouton* in B (see 1721n.). He quotes (pp. 39–40) a letter from Skeat to document a difference in usage, "the disproportionately large number in Fragment

B of line-fillers like *withoute wene, withoute drede*, and others" (p. 39). Finally, he bolsters his case with one of Lounsbury's arguments (1892:2.72–75)—about the un-Chaucerian usage of *do* as an auxiliary—for, as he points out (pp. 40–41), Lounsbury's examples come from Fragment B.

To show the dialectal differences (pp. 41–44), Kaluza presents very full catalogues of examples to show that "the rhymes of A and C correspond in all essential points to the dialect of Chaucer's genuine poems" (p. 41) but that "Fragment B was written in another, far more Northern dialect than A and C, and therefore it is impossible that it was written by the same author" (p. 42).

Under the heading of metrics (pp. 44–50), Kaluza argues first that while A and C preserve purity of rhyme (pp. 44–46), B has many irregularities—assonances, defective vowel-rhymes, and neglect of final *-e* in rhyme (pp. 46–49); on this latter point, he supplies lists of questionable rhymes in *-ay* : *-aye*, in *-y* : *-ye*, and in consonant : consonant + *-e*. Next he presents evidence for the presence of separated rhymes in A and C as a Chaucerian feature (p. 50). These are rhymes with at least one multi-word member, e.g. 1001 *countenauncis : daunce is*, and Kaluza develops this point more fully in Part II.

In Part II Kaluza maintains that Chaucer wrote both Fragments, A and C. He argues first from the general character of the translation in Fragments A and C, seeing them as parts of a close "translation" like *Boece*, rather than of a looser "adaptation" or "imitation" like *TC* or *SNT*; "for Chaucer," writes Kaluza (citing *LGWP* G 264-65, F 324-29, 417–30), "uses the verb *translaten* only about actual translations, and *maken*, by contrast, about all his other poems" (p. 57). Moreover, he argues, the translation is largely correct in these fragments (pp. 59–61), and he defends the lapses in Fragment C that Lindner had alleged (1887:167) by showing that they "are not very serious and are explained in part by the faulty transmission of the English text, in part by the variant readings of the French manuscripts" (p. 60). In this connection, we might note that Marsh (1860:257) speaks of

"Chaucer's Romaunt" as "an imitation rather than a translation," but that he does so on the basis of passages (*Rom* 2187–97, 2225–33, 2255–74, quoted p. 258) that come from Fragment B.

The argument from dialect is brief (pp. 62–63). Kaluza deals with a few questionable forms but concludes that "the dialect of Fragments A and C agrees in all points with Chaucer's" (p. 63). The argument from meter, however, is a full one, based principally on the comparison of rhyme-technique in the two fragments and in the genuine works of Chaucer. He emphasizes two forms of rhyme, "separated" and rich, which, he says, "appear in quite the same way and in quite the same relationship in the two fragments as in Chaucer's other works" (p. 63). The tabulation of separated rhymes (pp. 64–65) yields frequencies of four cases per 1000 lines in both *Rom* A and C, the same frequency as in *BD* and Group G of *CT*, while *PF*, *TC* 1, and Group D of *CT* each have three cases per 1000 lines, and other parts of Chaucer's works have lower frequencies (p. 65).

The analysis of rich rhymes occupies much greater space (pp. 65–82). Kaluza regards rich rhyme, like separated rhyme, as a device that Chaucer used very frequently, and his catalogue divides rich rhymes into a number of sub-types under five main types of rhyme-words: 1) homonyms, e.g., *Rom* 1191 *present* (time) : *present* (gift); 2) those in which a simple word rhymes with a compound form, e.g., *Rom* 7191 *holden : biholden*; 3) those in which rhyme words differ only in their affixes, e.g., *Rom* 6613 *accorde : recorde*; 4) "leonine" rhymes, in which the consonance of the two rhyme-words extends to the syllable(s) before the rhyme-syllable, e.g. *Rom* 6355 *enhabite* (verb) : *abite* (noun); 5) "intermittent" or "extended" rhymes, those in which the vowels of pre-tonic syllables are the same in both rhyme-words, e.g., *Rom* 7341 *a route : aboute*. The tabular presentation of results (p. 81) again shows nearly identical frequencies in Fragments A and C in all categories except 4), where Fragment C has nearly double the frequency of Fragment A; Kaluza accounts for this discrepancy by calling attention to the "frequent adoption of French rhyme-words," which lend themselves to leonine rhymes, "in the long-winded speeches of Fals-Semblant" (p. 81). Frequencies in Chaucer's other works are similar, with the highest frequencies in the third category.

Kaluza admits that such evidence, while having some force, still is insufficient to prove Chaucer's authorship. He therefore provides evidence that "as a rule we rediscover in Chaucer's genuine works the same rhyme-words that come to be used in Fragments A and C—insofar as they are not simply taken over from the French exemplar, and in part even these—and we find them for the most part in exactly the same combinations and in the same frequency" (p. 82). He presents the evidence in the form of a rhyme-index to Fragments A and C, with, of course, references to Chaucer's other works (pp. 82–126).

From the rhyme index he concludes (pp. 82–83, 123) that 69% of the rhymes in the two fragments (70% in Fragment A, 69% in Fragment C) are those in which "both rhyme-words are either adopted from the French poem or . . . occur elsewhere in Chaucer's works in exactly the same combination"; that 22% (21% in A, 22% in C) are those in which "only one of the two rhyme-words is adopted from the French poem and the other is also found elsewhere in Chaucer, or both rhyme-words appear in Chaucer, but in other combinations"; and that 9% (in both A and C) are those in which "only one of the two rhyme-words, or even none whatever, is confirmed at the corresponding point of the French original or in Chaucer's genuine works." In effect, he shows a close agreement between A and C and a high percentage of correspondence to either the French original or to Chaucer's works; when he separates out the correspondences to Chaucer's works, he still finds that 61% of all the rhymes in A and C recur in Chaucer's genuine works in the same combinations, while 22% recur in other combinations (pp. 123–26), but only 9% "are neither verified in Chaucer nor borrowed from the original" (p. 127).

Kaluza attempts to minimize the possibly adverse significance of this last group by "indicating similar forms in Chaucer," by correcting "any possibly faulty transmission of the manuscript" (p. 128), by noting those cases in Fragment A that Skeat (1887, 1889) had reclaimed for Chaucer, and by presenting (pp. 129–34) an inventory of Chaucer's bi-forms of the same word, forms that provided alternate means of achieving rhymes and that suggest the possibility that, if we did not know they were Chaucer's, some of the stranger among them might be labeled "un-Chaucerian" (p. 133). He is left (p. 135) with a group, in Fragment C, of seven loose rhymes in -*y* : -*ye* (see 6111–12n.); he justifies them by arguing that "in a translation . . . we may not place the same strict demands on the purity of rhyme that we do in an independent poem" (pp. 135–36) and that they may have originated with a scribe (p. 137).

Kaluza adds that A and C agree with Chaucer's genuine works in other metrical peculiarities: "in the frequency of rhyme-separation (division of the two lines of a couplet by means of heavier punctuation), of enjambments and of alliteration, and also in the line-rhythm as a whole" (p. 137).

The fourth and last of Kaluza's arguments for Chaucer's authorship of Fragments A and C concern style. After a specific refutation (pp. 138–40) of Lindner on line 5814 (see 5814n.), Kaluza points out that we need as broadly-based and as exhaustive a stylistic argument as possible. He notes also (pp. 141–42) that, as we have seen, Fick (1886*a*: 164–65) and Lounsbury (1892:2.77–160, 537–551) had adduced parallels between *Rom* as a whole and the genuine works of Chaucer. He feels (p. 142) that Kittredge (1892:25) errs in rejecting the evidence of literal translations of the French, as well as the evidence of all phrases which appear elsewhere in any fourteenth-century poem; Kittredge's arguments, he says (p. 143), have not shaken his "conviction about the great significance of these linguistic agreements for the question of the authorship." To bolster his case he supplies a catalogue of parallel passages between Chaucer's works and the two fragments, A (pp. 144–190) and C (pp. 190–241). He introduces this catalogue with a preliminary list (pp. 143–44), without citations but with cross-references to Lounsbury, of a number of words and phrases that act as line-fillers and that appear very frequently in A and C as well as in Chaucer's other works.

The catalogue itself, he believes, proves that the two fragments, A and C, agree completely with Chaucer's genuine works in language-usage. He explores three possibilities that might account for the agreement: 1) that "the author of A and C has imitated Chaucer's language-usage," 2) that "Chaucer has imitated the usage of the fragments," or 3) that "Chaucer and the author of Fragments A and C are one and the same person" (p. 242). He rejects the first possibility because the translation is a faithful one, and it would be impossible for a disciple of Chaucer to copy his style in a literal translation, to say nothing of the pointlessness of re-doing a translation that Chaucer had already done (pp. 242–43). The second possibility—that Chaucer imitated the translation of another—is unlikely in view of his own close knowledge of *RR* and of the assumption that he himself had translated it. And this second assumption, says Kaluza, is conceivable only in terms of the third, that Chaucer was himself the author of the two fragments (p. 243).

In his conclusion (pp. 245–48), Kaluza suggests a scenario for the composition of *Rom* as we have it. At the instigation of some patron, perhaps John of Gaunt, Chaucer may have begun the translation, have broken off at line 1705, and later, knowing the size of the task, have returned to work on the Fals-Semblant section (Fragment C) as an independent unit (p. 246; see 5811–7292n.). Alternatively, Kaluza suggests (p. 247), Chaucer may have translated the Fals-Semblant passage as a first essay and the opening 1705 lines later. In either case, both fragments may have come to the hands of another poet who tried to fill in the gap between A and C and thus produced B. Later still, the three fragments may have been copied by a scribe in the order that we have them (p. 248). In this scenario Kaluza assumes a date of around 1380 for Chaucer's composition (p. 1).

The response to Kaluza's work was largely favorable. Lindner (1893) and Richard Wülker

(1893) both approve of his methods and generally accept his conclusions. Work on Lydgate leads Joseph Schick (1893:683–84) to suspect that if Chaucer's translation of *RR* influenced Lydgate's *Reason and Sensuality*, then that translation must have been one other than our *Rom* (cf. Schick, ed. 1891); but he concludes nevertheless that Kaluza correctly divides *Rom* into three fragments, and he believes that after all Fragment A may be a survivor of Chaucer's translation. In 1901 J. H. Lange refers to Kaluza's work as epoch-making (p. 397 n.1).

Skeat in turn (1894;1899:1.1–20; cf. 1911: vi–vii) restates his conviction that Chaucer wrote Fragment A but not C (or B), the position taken in Skeat's brief response (1890) to Kaluza's discovery of Fragment A. He reviews (1894;1899:1.3–11) the work of Lindner and Kaluza and takes up again the internal evidence as it relates to Fragments B, C, and A. In the discussion of Fragment B he advances four tests for authorship instead of the seven he had used earlier. In response to Cook (1887) and Lounsbury (1892:2.20–34), he drops the tests of vocabulary and the rhyming of *here* with *there*; he treats final -*e* as a feature of dialect; and he makes "strange rhymes" a subhead under "assonant rhymes." In response, probably, to Kaluza's work, he advances a new test, "the proportion of English to French"; his results are parallel to Kaluza's (cf. 1893*a*:17 n.2) and show that while in A and C "the translation runs nearly line for line," in B the translator uses nearly 18% more lines than the French (1.4). Skeat uses these tests to show only that Chaucer is not the author of Fragment B.

On Fragment C, Skeat goes a long way toward agreeing with Kaluza, but he finds reasons for not attributing C to Chaucer (1.6–7). He adduces the questionable rhymes in -*y* : -*ye* (cf. Kaluza above and 6111–12n.) along with *hors : wors* (cf. 5919–20n.), *fare : are* (cf. 6045–46n.), *atte last : agast* (6105–06n.), *pacience : vengeaunce* (6429–30n.), and others. And he indicates that separated rhymes are significantly more frequent in C than in works undoubtedly by Chaucer. But the latter argument is less detailed than Kaluza's treatment (1893*a*:63–65) and ignores its conclusion that the frequency in C approximates that in A and in Chaucer's *BD*. Skeat's contrast between Fragment B's *Bialacoil* and Fragment C's *Fair-Welcoming* (see 5856n.) suggests only that Fragments B and C are not by the same author. And his reference (1.7) to Lindner's conclusion (1887) "that Chaucer certainly never wrote fragment C" is rather dated, since six years later (1893:104) Lindner had found that Kaluza argued in a convincing manner that A and C are Chaucer's; moreover, as we have seen, Skeat himself had argued earlier (1888*b*:xxv), against Lindner, that if any part of *Rom* is by Chaucer, it is the last fragment (our C). Thus Lindner and Skeat reversed their positions on Fragment C.

On Fragment A, Skeat supports Kaluza by noting that the rhymes in -*y* are kept separate from those in -*ye* and that there are no Northern forms, no merely assonant rhymes, and no other questionable rhymes that cannot be accounted for (1.8–11). Two years later (1896*b*:478), Skeat grants that "it is no longer possible to doubt the genuineness of Fragment A."

But in the same year, Karl Luick first calls attention to a questionable rhyme that Skeat had not noted, the Northern rhyme *love : behove* (lines 1091–92; see n.). Luick (1896: 268) feels that its presence justifies a lively doubt in Chaucer's authorship of A. Kaluza (1897) counters by noting other strange dialectal combinations in the rhymes of Chaucer's genuine works (cf. 1893*a*:133–34). In a brief exchange (1898), both Luick and Kaluza restate their positions, Luick attempting to place the burden of proof on Kaluza, Kaluza arguing that the external evidence (*LGWP*, Lydgate, Deschamps) creates the initial probability and that the internal evidence is preponderantly in favor of Chaucer as author of A. Emil Koeppel (1898:146n.) declares that his willingness to believe with Kaluza in the authenticity of Fragment A has of course been shaken by Luick's discovery but not yet abandoned. Skeat does not refer to this controversy when he calls Chaucer's authorship of Fragment A "as good as settled by my discovery . . . that Fragment A is

expressly quoted by Lydgate in his 'Complaint of the Black Knight,' l. 80, where he introduces the expression *softe as (any) veluët* from [*Rom*] 1420, where the original French version has nothing corresponding to *soft* or to *velvet*" (1899:66; cf. Skeat 1896*a* and the note to line 1420, below). Skeat adds a further parallel between *Rom* 1515–16 (see note) and *Complaint of the Black Knight* 111–12 (ed. Skeat 1897:249).

The focus of Skeat's article, however, is on two points relating to parallels between *Rom* and *The Kingis Quair*, by James I of Scotland. For the first he adduces verbal parallels to show that James was familiar with Fragment A (see 1080–1124n.). In a continuation two weeks later, he extends his argument by proposing that James was the author of Fragment B. He finds "the same phenomena" in Fragment B as in *The Kingis Quair*: "the occasional (not universal) use of final -*e*, many Northumbrian forms and rhymes, an artificial language, the southern prefix *y-* to past participles . . . and actually the staggering fact that the scribe has unconsciously preserved some Kentish forms, and even a Kentish rhyme" (1899:130). The same suggestion appears a year later in Skeat's book, *The Chaucer Canon* (1900:84–89). We shall return to this book in connection with Koch's denial of Chaucer's authorship.

Denial of Chaucer's Authorship: Koch. As we have seen, on the basis of a single Northern rhyme Luick rejected Chaucer's authorship of Fragment A and, in effect, of *Rom* entire. This position is argued more fully and tenaciously by John Koch, first in 1890 (see above), and then in a series of papers published over the next thirty years (see Bibliography). Koch (1900*a*) takes issue with Skeat and Kaluza over the authenticity of Fragment A—and thus of the entire *Rom*—by presenting a list of twenty doubtful rhymes (pp. 66–67), twelve of which he had adduced in 1890 (see notes to lines 7–8, 53–54, 55–56, 183–84, 415–16, 457–58, 481–82, 505–06, 579–80, 661–62, 887–88, 1091–92, 1341–43, 1673–74, 1705–06); in addition, he finds in Fragment A a greater frequency of unique rhymes than in *BD* or *HF* (p. 69), a number of metrical irregularities which contradict Chaucerian technique (lines 124, 657, 923, 1304, 1326, 1587), and some questions about the validity of Kaluza's evidence from rich rhymes and from parallel passages in A and C. On this last point (pp. 70–72), he culls examples from Kaluza that he finds superficial and "worthless as evidence of identical authorship"; he also cites Kittredge's strictures on arguments from vocabulary. He makes the point that if, as Kaluza believes, Fragments A and C have the same author, then those, like Skeat, who object to Chaucer as the author of Fragment C could object to Fragment A as well (pp. 72–73).

Skeat (1900:149–53) regrets that Kaluza maintains his thesis that Chaucer wrote both A and C. In continuing to defend Fragment A he examines Koch's list of twenty doubtful rhymes; he concludes that "they are quite of a different character from those . . . in . . . Fragment B or Fragment C, that eight of them "are mere mistakes, and tell the other way," and that "the objections practically fail" (p. 152). Further, he points out, as many before had done, the weaknesses of arguments from vocabulary (pp. 152–53).

Koch, in a second article (1900*b*) disputes Skeat's assertion (1899:66) that Lydgate borrowed from Fragment A in his *Complaint of the Black Knight* (cf. Skeat 1896*a*, 1897: xliv–xlv). Koch claims that Lydgate probably used *RR* itself or, possibly, another translation.

The controversy continues in two reviews, by Kaluza and Koch, of Skeat's *The Chaucer Canon* (1900). Kaluza (1901:865–66) summarizes the various positions, noting that the majority of Chaucer scholars share Skeat's thesis, that Skeat's examination of Fragment B shows Lounsbury's view to be untenable, and that Skeat has refuted Koch's view with little difficulty. Koch's attempt (1900*b*) to refute Skeat, he feels, has been unsuccessful. Incidentally, he notes that Koch has overlooked Ernst Sieper's discovery (1898:240–44) of the numerous accords between Fragment A and another Lydgate poem, *Reason and Sensuality* (cf. Sieper, ed. 1901–03:2.79–81).

Koch's review (1902), understandably, devotes much space to the debate with Skeat.

An interesting development of his attempt to refute the idea that Lydgate borrowed from (Chaucer's) *Rom* is his gradual veering toward the idea that Lydgate, rather than Chaucer, was the author of *Rom*. He picks up (p. 454) Kaluza's citation of Sieper and admits, without granting Chaucer's authorship, that Lydgate knew *Rom*. He then (p. 455) cites further parallels between Lydgate and *Rom*, parallels supplied by Hugo Lange (1901 and private letter), and he quotes Schick's observation (ed. 1891:lxii) that "the language of [*Rom*] often reminds one of Lydgate, both in its rhymes and in its vocabulary." He declares (pp. 455–56) that he will *not* conclude from these parallels that Lydgate is the author of Fragment A but that they offer "more similarities with the language of the monk of Bury than with that of Chaucer." The phrase "monk of Bury" reflects Lange's hint (1901: 405) about the coincidence of the eighteenth-century appearance of the Glasgow MS at Bury Saint Edmunds (see "Description of the Manuscript" below), where Lydgate was a monk.

It is useful at this point to distinguish between the positions of Lange and Koch. Lange (1911:338 n.2) was somewhat concerned that Hammond (1908:453) had misrepresented him as arguing "that the writer of Fragment B was John Lydgate." Hammond had some reason, however, since Lange had said that he had come across "various pieces of evidence which point to Chaucer's principal pupil, Lydgate, or at least a poet close to him, as the author of Fragment B" (1901:397). But two years later he backs away from this identification (1903:159), and still later (1911: 341) he denies any possibility that Lydgate could be the author of Fragment B because the rhyme and meter of B contravene Lydgate's technique. Lange also rejects Skeat's conclusion that King James I of Scotland was the author of B (1903:159). He agrees, however, that Fragment A, a performance superior to Lydgate's (1911:340–41), was written by Chaucer, and he clearly supports Skeat's refutation of Koch's twenty objections to the rhymes of Fragment A (1911:343–44; 1913; but see also 505n. below).

Nevertheless, Lange's early hints provided Koch with material for his conclusion that Lydgate or a pupil of his wrote not only Fragment B but the whole of *Rom* (Koch 1912: 107–09). For example, Lange had taken up Arnold's suggestion (1878*b*:67) that an eighteenth-century note in the Glasgow MS might confirm the view that MS is an East-Anglian transcript; this note (see "Provenance") indicates that MS was owned by a surgeon of Bury Saint Edmunds. Lange, although he grants that MS's appearance there was a mere accident, still wonders if it might not support the hypothesis of Lydgate's authorship (1901:405). But when Koch (1912:107) argues that the entire *Rom* was written in the region of Bury Saint Edmunds, he pushes Lange's hint too far. Moreover, he incorrectly attributes to Skeat the opinions of Arnold, whom Skeat quotes only to confute (1884:443). It was Arnold who first mentioned the 1720 note and who showed some confusion between Northern and East-Midland dialects, a confusion that Koch seems to perpetuate.

Koch returns to the authorship question in 1921, urged, as he was to say later (1925:206), to reply to Lange again. After a summary of earlier arguments (1921:163–68), he puts forward, somewhat tentatively, an argument based on the special vocabulary of Fragment A, and he suggests evidence of Northern rhymes in Fragment A as well as in B and C (pp. 171–73). As before, he associates Fragment A with the region of Bury Saint Edmunds and remains convinced that Chaucer was not the author (p. 174). As a final statement of Koch's view, this article is perhaps less clearly presented than his early formulations, especially those of 1890 and 1900 (cf. Peck's summary, 1988:26–27).

A subsequent adherent to Koch's view, Nesta Thompson (1926), is able to use the galleys of Tatlock and Kennedy's *Concordance* (1927) in examining the vocabulary of *Rom* and Chaucer's undisputed works; she also studies apocope (of final *e* within the line) in *Rom* and in Chaucer's works in "four-stress metre" (pp. 6, 50). She recognizes that these tests are not conclusive but records her "conviction that Chaucer had no hand in

[*Rom*] as we possess it today" (p. 1). She cites (p. 69) Pollard (1893:141–42) and Fansler (1914:130) for their expressions of skepticism about Chaucer's authorship, but she agrees (pp. 5–6) with A. D. Schoch that "perhaps no entirely satisfactory solution . . . will ever be reached, unless another manuscript of the *Romaunt* should be found with some indication of the author's identity" (Schoch 1906: 358). She cites Lounsbury (1892:1.377–78; cf. 2.81–82) in support of her belief that "the best test is . . . a certain something in the work of every great writer which differentiates him from every one else" (p. 70), but she admits that this test is "the strongest and at the same time the weakest." The fact that her conclusion about Chaucer's authorship differs completely from Lounsbury's may indicate the weakness.

Support of Chaucer as Sole Author of the Romaunt: Lounsbury *to Brusendorff.* We have seen that even after the uncritical assumption that Chaucer wrote the entire *Rom*, and in opposition to the growing skepticism about his authorship, there remain some who would claim all of it as his. Chief among these are Lounsbury (1892) and Aage Brusendorff (1925). We have looked at Lounsbury's work above. Even though his book appeared in 1892, he dismisses Kaluza's announcement of 1890 with the briefest recognition and does not even mention him by name. Nor does he appear subsequently to have dealt adequately with Kaluza's detailed distinctions among the fragments, although he pursues the matter, principally against Skeat and Kittredge, in the columns of the *Manchester Guardian* and the *New York Daily Tribune.* Although little fresh material appeared, it may be useful, in order to clarify the citations of Kaluza (1895:338–39) and Hammond (1908:453), to give a brief chronological summary of the controversy.

It arose in 1894 when the *Manchester Guardian* review of the first volume of Skeat's new edition took Skeat to task for not recognizing Lounsbury's arguments in favor of Chaucer's authorship of the entire *Rom* (Unidentified reviewer 1894*a*). Skeat (1894*b*) responded with references to his letters in *The Academy* (1890–92) and to the work of

Kittredge (1892). After the reviewer's rejoinder (1894*b*), Lounsbury entered the discussion with a letter to the *Manchester Guardian* (1894*a*); an article in the *New York Daily Tribune* (1894*b*) gives an account of the controversy, from Lounsbury's viewpoint, and reprints the letters of Skeat and Lounsbury. In the following year, Lounsbury published a long review of Skeat's edition in two issues of the *New York Daily Tribune*, where, in the second part of the review (1895:22), he restated his position on the authorship question. Sometime in 1894, Skeat published a further essay to show that Fragment B is not Chaucer's; "Prof. Lounsbury," he writes (1894*c*:675), "is still unconvinced. He will not admit two authors for the *Romaunt of the Rose*, still less would he admit that there are *three*."

Kaluza came to the defense of Skeat and Kittredge in a short article (1895), and the next year, in a full review of Skeat's edition, he devoted a short section to the controversy (1896:275–76). In both of these, he chided Lounsbury for some of his rhetorical excesses in accusing Skeat of lacking literary judgment as well as logic and of changing his stand to suit the latest findings of German scholars like Lindner and Kaluza.

Louise Pound, like Lounsbury in 1892, also leaves Kaluza unnamed when she refers to "certain German scholars" (1896:97, 101). After an opening defense of Lounsbury against Skeat, she presents additional evidence that *Rom* is Chaucer's. The evidence consists of a statistical analysis of the relative frequency of five sentence features: words (i.e., sentence length); predications; simple sentences; initial conjunctions; and interior conjunctions. She tabulates these features for three groups of works: the genuine works of Chaucer, "the group of works generally acknowledged to be spurious" (p. 99), and *Rom*; additionally, she compares the three fragments of *Rom* on the same basis. Her results show that the genuine and spurious works contrast significantly in all these features: the genuine works have shorter sentences, fewer predications per sentence, more simple sentences, fewer initial and interior conjunctions, but the genuine works

and *Rom* show nearly the same frequencies in all categories (pp. 99–101). Again, when she compares the three fragments to each other, she finds little difference among them; if anything, Fragment B is slightly closer to Fragment A than is Fragment C.

Hammond (1908:453) says that Pound's is the only published attempt to support Lounsbury's view but adds that "Miss Pound no longer maintains the thesis of this paper." There had, however, been some other support. George Saintsbury (1906:1.145–46) enters a very limited defense of Chaucer's authorship by objecting to Bradshaw's rhyme tests: "it *is* impossible to argue with persons who say that Chaucer never rhymes *Y* to *ye*, and then admit that he did in *Sir Thopas*." Henry B. Hinckley (1906) argues that Chaucer was influenced by the Northern forms of *Ywaine and Gawin*, that the Northern forms are not confined to Fragment B, and that, while the evidence is not conclusive, it "makes it probable" that *Rom* is entirely the work of Chaucer. Skeat (1906) replies in detail to Hinckley's allegation that Northern forms exist outside of Fragment B; he also points out that the other rhymes adduced exist in several Northern writers, not exclusively in *Ywaine and Gawin*. Hinckley restates his case (1907*a*) and suggests that Chaucer might well have used occasional Northern forms, since "great poets have sometimes used more than one dialect."

Cook (1919:24–25) suggests that in a specific passage of Fragment B (2837–50) there is reason to think that Chaucer is the translator; he finds that the rhymes are Chaucerian and that certain phrases correspond to Chaucer's usage. W. P. Reeves (1923) argues for Chaucer's authorship of the entire *Rom* by suggesting that Skeat's analysis of the break between Fragments A and B is wrong. MS *dide*, he says, is not an auxiliary as Skeat thinks (see 1705n.), but a form of *dyed*, as in TH[1]. Thus there is no syntactic break and no necessity to assume a change of author. Reeves does not deal with the rhyme or with any other of Skeat's arguments.

Brusendorff (1925), making use of Langlois's edition of *RR*, defends Chaucer's authorship by arguing that *Rom* is based on "a greatly contaminated [French] MS., showing readings from various subdivisions of groups I and II, not unlike such a MS. as Brit. Mus. Eg. 881 (κω)" (p. 319; for very different results from the same evidence, see Sutherland, below). Brusendorff elaborates his theory by suggesting that the Glasgow MS is at least twice removed from the Chaucerian original (p. 302). (For his views on the relationship of MS and TH[1] [pp. 296–302], see the Textual Commentary below.) To explain the Northern dialect of Fragment B, he assumes scribal changes (pp. 302–08) and a Northern reviser (p. 377). To account for the present state of the text, he starts from the notion of a "greatly contaminated MS" as "the French original of the ME. translation" (pp. 318–19) and goes on to examine Kaluza's division into three fragments, a division that is, he thinks, "really based on curiously weak evidence" (p. 320). Brusendorff feels that "the essential unity of the translation" (p. 348) is more likely than a "composite origin" (p. 326).

Nevertheless, he recognizes "that the text is of such an extraordinarily unsatisfactory kind as to demand an equally extraordinary explanation" (p. 326). To account for such anomalies as the shift from *knoppe* in Fragment A to *bouton* in Fragment B (see 1721n.) or from *Bialacoil* in Fragment B to *Fair-Welcoming* in Fragment C (see 5856n.), he posits "later interference . . . almost certainly due to the same man all through" (p. 348). This "reviser" (p. 349 and elsewhere) produced the immediate ancestor of the Glasgow MS. Brusendorff reconstructs the process as follows (pp. 382–83):

originally composed in the Standard English of the late fourteenth century [*Rom*] has only been preserved in a version, written down in the beginning of the fifteenth century by some person from the North Midlands, who had once learned the translation by heart, and who still knew its first 1800 lines or so almost perfectly; during the next 4000 lines, however, his memory constantly kept failing him, so that at last he had to break off abruptly and start again at an episode which occurred nearly 6000 lines further on in the translation, but which he remembered better, until

after some 1900 lines he had to break off finally, still almost 10000 lines from the end. While fully explaining the mixed dialect and the faulty rhymes as well as the gradually increasing expansion, the insertions and repetitions, this interpretation also accounts for the anticipations and transpositions, and for the errors through hearing.

Brusendorff characterizes his theoretical reviser as "a younger contemporary of Chaucer" (p. 415) who relied on his memory and thus produced the garbled state of the text as we have it.

In the remainder of his chapter on *Rom*, Brusendorff reviews the external evidence for Chaucer's authorship: Deschamps, *LGWP*, Lydgate (pp. 383–87); and he adds further citations of the use that Lydgate made of *Rom* and *RR* (pp. 387–92). In order to strengthen his case for Chaucer's authorship of *Rom*, he introduces parallels between *RR* and Chaucer's recognized works (pp. 392–414); some of these parallels, he believes, are with *Rom* rather than the original (pp. 402–07). He closes with suggestions for emendation of *Rom* (pp. 416–25); some of these appear in the notes.

Robinson (RB[1], p. 989; RB[2], p. 872) calls this "the boldest sort of emendation to restore this supposed Chaucerian original"; and he concludes that "Professor Brusendorff's hypothesis of a transmitter by memory is a rather desperate measure to save the Chaucerian authorship of the whole poem." David (RI) remarks, in his note to *Rom* 5486, that "the conclusion need not be that Fragment B is a garbled version of Chaucer's translation but that the translator was familiar with Chaucer's poetry and used it in appropriate places." Sutherland's work tends to confirm this assessment, since he also makes use of the corpus of variants in the Langlois edition to arrive at an entirely different textual theory. We shall consider his work in the course of a survey of those twentieth-century writers who consider *Rom* to be only partly by Chaucer.

The Twentieth Century. Despite the divergent efforts of Koch and Brusendorff, in the twentieth century the dominant opinion is that Chaucer is probably the author of Fragment A only. To a large extent this opinion reflects the influence of Skeat's edition, but before tracing that influence, it will be convenient to consider the contribution made by A. D. Schoch (1906).

Schoch presents some new data to document the differences among the three fragments (pp. 340–52): the frequency of mistranslation; variations in the translation of single words; departures from the original in the gender of characters; differences in the translation of French double negatives and of exact numbers; frequency of retention of rhyming terminations from the original; frequency of interlinear padding; and variations in the accuracy of treatment of the original. He finds a few agreements among the fragments but more differences.

While Schoch concludes that *Rom* really is comprised of three identifiable fragments, he is careful to avoid the inference that each is by a different translator, since such an inference must depend on a premise, difficult to prove, regarding a writer's consistency of usage. Observing that none of the fragments is absolutely consistent with Chaucer's usage elsewhere, Schoch points out that Lounsbury, Kaluza, Skeat, and Koch come to different conclusions regarding Chaucer's authorship of *Rom* or its parts because they apply different standards of consistency, Koch requiring absolute consistency with Chaucer's known works, Lounsbury allowing the greatest latitude. Schoch criticizes all of these writers for not explaining or defending their assumptions about what degree of inconsistency is allowable. He adds that "no entirely satisfactory solution of the difficulty [may] ever be reached" (p. 358).

Schoch suggests that opinion generally favors the views of either Skeat or Kaluza, not because those scholars offer weightier evidence or more cogent arguments, but because they represent the middle ground between the extreme positions of Lounsbury and Koch. Whatever the merits of this view, it is certainly true that after Skeat the major editors accept at least the possibility of Chaucer's authorship of Fragment A. Mark Liddell (1898, in GL) writes: "All that we can say at present is that A . . . may be part of the translation Chaucer says he made; that C is also possibly Chaucer's, but this assumption is less likely than the former" (pp. liv–lv). F. N. Robinson (1933, 1957), while noting, as do others, that the question of authorship "can perhaps never be positively decided on the internal evidence which appears to be alone available" (RB[1], p. 989; RB[2], p. 872), nevertheless makes the usual assessment: "Fragment A . . . accords well enough with Chaucer's usage in language and meter. . . . But Fragment B, on the testimony of the dialect alone, can hardly be Chaucer's; and the non-Chaucerian forms in Fragment C, though fewer than in B, would probably be held evidence enough for the rejection of an independent poem." Alfred David (1987) expresses a similar opinion somewhat more cautiously ("insofar as one can arrive at any consensus"; RI, p. 1103). John Fisher (1977; 1989), following Sutherland's textual and authorial theory (see below), likewise finds that only Fragment A "meets all the requirements of Chaucer's dialect, prosody, and style" (FI, p. 711).

The editors' consensus appears also in general treatments of Chaucer. Emile Legouis (1910; 1913:52) notes that "most commentators incline to think" that Fragment A is Chaucer's. Robert Dudley French summarizes the scholarship (1927; 1947:78–80) and concludes that "only Fragment A can certainly be attributed" to Chaucer (p. 81). John Speirs (1951:35) asks: "who else could have composed the first part at least" of *Rom*? This consensus has been little disputed, and those who write about *Rom* in other connections usually take Chaucer's authorship of Fragment A as a given.

Ronald Sutherland also feels that "there is every indication to believe Chaucer was the author of Fragment A" (1959:183). His conclusion, however, is based not on stylistic analysis but on comparison of *Rom* with French MSS of *RR*. Like Brusendorff (see above), he attempts to account for the peculiarities of *Rom* by finding their sources in the groups, families, or individual MSS of Langlois's classification. Unlike Brusendorff, who posits a single greatly contaminated

French MS as the basis for the ancestor of the fragmentary Glasgow MS, Sutherland posits French MSS of different families as sources for two different translations, Fragment A and Fragments B and C. Sutherland's surprising view that B and C were composed by a single translator is anticipated by Robinson's critique of Brusendorff: "It seems more reasonable to assign B and C to a second translator, perhaps a Northern Chaucerian, than to explain them as works of Chaucer corrupted in transmission" (RB[1], p. 989; RB[2], p. 872). While Sutherland concludes that the ancestor of Fragment A was done by "a Londoner who worked from a *Roman* H MS," he finds that the ancestor of Fragments B and C was composed by "a Northerner who worked from a *Roman* R MS" (1968:xxxiv). Manuscripts of these two translations, Sutherland thinks, were combined by a third person who introduced revisions based on the B and G families of *RR* MSS, and this revised version, he believes, was the common ancestor of the Glasgow MS and Thynne's edition of 1532 (1968:xxxvii).

Sutherland's theory, as it appears in 1968, differs in some details from his earlier explanation (1959), where he argues that Fragments B and C had a B MS (not an R MS) of Meun's poem as source, and that the latter portion of Lorris's poem (B₁) derived from "a source MS which, although not positively from the R family, was certainly of Group II" (p. 183). Also, in 1968 Sutherland elaborates his theory of the reviser to account for the presence of readings that correspond to the B and G families. For his treatment of one piece of evidence for the presence of a reviser, see 1816n.

While most twentieth-century scholars are content to assume that Fragment A is Chaucer's, few (e.g., Root 1906; 1922:55) accept Fragment C as well. Not until the work of Xiang Feng (1990) is there a systematic defense of Kaluza's proposition that Chaucer wrote Fragments A and C though not B. After countering Skeat's arguments against Chaucer's authorship of C (cf. Skeat 1890), employing newer forms of Kaluza's rhyme tests, and amassing "overwhelming evidence [for] the

close similarities between A and C, in both usage and style, as well as their equal distance from B," Feng concludes that "there is no reason why common authorship of A and C should be thought impossible" (1990:iii).

In Feng's view the most important of Skeat's arguments against Chaucer's authorship of C rests on six loose rhymes in -*y*/-*ye* (lines 6111, 6301, 6339, 6373, 6875, 7317; see SK 1.6; Skeat 1900:90–91; Feng 1990:22–23, 48, 58–67); Kaluza (1893*a*:106, 136) lists a seventh rhyme at line 7571, from a passage that appears only in TH[1]. Skeat's argument, based on Bradshaw, is that such rhymes do not appear in Chaucer (except intentionally in *Thopas*). Feng's counter-argument (1990:58–67) holds that Chaucer's mature practice of distinguishing -*y* from -*yë* in rhyme was fashionable among late fourteenth-century poets in the French tradition, including Gower, the *Pearl*-poet, Hoccleve, and Lydgate (except in his early work); that the distinction was not observed in all English poets or in current English speech; and that "it is not impossible that the six instances in Fragment C are the relic of Chaucer's early literary apprenticeship, when he has not yet caught the 'fashion' of avoiding -*y*/-*ye*" (p. 63). This argument reinforces Kaluza's (1893*a*:136), which justifies the rhymes as liberties in a close translation. Feng even suggests (1990:66), as Kaluza had done earlier (1893*a*:247), that Fragment C may have been translated before Fragment A.

Feng also gives considerable attention to the pronounced differences between Fragments A and C on the one hand and Fragment B on the other. In this context it is useful to note complementary results in the work of other scholars. Schoch (1906:353), for example, had found that while B tends to retain more rhymes in -*ance* : -*ence* and -*ise* than do the other fragments, "Kaluza's statistics show that B in general had less of a tendency to retain the riming words of his original than the other translators had." B. F. Huppé (1948), in turn, finds that Fragment B is less exact in the translation of scholastic terminology than is Fragment C (see 4456–69n., 7465–72n.). John Fleming (1967) suggests that, at a point where there is no parallel in the French original (2326 "Songes . . . make"), the translator of Fragment B may have used Chaucer's description of the Squire (*GP* 95, "He koude songes make"); if so, the fragment must be later than *GP* and by someone other than Chaucer (see 2325–28n., 2326n.).

To show the close similarities between A and C and their equal distance from B, Feng supplies "a set of new tests of the use and translation of rimes and rime words in the three fragments" (1990:69). He notes that these tests are lacking in Skeat and that they are flawed in Kaluza because of the shortcomings of his French text and because "none of his well-prepared lists of rimes and parallelisms includes data on Fragment B," without which "the evidence induced from his full citation of identical rimes and rime words, verbal repetitions, and parallel passages between A and C and between these and Chaucer's genuine works becomes much less persuasive than it should be" (p. 74).

Feng bases his new tests (p. 95), accordingly, on three indices that go beyond the material of Kaluza (and of Geissman 1952:262–85, as Feng notes): (1) Index of Rime Words in *Le Roman* and Their Translations (Appendix A); (2) Index of Cognate Rimes and Rime Pairs in *The Romaunt* (Appendix B); and (3) Index of Common Rimes in *The Romaunt* (Appendix C). Unlike Kaluza's and Geissman's, these indices cover all three fragments. The first index, the main one, includes "both the French rimes and their English translations," and Feng compiles it "from French into English, following the translation, so that the different styles of the translators may be clearly shown and properly examined" (1990:96). Since "the use of cognate rimes is an important aspect of Chaucer's style in the *Romaunt*," Feng compiles the second index "for convenient reference" (p. 96). The third index compiles common rimes in the three fragments of *Rom* and in *BD* (p. 266); as a supplement to the first two indices, it shows that "the *Book of the Duchess* and Fragments A and C (BD-A-C) share more COMMON RIMES and considerably more RIME PAIRS than any 3- and 2-

piece combinations [of BD, A, B, C] except A-B-C" (p. 116).

The first index provides the material for Feng's most important tests (p. 98), those based on rhymes and rhyme words. His results (p. 118) confirm the conclusion of Kaluza (1893*a*:17–18) and Skeat (SK 1.3–4) that B differs from A and C in having a significantly higher proportion of English to French lines (118.3:100) than do A (103.5:100) or C (102.9:100). Besides being prolix, B is less careful to preserve the French; it adapts a lower percentage of French rhyme words by means of English cognates for rhyme (12.5%) than do A (18.18%) or C (20.51%); again, this result confirms that of Kaluza (1893*a*:19–20), who accounts for the slightly higher frequency of rhyme-word retention in C by citing "the clearly theological discussion of Fals-Semblant" (p. 20).

Feng shows similar results in other tests (1990:98, 118). In general, whether they use cognates or non-cognates, Fragments A and C retain higher percentages of French rhyme words than does Fragment B. Conversely, another test shows the "percentage of French rime words left untranslated, or 'Chaucer's defeat'" (Test 7, p. 98; result 5, p. 118; cf. pp. 82, 117, and Geissman 1952:166); the percentage of "defeats" in Fragment B is nearly twice as large (30.5%) as that in A (15.66%) and over half again as large as that in C (18.97%).

Feng concludes that "in all major aspects of style of translation, A and C come very close to each other, in sharp contrast to B," and that "given the overwhelming evidence for a common authorship of A and C, one cannot but concede there is a strong possibility that C, as well as A, is by Chaucer" (1990:118, 121).

These conclusions clearly support Kaluza's of a century earlier, those that gave rise to Skeat's defense of the position that only Fragment A is Chaucer's. Feng is probably right in saying that Skeat's has been "the accepted view" (1990:1), but many of those who have accepted it have left open the possibility that C may be Chaucer's. Feng's work strengthens this possibility.

Summary

The authorship question—meaning the question of whether Chaucer wrote part or all of *Rom* as it exists in the Glasgow MS—cannot be decided on the basis of the external evidence that he made a translation of *RR*; and there is no external evidence that he wrote *Rom* itself. The internal evidence has evoked conflicting opinions. Koch denies Chaucer's authorship on the basis of evidence that leads Brusendorff to assume that the un-Chaucerian features are due to a scribe or to a North Midlands memorial version of an earlier translation by Chaucer. Thynne's inclusion of *Rom* in the 1532 *Works* is no guarantee of its authenticity, and the increasing doubt in the nineteenth century that it was Chaucer's led to the major investigations of Skeat and Kaluza. The partial consensus that emerged in the early 1890s—that at least Fragment A is Chaucer's—is still not capable of ultimate proof; but the inclusion of *Rom* in the collected works of Chaucer, where other works have been rejected as spurious, is itself evidence of its general acceptance as partly Chaucer's. Clearly, "for excellent reasons" (RB², p. 564), Chaucer scholars do not want to lose *Rom* and are willing to print it in its entirety even though part of it be inauthentic. As Larry Benson puts it (RI, p. xxvi), "all three parts of *The Romaunt of the Rose* are printed [in RI] because some may be genuine and because the *Romaunt* provides the student with a contemporary translation of a work that had an enormous influence on fourteenth-century literature in general and on Chaucer's works in particular."

These excellent reasons may bear further exploration (see below). First, however, we can look at the theories of date.

Date of Composition

The present discussion will consider primarily the date of composition of *Rom*, but since many think that Chaucer wrote a translation that is at least partly distinct from *Rom*, it will be necessary to touch on the question of whether and when he translated *RR*. For opinions on the date of the Glasgow MS and for theories on its makeup, see the section on "Description of the Manuscript" in the Textual Commentary below.

As with authorship, there is no certain evidence of the date of composition; in fact we are often in the position of trying to establish date on the insecure basis of an assumption about the author. As Pollard put it (1931:53):

Those who regard the present version as in whole or part textually Chaucer's must suppose it to have been written before his principles of versification were fixed, *i.e.* considerably earlier than 1369. If Chaucer's version be wholly lost or if some explanation can be accepted . . . as to how his text came to be so mutilated and degraded, we should be inclined to bring it towards the end of the 'seventies, partly to link it up with the *Hous of Fame* in the same metre, partly because the manner of the reference to it in the *Legende* [*LGW*] does not suggest that it was translated in Chaucer's youth.

This is a fair summary of the two main positions on the question of date; for other summaries, see Tatlock (1907:x) and Root (1906; 1922:55–56). There are, however, some variants of these two positions.

The earliest opinions assume Chaucer's authorship. We may begin with an apparent dating by John Bale (1557–59:2.58), who states that Chaucer translated the "*De arte amandi*" of "Ioannes Mone" and added the title "The Romaunt of thœ rose"; Bale concludes, "it [*Rom*?] is said to have become illustrious in fame in the year of our Lord 1390" ("Anno Domino 1390 claruisse fertur"). Bale offers no hint as to his source of information. The next suggestion of a date appears in William Thomas's revision of John Dart's Life of Chaucer (in the Preface to UR, folio f1): *RR* "seems to have been translated by *Chaucer* while he was at Court, and about the time of the Rise of *Wickliffe's* Opinions, it consisting of violent Invectives against the Religious Orders." Although the basis of this inference is doubtful, the implied date (mid 1370s) is one favored by later scholarship. The Dart/Thomas discussion places *Rom* in a list of Chaucer's works arranged chronologically, and in this list Rom appears ahead of all other works now regarded as genuine. Warton (1774–81:1.382), by contrast, refers to the *Book of the Duchess* ("his *Dreme*") as having been "written long before" *Rom.* (Furnivall's identification of the "Dreme" with the *Yle of Ladyes* [note, ed. Warton 1871:2.326] is almost certainly wrong; cf. UR, pp. 404, 572; for the origin of the confusion in SP"'s "Arguments," see Pearsall 1984*b*:80–81). Warton offers no evidence, and the dating is in fact exceptional, since most subsequent writers place *Rom* before *BD.* Tyrwhitt (1775:4.80) regards *Rom* as, "probably, one of [Chaucer's] earliest performances." So also do Sandras (1859:37), Ebert (1862:88, citing Pauli 1860:194), and Brink (1867:312). Like Sandras, Brink (1870: 16–18) finds confirmation for a date before *BD*, noting that *RR* had influenced *BD*, that Chaucer had more time for working on the translation before 1369 than after, that such a project was appropriate to apprentice years, and that if he had not carried it out then, he would hardly have done so later, when he began his independent creations. Brink regards *Rom* as the oldest of the poems that are mentioned in *LGWP* but grants that he cannot establish an exact date of composition (pp. 21, 25–26). Furnivall (1871:7) expresses a slight difference of opinion: "the best early parts of the *Romaunt* [are] perhaps too good to be Chaucer's earliest work." But Fick (1886*a*: 163–64; 1886*b*) accepts Brink's theory of an early date—and of Chaucer's authorship—as a sufficient explanation of the false rhymes in *Rom.*

Brink, however, changes his mind about author and date. He comes to think that Chaucer translated *RR* around 1380 and that, because the existing version in the Glasgow MS suggests an earlier date, it cannot be Chaucer's (1883–96:2.76–77; 1892:9–10). He bases his theory on *LGWP*, particularly G 344–48 and 254–65. As we have seen above (see "Authorship"), he takes the phrase "som persone" (G 346, F 367) to refer to John of Gaunt, the line "For he hath write many a bok er this" (G 348) to preclude an early date of composition, and the conjunction of "the Rose and ek Crisseyde" (G 344) to indicate

consecutive dates of composition for the two. We might note that Brink was among the first to take the G version of *LGWP* as later than the F (1892:13–19; cf. Koch 1890:81–87). For further consideration of *LGWP*, see below, "Chaucer and the *Roman de la Rose.*"

Kaluza (1893*a*:1) follows Brink in believing that Chaucer wrote his translation around 1380, but he believes that the existing version of *Rom* is Chaucer's. He adds a further detail to this case when he argues (p. 2) that the use of the present tense in the God of Love's indictment of the dreamer (*LGWP* F 322–26, "Thow . . . werreyest . . . misseyest . . . hynderest . . . lettest . . . holdest") shows that *Rom* was composed shortly before *LGWP.* This argument of course does not take into consideration the fact that the tense is used within the fictive time-framework of a dream.

Kaluza is aware that *Rom* and *BD* differ in their treatments of the same passages from *RR* (e.g. *BD* 420, *Rom* 1393 [Lc 1366]; *BD* 410, *Rom* 61 [Lc 57]), and he explains these differences (pp. 140–41) by assuming an earlier date for *BD.* Thus he argues that *BD* cannot contain any citation from the English translation, since that was later.

Kaluza (pp. 246–48) suggests a scenario for the composition of *Rom* which assumes that the "persone" mentioned in Alceste's plea (*LGWP* F 367, G 347) was a patron, perhaps John of Gaunt, and that the date was around 1380, when Chaucer enjoyed John of Gaunt's patronage. Either Chaucer translated the opening 1705 lines first and, later, the Fals-Semblant section, or he may have translated the Fals-Semblant section as a first essay and the opening section afterward. Later, another poet may have partially filled the gap by translating Fragment B; and still later, a scribe may have copied the three fragments as we now have them.

Koeppel (1898:146), in his defense of the authenticity of Fragment A against Luick's charge that it contains a Northern rhyme (see 1091–92n.), argues that Chaucer worked on it in his youth and that he took greater liberties in rhyme than he did later.

Skeat, in his earlier writings, believes that *Rom* is not by Chaucer and that it "belongs to the fourteenth century"; he dates it "as early as A. D. 1350" (1878*b*:143; 1880:xciv; 1884:451). But after Lindner's suggestion (1887) that there were two main fragments, before and after the gap at lines 5810–11, he changes to the view that the translation "scarcely belongs to the fourteenth century, as it contains many words supposed to be of later date" (1888*c*: xciv). Then after Kaluza's discovery of Fragment A (1890; 1893*a*), Skeat accepts Chaucer as the author of that fragment only, and he believes that "Chaucer's translation was evidently the work of his younger years" (1894; 1899:1.11). In his *Chaucer Canon*, he accepts the *OED* date of about 1366 for Fragment A because, he argues, "Chaucer was already familiar with *Le Roman* when writing The Book of the Duchesse in 1369" (1900:74); but he gives separate dates for Fragments B and C, which, he believes, are not Chaucer's. On the assumption that Fragment B is the work of an imitator whose use of final -*e* is not consistent, he guesses at a date of "about 1420" (p. 84). He finds that Fragment C "is quite complete in itself" (p. 92), that its "grammatical forms are fairly correct and not late," and that "this Fragment may have been written as early as 1390" (p. 93).

Koch consistently denies that *Rom* is Chaucer's, but he accepts the idea that Chaucer made an early translation (now lost) of *RR* (1890:12–13). To Koch, the God of Love's statement "Thou hast translated the Romaunce of the Rose" (*LGWP* F 329) implies a literal rendering which "would . . . suit the character of a youthful production" (p. 13). The coupling of *TC* and the *RR* translation in *LGWP*, he says, "need not at all allude to their having been composed about the same period" (p. 14). And he argues finally that Chaucer would hardly have had time in the later period for all that is ascribed to that period plus the *RR* translation (p. 14). Koch (1900*a*:62–63) reiterates this point of view and cites *Adam*, where *Bo*, not *RR*, is associated with *TC*. He adds that the reference to *RR* in *BD* 332–34, even if it does not prove that Chaucer's translation was earlier than *BD*, still makes probable a rather early composition of the (lost) poem.

Later (1921:172–73), Koch revises his dating of Chaucer's supposedly lost translation to the middle 1380s, when Chaucer first became acquainted with Deschamps and when, Koch thinks, Chaucer gave him a copy of a recently-translated section of *RR* (cf. Deschamps's "Autre balade"; text in Spurgeon 1925:3.v.16–17); Koch argues that Chaucer would hardly have given the copy if it had been an early attempt. Nesta Thompson, who agrees with Koch that *Rom* is not Chaucer's, dates Fragment A "at a late period, with *Sir Thopas*, or *Hous of Fame*" (1926:68).

Lange (1901:397) implies a later date for Fragment B when he suggests that Lydgate or a poet close to him was the author. Although subsequently (1911:340–41) Lange rejects this hypothesis, Koch (1912:109) adopts it to argue that *Rom* was composed no later than 1400; his argument assumes Schick's chronology of Lydgate's works (1891:cxii) and that certain works of Lydgate were influenced by *Rom: The Complaint of the Black Knight, The Temple of Glas*, and *Reason and Sensuality.* Lange (1914:477–49), on the basis of the phrase "lyved in langour" in *Rom* 214, 304 and *Piers Plowman* B 14.117 [118], suggests that Fragment A uses *Piers* B and was therefore composed after 1377, the presumed date of Version B.

Those who think that Chaucer translated the entire *Rom* tend to date it early or to be somewhat vague as to date. Lounsbury gives little indication of date except to label as conjecture the opinion of "biographers" that Chaucer began the translation in the period 1360 to 1367 (1892:1.59). Pound, in supporting Lounsbury's theory of Chaucer's authorship, writes that "the translation . . . could not have been consecutive work. It must have extended over a long period of Chaucer's life, and before its completion have seen many changes of mood and mannerisms that would naturally affect its style" (1896:101). Hinckley (1906:641) also argues that *Rom* "was the work of a single author, . . . Chaucer." He believes that the differences from his other works "would . . . be due to the fact that Chaucer made the translation very early—in 1360 or even earlier," and that the differences within *Rom* are due "to the restless experiments of . . . youth." For example, he excuses the imperfect rhymes by the supposition that "nothing is more likely than that Chaucer indulged in this licence more freely in his youth than in his age" (1907*a*:99). Brusendorff, however, thinks that Chaucer's translation was several years later than *BD* (1925:396), that he composed the entire *Rom* "in the Standard English of the late fourteenth century" but that the existing MS is "a version, written down [from memory] in the beginning of the fifteenth century by some person from the North Midlands, who had once learned the translation by heart" (p. 382).

In general, a twentieth-century consensus favors an early date, at least among those who think that Fragment A is possibly or probably Chaucer's. Thus Kittredge, who earlier had concluded that "the *Romaunt* is not Chaucer's, with the possible exception of the first seventeen hundred lines" (1892:65), assumes in a later study (1915:54, 60–61) that Chaucer had translated *RR* before he wrote *BD*. Root (1906; 1922:56) inclines toward the view that "Chaucer's translation belongs to the period of his youth," and similar opinions appear, for example, in French (1927; 1947:75), Kuhl (1945:33–34), and Speirs (1951:35, 40). Most of these views assume but do not necessarily make explicit the partial distinction between Chaucer's translation and the existing *Rom*.

Little fresh evidence has appeared since 1900. Langhans (1918:223–28) supports an early date by taking issue with Brink's and Kaluza's view of the evidence in *LGWP*. He argues (p. 225) that the placement of *HF* before *BD* (see *LGWP* F 414–29) "shows that it did not matter to the poet if Alceste enumerates his works according to their order of composition. The date of composition of [*Rom*] and the *Troilus* follows just as little from the fact that Love mentions both of them in his reproach to the accused poet."

Kuhl (1945:33–34) makes another new argument for an early date. He believes that the reference to the color red at *Rom* 1680 ("I love well sich roses rede"), where the French (Lc 1642–43) mentions no color, is a compliment to the House of Lancaster. If so, he writes, "evidence points to a time before . . . the death of the Duchess (1369)" since "Chaucer speaks of living roses," i.e. both Duke and Duchess, and since "critics generally agree that Chaucer translated only Fragment A, [which ends] just beyond where Chaucer inserts the lines on red roses." Lawton (1981; 1985:30) implies that Fragments B and C were composed in the fourteenth century when he suggests that, while Chaucer did not write those pieces, he did make use of them in composing *PardPT*.

The Nature of the Translation

As Caroline Eckhardt has observed (1984: 42–44), there has been little consideration of *Rom* as translation, although she herself offers a good discussion of this topic. Most opinions have been subordinate to other concerns, mainly authorship, and we have touched upon them in that connection. One other concern may be reported here. To rebut John Bale's claim (1557–59:2.58) that Jean de Meun ("Ioannes Mone") was an expatriate Englishman, and to champion French literary achievement, André Thévet writes (1584:499, 502; 1735 text in Spurgeon 1925:3.v.22) that Chaucer merely imitates *RR*, and "in order to embellish and enrich his [*Rom*], Chaucer has pillaged the prettiest buds from the Roman de la Rose."

Subsequent commentators may be classified, as we have seen, according to their view of authorship. Those who believe that Chaucer is the sole author of *Rom* tend either to praise it or to entertain a low opinion of translation as such (for the post-medieval disparagement of *translatio*, cf. Eckhardt 1984:62, who cites Nichols 1983:20–21). Puttenham (1589:49–50) lumps *Rom* and *TC* together as "but bare translations . . . yet . . . wel handled." Wilson (1845:618–19; see Brewer 1978:2.61) calls *Rom* "the longest and most desperate of [Chaucer's] Translations." "Only judicious translation," says Emerson (1850; ed. Ferguson et al. 1971:4.113–14). "Nothing but a translation," remarks Brink (1870:30), when he still accepted Chaucer's authorship.

Sandras finds *Rom* "remarkable for its fidelity . . . as good as the original, without surpassing it" (1859:132), and if occasionally Chaucer improves on Guillaume de Lorris's phrasing, just as often he fails to reproduce either the precision or the grace of his original (p. 38). Sandras asserts that *Rom* gives preference to French words and allows "Saxon" vocabulary only a small ("faible") part (p. 37). What seem to be interpolations he thinks will doubtless be found in complete manuscripts of *RR*. Sandras rejects Tyrwhitt's notion that part of Chaucer's translation has been lost. Rather, Chaucer deliberately set out to streamline Jean de Meun's massive work, to give it a certain symmetry (pp. 39–40). And while Chaucer excerpted passages, he did not otherwise alter them, except at lines 5739–44 (see note).

Lounsbury (1892:2.15), who claims that "some" (unspecified persons) call *Rom* "superior to the original," allows that the translation is "remarkable"; it is, he writes, "faithful" but not "servile" (2.16). Brusendorff (1925:425) recognizes more clearly that the translation has defects but still believes that from the "garbled fragments" that are left "we may get an idea of the trenchant quickness and power of [Chaucer's] original rendering."

Likewise various are the opinions of those who think that *Rom* is, entirely or in part, not Chaucer's. Child (1870) finds the translation "often in a high degree slovenly." Kittredge (1892:1) regards it as "at best respectable; . . . servile and loose by turns, and by no means free from blunders." Lindner (1887:166, 170) observes that the translation is rather faithful before the large gap at lines 5810–11 but not after. Kaluza (1890; 1893*a*:15) distinguishes two fragments (our A and B) in Lindner's first part, on the basis of fidelity in terms of word-for-word and line-for-line translation, and regards A and C as examples of close translation like *Boece*, rather than of looser adaptation or imitation like *TC* or *SNT* (1893*a*:57; Kaluza adapts the terms from Brink 1870:18). Root (1906; 1922:56) admires the "high degree of excellence" in Fragments A and C and finds their manner "easy and spirited"; but he allows that "they have not the power

of [Chaucer's] maturer work." Chesterton (1932; 1949:204), on the other hand, denigrates the translation as "somewhat dreary."

Most subsequent writers limit their discussion to Fragment A, since from the time of Kaluza and Skeat they have been reluctant to assume Chaucer's authorship of Fragments B and C.

Thus Rosemond Tuve (1933:181–82) uses the description of May at the beginning of the poem to support her point that *Rom* is the principal channel for the "courtly and sophisticated element" in Chaucer's seasons poetry. She finds that

the translation in the long May passage is very close (vv. 49ff.); we find here a different phraseology from that which he inherited from earlier English uses of the motif. There are conceits he is not to forget, and a kind of diction which will persist in his spring descriptions until his later period. Busk and hay will be "shrouded"; the ground will have a "queynt robe and fayr" ("cointe robe faire"). . . . The "erthe 'wexeth proud" ("s'orgueille"); . . . "love affrayeth alle thing" ("toute rien d'amer s'esfroie").

Tuve's emphasis is on a single motif, the description of seasons and months. Joseph Mersand (1939), who studies all of Chaucer's Romance vocabulary, shows that the Romance element is significant but limited. The frequency of Romance words in Fragment A of *Rom* is about 1 in 8 or 12.5% (pp. 32–33), nearly twice that for *BD*, with 1 in 14, or 7.14% (pp. 90–91). Even with the 35 new Romance words that Mersand finds in *Rom* (pp. 58–59), the frequency of 1 in 8 shows a predominantly English vocabulary; Mersand makes this point in the case of *BD* by noting that, in a work where we might expect a large Romance element, the low percentage, 7.14%, "speaks eloquently for the overwhelmingly Anglo-Saxon proportion of its vocabulary" (p. 91; contrast Sandras, above).

Erwin Geissman (1952) compares *Rom* (Fragment A) with *RR*, making use (pp. 153–55) of Langlois's text and corpus of variants; (pp. 157–58) of Kaluza (1893*a*); and (pp. 158–65, 278–85, 304–11) of Mersand (1939). He concludes that the translation is very close, but his analysis is curious in that he sees Chaucer's intention to translate literally as being "continually defeated by the requirements of meter and rime. He was forced," says Geissman, "to compromise with literalness, and the surprising result is a translation which fully and accurately renders the original but still usually retains the smoothness and freshness of an original composition" (p. 166). Eckhardt (1984:51), it may be noted, finds it unsurprising that such a result should appear in a translation by Chaucer, but surprising that the result should be seen as a series of defeats, of forced compromises. Nevertheless, with allowance for some exaggeration, Geissman's conclusion is unexceptional and follows the mainstream of opinion stemming from Kaluza.

An aspect of the translation that has received considerable attention is the use of doublets in *Rom*. Lounsbury calls attention to them as characteristic of Chaucer's style (1892:2.153–58); Kittredge (1892:61–63) rejects this idea because doublets appear in the French and in other Middle English writers. Geissman (1952:252–55), who finds that *Rom* not only preserves most of *RR*'s doublets but occasionally creates new ones where *RR* has a single adjective or noun, concludes that "they must be thought of as highly characteristic of Chaucer's style" (p. 255). Nordahl's (1978:24–31) systematic analysis of *RR*'s "tautologies binaires" in Fragment A (e.g., Lc 826 "Par druerie et par solaz" *Rom* 844 "By drury and by solas") reveals that Chaucer has faithfully recreated the emphatic function of the French doublets, by keeping them intact through borrowing or translation, as he does in over half of the cases, 58 of 104; by changing the construction of one element; by adding another element; or by reducing one element and strengthening the other. Nordahl finds only nine cases (out of 104) in which Chaucer has de-emphasized the French doublet, either through reducing it to a single element or eliminating it entirely.

The general emphasis on the fidelity of Chaucer's translation and on the strong influence of the French (cf. Brewer 1966:3) has been modified in recent years by a comple-mentary emphasis on the English quality of *Rom*. We have seen that Lounsbury identifies many words and phrases common to *Rom* and Chaucer's other works, and that Kittredge finds many of them to be common stock in Middle English metrical romances (see above, pp. 10–11). An inference that Kittredge does not develop is that, in using this stock, *Rom* shows a measure of native English influence that complements that of the French original. Recent writers who deal with the nature of the translation have been developing this idea.

Raymond Preston (1952:21–22) comments that the passage on the carole (*Rom* 759–68) has a "distinctively English relation to the dance that makes [it] the most interesting piece of translation in the whole of the *Romaunt*"; "the meter," he writes, "looks the same . . . as the French, but is not the same." He finds (citing lines 507–08, 531–32, 561, 677, 1031–32; 928, 1196, 1219, 1420) that in *Rom* "the translator [is] inclined to prune generally descriptive terms, and to add phrasing idiomatic in his own dialect." He also finds the English more concrete than the French in the descriptions of Beaute (lines 1009–16), Largesse's knight (lines 1207–10), and Courtesy's knight (lines 1270–72). "The first fragment," he concludes (p. 24), "is on the whole discreet and accurate: a better poem, in English, would have been a less faithful translation."

Shinsuke Ando (1970; cf. 1986) argues that while "Chaucer borrowed a great many French words and phrases . . . the influence on him of provincial English poetry is distinctly shown in his style and phraseology in *The Romaunt* [Fragment A]" (1970:65). In the descriptions that Preston used to show *Rom*'s greater concreteness, Ando finds words and phrases that appear also in the Harley lyrics and in tail-rhyme romances: e.g., *byrde in bour, rose in rys* (cf. Kittredge 1892:36), *as whyt as lylye, styf in stour, fetys, tretys, gente, lemman, doughty,* and rhyme-tags like *ywis : (is, this), nomen : (-)comen, of prys : (fetys, wys).*

Ando's evidence for native influence is obviously limited. Another limited study, by Merete Smith, focuses on OF loanwords in

Rom for "articles of dress and fabrics used for dress" (1982:89). On the basis of *MED* and *OED* citations, Smith concludes that, in view of the common assumption "that a large number of OF loanwords in ME were literary borrowings" (p. 89), "it is remarkable that only six out of . . . thirty-nine OF loanwords in the ME translation are in any likelihood new words" (p. 92). And only two of these six—*chapelet* (lines 563, 565, 845, 908, 2278) and *tyssu* (line 1104)—"seem to have gained currency in English during the Middle Ages" (p. 89). The other four "were nonce-borrowings" (p. 92): *kamelyne* (line 7365), *chevesaile* (line 1082), *mourdaunt* (line 1094), and *sukkenye* (line 1232). The study suggests that other OF loans in this category were already part of ME when *Rom* was composed.

Alexander Weiss (1985), who grants that Chaucer's translation (Fragment A) is "a close and careful one" (p. 203), nevertheless finds "greater simplicity and directness" in, for example, *Rom*'s passages on May (*Rom* 51–56, Lc 47–52) and on time (*Rom* 369–77, Lc 361–69). These qualities, he argues, promote clarity through such devices as the more frequent use of doublets (pp. 205–06; cf. Nordahl 1978), of structural repetition (p. 206), and of extended coordinate series (p. 207). Like Geissman (1952:178) and Preston (1952:22–23), he finds (pp. 207–10) that the ME is more concrete than the French, particularly in descriptive passages, and he adduces the descriptions of Hate (*Rom* 147–61, Lc 139–51) and Narcissus's pool (*Rom* 1417–22, Lc 1389–93). The most distinctive feature of Chaucer's translation, he feels, is the "conversational manner" that arises from "the particular combination of syntax and meter" (p. 210). He examines (pp. 211–16) such combinations in parallel passages from *RR* and *Rom* to show the effect of features like run-on lines, enjambment, initial metrical stress, and initial participial constructions. Weiss grants that *Rom* adapts many of these features from *RR*; in fact, his evidence strengthens the case for close—and idiomatic—translation in Fragment A.

Caroline Eckhardt, who likewise restricts her study of *Rom* as translation to Fragment A, argues that it is a very close translation: "the predominant quality . . . remains its fidelity to its source" (1984:62). Eckhardt provides a brief theoretical framework (p. 45), based on Steiner (1975), that includes an account of Saint Jerome's bipartite distinction between translating *verbum e verbo*, "necessary for Scripture," and *sensum de sensu*, "appropriate for other texts" (cf. Fleming 1986*b*:3, who draws attention to Jean de Meun's plea, in the Preface to his translation of Boethius, ed. Dedeck-Héry 1952:168, for clarity of meaning over word-for-word literality). She also describes Dryden's tripartite distinction, which adds "imitation," a species of translation that affords greatest license to the translator. Although Eckhardt does not specify the position of *Rom* within these categories, she does offer a balanced treatment of the French and native influence. She points out (pp. 46–47) that while many lines appear in English with little change from the French (see *Rom* 844, 899, 916, 957; cf. Nordahl 1978), "the resulting verses are completely natural in English." Even when greater changes are necessary, some element of the French, like rhyme or alliteration, may be maintained (pp. 47–48). The lament upon Time (*Rom* 381–94), whose "elegiac melancholy . . . sounds eloquently 'English,'" in fact contains "several lines [381, 389, 391, 392] that are translated verbatim" and "other lines [that] show very modest changes" (p. 48). As a result, Chaucer "allows the new version to remain perceptibly French in its English form" and achieves "the right balance between familiarity and distance, . . . a matter of the highest art" (p. 50).

At the same time, there is in fact a "new English tone" (p. 52) that can be seen in a set of slight differences from Guillaume de Lorris's poem:

The increase in the felt presence of the first-person narrator, the greater distinctness of the images and the heightening of their function as things seen, the expansion that leads to an informality of tone, the deviations from *courtoisie* toward colloquialism—all tend to impart to the *Romaunt* a fresh new narrative voice. (p. 60)

Eckhardt shows (pp. 52–54) that the emphasis on the first-person narrator is more than a matter of the linguistic necessity of a stated subject in English. At a significant point at the beginning of the poem, where Guillaume announces the subject, he does so in a passive construction (Lc 38 "ou l'art d'Amors est tote enclose"); but Chaucer uses the first-person active construction (*Rom* 40 "In whiche al the arte of love I close"), a "mode in which the agent is identified with the narrator, who thereby becomes the typical Chaucerian double agent of character from within the poem and literary designer from without" (p. 53). Eckhardt grants that the change may have been suggested by the rhyme, and she adduces other examples, some in which rhyme is not involved. Thus Guillaume's "Dames, cest essample aprenez" (Lc 1505) becomes Chaucer's "Ladyes, I *preye* ensample takith" (*Rom* 1539) where, Eckhardt suggests, "this verb too could have been left in the impersonal mode (as in, hypothetically, 'Ladyes, now ensample taketh')" (p. 53).

In dealing with *Rom*'s heightening of visual imagery, Eckhardt (pp. 54–57) notes that Chaucer sometimes introduces the first-person pronoun to produce this effect, as when Guillaume's "Une autre ymage i ot asise" (Lc 195) becomes Chaucer's "Another ymage set saugh I" (*Rom* 207). In general, she writes, "Chaucer . . . tends to emphasize the images as things seen by a spectator rather than as things existing in an indefinite or absolute state" (p. 54); and the spectator may be expressed in the first person (cf. *Rom* 1273, 1409), the third person (cf. *Rom* 947, 1401), or the infinitive phrase *to sene* (*Rom* 58, 158). There is also (p. 55) "a slight increase in the specificity and precision of the images themselves" (cf. *Rom* 128, 295, 568, 1270, 1372, 1514–16). One kind of specification (p. 56) is attachment to a possessor, as when "'i. chant' [Lc 661] becomes '*her* song'" (*Rom* 671; cf. 719, 780). A heightening of emotional qualities or human sensitivities occurs in changes in the descriptions of the birds, of Elde, and of Youth (*Rom* 71–73, 409–10, 1283–84).

A third characteristic of the new English tone comes from slight expansions, mostly of single lines (pp. 57–59). Eckhardt calls attention to the effective expansion in line 36—"Whether that it be, he or she"—which delays and thus supports the development in "building toward a very important statement" in lines 39–40: "It is the Romance of the Rose, / In whiche al the arte of love I close" (p. 58; see line 36n.). In this example, the introduction of the first-person pronoun in the last line further reinforces this development; and in another of Eckhardt's examples of expansion (*Rom* 503 "Hadde be unto me free"), Chaucer's added line has another such pronoun, *me*, that does not appear in Guillaume.

Eckhardt (pp. 59–60) documents a fourth change, the shift from courtly to colloquial diction, with an analysis of the opening lines (Lc, *Rom* 1–4). Her argument is that Chaucer seems not even to have tried to reproduce the rhetoric of the "multiple wordplay upon songe" in the rhyme-sequence of *songes / mençonges / songes songier / mençongier*, "as the English lines diminish in formal rhetorical complexity, they lose the almost incantatory reiteration of the word for dreaming, but they increase in naturalness and simplicity."

Eckhardt hedges her argument by noting constantly that these elements, while certain, are slight, and that "it is possible to find contrary examples" (pp. 60–61). Her caution stems from a circumstance to which she calls attention and which will be obvious from the discussion above; few attempt to clarify the relation between the medieval concept of *translatio* and the medieval activity of translation. She cites the work of Vance (1981), Shoaf (1979), and Nichols (1983:21) but notes (p. 63) that Huppé's call for "a thoroughgoing investigation of Middle English translation from the French (and Latin)" (1948:342) remains unanswered.

Two years before Eckhardt's article, Longo had explored the thesis that "Chaucer's understanding of translation was much broader and [more] complex than our own, one which is essentially related to the notion of the *translatio studii* or simply *translatio*, the progressive elucidation and appropriation of past works in the present" (1982:v). More recently, Fleming has touched upon the question of translation and *translatio* (1986b.1–4) in an examination of the phrase "smoky reyn" in *TC* 3.628. We shall turn to these two studies below, since they respond to the question: how did *RR* influence Chaucer?

Chaucer and the Roman de la Rose

Early commentators tend to deplore Chaucer's interest in *RR.* Tyrwhitt's attitude is probably characteristic of the late eighteenth century. He writes (1775:3.314): "If [Chaucer] translated the whole of that very extraordinary composition [*RR*], (as is most probable,) he coud scarce avoid being guilty of a much greater licentiousness, in sentiment as well as diction, than we find in any of his other writings." Brink (1870:17) finds the material of the French poem "not very edifying." And Cyples (1877; text in Brewer 1978:2.189, 191) criticizes *Rom* and *TC*, "objectionable writings of the sentimental kind," as "the worst example" of Chaucer's "want of sense in picking topics."

But there is no denying the importance of *RR* and its influence on Chaucer's work. Muscatine (1957) shows how fundamental that influence is, and Wallace, who calls *RR* "the great foundation text of the European Middle Ages, the secular tree of Jesse upon which all illustrious poets sit," asserts that "the study of Chaucer and Italy must begin . . . with a reading of the *Roman de la Rose*" (1985:67; cf. 1986:30–31). The following survey, however, will attempt no more than a selective review of the scholarship on the subject. The first section deals with the search for parallels, the second with the development of more general topics, including rhetoric, style, allegory, and the use of a first-person narrator.

There are some useful recent bibliographical materials. Peck's annotated bibliography of twentieth-century scholarship on *Rom* (1988) gives some attention to the influence of *RR* on Chaucer. Morris's *Chaucer Source and Analogue Criticism* (1985) indexes the sources and analogues of Chaucer's works, by author, title, and origin or genre. Luria (1982) has a good bibliography on *RR* that

includes a short section (pp. 75–84) on the poem's influence on Chaucer (see also Arden 1987:78–84).

Editors of Chaucer, beginning with Tyrwhitt (1775), identify many parallels with *RR*; the notes of SK, RB, and RI are particularly important (a list of lines from *RR* for which correspondences in Chaucer's work have been proposed appears in Dillon 1974: 196–201). The principal writers to deal with the specific topic of Chaucer's indebtedness to *RR* are Cipriani (1907) and Fansler (1914); Koeppel (1892) devotes special attention to parallels in Jean de Meun. Other scholars include *RR* in studies of Chaucer's debt to French writers (e.g., Sandras 1859, Muscatine 1957, Wimsatt 1975, and Braddy 1979). Those who deal still more generally with the sources of and influences on Chaucer inevitably consider *RR* (e.g., Lounsbury 1892:2.169–426, Schaar 1955). And there are useful studies of the sources of individual works—like Bryan and Dempster (1941) for *CT* and Wimsatt (1968) for *BD*—that touch upon the influence of *RR*.

The Search for Parallels

Tyrwhitt (1775) points out a number of parallels between *RR* and passages in the *Canterbury Tales.* He is the first to note (TR 4.196) that the description of the Prioress's table manners (*GP* 127–36) comes from La Vieille's recommendations (Lc 13378–85); that Fals Semblant's boast (Lc 11536) stands behind the statement (*GP* 256) that the Friar's purchase was better than his rent (TR 4.201); that the antifeminist parts of *RR* may be a source for *WBP* and *MerT* (TR 4.152–53, 263–64, 266); that *PhyT* derives more from *RR* (Lc 5559–628) than from Livy (TR 4.305); that *PardP* C 407 is equivalent to *RR* (Lc) 5083–84; that much of the stories of Nero and Croesus in *MkT* comes from *RR* (Lc 6155–6220, 6459–6589; TR 3.283–84); and that in *ManT* the exempla of the caged bird and the she-wolf, as well as the advice on holding one's tongue, derive from *RR* (Lc 13911–28, 7734–36, 7007–27; TR 3.303–04). Tyrwhitt compares other passages from *RR* and *CT* as well: *GP*

741 and Lc 7067–75 (TR 4.215), *KnT* A 1940 and Lc 522–630 (TR 4.223), *KnT* A 2895 and Lc 909 (TR 4.234), *MLP* B¹ 114 and Lc 8148 (TR 4.258), and *WBP* D 721ff. and Lc 9161–76 (TR 4.266).

Sandras (1859) is the first to consider the impact of *RR* on Chaucer's work as a whole. He finds that Guillaume de Lorris's influence is more pronounced in the poems written before the *Canterbury Tales*, and that in *CT* Chaucer draws upon Jean de Meun's material about women and about the mendicant orders (pp. 36, 132, 257). Chaucer, he believes, "yields to the taste of the court in imitating Guillaume de Lorris; but it is his own inclination that carries him along when he takes his inspiration from Jean de Meun. The imprint of the former is found only in compositions that are now without celebrity; the verve of the latter has penetrated completely into the work [*CT*] in which Chaucer defies oblivion" (pp. 39–40). Sandras also calls attention to how the general influence of Guillaume's portion of *RR* works through the poems of Machaut, Froissart, and other poets of the fourteenth century (pp. 75–81; cf. Wimsatt 1968).

Chaucer's principal "imitations" of the first part of *RR* are the dream-visions: *PF, BD, LGW,* and *HF.* Sandras treats *PF* (1859:65–72) in terms of a court of love. He recognizes general parallels with *RR*: the debt to Guillaume's Garden of Delight, reflected (for example) in the language of one of the inscriptions set over the gate to Nature's park (*PF* 127–33), and in the description of the temple of Venus (with parallel echoes of the *Teseida*). While recognizing Chaucer's use of Alain de Lille's *De planctu naturae*, Sandras also implies that there is a specific borrowing from *RR* (Lc 16752) in *PF* 379, where Nature is called God's vicar. The account of *BD* (1859:89–95, 289–90) takes into consideration the major sources in Machaut, Froissart, and *RR.* Sandras refers generally to *RR* and Machaut as the sources of the complaint against Fortune. He notes a direct reference to *RR* (*BD* 332–34), remarks that every detail in *BD* 397–415 is to be found in *RR* (see especially Lc 55–58, 5908–11), and reports the

correspondence of *BD* 659–63 with *RR* (Lc) 6622–25, 6661–62.

His comments on other works are few. He points out (pp. 46–47) that *TC* 4.519–20 is taken from *RR* (Lc 6352–53). He observes somewhat vaguely (pp. 106–07) that *For* has frequent "rapprochements" with *RR* and that *Pity* belongs to the same genre as Guillaume's part of *RR*; also (pp. 117–18) that the dissertation on dreams at the start of *HF* is analogous to that which begins *RR*, and that *HF* is elsewhere indebted to Jean de Meun (for example, the reference to Croesus at line 105). Oddly, in the brief account (pp. 113–16) of *LGW*, he omits the very important allusions to *RR* in the speeches of the God of Love, Alceste, and the dreamer (*LGWP* F 322–31, 440–41, 469–72). Perhaps because discussion (pp. 116–25) of this work and *HF* appears under the heading of "imitation of antiquity," the influence of *RR* receives little attention. The neglect is all the more serious because it inhibits a fuller understanding of the nature of Guillaume's allegory.

The second part of Sandras's book emphasizes the influence of Jean de Meun on the *Canterbury Tales.* Like Tyrwhitt, Sandras points to the description of the Prioress's table manners (p. 154); to the antifeminist tradition reflected in the Wife of Bath and in her Prologue (pp. 186–89); to the uses of *RR* made in *PhyT, MkT* (Nero), and *ManT* (pp. 230–32, 248). In addition Sandras identifies some specific verbal borrowings. He alleges (pp. 145–46) that Chaucer draws from *RR* (Lc 882–88) to describe the Squire's clothing (*GP* 89–90). He indicates (pp. 224–26) that all the antifeminist barbs found in *WBT* D 919–49 are to be found in Jean de Meun's portion of *RR* (for example, Lc 9915–22, 16317–18). He compares (p. 230) *PhyT* C 11–18 with Lc 16138–80 (also noted by Wright 1847–51: 2.247) and *PhyT* 225–26, 254–56 with Lc 2605–08.

In the 1870s and 1880s Skeat adduced nearly fifty more parallels, principally in *BD, HF,* and *PF.* These appear in his editions of various parts of Chaucer's works and are identified in a convenient handlist by Koeppel (1892:238–67), who gathers almost seventy previously unnoted parallels with Jean de Meun's work, most from *RR* but a few from Jean's *Testament*. Koeppel draws only from those portions of *RR* not translated in *Rom* in order, he says, not to encroach on Kaluza's (1891) parallel-text edition. Koeppel also lists most of the parallels adduced by Tyrwhitt; he acknowledges Sandras only once (p. 242), allowing that Sandras had preceded him in noting the source in *RR* for *TC* 4.519–20. Koeppel adduces many more instances for *TC*; among Chaucer's other works only in *WBPT* does he find a greater number of parallels with *RR*.

Lounsbury (1892:2.217–21) reviews Tyrwhitt's parallels (p. 219) and adds to them a comparison of *LGWP* 17–28 and *RR* (Lc 9603–06). He proposes that the confession of Fals Semblant had a general influence on Chaucer's portrait of the friar in *GP* and on the Pardoner's self-revelation in *PardP*. Like Koeppel, Lounsbury (p. 393) compares *GP* 429–34 with the list of physicians in *RR* (Lc 15929–31; but cf. Bowden 1948:200, 211n., who credits Pauline Aiken with the discovery of a more complete source in Vincent of Beauvais). In general, Lounsbury finds the influence of *RR* very substantial (p. 217), but, unlike Sandras and like Koeppel, he feels that Jean de Meun's influence was greater than that of Guillaume de Lorris (p. 220), that Chaucer particularly liked Jean's "keen observation . . . satire . . . wit" (p. 220), and that the influence was "intellectual" rather than "spiritual" (p. 221; cf. Hammond 1908:79).

Skeat's 1894 edition (SK) includes in its introductions and notes the material from Skeat's earlier editions of selections published in the 1870s, '80s, and early '90s and acknowledges the work of Tyrwhitt, Warton, Thomas Wright (1847–51), Koeppel, Lounsbury, and others. Skeat's new explanatory notes, if one may trust the listings made by Cipriani (1907; see below) and the index in SK (6.388), introduce some 40 new parallels between Chaucer's work and *RR*; see notes to *BD* 292, 410–12, 419, 835–37, 849, 1121, 1152–53; *PF* 122, 176ff., 214; *HF* 265, 392, 917, 1022; *TC* 3.1194; 4.6–7; 5.552, 1174; *LGW* 25, 125, 128, 227, 352, 917; *GP* 404, 885; *KnT* A

1625, 1999, 2388; *WBPT* D 293, 407, 1158; *FranT* F 792; *PhyT* C 79, 135, 165, 184, 203, 225; *NPT* B² 4516; *SNT* G 3.

Lisi Cipriani (1907), who does not include *CT* in her analysis, offers brief comments on *Form Age, For, Gent, ABC, Anel*, and *LGWP*, and fuller treatment of *BD, PF, Bo, TC*, and *HF*. Her method is to list for each poem in turn the line references to passages previously noted, mainly by Skeat and Koeppel, and to quote additional parallels that she has culled. Like Sandras, Cipriani argues that *RR*'s influence on *BD* appears both directly and through the intermediary of Machaut (pp. 554–55), and she finds (p. 561, this time ignoring Sandras) that in *PF* (120–40) the messages on the two gates echo not only Dante but the comparison in *RR* between the park and the garden (Lc 20237–596). She also adduces (pp. 564–68) thirteen new parallels with *RR* in the glosses of Chaucer's *Boece*, but these are actually drawn from Jean de Meun's French translation of the *Consolatio* and thus have accidental similarity to Jean's language in *RR*. For *HF* and *LGW* many of Cipriani's new parallels concern dreams and the dream-framework (pp. 585–86, 594–95).

Troilus and Criseyde receives Cipriani's most extended treatment (pp. 568–85). She reports (pp. 568–71) the view of Sandras (1859:35–37) and Kissner (1867:53–54), that Guillaume de Lorris's influence on *TC* was far greater than Jean de Meun's influence, and she records Brink's rejection (1870:73, 44) of this opinion. She develops Brink's argument (1870:84) that Guillaume de Lorris influenced the depiction of love in *TC* and that Jean de Meun influenced the depiction of Pandarus. After showing (pp. 571–74) the influence of *RR* on the first part of Boccaccio's *Filostrato*, where Troilo falls in love, she writes "that Chaucer has twice undergone the influence of the Romance of the Rose: once consciously and directly through the original, and once unconsciously and indirectly through the *Filostrato*" (p. 574).

Cipriani finds that the direct influence of *RR* "appears . . . nowhere more distinctly than it does in the *Troylus*" (p. 575). She argues partly from the linkage of "the Rose" and

"Criseyde" in *LGWP* (G 431; cf. F 441, 329–32) and mainly from new parallels that she has discovered. Some of her evidence is suspect (*RR* 5018–121, in the edition by Michel 1864: 1.146–49) because it comes from a passage that Langlois regards as an interpolation (at Ln 4400–01 [= Lc 4370–71]; see Langlois 1910:425). Thus her argument (pp. 575, 583) regarding ethical and religious traits drawn from Jean de Meun needs qualification. Her case for multiple avenues of relationship between *RR* and *TC* is nevertheless a good one.

Henry B. Hinckley (1907*b*) proposes a few new parallels in *GP, KnT, NPT, ClT, SqT, FranT*. Apart from the common spelling "Aristote" (p. 225; cf. *SqT* F 233 in the Petworth MS and Lc 8921, 18001), the parallels lack close verbal similarity. They include the following topics: (pp. 75–76) folly in love (*KnT* A 1799; Lc 3025–28); (p. 87) the invocation of Lucina as goddess of childbirth (*KnT* A 2083–86; Lc 10593–96); (p. 163) the abuse of papal bulls (*PardP* C 336; Ln 11222.58.5–9 [text in Ln 11222–23n. = Marteau 11703–07]); (p. 167) manual labor for the religious (*PardP* C 444–45; Lc 11353–61); (p. 183) the figure of testicles as relics (*PardT* C 952–53; Lc 7073–7106); (p. 227) the transformation of fern-ash to glass (*SqT* F 255; Lc 16066–71).

Dean Fansler (1914) offers the only book-length study of Chaucer's debt to *RR*. He adopts a topical organization (p. 7), with separate chapters on the influence of *RR* on Chaucer's "allusions to historical and legendary persons and places" (Chapter II); "mythological allusions" (III); style (IV); "situations and descriptions" (V); "proverbs and proverbial expressions" (VI); and "philosophical discussions" (VII). He acknowledges (pp. 1–5) the work of earlier scholars, including (p. 166) Mead (1901; for *WBP*), but not Hinckley (1907*b*).

Fansler's principal contribution, aside from the addition of some new parallels, is a critical examination of those previously cited. Thus, for example, in dealing with the topic of allusions in chapters 2 and 3, he calls into question (pp. 33–34) some of Skeat's citations of parallels to *PhyT*. He refines the parallel

between *BD* 1081–84 and *RR* where the names Penelope, Lucrece, and Livy occur along with the rhyme *Grece : Lucrece*; Skeat (SK 1.490) had cited Lc 8621–22 (for Penelope and the rhyme *Lucrece : Grece*) and Lc 8582 (for Livy); but Fansler (p. 38) shows a closer juxtaposition of the three names and the rhyme at Lc 8575–82. Where Koeppel and Skeat had adduced a number of parallels that involve Biblical and classical allusions, Fansler shows (pp. 40–47) that in some of these cases, *RR* is not necessarily the source or, often, not the sole source. He argues in greater detail (pp. 48–72) that, particularly in the case of Venus and Cupid, the parallels with *RR* show in many cases Chaucer's familiarity with classical sources or with French writers of the fourteenth century. "Clearly," he writes, "Chaucer followed no one author in the description of Cupid" (p. 68), and he suggests (pp. 69–71) parallels between Machaut's *Dit du vergier* and the God of Love in *LGWP*.

In his chapter "Chaucer's style as affected by the *Roman*," Fansler again calls into question much of the dictional material of Koeppel and Skeat. He classifies this material ("somewhat arbitrarily") under the headings: "(1) picturesque negation, (2) exclamations and imprecations, (3) figures of speech—allegory, simile, metaphor, anaphora, (4) rhymes and vocabulary, (5) various other devices of expression, such as the use of emphatic repetition in interrogative form, emphasis by a series of contrasts, the employment of extended lists of objects; catalogues, and transitional and summarizing sentences" (p. 74). Although Chaucer copies from *RR* no specific cases of "picturesque negation," what some call the figure of worthlessness (e.g., "not worth an hen"; *Rom* 6856, *WBT* 1112), Fansler believes that his "predilection for this trick of diction came from his reading of Jean de Meung; for by no other two writers is it so frequently used" (p. 77). Apart from this kind of influence on style, Fansler finds that "most of the parallels discussed are of little significance as showing *Roman* influence on Chaucer. . . . I am not inclined to regard more than eighteen of the correspondences . . . as standing in the relation of cause and effect" (p. 122). We may draw a similar conclusion from Fansler's examination of the topic "Proverbs and Proverbial Expressions." Again he accepts relatively few of the previously suggested parallels of this sort; such a conclusion is reasonable for proverbial material.

The case is quite different for the two chapters on "Situations and Descriptions" and "Chaucer's Philosophical Discussions," where, as we might expect, it is easier to isolate distinctive parallels. In these two chapters Fansler finds 507 lines "which we may in all reason suppose to have been directly imitated from the *Roman de la Rose*" (p. 229), more than twice the number—247—of reliable identifications in the four chapters on allusions, stylistic devices, and proverbial material (p. 230). According to Fansler, the largest borrowing of nature-description is in *BD*, but the dream-landscapes of *PF* and *LGWP* also show such influence (pp. 124–37). His analysis of personal descriptions (pp. 149–74) emphasizes parallels in Troilus, Pandarus, and certain figures from *CT*: the Squire, the Prioress, the Friar, the Pardoner, the friar in *SumT*, and, in particular, the Wife of Bath.

In addition to evaluating previously noted parallels, Fansler adds several new ones. He is the first, for example, to call specific attention (p. 31; cf. SK 5.230) to the spelling "Dalida" in both Chaucer and *RR* (*MkT* B² 3253 [cf. *BD* 738]; Lc 9176, 16647); to note (pp. 120–21) the multiple echoes of the line "Divers diverses choses distrent" (Lc 10654) in *RvP* A 3857, *MLT* B¹ 211, and *SqT* F 202; and to note (p. 99), conversely, the multiple sources of the figure of the sword of cold (*LGWP* F 127, *SqT* F 57) in Alanus de Insulis and Machaut as well as in *RR* (Lc 5912–14). He records (p. 27) the agreements in the two accounts of how Seneca died (*MkT* B² 3699–706; Lc 6181–92). He finds (p. 100) a parallel to the Nun's Priest's "Taketh the fruyt, and lat the chaf be stille" (B² 4633) in Fals Semblant's "J'en lés le grain et pregn la paille" (Lc 11186); but he misses Hinckley's parallel (1907*b*:155), a less likely but closer one in

Jean de Meun's *Testament*, line 2150: "Mès retiengnent le grain et jettent hors la paille" (line 2167, ed. Méon 1814:4.115); the figure itself is of course widespread, and in any case the Nun's Priest's purport is the opposite of Fals Semblant's. In *HF* 916–18, Fansler shows (p. 38) that Scipio's vision of "Helle and erthe and paradys" has a parallel in Nature's account of dreams, like Scipio's, of "anfer et paradys / et ciel et air et mer et terre" (Lc 18338–39).

In reviewing the work of previous scholars (pp. 1–6), Fansler had noted "the diversity of opinion on the relative influence of Guillaume de Lorris and Jean de Meung upon the English poet" (p. 1). His analysis enables him to conclude that "the proportional number of lines borrowed from [Guillaume] is as large as that from Jean" (p. 230). From Guillaume, Chaucer borrowed (p. 231) "not a few touches" of outdoor description, "many hints in the character of Troilus," and "some conventional situations and possibly a stylistic device or two"; from Jean he seems to have borrowed "all kinds of allusions and information," particularly in the discourses of Raison (on Fortune), Amis (on poverty, the Golden Age, domestic tyranny), La Vieille (on the wiles of women), Nature (on the "various natural phenomena of the earth and heavens . . . alchemy, astronomy, free-will, necessity, destiny, optics, dreams, true nobility and gentility"), and Genius (in his "earnest and vigorous exhortation to fecundity"). Fansler agrees too that Fals Semblant is the source for "many details for [Chaucer's] characterizations of the Frere and the Pardoner and his attacks on corruption in the clergy" (p. 232; for discussion of the relationship of the Pardoner and Fals Semblant, see Lawton 1981; 1985:29–35).

After Fansler, new parallels, or elaborations of those previously noted, appear principally in the annotations of the major editions; in this regard, special attention is due to Root's 1926 edition of *TC*. Full details of individual attributions will of course be provided in the notes of the relevant fascicles of the *Variorum Chaucer* edition. Extended quotations from *RR* as source for passages in *WBPT*, *PhyT*,

PardT, MkT, and *ManT* may be found in Bryan and Dempster (1941). Parallels appear also in studies of specific images, as in George Economou's article (1975) on the caged-bird motif in *CT* and *RR* (*ManT* H 163–74; *SqT* F 607–20; *MilT* A 3221–26; cf. *Bo* 3m2 and *RR* Lc 13911–36). Full treatment of the relation of *BD* to *RR* is provided by James Wimsatt (1968), who identifies (pp. 155–62) specific parallels, line by line, in the major and minor sources of *BD*.

From this brief review of the preoccupation with parallels between *RR* and Chaucer we turn to some writers who have highlighted one or another aspect of the relationship between the two.

Questions of Special Interest

Three approaches have been particularly productive in elaborating the relation between Chaucer and *RR*: the rhetorical, the stylistic, and the allegorical. The first of these has its roots in the historical study of rhetoric (cf. Baldwin 1928, Curtius 1953:62–78, Murphy 1974, and, for bibliography, Murphy 1971). The second stems from the branch of rhetoric that is concerned with style levels, while the third develops from the study of the rhetorical trope of allegory as well as from the allegorical reading of texts (see below). A final section, on the use of first person, surveys some recent work on the narrators in Chaucer and *RR*.

Rhetoric. On the general influence of rhetoric on Chaucer's work one should see Manly (1926), Naunin (1929), and Payne (1963; cf. Payne 1978). Naunin in particular makes comparisons with *RR* in his analysis of Chaucer's use of rhetorical figures (1929: 40–48). More to the point is the work of James V. Cunningham (1952). After only brief reference to rhetorical theory, he argues that *RR* influenced the descriptive portraits of *GP*. He thinks that "the literary form to which the Prologue to the *Canterbury Tales* belongs and of which it is a special realization is the form of the dream-vision prologue in the tradition of the *Romance of the Rose* and of the associated French and English poems of the

subsequent century and a half" (p. 174). Cunningham sees the elements of that tradition, aside from the dream-setting (which does not appear in *GP*), as including a more or less elaborate description of the seasonal setting, an author as character, a specific locale, a company of people (birds in *PF*), and a character who sponsors the further action of the poem (pp. 177–78). The portraits in both *RR* and *GP*, he argues, appear in succession with minimal transitions; the numbers of portraits are about the same— twenty-five in *RR* (including the wall-portraits and Deduit's company inside the garden) and twenty-one in *GP*; the lengths of the portraits vary within similar ranges; and they "are introduced by brief critical remarks in which the terms derive from the medieval arts of poetry" (p. 180; Cunningham does not develop this last suggestion).

Claes Schaar (1955) refers more specifically to arts of poetry, and he includes many comparisons between Chaucer and *RR*. He develops a topic—Chaucer's descriptive technique—that Fansler had introduced in his chapter on "Situations and Descriptions" (1914:123–74) and that Cunningham touched on in his discussion of the portraits. Schaar's brief introduction identifies Matthew of Vendôme (*Ars versificatoria*) and Geoffrey of Vinsauf (*Poetria nova*) as "the medieval theorists who pay most attention to the structure of description" (1955:2). In their doctrine, he notes, "amplification and abbreviation are concepts of fundamental importance," and *descriptio* is the most important method of amplification (p. 3). They devote their greatest attention to portrait-descriptions, less to "the theory and practice of the description of scenery" (p. 4). Schaar's method is to compare "the descriptive technique in Chaucer with that in other authors with a view to ascertaining possible influences" (p. 9), and, by emphasizing the importance of general influences as well as strict parallels, he distinguishes his procedure from that of "an older critical school, whose representatives searched assiduously for borrowings" (p. 6).

Schaar divides his book into three main chapters: "Description of Emotions," "The

Portraits," and "Landscape Description." He finds a greater degree of "emotive" description in Chaucer's early poems than in his sources or than in the later poems; "in Troilus and Criseyde this development reaches its summit" (1955:92). Schaar also finds that in *RR* Guillaume and Jean "are rather sparing with emotive description" (p. 123); but he limits his investigation to "such paragraphs as deal with emotions in the third person" (p. 17) and thus excludes, in particular, the Dreamer's first-person utterances. The third-person cases that exist (pp. 123–25) are mostly brief, but an outstanding exception (p. 123) is the record of Pygmalion's delight in his statue (citing Ln 20836, 21065–66, 21175ff.) and his agitation at its lack of response (citing Ln 20932). Schaar notes that Jean's tendency to avoid "emotive description in *exempla* . . . is similar to Chaucer's habits in this respect" (p. 124), and in the chapter on description in the portraits, he finds that Chaucer's "general averseness to portrayal in *exempla* with classical themes [as in *LGW*], and notably to concrete portrayal, may be a trace of the influence of Jean de Meun" (p. 295). Again he notes an exception in the Pygmalion story with its "very particularized description of the various garments and adornments ([Ln] 20937ff.)." In his analysis of Cunningham's comparison of the *GP* portraits with the double series at the beginning of Guillaume's *RR*, Schaar stresses the differences. Regarding the portraits of Chaucer's rascals and the images painted on the wall of the garden in *RR*, Schaar argues as follows (pp. 304, 306):

The essential feature in these portraits [of *GP*] is not caricaturish distortion but objective exactness and scrupulous accuracy. . . . The portraits in the *Roman* . . . are executed almost exclusively in types of technique which are uncommon in the Prologue. . . . Guillaume de Lorris does his best to make his figures as ugly and repulsive as possible. . . . To Chaucer, on the contrary, sharp outlines are of prime importance, and his task is . . . to give . . . an objective picture of a certain set of people.

As for Guillaume's portraits of those who inhabit the garden (Ln 796ff.), Schaar writes: "Guillaume . . . is concerned with the oppo-

site extreme . . . good and noble qualities. . . . We are far from the technique in Chaucer's Prologue, where idealization is much more restricted" (pp. 311–12). When Schaar seeks analogues for a tradition of objective description (pp. 312–13), he includes among his "isolated instances" of such description the portrait of Papelardie (Ln 420ff.), citing her "simple contenance," the fact that she was clothed and shod *like a nun* ("tot ausi con fame rendue"), her *feigned* ("feinte") prayers and her *appearance* ("semblant") of doing good works.

Schaar's procedure sometimes results in discrete discussions of the same passages in different contexts. In the chapter on descriptions of scenery, for example, two parallels between *RR* and Chaucer's works—the flowering-meadow parallel (Ln 8411ff.; *BD* 398ff.) and the allusion to "Argus, the noble countour" (Ln 12790ff.; *BD* 435ff.)—appear in different places. First, although Schaar questions certain previous identifications of parallels between *RR* and *BD*, he accepts these two (pp. 380–85). Later, in his discussion of sentence-structure (pp. 425–26), he cites these passages among the "long-winded and intricate patterns" in *BD*; in the first passage, where both *BD* and *RR* use *for*-clauses for elaboration, Schaar observes that *BD* is "less complicated . . . as compared with the *Roman*"; and he writes that the second (the "Argus") comparison "is more similar to the structure in the *Roman*." But on the next page he modifies this analysis by distinguishing the structure of the *BD* passage—where "the consecutive clause ['That thogh Argus . . .'] is interspersed with a complicated system of concessive, causal, and conditional clauses"—from that of *RR*—where "there is no consecutive link between the conditional link-clause ['Se maistre Algus . . .'] and the preceding description" (p. 427).

In a more general sense, Schaar finds that Chaucer's landscape descriptions are "impressionistic . . . in the earlier poems," where "the technique . . . has much in common with that in similar descriptions in Machaut's poems and the beginning of the *Roman de la Rose*" (p. 485). "The particular sensory variant of impressionistic description which involves a recording of the observer's perceptions is met with primarily in" *BD* and *LGWP*, among "the different categories of description," he concludes, "Chaucer's originality asserts itself best in the portraits" (p. 495).

In a much broader treatment, but with only brief attention to Chaucer, Douglas Kelly (1978*a*) examines the topic of "imagination" in medieval rhetoric and in French love poetry from *RR* to the fifteenth century. By imagination he means "the cognitive faculty known as *imaginatio*," the faculty that "governs the invention, retention, and expression of Images in the mind [and that] also designates the artist's Image, projected as it were into matter" (pp. xi–xii); further, he finds that Chaucer "described most clearly and succinctly the essential features of Imagination" (p. xii, citing *HF* 725–28). Kelly's view (pp. 195–99) is that Chaucer's use of *imaginatio* reflects the differing uses of it made by Guillaume de Lorris and Jean de Meun. Whereas "Guillaume de Lorris' fragment . . . is the first thoroughgoing representation of courtly love by poetic *imaginatio*" (p. 95), Jean "is concerned with simpler and more stringent moral values broadly valid for all humanity" (p. 78). In turn, "Chaucer's tendency to emphasize the decline of *fyn lovyng* into a worse state" represents an "inversion of Guillaume de Lorris' progress from rage to love," an inversion which "involves a concomitant lowering of the quality of Imagination to the farce, of the quality of courtly love to Jean de Meun's vision" (p. 196).

Style. Charles Muscatine's remarks about Chaucer's style (1957) anticipate Kelly's perception of the contrast between Guillaume and Jean and its effect on Chaucer. Recasting the classical and medieval terminology (high, low, and middle), Muscatine distinguishes three levels of style used by Chaucer and his French models: the courtly style (conventionalism), the bourgeois style (naturalism), and the mixed style.

The courtly style, Muscatine observes, is employed by Guillaume de Lorris. "The style, designed to evoke invisible worlds, is equally well adapted to describe an earthly paradise and a human soul. The Garden of the Rose is both of these at once" (p. 40). Muscatine finds in Jean de Meun's portion, on the other hand, "the realistic style of the bourgeois tradition" (p. 59), which serves as an effective vehicle for Jean's philosophic naturalism (pp. 74–79). For Muscatine, the significant point is that (p. 96), even "had Chaucer never borrowed a line from Jean":

the French poet for the first time clearly outlines the configuration of styles that Chaucer was to find most congenial. . . . This configuration—the juxtaposition of realism and courtly convention in a meaningful relationship to each other—implies a broadness of spirit characteristic of both poets. . . . This configuration, in various versions, becomes a leading trait of European literary style.

Muscatine argues further that in Jean "the relationship between style and meaning . . . is a functional one" (p. 96); this "functionalism of style" is the main theme of Muscatine's discussion of Chaucer (p. 97).

In *BD* Muscatine sees "the emergence of Chaucer's central stylistic problem: this strain of realism in the midst of conventional elevation, with the attendant problem of their mutual adjustment" (p. 107). The theme of *PF*, Muscatine says, is Jean de Meun's theme: "the comic, contradictory variety of men's attitudes toward love" (p. 116). But Chaucer's "use of the Narrator's naïve personality to promote imaginative surrender to the dream world" is a "device . . . learned from Guillaume de Lorris" (p. 123).

In *TC* Muscatine sees a consummate blending of these styles. "Medieval realism . . . jostles courtly convention all through . . . the *Troilus*" (p. 130). "The whole meaning of the poem depends as fully on the style and ethos represented by Jean de Meun as on the values of Chrétien and Guillaume de Lorris" (p. 131). "By juxtaposition of scenes and passages alternatingly conventional and naturalistic . . . Chaucer creates a pervasive, literary, structural irony" (p. 132). "Troilus represents the courtly, idealistic view of experience" (p. 133), "Pandarus . . . provides a view of courtly love under the aspect of realism" (p. 139), and Criseyde combines the two natures: "Her ambiguity is her meaning" (p. 164). "The style of the poem is . . . medieval and conservative, but developed and deployed with critical energy. Its naturalism is the inherited style made newly acute. It can explore recesses of phenomenal and social experience well beyond the scope of Jean de Meun" (p. 165).

In *CT* Muscatine again finds a "tension between phenomenal and ideal" (p. 168). He points out that in *GP* Chaucer's "modifications of convention both within and between the portraits produce not only the 'real life' of naturalistic criticism, but also the tension . . . that supports his deepest meaning" (p. 171). Muscatine's selective analysis of the tales themselves—organized in terms of three styles: conventionalism (*KnT* and *ClT*), naturalism (*RvT, WBP,* and *CYT*), and "the mixed style" (*MilT, MerT, NPT*)—is designed to lead up to his argument that *CT* "as a whole is an example of the mixed style" (p. 222), that "virtually all the *Canterbury Tales* have some mixture of styles," but that "there are a number of tales in which, as in [*PF* and *TC*], the mixed style is on display and becomes part of the subject of the poem. These [*MilT, MerT, NPT*] are the tales which seem most 'Chaucerian'" (p. 223).

D. W. Robertson (1962) takes a very different approach to the Gothic style of Chaucer and *RR*. Robertson (pp. 206–07, citing Friedman 1959) questions the appropriateness of the term "bourgeois realism" (cf. Muscatine above) to describe Jean's style. He prefers the term verisimilitude (pp. 184–86) for what he regards as surface embellishment that does not affect the meaning inherent in the figures and actions depicted by medieval artists. His analysis of *RR* emphasizes its development through "symbolic actions involving iconographically described characters in an iconographically described setting" (p. 197), and he adduces illustrations that emphasize the traditional significance of visual details. "Jean de Meun," he writes, "is just as fond of iconographic detail as was Guillaume, but his continuation shows a much greater flexibility in the use of exemplary materials" (p. 203).

In Chaucer also, Robertson argues, "iconographic descriptions made up of elements to

which conventionally established areas of meaning were attached are frequent[,] not only in the formal allegories but also in *The Canterbury Tales*. . . . The garden of the Merchant's Tale . . . is clearly a variant of the Garden of Deduit in the *Roman de la Rose*. . . . Even more significant," he continues, "is Chaucer's tendency to mingle details of an iconographic nature with other details which produce an effect of considerable verisimilitude" (p. 242). The portrait of the Prioress, for example, shows how Chaucer borrowed "two bits of iconographical material whose significance had been established by Jean de Meun: the table manners [Lc 13355–426] and the motto [*Amor vincit omnia,* Lc 21297–306; cf. Finlayson 1988]. To these he added materials of his own with similar implications, in order to form a picture with a certain amount of verisimilitude, and he couched the whole in schemes and tropes designed to emphasize the principal idea" (p. 247), that the Prioress is "a peculiarly striking exemplar of false courtesy, nourished . . . by sentimentality" (pp. 246–47). This use of iconographic motifs with verisimilar detail, and the aesthetic theory which underlies it, relates in Robertson's thought to the topic of allegory. We turn now to that topic.

Allegory and Convention. The earliest statement regarding the influence of *RR*'s allegorical technique on Chaucer appears in Fansler's observation that "the kind of allegory in the *Roman* which seems to have been most used by Chaucer was nothing more than personification of abstractions" (1914:83). C. S. Lewis (1936), who assumes that allegory *is* personification, offers the first and perhaps the most influential statement about Chaucer's perception and use of *RR*'s allegory. Lewis's special interest is "the allegorical love poetry of the Middle Ages," and he sees the allegorical form as "that of a struggle between personified abstractions. . . . It is essential to this form," he writes, "that the literal narrative and the *significacio* should be separable" (1936:1). The same conception underlies Lewis's understanding of *RR* and of its relationship to Chaucer. He sees "the development of allegory" as a way of representing human psychology and thus of supplying "the subjective element in literature" (p. 113), the element that Guillaume de Lorris embodies in his personified abstractions. But he feels that Jean de Meun is not at heart "an allegorist. . . . He utterly lacks . . . Guillaume's architectonics and sense of proportion. . . . It is not the allegorical narrative which swells [the poem] to its prodigious length; it is the digressions" (pp. 137–38). Moreover, Jean's narrative details often have no cogent allegorical significance and therefore violate the genre that he pretends to work in. Thus "what Jean really does is to substitute a third-rate literal story for a first-rate allegorical story, and to confuse the one with the other so that we can enjoy neither" (p. 141).

Lewis's concept of allegory also leads him to see Chaucer's love poems as influenced by but different from Guillaume's *RR* (pp. 166–67):

They are all recognizable descendants of it, but none of them is a poem of the same type. . . . In Chaucer we find the same subject-matter, that of chivalrous love; but the treatment is never truly allegorical. . . . In his greatest work [*TC*], we have the courtly conceptions of love, which Chaucer learned from the French allegory, put into action in poetry which is not allegorical at all. Chaucer achieves the literal presentation; but it is Guillaume's allegory which has rendered the achievement possible.

A number of scholars have reacted to Lewis's characterization of allegory, particularly his insistence on personification: see Bronson (1947), Frank (1953), Muscatine (1953), and Bloomfield (1963). For present purposes, the more important issue is the view, common long before Lewis's expression of it, that the two poets of *RR* differ radically in their treatments of and their attitudes toward their subject matter. There is a tendency among those who see opposition between Guillaume and Jean to regard Guillaume's portion of the work as "autobiographical," that is, as representing experience, common or individual. Lewis's analysis of allegory as supplying "the subjective element in literature" (1936:113) is an example; Muscatine's

study of the origins of psychological allegory in *RR* (1953:1163) is another (cf. Van Dyke 1985:71, 77). Underlying this kind of view is the assumption that Guillaume celebrates idealized, refined love, whereas Jean focuses on the purely sexual and procreative aspects of love (cf. Dahlberg 1971:3).

A fundamental challenge to this view appears in the work of D. W. Robertson, who feels not only that Jean understood Guillaume but that both poets present Amant, from beginning to end, as a foolish lover (cf. Fleming 1969, 1984). Robertson first enunciates this position in 1951, when he characterizes *RR* as "a humorous and witty retelling of the story of the Fall" (p. 43; cf. Dahlberg 1961). Later (1962:91–98) he states this position more fully, and he elaborates it, partly through an examination of the kinds of allegory (pp. 286–317). For the concept of allegory as a feature of rhetoric, as "the art of saying one thing to mean another" (p. 57), Robertson cites the authority of the character Reason in *RR* (Ln 7153–80)—"the source of instruction on the subject of poetic appreciation" (p. 61); it is she who tells the Dreamer-Lover that the poets' "integuments" conceal many of the "secrets of philosophy." Robertson employs this concept of allegory to interpret (pp. 91–104) the pattern of action in *RR* as the abuse of beauty and its concomitant distortion of reason, a significant pattern that he finds also in Chaucer's poetry, e.g., *KnT*, *MerT*, and *TC* (pp. 105–112, 476–78). "The *Roman* is a humanistic and poetic expression of ideas which Chaucer could have his parson in the *Tales* state in a straightforward way, but which he, as a court poet, could state most effectively in ways suggested by the *Roman* and by other poems like it" (p. 104).

Robertson also offers (1962:317–36) a full exposition of the method of Scriptural exegesis in reading Chaucer; his discussion, however, does not treat the influence of *RR* on Chaucer but rather traces their participation in a common, exegetical tradition. Still, as we have seen, three of Chaucer's exegetes—the Wife of Bath, the friar in *SumT*, and the Pardoner—have distinct antecedents in La Vieille and Fals Semblant (cf. 1962:318, 327,

380–81). Robertson finds that the exegetical theme of spiritual oldness present in La Vieille and Fals Semblant likewise inheres in the literal figures of their Chaucerian progeny— the Wife of Bath, the Pardoner, and January of *MerT* (pp. 379–82; cf. Miller 1955). Similarly, such works as *KnT*, *MerT*, *FranT*, *BD*, *PF*, and *TC* reflect the garden-setting of *RR* and its Biblical progenitors in Genesis and the Song of Songs (pp. 386–88; cf. Robertson 1951 and Tuve 1966:232–80, esp. 262–63n.).

Another discussion that considers shared tradition as well as linear influence is offered by James Wimsatt (1970), who examines the conventions of love narrative employed in *RR* and in Chaucer's works, especially in *BD* and *TC*, for which *RR* seems to be the principal exemplar of the conventions (pp. 65–82). He observes (p. 83) that each poem manipulates the conventions to produce a different narrative result. A quite different effect is achieved, Wimsatt states (p. 85), in the story of May and Damian in *MerT*, which travesties the conventional narrative typified in *RR* by making the source of love physical rather than psychological. Further, Wimsatt refines previous analyses of the parallels between Pandarus and Lady Reason when he sees that Pandarus's true role is primarily as "a counterpart to Friend of the *Romance of the Rose*" but that "he often parades as Reason or Lady Philosophy" (p. 100).

Maureen Quilligan (1981) traces alteration of another kind in her treatment of *RR*'s influence on Chaucer's *PF*. Like Wimsatt (1970:65), she sees movement away from *RR*'s allegorical mode toward a more realistic mode of presentation; psychological allegory gives way to a "dreamworld . . . peopled by real creatures whose language is subordinate to personality (though this personality be the character of a class type)" (pp. 175–76, 180). The most important aspect of this change, at least within the framework of Quilligan's novel theory of allegory (it is, she argues, an outgrowth of wordplay), lies in Chaucer's substitution of language that is designed to be heard for language that is designed to be read, the latter being the language of allegory, in which the word must be cousin to the deed

(cf. Lc 7033–7154), the former being the language of literary realism (cf. *GP* 725–42; *MilP* A 3167–86, *ManT* H 207–20). After considering the debate between Reason and Amis on the proper naming of the sexual organs, Quilligan writes (pp. 185–86) that Chaucer's *PF*

takes Jean's concern about language (the conflict between euphemistic and natural-reasonable diction) and dramatizes it with a chorus of [bird] voices that renders audible the community of creatures served by the ideal of a "commune profit" [*PF* 75]. . . . The language of . . . Jean [de Meun] is meant to illuminate and instruct us in our true social responsibilities within a God-centered cosmos. . . . Language for [him] is a force that must move society toward the Word at the center of the universe. . . . To accept that in the *Parlement* Chaucer has deallegorized his sources by transforming their silent textuality into audible mimesis should not obscure the fact that for [Chaucer as well as Jean] it was critically possible and morally vital to perceive that Word in the world.

John Longo (1982), who sees Guillaume's *RR* as a *translatio* (adaptation) of Ovidian materials (p. 79), and Jean's continuation "as a gloss on [Guillaume's] poem" (p. 169), finds that Chaucer's *LGWP* is in its turn a further *translatio* of *RR*. Whereas in the French poem Amours declares *RR* to be "his definitive *ars amatoria*," in the English poem the God of Love condemns *RR* as a *remedia amoris*. "Chaucer's rewriting of Ovid here . . . flushes out Jean's own ironic presentation of his poem as a mirror for lovers. . . . The Prologue to *LGW*, and the God's anger at Chaucer's *Romaunce*, identify Chaucer as the *Roman*'s heir, the recipient of the *translatio studii* [see Curtius 1953:28–29; Kelly 1978*b*] in vernacular verse" (pp. 215–16).

Longo finds two other noteworthy "translations" of *RR* in Chaucer's work. Having earlier noted that in Jean de Meun's continuation the God of Love calls *RR* "a mirror for lovers" (p. 170; Lc 10621), Longo reads *TC* as Chaucer's own mirror for lovers (pp. 281–370); in it, he writes, "Chaucer's Boethian narrator finds his enlightenment precisely through his engagement with his 'olde bookes' in the process of *translatio*," and "in borrowing this

Boethian movement Chaucer is even more insistently rewriting the *Roman de la Rose*" (p. 287). For a specific instance of such rewriting, see John Fleming (1986*b*). And in *FranT*, Longo argues (pp. 403–26), the *translatio* of Boccaccian material regarding freedom and *maistrie* in love reflects Jean's treatment of the topic in the speeches of Amis (Lc 8417–24, 9394–424) and La Vieille (Lc 13929–65; cf. Robertson 1974:13–16). "At one level, the *Franklin's Tale* is a study in what happens when people try to live as Amis recommends. As such it is Chaucer's 'reading' of this part of the *Roman de la Rose*" (p. 420).

Steven Wright (1986) attempts "to point out ways that the influence of the *Roman* on . . . Chaucer was literary, with literary consequences" (p. 2). By literary influence Wright means parallels in structure and situation, a "level of influence that might be expressed in the literary devices that establish the tone of a work, such as in Chaucer's debts to Jean's ironic allegory" (p. 27, citing Diekstra 1981; Wright also cites, p. 25, Cunningham's work, discussed above). Wright sees Jean not only as mocking "Guillaume's courtly allegory by introducing realistic touches of different kinds," but as mounting "its most sophisticated attack on Guillaume's courtly allegory by mocking the devices of allegory themselves" (p. 171; cf. Quilligan 1979:244). Wright argues that "Jean de Meun taught Chaucer the hidden suppositions of the allegorical mode as Guillaume de Lorris . . . had used it," that "it was Jean de Meun's manipulation of Guillaume's allegory that seems to have provided Chaucer with his model when his ends required a complex deflation of allegorical devices or allegorical meaning" (p. 172).

Thus Wright (following David 1976:243 n.10) regards Jean as the greater influence on Chaucer, even in a poem like *BD*, which clearly owes much to Guillaume (de Lorris and de Machaut). Just as "Jean deflated Guillaume's delicate allegory," so too Chaucer's *BD* deflates Machaut's "preposterously ideal world by exposing the actual literal meaning of its images" (pp. 117–18). Similarly, Wright believes, allusions to *RR* suggest that the "authority" assumed by the dreamer when he meets the Black Knight (p. 131) is deflated in the face of the Black Knight's "experience" (pp. 151–58; cf. David 1976:135–58).

The influence of *RR*, Wright finds, is much the same in *SqT*, *MerT*, *PardT*, and *NPT*. In *SqT* F 604–20 the "famous Boethian image" of the bird in the cage (cf. Lc 13911–16; Boethius, *De Cons. Phil.* 3m2) "literaliz[es]" the Garden of Deduit (p. 179). Likewise, Wright argues, Chaucer's description of Pertelote (*NPT* B² 4061–65) draws from Guillaume de Lorris's description of Leesce (Lc 830–33) but treats that material "in a way that Jean de Meun's part of the *Roman* had suggested to him" (p. 230).

In Wright's long analysis of *MerT* (pp. 179–216), the Guillaume-Jean relationship is again fundamental, but in a different way. Chaucer does not set Jean against Guillaume but in effect sets the two of them against a third, more radical viewpoint. The garden in *MerT*, "deliberately reminiscent of Guillaume's Garden of Deduit," becomes in the hands of Chaucer's narrator "a debased and brutal version of Jean de Meun's own ironic handling of Guillaume de Lorris. . . . In the *Merchant's Tale*, the narrator's brutally ironic treatment of January is an attack on both Guillaume's courtly allegory and on Jean's 'cosmic' allegory" (pp. 180–81). "Chaucer used [the narrator's] voice to present a cynical account of 'idealism'" (p. 189), one that eliminates the "grander scope of Jean's part . . . from the narrator's vision; I suspect this tells us something about Chaucer's vantage on the action of the *Merchant's Tale* and about Chaucer's reading of Jean's part of the *Roman*" (p. 208).

Guillaume de Lorris does not figure in Wright's treatment of *PardT*, which finds that "the patterning of the action" between the Pardoner and Harry Bailly at the end of the tale is "almost certainly grounded in Faux-Semblant's murder of Malebouche in the *Roman*" (p. 218). Wright also argues (pp. 225–27) that the Host's verbal play with "coillons" and "relics" (*PardT* C 952–55) recalls Reason's use of the same terminology when she refutes Amant's accusation of dirty talk (Lc 7079–85); the Pardoner, like Amant and Amors, tries to remake things with words (p. 227), and Harry Bailly, like Reason, resists that sort of fraud (p. 228).

F. N. M. Diekstra argues that Chaucer imitates *RR*'s use of irony (1988:12), particularly the technique of irony "achieved through the juxtaposition of units that are not in themselves ironical" (p. 17). He finds this technique even in Guillaume de Lorris's portion of *RR* where, he points out (p. 13), the narrator's announcement that the romance is going to "improve" (Lc 2060 "li romanz des or amende") immediately precedes commandments of the God of Love that "introduce the Lover to a life of unredeemed hardship" (cf. Lc 2074*a*–2580). Chaucer, Diekstra finds (pp. 17–25), employs similar techniques: juxtaposing incongruous scenes in the early poems; putting incongruous argument into the voices of characters like the Wife of Bath; presenting alternative hyperbolic parallels to Chantecleer's downfall; mingling narrator's and character's voices, as in the defense of worldly activity in the *GP* portrait of the Monk. Diekstra's sense of irony clearly differs from that of Wright, who links "Chaucer's debts to Jean's ironic allegory" (1986:27, citing Diekstra 1981) with the idea that Jean's portion of *RR* is an "ironic reworking of Guillaume de Lorris's part."

The Use of First Person. Another approach to the influence of *RR* on Chaucer is the study of the first-person narrator, a device employed in "all of Chaucer's literary sources at this period, and of some of his major philosophic ones" (Finlayson 1990:205–06). For the possible sources of first-person narration in *RR*, see Charles Muscatine (1953), Paul Zumthor (1972:172–73, 371), and John Fleming (1984: 84–85; cf. Dahlberg 1977). The genre of dream vision is perhaps the most obvious source of the first-person narration in both *RR* and Chaucer (on the dream vision, see Spearing 1976; Lynch 1988, particularly 2–4; Russell 1988; Kruger 1992). Barbara Nolan (1977) points out that writers of dream visions often employ a "fallible 'I'" as a device that "could provide . . . one way of 'seeing' the visionary world," and she declares that "the master who brought the technique to a point of perfection was Guillaume de Lorris,"

whose "handling of the narrator in relation to his dream world and his audience's reason exerted so powerful an influence on later poets that an understanding of his method is an essential preparation for approaching all subsequent questing narrators" (pp. 140–41). Nolan describes that method as follows (p. 141):

In those vision quests like the *Roman de la Rose* which depend heavily on the spiritual condition of the narrator in relation to his experience, the audience must be aware simultaneously of two visions. They are expected to see both the visionary world as it is seen by the stumbling narrator and the same world in its universal or spiritual significance. They, together with the poet, . . . observe with ironic detachment and amusement (and sometimes sympathy) the disparity between the two visions.

David Lawton (1985) suggests that the narratorial voice "developed by Chaucer" owes "its greatest debt . . . to the dreamer *persona* in the *Roman de la Rose*" (p. 13), and that in this regard the influence of *RR* on *BD* and *LGW* far exceeds that of the more obvious models in the French *dits amoureux* (pp. 48, 57). He observes that *RR* "is awarded pride of place" both in the Prologue to *LGW* and in *BD* (lines 333–34), where "Chaucer's narratorial *persona* begins his career with his colours nailed to the bedroom wall" (p. 57). Lawton gives greatest credit to Jean de Meun's "debunking [of] the narrator" (p. 70; cf. Hult 1984:250, 266–67), and to Jean's direct interventions (Lc 15105–272), especially to defend his poem against charges of antifeminism, which are, Lawton states, "a major source of a Chaucerian repertoire" (p. 71). Nevertheless, Lawton allows that "Jean's continuation, different as it is, develops hints in Guillaume, and Chaucer's debt to the first part of the poem is immense" (p. 62). The debt includes the distinction between poet and dreamer (p. 63, citing Spearing 1976:33) and the use of past tense by a present voice (pp. 64–65; cf. Vitz 1973:53–54, 62–64). From Guillaume and Jean, Chaucer learned how to to exploit the time frames and hence perspectives that separate the callow dreamer, the maturer narrator, and the wiser poet, often making it difficult to determine which of the three voices is speaking.

The dream-vision narrator would seem to serve as a model for some of Chaucer's other narrators. Lawton sees *HF* as the transition to the non-dream poems; with this poem's "Geffrey," he argues, Chaucer creates a narratorial *persona* that will allow him to abandon dream fiction. "The reconditioned dreamer becomes an apocryphal author" (1985:75) or a performer concealed, as in *TC*, "behind an apocryphal source, 'Lollius'" (p. 76). In support of this position, Lawton (p. 79) invokes the narrator's disclaimer in *TC* 3.1324–27 ("though I kan nat tellen al, / As kan myn auctour . . . / Yet have I seyd . . . / al holy his sentence"):

> The narrator . . . like Jean de Meun in the *Roman* . . . can profess a detached attitude to love which is not devoid of clerkly suspicion while at the same time invoking the antecedent authority of his text [3.1196, 1199] . . . just as Jean de Meun maintains a pose of fidelity to the prior events of his dream, to license representation of scenes of sexual fulfillment. At the same time the clerkly disengagement from love, like Jean's detachment from his younger self, allows a passage condemning "feynede loves" in the poem's epilogue (V 1848), and implicitly anticipates the potential for this judgment. The dialectic of the reconditioned dreamer-poet with his youthful dream is transposed into that between the translator-poet and his ancient text.

Diekstra (1988), in his "attempt to read the *Romance* through the eyes of Chaucer" (p. 12), raises the question of how the inner voices—e.g. those of Fals Semblant, Raison, or Amis in *RR*, or of the tale-tellers like the Pardoner in *CT*—relate to the voice of the poet. It is a question as old as the debate over *RR* in the early fifteenth century (see Fleming 1965; Potansky 1972; Hicks, ed. 1977; Baird and Kane, trans. 1978; Badel 1980), when Christine de Pisan and Chancellor Gerson attributed the opinions of the characters to Jean de Meun, and Pierre Col distinguished them from Jean's. Diekstra rejects "the views of commentators who have discovered anti-

social, antiascetic, antifeminist and heretical views in the poem and ascribed them to Jean de Meun" (pp. 18–19):

> The typical device by which Jean de Meun's allegorical personifications express their unorthodox views is that of the encapsulated speech. It is never the author speaking in his own voice, but a dramatic presentation, a reported monologue. [In] the Jealous Husband . . . we have a speech at two removes from the author's voice. . . . The effect . . . is that we are drawn to the manipulating figure of the poet to supply us with the unifying answer to the diversity of views. . . . The result is that our attention becomes author-directed. . . . This effect may be held responsible for the critical error of attributing the characters' views to himself.

As for Chaucer, Diekstra suggests (p. 19) that his "greater interest in authenticating realism has led us to show greater curiosity towards his characters. Yet it is instructive occasionally to remind ourselves that in many cases they have evolved from the flat abstractions of the *Romance* and cannot bear the weight of too much novelistic analysis."

John Finlayson (1990:188) suggests that a comparison of Chaucer's narrators "with the narrative voices of the *Roman*, the source which seems to have influenced him and provided matter throughout the whole of his production, may clarify somewhat the continuing debates on the characteristics of the narrators, their function within the dream poems, and their relation to other narrative voices." In *RR*, he writes, there are "two authors, but more than two narrative voices or stances, and the continuation by Jean de Meun has a varying relationship both to the matter of Guillaume and to his dramatized autobiographic stance" (p. 188). He cites Vitz's work (1973) on multiple "I"s and argues that "even in Guillaume . . . there is a multiplicity of narrative voices or stances" (p. 190); and he finds that "Jean's continuation . . . multiplies considerably the number of narrative voices or stances. . . . The relation of Jean de Meun to the Lover, whether as the young Guillaume or as an allegorical concept, is closer to that of the *Troilus* narrator to his characters and his sources" (p. 193).

Finlayson's analysis of Chaucer's narrators in comparison with *RR* leads to the following conclusions (p. 208):

In the *Book of the Duchess* and the *Parliament of Fowls* the narrator as *persona* is much less "present" than is often assumed, . . . the narratorial voice is more usually neutral, and . . . for major and, indeed, central parts of the poem there is *no* first person presence. . . . The *House of Fame* is radically different in that the narrator is, on the level of *literalis*, the only constant or uniting factor. . . . In this he most nearly resembles Jean de Meun's narrator, who at times is autobiographical, at others is the Lover, and very frequently disappears from the text in any role to be replaced by the dialogues and monologues of allegorical *personae*. Where Chaucer differs from both Guillaume and Jean is in one feature—that his narrator-*persona* is more comically "humanized" and, at the same time, "detached" from his matter, even in the *House of Fame* where he is the observer of his own experience. But this "humanization" is only occasional, not continuous or consistent.

TEXTUAL COMMENTARY

The basis of the text is the unique Glasgow manuscript (MS), except for those portions where it is defective and where the Thynne print of 1532 (TH[1]) is the sole authority. We discuss first the manuscript and its relationship to TH[1], then the printed editions, and finally the present edition.

Description of the Manuscript

The sole manuscript (MS) of *The Romaunt of the Rose*—Glasgow University Library, Hunter 409 (formerly Hunterian Museum V. 3. 7)—is fully described by Young and Aitken (1908:329–331). One need correct only their statement that MS originally had 262 folios, probably an error for 162, that is, the present 151 folios plus the eleven missing leaves (see below). MS was rebound in 1963 by Douglas Cockerell and Son of Cambridge, and a binder's note signed by S. M. Cockerell ("SMC") appears inside the back board; it reads in part:

Book taken down, some leaves flattened and mended with vellum, end papers repaired, linen joints, resewn on five double cords to the old marking up with the quires in the same order as before, thread headbands, spine covered with brown morocco, boards repaired and replaced, gold lettering, previous lettering piece mounted on the inside of the back board.

Contents

As Young and Aitken note (1908:329), MS contains only *Rom.* Peck errs in writing that in "MS the *Romaunt* is followed by *Troilus and Criseyde*" (1988:2). This sequence does appear, however, in TH[1] and the early printed editions.

Date

Although most commentators do not actually cite evidence, their basis for dating MS is clearly paleographical. Furnivall (1868:110 and note, ed. Warton 1871:2.317) states simply that MS is from the fifteenth century. Skeat, at first vague—"considerably later" than 1350 (1880:xciv; 1884:451)—subsequently specifies "about 1440–50" (1888c:xciv). He then offers greater precision (1894; 1899:1.13), "hardly later than 1440," a date for which he acknowledges the help of "experts . . . Mr. [E. A.] Bond and Mr. [E. M.] Thompson at the British Museum." Further, he suggests the possibility of a lost original (O) of MS and TH[1], "written out not much later than 1430" (see below, on the relationship of MS and TH[1]). In 1900 (p. 84) he again says that MS "cannot well be later than 1440." Lange (1901:397) accepts this date and the idea of an earlier version.

Young and Aitken (1908:329), however, give the date as "Early Cent. XV." Citing them, Brusendorff (1925:296) writes that MS is "carefully executed in a style of writing and illumination dating from the first quarter of the XV century or so." He adds that "Skeat's date towards 1440 . . . is almost certainly too late." Fisher (FI, p. 970) likewise dates MS "from the first quarter of the fifteenth century." Sutherland (SU, p. ix, n.1) indicates a date between 1400 and 1440. The editions of Robinson (RB) and David (RI) do not assign a date.

Provenance

There are no certain indications of the early provenance of MS, but evidence for its whereabouts in the sixteenth century does exist. On the left side of the upper margin of fol. 1r, in what Young and Aitken (1908:329) describe as an early sixteenth-century hand, is written: "Thomas Griggs, possessor huius libri" ("Thomas Griggs, owner of this book"; neither Young and Aitken nor SK 1.13 identify Griggs). Further, MS must have been in London before 1532. Blodgett (1979, 1984; see below) has shown that William Thynne used MS as printer's copy for TH[1]. Thynne's son Francis reports (1599; 1875:12; cf. Carlson 1989:214–15) that some twenty-five of his father's manuscripts were "partly dispersed aboute xxvj yeres a-goo [i.e., ca. 1573] and partlye stoolen oute of my howse at Popler." We do not know that MS was among these, but Blodgett's discovery makes it a strong possibility. A further connection with the Thynne family may appear in a marginalium on folio 60r, where among some isolated words in a sixteenth-century hand appears the name "Ihon thin" (cropped) or, possibly, "Ihon thiu." The former reading suggests an association with a nephew of William and cousin of Francis, and builder of Longleat House, where there are other Chaucer manuscripts (Blodgett 1984:39–40).

There are other sixteenth-century suggestions of London or legal associations. On fol. 139r is a marginalium, "in brown crayon, in an early XVI. Cent. hand" (Young and Aitken 1908:330), that reads: "my lorde Mont Joy | my lady yō"; Young and Aitken (1908:331) believe that "Lord Mountjoy . . . is possibly Charles Blount, fifth Baron Mountjoy, who died 1545, or his father William Blount, fourth Baron Mountjoy, who died 1534," and they refer to the *DNB* (2:701–02, 721–22). Another marginalium (fol. 134r) of the same period uses legal phraseology: "Thes Indenture made the sekond | Daye of June In the iij and fourthe | yeare of the Raygne of Kynge | Felyppe and quene mari bye | the grace of god kynge of Ingland | flanco (?) mapler"; the indicated year is 1556–57 (Cheney 1945;

1970:24). Another legal association appears on the verso of the final text leaf (fol. 150v) in the repetition, in an engrossing hand, of part of line 7311—"I take youre silf to Recorde"—next to the phrase, in secretary hand, "flytewoddes chamber." The signature "William Ball" appears twice, once above and once below the phrase "flytewoddes chamber." Several Fleetwoods were associated in the sixteenth century with the Inns of Court; the most famous of them, William Fleetwood (1535?–1594), recorder of London, was a bencher of the Middle Temple, and his father and two sons, as well as other relatives, also appear in the Middle Temple Records from 1553 to 1604 (ed. Hopwood 1904:1.94, 109, 175, 177, 230, 267, 276, 332–33, 374, 400, 413; 2.443; on the family relationships, see Burke and Burke 1844:199–201, and Buss 1920: vi.9–10).

Finally we may note three names on folio 151r–v, a vellum fragment (140mm x 134 mm) that follows the text. On the recto appear the names Robert Brunefeld and, lower, Henrye Beakyns. Young and Aitken, perhaps correctly, transcribe the first name as "Robert bromfeld" and date the hand as sixteenth century (1908:330). On the verso appears the name "Edm*und* Sexten" in a hand of the late sixteenth century (for full transcript see Young and Aitken, p. 330).

The associations collected here prove nothing about the original provenance of the MS. They do, however, indicate a learned milieu that would lead eventually to the antiquarian Thomas Martin, whose name appears on an original vellum fragment of a fly-leaf (iv, 1r) before the text: "Tho: Martin Ex dono doṁ Iacobi Sturgeon | de Bury scī Edmundi in agro | Suffolc: Artis Chirurgicae | Periti | Nov: 9 | 1720." ("Thomas Martin, from the gift of mister James Sturgeon of Bury St. Edmunds in the county of Suffolk, expert in the practice of surgery, Nov. 9, 1720"; on Thomas Martin of Palgrave see *DNB* 12:1182–83). This note once aroused untenable conjecture that MS may have been an East Anglian transcript (see pp. 17–18). Skeat (SK 1.13) says that the note is "by A. Askew (from whom [William] Hunter bought the

MS.)"; but Young and Aitken (1908:331), who do not identify the hand, note that "Dr. Anthony Askew (1722–74) . . . was born two years after [the] date" in the inscription.

Young and Aitken (1908:329) ascribe to Martin a note on one of the paper fly-leaves inserted at the beginning of MS (iii, 1r); it reports that an initial leaf is missing from MS (see below, "The Missing Leaves"). They also state (p. 330) that Martin numbered the first 400 lines and wrote next to line 7688 "7690. Urry. p. 268."

Thus the provenance is fairly clear from the early eighteenth century to Dr. William Hunter's acquisition and his bequest (after his death in 1783) to the Hunterian Museum and, eventually, to Glasgow University (see Young and Aitken 1908:ix–x).

The Missing Leaves

Editors since Robert Bell have called attention to the fact that eleven leaves are missing from MS. These leaves must have been present in the sixteenth century when, as Blodgett argues (1979, 1984; see below, "The Printer's Marks"), MS served as printer's copy for Thynne's 1532 edition. Brusendorff (1925:298 n.3) mistakenly infers that MS still contained these leaves in the eighteenth century, "when somebody numbered the first 400 lines correctly" and made the notation "at 7688 (f. 150): '7690. Urry. p. 268.'" That "somebody" was probably Thomas Martin (see above, "Provenance"). On a paper fly-leaf at the front of MS (iii, 1r) is a note that Young and Aitken (1908:329) likewise ascribe to Martin: "This fair copy of Chaucers Romant of the Rose is curtaild of the first Leaf, not unlikely for the sake of some fair Imbellishment wch was Illuminated at the Beginning of the Book. It begins at the 45th Line, in Urreys Edition (pag. 215) so mokil prise, &c." Below this note, moreover, there is pasted a cutting from an eighteenth-century sale catalogue: "CHAUCER'S ROMANT OF THE ROSE; a most beautiful MSS on vellum, exceedingly well preserv'd, with the Initials neatly illuminated with Flowers, and other Devices in Gold and beautiful Colours, in 297 pages." Martin's

observation, combined with the catalogue count of pages (= 149 leaves), proves that the eleven missing leaves were detached from MS sometime before ca. 1721. Young and Aitken (1908:329) identify the missing leaves in terms of the collation of quires, but they have some errors in leaf numbers and line numbers. The accompanying table notes the corrections.

Quire, lea(f,ves)	Line numbers	Total lines	Lines per page
1,1	1–44	44	20 + 24
1,8	333–380[a]	48	24
4,6–7	1387–1482[b]	96	24
7,3	2395–2442	48	24
10,4–5[c]	3595–3690	96	24
20,3–6[d]	7383–7574[e]	192	24

[a] Young and Aitken (Y&A), following the 18th-century line numbers, have 333–379.

[b] Y&A have 387–1482.

[c] Y&A have 10,4–6 (three leaves); but 96 lines occupy two leaves, not three.

[d] Y&A have 20,4–6 (three leaves); but 192 lines occupy four leaves, not three.

[e] Y&A have 7387–7576.

The Misplaced Leaves

Toward the end of MS, lines 7109–58 appear before lines 7013–7108, and lines 7159–7206 after lines 7207–7302 (see 7013–7302n.); these transpositions are the result of misplaced leaves, not in MS itself but in the exemplar from which MS was copied, either directly or at some remove. The evidence lies in the fact that the transposed sections do not begin at new leaves but about two-thirds of the way down a MS page, anywhere from the sixteenth to the nineteenth line. That they do so consistently argues for a page length in the exemplar about the same as that in MS, 24 lines.

The two major explanations of the transposition, those of Skeat (1891, 1894: 1899: 1.12, 1911:vi–ix) and Young and Aitken (1908: 330), are essentially the same. Skeat's is a fuller account and extends to a theory about how the three fragments came to be put together (see the next section). He notes (1891; I have introduced corrections of typographical and arithmetical errors) that Fragment C

was copied from an original which usually had 24 lines, but rarely 25 lines, on a page. . . . This fragment consisted of 3 sheets [i.e., quires] of 16 pages each, with 24 lines to the page; followed by a fourth sheet, having 12 pages of 24 lines and 4 pages of 25 lines, which sheet was so transposed as to bring the *middle* pair of leaves next to the *outer* pair of leaves. After which came 14 more leaves, 4 having 24 lines, and 10 having 25 lines. Total 3 x 16 x 24 + 12 x [2]4 + 4 x 25 + 4 x 24 + 10 x 25 = 1182 [1886] lines, as extant [in the printed editions].

Similarly, Young and Aitken (1908:330) point out that "the displacement of lines in quires 19 and 20 [of MS] is due to the original having had the leaves of its penultimate quire disarranged in the binding." They give a table showing the sequence of quires and lines in quires 19–20 of MS, and a chart (p. 331) of the sequence of quires, leaves, and lines in the ancestor of MS.

We should note that Skeat uses "quire" and "sheet" interchangeably to mean a sheet folded in octavo (1894; 1899:1.12; cf. McKerrow 1928: 25). In the account below, I use "sheet" to mean a pair of leaves in folio (cf. Boyd 1973:12).

Although it is customary to speak of misplaced leaves in the plural, one may think of the transposition as one in which a single sheet was misplaced. The quire was composed of four sheets, each folded to form a pair of leaves; when nested, they made up a quire of 8 leaves or 16 pages. If we number the sheets I to IV, from outside to inside of the quire, then it was Sheet IV that was misplaced from the inside position to second position, between Sheets I and II. The chart (based on Young and Aitken) shows the original order of the leaves as well as the misplaced order; Skeat's alphabetic designations of the pages appear in parentheses. The line numbers differ slightly from those in Skeat and in Young and Aitken, since after line 7172 Skeat adds two lines that change his line count by +2 for the rest of the poem; Young and Aitken use Skeat's numbering.

Original order   *Transposed Order*   *Block Size*

```
4 ——————— 5      3 ——————— 6
3 ——————— 6      2 ——————— 7
2 ——————— 7      4 ——————— 5
1 ——————— 8      1 ——————— 8
```

Original order	Transposed Order	Block Size
1r (A) 6965–6988	1r (A) 6965–6988	
1v (B) 6989–7012	1v (B) 6989–7012	
2r (C) 7013–7036	4r (G) 7109–7133)	} 50
2v (D) 7037–7060	4v (H) 7134–7158)	
3r (E) 7061–7084	2r (C) 7013–7036)	
3v (F) 7085–7108	2v (D) 7037–7060)	} 96
4r (G) 7109–7133	3r (E) 7061–7084)	
4v (H) 7134–7158	3v (F) 7085–7108)	
5r (I) 7159–7182	6r (L) 7207–7230)	
5v (K) 7183–7206	6v (M) 7231–7254)	} 96
6r (L) 7207–7230	7r (N) 7255–7278)	
6v (M) 7231–7254	7v (O) 7279–7302)	
7r (N) 7255–7278	5r (I) 7159–7182)	} 48
7v (O) 7279–7302	5v (K) 7183–7206)	
8r (P) 7303–7326	8r (P) 7303–7326	
8v (Q) 7327–7350	8v (Q) 7327–7350	

The transposed blocks consist of even-numbered groups, and couplets are not split. Except in the case of leaf 4, the blocks are in multiples of 24, the standard page length. On leaf 4 the block is 50 lines long (lines 7109–58), and we must assume, with Skeat, that this leaf had 25 lines on each side.

Although Skeat was the first to explain the transposition, he was not the first to observe it. Tyrwhitt (1775), in a note on Chaucer's *Retraction* (TR 3.314), points out the misplacement as it appears in Urry's edition, where, he says, "we have a strong proof of the negligence of the first editor [i.e., William Thynne], who did not perceive that two leaves in his Ms. were misplaced. . . . The later Editors have all copied this, as well as many other blunders of less consequence, which they must have discovered, if they had consulted the French original." In 1855 Jephson (BE 7012n., 7013–7302n.), without acknowledgement of Tyrwhitt, notes that "In the MS. and in Speght . . . several passages have been transposed," and he states that he has "restored [them] to their proper order . . . by a reference to the original French."

Norgate (1894) says that Robert Bell (i.e., BE) "seems to have had the credit of having been the first to detect and rectify the . . . error"; but Norgate finds that John Bell's edition of 1782 was the first to make the correction, on the basis of Tyrwhitt's hint, and that the correct order appears also in the editions of Anderson (1793), Chalmers (1810), Singer (Chiswick edition, 1822), and in the Moxon edition (1843) and the Aldine editions of 1845 and 1846 (cf. Hammond 1908:132–42; on John Bell's ed., see also Bonnell 1987). Kaluza (1893*a*:3) was aware of Tyrwhitt's observation but thought that the first corrected edition was that of Chalmers. Skeat may have caused some confusion when he wrote (1894; 1899: 1.12), "this displacement . . . was first noticed in Bell's edition." If he meant John Bell, he was partly right, but he probably meant Robert Bell (1855), since two pages later he refers to Robert Bell as "Bell," and he does not mention Tyrwhitt (cf. Hammond 1908: 450, 133).

The specific displacements are also noted by Lounsbury (1892:2.10), in KA SKt RB SU FI (7012n.), and in RIt (7013–7302n.). Sutherland (SU, p.xxxiii–xxxiv) finds a possible cause for the misplacement in French MS Be, which omits a folio "at exactly the line where this mix-up begins." His argument assumes that someone read "the *Romaunt* and Be at the same time" and that "when he came to ME 7013, the beginning of a new folio, he noticed

that it did not correspond to his French" and shuffled first one folio forward, then another, "in an attempt to harmonize."

Theories on the Makeup of the Manuscript's Original

Skeat's analysis (1891) of the misplaced leaves in Fragment C is part of his theory about how the three fragments came to be put together. Lindner (1887:167–72; see "Authorship" above) had already called attention to the gap after line 5810 and concluded that MS was copied from two separate manuscript fragments by different authors. Skeat, as we have seen, developed his theory on the basis of Kaluza's identification of three fragments. First, he regards Fragment C (5811–end) as a set of five quires, four of 16 pages each and one of 14. This analysis later leads him to the conclusion (1911:vii) that "Fragment C was originally an independent poem, and existed *at first* in a different MS., in which it began with the *first page* of that MS."

Skeat (1891; cf. SK 1.13) offers a similar analysis of Fragment A (lines 1–1705) to suggest that its original ancestor existed as an independent manuscript. He conjectures that this manuscript contained 68 pages, usually with 25 lines to the page but on five pages 26 lines, and that it was made up of four quires plus one gathering of only four pages; thus it would contain 1705 lines. Skeat has no explanation for Fragment B, but he supposes (1911:vii) that the parent of MS, and (he assumes) of TH[1], "was made up of two distinct parts at least, which may be called M and N. M contained Fragments A and B, which had been brought together by some process to which we have but little clue. . . . But N was complete in itself, and existed independently. It . . . was executed by some rather ingenious translator . . . who selected *a particular episode* . . . and thus [gave] us a poem which is complete in itself."

Kaluza had proposed a partly similar theory (1893*a*:245–48; see above, "Authorship") that sees Fragments A and C as independent units but both by Chaucer; however, Kaluza does not, like Skeat, try to reconstruct the collation of the parent manuscript. According to him, Fragment C, the Fals-Semblant section, may have been composed as a first essay; or Fragment A may have been the first attempt, broken off when the size of the task became apparent, and Fragment C the selection of a discrete, manageable unit for further translation. Either way, he reasons, another poet may have tried to fill the gap and thus produced Fragment B. This theory would make Chaucer's fragments at least the great-grandparents of MS, since the grandparent would include the work of the second poet, and the parent would introduce the transpositions in Fragment C.

Brusendorff's theory (1925) of the way that MS arose is quite different since, as we have seen, he argues that its ancestor was a complete translation by Chaucer, one based on a contaminated French manuscript (p. 319); this ancestor, he assumes, is at least the grandparent of MS (p. 302). And he believes that the parent would be the product of a memorial reconstruction that was later worked over by a reviser (pp. 349, 377, 382). Whatever the merits of Brusendorff's theory, it does not account, as he claims (p. 383), for the transpositions.

We touched on Sutherland's theory (1968) in the discussion of authorship above. He reasons (p. xxxvii) that French manuscripts of the H and R families were sources for two different translations; that manuscripts of these two translations were combined by a third person who introduced revisions based on *RR* manuscripts of the B and G families; and that this revised version was the common ancestor of MS and Thynne's edition of 1532. Sutherland's identification of correspondences between *Rom* and families of French manuscripts is useful. But, like his predecessors, he has been unable to do more than offer a scenario that has elements of possibility without clear proof of probability. His genealogy is suspect, for example, when we consider Blodgett's proof, in the printer's marks, of TH''s dependence on MS. It is probably significant that Brusendorff and Sutherland, both working with Langlois's manuscript collations, come to quite different conclusions.

The Manuscript Hands: The Scribe (MS₁)

This and the next section deal with the hands of the text. Extra-textual marginalia are the subject of a separate section below. The main scribe's hand is readily legible (see frontispiece; Brusendorff 1925, plate V, provides a reproduction of fol. 32v) but does have a few peculiarities. (For grammatical anomalies in the use of final -*e*, questionable rhymes, and certain dialectal forms that relate more to authorship than to scribal practice, see the notes and the discussion of authorship; but where such features exist without significance for rhyme or meter, they may reflect the casual usage common among fifteenth-century scribes.) One peculiarity is the rare appearance of the spelling *ij* for long *i*: *sijknesse* in lines 2295, 2644; and *wijs* in line 4621. Dr. Jeremy Smith, in a private letter, suggests that these spellings show vowel doubling to mark length; he cites *LALME* 1.547 for a geographical distribution in the South Midlands. *MED siknes(se* n. indicates that that word was variously pronounced, with long and with short *i*.

Abbreviations in the text of MS, mostly conventional, include an inconsistent use of the crossed -*ll*. As Wright (1960:22) observes of fifteenth-century book hands, -*ll* is used "presumably but not certainly to indicate the presence of final *e* (it may however have become merely a scribal mannerism)." In MS, -*ll* appears several times. BE and MO generally transcribe it as -*lle*, but such a transcription is not always warranted. On folio 18v (see frontispiece), for example, one finds *wel* (lines 933, 941) and *well* (line 945, rhyming with *st[e]ell* "steel"). At lines 3269–70, *calle* rhymes with *alle*. The spelling *wall* often appears where one expects no final -*e*, and I thus transcribe such cases as *wall*; see, e.g., lines 302, 3918, 4054, 4186, 6290, and see 4200n.

In some instances -*ll* seems to represent an abbreviation for -*lles*. These I expand silently, and without collation (at line 3429, the crossbar ends in a looped downward stroke):

> *ell to* elles: in lines 300, 410, 485, 1231, 2964, 3429, 4429

iowel *to* jowelles: in line 2092
devel *to* develles: in line 4549

Another inconsistency appears in the scribe's uses of *him* and *hem*, normally the grammatical forms for "him" and "them." But *hem* for the singular and *him* for the plural occur often enough in Fragments B and C to suggest that they may be scribal bi-forms rather than errors. I keep the MS forms in the text and have not collated them as substantive variants where *him* appears for the plural and *hem* for the singular; but I supply notes in such cases. For *hem* as singular, see lines 2854 (and note), 4267, 4498, 5107; for *him* as plural, see lines 1922 (and note), 2218, 2221, 4948, 5419, 5420, 5425, 5427, 5436, 5503–04, 5997, 5999, 6041, 6677, 6925, 7252–53. *MED him* pron., 1a. (b), shows only one example of the sing. in *-e* but, s.v. *hem* pron. pl., seven examples of the pl. in *-i-*. *LALME* (4.13; 1.316) shows primary distribution of *him* as pl. in Ely, secondary in Devon and Sussex, tertiary in Cambridge and Norfolk; for *hem* as sing., *LALME* (4.198) shows primary distribution in Cambridge and East Anglia, tertiary in Ely, Lincoln, and the West Riding of Yorkshire.

It will be convenient here to characterize the kinds of variants that the scribe was prone to create (see also "The Manuscript Hands: The Corrections" below). Of the 535 readings counted as variants from the text of the present edition, 5 will not be considered here because they were not introduced by the original scribe but by a second scribe who supplied whole lines omitted by the first scribe. The lines omitted (an asterisk marks those supplied, with variants, by the second scribe) are 892, 1553, *1892, 1984, 2036, 3136, *3490, 4856, 5624, 6190 (corrected MS₁), 6205, 6318, 6372, *6688, *6786, 7035 (corrected MS₁), *7092, 7109, 7592 (corrected MS₁). Of the remaining variants, 351 involve substitution of one word for another; but of these instances 67 result from mere omission of a letter or letters to create the new word (e.g., *tresour* for *tressour* at line 568 [see note]), 37 from addition of a letter (e.g., *preyse* for *pryse* in line 887 [see note]), 2 from the transposition of letters (*lefte* for *felte* in line 1814

and *pleyne* for *pleyen* in line 3745), and 2 from the spacing of letters (*in fortune* for *Infortune* in lines 5493 and 5551). I also count among substitutions miswritings that produce gibberish (in some cases one may argue that the intended word remains recognizable and therefore belongs with miswritings not counted as variant): at lines 310, 508, 716, 884, 933, 1058, 1117, 1130, 1188, 1263, 1313, 1379, 2342, 2343, 3864, 4372, 4709, 5585, 5740, 7255. MS transposes words only 5 times: at lines 1134, 3525, 4191, 4921, and 4952. In 123 instances MS omits words and in 25 instances adds words (dittography in lines 2025 [corrected], 2772, 4540, 4641, 4692). In most cases the variants are trivial. The more interesting ones are in lines 444, 478, 865, 923, 1201, 1282, 1334, 2285, 2341, 2473, 2992, 3294, 3450, 3489, 3943, 4576, 4705, 4871, 4935, 4943, 5117, 5223, 5585, 5586, 5701, 7022, 7056, 7098, 7178, 7219. See further "Relation of MS to the Present Edition," below.

Rubrics appear, principally as speech headings, from fol. 90r to 102v (see 4614–15n.); these follow a pattern of rubrication found in manuscripts of *RR*. The scribe (possibly a later hand) also used red ink to cancel a repeated line (line 5835, fol. 115v), to underline the word *Iustinian* (in line 6615, fol. 132r), and to underline the running title *Falssemblant* (fols. 115v–150r).

The Manuscript Hands: The Corrections

Throughout MS there are corrections, some of them in the hand of the scribe (MS₁), some in later hands (MS₂). The notes detail these corrections; here I classify them according to the different hands.

MS₁. The scribe has made the bulk of the corrections. Kaluza (KA), who notes nearly all of them, clearly identifies four cases as "written in the margin by the same hand" (at lines 6190, 6609, 7035, 7592). All except that at line 6609 consist of complete lines; line 6609 involves the single word *eke*. In these cases, the writing is obviously in the same carefully executed book hand as the rest of the text. In none of the other cases, listed below, does Kaluza identify the hand; his silence implies MS$_1$. The ink is the same, but the smaller characters show less shading and in some cases more cursivity than those in the rest of the text: in lines 519, 929, 946, 1179, 1250, 1642, 1790, 1792, 2758, 2893, 3184, 3295, 3780, 3956, 3965, 3973, 4191, 4470, 4680, 4810, 5119, 5149, 5188, 5680, 5910, 6273, 6281, 6328, 6538, 6552, 6705. Kaluza does not note the correction at line 6705. For a questionable case, see 1792n. For an example of expunctuation, perhaps by the scribe, see line 4692.

MS$_2$. This heading covers a number of different hands. In the collations I list them all as MS$_2$, but in the notes I give them the sub-headings of the lists below.

MS$_{2a}$. Lines 1892, 1984, 2036, 3490. This is a book hand very similar to that of the scribe; in fact, Brusendorff (1925:296–97) thinks that it is the same hand but a different ink. Kaluza (KA), however, thinks that each of these was "written by a later hand on a line originally left blank." David (RI), who rejects line 1892 as spurious, accepts the other three lines, although he notes (RIt) that line 3490 "may be spurious"; see notes. Individual characters differ somewhat from those of MS$_1$ (e.g., *a e h l m o T t*), and their lateral density is greater.

MS$_{2b}$. Line 5624 only. This is a more cursive book hand than either MS$_1$ or MS$_{2a}$. Kaluza (KA) states simply "written by a later hand on a line originally left blank." Brusendorff (1925:297–98) thinks that this is the same hand as 2c (see below). David (RI) accepts this line for his text and notes (RIt) that it is "written by a later (but probably fifteenth-century) hand."

MS$_{2c}$. Lines 6688, 6786, 7092. In line 7092, the last word (*dome*) is in still another hand. A sprawling secretary hand (sixteenth century) has entered these spurious lines in spaces originally left blank (KA). In the case of line 6688, the words are a partial repetition of the previous line. Brusendorff (1925: 297–98) thinks that these lines and line 5624 are by the same hand that "collated the MS. with Thynne's edition" [he refers to marks that Blodgett (1975, 1979, 1984) has identified as printer's marks made when MS was prepared

as copy for TH^1; see below]. David (RI) rejects all three lines from his text; see notes.

MS$_{2d}$. Under this heading I group corrections by various later hands: at lines 933 (see frontispiece; not noted in KA), 958, 3046, 3958, 6180, 6609. Kaluza (KA) does not designate the corrections made at lines 3046, 3958, and 6180 as made by a later hand. Line 6609 has a duplicate correction; MS$_1$ has the word *eke* in the margin, and MS$_{2d}$ inserts it above the line (KA does not report the supra-linear insertion; Brusendorff (1925:296 n.2) says that MS$_1$ made both additions of *eke*).

Other Marginalia

There is a series of paragraph signs (¶), possibly but not necessarily by the hand that made the printer's marks (see below). In any case, they do not present a consistent enough pattern of correspondence to the paragraph indentations of TH^1 to be significant. In general, MS has no indentations but shows paragraphing by large capitals; at such points, TH^1 leaves a line space and indents. In the following cases, MS has not a large capital but a paragraph sign that corresponds to a paragraph indentation in TH^1: at lines 223 (instead of 224, where TH^1 has an indentation), 414 (instead of 413, where TH^1 has a ¶ and an indentation), 449, 475, 847, 2239. Other paragraph signs appear, however, that do not correspond to indentations in TH^1: at lines 795 (where it looks as though there is a stroke through the ¶, perhaps for cancellation), 2229 (where the line does not even begin a sentence), and 2278 (where only a new page begins in TH^1).

MS also contains two incomplete sets of line numbers. The first is a set in ink by Thomas Martin of Palgrave, an eighteenth-century owner (see "Provenance," above). He follows Urry's numbering from line 45 to line 330 and, after a missing leaf, from line 380 (*sic for* 381) to line 400; he omits further numbering until near the end (fol. 150r) where, opposite line 7688, appears the note "7690. Urry. p. 268." Urry's line count follows the text as it appears in TH^1–SP^3 and is in fact +2 because of TH^1's two inserted lines (see below).

The other series is in pencil, in a modern hand like that of the folio numeration; it runs from line 410 to line 480 (fols. 7v–9r) and reappears at line 1049 (23r) and line 1483 (28r). On 146r, opposite lines 7206, 7303—consecutive lines on either side of the last misplaced-leaf discontinuity (see above)—appear the numbers 7210, 7307. Other numbers, also +4 over the standard numbering, appear on 147r (7339 = 7335), 147v (7386 = 7382), and 148r (7579 = 7575). These numberings correspond to those of the Aldine edition of 1845, which is +4 at the same points. None of the collated editions with line numbers is +4 at these points; those that follow the text of TH¹–SP³ (UR FU) are +2 because of TH¹'s inserted lines at 7109A, 7110A (see notes), MO is +2 because of numbering errors, and SK is +2 because of his two inserted lines (see 7172–73n.).

There are other marginalia in pencil: on fol. 17r, where the phrase "In Guild Hall" appears in an eighteenth-century hand (Young and Aitken 1908:331); on 19r, where a large flourished capital *B* appears in the right margin; on 85v, where the word "coll," in the left margin, duplicates the printer's mark "coll" of the right margin; and on 86r, where there is a series of flourished capitals and the word *They*. All these may well be in the same hand.

Other inscriptions are mostly in ink. For those identified with former owners of MS, see above, "Provenance." Among the remaining marginalia the more legible are as follows:

On 27r, in the bottom margin following line 1362, appears a missing-word puzzle in a hand that Young and Aitken (1908:329) date as "later XVI. Cent":

I had my	And my	
I lente my	To my	
	frynde	sylver
I asked my	Of my	
I loste my	And my	

As Kaluza observes (KA 1362n.), one "must transpose *frynde* and *sylver*"; he reprints the puzzle so corrected.

On 32r, upper right, appears the name "Teofile" (?; Theophilus?), followed by a dec-

oration. Young and Aitken do not record this name, but the hand seems to be the same as that of the four-line passage at the bottom of the page, which they date as seventeenth century. The four lines repeat lines 1697–1700, the last two of 32r and the first two of 32v (for text, see 1697–1700n.). The same hand has repeated the running title, "Faulssemblaunt," opposite line 6684.

Another hand, or hands, has copied this same running title, which appears in the scribe's hand from 115v to the end of MS: "Falssembant" (decorated, 126v, upper left); "Falssemblante" (134r, top); "Fallssembant" (135v, upper left). Despite the spelling variants, these may be by the same hand; it is similar to 2c, the sixteenth-century secretary hand that supplies the spurious lines 6688, 6786, and 7092 (see above, "The Manuscript Hands: The Corrections").

Other marginalia appear in a similar hand, and we may look at these as a group. On 71r, top margin, appears the phrase "Be It better or by it worsse"; in right margin, opposite line 3691, "Father and . . . ."; opposite lines 3695–3700, "Father and mother / my dewly loyll consyd [cropped] / And I haue / Jhames bynge Ihon Rygeman"; opposite lines 3702–04 are three lines that are difficult to read except for the phrase "For we haue" in the first line. The uncertain spelling of this hand reappears on 126v, not only in the "Falssembant" [*sic*] repetition that we have noted above, but in the word "Somtine" [*sic*], in the left margin opposite line 6351, a repetition of the opening word of the page, "Somtyme." The same hand has inscribed a large capital "T," patterned after those of the MS scribe, to the right of line 6360.

There remain few other intelligible marginalia. On 134r, lower than the "Falssemblante" repetition and the Mapler indenture that we looked at above (see "Provenance"), appear less intelligible phrases: "Thes Indenture mayde / oblygayccon / Inprimis / in th.. ij / yere iij voyir (?) / iiij and ." On 122r, bottom margin, another sixteenth-century hand writes "In In the yᵉre of lorde god / Anno" (for "Anno," Young and Aitken [1908:330] read "Amne," perhaps correctly). On folio 139r, a few lines lower down than the Mountjoy inscription (see "Provenance") in the right margin, and in still another sixteenth-century hand, is the Latin line "adue*rs*us est ille qui nemine*m* amet."

Several marginalia refer to the text. At 43r, to the right of line 2213, "Wherfore be wise and aqueyntable," appear the words "no*a* bene" (nota bene). To the right of lines 2259–60 stands a pointing-finger symbol. A hand appears to the right of lines 4703–05, which begin the oxymoronic definition of love taken from Alanus de Insulis; the hand rests on a decorative device in the shape of a capital "A." The abbreviation "nō" (nota) appears to the right of line 5852, "With his Normans full of janglyng."

Another form of vague reference to the text occurs in the form of heavy marks in black ink on 145r and 146r. The first of these, which looks like an elongated "E" with four horizontal arms rather than three, occurs at 145r:16–18 (lines 7302, 7159–60) and seems to relate to the misplaced-leaf discontinuity at that point. The other two are in the form of a rectilinear capital "T." One appears at 145r:23 (line 7165), opposite the opening line of the next paragraph after the discontinuity. The other appears at 146r:20 (line 7306), four lines after the discontinuity at lines 7206, 7303, the one marked in pencil at a later period (see above and the notes to lines 7165, 7302, 7306).

Marginalia on many pages of MS arouse little interest. Some are illegible words, and others seem to be scribbles or doodles, mainly in a sixteenth-century secretary hand and in a brown ink. Some are smudged by wiping when the ink was wet (63r, 70r, 72r, 107r, 114r, 125r); some are the forms of capital letters (46r, 55v, 56r, 92r), of the sigmoid final -*s* of secretary hand (63r, 77r), or of the conventional pointing hands referred to earlier (46r, 56r, 92r); and some are amounts, like "x ^{li}" (60r, 63r). The rest consist of isolated words, some cropped (3r, 50r, 59r, 60r).

The Printer's Marks (MS$_{2e}$)

There are marks in MS that correspond to the page and column breaks of TH[1]. James

Blodgett (1975, 1979, 1984) identifies them as printer's marks; he gives credit for the original suggestion (1979:101) to A. I. Doyle and Alfred David. Blodgett writes (1984:39; cf. 1979:98) that the whole of MS is "counted off in marks characteristically used by Tudor printers to prepare copy" and that "the marks reflect the layout of the columns in Th":

Numbers in a series from one to twelve correspond to the twelve pages within each signature of folios in sixes that, with the exception of one folio in fours and one in nines, make up Th. The book is printed two columns to a page; thus between each number in the series there is also the notation "coll" to indicate the first line of the second column on each page in Th. The relationship between these printer's marks and the corresponding texts in Th proves that Thomas Godfrey, the printer of Th, used Gl [MS] as his copy for the *Romaunt*.

The typical mark consists of two dashes, left and right, between the line that stands before the break and the line that stands after the break; a marginal letter (or letters) indicates a new signature (see the frontispiece marginalium and 949n.), a number indicates the page within the signature, and the notation "coll" marks the second column of a page. Blodgett carefully notes the exceptions to this pattern (1979:98–101); none of them, however, invalidates his conclusion. In addition (1979:100–01), Blodgett clarifies the words "lat a lyn" (17v; see 892n.) as an instruction to the compositor of TH[1] to leave a space for a line to be supplied. Brusendorff (1925:298) had earlier noted these marks and their correspondence to TH[1] but had not drawn the conclusion that they were printer's marks. In the notes I record as *marginalia* those marks that offer more than routine interest. For the textual significance of the printer's marks, see below, "The Glasgow MS and the Thynne Print."

Some marks of punctuation, perhaps in the same hand as the printer's marks, may be mentioned here. First, there are a few paragraph signs (¶), and these sometimes correspond to indentations in TH[1]; they are recorded above, in "Other Marginalia." Second, at lines 2113,

2120, and 2122, a later hand, perhaps 2e, has added commas that match virgules in TH[1]. Finally, at line 2118, perhaps the same hand has added parentheses that also appear in TH[1]. See notes.

The Glasgow MS and the Thynne Print

Blodgett's explanation of the printer's marks in TH[1] alters what had been the prevailing view, that MS and TH[1] derive independently from a common ancestor (cf. Lounsbury 1892:2.10 and Robinson 1957:924). Skeat (SK 1.11) thinks that MS and TH[1], "nearly duplicate copies, [are] both borrowed from one and the same original"; Brusendorff (1925:298, 301n.) argues that MS and TH[1] are not "sister codices" but share a more distant ancestor (cf. Sutherland 1968:ix, David 1969:666–67).

But Max Kaluza had already suggested (1893a:2) that TH[1] may have come from MS, and he pursues that hypothesis (1893b:109–10) in arguing against Skeat (cf. SK 1.14) that the extra four lines at the end of TH[1] (see 7691–92n., 7692n.) are Thynne's addition and not, as Skeat thinks, an entirely correct version of the Fr. "Thus," he concludes, "in my view, Thynne's exemplar stopped at the same point as G; of course we cannot exclude the possibility that O [the original of both exemplars] ended there, and so the dependence of Th on G cannot be proved for certain" (p. 110). Kaluza also argues that TH[1] supplies other lines from the French original (see notes to lines 6205, 6317–18, 6786, among others).

Brusendorff (1925:297 n.3) removes the caution from Kaluza's statement and then criticizes it: "Kaluza thinks . . . that Thynne actually printed his ed. from the Glasgow MS. and himself composed all lines not in this codex. But this is an entirely arbitrary view, nor does the Glasgow MS. look like having been through a Tudor printer's hands." Brusendorff knew, of course, about the marks later identified by Blodgett as printer's marks, but he thought that they were signs of a later collation of "the MS. with Thynne's edition," one that "seems to have been done when the MS. was complete" (1925:298 n.3). Alfred David, who adopts Blodgett's position, sup-ports the "notion that Thynne's editing accounts for most of the discrepancies between" MS and TH[1] (RI, pp. 1198–99). David points out that the pattern of Thynne's editing does not show a "more or less random distribution of the variants between" MS and TH[1], as one might expect "if Thynne had merely reproduced a manuscript similar to G." Instead, they are more frequent toward the beginning of *Rom*: "11 percent of the lines before 1300 show variation but only 4.7 percent of the lines after that point. The inference is that Thynne's interest and editorial initiative began to decline after some 1200 lines" (p. 1198).

Relation of MS to the Present Edition

Perusal of the collations will show that MS has 535 variants from the present edition, 41 of them unique and 285 shared with TH[1]. These variant counts do not include lapses in MS that result from physical damage. Two erasures, however, are counted as variants (at lines 103–04), though what was erased cannot be identified. Unique readings in MS reflect the state of the manuscript prior to correction either by the original scribe or by later hands. MS has so few unique variants because KA is essentially a transcription of MS that incorporates the various scribal corrections (KA mistranscribes a variant at line 6874, which therefore remains unique). Most of the corrections listed above in "The Manuscript Hands: The Corrections" involve alteration of unique readings. For analysis of kinds of variants found in MS, see above, "The Manuscript Hands: The Scribe (MS$_1$)."

Many spelling lapses are not counted as variants though they are recorded in the collations. Those corrected in MS are at lines 946 (*steel*), 1179 (*heere*), 5119 (*thou > thow*), and 6705 (*hat > hath*). Those uncorrected in MS may be subdivided into spelling variations not adopted in the present edition, and miswritings that do not obscure the intended words. The former appear in lines 149, 292, 739, 859, 906, 958, 1214, 1695, 1721 (see note for the 22 other instances of this particular variation), 1933, 1965, 2215, 2372, 2709, 3186,

4366, 5612. The latter appear in lines 415, 1206, 1496, 1624, 1932, 2271, 2644, 2699, 3799, 3965, 4332, 4643, 4815, 6019, 6340, 6374, 6601, 6796, 6893 (see note), 7007. I have counted as unique variants a few similar slips (corrected in MS) that arguably create a different recognizable word: at lines 929 (*other*), 1250 (*lordis*), 1792 (*nedes*), and 5188 (*thee*). It should be noted too that where both MS and correction in MS disagree with the present edition, I count each disagreement independently: at lines 1892, 3490, 4191, 6688, 6786, 7092. I also count as variant a few readings that might as easily be disregarded as spelling variations: see lines 5983, 6543, 6728; and cf. treatments of *werye/werrien* and *werrey* in lines 2078, 3251, 3699, 3917, 6926, 7018 (also *wery* in line 6264). Finally, while I collate variations in the headings and rubrics that appear in the present edition, these are not counted as variants in the analysis of the individual texts.

Descriptions of the Printed Editions

I have not collated texts that derive from Urry (J. Bell 1782, Anderson 1793), or from the black-letter prints (Chalmers 1810, the Chiswick edition 1822, Moxon 1843). Neither have I collated the early Aldine edition (1845), which derives from the Chiswick text; or the edition of Gilman (1880), which derives from Morris (1866). For general information on these editions, see Hammond (1908:132–43, 450).

There are two main lines of dependence in the textual tradition: on MS directly (TH[1] BE MO KA SK GL RB[1,2] RI) and on MS through TH[1] (TH[2]-UR FU SU FI). For general information on the collated editions, see Hammond (1908:116–49), Skeat (SK 1.29–46), Muscatine (1963), Hetherington (1964), Brewer (1969, Introduction), Brewer (1978:1.33–38), and Ruggiers (1984).

Thynne 1532 (TH[1])

As noted above ("The Glasgow MS and the Thynne Print"), Blodgett (1984:39), on the evidence of printer's marks, concludes that MS was the copy text for TH[1]. The dependence of TH[1] on MS is also reflected in the relatively large number (285) of their agreements against the present edition. If MS were not deficient in the 524 lines from the missing leaves, this number would probably be higher. A major reason for the differences between MS and TH[1] is that Thynne often emends the MS readings. Not only does TH[1] agree with the present edition against MS in 228 readings, TH[1] also has 285 variants where MS and the present edition agree, 21 variants where MS is Out owing to damage, and 23 variants that differ from variants in MS (but one of these 23, at line 3490, involves an agreement with MS[2] and the present edition). TH[1] diverges from MS 536 times and has 612 variants from the present edition.

Blodgett (1984:49) finds 685 such divergences, a count that presumably includes non-substantive variation either unrecorded in the present collations or not counted as substantive variation. Indeed, my own count includes several variations that might be regarded as non-substantive. For example, TH[1] substitutes a weak preterite for a strong one in MS (in lines 332, 691, 3083, 3498). MS *flee* is rendered fairly consistently in TH[1] as *flye* (see lines 951, 2752, 3149, 4697, 4783, 5471, 6268). TH[1] prefers *eyther* to MS's *outher* (see lines 250, 1624, 3308, 5490), *natheles* to *netheles* (see lines 5889, 6073, 6195), and *tymes* to *tyme* as a plural form (see lines 6072, 6492, 7684). Other common substitutions may be found in lines 134, 1071, 1094, 1398 (cf. lines 2371/72), 1562, 1798, 2880, 2958, 5403, 5559, 5680, 6329, 6986, 7430. See also lines 1313 and 1379.

Before Blodgett's argument that TH[1] was printed from MS, these divergences were taken as evidence that TH[1] was printed from a copy (now lost) that was more correct than MS. David (RI, pp. 1198–99) considers it more likely, however, that "Thynne edited G [= MS], just as modern editors have done, with the aid of the French original and according to his notions of Chaucerian usage" (citing Kaluza 1893*a*:2–3, 254, and 1893*b*:106–11). He points out that Thynne's variants from MS are over twice as frequent in the first 1300 lines as thereafter, a finding that implies that "Thynne's interest and editorial initiative began to decline after some 1200 lines" (p. 1198). In a typical (in this case, non-substantive) variation, TH[1] has the prefix *y*- in past participles twenty-one times to MS's one (Blodgett [1984:47] says TH[1] has twenty-two instances and MS none), and of these twenty-one, nineteen occur before line 2000 (Blodgett says twenty appear before line 1610); David infers that Thynne added the prefix, "mainly in the first 2000 lines, because he considered it to be a hallmark of Chaucer's style and found it a convenient device to add a metrical beat to a line" (p. 1198). Other instances where one might detect editorial activity in TH[1] unprompted by *RR* occur in lines 103, 163 (but see 163n.), 688, 1749, 1757, 1758, 2234, 3227, 3552, 3779, 4063, 4191, 4269, 5505, 5633, 5675, 6037, 6393, 7098, 7133. TH[1]'s disagreements with the present edition that may result from the same kind of editing appear in lines 1062–65, 1172, 3761, 4208, ?4372, 4709, 5446, 6361–62, 7109–10, 7137.

Most of TH[1]'s corrections repair obvious errors in MS, but many do seem to reflect Thynne's consultation of a text of *RR* (Blodgett 1984:47–50). Blodgett (p. 49) adduces examples of small variants (see notes to lines 296, 421, 673, 1068) to which one might add many others where there is at least some suggestion that a text of *RR* was used (e.g., in lines 147, 185, 293, 310, 478, 508, 568, 887, 980, 1520, 1604, 7323). In two instances (at lines 1080 and 7022) TH[1] produces readings that do not agree with the present edition but seem to show the influence of *RR*. The clearest evidence for the use of *RR* lies in the fact that, in twelve of the thirteen individual lines where MS has either nothing or a different version, Thynne has supplied lines that seem to be based on *RR* (Blodgett, pp. 49–50; both MS and TH[1] omit line 6372, MS leaving a blank space). Of the seven cases where MS has nothing, there is no gap in two (lines 892, 1553) and a blank line in five (lines 3136, 4856, 6205, 6318, 7109). In one of the five cases where MS differs (line 7692, the last line in MS), TH[1] has altered the line and added a four-line conclusion based loosely on the French original (see 7692n.). And in

each of the four other cases (lines 1892, 6688, 6786, 7092), MS left a blank line and a later hand supplied a spurious version; Blodgett (1984:50) cites Kaluza (notes to KA) for the suggestion that these lines "may have been blank at the time Thynne prepared his edition and that the versions in Th can best be understood as Thynne's translations of the French equivalent." While this latter suggestion may serve for lines 6688, 6786, 7092, it does not do so for line 1892, where there is no equivalent in the Fr. (see 1892n.) and where the hand is probably earlier than 1532.

TH[1] has no unique variants, but it shares only with FU, a transcription of TH[1], four variants (at lines 2075, 4926, 5054, 6010) and five obvious typographical errors—at lines 314 (*fulfylfed*), 5325 (*amorours*), 6553 (*msisters*), 7289 (*parceyned*), 7594 (*my selu*). There are, of course, other typesetting errors in TH[1]: e.g., turned *u* (in lines 1219, ?3777, 4926, 5238), *s* for *l* or *f* (in lines 847, 1448, 3626), faulty spacing of letters (in lines 343, 1652, 2484).

A few other variants in TH[1] are noteworthy. Readings in lines 3643 and 3676 suggest that Thynne was working from pages no longer extant in MS. There are plausible miscopyings that survive in several subsequent editions in lines 4495, 4859, 6197. A curious change of pronoun gender occurs in line 7531.

Thynne 1542 (TH²)

TH[2] was printed from TH[1] but diverges from it 155 times, agreeing with the present edition in thirteen readings (at lines 343, 1605, 2075, 2224, 3767, 4846, 4955, 5010, 5054, 5555, 6010, 6296, 7025), and substituting a variant different from that in TH[1] five times (at lines 196, 1745, 2934, 4242, 4926). TH[2] has 732 variants from the present edition. Most of its new variants are unique and evidently result from typesetting error. I do not count as variants typesetting lapses in which the intended words are readily apparent: *Rygh* (30), *mygh* (5665), *unstabale* (5803), *tankynges* (6041), *scatche* (6649), and *eueneme* (7470); perhaps to be included in this group are readings in lines 156, 2327, 4674, 4712, 6042. Only fourteen of the variants first printed in TH[2] reappear in later editions: at lines 568, 825, 970, 1086, 1368, 3274, 4926, 5257, 5447, 5712, 5977, 6026, 7437, 7480. Only a few of TH²'s new variants suggest editorial judgment or misjudgment: at lines 40, 150, 725, 733, 734, 2934, 5723, 5725, 6368, 7625.

Thynne 1550? (TH³)

The edition is undated; Skeat (SK 1.29) suggests "about 1550." Pollard and Redgrave date it "1545?" (*STC* 1926:111), but later writers prefer 1550 or 1551 (Muscatine 1963:23) or ca. 1550 (Hetherington 1964:14); and the second edition of *STC* (1976–86:1.228) gives "1550?" as the date.

The evidence from *Rom* suggests that TH³ was printed from TH¹ rather than from TH² (cf. Pearsall 1984*a*:113). While TH³ abandons TH¹ to join TH² in four agreements with the present edition (at lines 2075, 3767, 5054, 6010), and while it shares five variants first printed by TH² (at lines 568, 825, 4926, 5977, 6026), TH³ fails to reproduce TH²'s other 146 divergences from TH¹. TH³ introduces its own alterations. It corrects TH¹ and TH² to agree with the present edition at lines 847, 1219, 1814, 2298, 2574, 2752, 3777, 4272, 5238, 5458, 6035, 7178, 7392. It substitutes a variant different from that in TH¹'² at lines 2092 and 5638. And it introduces 119 new variants where TH¹ agrees with the present edition. TH³ diverges from TH¹ in 142 readings and from the present edition in 717 readings.

Most of the new variants in TH³ result from carelessness. The sorts of typesetting error that occur may be seen in missettings that do not create true variants or obscure what the intended words are: *pent* (rhyming with *queynt*, 1436), *witheuten* (1572), *beboueth* (2072), *h .. e* (2165: two graphs between *h* and *e* are set above the line; the word rhymes with *lere* in line 2166), *shalde* (3071), *Lordiges* (5877), *bhlt* (7032), *Abstyuaunce* (7354). Some changes in the text suggest editing: e.g., at lines 1803, 2092, 3088, 3105, 4041, 4164, 4235, 4239, 4525, 5520, 5977, 6682, 6787, 7285. However, similar alterations elsewhere are clearly inadvertent: at line 5205 TH³ spells *continue* where the rhyme demands the

alternative *contune* (see note); at lines 5209 and 6805 TH³'s readings disturb the rhyme scheme even more flagrantly.

Stow 1561 (ST)

ST's text of *Rom*, evidently set from TH³, has 776 variants from the present edition. ST departs from TH³ in 63 substantive readings but returns to earlier readings only six times: with the present edition at lines 6712 and 7485 (both by omission) and with TH² at lines 1086, 1368, 5257, and 5447. ST introduces new readings in all its other substantive divergences from TH³; three of these (at lines 3429, 4550, 6169) replace variants in TH³ with new variants. Many of the new readings doubtless result from typesetting error. Consider, for example, the omissions at lines 201, 651, 706, 1740 (of a rhyme word), 2027, 2083, 2115, 6965; the colophon too omits a word. Also, non-substantive spelling errors at lines 1043 (*valous*), 1047 (*clepled*), 2133 (*nygh* for *nyght* in rhyme position), and 7494 (*amenne*) suggest inadvertent typesetting as the cause of variants at lines 311, 917, 1795, 2108, 2369, 3041, 3183, 4050, 4355, 4424, 4665, 4779, 5867. Misspacing of letters creates a variant at line 1777 (cf. ST's convergence with TH² at line 5447). On the other hand, ST also corrects typographical errors in TH³ at lines 1572, 2072, 2165, 3071, 5877, 7032, 7354, 7678; and its alteration of line 6806 (see TH³ at line 6805) seems clearly an editorial amendment. Its other substantive divergences from TH³ are at lines 262, 732, 753, 881, 967, 1919, 2378, 3156, 3164, 3290, 3296, 3312, 3571, 3595, 3662, 3695, 3891, 4143, 4335, 4368, 4841, 4903, 5150, 5843, 6103, 6111, 6351, 7022, 7166.

Speght 1598 (SP¹)

SP¹ is a page reprint of ST; both have 108 lines per page, the same distribution of multi-line capitals, and the same format as well as wording of the colophon (cf. Pearsall 1984*b*:79). Nevertheless, SP¹ diverges from ST's text of *Rom* in 147 readings, joining the present edition 85 times, substituting a different variant from the one in ST 7 times (at lines 323,

2092, 4468, 4550, 5117, 5638, 5741), and introducing 55 variants where ST agrees with the present edition. SP¹ has 746 variants from the present edition.

In 12 instances SP¹ is the first text to print the reading of the present edition: at lines 1034, 2176, 2902, 3525, 4861, 5283, 5471, 5620, 6466, 6549, 7145, 7314. Of SP¹'s 73 other agreements with the present edition against ST, 72 are shared with TH¹˒², only 24 (and none exclusively) with TH³; at line 2224 SP¹ joins only TH², and at line 5447 only TH¹˒³. In several instances SP¹ may revert to the earlier reading through typesetting error: omission of words or letters occurs at lines 967, 1034, 1107, 1795, 3168, 3695, 4164, 4283, 5283, 5471, 5620, 5648, 5977, 6351, 6528, 6697, 6959; transposition of words or letters at lines 2020, 3031, 3170, 3525, 3595, 4476, 6247 (roman numeral), 6428, 7104; respacing of words or letters at lines 1777, 5447, 6549; substitution involving *s/f* at lines 2902, 5864, 7314. On the other hand, SP¹ emends ST by making additions of words or letters at lines 112, 310, 1552, 1740, 1881, 2082, 2083, 2099, 2115, 2176, 2224, 2374, 2752, 3164, 3171, 3222, 3234, 4143, 4759, 4785, 5423, 5965, 6111, 6324 (rhyme), 6329, 6466, 6683, 7145, 7285, 7539; and by substituting words at lines 824, 881, 917, 1108, 1919, 2108, 2628 (common substitution?), 3183, 3296, 4018, 4041, 4050, 4774, 4779, 4841, 4861, 5209 (rhyme), 5438, 5492, 5867, 6512, 7022, 7377.

Of the 62 divergences of SP¹ from ST that do not agree with the present edition, 55 are readings printed for the first time in SP¹ (45 of these are unique variants). The other 7 agree with TH¹˒²: at lines 2092, 2298, 2752, 4550 (=TH³), 5458, 5638, 7392. Of course, some of these variants probably result from typesetting error. Such error is obvious in readings not treated here as genuine variants: at lines 3401 (*hs*), 4174 (*Lage*), 4628 (*fhe*), 5426 (*wordely*), 6621 (*aperr*), 6868 (*Vntounsailed*), 7326 (*cousaile*), 7355 (*wicken T.*). Variants resulting from omission of words or letters appear at lines 679, 2064, 2298, 3127, 3579, 4680, 5060, 5458, 6797, 7042, 7392; and line 4407 is Out. Transposition of words or letters occurs at lines 2977 and 6068. SP¹ differs from ST by

adding words or letters at lines 323, 972, 1698, 3181, 4241, 4289, 4468 (cf. TH¹˒²), 6042, 6469, 6957. It makes substitutions of words or letters at lines 206, 256, 528, 687, 764, 791, 1350, 1564, 1595, 1674, 1966, 2029, 2092, 2116, 2198, 2547 (turned *n*), 2752, 2942, 3297, 3353, 3397, 4273, 4291, 4550, 5062, 5117, 5326, 5638 (common substitution?), 5741 (*s/f* substitution), 6398, 6786, 6927, 6942, 6952, 7041, 7212, 7253, 7685. The reading at line 6786 suggests editing; cf. the correction of typographical error in ST (see above) at lines 1043, 1436, 2133, 2953, 7494. SP¹ also introduces modernized spelling (not counted here as variant) in lines 2067 and 3235 (*surprised*).

Speght 1602 (SP²)

SP²'s text of *Rom* seems to have been printed from ST rather than from SP¹. SP² departs from SP¹ in 231 readings, and in 112 of these instances it returns to the reading of ST (even to spoil the rhyme in line 5209 and to preserve a typographical error in line 7494, *amenne*). Conversely, SP² preserves only 34 of SP¹'s departures from ST. SP² joins the present edition against SP¹ in 77 readings, substitutes twelve variants that differ from variants in SP¹ (in lines 72, 1201, 2046, 2092, 4468, 4550, 4561, 5051, 5521, 5638, 7145, 7634), and adds 141 variants where SP¹ agrees with the present edition. SP² has 810 variants from the present edition.

SP²'s 22 agreements with the present edition independent of ST and SP¹ appear in the following lines (asterisks mark readings that first appear in SP²): 248, 590, *1313, 2964, 3041, 3083, *3231, *3676, 3891, 4298, 4631, *4657, 4665, 4800, 4846, *4858, 4903, *5493, *5551, 6713, *6823, 6900. In five of these readings SP² agrees with TH¹˒², but the agreements are likely accidental: in 96 other departures from both SP¹ and ST, SP² fails to agree with TH¹˒². Of these 96 variants printed first by SP² (MS provides precedent only at line 2709) twelve are unique: at lines 68, 72, 126, 149, 173, 216, 236, 569, 603, 1201, 2766, 3399 (dittography). Among the others, omission of words or letters accounts for twenty variants: at lines 110, 423, 1496, 2683, 2853,

3319, 3793, 4034, 4561, 4698, 5071, 5184, 5254, 5308, 5317, 5593, 5613, 5880, 5924, 6297 (line Out). Addition of words or letters produces twelve variants: at lines 1541, 2046, 2709, 3046, 3174, 3249, 3283, 3435, 3463, 5634, 6298, 6901. Transposition of words appears in lines 1171 and 6194. The 50 other new variants involve substitution of words or letters (e.g., at lines 230, 369, 413, 417, 547, 642, 664). Many of these substitutions seem inadvertent; more piquant cases may be found in lines 3174, 3811, and 7688. Typesetting error clearly appears in spellings not recorded as separate variants in the collations below; these appear in lines 1 (*sweueueninges*), 526 (*Euiron* for *Enuyron*), 839 (*egise*), 5877 (*gooddes*).

As many have noted (e.g., Pearsall 1984*b*: 83–90), Francis Thynne's *Animadversions* (1599) prompted much of the editorial activity in SP^2 (see notes to lines 149, 562, 1106, 1250, 2342, 6068, 6279, 6861). There is editorial activity of another kind as well. In SP^2 149 passages are marked by the image of a pointing hand printed in the margin: this image appears next to lines 203, 265, 279–80, 343, 412, 1171, 1174, 1179, 1288, 1794, 1820. 1935, 2109, 2119–20, 2151, 2161, 2181, 2182, 2191, 2199, 2223, 2227, 2241, 2253, 2255, 2275, 2287, 2291, 2295, 2308, 2331, 2349, 2351, 2367, 2379, 2383, 2385, 2478, 2522, 2573, 2603, 2631, 2671, 2685, 2737, 2741, 2748, 2775, 2777, 2783–84, 2887, 2905, 2919, 2933–34, 3146, 3177, 3237, 3240, 3297, 3303, 3387, 3463, 3541, 3544, 3684, 3786, 3802, 3914, 3931, 3955, 4030, 4032, 4254, 4329, 4353, 4357, 4359, 4387, 4461, 4475, 4477, 4531, 4753, 4783, 4809, 4831–32, 4841, 4879, 4929–30, 5023–24, 5049, 5051, 5089, 5106, 5123, 5216, 5221, 5225, 5234, 5237, 5239, 5241, 5259–60, 5265, 5293, 5295, 5325, 5357, 5367, 5456, 5520, 5541, 5547, 5581–82, 5593, 5653, 5671, 5693, 5697, 5722, 5759, 5763, 5787, 5795, 5805, 5887, 5907, 5920, 6147, 6192, 6227, 6253, 6259, 6502, 6525, 6534, 6599, 6653, 6661, 6821, 7085, 7385, 7465, 7505, 7511, 7543, 7607, 7617–18.

Speght 1687 (SP³)

SP^3 clearly was printed from SP^2 (even punctuation is much the same in the two editions),

but it is not a page reprint, as Pearsall says (1984*b*:91); counting blank lines, SP^2 has 116 lines per page, SP^3 134. SP^3 departs from SP^2 in only 47 readings. In fourteen of these instances it agrees with the present edition (and with SP^1 except where otherwise indicated): at lines 68, 110, 126, 149, 173, 201 (TH$^{1-3}$), 216, 236, 262 (TH$^{1-3}$), 569, 603, 2020, 3399, 5452 (unprecedented). SP^3 also corrects SP^2's typographical error (*sweueueninges*) in line 1 and introduces such an error at line 7516 (*ninne* for *inne*). SP^3 substitutes four variants for variants in SP^2 (at lines 72, 1201, 2766, 3895) and adds 29 variants where SP^2 agrees with the present edition. SP^3 has 825 variants from the present edition. Of the 29 new variants, 27 are unique: at lines 341, 428, 621, 1600, 1657, 1721, 1885, 2336, 2439, 2504, 2766, 2767, 2896, 3347, 3367, 3851, 3869, 3895, 4286, 5420, 6158, 6159, 6233, 6513, 7381, 7413, 7681. The other two are at lines 2195, 3979. SP^3 follows SP^2 in marking sententious passages; it differs only in the style of marking (star at the head of an indented line) and in the failure to mark lines 4929–30, 5697, and 7617–18. For a general description of SP^3, see Alderson (1970:40–52) and Pearsall (1984*b*:90–92).

Urry 1721 (UR)

Alderson (1970:97–103, 121–35) has a full account of UR, the first edition in roman type rather than black letter. The text was prepared by John Urry and his successor Thomas Ainsworth, the glossary by Timothy Thomas. In *Rom* UR differs from SP^3 in 1005 readings: UR agrees with the present edition in 175 of these readings, offers a different variant in 94 others, and adds 736 variants where SP^3 agrees with the present edition. UR, with 1386 variants from the present edition, offers what is easily the most idiosyncratic text of *Rom*.

UR's closest affiliation is with SP^2. UR agrees with SP^3 against SP^2 only eleven times, and SP^1 shares all but two (marked *) of these agreements: at lines 68, 72, 126, 149, 173, 216, 236, 603, *1738, *2195, 3399. Conversely, UR agrees with SP^2 against SP^3 29 times (again with SP^1 sharing all but two): at lines *110, 262, 341, 428, 621, 1600, 1657, 1721, 1885,

*2020, 2336, 2439, 2504, 2767, 3347, 3367, 3851, 3869, 3895, 4286, 4999, 5420, 5452, 6158, 6159, 6233, 6513, 7413, 7681 (cf. too readings at line 2766). The relative influence of SP[1] can perhaps be measured by its 92 agreements with UR against SP[2] (including the nine shared with SP[3]); especially noteworthy are those at lines 972, 1595, 2176, 4291, 5283, 5471, 6297, 6713, 6786, 7688. But SP[2] in turn has 120 agreements with UR against SP[1].

UR also shares with earlier editions 24 readings that do not appear in SP[1-3]: at lines 63, 142, 651, 721, 970, 1034, 2027, 2369, 2378, 3274, 3429, 3571, 4335, 4355, 4958, 5333, 5438, 5620, 5712, 5867, 6296, 6546, 7049, 7314. Among these readings, which show mostly trivial convergences, TH[2] appears 22 times, TH[1] 18 times, TH[3] 12 times, and ST only 5 times (ST and UR also have in common a typesetting error, spelling *compendouly* at line 2953). Alderson states that Urry had a copy of TH[2] (1970:93) and made use of ST for collating (p. 98); the evidence of UR's text of *Rom*, however, is too scant to support any conclusion concerning Urry's use of those editions. The data are especially inadequate given the great latitude that Urry gave himself as editor. After all, given that he introduced 871 readings never before in print, he is likely to have invented other readings that simply happen to appear in previous editions (accidental convergence). Of the readings first printed in UR, 61 agree with the present edition (17 of which are supported by MS), 99 are variants that appear in editions subsequent to UR, and 711 are unique. One variant is shared only with MS (at line 1652), hardly proof that Urry had access to MS.

Alderson writes of the extent and nature of UR's editorial changes (1970:121–29; cf. Constance Wright 1990:312, 317–18). The 61 agreements with the present edition show UR's bases for emendation: the correction of obvious errors (e.g., in lines 3694, 3697, 4793, 4812, 4813, 5021, 5253, 6064, 7623); regularization of meter (e.g., in lines 865, 1831, 2746, 4357, 4634, 5379, 5546, 6810); and occasional use of the French text (e.g., in lines 860, 2141, 2622, 2650, 3522, 4032, 5116, 5282, 5953). Even in the cases where UR originates a

reading that has not been accepted, it has occasionally pointed the way to an acceptable reading (e.g., in lines 2341, 2499, 2763, 2836, 2992, 3179, 3448, 3902, 4689, 4940, 5287, 5301).

Meter is a major concern in UR, one that predominates in the 711 unique variants (e.g., in lines 3, 20, 37, 65, 98, 103, 111, 124, 129, etc.). This concern appears also in the frequent use of the *y-* prefix for an extra syllable. While other editors sometimes add *y-* to past participles, UR does so with other verb forms as well: e.g., 264 *yhapith*, 282 *yknew*, 290 *yhad* (pa. t.), 297 *ybrennid* (pa. t.), 298 *yse* (inf.), 319 *ywas*. I collate none of these cases. Similarly, UR uses *-in* to give an extra syllable to singular verb forms; for these false plurals, see 49n.

Bell 1855 (BE)

This edition of *Rom* is the first since TH[1] to use MS as its base text. The Introduction claims that the text of MS "has been carefully re-produced" and that "Speght's edition" was used to supply the deficiencies of the missing leaves (BE, p. 12). Analysis of BE readings clearly supports both claims. BE, which has only 482 variants from the present edition, preserves 287 of MS's variants and substitutes only 24 variants for variants in MS (at lines 188, 1750, 2177, 2499, 2669, 2709, 3319, 3450, 3710, 4191, 4372, 4940, 5117, 5403, 5491, 5977, 6318, 6491, 7022, 7092, 7109, 7255, 7315, and 7634). BE joins the present edition without MS in 222 readings and is the first edition to print these readings at lines 103, 190, 526, 1117, 1663, 2413, 2569, 2763, 3150, 3448, 3902, 4366, 4467, 4705, 4709, 4721, 4722, 4732, 4755, 4796, 4933, 4935, 5271, 5314, 5433, 5569, 5699, 5741, 5781, 5959, 6824, 6851, 7056, 7387, 7430, 7661. BE also prints 171 variants where MS either agrees with the present edition or is Out owing to loss of leaves.

BE's 49 unique variants are about evenly divided between obvious errors (e.g., at lines 188, 1565, 2151, 3429, 5200, 5491, 5753, 5864, 6206, 6645, 7390, 7438, 7575, 7642), and changes that may have been deliberate (at lines 2283, 2349, 2905, 3654, 4374, 4396, 5563, 6539, 7147). Some changes impair the meter (at lines 3283, 6184, 6758); some seem intended to improve it (at lines 370, 2823, 4449, 5172, 7444), once at the expense of sense (line 3612). Some changes show uncertainty in morphology (at lines 700, 2306, 2386, 6491, 7474), idiom (at lines 143, 4423), or sense (at lines 2354, 2626, 3008, 3359, 5440, 7574, 7593). Some emendations are reasonable but have not been adopted elsewhere (at lines 2177, 7255). BE suggests but does not incorporate an emendation in line 7109. Variant readings printed first in BE and then in subsequent editions are to be found in lines 149, 683, 1063, 1466, 1760, 1969, 2621, 3462, 3548, 3886, 4191, 4280, 4574, 4940, 5670, 5921, 6221, 6346, 6523, 7092, 7110, 7315.

It is not entirely clear which edition of Speght was used to correct MS. Examination of lines for which MS cannot have been the source (1–44, 333–80, 892, 1387–1482, 1553, 2395–2442, 3136, 3595–3690, 4856, 6205, 6318, 6372, 7383–7574) shows that if BE shares a variant with any of the three, it does so with all of them, except at line 7539, where BE agrees with SP^{2,3} but not with SP^1. BE also reproduces their five-line ending to the poem. If we examine spelling variants in the sections with missing lines, we reach no clearer conclusion; BE sometimes follows SP^{2,3}, sometimes SP^1, sometimes all three, sometimes none. Examples from the opening lines will illustrate:

Title Romaunt SP^2-BE; Romant SP^1
1 men SP^{2,3} BE; menne SP^1 UR
   seyen BE; saine SP^1 UR; sain SP^{2,3}
2 Ther SP^1 UR BE; There SP^{2,3}
   lesynges BE; lesings SP^1; lesinges SP^2-UR

In lines 1401–10, BE's spellings agree with SP^1 in seven cases, with SP^{2,3} in two, with all in thirty-three, and with none in thirteen.

Many of these spelling agreements are probably coincidental, but there is further evidence that BE used all three of Speght's editions. At lines 2902, 3525, and 7145 (with UR), SP^1 is the only edition to anticipate BE (though perhaps coincidentally; cf. lines 3654, 3767, 6296) in printing the reading of the present edition. At lines 3231, 3319, 4846 (with TH^2), 4858, 5493, 5551, and 6823 BE's agreements with the present edition have precedent only in SP^2-UR. At line 4657 only

SP^{2,3} precede BE in printing such a reading. Variants that BE shares with SP^{2,3} (and with UR where starred) but not with SP^1 are found at lines 119, *664, 2374, *2752, *3170, *3249, 3264, *3406, *3463, *4468, *4774, *4986, 5309, 5593, 5732, 5824, 6329, 6512, 7539, *7634. By contrast, BE shares a variant with SP^1 but not with SP^{2,3} (or UR) only at line 2092. At line 72 BE is variant with SP^{1,3} (and UR) but not with SP^2; at line 2195 BE joins only SP^3 UR; at line 3979 BE agrees with SP^3 but not with SP^{1,2} (or UR). Jephson's note to line 4291 says that "the printed editions read *expert*"; but the only editions available to him that so read are SP^1 and UR. On the other hand, BE has the form *moveresse* (rather than *Mynoresse*) at line 149, and Jephson quotes "Speght" in support; but Speght's note on this point did not appear until SP^2 (see 149n.). We cannot even be certain that Jephson did not occasionally confuse his sources; at line 1885, he reports, incorrectly, that "the MS. reads *thought*"; in fact, only SP^3 so reads. See, further, the notes to lines 3264, 3319.

Given the 107 unprecedented readings in BE, its few unusual agreements with SP^1 may be accidental (cf. BE's unique convergence with TH^2 in line 5010). Indeed, BE's relationship with SP^1 is attenuated further when one considers the evidence for the influence of UR on BE. With two minor exceptions, UR is the only edition to anticipate 24 readings printed in BE: at lines 970 (TH^2), 1831, 1976, 2116, 2499, 2622, 2669, 2690, 2709, 2921, 3522, 3697, 3710, 3733, 4702, 4793, 5021, 5107, 5253, 5953, 5976, 5977, 6296 (TH^2), 6298.

Whatever BE's use of "Speght," there is probably a greater degree of editorial conflation in BE than the introductory claim might lead us to expect. Nevertheless, BE's editorial practice is remarkably judicious, in its return to MS as base, in its use of intermediary texts, and, as we see by way of Jephson's notes, in the frequent comparison of the text with the French original.

Morris 1866 (MO)

Like BE, MO uses MS as base (MO 1.ix); hence MO agrees with MS in 333 variants from the present edition and follows corrections in MS in 38 instances. MO corrects MS in 163 other instances and introduces 128 variants where MS either agrees with the present edition or lacks text owing to damage. MO also substitutes a variant for a variant in MS 28 times: at lines 537, 1201, 1689, 1750, 2177, 2669, 3141, 3179, 3490, 3864, 4191, 4207, 4372, 4796, 4935, 4940, 5117, 5408, 5470, 5700, 6318, 6361, 6653, 7092, 7109, 7255, 7315, 7634. MO has 461 variants from the present edition. It should be noted that after line 4658, where speech divisions break up several lines, MO misnumbers the lines as follows (cf. SK 1.16; Lounsbury 1892:2.6; Kaluza 1893*a*:13):

4659–5694 +3	6006–6016 +4	6217–6371 +3
5695–5706 +5	6017–6205 +3	6372–7692 +2
5707–6005 +3	6206–6216 +4	

In the present discussion all line references are to the standard numeration.

Where MS is Out owing to damage, Morris clearly had to make use of a printed text. Evidence that he consulted TH[1] is not surprising; less expected is the evidence that he made even more use of TH[2]. In lines missing from MS (1–44, 333–80, 1387–1482, 3595–3690, and 7383–7574), TH[1] and TH[2] have 352 divergent spellings/readings. MO agrees with TH[2] in 247 of these, with TH[1] in 98, and with neither in 7. (MO also diverges from 56 spellings in which TH[1] and TH[2] agree.) Moreover, MO's italicized emendations show even more clearly that TH[2] is the base text for these lines in MO. In a number of instances, for example, MO adds an italic final *e* where TH[1] already has final *e* but TH[2] does not. We may note too the substantive agreements of MO and TH[2] against TH[1] in lines 343, 7437, and 7480. Conversely, MO italicizes final *e* once (rasoure, line 7418) where TH[2] already has it and TH[1] does not; and agrees with TH[1] against TH[2] in substantive readings at lines 1, 27, 38, 40, 355, 2416, 2431, 3661, 7483, and 7532. One may note finally that MO does not always italicize emendations, and that MO's spelling practices show clear preferences but are hardly uniform.

It does not seem improbable that Morris also consulted other editions from time to time. Interesting in this regard are the readings in MO that have precedent only in UR. See the collations for lines 129, 532, 581, 860, 1924, 1978, 2746, 3179, 3439, 3891, 3967, 4032, 4207, 4222, 4357, 4758, 5352, 5535, 6349, 6543, 6808, 6810 (cf. 5906). MO also includes readings initiated in BE: at lines 103, 149, 1063, 1117, 1466, 1663, 1760, 2569, 2763, 3150, 3448, 3548, 3902, 4280, 4467, 4574, 4705, 4709, 4721, 4722, 4732, 4755, 4933, 4940, 5314, 5433, 5569, 5699, 5741, 5781, 5959, 6523, 6851, 7056, 7092, 7110, 7661 (cf. 119, 526, 2621, 3525, 4335, 4657, 5010, 6549, 7315). To these readings may be added those for which only UR and BE provide precedent: at lines 1831, 1976, 2921, 3522, 3697, 3733, 4793, 5253, 5953, 6298 (cf. 1453, 2176, 2298, 3231, 4846, 5493, 5551, 6296, 6466, 7145, 7634).

In many of these readings, of course, Morris may have arrived independently at the same editorial decisions. His independence is apparent in the 96 readings that appear first in MO. Of these, thirteen are in agreement with the present edition (at lines 1733, 2992, 3482, 3519, 3895 [*trechorus*], 4722, 4921, 5051, 5403, 5977, 6372, 7041, 7366) and fifteen are variants shared by editions subsequent to MO (at lines 645, 1125, 1848, 2349, 3431, 4000, 4089, 4175, 4314, 4796, 5376, 5408, 6460, 6469, 7546). The other new variants are unique: MO adds words at lines 448, 728, 1261, 1689, 2007, 2035, 2177, 2204, 2220, 2309, 3068, 3141, 3266, 3495, 3505, 3845, 4348, 5906 (cf. UR), 6653, 6851, 7151, 7600, 7615; substitutes words (sometimes by changing a letter or two) at lines 537 (2), 1201, 1302, 1640, 2345, 2365, 2970, 2985, 3013, 3128, 3160, 3267, 3363, 3618, 3659, 3864, 3972, 4000, 4099, 4170, 4372, 4445, 4554, 4683, 4935, 5081, 5144, 5470, 5572, 6007, 7109, 7255, 7287; transposes words at lines 629, 1812, 2695, 2696, 3962, 5700, 6582, 7442, 7553; and omits a word at line 2188.

The Modern Transcriptions:
Kaluza 1891 (KA) and Furnivall 1911 (FU)

Furnivall chose Kaluza to prepare the Chaucer Society's parallel-text edition of the French *RR* and the MS text of *Rom* (Kaluza 1893*a*:9); Furnivall himself was to prepare the transcription of TH[1]. As it turned out, Kaluza completed his far more exacting task twenty years before Furnivall's transcription appeared posthumously with an introduction by Skeat. Because FU is inconsequential (a facsimile of TH[1] entire, with an introduction by Skeat, was published in 1905), I will deal with it first, and in short order.

Skeat provides (FU, p. xi) a list of 39 errata in FU (including 14 substantive variants) and says, "I have not observed many inaccuracies, and it is extremely unlikely that they can amount to much" (FU, p. v). By my own count FU differs from TH[1] in 133 spelling variations and 33 substantive variants. The substantive variants, except for those at lines 243, 3602, 5150, 5965, and 6346, are unique: at lines 307, 329, 360, 428, 1080, 1214, 1270, 2768, 3019, 3030, 3719, 4044, 4802, 4891, 4892, 5190, 5194, 5330, 5991, 6112, 6199, 6377, 6378, 6381, 6412, 6999, 7054, 7669. The chief utility of FU is that it numbers the lines of TH[1]'s text (without, however, indicating the displacements involving lines 7013–7110 and 7159–7304).

Kaluza's transcription of his copytext, by contrast, shows only eight substantive disagreements (MS/KA): at lines 3519 (*lefeth/leseth*), 4314 (*of*/om.), 4926 (*in*/om.), 5376 (*his/this*), 6757 (*his*/om.), 6851 (*Of/Or*), 6874 (*His/Hir*), 7092 (*juste the ju dome / juste their dome*). See also the note to line 6688. Some of these lapses in KA's transcription reappear in later editions; see the collations and notes. So too do KA's mistranscriptions of spellings in MS (or TH[1] for passages not in MS): MS vs. KA GL RB[1,2] RI in lines 1708 (*But/Bot*), 2447 (*gret/greet*), 4948 (*thurgh/thourgh*), 5056 (*lyf/lif*), 7046 (*thurgh/thourgh*), 7652 (*distroie/destroie*); TH[1] vs. KA GL (except where starred) RB[1,2] RI, in lines 24 (*wonte/wont*), 30 (*Right/Ryght*), 337 (*wo/woo*), 3615 (*dout/doute*), 3616 (*about/aboute*), 3685 (*his/hys*), 7410 (*His/Hys*), *7456 (*prechours/preachours*), 7516 (*gilty/gylty*), 7518 (*right/ryght*).

KA is useful for its parallel French text, based on Michel's, itself derived from Méon's, which was based on MS Za (Ln 1.46–47).

Kaluza also has variants from MSS Fo, λο, κω, Ly, and Jb, as well as from the 1878 facsimile of Jean Du Pré's edition of 1493 (KA, p. 2). Despite the limitations of this text—Langlois's study of the MSS (1910) had not appeared, let alone his edition—it reveals some of the problems one faces in establishing something like an exemplar for the Middle English.

KA's apparatus (footnotes) indicates the emendations that Kaluza would make to the text of MS, and it includes spellings and readings in UR BE MO (these are presented as "corrections" [p. 3] but sometimes seem no more than a record of variation, especially where KA records forms in which these editions diverge from each other as well as from MS). KA's footnotes also record some variants and spellings in TH[1] and emendations either suggested by Skeat (cited in square brackets) or adopted in his edition (printed the following year).

Skeat 1894 (SK)

Though based on MS, SK departs from it 881 times, not counting 32 instances in which SK agrees with corrections in MS rather than with its first readings. In 463 instances SK agrees with the present edition against MS. In 375 instances SK disagrees with readings shared by MS and the present edition; in 43 instances SK has variants that differ from variants in MS. SK, which adds 26 variants where MS is Out owing to damage, thus has 473 variants from the present edition, sharing 29 of these with MS: at lines 190, 211, 472, 978, 1581, 1683, 1696, 2473, 2541, 2682, 2752, 2783, 2828, 2836, 2950, 3294, 3489, 3588, 3717, 4416, 4527, 4576, 4871, 5162, 5284, 5301, 6002, 6911, 7316.

Skeat believed that MS and TH[1] were collateral authorities, and for this reason he collated TH[1] "throughout" (SK 1.11–15). Consequently, SK shares with TH[1] 83 variants that do not appear in MS, and 186 readings not in MS but adopted in the present edition (again, ignoring the 32 instances in which MS corrects itself). Often SK abandons TH[1] as well as MS. SK introduces 170 unique variants (to which one may want to add a reading in line 5590) and 80 variants without precedent but adopted by subsequent editors; also SK is the first text to provide 138 readings adopted in the present edition. To these interventions one may add SK's 56 variants and 20 agreements with the present edition that have precedent only in UR (mostly trivial adjustments made with an eye to repairing meter). In footnotes KA records 48 of these UR readings; in footnotes SK expressly claims authority for 9 of them and never makes reference to UR (see, however, SK's explanatory note to line 2141, which records an UR reading not noted in KA).

Skeat does adduce BE and MO (SK 1.12, 15–16) but in footnotes cites only MO's text, at lines 1125, 3482, 4175, and 6372 (where only MO precedes SK) and at lines 3891, 4222, 4254, 4357, 4758 (where readings in SK have precedent only in UR MO). Other such precedents appear in lines 1848, 2349, 2992, 3431, 3519, 3895, 4089, 4722, 4921, 5408, 5977, 6460, 6469, 7041, 7366, 7546 (MO only) and in lines 532, 860, 1924, 1978, 2746, 4032, 5352, 6543, 6808, 6810 (UR MO only); KA records MO as authority for fifteen of the readings, but SK claims responsibility for three of them. BE alone anticipates SK at lines 683, 3886, 4191, 4366, 4796, 4935, 5271, 5670, 5921, 6221, 6346, 6824 (four of these are noted in KA); UR BE at lines 2622, 2690, 2709, 5021, 5976 (BE noted consistently in KA). SK fails to recognize either BE or MO when both editions offer the only precedents for SK's readings at lines 526, 1063, 1117, 1663, 2569, 2763, 3150, 3448, 3902, 4467, 4574, 4705, 4709, 4721, 4722, 4732, 4755, 4933, 5314, 5433, 5569, 5699, 5741, 5781, 5959, 7056, 7661. Indeed, Skeat claims credit for the emendations at lines 2763 and 3448. KA, which records several of these BE/MO readings, alone precedes SK in a variant at line 6757.

A few final observations. SK evidently is based on KA rather than MS itself, following KA's mistranscriptions (without comment) at lines 3519, 6757, 6851, 6874; cf. lines 4314 and 5376, where SK inadvertently agrees with MS against KA and records KA's mistranscription as an error in MS. Also, SK's addition of two lines after line 7172 affects the numbering

of lines after this point in SK (all references above are to the line numbering of the present edition). Beneath lines 1–1705 SK prints the corresponding lines of Méon's French text of *RR.* Skeat discusses *Rom* in SK 1.1–20. A. S. G. Edwards' general assessment of Skeat as an editor has only a few comments on his edition of *Rom* (1984:178, 189, 282, 285).

Liddell 1898 (GL)

The text of *Rom* in the Globe edition (GL) was prepared by Mark Liddell, who says (p. lv) that it is based "almost solely upon the Glasgow MS." Nevertheless, GL departs from MS in 660 readings, agreeing with the present edition 425 times, substituting 31 variants for variants in MS, and printing 204 variants where MS agrees with the present edition. GL, which shares 79 variants with MS and adds 16 variants where MS is Out owing to damage, has 329 variants from the present edition.

Like SK, GL seems actually to be based on KA rather than on MS (see readings at lines noted in the discussions of KA and SK, above); nevertheless, in textual notes GL cites MS (as G and as MS.). GL also makes frequent reference to TH[1] (as Th.; MSS. = G and Th.), KA (always emendations suggested in KA's textual notes), and SK. The rare citations of readings in UR (at line 2141), BE (at lines 3429, 6372) and MO (at lines 3137, 3482, 6372) probably are adduced from notes in KA and SK. On the other hand, Liddell makes use of some non-textual information in BE (see GL, note to line 5811) and shares readings that previously appeared only in UR, BE, or MO: in UR at lines 1771, 2141 (noted in KA and SK), 2314, 2727, 3146, 3439 (with MO), 3513 (noted in KA), 3679 (noted in KA), 5107 (with BE; cf. SK), 5947 (noted in KA), 5978 (cf. notes in KA and SK), 6287, 6487; in BE at line 1969 (noted in KA) and colophon; in MO at lines 1733, 5403. These convergences, of course, may be accidental; cf. GL's unique convergences with SP[1] in lines 256, 2116, 6469 and GL's agreements with TH[3]-UR in lines 4525 and 6097.

Liddell exercised considerable independence as an editor. GL introduces 104 unique readings in *Rom*, 19 new variants adopted by later editors (at lines 586, 602, 1043, 1065, 2333, 2365, 2592, 2992, 3040, 3175, 3385, 3482, 3769, 4137, 4357, 4732, 4793, 5069, 5502, 5590), and 39 readings adopted in the present edition (at lines 22, 211, 472, 978, 1007, 1026, 1581, 1683, 1696, 1750, 2473, 2682, 2709, 2710, 2752, 2783, 2828, 2934, 2950, 3450, 3489, 3490, 3502, 3588, 4416, 4527, 4689, 4871, 5028, 5284, 5287, 5491, 5585, 5586, 6002, 6359, 6361, 6606, 6911). These adjustments reveal tendencies to emend for meter (e.g., at lines 801, 816, 1206, 1261, 5389, 5418), to work with construction and punctuation (e.g., at lines 520, 749, 1496, 3294), and to consult the French (e.g., at lines 22, 37, 1978, 2024, 6371–72, 6653, 7116).

Despite this evidence of Liddell's independence, he seems to acquiesce in many of the readings proffered in SK. GL has 39 variants for which SK is the only predecessor (in another 19 variants only UR SK anticipate GL); furthermore, SK introduces 96 readings with which GL and the present edition agree (see, in addition, lines 4955, 5452, 5555, 7314), and in 16 other such cases only UR SK precede GL. SK shares 21 of GL's 29 agreements with TH[1] against MS and the present edition, but only six of GL's 55 agreements with MS and TH[1] against the present edition.

Robinson 1933 and 1957 (RB[1,2])

F. N. Robinson based his two editions of *Rom* on MS but with many adjustments. In RB[1] the text of *Rom* departs from MS in 649 readings, agreeing with the present edition 515 times, adding variants where MS and the present edition agree 123 times, and substituting a different variant in eleven instances (at lines 189, 2564, 3482, 4032, 4846, 5051, 5223, 5403, 5590, 6355, 6361). Where MS is Out and TH[1] serves as base text, RB[1] diverges from the present edition in three readings: at lines 37, 7387, 7456. Thus RB[1] has 146 variants from the present edition. It converges with MS against the present edition nine times (at lines 190, 2025, 3489, 3588, 3717, 4207, 4416, 4576, 5162), but it also originates eight readings with which the present edition agrees (at lines 2775, 2836, 3294, 4725, 6653, 7022, 7316,

7634). RB[1] introduces variants that are without precedent at lines 1137, 1913–14, 2645, 3429, 4032, 4846, 5393, 5421, 7137, 7593, 7614.

Like Skeat, Robinson regarded TH[1] as an independent text, even though closely similar to MS (RB[1], p. 1043; RB[2], p. 924). RB[1] joins TH[1] against MS in 287 readings (229 of which are in agreement with the present edition) and often cites TH[1] in textual notes. As one might expect, Robinson also consulted KA, SK, and GL; they appear frequently in his textual notes, and his four references to UR (notes to lines 256, 2141, 4634, 6359) are probably derived from them. So too may be three of his references to MO (notes to lines 3137, 3482, 6372), but for his note to line 3179 he must have consulted MO. RB[1]'s convergences with UR at lines 1623, 3967, 4634, and 6843 are doubtless coincidental (though KA does record UR's readings at lines 4634 and 6843), and probably so are convergences with MO at lines 3967 and 4000 (both noted in KA), and line 4657. KA provides the only precedent for a reading in RB[1] at line 4926.

When in disagreement with both MS and TH[1], RB[1] tends to reflect editorial decisions made in SK and/or GL. In 20 variants SK and GL are either the only texts to precede RB[1] or the only ones (starred) that Robinson is likely to have consulted: at lines 149, 240, 541, *746, 1860, *2049, 2532, *2617, *3846, 3942, *3979, *4291, 4358, 5223, 6009, 6482, 6707, 6819, 6974, 7456 (cf. line 6757, where only KA joins this group). Where SK and GL differ, RB[1] tends to favor SK, converging with SK in 63 agreements with the present edition and in 22 variants; by contrast, RB[1] joins GL in 35 agreements with the present edition and in 15 variants.

As in SK, spelling "is corrected to conform to grammatical standards" (RB[2], p. 924), especially in respect of final -*e*. But Robinson, noting that most of *Rom* is not Chaucer's, and that his part of it is youthful work, takes a less fastidious approach than did Skeat to meter and vagaries of spelling in *Rom*.

RB[2] resets the text of RB[1], with eleven differences: correction of typographical errors in lines 1932, 2025, 2165 (*Fo > For*), 4032; and introduction of typographical errors in lines

187, 473, 2201 (also in RI), 3977 (an egregious error owing to eyeskip), 4720, 6599, and 7423. None of these changes is addressed in textual notes (but see RB²'s textual note to line 3979).

Sutherland 1968 (SU)

Sutherland based his text of Rom on TH¹ because he believed, as his modern predecessors did, that TH¹ was cognate with and not a descendant of MS (SU, pp. v–vi, ix, xxxvii), and because he regarded TH¹ as having not only a fuller text than MS but a sounder one as well. Nevertheless, SU departs from TH¹ in 380 readings, to anticipate the present edition 307 times (joining MS in 62 instances), to add 57 variants where TH¹ agrees with the present edition, and to substitute 17 variants different from variants in TH¹. Thus SU has 362 variants from the present edition. SU is the first text to anticipate a reading of the present edition at line 6355.

SU's departures from TH¹ include 59 new readings, several resulting, apparently, from inadvertent error (an asterisk marks readings annotated in SU): unique readings at lines 78, *535, 729, 758, 973, 1627, *1644, *1779, 1977, 2324, 2896, 3166, 5369, 5720, *5906; readings adopted later only by FI, at lines 859, 1283, 1315, 2079, 2085, *2323, *2551, 2817, *2988, 3133, 3164, 3362, *3490, 3493, *3774, *4075–84, *4174, *4291, 4388, 4439, 4753, *4764, 4842, 4878, 4881, *5165, *5166, 5192, 5207, 5210, *5401, *5638, 5803, 5902, 5977, 5990, 6179, *6372, *6653, 6871, *7178, 7275, 7594, *7634. To these instances one might add a few in which SU is preceded by texts that Sutherland probably did not consult: at lines *2621 (note points only to RB's approximation of SU's reading), 3183, and 7455.

Sutherland's textual notes adduce with great frequency MS, TH¹, SK, GL, and RB. His few references to UR, BE, and MO are taken at second hand: see his notes to lines 3429, 3482, 3891, 4634, 6372. Emendations suggested in KA are cited in his notes to lines 379, 960, 1015, 1026, 1031, 1058, 1244, 1683, 1775, 2074, 2551, 4177, 6041, 6042, 6317–18, 6606. Where SU abandons TH¹ and MS to

follow SK, GL, or RB, the tendency is to prefer RB, in 79 instances (four times against both SK and GL: at lines 2775, 2836, 4634, 7316); then SK, in 71 instances (seventeen times against GL and RB: at lines 256, 356, 645, 2309, 3482, 4096, 4177, 4181, 4846, 5287, 5292, 5301, 5309, 5353, 5670, 5762, 6606); then GL, in 35 instances (six times against SK and RB: at lines 2992, 3588, 4416, 4732, 4793, 5107; see also 2341n., 5401n., 5638n.).

Fisher 1977 (FI)

Fisher (p. 970) accepts earlier opinion that the text of *Rom* in MS "is not as complete or correct" as that printed in TH¹; hence TH¹, he states, serves as the base text for FI. Collation shows, however, that FI is far less close to TH¹ than to SU. FI, which shares exclusively with SU 44 readings (see description of SU above) and a heading before line 4431 (see collations below), departs from SU in only 100 readings and rejoins TH¹ in only 20 of these instances: with MS and the present edition at lines 78, 729, 758, 973, 1627, 1977, 2324, 2896, 3166, 5369, 5627, 5720, 5906; with variants in MS at lines 3902, 5546, 5641; and at lines 146, 1043, 1447, 2641. Since in nine instances FI, SU, and TH¹ are each independent of the other (at lines 535, 1644, 1779, 2473, 2621, 3774, 4357, 4634, 4732), FI preserves 351 of SU's 380 departures from TH¹ and introduces 71 disagreements with readings shared by SU and TH¹. Thus FI diverges from TH¹ in 422 substantive readings.

FI agrees with the present edition against SU in 54 readings, offers a different variant from that in SU twice (at lines 1447, 2621), and adds 44 variants where SU agrees with the present edition. FI thus has 352 variants from the present edition. FI agrees with MS and the present edition against TH¹ and SU at lines 225, 295, 314, 408, 497, 520, 521, 523, 794, 904, 947, 1061, 1168, 1221, 1231, 1263, 1611, 1648, 1736, 2880, 3774. When FI disagrees with MS, TH¹, and SU, support for FI's reading comes most often from SK (unique precedent marked with an asterisk): with the present edition at lines 66, 103, 485, 535, 1018, 1233, 1644, 1779, 1994, 3337, 3491,

3710, 3851, 4476, 4732, 5379; against the present edition at lines *249, *261, *296, 307, *536, 583, 683, *688, 775, 791, *806, 932, 1010, *1134, *1222, 1934, *1965, 2049, *2074, 2617, *4634, 4960, 5068, 5641, 6500. GL and RB support corrections not in SK or MS at lines 1733, 2950, 3502; GL is sole support for a variant at line 4357; RB for a variant at line 2621. FI introduces unique variants at lines 138 (cf. SK), 307, 1031, 2473, 2786, 3338, 3555, 3995, 4324, 5236, 6054, 7146. Not counted among these unique readings is a typographical error at line 6226 (*wordly* for *worldly*) and a unique spelling at line 6197 (*resour* for *rasour*, a spelling intended as an easy emendation of MS *resoun* but unattested in *MED* and *OED*). At line 4576 FI provides the first precedent for a reading adopted in the present edition. In Fisher's second edition "the text and notes remain as they were in the first edition" (1989, p. vii).

David 1987 (RI)

In the Riverside Chaucer *Rom* is edited by Alfred David, who accepts, and gives a full explanation of, Blodgett's discovery that MS was printer's copy for TH[1] (see above, "The Glasgow MS and the Thynne Print"); in particular, he emphasizes the point that TH[1] can "no longer be taken as a primary authority except where it preserves the text of eleven leaves and a few marginal words now lost" from MS (p. 1198). Accordingly, he omits from his text a series of twelve lines (892, 1553, 1892, 3136, 4856, 6205, 6318, 6372, 6688, 6786, 7092, 7109; see notes) that appear in TH[1] but not in MS; in each case RI shows the lacuna by a line of dots and supplies the TH[1] version in a footnote. It may be noted, furthermore, that in passages missing from MS owing to damage, RI never joins TH[1] against the present edition; rather the two editions agree in nineteen emendations of TH[1]: at lines 3, 22, 343, 379, 1398, 1400, 1447, 1448, 3626, 3643, 3676, 7387, 7392, 7407, 7430, 7471, 7485, 7486, 7531.

RI, of course, like the present edition, emends MS numerous times. RI departs from MS in 564 substantive readings: to anticipate the present edition in 509 instances (37 of which involve corrections already introduced in MS); to substitute a variant different from that in MS eight times (at lines 2564, 3482, 4657, 4846, 5051, 5403, 5590, 6606); and to print variants where MS agrees with the present edition 47 times. In addition to omitting the twelve lines not present in MS (listed above), RI preserves six MS readings not adopted in the present edition (at lines 2499, 2541, 3717, 4207, 4416, 6810); RI thus has 73 variants from the present edition. In 235 readings RI joins TH[1] against MS; 220 of these readings agree with the present edition and fifteen do not (at lines 264, 446, 1062, 1080, 1146, 1147, 1359, 4208, 4358, 5403, 5889, 6073, 6195, 6600, 6880). RI diverges from 271 readings shared by MS and TH[1] to join the present edition. In another eighteen instances RI reads with the present edition and not with competing variants in MS and TH[1]: at lines 103, 189, 526, 535, 1233, 1313, 1652, 1750, 3150, 3433, 3450, 4294, 4372, 4709, 6359, 6361, 7022, 7661.

RI has 40 variants from the present edition supported neither by MS nor by TH[1]. RB agrees with 32 of these readings (an asterisk marks those supported only by RB): at lines 586, 746, 749, 791, 1623, 2049, *2201, 2477, 2564, 3482, 3769, 3774, 3942, 3967, 4137, 4291, 4358, *4846, 4892, 5051, *5421, 5590, 5627, 6482, 6500, 6682, 6707, 6819, 6901, 6974, 7456, *7614. RI has a unique reading in line 2610; the other variants (unique support indicated) are in lines 1063, 4314, 4657, 4764 (GL), 5069 (GL), 5107, 6606. GL agrees with 20 of the 40 variants, SK with 23. Given RI's special closeness with RB it may be useful to note that RI diverges from RB[1] in 116 readings and from RB[2] in 121 readings; among these instances RI fails to rejoin MS only at lines 190, 1063, 2025, 2610, 3489, 3588, 4314, 4576, 4657, 4764, 5069, 5162, 6606. Finally, it may be noted that RI marks the lacuna at lines 7172–73 by a line of dots (see note).

The Present Edition

The base of the text is MS, supplemented by TH[1] where MS is defective. The reasons for choosing MS as base appear above in "The Glasgow MS and the Thynne Print." The collations record substantive variants from the base line as it appears in the text; a few spelling variations (so marked and not counted as variants in the textual analysis) have been included (see the accompanying notes). Combined textual and explanatory notes follow the Collations; explanatory notes follow the textual notes, separated by the symbol §.

In the text, the marginal folio numbers with *r* (recto) or *v* (verso) indicate MS as base, while those with column letters (*a, b* for the two recto columns; *c, d* for the two verso columns) indicate TH[1] as base; in the latter case, all text from TH[1] appears in square brackets, as do all other emendations. In general, these bracketed portions include the 524 lines of the eleven leaves that are missing from MS (lines 1–44, 333–80, 1387–1482, 2395–2442, 3595–3690, 7383–7574), as well as the twelve lines that do not appear, or that appear in spurious versions, on MS leaves that still exist (lines 892, 1553, 1892, 3136, 4856, 6205, 6318, 6372, 6688, 6786, 7092, 7109). There is of course a distinction to be drawn; the lines from the missing leaves were there when TH[1] used MS as copy text, while the other twelve were not, or existed in later hands. Thus, as we have seen, RI regards all twelve of these lines as spurious, omits them from the text, and supplies them in the notes. In the present text, TH[1]'s version appears for ten of the twelve; in the other two cases, SK's version appears for line 6318, MO's for line 6372. In the case of line 7109, TH[1]'s version appears with SK's emendations. Although these twelve lines appear in the text, bracketed, they must be regarded as conjectural.

In the collations, the order of the twenty sigils is chronological, as follows: MS TH[1] TH[2] TH[3] ST SP[1] SP[2] SP[3] UR BE MO KA SK GL FU RB[1] RB[2] SU FI RI. I abbreviate strings of sigils that are inclusive. Thus TH[1]-SP[3] designates the string TH[1] TH[2] TH[3] ST SP[1] SP[2] SP[3]. SP[1] SP[3] means that the variant occurs in SP[1] and SP[3] but not in SP[2], while SP[1-3] indicates the presence of the variant in all three of Speght's editions.

From the text and collations it is possible to reconstruct the base text. More often than one would like, the emendations are conjectural. Where only a single authority exists, emendation on the basis of recension is manifestly impossible, as it would be even if MS and TH[1] were independent authorities (Greg 1927:21; cf. Kane 1965:3, Donaldson 1970b). Thus the criteria for emendation need explanation. Paleographical considerations are primary. There are relatively few emendations for metrical reasons alone, but many are based on the French text. In the case of *Rom*, there is a special reason for this decision, since the question of authorship has not been settled. To emend freely for meter assumes Chaucer's authorship, the very question that, in the absence of external evidence, one must approach on the basis of the unemended text. Emendation on the basis of the French, however, involves less such begging of the question, for it does not necessarily assume Chaucer's authorship.

The present text does not normalize MS's many "ungrammatical" features, chief of which is its irregular use of final -*e*, a phenomenon that far exceeds the "normal" irregularity in Chaucer's practice (see McJimsey 1942). These irregularities fall into several categories: the absence of -*e* in the wk. pa. t. sg.; the presence of -*e* in the wk. pa. part.; the presence of -*e* in the str. pa. t. sg.; the absence of -*e* (or -*en*) in the inf., pres. pl., or str. pa. part.; the ahistorical addition of -*e* to an inf. or pres. pl. in -*n*; the ahistorical presence or absence of -*e* in nouns; the absence of -*e* in weak or plural adjectives; and the presence or absence of -*e* in adverbs. See also Lounsbury (1892:2.66–72); Kittredge (1892:6–11). The result of these considerations is a text that is not made to appear "Chaucerian" but that represents a mid-15th-century version of a text whose ancestor may have been, in part, by Chaucer.

The Romaunt of the Rose

And it was peynted wel and thwyten
And oueral dyapred and writen
With ladyes and with Bachelers
ffull lyghtsom and glad of cheris
These bowes two helde swete lokyng
That semede lyk no gadelyng
And ten brode arowis hilde she there
Of which v. in his righthond were
But they were shauen wel and dight
Nokked and fethered right
And all they were with gold bygoon
And stronge peynted euerychoon
And sharp forto keruen well
But yren was ther noon ne stell
ffor al was golde men myght it see
Outake the fetheres and the tree
The swiftest of these arowis fyue
Out of a bowe forto dryue
And best fethered for to flee
And fairest eke was clepid Beaute
That other arowe that hurteth lasse
Was clepid as j trowe symplesse
The thridde cleped was ffraunchise
That fethred was in noble wise

Glasgow University Library Manuscript, Hunter 409, folio 18v (lines 933–56).

[The Romaunt of the Rose]

[Many men sayn that in sweveninges	TH¹:	This maye I drawe to warraunt
Ther nys but fables and lesynges;	128a	An authour that hight Macrobes,
But men may some sweven[es] sene		That halte nat dremes false ne lees,
Whiche hardely that false ne bene		But undothe us the avysioun
But afterwarde ben apparaunt.	5	That whilom mette kyng Cipioun. 10

Title: **The]** om. FI *Out:* MS *Lines 1–44* Out: MS (*leaf missing*); *supplied from* TH¹ 1 **men]** man
TH² 3 **But]** B. yet UR **swevenes]** sweuen TH¹-KA FU 4 **that false ne]** n. f. SK

Title: I use the conventional form of the title, with the spelling *Romaunt*. MS has no running titles, and since the opening leaf is missing (see Introduction, "The Missing Leaves"), no title appears as a heading or at line 39; elsewhere the form *Romance* appears (in lines 2148, 2154, 2168, 2170). Although TH¹ uses the spelling *Romaunce* in the heading of the opening page as well as on eight other pages (128r–129r, l30v–l32v), all the other page headings, as well as the colophon (168v), read *Romaunt*; in lines 39, 2154, 2168 TH¹ has *Romance*, in line 2170 *Romaunce*, and in line 2148 (see n.) *Romaunt*. Except for SP¹ (*Romant* in titles), subsequent editions favor the spelling *Romaunt*, a form that provides a convenient way of distinguishing the ME translation from the Fr. original. Cf. Hetherington (1964:9).

1–44 The opening leaf is missing in MS, and these lines are supplied from TH¹ (KA SKt GL RBt SU FI RIt). BE supplies them from "Speght" (BE, p. 12), MO from TH² or TH¹. See above, "The Missing Leaves" and "Descriptions of the Printed Editions."

1–20 On the significance of dreams, editors refer to their notes to *HF* 1–52 (BE SK RB RI) and (RB RI) to *NPT* B² 4112–4347; David (RI) also cites *TC* 5.358–85 and note, and he observes that "the significance of dreams is a recurrent topic in Chaucer's poetry." See also Ln 1–2n., Dahlberg (1971:357–58).

1–2 Skeat (SK) scans: "Many | men seyn | that in | swev'níng-es. . . . lesíng-es." In general, throughout Fragment A, Skeat recommends, "apply the usual rules of Chaucerian pronunciation."

3 **swevenes:** "read:—swev'nes" (SK). This is KA's suggested emendation for TH¹'s singular *sweuen* ("dreame" SPg et al.). SK GL RB¹-RI adopt it on the bases of the Fr. plural *songes* and the plural verb *bene* in line 4.

4 **hardely:** "read . . . as *three* syllables" (SK).

that false ne bene: Skeat (SK), emending to *ne false been*, reads "'fals-e' as two" syllables. Liddell (GL; noted in RBt) suggests "? to falseen ben" and cites the Fr. *mençongier* (Lc 4 "deceivers"), a form that Liddell takes as the verb; Ln glosses it as a noun, "trompeurs" (Tobler-Lommatzsch 1925– :5.1397 quotes the Fr. line, s. v. *mençognier* adj. and subst.).

5–6 **apparaunt : warraunt:** RBt allows that added *-e* (in BE SK) may be valid. Cf. lines 929–30 in RB.

7–8 **Macrobes : lees:** Koch (1890:11; 1900a:66) argues against Chaucer's authorship by noting the different form *Macrobeus*, rhyming with *us*, at *BD* 283–84; Kaluza (1893a:128), arguing for Chaucer's authorship of Fragment A, notes that the form *Macrobes* follows the Fr. (Lc 7–8 *Macrobes : lobes*). This is the first in a series of rhymes that Koch uses as evidence that Chaucer is not the author of Fragment A; for others see lines 53–54, 55–56, 183–84, 415–16, 457–58, 481–82, 505–06, 579–80, 661–62, 887–88, 1091–92, 1341–42, 1673–74, 1705–06, and notes. For counter-arguments, see Kaluza (1893a:126–29) and Skeat (1900:149–53).

7 **Macrobes:** Macrobius (flourished ca. 400 A.D.), author of commentary on Cicero's *Somnium Scipionis*, as noted first in URg, s.v. *Cipioun*. Jephson (BE 4.189; *PF* 31n.) summarizes the content of Cicero's *Somnium*. RI notes that Macrobius's commentary was "the source of much medieval dream lore"; see Peden (1985). On the relationship to *RR*, see Dahlberg (1961). Ln (6–7n.) quotes Chrétien de Troyes' citation of Macrobius in *Erec et Enide* 6738 (6676, ed. Roques 1966). For fuller analysis of the commentary, see the notes to *PF* 31 in SK RB RI. See also 9–10n. below.

8 **halte:** "the contracted form of *holdeth*" (BE).

lees: "lies" (URg et al.); "false" (TRg et al.); "deceptive" (SK). The form is that of a noun, not of an adjective.

9–10 "But explains to us the vision that king Scipio formerly dreamt" (SK). Skeat (SK 1.505–06; *PF* 31n.) records other allusions in Chaucer to the dream of Scipio: *NPT* B² 4313- 14, *BD* 284–87, and *HF* 514; David (RI) adds *HF* 916–18 (see 10n.) and (RIf) cites Chaucer's summary of the dream in *PF* 36–84; see also *PF* 96–97, 109–11. RB notes that, in *BD* and *NPT*, "Chaucer speaks of Macrobius as if he were the author of the Somnium, an impression he might have derived from this line of Lorris," but that, in *PF* 31, "he names *Tullyus* as the author." FI also notes Chaucer's "mistaken reference in *BD* . . . which he corrected in *PF*." RI notes further that "Guillaume de Lorris, whose reference echoes Chrétien de Troyes's Erec (see Langlois's n.), may have known Macrobius only as a name" (see 10n.).

9 **undothe:** "explain[s]" (URg et al.), "either 'expounds' or 'relates'" (RB). RB RI cite the Fr. *escrist* (Lc 9 "wrote"), and RI notes the variant *espont* ("expounds"), from MSS Ga Ra (Ln 9t), "which corresponds to the English."

10 **kyng Cipioun:** David (RI), noting that this phrase translates the Fr. *roi Scypion* (Lc 10), observes that "Scipio was not a king" and that "this passage doubtless lies behind the same mistake in *BD* 286 and *HF* 916–18

And whoso saith or weneth it be
A jape or els nycete
To wene that dremes after fal,
Lette whoso lyste a fole me cal,
For this trowe I, and say for me,   15
That dremes signifiaunce be
Of good and harme to many wightes
That dremen in her slepe a-nyghtes
Ful many thynges covertly
That fallen after al openly.   20
   Within my twenty yere of age,
Whan that Love taketh his [cariage]
Of yonge folke, I went soone
To bedde, as I was wonte to done,

And faste I slepte; and in slepyng   25
Me mette suche a swevenyng
That lyked me wonders wele.
But in that sweven is never a dele
That it nys afterwarde befal,
Right as this dreme wol tel us al.   30
   Nowe this dreme wol I ryme aright
To make your hertes gaye and lyght,
For Love it prayeth and also
Commaundeth me that it be so.
And if there any aske me,   35
Whether that it be, he or she,
Howe this booke whiche is here
Shal hatte, that I rede you here,

---

11 **or**] and UR   12 **els nycete**] e. a n. UR SK FI   20 **al**] *om.* UR   22 **cariage**] corage TH¹-SK FU   25 **slepte**] sleep SK   27 **lyked**] lyke TH²   **wonders**] wonder GL   37 **Howe**] And h. UR; H. that SK; H. wil I GL   **whiche**] the w. SK RB¹·²   38 **that**] which t. UR   **you**] *om.* TH²

(see n.)." At *BD* 287, Chaucer mistakenly identifies Scipio the dreamer as "the Affrikan"; and Fisher thinks that "the failure [at *Rom* 10] to specify that Scipio the Younger dreamt of his ancestor Scipio Africanus led to Chaucer's initial confusion." In *PF* 96–97, 109–11, Chaucer has the correct relationships among "Affrican," "Scipion," and "Macrobe."

12 **els:** SP²·³ have *else*, BE MO SK GL RB RI *elles*, FI *eles*. KA notes the historical (OE) form *elles* in BE MO. In the case of SK FI, who add *a*, a disyllable is not necessary for meter.

22 **taketh his cariage:** SK reads the unemended phrase *taketh his corage* as "assumes fresh confidence from the support of the young, is encouraged by the young, receives their tribute." This last sense would seem to support Liddell's emendation, *cariage* (below), rather than the reading *corage*.

    cariage: "toll" (GL et al.), "feudal tax" (RIf; see *MED cariage*, 4. [a]). Liddell's emendation (in GL) is based on Fr. *paage* "toll" (Lc 22). SK notes that "*paage* is the mod. F. *péage*, toll, lit. 'footing.'" RIt notes that TH¹'s reading *corage* "could only arise from the rarer word [*cariage*], a literal equivalent of the French."

24 **as I was wonte to done:** SK notes the same phrase in *HF* 113. With other subjects and infinitives, the phrase is common in Chaucer.

25 **slepte:** Skeat (SKt) notes this form in TH¹, but he prefers the strong pa. t., *sleep*, for meter.

26 **suche:** Skeat (SKt) notes this form in TH¹ and emends the text to *swiche*, a Chaucerian form that he prefers throughout Fragment A (1–1705).

27 SK suggests "That hit me lyked wonder wel," and GL adopts the form *wonder*. Skeat (SK) takes the phrase *wonder wel* as "wonderfully well"; he notes that "this use of *wonder* is common," refers to *CYT* G 751, 1035, and notes that the *-s* of TH¹'s *wonders* is an adverbial suffix. SP²·³ BE modernize to *wondrous*, UR MO to *wond(i,e)rous*. According to *OED* (*Wondrous* adj. and adv.), the modern form is "an alteration of *wonders . . .* by substitution of suffix *-ous*, after *marvellous*."

30 **Right:** MO and KA mistranscribe as *Ryght*, and the spelling persists in GL RB¹·² RI.

31 **Nowe:** In notes, SU FI mistakenly indicate that TH¹ reads *Howe*.

36 **Whether:** Probably the pronoun "which of two," rather than the conjunction; TH¹ has a virgule between *be* and *he*.

37 The faulty metrics of this line have encouraged emendation. GL's is based on the Fr. (Lc 35 "je veil" "I wish"), which RBt and RIt also adduce. However, David (RIt) observes that "many lines in G [= MS] do not count out to eight syllables. In view of the different emendations, it seems best to follow the copy-text." At this point, TH¹ (not MS) is the copy-text.

38 **hatte:** "was called" (SPg et al.); SK respells as *hote*, "a less ambiguous spelling than *hatte*," and compares *WBP* D 144. Hinckley (1906) thinks *hatte* a Northern form; Skeat (1906) notes that it does not occur in rhyme, that it appears only in TH¹, and that "it is wrong."

    rede you here: "advise you to hear" (Kaluza 1893*a*:67, SK RI). David (RI), following Kaluza, thinks that "an alternative meaning, 'read to you here' is less likely because it violates the convention of *rime riche* (see GP I[A].17–18n.)."

It is the Romance of the Rose,
In whiche al the arte of love I close.
   The mater fayre is of to make;
God graunt me in gree that she it take
For whom that it begonnen is!
And that is she that hath, ywis,]
So mochel pris, and therto [she]
So worthy is biloved [to be]
That she wel ought of pris [and right]
Be cleped Rose of every wi[ght].
   That it was May me thought tho—
It is fyve yere or more ago—

40

44

MS:1r

50

That it was May, thus dremed me,
In tyme of love and jolite,
That al thing gynneth waxen gay,
For ther is neither busk nor hay
In May, that it nyl shrouded bene
And it with newe leves wrene.
These wodes eek recoveren gr[e]ne
That drie in wynter ben to sene,
And the erth wexith proude withall
For swote dewes that on it fall,
And the pore estat forgette
In which that wynter had it sette.

55

60

---

40 **close]** glose TH²   42 **me]** *om.* UR SK   44 *Lines 1–44 Out:* MS   45 **she]** *om.* MS (*leaf torn*)   46 **to be]** be SK; *om.* MS (*leaf torn*)   47 **and right]** *om.* MS (*leaf torn*)   48 **wight]** wi MS (*leaf torn*)   57 **grene]** gr ne MS (*thin spot in vellum*)   61 **And the]** A. al t. SK GL

---

39 **Romance:** SKt observes that TH³ has the spelling *Romaunte*. Other eds. have *Romaunce* (TH² MO), *Romaunt* (ST-BE); see note on title. *MED romaunce* n. does not list the forms in *-nt-*.

40 **arte of love:** "The poet here adopts the title of Ovid's *Ars Amandi*; but the two poems are composed on entirely different models" (BE).

42–48 BE SK RB observe that allusions to "she" and "Rose" are translated from the Fr. and "have therefore no special significance" (SK). RB adds that "the person intended by Guillaume de Lorris is unknown."

42 **gree:** "good parte" (SP²³g) rather than "estate" (SP¹g). URg distinguishes the two senses, "pleasure" and "degree," and TRg notes the separate origins, through Fr. *gré*, in Latin *gratum* "pleasing" and *gradum* "step." See *MED gre* n. (1), n.(2).

45–48 Folio 1 of MS is damaged; on the recto, the ends of these lines are missing and supplied from TH¹ (KA). BE supplies the lines from "Speght."

45 BE SKt note that MS begins at this line.

49 SK compares *BD* 291.

    thought: UR has *thoughtin*, where the *-in* indicates a metrical syllable rather than a plural ending (Alderson 1970:122); in such cases, I regard the variants as non-substantive and do not collate. Examples of such seemingly plural forms occur in UR at lines 294, 398, 517, 676, 6557 (mightin); 654, 7551 (thoughtin); 3079, 3411, 4615, 6369 (madin); 3228 (haddin); 4432 (shuldin); 4491 (wollin); 5049 (preisin); 5182 (woldin); 5327, 6969 (lovin); 5624 (sparin); 6303 (fallin); 6967 (delin); 6972 (makin); 6982 (repairin).

53–54 **gay : hay:** Koch (1890:11; 1900a:66) thinks the rhyme un-Chaucerian because Chaucer usually has *hawe* or *hegge*; *haye* occurs only once in the pl. (*TC* 3.351 *hayis : May is*); but Kaluza (1893a:128) points out that *hay(e)* follows the Fr. *haie* (Lc 50). See 7–8n.

56 **wrene:** "cover" (SPg et al.), "hide" (URg), "covered" (FI). The form is probably the infinitive rather than the pa. part. Jephson (BE) points to OE *wrēon* and quotes the Fr. (Lc 51 "qui en may *parer* ne se veille" "that in May does not want to adorn itself"). SK compares "wrye" in *SumT* D 1827; but this, Chaucer's usual form, Koch (1900a:66) observes, would here produce a defective rhyme. URg notes that the infinitive *wrie* occurs at *Rom* 6795.

57–62 SK RI compare *BD* 410–15; SK RB RI compare *LGWP* F 125–29 (G 113–17), to which RI has a relevant note.

57 **grene:** KA notes that the first *e* is illegible and that there are "two small holes in the parchment." Although the "holes" do not go through, the vellum is very thin, and the illegible medial *e* backs up on the illegible medial *n* of *chelaundre* (line 81) on folio 1v.

59–70 For the idea of the earth's pride in a robe of grass and flowers, Ln (59–66n.) quotes Alanus de Insulis, *De planctu naturae* (see *PL* 210:447D–448A).

59 **And the erth:** KA suggests *erthe*, and SK scans "And th'erth-e."

61 **pore estat:** Kaluza (1893a:140–41) notes the differing treatments of the Fr. *povreté* (Lc 57) here and in *BD* 410 *povertee*, and he uses the differences as an argument for dating *BD* earlier than *Rom*. Brusendorff (1925:397–98) makes a similar argument.

    pore: GL suggests *povre* in a note.

And than bycometh the ground so proude
That it wole have a newe shroude,
And makith so queynt his robe and faire   65
That it ha[th] hewes an hundred payre
Of gras and flouris, ynde and pers,
And many hewes ful dyvers.
[That is the robe I] mene, iwis,   1v
[Through whiche th]e ground to preisen is. 70
　[The briddes that ha]ven lefte her song
While thei [suffr]ide cold so strong

In wedres gryl and derk to sight
Ben in May, for the sonne bright,
So glade that they shewe in syngyng   75
That in her hertis is sich lykyng
That they mote syngen and be light.
Than doth the nyghtyngale hir myght
To make noyse and syngen blythe.
Than is blisful many sithe   80
The chelau[n]dre and papyngay.
Than yong folk entenden ay

---

63 **bycometh**] become TH³-SP³   65 **makith**] make UR   66 **hath**] had MS-KA FU SU   68 **hewes**]
hilles SP²   69 **That is the robe I**] *om.* MS (*leaf torn*)   70 **Through whiche the**] e MS (*leaf torn*)
71 **The briddes that haven**] ven MS (*leaf torn*)   72 **suffride**] ide MS (*leaf torn*); han s. TH¹-SP¹ SP³-MO SK
FU SU FI; had s. SP²   **so**] ful TH¹-UR FU SU FI   76 **hertis**] herte TH¹-UR SK FU SU FI   78 **Than**] That SU
80 **sithe**] a s. TH¹-UR SK FU SU FI   81 **chelaundre**] chelau dre MS (*thin spot in vellum*)   **papyngay**] the
p. TH¹-MO SK-FU SU FI

63　RB compares Alanus de Insulis, *De planctu naturae* (see *PL* 210:447ff.).

65　**queynt:** General glosses include: "strange" (SPg et al.); "neat" (URg et al.); "artful" (TRg BEg RBg); "curious"
(SKg et al.); "(curiously, skillfully, elaborately) contrived" (RBg, Davis 1979, RIg); "elegant" (SKg₂ et al.). Here, "curious, dainty" (SKg); "intricate" (FI); "elegant (pleasing)" (Davis 1979, RIg). On the idiom *maken it queynt*, see 2038n.

66　**hath:** KA's suggestion for MS *had* follows the Fr. *a* (Lc 62) and is consistent with *bycometh* (line 63) and
makith (line 65). SU allows that the emendation is "perhaps" right.

67　**ynde and pers:** "*Indian* and *Persian*" (URg); BE FI note that these colors derive their names from the
countries of India and Persia. BE quotes the Fr. ("indes et perses") from Méon (ed. 1814; cf. BE, p. 7); Ln Lc 63 have
"blanches et perses." For the variant *indes* see Ln (63t) and the Fr. text in KA. SU locates it in MSS Za M N L and
argues that since these "constitute more than fifty MSS, the reading *indes*, if it be not the original, must have been
close to the original" (SU Fr. 63n.). The phrase "ynde, ne perse" occurs elsewhere in *RR* (Lc 891), but only in the H
family (Ln 892t).

　　ynde: SPg defines *ynde* as "blacke" but *inde* as "azure colour"; URg shows the latter sense for both forms
and "black" as a possible meaning for *ynde*. TRg BE SK FI specify azure hue, but RIf glosses "indigo blue." SK
adduces *Cursor Mundi* 9920 (ed. Morris 1874–93:570; Vespasian MS, "Es al o bleu, men cals Ind").

　　pers: "skie colour" (SPg et al.), to which URg et al. add "Blewish-gray." URg and SK adduce *GP* 439.

69–72　Folio 1 is damaged; on the verso, parts of these lines are missing and supplied from TH¹ (KA SKt SU FI RIt).

71–131　David (RI), expanding RB's note, points out that the description of birds, landscape, and river, as well
as of the garden (136ff.), parallels many others in medieval poetry. RB refers to Ln 78n. and its citation of Johnston
(1908); see *Floire et Blancheflor*, lines 1979–2051 (ed. Leclanche 1980; = lines 1744–1810, ed. Pelan 1937). Ln cites a
14th-century marginal reference in MS Me to Matthew of Vendôme's description, in his *Ars versificatoria*, of a
tranquil place ("loci placidi descriptione"; Faral's ed. [1924:148–49] lacks 103 lines on plants and trees), a description
which, Langlois thinks, Guillaume de Lorris may have known. David cites Curtius's study (1953:195–200) of "the
topos of the *locus amoenus* (pleasance) in Latin poetry," and he notes that Curtius (202n.) cites Langlois's reference
to Matthew of Vendôme "as evidence of dependence on Latin rhetorical tradition" (RI); David notes further that
Thoss (1972:113–38) "gives contrary evidence that [Guillaume's] description derives independently from vernacular
tradition and departs in significant ways from Matthew of Vendôme's model."

71　**briddes:** BE MO SK RI have this spelling of TH¹'s *byrdes*. RIt notes that "the word is torn off in G [MS],"
and that "G's spelling is regularly *briddes*, modernized in Th to *brydes*."

　　haven: KA saw only en in MS, but the *v* is also visible. RIt notes that "*han* is metrically preferable, but -*en*
is visible in G."

72　**suffride:** MS has space for the five missing letters but not for TH¹'s auxiliary *han*. As KA notes, "the lower
parts of *s, ff, r* are still visible in the MS."

73　**gryl:** SP and UR gloss as "cold," but TRg has "horrible." SK—citing *Promptorium Parvulorum*, "*Gryme*,
grill, or horrybile"—glosses "keen, rough." *MED grille* adj. 2. (d) gives "inclement."

78　**Than:** FI ascribes the variant *That* to TH¹, but it appears only in SU, in error.

81　**chelaundre:** KA saw only part of the *u*, but with back-lighting the letter is quite visible in MS. Cf. 57n.
§　SP TR gloss as "goldfinch," URg adding "a sort of lark"; later eds. propose a lark, or a kind or variety of lark. *MED*
defines *chalaundre* n. as "the calander lark (Melanocorypha calandra)," and *gold-finch* n. as "the European

For to ben gay and amorous,
The tyme is than so [saverous].
Hard is the hert that loveth nought   85
In May, whan al this mirth is wrought,
Whan he may on these braunches here
The smale briddes syngen clere
Her blesful swete song pitous.
And in this sesoun delytous,   90
Whan love affraieth al thing,
Me thought a-nyght in my sleping,
Right in my bed ful redily,   2r

That it was by the morowe e[rly],
And up I roos and gan me clot[he].   95
Anoon I wisshe myn hondis both[e].
A sylvre nedle forth y droughe
Out of an aguler queynt ynoughe
And gan this nedle threde anon,
For out of toun me list to gon   100
The song of briddes for to here
That in thise buskes syngen clere.
And in [the] swete seson that [lefe] is,
With a threde bastyng my slev[i]s,

---

84 **saverous]** fauerous MS MO KA   85 **the]** his TH¹-BE SK FU SU FI   89 **swete]** s. swete TH²
91 **affraieth]** affirmeth TH¹-UR FU   92 **a-nyght]** one night TH¹-UR FU SU FI   94 **erly]** e MS (*leaf torn*)
95 **clothe]** clot MS (*leaf torn*)   96 **bothe]** both MS (*leaf torn*)   98 **an]** *om.* UR   101 **song]** sowne
TH¹-UR SK FU SU FI   102 **in thise]** on t. TH¹·² SK FU SU FI; on the TH³-UR   103 **And in the]** A. i. MS (*with erased space following*) KA; That i. t. TH¹-SP³ FU SU; I. t. UR   **lefe]** swete MS KA   104 **slevis]** sleu s MS (i *erased*)

---

goldfinch (Carduelis carduelis)." SK gives etymology (OF *calandre* < Lat. *caradrius*, Gk. χαραδριός) and compares *Land of Cockaigne* 97 (quoted in *MED*).

    papyngay: "parrot" (URg et al.). Jephson (BE) suggests the gloss "jay" because the parrot is alien to European scenery, but Skeat (1878c:4.15) rejects this proposal. SK compares *Tb* B² 1957.

    84 **saverous:** TH¹'s emendation corresponds to a Fr. variant *savoureus* that Ln (80t) and SU (Fr. 80n.) record in MS Ca; the usual Fr. reading is *doucereus* (Lc Ln 80). SKt incorrectly reports the MS reading (*fauerous*) as *sauerous*. Cf. 2902n.

    85–89 Muscatine (1957:32) remarks that here *RR* has "brought out the best in the translator, Chaucer."

    85 **the hert:** KA cites line 3541 "His herte is hard" as a parallel to the TH¹ variant.

    91 **affraieth:** While MS is clear, it also reveals the possibility, through recto-verso shadow, of TH¹'s misreading, *affirmeth*; one might read an *i* instead of *r*, but the "dot" (stroke) is the shadow from the recto character *d* in *and* of line 67. In support of MS *affraieth*, BE SU RI note the Fr. *s'esfroie* (Lc 85 "que toute rien d'amer s'esfroie" "that everything is stirred to love"), and GL compares *BD* 296 "That had affrayed me out of my slep."

    94–96 Folio 2 is damaged; on the recto, the ends of these lines are missing and supplied from TH¹ (KA RIt).

    96 **wisshe:** SP¹ has *wash*, an alternate β-form of the str. pa. t. sg. (see *OED Wash* v.) and thus not a substantive variant.

    97–98 **droughe : ynoughe:** SK adduces "the rime *drow, y-now*" in *LGW* 1458–59 to justify dropping *-e*.

    97 *Marginalium:* 4 MS₂ₑ. The first of the printer's marks (see above, "The Printer's Marks"). It is an instruction to the printer of TH¹ to begin Sig. 2A2v (= p. 4 of the 12 pages in Sig. 2A, a signature of folios in sixes). Since Blodgett (1979:98–101) describes these marks in detail, I omit further notes on the routine sequence of printer's marks but call attention to those of special interest. See 145n., 892n., 949n. (and frontispiece), 1517n., 2609n.

    98 **aguler:** "needle-case." URg et al. cite the Fr. *aguillier* (Lc 92); SK RB report further that the word "seems not to be recorded elsewhere in English" (RB). Cf. *MED aguler* n. For the use of the needle, see line 104 and n.

    queynt: "neat" (SKg). Cf. 65n.

    101 **song:** In support of *sowne*, SU FI compare the Fr. *sons* (Lc 95), which both Ln and Lc gloss as "chants."

    103 **And in the swete:** KA notes the erasure in MS between *in* and *swete* and suggests inserting the word *that*. The erased space—9 mm—is the right size for *the*, with which TH¹ has emended.

    that lefe is: BE notes that the MS line "is evidently corrupt." KA notes that in MS "the last letters of *that* and *swete* are written over an erasure"; however, the erasure underlies only the last letter of *that* and the first two of *swete*. GL RIt also note the erasure.

    lefe: The eds. all follow TH¹ in this emendation; T. Thomas (URg, s. v. *lefe*) would further emend *lefe* to *love*. KA suggests "read *leef*" and notes the wk. forms *lefe* (UR BE), *leve* (MO); SK RB RI adopt KA's *leef*, for the str. form of the adjective. GL suggests *newe*, on the basis of the Fr. (Lc 97 "novele"). RB RIt also note the Fr.; David (RIt), expanding RBt, notes: "the reading *leve is* would make the best rime (: *slevis*), and that may well be the pronunciation intended, though *leef* cannot be construed as a weak adjective." § FI offers the gloss "lief (dear), but *double entendre*, in English, with leaf."

    104 **bastyng my slevis:** "Sewing slightly [my sleeves]" (TRg). Jephson (BE) thought that the activity was that of sewing detached sleeves to the body of the garment. RB FI RI, following the Fr. text (Lc 98 "Cousant mes

Alone I wente in my plaiyng, 105
The smale foules song harknyng;
They peyned hem, ful many peyre,
To synge on bowes blosmed feyre.
Joly and gay, ful of gladnesse,
Toward a ryver gan I me dresse 110
That I herd renne fast by,
For fairer plaiyng non saugh I
Than playen me by that ryvere,
For from an hill that stood ther nere
Cam doun the streme ful stif and bold. 115
Cleer was the water and as cold
[As any welle is, sot]h to seyn;
[And somdele lasse] it was than Seyn,
[But it was stray]ghter wel away.
[And never sau]gh I, er that day, 120

The watir that so wel lyked me;
And wondir glad was I to se
That lusty place and that ryvere.
And with that watir, that ran so clere,
My face I wysshe. Tho saugh I well 125
The botme paved everydell
With gravel, ful of stones shene.
The medewe softe, swote, and grene,
Beet right on the watir syde.
Ful clere was than the morowtyde 130
And ful attempre, out of drede.
    Tho gan I walk thorough the mede
2v Dounward ay in my pleiyng,
The ryver syde costeiyng.
And whan I had a while goon 135
I saugh a gardyn right anoon,

---

107 **They]** That TH¹-UR SK-FI   **many]** m. a TH¹-BE SK FU SU FI   110 **gan I]** g. SP² UR; I g. SK   111 **That]** Which t. UR   112 **plaiyng]** playen TH³ ST SP²-UR   117 **As any welle is soth]** h MS (*leaf torn*)   118 **And somdele lasse]** om. MS (*leaf torn*)   119 **But it was strayghter]** ghter MS (*leaf torn*)   **wel away]** weleaway SP²·³ BE MO   120 **And never saugh]** gh MS (*leaf torn*)   124 **And]** om. UR   126 **paved]** I ipaued SP²   128 **medewe]** medowes TH¹-UR FU SU FI   129 **on]** upon UR; up on MO   133 **ay]** evir UR   134 **The ryver]** T. ryuers TH¹-SP³ FU SU FI; Nigh to the River's UR

---

manches a videle" "sewing my sleeves in zig-zag") and Ln 98n. ("*Cousdre a videle*, lacer"), explain that "the sleeves were fashionably sewn or laced" (RI). RB RI note Langlois's article on the subject (1904), and they both refer to line 570 below, where Idleness's sleeves are "sewid fetously." FI (98n.) observes that "the figure of unlaced sleeves for emotional disorder persisted as late as 'the ravell'd sleave of care' in *Macbeth* II.ii.34." Caie (1974:321) adduces evidence on tightly stitched clothing—from *Rom* 2263-64, *ParsT* I 415-30, and St. Jerome—"to support the contention that Amant's sleeve-basting signifies his conscious attempt to seek out *fol amour*." § KA notes TH¹'s *sleuys* and the "*i* erased in the MS."

107 **They:** In support of MS, RIt cites the use of the personal relative *qui* in the Fr. (Lc 101).

117–20 On the verso of folio 2, the beginnings of these lines are missing and supplied from TH¹ (KA SKt SU FI RIt).

118 **Seyn:** The river Seine (SK et al.).

119 **strayghter wel away:** This phrase translates the Fr. *plus espandue* (Lc 113 "more spread out," broader; cf. SK et al.), but FI reads *strayghter* as "either 'narrower' or 'straighter,'" and notes that "the Seine is famous for its meandering course." RI clarifies the sense of *strayght* "spread out" in the adjective's origin "from the pp. of *strecchen*" (see *MED streight* adj.).

wel away: "far, much," rather than, as in URg BE MO, the "interjection expressive of sorrow" (BE), which is of different origin (see *OED Wellaway*); Jephson (BE) thinks that the phrase is a line-filler. SK notes that the intensifying adverbial sense appears in *Piers Plowman* B 12.263 [265] ("wel away . . . swifter") and B 17.42 [45] ("wel away worse").

121 **The watir:** Only the lower parts of these letters are visible in MS (KA).

that: "Perhaps om. *that*" (SKt).

128 **swote:** "sweet-smelling, cf. *CT* I[A].1n." (FI); in that note, FI reports that "the unmutated form of *swete*, *swote* or *soote*, was generally used to translate Lat. *suavis*; *swete* was used to translate *dulcis*."

129 **Beet:** "beat, struck, i.e. bordered closely" (SK); later eds. have similar glosses. SK RB FI note the Fr. *bastoit* (Lc 123 "struck").

131 **attempre:** "moderate" (SP²·³g URg), "temperate" (TRg et al.), "mild" (MOg et al.); SK adduces *BD* 341.

134 **costeiyng:** "to walke" (SPg, s.v. *costay*); "to coast along, to pass by the side of" (URg); "to go by the coast" (TRg); "coasting, going by the shore or coast (MOg); "coasting (following the coast)" (FI, noting the Fr. *costoiant* [Lc 128]); "following the edge of the water" (RIf).

Ful long and brood; and everydell
Enclosed was, and walled well,
With high walles enbatailled,
Portraied without and wel entailled   140
With many riche portraitures.   3r
And bothe the ymages and the peyntures
Gan I biholde bysyly,

And I wole telle you redyly
Of thilk ymages the semblaunce   145
As fer as I have in remembraunce.
    Amyd saugh I Hate stonde,
That for hir wrathe, yre, and onde,
Semede to ben [a] Mynoresse,
An angry wight, a chideresse;   150

---

138   **Enclosed]** Enclos it SK; E. it FI   141   **riche]** full r. UR   142   **the ymages]** yet y. TH³-SP³; y. SK   **the peyntures]** p. TH¹-UR SK-FI   143   **Gan]** Can BE   146   **in]** *om.* TH¹-BE SK-FU FI   147   **Hate]** a hate MS MO KA   148   **yre]** and y. TH¹-UR FU SU FI   149   **ben a Mynoresse]** b. an M. MS KA; me moneresse SP²; b. an moveresse BE MO; b. a moveresse SK GL RB¹·²   150   **An angry wight]** And a. with TH²

---

138   **Enclosed was:** SK's emendation follows KA's suggestion. KA SKt RBt note line 1652 "enclos is" (TH¹ *enclosis*), but there MS reads "enclosid is."

140–42   RB RI, following Ln (132n.), note that the images are wall-paintings rather than statues. The words *entailled* (line 140), *entayle* (line 162) (Lc 132 "entaillié," line 152 "taille") suggest sculpture; but the word *peynte*, in various forms based on the Fr., occurs more often (lines 175, 181, 289, 301, 478, 609). In particular, see lines 475–78, which state that "Alle these thingis . . . With gold and asure . . . Depeynted were upon the wall." (On the colors gold and azure, see 477n.) At line 609, in a departure from the Fr. (Lc 597 "les ymages qui i sont pointes" "the images which are painted there"), the ME text has both *entaile* and *peynte*. The concept of images *both* carved and painted seems to follow the text in both Fr. and ME, and the tradition of Fr. MS illustrations shows either technique; see Fleming (1969:32–33).

140   **entailled:** "carued" (SPg et al.); SP²·³g et al. specify a French etymology, URg an Italian one (see 1081n.).

145   **Marginalium:** coℏ MS₂ℂ. This mark is an instruction to the printer of TH¹ to begin the second column of signature 2A2v (= p. 4 of the signature). This pattern of column markings between page numbers continues through MS; cf. 97n.

146   **in:** KA compares line 996 "As fer as I have remembrance" with the TH¹ variant. In support of *in*, SU compares the Fr. (Lc 138 "si com moi vient a remenbrance" "as it [the appearance] comes to my memory").

147–478   SK, noting that "the descriptions of allegorical personages . . . are clearly imitated from . . . Latin poets," compares "the celebrated description of Envy in Ovid, Metam. ii. 775, and the like." FI (140n.) says that the images "are icons of the qualities antithetic to the courtly virtues."

148   **hir:** RI notes that the portraits are all "female because of grammatical gender," that "the translation follows the original," but that "in English the same personifications could be male as *Envye* and *Coveitise* are in Piers Plowman, B 5.75, 186."

    onde: "envy" (FI RIf), "anger, wrath" (*MED onde* n.[1]). The early glossaries (SP¹ "breath," SP²·³ UR "breath . . . also fury") confused this word (from OE *anda*) with its cognate, *MED onde* n.(2), "breath," from ON *andi*; TRg notes the OE origin and defines as "zeal, malice." Cf. *OED onde, ande.*

149   **to ben:** KA suggests omitting *to* and compares lines "173, 214, 305 etc."

    Mynoresse: Minorite or Franciscan nun (FI RI; RI cites *MED menouresse*); a follower of St. Clare (BE). Cf. Sutherland (1959:179; 1968:xvii), who thinks that the word "has no clearly defined meaning." The reading may anticipate the Fals-Semblant passage and reflect the Chaucerian anti-mendicant position, but the origin of the form (see Brusendorff, below) may have been in Fr. *meneresse* (Lc 141, one who leads [astray], who provokes [Lcg]; "agitator, ringleader" [FI]); such is the reading of at least two MSS (Ln 141t), including B.N. fr. 1573 (Ln's Ha), upon which Lc is based (Lc 1.xxxix). Ln and earlier versions of the Fr. text read *moverresse* ("*provocatrice,*" agitator [Lng]), the source of the emendations.

    Francis Thynne (1599;1875:74) first suggested the emendation *moveresse* "a mover or styrrer to debate," on the basis of Fr. *moverresse*, "in the oldest written copye . . . in Englande." Speght, who makes a general acknowledgment of Thynne's help (1602:sig. a3v, "To the Readers"), changed his text to *moneresse* [*sic for* moueresse] and used Thynne's note in his glossary, s. v. *Minoresse*. SP³ oddly reverts to *mynoresse* in the text but keeps the glossarial note (s.v. *minoresse*): "the right reading is moueresse, as we have now printed it." In URg T. Thomas lists UR's *minoresse* as *Mineresse* and guesses that the form "may be the fem. of *Miner*, an underminer"; but Thomas also quotes from Speght the argument for *moveresse*. So does Jephson (BE), and he and Skeat (SK) mistakenly credit Speght with the reading; Skeat compounds the error by saying that Speght introduced it in 1598.

And ful of gyle and felle corage
By semblaunt was that ilk ymage.
And she was nothyng wel arraied,
But lyk a wode womman afraied.
Frounced foule was hir visage   155
And grennyng for dispitous rage;
Hir nose snorted up for tene.
Ful hidous was she for to sene;
Ful foule and rusty was she, this.
Hir heed writhen was, ywis,   160
Ful grymly with a greet towayle.
  An ymage of another entayle
A lyft half was hir [faste] by.
Hir name above hir heed saugh I,
And she was called Felony.   164
  Another ymage that Vilany
Clepid was saugh I and fonde
Upon the wal on hir right honde.
Vilany was lyk somdell

That other ymage, and, trustith wel,   170
She semede a wikked creature.
By countenaunce in portrayture
She semed be ful dispitous
And eek ful proude and outragious.
Wel coude he peynte, I undirtake,   175
That sich ymage coude make.
Ful foule and cherlysshe semed she,
And eek vylayneus for to be,
And litel coude of norture
To worshipe any creature.   180
  And next was peynted Coveitise,
That eggith folk in many gise
To take and yeve right nought ageyne,
3v   And gret tresouris up to leyne.
And that is [she] that for usure   185
Leneth to many a creature
The lasse for the more wynnyng,
So [coveitous] is her brennyng.

---

156 **dispitous]** disputous TH² 163 **faste]** *om.* MS BE-KA 169 **Vilany]** This V. UR 173 **dispitous]** spitous SP² 176 **sich]** s. an TH¹-UR FU SU FI 182 **many]** m. a TH¹-UR FU SU FI 185 **she]** *om.* MS BE-KA 187 **more]** morwe RB² 188 **coveitous]** coueitise MS MO KA GL; coveit BE

Hammond (1908:508) gives proper credit to F. Thynne and the right date for Speght's emendation. Brusendorff (1925:308–09) refers to F. Thynne and observes that the MS reading "is still thought a scribal mistake for *moveresse*"; he also states that the reading *meneresse*, in "at least two French MSS. and one old edition, . . . was presumably taken over into the English text . . . and later corrupted into *mynoresse*." RB SU correctly report that GL reads *meveresse*, but RIt notes that the 1928 print of GL revised to *moveresse*. RB RI repeat Brusendorff's theory regarding the origin of *mynoresse*. SU restores MS *mynoresse* on the basis of Fr. *meneresse*, the reading of the Fr. text in SU, which, like Lc, is based at this point on B.N. fr. 1573.

155–57   R. Benson (1980:15–20, 30, 103–08) analyzes this passage, among others, as an example of "the use of gesture" in Chaucer. Most of the passages in *Rom* have to do with the wall-portraits, the characters in the garden, and the Dreamer's reactions in his encounters with the God of Love, Bialacoil, and the Rose.

155   **Frounced:** BE quotes the Fr. (Lc 147 "froncié" "wrinkled").

159   **she, this:** GL notes "a similar repetition of subject in v. 880."

162   **entayle:** "graued worke" (SP²³g); "Carving, Sculpture" (URg); "shape" (TRg), to which SKg adds "figure, . . . description"; Davis (1979) "fashion."

163   **faste:** It is a reasonable conjecture that this word appeared in the original of MS, not so much because the meter is deficient without it as because the phrase *fast(e) by* appears often, as KA notes ("111, 208, 224 etc."). In line 224, "fast by" translates the same Fr. prep., *delez* "beside," that is the parallel form in this line.

166   **Another ymage:** GL compares lines 162, 170, 207.

176   **ymage:** RIt notes that "Thynne [TH¹] supplied the article [*an*] because he did not pronounce the final *-e* and put the stress on the first syllable."

183–84   **ageyne : leyne:** Koch (1900*a*:66) thinks that the rhyme is questionable because Chaucer's usual form is *leye*.

185   **she:** TH¹'s emendation follows the Fr. "c'est cele" (Lc 173 "it is she"). Jephson (BE) thinks that the unemended line, without *she*, "appears to be in accordance with the idiom of Chaucer's time."

  usure: On the practice of usury, BE cites Ps. 15 [Vulgate 14].5 and *PrT* B² 1681.

188   **coveitous:** The MS reading, the noun *coueitise*, is probably an error for the adjective *coveitous*, but the line might be construed in the sense "So (much) is covetousness her burning (desire)." For forms, see *MED coveitise* n., *coveitous* adj.

And that is [she] that penyes fele
Techith for to robbe and stele 190
These theves and these smale harlotes;
And that is routh, for by her throtes
Ful many oon hangith at the laste.
She makith folk compasse and caste
To taken other folkis thyng 195
Thorough robberie or [myscounting].
And that is she that makith trechoures,
And she makith false pleadoures
That with hir termes and hir domes
Doon maydens, children, and eek gromes 200

Her heritage to forgo. 4r
Ful croked were hir hondis two,
For Coveitise is evere wode
To gripen other folkis gode.
Coveityse, for hir wynnyng, 205
Ful leef hath other mennes thing.
    Another ymage set saugh I
Next Coveitise fast by,
And she was clepid Avarice.
Ful foule in peyntyng was that vice; 210
Ful [fade] and caytif was she eek
And also grene as ony leek.

---

189 **she that]** that MS BE-KA; she for TH¹-UR SK-FI   190 **Techith]** That t. MS-UR MO-FI   193 **the]** *om.* UR   196 **or myscounting]** o. myscoueiting MS TH¹ TH³-KA FU; and myscouetyng TH²   198 **makith]** that m. UR SK   201 **to]** alas UR; *om.* ST-SP²   205 **Coveityse]** For c. UR   206 **hath]** had SP¹   208 **Next]** N. unto UR   211 **fade]** sade MS-SK FU

189–91 See 189–90n. and cf. the Fr. (Lc 176–77 "c'est cele qui semont d'embler / les larrons et les ribaudiaus" "It is she who incites thieves and rascals to steal"), which suggests that the subject of *Techith* (line 190) must be the singular relative pronoun *that* (with the missing antecedent "she") and that the verb *Techith* governs the infinitive construction "thieves and harlots to rob and steal many pennies."

189–90 **she that penyes fele / Techith:** I adopt RI's emendation. Earlier, BE had omitted *That* from line 190 as "evidently redundant." David (RIt) notes Fr. *semont d'embler* (Lc 176 "incites [thieves] to [the act of] stealing"); he reasons that MS *That* in line 190 may have appeared "through dittography" and that its "omission . . . yields better sense than the substitution of *for* in line 189." As David observes, "*Coveitise* is the one that teaches thieves to steal many pennies, not to steal *for* many pennies." See 189–91n.

189 **she that:** KA implies incorrectly that UR's reading is "she that"; it is "she for."

191 **These . . . these:** RB RI note the generalizing sense. They compare line 411 (see 411n.) and adduce *KnT* A 1531 and notes.

harlotes: This word is "used indifferently of loose persons of either sex" (URg), a fact noted also in TRg BE, with reference to *GP* 647, where their notes refer to *Rom* 6068; see note below.

196 **myscounting:** "embezzlement" (RIf), false accounting. Tyrwhitt (TRg, s. v. *Miscoveting*) suggests this emendation, as does KA (noted in GL), and cites the Fr. *miscompter*, noted by SK GL RBt RIt. *Miscompter* appears, in certain Fr. MSS, in lines that parallel this one (Ln 181–82 "Rober, tolir et bareter [var. MS He et maiscompter], / E bescochier e mesconter [var. MSS H En nul pris n'en puet on monter]" "to rob, to ravish and cheat [var. account falsely], to swindle and account falsely [var. one can gain nothing from that activity]"). Cf. the Fr. texts in KA, SU, Lc (all 181–82).

197 **makith:** SK notes that the word is "pronounced *mak'th*" and that " *'th* for final *-eth* is extremely common throughout all parts of this poem."

199 **hir . . . hir:** David (RIt, for line 716) observes that in this line one finds "the sole exception" to MS's practice, in Fragment A, of using *her* for the third person plural genitive pronoun, and he suggests that, since Fragment A uses *hir* for the third person feminine genitive and accusative singular, this case is "perhaps influenced by *she* in the preceding line." See 716n.

206 **thing:** "pl. goods (A.S. *þing*, pl.). Cf. l. 387" (SK). Cf. also line 390, among others.

207–23 BE states that "this description of Avarice appears to be the original of Buckhurst's 'Misery.'" Thomas Sackville (Lord Buckhurst) composed the Induction to *The Mirror for Magistrates*, from which BE quotes lines 253–59 (ed. Campbell 1938:307; cf. 301–30n., 311n., 349–68n.). SK distinguishes between Avarice, "i.e. Penuriousness," and Coveitise, "i.e. Covetousness of the wealth of others," and compares "the description of Avarice in Piers Plowman," B 5.188 ff., where the text reads "Coueitise."

208 **fast:** GL errs in reporting the MS spelling as *faste*.

211 **fade:** "faded" (RB), to which FI adds "wasted." GL emends with a word of French origin to translate Fr. *maigre*, and compares line 311; see 311n. GL errs slightly in reporting MS as spelling *sad*.

212 **ony:** This form appears consistently throughout MS. TH¹-UR SK FU SU FI select the Chaucerian form *any*. *MED anī* lim. adj. identifies the type *anī* as a regional variant "derived from the inflected trisyllabic forms of OE [ǣnig] by normal shortening of the vowel," while East Midland *ōnī* has "the vowel of OE *ān*."

So yvel hewed was hir colour
Hir semed to have lyved in langour.
She was lyk thyng for hungre deed, 215
That ladde hir lyf oonly by breed
Kneden with eisel strong and egre;
And therto she was lene and megre.
And she was clad ful porely,
Al in an old torn courtpy, 220
As she were al with doggis torne;
And bothe bihynde and eke biforne
Clouted was she beggarly.
A mantyl henge hir fast by,
Upon a perche weike and small; 225
A burnet cote henge therwithall
Furred with no menyvere,
But with a furre rough of here,
Of lambe-skynnes hevy and blake;

4v It was ful old, I undirtake, 230
For Avarice to clothe hir well
Ne hastith hir never a dell.
For certeynly it were hir loth
To weren ofte that ilk cloth,
And if it were forwered, she 235
Wolde have ful gret necessite
Of clothyng er she bought hir newe, 5r
Al were it bad of woll and hewe.
This Avarice hilde in hir hande
A purs that henge by a bande, 240
And that she hidde and bonde so strong,
Men must abyde wondir long
Out of that purs er ther come ought,
For that ne cometh not in hir thought;
It was not, certein, hir entent 245
That fro that purs a peny went.

---

214 **to**] *om.* SK   216 **lyf**] *om.* SP²   220 **an old**] a TH²   225 **perche**] benche TH¹-SP³ FU SU; benche both UR   230 **ful**] so SP²·³   234 **ofte**] of TH³-UR   236 **ful**] *om.* SP²   **necessite**] nycete TH¹-UR FU   240 **that**] which t. UR   **henge**] h. doun SK GL RB¹·²   243 **that**] the TH¹-UR SU FI   244 **not**] *om.* TH¹-UR FU SU FI

---

214   **to:** KA recommends omission of this word and compares lines 173, 149, 305.
 lyved in langour: Lange (1914:477–79) calls attention to this phrase here, at line 304, and in *Piers Plowman* B 14.117 [118]; he suggests that Fragment A used *Piers* B and was composed after 1377, the presumed date of the B version.
216   **lyf:** Timothy Thomas (URg, s. v. *Lad*) suggests that Urry emends the text here, noting that Skinner (1671) quotes the line without *lyf* (i. e., follows the reading of SP²) and supposes that *lad* here means "lived."
220   **old:** Liddell (GL) notes that "Th." omits this word, and he quotes the Fr. (Lc 208 "Cote avoit viez et derompue" "She had a coat [that was] old and torn") to support its presence; TH¹, however, has the word; only TH² omits it.
 courtpy: Short coat or cape (SK FI); jacket (RIf). TRg and SK compare *GP* 290; for early glosses see the note to this line in Andrew (1993:274–75).
223   **Clouted:** "patched" (MOg et al.), "wrapped in rags" (RIf). *MED clouten* v.(1) quotes this line under sense 2, "to wear patched or ragged clothes."
224   **fast by:** See 163n.
225   **perche:** As BE notes, this horizontal pole for hanging clothes is "often to be seen in illuminations in manuscripts"; see Dahlberg (1971, Fig. 5). RIt explains TH¹'s variant *benche* as resulting "from the printer's misreading the ligature between *r* and *c*."
226   **burnet:** "wollen" (SPg); "[apparently] a rich Stuff worn by Persons of Quality, which was therefore forbid to be used by Monks" (URg, quoting Matthew Paris and citing lexical sources); "Cloth died of a brown colour" (TRg), either "coarse" (RIf; "probably like that of a cordelier's gown" [BE]) or "fine" (MOg). *OED* and *MED* support the idea that the brown woolen cloth was fine not coarse. See also 4756n.
227–29   BE and SK note that gowns were nearly always trimmed with fur; "in this case," adds SK, "only a common lambskin fur was used, instead of a costly fur such as *miniver*."
227   **menyvere:** A fine fur, "white" (URg); pale, "like ermine" (FI); gray (RIf). Since the usual sense is "the fur of some kind of squirrel" (*MED meni-ver* n.), the color was probably pale to gray, rather than ermine-white. KA notes that in MS the *u* of *menyuere* is "altered to *v*."
233–34   RB quotes the Fr. (Lc 221–22 "car sachiez que mout li pesast / se cele robe point usast" "for know that it was a great burden to her if she used the dress at all") and notes that "the English does not quite correspond."
236   **necessite:** TH¹'s *nycete* is "a probable error" (SU).
240   **henge:** "Perhaps *hengde*" (GL). Both weak and strong forms existed; see *MED hongen,* v. SK supports *heng doun* by comparing *CYP* G 574.

And by that ymage nygh ynough
Was peynted Envye, that never lough
Nor never wel in hir herte farede,
But if she outher saugh or herede   250
Som gret myschaunce or gret disese.
Nothyng may so moch hir plese
As myschef and mysaventure;
Or whan she seeth discomfiture
Upon ony worthy man falle,   255
Than likith hir wel withalle.
She is ful glade in hir corage
If she se any grete lynage
Be brought to nought in [shamful] wise.
And if a man in honour rise,   260
Or by his witte or by his prowesse,   5v

Of that hath she gret hevynesse,
For, trustith wel, she goth nygh wode
Whan any chaunge happith gode.
Envie is of such crueltee   265
That feith ne trouth holdith she
To freend ne felawe, bad or good.
Ne she hath kynne noon of hir blood
That she nys ful her enemye.
She nolde, I dar seyn hardelye,   270
Hir owne fadir farede well.
And sore abieth she everydell
Hir malice and hir maletalent,
For she is in so gret turment
And hath such [wo] whan folk doth good   275
That nygh she meltith for pure wood.

---

248 **never]** euer TH³-SP¹   249 **hir]** *om.* SK FI   250 **outher]** eyther TH¹-UR FU SU FI
252 **Nothyng]** N. ne UR   256 **Than]** That SP¹ GL   **wel]** right w. UR; ful w. SK SU FI   259 **shamful]**
shynful MS BE-KA   261 **by his prowesse]** h. p. UR; b. p. SK FI   262 **hath she]** s. h. ST-SP² UR
264 **chaunge]** chaunce TH¹-UR SK FU-RI   266 **holdith]** ne h. UR   271 **Hir]** That her UR   272 **abieth]**
abydeth TH²   275 **hath such]** hate s. TH¹-BE FU   **wo]** *om.* MS-KA FU   **whan]** w. that UR

247–300   Following BE's lead, SK RB RI note that the portrait of Envy is based on Ovid, *Met.* 2.775–87; SK also compares *Piers Plowman* B 5.76 [75] ff.

248   **peynted:** SK adopts KA's recommendation to "read *peynt.*" GL notes that the change avoids "slurring *envye*" but that "*peynted* is the form in ll. 301, 349, 450, 807 [892?], 935 [933?]." See also line 1600.

249–50   **farede : herede:** KA prefers *ferde : herde*, as in lines 499–500, 673–74, so spelled in most editions. Cf. line 271 *farede* and n.

249   **hir:** On KA's suggestion, SK FI omit *hir*. KA compares lines 691, 1486.

250   **outher:** As at lines 1624, 3308, 5168, 5490, TH¹ chooses the form *eyther*, little more than a var. sp. but of distinct origin, from OE *ǣgþer*, rather than *āhwæþer*. On a third variant, MS *other*, from OE *ōþer*, cf. 5168n. See *MED either, outher, other* conj.

255   "Perhaps read *On . . . to falle*" (SKt).
   ony: See 212n.

256   **Than:** SP¹'s *That* may be an error—SP² reads *Then*—but GL and RBt justify the same reading on the basis of Fr. *ice* (Lc 244 "that"). RIt notes the same parallel but RI retains *Than*.
   wel: RBt notes that "Skeat inserts [*ful*] and Urry *right* for meter"; GL, on the basis of the Fr. *a veoir*, states that "if anything is to be added to the verse, it should be *to se* after *wel.*" SU FI RI note the parallel between *ful* and Fr. *mout*, but RI does not so emend. The single word *wel* can translate *mout*.

257–59   BE suggests that these lines may have been intended "as a sarcasm on those writers who, like Boccaccio, made the fall of princes the subject of their verse." He adduces, besides Boccaccio, *MkP* B² 3162 ("Of whiche I have an hundred in my celle"), and *The Mirror for Magistrates* (cf. 207–23n).

259   **shamful:** TH¹'s emendation; KA notes it in UR. In support, RIt adduces the Fr. (Lc 247 "aler a honte" "come to shame"). MOg defines MS *shynful* as a spelling of "*shyndful*, adj. disgraceful, shameful."

261   KA recommends omitting the first *or*; UR SK FI adopt other omissions for meter.

264   **chaunge:** TH¹'s *chaunce* may improve the sense but is unsupported (Lc 252 "estre iriee quant biens avient" "be angry when good things happen").

266   **ne:** GL notes, wrongly, that "MSS. omit" *ne*.

271   **farede:** KA suggests *ferde* and compares line 249; SK GL RB FI RI so normalize. See 249–50n.

273   **maletalent:** "ill will, evil intent" (URg et al.), "evil disposition" (RI). SK adduces line 330 and compares *talent* in *PardT* C 540; SKg cites O.F. *mal talent*.

275   **hath:** Jephson (BE) thinks that MS *hath* is "probably a clerical error"; but it follows the Fr. (Lc 263 "et a tel duel" "and has such woe"). RIt suggests that TH¹'s *hate* arose from "reading *such* as the object."
   wo: KA recommends inserting this word; cf. the Fr. *duel* (see above).

276   **meltith:** "Read *melt'th* or *melt*" (SKt).

Hir herte kervyth and so brekith
That God the puple wel awrekith.
Envie, iwis, shal nevere lette
Som blame upon the folk to sette.　280
I trowe that if Envie, iwis,
Knewe the best man that is
On this side or biyonde the see,
Yit somwhat lakken hym wolde she;　284
And if he were so hende and wis　6r
That she ne myght al abate his pris,
Yit wolde she blame his worthynesse
Or by hir wordis make it lesse.
I saugh Envie in that peyntyng
Hadde a wondirful lokyng,　290
For she ne lokide but awrie

Or overth[w]art, all baggyngly.
And she hadde [a foule] usage;
She myght loke in no visage
Of man or womman forthright pleyn　295
But shette hir [oon eie] for disdeyn,
So for envie brenned she
Whan she myght any man se
That fair or worthi were, or wise,
Or elles stode in folkis pryse.　300
　　Sorowe was peynted next Envie
Upon that wall of masonrye.
But wel was seyn in hir colour
That she hadde lyved in langour;
Hir semede to have the jaunyce.　305
Nought half so pale was Avarice

---

277 **kervyth**] so k. UR　**so brekith**] to-brekith SK　286 **al**] *om.* UR　292 **overthwart**] ouerthart MS BE-KA GL　293 **a foule**] a full f. UR; eek a f. SK; *om.* MS KA　295 **or**] ne TH¹-UR FU SU 296 **hir**] *om.* SK FI　**oon eie**] eien MS BE-KA　299 **fair or worthi**] fairer o. worthier MS BE-KA 305 **to**] *om.* SK

---

for pure wood: "for very madness" (BE). On the construction of prep. with substantival adj., Jephson (BE) and later eds. compare *MilP* A 3120 and *KnT* A 2142–44. SK RB RI note that *for wood* occurs also at *HF* 1747; and SK notes the phrase at *LGW* 2420, "unless *For-wood* is there a compound adjective." RB RI further compare *for hor, Rom* 356; *For moiste, Rom* 1564; *for pure ashamed, TC* 2.656.

277–78　"The meaning is, that God avenges those whom Envy hates, by making her own envious mind the source of her misery" (BE). BE refers to illustrations of the last judgment, where sinners are punished by their own passions.

290　**lokyng:** "appearance" (SKg FI, citing Fr. *esgardeüre* [Lc 280]).

292　**overthwart:** KA's correction. SKt regards both MS *ouerthart* and TH¹ *ouertwharte* as misprints, but probably only the former is so; see *MED overthwert* adv. for forms. As for sense, this passage appears in *MED* under 2. (c) "angrily, furiously"; but SKg RIf have "askance (sidewise)," the basic sense in *MED* 1. (a) "crosswise, transversely."

　baggyngly: "askant, sideways" (SK); "askant" (RB¹); "askance" (RB² FI); "with a leer" (*MED* RI). The glosses of SP ("[*tumide*] swellingly, disdainfully") and UR ("haughtily, disdainfully") assume a derivation from *baggen*—*MED* v.(1),(b) "to swell or bulge"—rather than from *baǧǧen*—*MED* v.(3),(c) "to leer, to squint." TRg cites the Fr. *en lorgnoyant* (*sic*; a var. not recorded by KA Fr., Ln, Lc, SU Fr.) and defines as "squintingly." GL RB RI cite the Fr. *borgneiant* (Lc 282 "borneant"), which both Ln and Lc gloss as "regarder de travers"; GL cites Cotgrave's definition (1611), "to loure." SK GL compare *BD* 623 *baggeth* which SK takes as "looks askant," RIf as "squints." As RI notes, "*MED* [*baǧǧingli* adv.] cites this as the sole instance."

293　**a foule:** TH¹'s emendation. RIt notes the basis in Fr. *mauvés* (Lc 283).

296　**oon eie:** TH¹'s "one eye" is noted in UR by KA. In support, GL FI RIt cite the Fr. (Lc 286 "un oil" "one eye"); cf. Blodgett (1984:49) on TH¹'s use of the French.

298　**se:** UR MO SK GL FI have *yse(e)*, "perhaps correctly" (RBt). GL compares line 1401, where MS has *y se.*

299　**fair or worthi:** TH¹'s emendation. RIt notes the basis in Fr. (Lc 289 "ou preuz ou biaus ou genz" "either worthy or fair or noble").

300　**elles:** MS has *ell*, which UR-MO SK GL RB FI RI read as *elles.* All other instances of MS *-ll* as abbreviation for *-lles* are listed above, "The Manuscript Hands: The Scribe (MS₁)."

301–30　Jephson (BE) thinks that "Buckhurst's [Thomas Sackville's] description of Sorrow, in the Induction to *The Mirror for Magistrates*, is evidently imitated from this fine passage" (see lines 71–126, ed. Campbell 1938:300–02). Without mentioning BE, Koeppel (1898) quotes verbal parallels (*Rom* 312, Induction 90–91; *Rom* 336–38, Induction 123, 87) and thinks that Sackville had this passage in front of him. Cf. 207–23n., 311n., 349–68n.

304　**lyved in langour:** See 214n.

305　**to have:** KA recommends deletion of *to*; SKt reads *have* as two syllables. GL suggests: "Either omit *to*, or read *to have* as two syllables."

Nor nothyng lyk of lenesse;
For sorowe, thought, and gret distresse,
That she hadde suffred day and nyght,   6v
Made hir ful [yelwe] and nothyng bright,   310
Ful fade, pale, and megre also.
Was never wight yit half so wo
As that hir semede for to be,
Nor so fulfilled of ire as she.
I trowe that no wight myght hir please   315
Nor do that thyng that myght hir ease;
Nor she ne wolde hir sorowe slake
Nor comfort noon unto hir take,
So depe was hir wo bigonnen,
And eek hir hert in angre ronnen.   320
A sorowful thyng wel semed she,
Nor she hadde nothyng slowe be
For to forcracchen al hir face
And for to rent in many place
Hir clothis, and for to tere hir swire,   325
As she that was fulfilled of ire.
And al to-torn lay eek hir here

Aboute hir shuldris here and there,
As she that hadde it al to-rent
For angre and for maltalent.   330
And eek I telle you certeynly
Hough that she wepe ful tendirly.
[In worlde nys wyght so harde of herte   TH¹:
That had sene her sorowes smerte   129c
That nolde have had of her pyte,   335
So wo-begone a thyng was she.
She al to-dassht herselfe for wo   TH¹:129d
And smote togyder her hondes two.
To sorowe was she ful ententyfe,
That woful rechelesse caytyfe.   340
Her rought lytel of playeng
Or of clypping or kissyng;
For [whoso] sorouful is in herte,
Him luste not to play ne sterte,
Ne for to dauncen, ne to synge,   345
Ne may his herte in temper bringe
To make joye on even or morowe,
For joy is contrarie unto sorowe.

---

307   **Nor]** No FU; Ner FI   **lyk]** alike UR; l. as SK GL FI   310   **hir]** he TH³ ST   **ful]** *om.* TH¹-UR FU
yelwe] yolare MS MO KA   311   **fade]** sade ST-UR   314   **of]** with TH¹-BE FU SU   323   **forcracchen]**
cratchen TH¹-ST FU SU FI; scratchen SP¹⁻³; bescratchin UR   329   **As]** And FU   332   **wepe]** wept TH¹-UR FU
SU FI   333   *Lines 333–380   Out:* MS *(leaf missing); supplied from* TH¹   334   **had sene]** h. he s. GL
341   **rought]** wrought SP³   342   **or kissyng]** o. of k. UR SK GL   343   **whoso]** who so TH¹ TH²-BE KA GL
FU   344   **luste]** liste SK   348   **unto]** to UR

---

307   **Nor:** FI has *Ner*, perhaps in error; but, for *ner* as the weakened form of *nor*, see *MED ner*, conj. RIt notes
TH¹'s *Ne* (in TH²-UR SU as well), which I do not collate as a substantive var.

310   **ful:** SU FI support retention of this word by noting the Fr. *mout* (Lc 301 "l'avoient mout fete jaunir" "had
very much made her grow yellow").

    yelwe: TH¹ prints *yelowe*; BE and GL, *yolwe*; (*OED yellow* gives β-forms in *-o-*). MOg does not list the
form *yolare*.

311   **fade:** BE notes that "Speght reads *sad*; but *fade* is perhaps right, and may mean *faded*; or from the
French *fade*, insipid." The French word is the origin of both senses; see *MED fade* adj. 1., 3. SK glosses the word as
"withered" but quotes *William of Palerne* 891, "þi faire hewe is al fade," a line that *MED* quotes under sense 1, "Of
color . . . : lacking in brilliance; pale, discolored, dim; dull." In support of this sense, David (RIt 211) notes that
Liddell (GL 211n.) "is incorrect in saying that *fade* also translates *maigre* in 311, where it is a synonym for *pale*"; see
the Fr. (Lc 302 "et maigre et pale devenir" "and become lean and pale"). Cf. 211n. SK (like BE; see 301–30n.) also
compares the description of Sorrow in Sackville's Induction; see line 81 "Her color pale" (ed. Campbell 1938:301).

323   **forcracchen:** "to scratch excessively" (SKg); FI notes that "'for' is an intensifier."

324   **rent:** A var. sp. of *rend*; see *MED renden* v.(2), *OED rend* v¹. As SU notes, SK spells *rende*.

325   **swire:** "neck" (SPg et al.), "throat" (GL RB FI); the gloss in RIf, "face," seems indebted to the Fr.
counterpart, "chiere" (Lc 315). GL RB RI note that *swire* has no parallel in the Fr.; David (RI) thinks that the phrase
tere hir swire was "added for rhyme."

333–80   A leaf is missing from MS, and these lines are supplied from TH¹ (BE KA SKt RBt SU FI RIt). See
above, "The Missing Leaves."

340   **rechelesse:** "negligent, careless" (URg, s.v. *Reche*); "hopeless" (FI). Perhaps rather, "uncaring, . . .
indifferent" (*MED recheles* adj., 1. [d]).

342   **kissyng:** KA recommends *of kissyng*.

344   **luste:** From *lust* n. + OE *lystan*; SK's *liste* derives from OE *lystan* (see *MED lusten* v., *listen* v.[1]).

348   **contrarie:** BE SK have *contraire*; GL retains TH¹'s *contrarie* but notes: "Perhaps read *contraire*; cp. 991."

Elde was paynted after this,
That shorter was a foote, iwys, 350
Than she was wonte in her yonghede.
Unneth herselfe she might fede.
So feble and eke so olde was she
That faded was al her beaute.
Ful salowe was waxen her colour; 355
Her heed, for hore, was whyte as flour.
Iwys, great qualme ne were it none,
Ne synne, although her lyfe were gone.
Al woxen was her body unwelde,
And drie and dwyned al for elde. 360
A foule, forwelked thyng was she
That whylom rounde and softe had be.

Her eeres shoken faste withall,
As from her heed they wolde fall.
Her face frounced and forpyned, 365
And bothe her hondes lorne, fordwyned.
So olde she was that she ne went
A foote, but it were by potent.
The tyme, that passeth nyght and daye
And restlesse travayleth aye, 370
And steleth from us so prively
That to us semeth sykerly
That it in one poynt dwelleth ever,
And certes it ne resteth never
But gothe so faste, and passeth aye, 375
That there nys man that thynke may

---

353 **eke]** *om.* UR   355 **was]** *om.* TH²   356 **for hore]** for-hoor SK SU FI   360 **drie]** due
FU   363 **eeres]** heeres TH³·BE   369 **passeth]** passed SP²·³   370 **restlesse]** restlesly BE   371 **so]**
om. UR   372 **semeth]** s. so GL

349–68   BE states that "from this description Buckhurst [Thomas Sackville] has . . . taken his picture of Old Age." See the Induction to *The Mirror for Magistrates*, lines 295–336 (ed. Campbell 1938:308–10). Cf. 207–23n., 301–30n., 311n.

356   **for hore:** "for hoarness" (BE); "because (of being) hoary" (RB); "because of age" (RIf). For the construction, see 276n. RI (cf. *MED hor* adj. 2. [d]) calls this "the sole instance of *hor* as a substantive" and, like BE, calls attention to line 276, "for pure wood." RB suggests that the phrase is "possibly to be read *for-hor*, 'very hoary.'"

357   **qualme:** To SPg's "griefe" URg adds "sickness"; SKg et al. gloss as "evil, plague."

358   **synne:** "pity" (RB), "pity, shame" (RIf); both cite the Fr. parallel, *pechiez*, literally "sin" (Lc 349).

360   **dwyned:** "consumed" SP¹g, to which SP²·³g add "dried," URg "Wasted, . . . pined away." URg notes OE *dwinan*, "whence Dwindle." BE adds "dwarfed" and notes that the word *dwiny* "is still [1850s] in use in East Anglia." RIf has "withered," though *MED dwinen* v. quotes the line under sense (a) "shrunk, dwindled," rather than under sense (b) "faded, withered," used of plants. SK compares *fordwyned* in line 366.

361   **forwelked:** "(*marcidus* ["faded, withered"]) dried vp" (SPg); "Full of whelks" (URg); "Much wrinkled" (TRg et al.); SK compares *welked, PardT* C 738.

363   RB notes that "the English departs from the original." KA RB RI quote the Fr. (Ln 355 "Les oreilles avoit mossues [var. (Lc) velues]" "She had mossy [var. shaggy] ears"). That is, her ears were shaggy or (?) wrinkled (the var. *velues* means "shaggy, hairy" and is related to the word *velvet*). For *mossues*, RB offers the glosses "wrinkled? hairy?" and RI has "wrinkled." RI calls attention to Ln's note, which explains that the adjective *moussu* "is often applied, in the middle ages, to old people, to describe the roughnesses of the facial skin, particularly that of the ears." It may also, says Ln (citing the late-13th-century *Merveilles de Rigomer* 15577, 15792), describe "the dirt on chests or heads that have not been washed or combed for a long time."

366   **hondes:** The standard Fr. reading is *denz* (Lc 356 "teeth"); *Rom* clearly reflects the variant *mains*, which is recorded by KA (Fr. 356n.) and Ln (356t) and noted by Brusendorff (1925:312), SU (Fr. 356n.), RB RI. Sutherland, however, thinks that "*denz* was responsible for ME 365, and ME 366 was produced by the translator to fill out the rime. Then again," he continues, "this may be an instance of a double reading, the ME ending up with elements from two different sources."

368   **potent:** "staffe or cruch" (SPg et al.); SK compares *SumT* D 1776.

369–99   Ln (363–34n., 373–76n., 377–81n.) quotes Ovid, *Ex ponto* 4.2.42, 4.8.49–50; *Fasti* 6.771–72; *Ars amatoria*, 3.62–64; *Met.* 15.179–85, 234–36; and the Latin proverb, "Transit ut aqua fluens tempus et hora ruens" ("time passes away like flowing water and the falling hour"). SK RB RI compare *MLH* B¹ 20–24. In notes on that passage, SK adduces *ClT* E 118–19; to those already cited, RB adds Seneca, *Epist.* 1.1.1, 19.8.32, and notes that such "observations on the passage of time, often with comparison to the river, were commonplace or even proverbial"; and Eberle (RI) adds Whiting (1968: T307).

What tyme that nowe present is
(Asketh at these clerkes this),
For [er] men thynke it, redily
Thre tymes ben passed by;]   380
The tyme, that may not sojourne,   MS:7r
But goth and may never retourne,
As watir that doun renneth ay
But never drope retourne may;
Ther may nothing as tyme endure,   385
Metall, nor erthely creature,
For all thing it frette and shall;
The tyme eke, that chaungith all
And all doth waxe and fostred be,
And al thing distroieth he;   390
The tyme that eldith our auncessours
And eldith kynges and emperours
And that us alle shal overcomen,
Er that deth us shal have nomen;

The tyme, that hath al in welde   395
To elden folk, had maad hir elde
So ynly that, to my witing,
She myght helpe hirsilf nothing,
But turned ageyn unto childhede.
She had nothing hirsilf to lede   400
Ne witte ne pithe in hir holde
More than a child of two yeer olde.
But natheles I trowe that she
Was faire sumtyme, and fresh to se,
Whan she was in hir rightful age,   7v
But she was past al that passage   406
And was a doted thing bicomen.
A furred cope on had she nomen;
Wel had she clad hirsilf and warme,
For colde myght elles don hir harme.   410
These olde folk have alwey colde;
Her kynde is sich whan they ben olde.

---

378 **clerkes]** grete c. UR   379 **er]** *om.* TH¹-KA FU   380 *Lines* 333-380 *Out:* MS   382 **may never]** n. m. SK   386 **Metall]** Ne m. UR   387 **it]** is TH³-UR   396 **elden]** elding UR   401 **in]** within UR; inwith SK   408 **cope]** cappe TH¹-UR FU SU

378–80 BE MO punctuate the three lines as a parenthesis (cf. FI), and Jephson (BE) thinks the passage corrupt; RB RI resolve the construction by closing the parenthesis at the end of line 378.

378 **Asketh at:** For the idiom, BE compares the phrase *spier at,* "used in Scotland and the north of England." See also *TC* 2.894, 3.1682, 4.555; *SNT* G 542; *CltT* E 653.

379–80 "It is here asserted," SK notes, "that no one can think of the present moment; for while he tries to do so, three moments have fled." GL paraphrases: "three moments are gone while one is thinking about it."

379 **er:** The emendation follows KA's suggestion, based on the Fr. *ainz* or *ençois* (Lc 370a "qu'ençois que l'en l'eüst pensé" "that before one had thought"; noted by RBt RIt). GL has *or,* a var. sp.; see *MED er* conj.(1).

380 **Thre tymes:** SK notes the Fr. (Lc 370b ".III. tens" "three moments").
     passed: KA notes *ypassed* in UR MO; RIt in SK GL FI; it appears in SU as well.

387–88 **shall : all:** SKt attributes the spellings *shalle : alle* to MS; accordingly, SK and other eds. except BE MO normalize to *shal(l).* The actual reading is -*ll,* regarding which see the discussion of crossed -*ll* above, "The Manuscript Hands: The Scribe (MS₁)."

387 **thing:** "pl., as in 206" (SK). Cf. line 390.
     frette: SK RB FI RI normalize to *fret* "for *freteth,* devours" (SK). SK RB RI adduce Ovid, *Met.* 15.234 "Tempus edax rerum" ("Time the devourer of things").

389 **doth waxe and fostred be:** d. w. "causes . . . to grow" (BE) a. f. b. "and be nourished" (FI).

395–98 "The sense is:—'Time . . . had made her grow so extremely old that, as far as I knew, she could in no wise help herself'" (SK).

396 **had maad:** "the verb agreeing with *the time,* repeated at the beginning of each of the five preceding clauses" (BE).
     elde: "Bell and Morris here print *elde* with a capital letter, shewing that they did not make out the sense. But it is here a *verb,* as in 391, 392" (SK). See 395–98n.

401 **in:** KA RBt note UR's *within.* RBt also notes SK's *inwith,* which SK states is "common in Chaucer"; *Concordance* has 16 entries for *inwith,* around 300 for *within.* SK comments, "the occurrence of *pith,* just before, probably caused the scribe to omit *with.*"

410 **elles:** See 300n.

411 **These:** See 191n. Ln, KA Fr., and SU Fr. print *Ces* (line 405), the reading in most of the Fr. MSS; Lc (403) has *que* ("since") from MS Ha.

Another thing was don there write
That semede lyk an ipocrite,
And it wa[s] clepid Poope Holy. 415
That ilk is she that pryvely
Ne spareth never a wikked dede
Whan men of hir taken noon hede,
And maketh hir outward precious
With pale visage and pitous, 420
And semeth a [simple] creature;
But ther nys no mysaventure
That she ne thenkith in hir corage.
Ful lyk to hir was that ymage,
That makid was lyk hir semblaunce. 425

She was ful symple of countenaunce,
And she was clothed and eke shod
As she were, for the love of God,
Yolden to relygioun, 8r
Sich semede hir devocioun. 430
A sauter helde she fast in honde,
And bisily she gan to fonde
To make many a feynt praiere
To God and to his seyntis dere.
Ne she was gay, ne fresh, ne jolyf, 435
But semede to be ful ententyf
To gode werkis and to faire,
And therto she had on an haire.

---

413 **don there**] d. their SP²·³; down t. UR   415 **was**] wa MS KA   **Poope Holy**] Papelardie UR   417 **spareth**] spared SP²·³   421 **simple**] semely MS BE-KA   423 **hir**] *om.* SP²·³   424 **that**] thilke TH¹-UR FU SU FI   428 **for**] of SP³; fore FU   429 **Yolden**] Yholdin UR   435 **ne fresh**] f. TH¹-BE SK FU-FI   436 **to**] *om.* SK

413–48   BE suggests that the portrait of Poope Holy "appears to be the original of Spenser's description of Hypocrisy, in the *Faery Queen*," 1.1, st. 29.

413   **don . . . write:** "caused to be written" (BE et al.). On *write*, RB notes that the word is "here used of portrayal in painting"; hence, "portrayed" (BE), "described" (SK), "painted" (FI). GL RB RI call attention to the Fr. *escrite* (Lc 405), which, as RI notes, Ln "glosses as 'indicated by an inscription.'"

415–16   **Poope Holy : pryvely:** Koch (1900*a*:66) regards the rhyme as questionable and the name *Poope Holy* as a meaningless translation of Fr. *papelardie* (see 415n.); he notes that the same Fr. word appears correctly at line 6796 as *pap[e]lardie* and that this appearance in Fragment C, which Kaluza ascribes to the same author as Fragment A, puts Chaucer's authorship of Fragment A into question.

415   **Poope Holy:** "Hipocrisie" (SP¹g URg), "hipocrite" (SP²·³g). SK notes: "properly an adjective, meaning 'holy as a pope,' hence, hypocritical. Here used as a sb., as equivalent to 'hypocrite,' to translate F. *Papelardie*." For parallels, SK cites the adjectival use in *Piers Plowman* C 7.37 [6.37] and the later appearances in "Dyce's Skelton, i. 209, 216, 240, 386; Barclay, Ship of Fools, ed. Jamieson, i. 154; and Polit. Poems, ed. Wright, ii. 251." As RI notes, the *Piers Plowman* parallel appears also in the B-text at 13.284 [283]: "Was noon swich as hymself, ne noon so pope holy"; RI reports that Lange (1914:481–82; cf. 479–82) "takes this as evidence of direct influence of Piers Plowman on the Romaunt." RB RI cite the Fr. *Papelardie* (Lc 407) and its etymology from *paper*, "eat," and *lard*, "bacon"; "the original meaning appears to have been 'glutton'" (RB). Both state that "the English word is apparently a folk etymology" (RI).

421   **simple:** KA notes *simple* in UR. SU (Fr. 415n.) notes the Fr. *seinte* (Lc 413 "et semble seinte criature" "and seems a saintly creature") and suggests that "perhaps *seinte* explains how *semely* got into the Glasgow MS." The var. *simple* appears in several MSS of *RR*: see Ln (415t), KA (Fr. 415n.), and SU (Fr. 415n.). Cf. Blodgett (1984:49) on TH¹'s use of the French.

429   **Yolden to relygioun:** BE SK FI RIf gloss variously for the sense "given (dedicated, devoted) to a monastic (religious) life," i.e., says FI, "dressed like a nun." RI notes that "illustrations portray her as a nun" (see Dahlberg 1971, Fig. 9). Skeat refers to his note (1886*b*:2.135–36) to *Piers Plowman* C 11.88 [10.88]: "the word *religion* was frequently used to signify a religious order."

435   **ne fresh:** KA notes the omission of *ne* in UR BE. RIt states that "the omission does not greatly improve the meter and breaks the parallelism of the three negatives."

436   **semede to be:** As at line 149, KA suggests omission of *to*, and compares "149, 173, etc." MS omits *to* from this phrase only at line 173; at line 313, it has *semede forto be*.

437   **faire:** GL suggests that the translator carelessly misread the Fr. verb *faire* (Lc 427 "bones ovres feire" "to do good works") as the English adjective.

438   **haire:** "heare cloth" (SP²g-TRg); "hair-shirt" (BE et al.), "sleeveless . . . worn as a penance" (GL). BE SK GL adduce Fr. *haire* (Lc 428), which, as SK notes, has a West Germanic origin, as does OE *hære*, "a derivative from *hær*, hair." SK adduces *SNT* G 133 and *Piers Plowman* C 7.6 [6.6].

Ne certis she was fatt nothing,
But semed wery for fasting; 440
Of colour pale and deed was she.
From hir the gate ay werned be
Of paradys, that blisful place;
For sich folk maketh lene her [face],
As Crist seith in his evangile, 445
To gete prys in toun a while,
And for a litel glorie veigne
They lesen God and his reigne.
　And alderlast of everychon
Was peynted Povert al aloon, 450
That not a peny hadde in wolde
All though she hir clothis solde,
And though she shulde anhonged be; 8v
For nakid as a worme was she.
And if the wedir stormy were, 455
For colde she shulde have deyd there.
She nadde on but a streit olde sak,

And many a cloute on it ther stak;
This was hir cote and hir mantell. 460
No more was there, never a dell,
To clothe hir with, I undirtake;
Grete leyser had she to quake.
And she was putt, that I of talke,
Fer fro these other, up in an halke. 465
There lurked and there coured she,
For pover thing, whereso it be,
Is shamefast and dispised ay.
Acursed may wel be that day
That povere man conceyved is, 470
For, God wote, al to selde, iwys,
Is ony povere man wel fedde
Or wel araied or [wel] cledde
Or wel biloved, in sich wise
In honour that he may arise. 475
　Alle these thingis, well avised,
As I have you er this devysed,

442　**gate**] gates TH¹-UR FU SU FI　　**ay**] shal SK　　444　**face**] grace MS-KA FU　　446　**gete**] g. hem TH¹-UR SK FU-RI　　448　**and**] a. eke TH¹-UR SK-FI; a. al MO　　451　**wolde**] holde TH¹-UR GL FU SU FI　　452　**All though**] Although that UR SK　　456　**shulde**] myght TH²　　472　**or wel cledde**] o. c. MS-SK FU　　473　**Or**] Of RB²

442　**gate:** "perhaps plural" (GL), as in TH¹'s emendation.
　　ay: Skeat (SKt) thinks that this word makes no sense and suggests (SK) that *ay* may be a form of *aȝ*, ought, from OE *āh*; but he bases his emendation on the Fr. *ert* (Lc 432), a form of the 3 sg. future of *estre*, from Lat. *erit* (cf. Lng 5.203). RB rejects Skeat's derivation of *ay* and reads the word as *ever*.
　　444　**face:** KA's suggested emendation follows the Fr. *vis* (Lc 434–5 "car iceste genz font lor vis / ameigrir" "for these people make their faces become thin"; noted in GL RBt SU FI RIt), which translates the Biblical source, Matt. 6.16 (Vulgate "exterminant enim facies suas"; Douay "For they disfigure their faces").
　　445　**evangile:** Matt. 6.16, as BE SK RB RI note; see 444n.
　　446　**prys:** FI's gloss ("praise [price, prize]") offers two words that are related in origin (see *MED pris* n.(1), *preis(e* n.). Perhaps "esteem, reputation" (cf. *MED pris* n.(1), sense 9).
　　447　**veigne:** Probably a sp. var. of the β-forms in *-e-* (see *OED Vain* adj.), perhaps by analogy with the rhyme-word *reigne* and with forms like *feign* (see *MED feinen* v.).
　　448　**God and his reigne:** To support the MS omission of *eke*, RIt notes the Fr. (Lc 438 "Deu et son raine" "God and his kingdom"). KA notes the emendations of UR and MO.
　　451　**wolde:** "possession" (SKg et al.). GL adopts TH¹'s *holde* (with the same sense) but compares line 395. Conversely, RB has *wolde* but allows (RBt) that *holde* is perhaps correct here.
　　454　**nakid as a worme:** GL and SK compare *ClT* E 880 "lyk a worm."
　　456　**deyd:** Following KA's suggestion, SK RB RI normalize to *deyed*. Other eds., except BE-KA, adopt TH¹'s *dyed*. For forms, see *MED dien* v.
　　457–58　**sak : stak:** Koch (1900a:67) questions this as a Chaucerian rhyme because *stak*, here intrans., is trans. in Chaucer; he adduces *TC* 3.1372. Cf. 7–8n.
　　464　**halke:** "corner" (SPg et al.), "nook" (RIf); Skeat refers to "[*SNT*] G 311."
　　468　RB RI compare Job 3.3.
　　471–72　**fedde : cledde:** TH¹-UR RB FI add the prefix *y-* (or *i-*) to the first word, TH¹-UR MO SK FI to the second.
　　471　**ony:** See 212n.
　　472　**or wel cledde:** As SU FI RIt note, KA's suggestion to insert *wel* follows the Fr. *bien* (Lc 459 "ne bien vestuz ne bien chauciez" "neither well clothed nor well shod").

With gold and asure over all,		9r	The gardeyn was not daungerous	490
Depeynted [were] upon the wall.			To herberwe briddes many oon;
Square was the wall and high sumdell;			So riche a [yerd] was never noon
Enclosed and barred well,	480		Of briddes songe and braunches grene.
In stede of hegge, was that gardyne;			Therynne were briddes mo, I wene,
Come nevere shepherde therynne.			Than ben in all the rewme of Fraunce.	495
Into that gardyn, wel wrought,			Ful blisful was the accordaunce
Whoso that me coude have brought			Of swete and pitous songe thei made,
By laddr[e] or elles by degre,	485		For all this world it owght glade.
It wolde wel have liked me.			And I mysilf so mery ferde,
For sich solace, sich joie and play,			Whan I her blisful songes herde,	500
I trowe that nevere man ne say			That for an hundreth pounde [nolde] I—	9v
As was in that place delytous.			If that the passage opunly

---

478 **were]** newe MS BE-KA   **upon]** on TH²   482 **nevere]** n. no UR   485 **laddre]** laddris MS-KA
FU SU   489 **was]** *om.* SK   492 **yerd]** yeer MS-KA FU   497 **swete and]** s. TH¹-SP³ FU SU; the s.
UR   498 **owght]** o. to UR   501 **nolde]** wolde MS-KA FU

---

477   **gold and asure:** Ln (132n., 1323n.) notes that the garden wall in *Floire et Blancheflor*, as here in *RR*, is painted "a or et a asur" (line 1984, ed. Leclanche 1980). RB (140n.) and RI (140–42n.) report Ln's parallel.

478   On the wall paintings, BE compares *BD* 332–34 ("And alle the walles with colours fyne / Were peynted, bothe text and glose, / Of al the Romaunce of the Rose.") and the note (BE 6.146) on the architectural function of medieval wall painting.
    were: TH¹'s emendation, suggested by KA, translates the Fr. *furent* (Lc 463).

480   **barred:** TH¹-UR MO SK FU RB FI add the *y-* prefix. As GL notes, "the [unemended] verse has apparently but three accents."

481–82   **gardyne : therynne:** David (RI) notes that "*Gardyn* rhymes six times in Fragment A but nowhere else in Chaucer nor in Fragments B and C" (see also lines 511–12, 601–02, 699–700, 1279–80, 1379–80). "Within the line," he observes, "Chaucer normally stresses the first syllable (except possibly MerT IV [E] 2136)." David refers to Koch (1900*a*:66; cf. 1890:11), who, arguing against Chaucer as author, takes this as one of twenty examples of "false or at least questionable rhymes in a poem of little more than 1700 verses [i.e., Fragment A] . . . a percentage otherwise unheard of in Chaucer" (1900*a*:67). In arguing for Chaucer as author of Fragment A, Kaluza (1893*a*:128) says that *gardyn* comes from the Fr. But that is literally the case only where it translates *jardin* (Lc 498, 589, 1352); in the other three cases it translates *vergier* (Lc 467, 688, 1256). Cf. 1348n., 3234n.

482   **shepherde:** SK takes as trisyllabic and compares *GP* 603 "herd-e." RI notes the Fr. parallel *bergiers* (Lc 468).

483   **wrought:** UR MO SK GL RB-FI add the prefix *y-*. SU compares line 480.

485   **laddre:** KA's suggested emendation for MS *laddris*. RBt RIt note that it follows the Fr. *eschiele* (Lc 471), and KA SKt compare *Rom* 523 "laddre."
    elles: See 300n.

490   **daungerous:** "coy, shy; Niggardly, sparing; Difficult, scrupulous" (URg); "stingy" (SK RB); "reluctant (aloof)" (FI); "reluctant, disdainful" (RIf). SK contrasts this word, normally applied to humans, with *riche*, in line 492. RB quotes KA (Fr. 479), "dangereus ne chiches," and notes that Ln (479) has "desdeigneus" ("disdainful"); so does Lc (477). David (RI) notes that *dangereus* is a var. (Ln 479t lists MSS Ga Ra; SU Fr. lists Go); he compares *Rom* 591 and refers to his note to line 3018. See 3018n.

492   **yerd:** KA recommends this reading and compares lines 634, 656, 1582, 1591. SU calls TH¹'s *yere* "a probable error."

501–04   GL paraphrases: "I wouldn't take a hundred pounds not to enter."

501   **hundreth:** A var. sp.; see *MED*, s.v. *hundred* card. num. All eds., except BE-KA GL, normalize to *hundred*.
    nolde: Skeat (SK) emends MS *wolde*, supposing that "the [ME] scribe stumbled over the double negative" (see 501–04n.); he also adduces the Fr. double negative (Lc 487/489 "que n'en preïsse pas . . . que enz n'entrasse et ne veïsse" "that I would not have taken . . . not to enter and see"). RBt agrees that "the correction seems necessary."

90

Hadde be unto me free—
That I nolde entren for to se
Th'assemble—God kepe it fro care— 505
Of briddis whiche therynne ware,
That songen thorugh her mery throtes
[Daunces] of love and mery notes.
Whan I thus herde foules synge,
I felle fast in a weymentyng, 510
By which art or by what engyne
I myght come into that gardyne;
But way I couthe fynde noon
Into that gardyne for to goon.
Ne nought wist I if that ther were 515

Eyther hole or place [o-]where
By which I myght have entre.
Ne ther was noon to teche me,
For I was [al] aloone, iwys,
[Ful] wo and angwishis of this, 520
Til atte last bithought I me,
That by no weye ne myght it be
That ther nas laddre or wey to passe,
Or hole, into so faire a place. 524
Tho gan I go a full grete pas, 10r
E[n]vyronyng evene in compas
The closing of the square wall,
Tyl that I fonde a wiket small

---

505   **kepe it fro care**] i. k. and were SK   506   **whiche**] w. that UR   508   **Daunces**] Daunws MS MO
KA   509   **foules**] the foulis UR   512   **into**] in SK   513   **fynde**] ne findin UR   516   **hole or**] a h. o. a
UR   **o-where**] where MS-KA GL FU   519   **al**] om. MS (MS, *corr.*)   520   **Ful wo**] For w. MS-KA FU; For-wo
GL   **angwishis**] anguisshe TH¹-SP³ FU SU; for anguishe UR   521   **atte**] at TH¹-SP³ FU SU   523   **That**] om.
UR   **or**] ne TH¹-UR FU SU   526   **Envyronyng**] Euyronyng MS KA; Enuyron TH¹-UR FU   528   **wiket**]
wicked SP¹

505–06   **kepe it fro care : ware:** Presumably because *ware* is a Northern form and therefore un-Chaucerian
("*a false spelling*," SKt), Skeat, as noted in GL, regards the rhyme as false; and Koch (1890:10; 1900*a*:66) cites it as
evidence that Chaucer is not the author of Fragment A. Skeat had suggested emending *ware* to *fare* (1887:vii) but
does not so emend in SK; as Koch points out, *ware* follows the Fr. *estoient*. Instead, SK adopts the usual Chaucerian
spelling *were* in line 506 and emends line 505, preserving the Fr. (Lc 490 "guerisse" "preserve") with *were*
("defend"); Kaluza (1893*a*:128) endorses the change. Skeat reasons that the scribe, perhaps not recognizing
Chaucer's *rime riche*, thought the repetition of *were* a defect and altered the first *were* to *care*, then "altered [the
second] *were* to *ware*, to give a rime to the eye." For *rime riche* in Chaucer, Skeat adduces *GP* 17–18 (*seke* "seek" :
seeke "sick"); he also notes that *were* "defend" and *were* "were" both rhyme with *spere*, the first at *KnT* A 2549–50,
the second at *HF* 1047–48. Chaucer, he concludes, "would therefore have had no hesitation in riming these words";
he compares the rhyme *were : where* at *Rom* 515–16. Koch (1900*a*:66) thinks that, since the MS reading follows the
Fr., there is no need for Skeat's emendation.

Skeat (1900:150–51) calls the reading of MS "a supposed 'correction'" that "may have been made here by the
Northern continuator, or author of Fragment B, in whose eyes the repetition of *were* seemed meaningless, and for
whom such a rime as *care, war* would be good enough." Lange (1910; 1911) thinks that Skeat's hypothesis is
untenable because "*rimes riches* could not have been in any way noteworthy for [the continuator] and already
appear in Fragment A before ll. 505–6" (1911:345). Lange thinks that the original reading was *it kepe fro were* ("keep
it from sorrow" [RIt]) and that the scribe of the Glagow MS altered *were* (see *OED Were* sb.³) to the more usual *care*,
similar in appearance and sense (1911:344; cf. Lange 1912:484); RBt RIt cite Lange's suggestion. Modern eds.
recognize the un-Chaucerian rhyme, but "the MS reading is retained by all editors save Skeat as a possible dialectal
variant" (RIt).

512   **into:** SK's *in* follows KA's suggestion.

516   **o-where:** SK's emendation, which adapts KA's suggestion "Perhaps read *anywhere* for *where*," avoids a
redundancy: "*where* would mean 'by which'" (SK), words that appear at the beginning of the next line. GL's
suggestion, "Perhaps read *there* for *where*," has support in the Fr. (Lc 503): "ne leu par ou l'en i entrast" "or place
where one might enter there").

519   **al:** "written above the line" (KA), by MS₁. See, further, "The Manuscript Hands: The Corrections."

520   **Ful wo:** KA suggests this emendation. Liddell (GL) grants that *For-wo* ("very weary") is "perhaps [a]
mistake for *ful wo*." Robinson (RBt), who cites GL, adduces his note to *KnT* A 2142 "on *for-* as a prefix." The Fr.
parallels *Rom*'s adjectival syntax (Lc 506 "Destroiz fui et mout engoiseus" "I was distraught and very anxious"), but
not precisely since *mout* modifies *engoiseus* rather than *Destroiz*.

angwishis: KA suggests normalizing the final -*is* to -*ous*, and eds. so emend, either with -*ous* (SK FI) or
-*us* (RB RI). For -*is* as a var. sp., see *MED -ous* suf. Skeat calls *angwishis* a "false spelling" and uses the form
anguissous, which he finds in *ParsT* I 304 (so Hengwrt; Ellesmere *anguissous*; see Ruggiers [ed. 1979:965, 1018]).

91

So shett that I ne myght in gon,
And other entre was ther noon. 530
   Uppon this dore I gan to smyte,
That was fetys and so lite,
For other weye coude I not seke.
Ful long I shof, and knokkide eke,
And stood ful long and [oft] herknyng 535
If that I herde ony wight comyng,
Til that [the] dore of thilk entre
A mayden curteys openyde me.
Hir heer was as yelowe of hewe
As ony basyn scoured newe, 540
Hir flesh tendre as is a chike,
With bent browis smothe and slyke;
And by mesure large were
The openyng of hir yen clere,
Hir nose of good proporcioun, 545

Hir yen grey as is a faucoun,
With swete breth and wel savoured,
Hir face white and wel coloured,
With litel mouth and rounde to see. 10v
A clove chynne eke hadde she. 550
Hir nekke was of good fasoun
In lengthe and gretnesse, by resoun,
Withoute bleyne, scabbe, or royne;
Fro Jerusalem unto Burgoyne
Ther nys a fairer nekke, iwys, 555
To fele how smothe and softe it is.
Hir throte also white of hewe
As snawe on braunche snawed newe.
Of body ful wel wrought was she;
Men neded not in no cuntre 560
A fairer body for to seke.
And of fyn orfrays hadde she eke

---

531 **this]** the TH² 532 **fetys]** so f. UR MO SK GL 535 **and oft]** a. of MS BE-KA; al TH¹-UR FU; oft
SU 536 **that]** *om.* UR **ony]** a SK FI 537 **that the]** that MS BE KA GL; thilke MO **thilk]** that
MO 541 **tendre]** as t. SK GL RB¹,² 542 **smothe]** both s. UR 543 **by]** thereto b. UR 546 **is]** *om.*
SK 547 **savoured]** fauoured SP²-BE 553 **scabbe]** or s. UR 554 **unto]** to UR 555 **fairer]** fayre
TH² 557 **also]** a. so UR 560 **neded]** neden TH¹-UR FU SU FI

531–84 "On the conventional details in this and other portraits," RI refers to Wilcockson's note to *BD*
817–1040 and cites Brewer (1955).
  532 **fetys:** KA notes *so fetys* in MO; RBt grants that it is perhaps correct.
  533 **coude:** SU states that this form is "possibly closer to Fr. *soi*" (Lc 518 "knew [how]") than is TH¹'s *coulde*.
  535 **oft:** To support this emendation, SK GL RBt RIt cite the Fr. (Lc 520 "par maintes foiz" "many times").
  536 **ony:** See 212n.
  537 **the:** KA notes TH¹'s emendation in UR; as noted in RIt, it reflects the Fr. *Le* (Lc 522 "Le guichoit" "the
wicket").
  540 **ony:** See 212n.
    basyn: RI notes Ln's gloss of the Fr. *bacins* (Lc 525) as a copper basin.
  541 **tendre:** KA suggests the emendation *as tendre*.
  544 **The openyng of hir yen:** RB RI, noting that this phrase corresponds to Fr. *li entr'ieuz* (Lc 528, lit. "the
between-eyes", i.e., the space between the eyes), point out that Ln (530n.) gives other examples in which a "large
entrueil" is a mark of beauty. RI cites *TC* 5.813–14.
  546 **grey:** Jephson (BE) notes that "it is not very easy to determine the exact colour meant." He cites the Fr.
vair (Lc 531 "vers") and notes that "the eyes of a falcon are certainly of that olive-green colour, which, in human
eyes, is called black." But Ln glosses *vairs* as "blue (in speaking of eyes)"; and *OED Vair* sb. suggests the color gray,
from the fur of a gray and white squirrel. David (RI) notes that gray was "a favorite color for the eyes"; he compares
Rom 822, 862, and refers to *GP* 152 "greye," where Ridley (RI) notes that "the color intended is uncertain."
    is: KA suggests omission of *is*.
  554 **Burgoyne:** "Burgundy" (SK 6.363 et al.). The word, which has no parallel in the Fr., is "supplied . . . for
rhyme" (RI).
  557 **also:** "as. Perhaps read *was also*" (GL).
  562 **orfrays:** Cf. the Fr. *orfrois* (Lc 554), a "head ornament made of material embroidered with gold" (Lng) or
a "cloth intermingled with gold threads, a lace" (Lcg). There has been a great deal of commentary on this word.
Francis Thynne (1599;1875:33–35) corrects the gloss in SP¹, "goldsmiths worke," with the glosses "frised or perled
cloothe of gold" (p. 33) or "a weued clothe of golde" (p. 35), which are supported with various quotations. One of
these, from Matthew Parker's Life of Boniface, Archbishop of Canterbury, seems to support the notion of woven
cloth of gold ("ornamentisque ecclesiasticis . . . ex lana tenuissima et auro artificiosè intexto fabricatis" "ecclesiastical

A chapelet—so semly oon
Ne werede never mayde upon—
And faire above that chapelet   565
A rose gerland had she sett.
She hadde [in honde] a gay mirrour,
And with a riche gold tre[s]sour
Hir heed was tressed queyntly,

Hir sleves sewid fetously.   570
And for to kepe hir hondis faire
Of gloves white she had a paire.
And she hadde on a cote of grene   11r
Of cloth of Gaunt. Withouten wene,
Wel semyde by hir apparayle   575
She was not wont to gret travayle,

---

564 **werede never]** n. w. TH³-UR   567 **in honde]** also UR; *om.* MS-SP³ BE-KA FU   568 **tressour]** tresour MS TH²-KA GL   569 **tressed]** dressed SP²; t. full UR

---

garments . . . made from the thinnest wool and from gold skillfully woven in"), but the "weaving-in" might be a form of embroidery. The idea of (woven) cloth of gold—with commentary taken from F. Thynne—persists in the glossaries of SP²-UR and in Thomas Blount's *Glossographia* (1656), although URg also reflects SP¹'s gloss in another quotation from Blount: "the Jackets or Coat Armors of the King's Guard were also termed *Orfrais*, because they were covered with Goldsmith's work" (Blount attributes this definition, correctly, to Cotgrave 1611).

The sense "gold embroidery" appears first in Tyrwhitt (TRg), who cites Du Cange, s.v. *aurifrigia*; F. Thynne, Speght, Blount, and Thomas had all taken Latin *aurifrisium* as "cloth of gold," but Du Cange's article supports only the notions of gold fringe and gold embroidery. Jephson (BE) quotes Speght's definition, but he disagrees with the sense "cloth of gold," citing French usage for the idea of gold trimming and Blount for the sense "jackets . . . covered with goldsmith's work." SK offers both alternatives, "gold embroidered work, cloth-of-gold"; compares *Rom* 869, 1076; and gives further citations. For further references, see the *loci* cited. Two recent glosses record both traditions—"embroidered cloth of gold" (FI) and "gold embroidery" (RIf); but it is clear from the range of quotations in *MED orfrei* n. that the latter sense, "rich embroidery, braid, or fringe, esp. of gold," is to be preferred.

563–64 **so semly oon / Ne werede never mayde upon:** "Some lines lost?" (SKt). SK accordingly punctuates with colon before and semi-colon after the phrase. Other eds. punctuate with semi-colon and period (BE MO RB FI). The punctuation here, from RI, maintains syntax, but the sense does not exactly parallel the Fr. (Lc 550–52 "onques nule pucele n'ot / plus cointe ne plus deguisé, / ne l'avroie hui bien devisé "no young girl ever had one more elegant or distinctive; nor would I now have described it well").

564 **upon:** "adverb," notes Liddell (GL), who compares *Rom* 1085 and *WBP* D 568, an error for D 559 ("wered upon"), which RB cites as a parallel construction.

566 **rose gerland:** Jephson (BE) notes that "the custom of wearing garlands of leaves and flowers was very general in the middle ages" and that "it was evidently derived from classical times"; for Chaucerian parallels, he cites *GP* 666, *KnT* A 1054, 1507.

567 **hadde in honde a:** "Insert *in honde* after *hadde*; cf. l. 431, 239" (KA); emendation is made on the basis of the Fr. (Lc 555 "En sa main tint un miroër" "In her hand she held a mirror"; noted in GL et al.).

mirrour: SK has *mirour*, the usual Chaucerian form with single medial *-r-*; the normalization is based on the Fr. *miroër* (Lc 555). Skeat has no textual note here, but he notes the form *mirrour* in MS TH¹ at the other five *loci* in Fragment A (lines 1585, 1601, 1605, 1642, 1649), where he also respells as *mirour*. At line 2806 he does not normalize.

568 **tressour:** TH¹'s emendation. KA recommends the same reading, which SK FU-RI adopt here but not at line 3717 (see note). Cf. the Fr. (Lc 556 "treçoër"). TRg cites Du Cange, *Tressorium* (s.v. *Trica*), for the sense "an instrument used in tressing the hair; or an ornament of it, when tressed." Although I collate MS *tresour* as an error, it is possibly a var. sp. of *tressour* (for forms, see *OED tressure* sb. "a ribbon or band worn round the head"). FI glosses *tressour* as "ribbons or threads of gold to be plaited with the hair." Skeat compares *Sir Gawain and the Green Knight* 1739 and notes that the form *tressour* (from OF *tresseor, tressoer*, from Lat. *trictātōrium* [*OED*]) "differs from the heraldic term *tressure* (Lat. *tricatura*) in the form of the suffix." *Concordance* lists this line under *tressure.*

569 BE suggests that this line "may possibly mean that her head was ornamented with gold and silver coins, a fashion still observed in many countries on the continent."

570 **sewid fetously:** sewn "hansome[ly]" (SPg, s.v. *fetis*), to which URg adds "neat[ly], decent[ly]," TRg "properly," and SKg "trimly." See also 98n. and 104n.

574 **Gaunt:** Ghent (BE et al.), "in modern Belgium, celebrated for its fine weaving" (FI). BE notes that the English spelling represented the French pronunciation and that "Ghent and Ypres were the great manufacturing towns of the middle ages"; BE and SK compare *GP* 447–48.

For whan she kempte was fetisly,
And wel arayed and richely,
Thanne had she don al hir journe,
For merye and wel bigoon was she.   580
She ladde a lusty lyf in May;
She hadde no thought, by nyght ne day,
Of nothyng but if it were oonly
To graythe hir wel and uncouthly.
    Whan that this dore hadde opened me 585
This may semely for to see,
I thanked hir as I best myght
And axide hir how that she hight,
And what she was I axide eke.
And she to me was nought unmeke,   590
Ne of hir answer daungerous,
But faire answeride and seide thus:
"Lo, sir, my name is Ydelnesse;
So clepe men me, more and lesse.

Ful myghty and ful riche am I   595
And that of oon thyng, namely,
For I entende to nothyng   11v
But to my joye and my pleyng
And for to kembe and tresse me.
Aqueynted am I and pryve   600
With Myrthe, lord of this gardyne,
That fro the lande of Alexandryne
Made the trees hidre be fette
That in this gardyne ben sette.
And whan the trees were woxen on hight, 605
This wall, that stant heere in thi sight,
Dide Myrthe enclosen al aboute.
And these ymages, al withoute,
He dide hem bothe entaile and peynte,
That neithir ben jolyf ne queynte,   610
But they ben ful of sorowe and woo,
As thou hast seen a while agoo.

---

581 **ladde**] had UR MO   583 **if**] *om.* UR SK GL FI   586 **may**] Maidin UR SK SU FI; mayde GL RB[1,2]
RI   590 **she**] *om.* TH³-SP¹   597 **entende**] entending UR   601 **lord**] the Lorde UR   602 **of**] *om.* GL
RB[1,2]   603 **the**] *om.* SP²   **hidre be**] h. to b. TH²; b. h. SK

579–80 **journe : she:** In arguing against Chaucer as author of Fragment A, Koch (1890:11; 1900*a*:66)
questions this rhyme and notes that Chaucer has *journey : wey* at *ClT* E 783–84; arguing for Chaucer's authorship,
Kaluza (1893*a*:128) notes that *journe* comes directly from the Fr. (Lc 568 "jornee").
    579 **journe:** "day's work" (TRg et al.). BE RB note the Fr. *jornee* (Lc 568); and RI adds that Lange (1914:480)
cites a parallel to *Piers Plowman* B 14.136 ("And til he haue doon his deuoir and his dayes iournee").
    580 **wel bigoon:** "In good humour, or plight; Fortunate" (URg); "In a good way" (TRg); "well contented,
joyous, merry" (SKg); "carefree" (FI); "happy, cheerful" (*MED bigōn* v., 3. [b]). Skeat (SK) notes that the phrase can
mean "richly adorned," as in Gower's *Confessio Amantis* 4.1313 (ed. Macaulay 1899–1902:2.336), "With Perle and
gold so wel begoon," but he emphasizes, comparing line 693, that "it is here equivalent to *mery*." For the basic
sense of *bigoon* "cover" (*MED* 1. [a])—parallel to Gower's sense—see line 943 "with gold bygoon."
    583 **if:** SU notes that SKt "drops *it*," an error for "drops *if*."
    586 **may:** KA suggests *mayde* and compares *Rom* 564; SKt compares line 538 for his form *mayden*; and SU
adduces the Fr. *pucele* (Lc 574). MS *may*, which also parallels the Fr. (see *MED mai* n.(1), *maid(e* n. & adj., *maiden*
n.), leaves the meter defective.
    593 **Ydelnesse:** BE RI note the Fr. *Oiseuse* (Lc 580), "represented as porter to the Garden of Love, because it
is generally when the mind is unoccupied with other things that love finds an entrance" (BE). Ln (582n.), as RB RI
note, compares Ovid, *Remedia amoris* 139 "Otia si tollas, periere Cupidinis arcus" ("If you take away idleness,
Cupid's bow is broken"). Eds. cite, as Chaucerian parallels, *KnT* A 1940 (SK GL RI) and *SNP* G 1–7 (GL RI).
    602 **of Alexandryne:** SK suggests omitting *of* (cf. GL RB) because in the Fr., as RI explicitly notes, "the word
[Alixandrins] is an adjective" (Lc 590 "la terre Alixandrins"). § "Alexandryne" ("of Alexandria" SK) indicates the
east. BE SK FI note the Eastern origin of many fruit trees, of the damson, specifically, from Damascus (BE SK); also
noted is the traditional association of the East with "the sybaritic life" (FI) or "Eastern luxuries" (RIf).
    603 **hidre be fette:** Skeat suggests that "*be* . . . is better omitted"; for the idiom *made hider fet*, he adduces
his note to *ClT* E 1098, where he refers to *KnT* A 1913, *MLT* B¹ 171, and "Royal Wills, ed. Nichols, p. 278." GL RBt
concur; GL compares *Rom* "607, 609, where the infinitives are passive, Fr. 'fist . . . faire,' 'fist portraire,'" and RB cites
the parallel to this line in Fr. "Fist . . . aporter" (Lc 591).
    610–11 SK RB note that "the images and pictures on the outside of the wall were made repellent, to keep
strangers aloof" (SK).
    610 **queynte:** "graceful" (SKg). Cf. 65n.

And ofte tyme, hym to solace,
Sir Myrthe cometh into this place,
And eke with hym cometh his meynee, 615
That lyven in lust and jolite.
And now is Myrthe therynne to here
The briddis, how they syngen clere,
The mavys and the nyghtyngale,
And other joly briddis smale. 620
And thus he walketh to solace 12r
Hym and his folk, for swetter place
To pleyn ynne he may not fynde,
Although he sought oon intyl Ynde.
The alther-fairest folk to see 625
That in this world may founde be
Hath Mirthe with hym in his route,
That folowen hym always aboute."
Whan Ydelnesse had tolde al this,
And I hadde herkned wel, ywys, 630
Thanne seide I to Dame Ydelnesse,
"Now, also wisly God me blesse,
Sith Myrthe, that is so faire and fre,
Is in this yerde with his meyne,
Fro thilk assemble, if I may, 635

Shal no man werne me today
That I this nyght ne mote it see.
For wel wene I there with hym be
A faire and joly companye
Fulfilled of all curtesie." 640
And forth withoute wordis mo
In at the wiket went I tho,
That Ydelnesse hadde opened me,
Into that gardyne faire to see. 644
    And whan I was inne, iwys, 12v
Myn herte was ful glad of this,
For wel wende I ful sikerly
Have ben in paradys erthly.
So faire it was that, trusteth wel,
It semede a place espirituel. 650
For certys, as at my devys,
Ther is no place in paradys
So good inne for to dwelle or be
As in that gardyne, thought me.
For there was many a bridde syngyng 655
Thoroughout the yerde al thringyng.
In many places were nyghtyngales,
Alpes, fynches, and wodewales, 658

---

613 **tyme**] timis UR   615 **cometh**] come UR   621 **walketh**] walked SP³   627 **Mirthe**] Sir M.
UR   629 **had tolde**] t. h. MO   642 **wiket**] wicked SP²·³   645 **whan**] w. that UR   **inne**] ther-inne MO
SK SU FI   651 **as**] *om.* ST-SP³ BE   657 **were**] *om.* UR   658 **Alpes fynches**] And A. and F. UR

---

619   **mavys:** "song thrush" (FI RIf). See 665n.
624   **oon:** "one; i.e. a place" (SK)
    intyl Ynde: "as far as India" (SK). Lounsbury (1892:2.119) notes that the phrase is not in the Fr.; he
thinks that it is special to Chaucer (cf. *PardT* C 722) and hence provides evidence of Chaucer's authorship. Kittredge
(1892:21–22) shows, however, that the use of India "as a limit of remoteness" is "a commonplace." Cf. RB's note to
PardT C 722; also RI's note to *WBP* D 824 ("Denmark unto Ynde").
625   **alther:** SP²·³, s.v. *alder*, gloss "all alone, onely, cheefe"; URg corrrectly has "of all," a "*gen. pl.*" (SKg).
645   **inne:** FI errs slightly in attributing the spelling *in* to MS as well as to TH¹. GL RBt grant that SK's
emendation *therin(ne)* may be appropriate; SU adduces Fr. *enz* (Lc 631 "inside") and *Rom* 617 *therynne*.
648–50   RB calls the comparison "familiar" and refers to examples in Ln (635n.). Lc (note to 632ff.) cites
Curtius (1953:195–200) on the theme of the *locus amoenus* and its literary tradition. RI cites Giamatti (1966:11–93)
"on the relation of medieval earthly paradise to classical and Christian tradition" and (pp. 60–66) "on
the *Roman de la Rose.*" See also Robertson (1951:40–43) on the garden in *RR*.
648   **paradys erthly:** "The Garden of Eden, as distinct from the celestial paradise" (RI).
649   **trusteth wel:** "This expression occurs frequently; it means, 'Be assured'" (BE).
655–56   **syngyng : thringyng:** SK identifies the rhyme as "only a single one, in -*ing*."
657–65   "There is no exact correspondence between the English and French lists of birds; the choice of names
by both poets was to some extent determined by rhyme and meter" (RI).
657   **places:** As RBt notes, Lange (1913:161) suggests *place*; for support, Lange adduces line 324 "in many
place" (rhyming with *face* [line 323]) and the Fr. singular (Lc 643 "un leu" "one place").
658   **Alpes:** Bullfinches (URg et al.); SK, quoting "Ray's Collection of South and E. Country Words (1691),"
states that the alp is "also called *an awp*, or, corruptly, *a nope*." MED *alpe* n., less confident, offers the definition "a
songbird of some kind; ?a bullfinch, ?a thrush" and quotes the *Promptorium Parvulorum* definition ("a bryde:
Ficedula") and the *Camden Series* (25,54,89 10 fn. "*Ficedula*: a wodewale or an alpe"). See *wodewales* below.

That in her swete song deliten
In thilke places as they habiten. 660
There myght men see many flokkes
Of turtles and laverokkes.
Chalaundres fele sawe I there,
That wery, nygh forsongen were.
And thrustles, terins, and mavys, 665

That songen for to wynne hem prys,
And eke to sormounte in her songe
That other briddes hem amonge.
By note made faire servyse 13r
These briddes that I you devise; 670
They songe her songe as faire and wele
As angels don espirituel.

---

660 **places]** place SK   662 **and]** a. of UR SK GL   664 **wery]** very SP²-BE   668 **That]** These SK

---

wodewales: See *Alpes* above, and line 914 below. Usually identified as the modern *witwall* (URg et al.); but, as SK notes, "there is often great confusion in such names." Thus UR glosses *witwall* as "Golden Ousel, a Bird of the Thrush-kind"; TRg as "Widewael. Belg. *Oriolus*. . . . a sort of Woodpecker"; and BE, reflecting both, as "Belgian *widewael*, . . . the oriole, or golden ouzle, a bird of the thrush kind." SK notes that "in the Prompt. Parvulorum, the *wodewale* is identified with the *wodehake*, woodpecker," that "Hexham explains Du. *Weduwael* as 'a kinde of a yellow bird,'" and that "the true *witwall* is the Green Woodpecker (*Gecinus viridis*)." According to *OED Woodwall* 1 ("a singing bird"), the identity in early quotations is uncertain; both *Woodwall* and *Witwall* are used for both the Golden Oriole (*Oriolus galbulus*) and the Green Woodpecker (*Gecinus viridis*); additionally, *Witwall* is used for the Greater Spotted Woodpecker (*Dendrocopus major*). Later eds. tend to be cautious: "orioles (?)" (GL); "a small songbird of uncertain identity, 'probably (as later) the Golden Oriole'" (RI, quoting *OED Woodwall*); "woodpeckers (?), song birds (?)" (RIf). FI (cf. SK), opts for "green woodpecker."

661–62 **flokkes : laverokkes:** Koch (1900a:67) questions this as a Chaucerian rhyme because one expects *larke* in Chaucer (*HF* 546). Cf. 7–8n.

662 **and:** KA reports *and of* in UR.

laverokkes: "A sort of Bird; a Lark" (URg, citing Skinner 1671). BE notes that "the lark is still [1850s] called the laverock in Scotland, and the north of England and Ireland." SK gives etymology: OE "*lāwerce, lāferce*, became *laverk*; then the final *k* was exchanged for the diminutive suffix *-ok*." On the [k], *MED lark(e* n. notes the inflected form *lafercan-* of the OE feminine wk. n. and compares Old Icelandic *lævirki*.

663 **Chalaundres:** Calendar-larks; see 81n. BE notes that "the chelaundre is, in the glossaries [of SP UR TR], interpreted the goldfinch," but that the Fr. [Lc 647, 649] has "*chardonneraus*, goldfinches . . . besides the *calendres*, which were a kind of lark."

664 **wery:** "weary" (SK, citing the Fr. [Lc 650 "lassees"]).

forsongen: "weary with singing" (SP²g et al.).

665 **thrustles, terins, and mavys:** As with other bird-names, there is uncertainty. Only the *mavys* appears in the Fr. (Lc 652 "melles i avoit et mauvis"), where Ln glosses *melles* as "merles," i.e. "blackbird, *Turdus merula*" (*OED Merle*). UR glosses the *mavis* as "a thrustle or song-thrush," and TR glosses both *throstel* and *mavis* as "thrush." Jephson (BE) says that "the mavis is the song-thrush, which differs from the throstle, or thrustle, in being smaller and darker coloured. It is still," he writes in the 1850s, "called the *maywish* in Norfolk." Skeat glosses *thrustles* as "throstles, thrushes"; cites *PF* 364; and says that "if we take the *mavis* to be the song-thrush, *Turdus musicus*, then the throstle may be distinguished as the missel-thrush, *Turdus viscivorus*. But," he notes, "the mavis is also called throstle. In Cambridge," he adds, "the name is pronounced *mavish*." RIf follows Skeat in distinguishing between the *thrustle* as thrush and the *mavys* as song-thrush. *MED māvis* gives the first meaning as "the song-thrush (Turdus musicus)" but the second as "?also, missel thrush (Turdus viscivorus)."

T. Thomas (URg) records Skinner's dubious conjecture (1671) that *terins* "signifies Teals"; and he rejects the sense "tern," which, he says "is a sort of Gull; but in this place it seems to signify some singing bird." In support of this last surmise, TRg adduces "Fr. *Tarin*" and cites Cotgrave (1611); SK elaborates: "Cotgrave has: '*Tarin*, a little singing bird, having a yellowish body, and an ash-coloured head'; by which . . . he means the siskin [so FI RIf], otherwise called the aberdevine." SK also cites Littré's identification of *Tarin* as the *Fringilla spinus*.

668 **That other briddes:** Chaucer uses the phrase *that other* with a plural noun elsewhere (see Plummer 1995:148–49). GL RB RI cite *Rom* 991 ("that other fyve"), but the case is not parallel; as adj., *five* modifies pl. nouns, but as noun, it is singular unless inflected with *-s* for plural.

669–70 **servyse:** Jephson (BE) calls attention to the "servyse" of the birds as "their worship of the great sustaining and reproductive principle of Nature." He refers to *The Court of Love* 1352–1428 (ed. Skeat 1897:445–47); to his note on the passage (BE 4.179), where he adduces the Boethian meter on love as a universal bond (cf. *Bo* 2m8); and to the presence of birds in such allegories as "*Florence and Blancheflor*" and *PF*.

672 "As spiritual (or heavenly) angels do" (BE SK).

And trusteth wel, [whan] I hem herd,
Ful lustily and wel I ferde,
For never yitt sich melodye   675
Was herd of man that myght dye.
Sich swete song was hem amonge
That me thought it no briddis songe,
But it was wondir lyk to be
Song of meremaydens of the see,   680
That, for her syngyng is so clere,
Though we mermaydens clepe hem here
In English, as is oure usaunce,
Men clepe hem sereyns in Fraunce.
    Ententif weren for to synge   685
These briddis, that nought unkunnyng
Were of her craft, and apprentys,
[But] of song sotil and wys.
And certis, whan I herde her songe
And sawe the grene place amonge,   690
In herte I wexe so wondir gay
That I was never erst, er that day,
So jolyf nor so wel bigoo,   13v

Ne merye in herte, as I was thoo.
And than wist I and sawe ful well   695
That Ydelnesse me served well,
That me putte in sich jolite.
Hir freend wel ought I for to be,
Sith she the dore of that gardyne
Hadde opened and me leten inne.   700
    From hens forth hou that I wrought
I shal you tellen, as me thought.
First, wherof Myrthe served there,
And eke what folk there with hym were,
Without fable I wole discryve.   705
And of that gardyne eke as blyve
I wole you tellen aftir this
The faire fasoun all, ywys,
That wel wrought was for the nones.
I may not telle you all at ones,   710
But, as I may and can, I shall
By ordre tellen you it all.
    Ful faire servise and eke ful swete
These briddis maden as they sete.

---

673 **wel]** me TH¹-UR FU   **whan]** that MS MO KA; than GL   674 **lustily]** lusty TH¹-UR FU   **wel]** full
w. UR   677 **was]** as w. UR   679 **was]** *om.* SP¹   683 **is]** in BE SK FI   687 **her]** the SP¹   688 **But]**
For MS BE-KA   **song]** hir s. SK FI   **wys]** eke w. UR   691 **wexe]** wext TH¹-UR FU SU FI   692 **erst]** *om.*
UR   700 **me leten]** let me UR; m. leted BE   706 **of]** alle UR; *om.* ST-SP³   712 **it]** *om.* TH²

---

673 **wel:** Against TH¹'s *me*, RBt SU FI RIt cite the Fr. *bien* (Lc 663 "et bien sachiez" "and know well").
    whan: TH¹'s *whan*, reported by KA in UR BE, follows the Fr. *quant*, as noted in RBt SU RIt, Blodgett
(1984:49). GL's *than* has the same sense (*OED Then* adv., sense 6).
676 **man that myght dye:** "mortal man" (BE et al.); RI notes the Fr. (Lc 666 "ome mortel").
680–84 On the song, and name, of the mermaidens, SK says that "Chaucer takes no notice of G. de Lorris'
notable etymology, by which he derives *Seraines* [Sirens] from the adj. *seri*"; Skeat quotes Cotgrave (1611) on "'Seri,
m. *ie*, f. Quiet, mild, calm, still; fair, clear.'" Although the translation obscures the etymology, it preserves part of the
sense; RI explains that, according to the Fr. (Lc 670–72) "'sereines' (Sirens) get their name because their voices are
'series' (clear) and 'saines' (pure)." RI notes further that "Lat. 'serenus' is rendered as *cler* in Bo 1.m4.1 and 2.m4.18."
684 **clepe:** RBt suggests that SK's *clepen* may be correct; but SK has *we . . . clepe* two lines earlier.
    sereyns: BE notes that "*Sereyn* means . . . a siren" and cites *Odyssey* 12.37 [12.39]. SK quotes Cotgrave
(1611): "'*Sereine*, f. a Mermaid.'" GL RB RI note that "in Bo 1.pr1.69 Chaucer translates Lat. 'Sirenes' as
mermaydenes" (RI).
687 **apprentys:** SP glosses *aprentise* as "skill"; URg (cf. TRg and FI) as "An Apprentice, A novice," citing this
line; like SK and Davis (1979), RIf glosses as an adjective, "unskilled, like an apprentice." Both the Fr. (Lc 674–75 "li
oiselet, qui aprentif / ne furent pas ne non sachant" "the little birds, who were neither unskillful nor ignorant") and
the ME constructions favor the adjectival reading.
688 **But:** KA incorrectly attributes this reading to BE. The entire line has no parallel in the Fr.
690 **amonge:** URg, s.v. *Emong*, notes that this word "is frequently used Adverbially, and signifies Commonly;
Sometimes, now and then;" and, citing this line, that it can mean "In common, or together with others" or "Likewise,
also." TRg supports this meaning here and at line 3881. FI gives "as well" in this instance.
692 **erst:** For the idiom, RB RI compare the notes to *KnT* A 1566, where they adduce *NPT* B² 4471 and *ClT* E
336 for the use of "*erst*, superlative, where the comparative would be more natural" in Modern English.
693 **wel bigoo:** "the opposite of 'woe begone'; as in l. 580. Cf. 'glad and wel begoon'; Parl. Foules, 171" (SK).
FI defines *bygo* as "contented," a gloss that applies rather to the entire phrase.
700 **leten:** "pp. of *leten*, to let" (SK).
705 **Without:** MO's *Withoute*, noted in KA, "improves the line: 'Without-e fabl' I wol descryve'"(SK).
714 **sete:** "sat" (SK). Skeat notes that the form is the correct descendant from OE *sēton*, pa. t. pl.

Layes of love, ful wel sownyng,   715
They songen in their [jargonyng].
Summe high and summe eke lowe songe 14r
Upon the braunches grene spronge.
The swetnesse of her melodye
Made al myn herte in reverye.   720
And whan that I hadde herde, I trowe,
These briddis syngyng on a rowe,
Than myght I not withholde me
That I ne wente inne for to see
Sir Myrthe; for my desiryng   725
Was hym to seen, over all thyng,
His countenaunce and his manere;
That sight was to me ful dere.
    Tho wente I forth on my right honde
Doun by a lytel path I fonde   730
Of mentes full, and fenell grene;
And fast by, without wene,

Sir Myrthe I fonde; and right anoon
Unto Sir Myrthe gan I goon,
There as he was, hym to solace.   735
And with hym in that lusty place
So faire folk and so fresh had he
That whan I sawe, I wondred me
Fro whenne[s] siche folk myght come,
So faire they weren, all and some;   740
For they were lyk, as to my sight,   14v
To angels that ben fethered bright.
    This folk, of which I telle you soo,
Upon a karole wenten thoo.
A lady karolede hem that hyght   745
Gladnesse, blisfull and the light.
Wel coude she synge and lustyly—
Noon half so wel and semely—
And couthe make in song sich refreynynge,
It sat hir wondir wel to synge.   750

---

716   **jargonyng**] yarkonyng MS BE-KA   717   **eke**] om. TH²   720   **reverye**] reuelrye TH¹-UR FU SU FI; reverdye SK RB¹·²   721   **hadde**] om. TH³-SP³   725   **Sir**] Her TH²   **for**] f. all UR   728   **to**] unto UR; tho t. MO   729   **Tho**] The SU   732   **And**] As ST-UR   733   **Sir**] Her TH²   734   **Sir**] her TH²   **goon**] to gon UR   739   **whennes**] whenne MS BE-KA   743   **This**] These TH¹-UR FU SU FI   746   **blisfull**] the b. UR SK GL RB¹-RI   **the light**] l. TH¹-SP³ FU   749   **And**] om. GL   **couthe**] om. SK RB¹-RI

---

716   On "the allegorical use of birds in the 'Courts of Love,'" Jephson (BE) refers to his introductions to *The Court of Love* and *PF*. See 669–70n.

   their: David (RIt) notes: "G's [= MS's] *their* is a unique instance of a Northern pronoun in Fragment A. The 3rd pers. pl. gen. pro. in G is consistently *her*; the 3rd pers. fem. gen. and acc. [sing.] is *hir*. The sole exception is 199, which twice reads *hir* for the 3rd pers. pl., perhaps influenced by *she* in the preceding line. Th [= TH¹] reads *her* for both these pronouns." David calls attention to the exchange between Hinckley (1906; 1907*a*) and Skeat (1906), one in which Hinckley adduces this form in support of his argument that Chaucer may have been influenced by the Northern poem *Ywain and Gawain*.

   jargonyng: MS *yar-* arose presumably from *iar-* (so TH¹) and a consequent scribal confusion between i/j and i/y. § With the sense, "chattering" (SK FI), "twittering" (RIf), SK FI compare Modern English *jargon*.

   720   **reverye:** "gladness, joy in the spring season" (RIf); "delight, ?wild delight" (*MED reverie* n.[1] [a]). The semantic element "spring season" is less appropriate to *reverye* than to the Fr. *reverdie* (Lc 706 "joy"), with its notion of "re-greening" (see Tobler-Lommatzsch 1925- :8.1106; 8.342–43, s.v. *resverie*; *raverdie*). Of the two emendations, *reverdie* and *revelrye*, neither has clear support. Skeat (SKt), followed by RBt, bases his *reverdie* on the Fr., but, as Robinson admits, "the NED records no other case of *reverdye*, and perhaps the MS. reading, *reverye*, should be retained." SU, on the assumption of TH¹'s authority, argues that "Th. *reuelrye* is a good reading for Fr. *reuerdie* (= 'joy, delight')." David (RI) retains MS *reverye*; he notes, with Robinson, that Fr. *reverdie* "is unattested in English" and that TH¹'s *revelrye* appears in variation with *reverie* at *RvT* A 4005.

   728   sight: KA recommends a final *-e*, and SK GL RB FI RI so emend. SKt regards the MS form as wrong, but the basis seems more metrical than morphological, since the historical form (OE *sihþ, gesiht*, str. fem.) had no *-e* in the nominative singular.

   735   "Where he abode, to amuse himself" (SK).

   739   **whennes:** TH¹ has *whence*.

   744   **karole:** "a . . . daunce" (SPg et al.). BE SK GL FI RI note that a carol was a ring dance with song accompaniment. SK notes the verb *karolede*, with the sense "sang," in the next line, and adduces *Rom* 765, 781; *BD* 849; and Robert Mannyng of Brunne, *Handlyng Synne* 9138 (=9142?, ed. Sullens 1983); see also *MED carole* n., *carole* v.

   745   **karolede:** "sang a song to accompany the dance" (FI; cf. RIf). RI notes the Fr. *chantoit* (Lc 727). SPg reports that as a noun *carol* can mean song; for which, URg suggests, "beginning and ending [are] alike." See also 744n.

   746   **blisfull:** KA and SK note UR's insertion of *the* before *blisfull*; SK compares line 797.

   749   The collations record ways of emending the hypermetrical line. KA recommends *made* for "couthe make." SK RBt RIt suggest that *couthe* may have been repeated from line 747.

Hir voice ful clere was and ful swete.
She was nought rude ne unmete
But couthe ynow of sich doyng
As longeth unto karolyng,
For she was wont in every place 755
To syngen first, folk to solace,
For syngyng moost she gaf hir to;
No craft had she so leef to do.
　Tho myghtist thou karoles sene,
And folk daunce and mery bene, 760

And made many a faire tournyng
Upon the grene gras springyng.
There myghtist thou see these flowtours,
Mynstrales, and eke jogelours, 764
That wel to synge dide her peyne. 15r
Somme songe songes of Loreyne,
For in Loreyn her notes bee
Full swetter than in this contre.
There was many a tymbester,
And saillouris, that I dar wel swere 770

---

752 **unmete]** yet u. UR　753 **of]** for ST-UR　758 **No]** Ne SU　760 **daunce]** ther d. SK
761 **made]** make SK GL SU FI; *om.* TH²　764 **eke]** the SP¹

---

　make: "invent," suggests RIf, a sense well attested in ME (cf. *faire* in Fr.), but the parallel Fr. passage (Lc 730–31 "ne nule plus avenanment / ne plus bel ses refrez feïst" "and no one did her refrains more agreeably or beautifully"), indicates that the verb *make* is to be taken as "perform" rather than "compose."
　refreynynge: Since a *refrain* is "the burden of a song" (URg BE), i.e., "a regularly recurring phrase in a poem, esp. at the end of a stanza" (*MED refrein(e* n.), the gerund *refreynynge* means the singing of a refrain (TRg SK). Other glosses vary the sense: "Upholding a Song" (URg); "add[ing] refrains to her song" (FI). *MED* records no verb *refreinen* "to sing a refrain" and only this example of the gerund in the sense "the act of singing a refrain" (*MED refreininge* ger. [1]).
　761　**made:** RBt RIt, citing Fr. *faire* (Lc 743), note that the emendation *make*, suggested by KA, is perhaps correct.
　763–92　"The flute players, minstrels, timbrel players, and dancers are professional entertainers hired by Mirth, as distinct from the aristocratic dancers in the *karole*" (RI).
　766　**songes of Loreyne:** As RB notes, Ln (750–52n.) quotes a passage from *Galerent* (1171–72 "Chançons gascoignes et françoises, / Loerraines et lais bretons"). SK (768n.) reports Warton's error in saying that "there is not a syllable of these songs . . . in the French" (1774–81:1.369), noting that Warton "consulted a defective copy," probably the 1735 ed. of Lenglet du Fresnoy (see BE, in 770n. below; cf. 1250n.).
　Loreyne: Lorraine, in "eastern France" (FI) or "northern France" (RIf), is about 300 kilometers east-southeast of Paris, between Alsace to the east and Champagne to the west.
　767–68　"The palm of skill in song is here given to Loraine, in preference to the more western departments of France" (BE). See 768n.
　768　**in this contre:** SK FI RI note that Fr. reads "in any country" (Lc 750 "en nul raigne"). BE identifies *this contre* as "the more western departments of France," GL and RB as Orléans. RI suggests that "the translation perhaps refers to England."
　769　**tymbester:** SK notes the fem. agent-suffix *-ster*, as in *spinster*, *Webster*, *Baxter*. The word translates Fr. *timberesses* (Lc 752) "a player on a *timbre*" (SK), a reading that, as BE notes (quoting TRg), is not in the 1735 ed. of Lenglet du Fresnoy and that appears differently in the 1529 ed. of Clément Marot. See 770n., 772n. § BE quotes the 1529 ed.—which has "batelleurs et batelleuses" who throw "ung bassin" in the air and catch it on a finger—as well as the Méon ed. (1814), which, like the modern eds., has "timberesses" who throw "le tymbre" on high and catch it on a finger; Jephson (BE) concludes that "the *tymbester* was a kind of mountebank (bateleur), one of whose feats was throwing up *tymbres*, or basins, and catching them on one finger." Skeat, however, notes that "there is . . . no reason for explaining *timbre* as a basin" and that the mistake arose from the 1529 ed.; "no doubt it had that sense," he says, citing Cotgrave (1611), "but not here." Jephson's conclusion that the timbester was a juggler might follow from the French text but not from the Middle English, where those who cast up the "tymbres" (line 772) are the "saillouris" (line 770).
　On the sense—player on a sounding instrument (SPg URg); female player on a timbrel or tambourine (SK FI RIf)—Skeat notes that TRg "confuses the matter by quoting Lye [*Etym. Ling. Angl.*], who mixed up this word with *tombestere*, a female tumbler."
　770–71　**that I dar wel swere / Couthe her craft:** The word *that*, Liddell (GL) suggests, "possibly belongs before *couthe*," and he adduces the support of the Fr. "qui moult savoient" (Lc 753 "who knew a lot about").
　770　**saillouris:** "dancers" (TRg et al.). TH¹'s form, *saylours*, noted in SKt, is adopted by all eds. except BE-KA GL RB RI. Jephson (BE) quotes Tyrwhitt's observation (TRg) that Chaucer's lines have no basis in the 1735 ed. of *RR*

Couthe her craft ful parfitly.
The tymbres up ful sotilly
They caste and hente full ofte
Upon a fynger faire and softe,
That they failide never mo. 775
Ful fetys damysels two,
Ryght yonge and full of semelyhede,
In kirtles and noon other wede,
And faire tressed every tresse,
Hadde Myrthe doon, for his noblesse, 780
Amydde the karole for to daunce.
But herof lieth no remembraunce
Hou that they daunced queyntly.
That oon wolde come all pryvyly
Agayn that other, and whan they were 785
Togidre almost, they threwe yfere
Her mouthis so that thorough her play

It semed as they kiste alway;
To dauncen well koude they the gise. 15v
What shulde I more to you devyse? 790
Ne bode I never thennes go
Whiles that I sawe hem daunce so.
  Upon the karoll wonder faste
I gan biholde, til atte laste
A lady gan me for to espie, 795
And she was cleped Curtesie,
The worshipfull, the debonaire;
I pray to God evere falle hir faire!
Ful curteisly she callede me,
"What do ye there, beau sir?" quod she, 800
"Come and, if it lyke yow
To dauncen, dauncith with us now."
And I, without tariyng,
Wente into the karolyng.

---

193 **hente**] h. them UR; h. hem SK   775 **failide**] ne f. UR SK GL FI   782 **herof**] therof TH²
791 **bode**] could SP¹; bede SK RB¹·² FI RI   794 **atte**] at TH¹-SP³ FU SU   798 **to**] *om.* SK   801 **Come**]
Comith UR; C. neer SK; C. here GL

---

and that, on the basis of Marot's ed. of 1529, "quoted by Junius, *Etym. Ling. Angl.* in v. *Timbestere*, . . . it is plain that the author is speaking of *jugglers* rather than *dancers*." But the words for *jugglers* ("batelleurs et batelleuses") do not appear in the modern eds. of *RR*, which have *tableteresses* and *timberesses*; see 769n. Skeat gives etymology and citations, both of which appear more fully in *MED sailen* v.(2) and *saillour* n.

772 **tymbres:** See 769n. Most agree that the *tymbre* is a percussion instrument, the timbrel or tambourine (SK [769n.] RIf *OED Timbre* sb.¹). URg defines the *timbre* as "a small bell," and TRg as a "bason"; cf. *OED Timbre* sb.²·³. Jephson (BE) follows TRg and, on the basis of the 1529 ed. of *RR* (see 769n.), thinks of the instrument as a basin "like our *timbrel*, which is, in fact, a brazen basin"; this sense does not appear in *OED Timbrel* sb.¹. For occurrences of the term, Jephson (BE 4.249, *Flower and Leaf* 337n.) cites the list of musical instruments in Guillaume de Machaut's *Le Temps Pastour*, and SK cites English passages, which appear in *OED Timbre* sb.¹.

773 **hente:** SK's emendation follows the suggestion of KA, who notes UR's reading. RBt RIt note that Liddell (GL) suggests *casten and [hem] hente*. Liddell grants that the line is "perhaps a 3-beat line," and he compares lines 480, 801; the latter, however, is a headless four-beat line.

782 **lieth:** SKt notes this form and (unnecessarily) prefers *lyth* in his text; cf. 197n.

791 SK GL RIt call attention to the Fr. (Lc 771–72 "mes ne me queïsse / remuer" "I would never seek to go away" [SK]) in support of the emendation *bede* (see below). GL notes that "the same Fr. is differently rendered at 1854," a line from Fragment B and probably of different authorship.

    bode: SK states that *bode* "gives no sense," notes that "*e* and *o* are constantly confused," and quotes Gower, *Confessio Amantis* 4.2905 "That I ne bede never awake" (ed. Macaulay 1899–1902:2.379). Liddell (GL) thinks *bode* a "mistake for *bede*, or *bad*," and compares line 808, *bad*. RBt calls it "apparently corrupt," and SU comments that the emendation to *bede* is perhaps correct. SK takes *bede* as "the pt. t. subj. of *bidden*, to pray." *MED* uses the emended line as a pret. example of ME *bēden* "offer" (from OE *bēodan*; *bead*) in sense 6 "ask for, request; pray," a sense influenced by ME *bidden* (from OE *biddan*; *bæd*). This sense reflects the Fr. (*queïsse*); MS *bode* may be the pa. t. of ME *bīden* (from OE *bīdan*; *bād* "await") in the sense "expect" (*MED* 7).

798 **to:** KA, citing line 1255, recommends omission of this word, for meter, as RBt SU note.

800 **sir:** GL RB RI adopt the spelling *Ser*, KA's transcription of the MS abbreviation, a long *s* with a flourished diagonal stroke through the stem. This abbreviation is common for s-vowel-r in Latin MSS (Capelli 1967:xxxix), where the sequence *ser* is of course far more frequent than *sir*. But the latter, TH¹'s transcription of the MS abbreviation, is clearly justified in this case. Cf. line 3101, where the same abbreviation occurs with the same variant transcriptions.

801 **Come:** In support of adding *here*, GL cites the FR. (Lc 783 "ça venez"), as do RBt RIt.

I was abasshed never a dell, 805
But it to me liked right well
That Curtesie me cleped so
And bad me on the daunce go.
For if I hadde durst, certeyn
I wolde have karoled right fayn, 810
As man that was to daunce right blithe.
Thanne gan I loken ofte sithe
The shap, the bodies, and the cheres, 16r
The countenaunce and the maneres
Of all the folk that daunced there, 815
And I shal tell what they were.
  Ful faire was Myrthe, ful longe and high;
A fairer man I nevere sigh.
As rounde as appille was his face,
Ful rody and white in every place. 820
Fetys he was and wel beseye,
With metely mouth and yen greye,
His nose by mesure wrought ful right.

Crispe was his heer and eek ful bright,
Hise shuldris of a large brede, 825
And smalish in the girdilstede.
He semed lyke a portreiture,
So noble he was of his stature,
So faire, so joly, and so fetys,
With lymes wrought at poynt devys, 830
Delyver, smert, and of grete myght;
Ne sawe thou nevere man so lyght.
Of berde unnethe hadde he nothyng,
For it was in the first spryng.
Ful yonge he was, and mery of thought, 835
And in samette, with briddis wrought
And with gold beten ful fetysly, 16v
His body was clad ful richely.
Wrought was his robe in straunge gise
And al toslytered for queyntise 840
In many a place, lowe and hie.
And shode he was with grete maistrie,

---

806 **to]** *om.* SK FI   811 **right]** *om.* SK GL   816 **tell]** tell you GL   824 **his]** her ST   825 **a]** *om.* TH²-UR   837 **ful]** *om.* SK

---

811 **right:** KA suggests omitting this word.

813 **shap:** In MS, a macron, the usual sign of abbreviation, appears over the *p.* In the Hengwrt manuscript of *CT,* such a macron apparently stands for final -*e*; see Ransom (1993:124).

816 **tell:** KA suggests insertion of *you* after *tell.*

817–1302 Jephson (BE 1272n.) writes, of the dancers in the *karole*: "The reader will observe that each of the personified qualities is accompanied by a lover, to show that different persons are attracted by different peculiarities."

817 **high:** FI notes the difference from the corresponding Fr. *droiz* "straight" (Lc 799).

818 **sigh:** "the past tense of the verb *to see*" (BE). For forms, cf. *MED sēn* v.(1).

824 **Crispe:** "curled" (SPg et al.). BE compares the Squire's "lokkes crulle as they were leyd in presse" (*GP* 81).

826 **girdilstede:** "waist" (URg et al.), "belt line" (RIf). URg and TRg note the etymology from OE *gyrdel* "belt" and *stede* "place."

830 **at poynt devys:** With "the utmost exactness," from Fr. *A points devisez* (URg, citing Skinner 1671). Jephson (BE 6.222 n. 3 on *HF* 917) also cites Skinner but objects that "this supposed French phrase has all the appearance of being made for the nonce," and he offers his own alternative: "a corruption of the Fr. *point de vice,* without fault." However, *MED point-devīs* n. derives the compound "from OF phr. **a point devisé* ["described exactly"], with ppl. taken as n." FI RIf gloss "[to] perfection."

831 BE compares the description of the Squire (*GP* 84).

836 **samette:** SP UR gloss "sattin"; TRg has "a rich silk" and cites Du Cange, s.v. *Examitus.* SK FI RIf have, variously: "(a very) rich silk." SK points to its etymology; Onions (1966) reports that Latin *examitum* comes from Greek *hexa-* "six" + *mitos* "thread" and observes that "the ref. to sixth thread is variously explained." Cf. *MED samit* n.

840 **toslytered:** cut with slashes to reveal the lining (BE et al.); Fr. *decopee* (Lc 823). SK notes that "*sliteren* is the frequentative form of *sliten,* to slit." § BE refers to pictures that show "doublets and hose of crimson velvet slashed so as to discover white satin underneath." SK notes that "slashed or snipped sleeves, shewing the colour of the lining beneath them, were common in the Tudor period." David (RI) reports that the practice "was fashionable, especially in the late fourteenth century," and he compares *ParsT* I 418 and *Mum and the Sothsegger* 3.162–66 (ed. Day and Steele 1936). Cf. 843n.

With shoon decoped, and with laas.
By drury and by solas
His leef a rosyn chapelet   845
Hadde made, and on his heed it set.
    And wite ye who was his leef?
Dame Gladnesse there was hym so leef,
That syngith so wel with glad courage
That from she was twelve yeer of age   850
She of hir love graunt hym made.
Sir Mirthe hir by the fynger hadde
Daunsyng, and she hym also;
Grete love was atwixe hem two.
Bothe were they faire and bright of hewe. 855

She semede lyke a rose newe
Of colour, and hir flesh so tendre
That with a brere smale and slendre
Men myght it cleve, I dar wel [seyn].
Hir forheed frounceles al [pleyn];   860
Bent were hir browis two,   17r
Hir yen greye and glad also,
That laugheden ay in hir semblaunt
First or the mouth, by covenaunt.
I not what of hir nose descryve;   865
So faire hath no womman alyve.
Hir heer was yelowe and clere shynyng;
I wot no lady so likyng.

---

844 **by solas]** eke b. s. UR   847 **leef]** sefe TH^{1,2} FU   851 **hym]** to h. UR   853 **Daunsyng]** A d. UR; In d. SK SU FI   854 **was]** there w. UR   857 **colour]** colours TH^1-UR FU SU FI   858 **slendre]** tendre TH^1-UR FU   859 **Men]** Mon SU FI   **seyn]** seye MS-SP^3 BE KA FU   860 **frounceles]** frouncels TH^2 **pleyn]** pleye MS-SP^3 BE KA FU   861 **browis]** eye-browis UR; browne b. GL   865 **not]** wot not MS-SP^3 BE-KA FU   **descryve]** I shal d. MS-SP^3 BE-KA FU

---

843 **shoon decoped, and with laas:** RI cites the Fr. (Lc 825 "sollers decopez, a laz" "shoes cut in patterns, with laces"). The word *decoped* transliterates the Fr. *decopez*, which, as SK notes, is translated as *toslytered* in line 841. The sense is much the same, but Jephson (BE) takes it as "stamped in a pattern" rather than as "cut" (SK), "slashed" (SK FI), or "cut in open-work patterns" (RIf). However, Jephson adduces notes to *MilT* A 3318 in TR, Wright (1847–51), and BE that favor the sense "cut" rather than "stamped." Skeat notes that "the shoes were slashed like the dress" (see 840n.); he compares *Piers Plowman* C 21.12 [20.12] "galoches ycouped" and his note (1886*b*.2.249–50) thereto; and he refers to his note to *MilT* A 3318.

844 **drury:** KA notes MO's spelling, *druery* (also in SK GL RB FI RI), which echoes more closely the Fr. *drüerie* (Lc 826). SP^1 UR gloss "sobriety, modesty," to which SP^{2,3}g add "comlinesse"; but TR, citing Du Cange, s.v. *Drudaria*, glosses more accurately as "courtship, gallantry"; cf. SKg GLg ("affection"), GLg RIf ("love"), FI ("love service"). Cf. 5064n.

853 **Daunsyng:** KA, who notes UR's reading, recommends *In daunsing*. SU FI cite the Fr. (Lc 835 "a la querole").

858 **slendre:** TH^1's *tendre* is "probably a printer's error" (SU).

859–60 **seyn : pleyn:** RIt implies, incorrectly, that the lemma is the MS reading. BE suggests that *pleye* appears "by poetical licence for *pleyne*, to suit the rhyme." SK proposes that "the scribe has omitted the stroke for *n* above the vowel." The emendation follows the Fr. *plein* (Lc 842 "smooth"). SK cites the Fr. parallel as *poli*, and RIt cites the reading *blanc, poli* (Ln 844 "white, gleaming"), with *bel et plein* as variant; the Lc reading is that of the H family of MSS (Ln 844t).

861 **browis:** GL's *browne browis* follows the Fr. (Lc 843 "les sorciz bruns et enarchiez" "the eyebrows brown and arched"; noted by GL RBt RIt) and reflects KA's suggestion, "insert *Broun and* before *Bent*."

864 **by covenaunt:** by "agreement" (SKg). "This is a most exquisite trait," says Jephson (BE). "The eyes and mouth of Gladnesse seemed to have made a covenant that the former should laugh before a smile appeared upon the latter." The phrase is a literal translation of the Fr. *par covent* (Lc 846), which Ln (s.v. *couvent*) glosses as "régulièrement, nécessairement," Lcg (s.v. *covent*) as "régulièrement, convenablement, d'une façon satisfaisante."

865 **not . . . descryve:** KA notes UR's emendations. The changes improve the meter and bring the line closer to the Fr. (Lc 847 "Je ne vos sai dou nés que dire" "I don't know what to tell you about her nose"). RIt quotes SK: "If the reader prefers to keep *eleven* (or *twelve*) syllables in this line, I am sorry for him." FI's report of MS and TH^1 is inaccurate: "GT *I wot not of.* T *nose I shal discryve.*"

866–67 Between these two lines there are "two lines lost" (SKt). RI quotes the missing lines from the Fr. (Lc 849–50 "Ele ot la bouche petiteite / et por beisier son ami prete" "She had a tiny mouth ready to kiss her lover").

868 **likyng:** "Agreeable" (URg et al.), "Pleasing" (TRg et al.). The Fr. is not parallel, as RB RI note in quoting the line from Ln (854 = Lc 852 "Que vos iroie je disant?" "What shall I go on telling you?"); but Kaluza (Fr. 848) finds a parallel to the ME in MS κω (KA's E: "Je ne sai dame si plaisant" "I don't know a lady so pleasing"). KA notes a

Of orfrays fresh was hir gerland;
I, which seyen have a thousand, 870
Saugh never, ywys, no gerlond yitt
So wel wrought of silk as it.
And in an overgilt samet
Cladde she was, by grete delit,
Of which hir leef a robe werede; 875
The myrier she in hir herte ferede.
    And next hir wente, [on] hir other side,
The God of Love, that can devyde
Love, and as hym likith it be.
But he can cherles daunten, he, 880

And maken folkis pride fallen;
And he can wel these lordis thrallen,
And ladyes putt at lowe degre,
Whan he may hem to p[r]oude see. 884
    This God of Love of his fasoun 17v
Was lyke no knave ne quystroun;
His beaute gretly was to [pryse].
But of his robe to devise
I drede encombred for to be;
For nought clad in silk was he, 890
But all in floures and in flourettes,
[Ypaynted al with amorettes], TH¹:132c

---

869 **Of]** *om.* TH²   870 **seyen have]** h. s. TH²; that s. h. UR   876 **hir]** *om.* UR SK   877 **And]** *om.*
UR   **on]** in MS BE-KA GL   879 **and]** *om.* SK   **be]** to be SK   881 **maken]** many ST SP²-UR
884 **proude]** poude MS KA   886 **ne]** n. no UR   887 **pryse]** preyse MS BE-KA GL   888 **robe]** robis
UR   891 **in flourettes]** f. TH¹-UR SK FU SU FI   892 *Out:* MS (*no gap*) KA RI

---

further variant in MS Fo (KA's B: "Je ne sai fame miuz plesant" "I don't know a woman better pleasing") as well as
Michel's reading, the same as that of Ln and Lc. Since Ln does not collate κω and Fo (Ln 1.50–52), those variants do
not appear in his collation (Ln 854t).

869 **orfrays:** "gold embroidery" (SK FI RIf). See 562n. Referring to line 872, SK notes that "in this case, the
gold seems to have been embroidered on silk."

873 **samet:** Cf. 836n.

875–76 **werede : ferede:** All eds. except BE-KA GL have *werde : ferde*. *Werede* is a normal form (from OE
werian), but *ferede* is not; cf. 249–50n., 271n., lines 499–500, 673–74.

886 **quystroun:** "scullion" (TRg SK GL RIf), "garçon de cuisine" (TRg), "kitchen boy" (SK FI). Earlier, SP and
UR had glossed the word as "beggar." BE, accepting TR's gloss, notes that URg's citation of Du Cange, *quaestionarii*,
implies (wrongly) a derivation "from *quester*, quêter, to beg." SK cites Godefroy (1881–1902) and a passage from
King Alisaunder, cf. *MED quistroun* n.

887 **pryse:** A transliteration of the Fr. (Lc 873 "prisier" "value"). In arguing against Chaucer's authorship of
Fragment A, Koch (1890:11; 1900a:66) draws attention to the poor rhyme of MS *preyse*, which Chaucer elsewhere
rhymes with *reyse* (*LGW* 1524, *WBP* D 705, *TC* 2.1583); arguing for Chaucer's authorship, Kaluza (1893a:128) notes
that the emended form *pryse* follows the Fr. The forms are closely related—*MED preisen* v. < OF *preisier* "praise,"
var. *prisier*, *MED prisen* v. [1] from OF *prisier*—and the senses overlap (RIf glosses *pryse* as "praise").

891 **flourettes:** URg defines as "fine flower-work, embroidery," but TRg's more literal gloss, "small flower[s],"
is followed by subsequent commentators. SKg adds "buds."

892 *Marginalium:* lat a lyn MS₂ₑ. First noted by Blodgett (1975:62; see RI), who (p. 93) credits A. I. Doyle with
the explanation. The hand is the same as that which has made the printers' marks for TH¹. Here, it has placed a pair
of horizontal dashes, left and right between lines 891 and 893, to mark the omission of the line in MS, and has
written the phrase "lat a lyn," which David (RIt) reads as "probably 'let [i.e., leave] a line.'" David cites Blodgett
(1979:100–01; cf. 1975:62), who would "read the notation as Thynne's instruction to the compositor to leave a space
for a line to be supplied by Thynne. In Th [= TH¹] a line does make good the omission." David notes further that "a
line is left empty at the bottom of the page"; see 908n.

Ypaynted al with amorettes: KA et al. (but not RB) note that TH¹ supplies the line, which is missing in
MS. RI rejects the line as spurious, shows the lacuna by a line of dots, and prints TH¹'s line in a footnote. On this and
other cases where RI rejects a line that has no basis or a doubtful basis in MS, see "The Present Edition" in
Descriptions of the Printed Editions.

with amorettes: Variously interpreted: with "louers fauours" (SP²,³g), with "love-stories" (URg), "by
amorous young ladies" (BE), "with love-knots" (SK FI), "by amorous girls" (GL), "by beautiful girls" (RB), (by, with)
"pure lovers or love-knots" (RIf).

Jephson (BE) cites the Fr. (Lc 877–79, 882–83): "ainz avoit robe de floreites, / fete par fines amoreites./ A
losenges, a escucius, / . . . / fu sa robe de toutes parz / portrete" ("rather had a gown of little flowers, made by pure
love[r]s. With lozenges, with little shields . . . his gown was covered in every part"). Jephson concludes, on the basis
of Fr. *par*, that ME *with* means "by." Skeat, who finds "the Fr. text . . . obscure," grants that *par* may mean "by," but
he argues that "if '*with* means *by*' here, it must have the same sense in l. 894, which would mean that birds, leopards,

103

And with losynges and scochouns,   MS:17v   Ne flour noon that man can on thynke;
With briddes, lybardes, and lyouns,   And many a rose-leef ful longe   905
And other beestis wrought ful well.   895   Was enterme[d]led theramonge.
His garnement was everydell   And also on his heed was sette
Portreied and wrought with floures,   Of roses reed a chapelett;
By dyvers medlyng of coloures.   But nyghtyngales, a full grete route,   18r
Floures there were of many gise   That flyen over his heed aboute,   910
Sett by compas in assise.   900   The leeves felden as they flyen.
Ther lakkide no flour, to my dome,   And he was all with briddes wryen,
Ne nought so mych as flour of brome,   With popynjay, with nyghtyngale,
Ne violete, ne eke pervynke,   With chalaundre, and with wodewale,

---

904 **man]** men TH¹-UR FU SU   906 **entermedled]** entermelled MS BE-KA GL (*var. sp.*)

---

and lions all lent a hand in painting" (cf. David below). He notes that the word *amourettes* occurs again at line 4755, where it means "young girls, sweethearts"; but, he cautions, "we must remember that it is there employed by a different translator." To support his reading, "with love-knots," he adduces James I's "*Kingis Quair*, st. 47, which," he claims, "was probably imitated from the present" passage (cf. Skeat 1899:66). Liddell (GL) accepts BE's reading and adduces *TC* 4.80 (wrong reference; *TC* 5.548?) in support of *with* in the sense "by," a sense that, he says, "is common in Middle English."

Robinson (RB) favors "by beautiful girls"; he reviews Skeat's objections and adduces Ln's citation (879ff. n.) of *Jugement d'Amours*, v. 169–71: "Cotes orent de roses pures / Et de violetes ceintures / Que par soulaz firent amors" ("They had tunics of bright roses and, of violets, belts that love made by way of comfort"). This passage has contrasting prepositions—*de* (with) and *par* (by)—that parallel those in *RR*—*par* (by) and *a* (with); but, since Robinson did not note that the ME line was supplied by TH¹ and since he assumed that TH¹ had parallel authority with MS, the significance of this observation remained for David (RI) to clarify. In defending the reading "by pure lovers," David points out that "Thynne . . . construes 'amoretes' as an ornament of the robe like the *scochouns*, *briddes*, etc., in the lines following. . . . The translation in Thynne misses the distinction between Fr. 'par' (was made *by*) and 'a' (made *with*) in 'A losenges, a escusiaus.'" David adds: "That the ME translator understood the word [*amoretes*] in its true sense is suggested by 878–79, where *The God of Love . . . can devyde Love* translates 'depart Amoretes.'" David refers further to lines 4755–56, where *amourettes* means "young girls, sweethearts." As David notes, *MED amorette* n. follows Skeat with the gloss "Love-knot"; since this gloss is the only one in *MED*, it serves there for line 4755 and for the *Kingis Quair*.

893 **losynges:** squares, square figures (SPg), a word of French origin (SP²g et al.); "Scutcheons of Arms, born by Ladies in a Lozenge" (URg); "quadrilateral figure[s] of equal sides but unequal angles, in which the Arms of women are usually painted" (SKg).

  scochouns: "Scutcheons of Arms . . . Fr. *Ecusson*, a Coat of Arms" (URg et al.); SK adds, "painted shields."

894 **lybardes:** "leopard[s]" (URg, s.v. *Libart*).

896–98 "i.e., Cupid's garment itself and the decorations on it were wrought of varicolored flowers" (FI).

900 **by compas:** "[by] circlet, wreath" (SKg); "[by] plan" (FI); "by design" (RIf); "round about" (Davis 1979).

  assise: "order" (SPg; of French origin, SP² et al.); URg adds "Place, site, situation" (cf. TRg, p. 253); "position" (SKg et al.).

906 **entermedled:** MS sp., *entermelled*, derives from CF, *entermedled* from AF; see *MED entermedlen* v. In support of *entermedled*, SKt compares line 898, *medlyng*.

908 KA notes that, after this line, MS leaves a blank line at the foot of folio 17v; see 892n.

  roses reed: Fr. has only *roses* (Lc 896), with no color. As RB² RI note, Kuhl (1945:33–34) sees in the emphasis on red roses, here and at line 1680, a reflection of Chaucer's connection with "Blanche of Lancaster and John of Gaunt whose family emblem was the red rose" (RI). David observes, however, that "it is altogether natural to assume that the rose of love is red." Kuhl suggests further that *Rom* was composed before the death of Blanche, Duchess of Lancaster (1369), and thus before *BD*.

909 **nyghtyngales, a full grete route:** Roscow (1981:49) finds here an example of "the tag order [in which a word or words are added—as a "tag"—after the close of a syntactic structure] of partitive expressions acting as postmodifiers," as in *BD* 295, *SqT* F 382, *PrT* B² 1686–87.

911 **felden:** caused to fall, felled, knocked off (TRg et al.; see *MED fellen*, v. l). *Nyghtyngales* (line 909) is the subject.

913–14 See 81n. and 658n.

With fynche, with lark, and with archaungell. 915
He semede as he were an aungell
That doun were comen fro hevene clere.
  Love hadde with hym a bachelere,
That he made alleweyes with hym be;
Swete-Lokyng cleped was he. 920
This bacheler stode biholdyng
The daunce, and in his honde holdyng
Turke bowes two had he.

That oon of hem was of a tree
That bereth a fruyt of savour wykke. 925
Ful crokid was that foule stikke,
And knotty here and there also,
And blak as bery or ony slo.
That [other] bowe was of a plant
Without wem, I dar warant, 930
Ful evene, and by proporcioun
Treitys and long, of ful good fasoun.

---

917 **doun**] doen ST   920 **Swete**] And s. UR   **cleped**] clepyng TH²   923 **had**] full wel deuysed h. MS-SP³ BE-KA FU; well devised h. UR   925 **a**] *om.* UR   929 **other**] othe MS (MS₁ *corr.*)   932 **of ful good**] and o. g. UR; o. g. SK GL FI

---

915 **archaungell:** Identification is uncertain. As Jephson (BE) notes, the gloss in URg ("the herb so called, a dead nettle") is inappropriate, although there is such a plant, the angelica (*MED archangel* n.[2]). Jephson, relying on the Fr. (Lc 901 "mesanges"), suggests "titmouse" (GL cites Cotgrave 1611 for the French), but *archaungell*, as SK RB RI make clear, has no such meaning elsewhere. FI glosses the word as "evidently titmouse, Fr. *mesanges*." Robinson and David (RI) review two suggestions: Thompson's (1938), that the word is "a corruption of *acanthyllus* 'goldfinch'" (RI); and Kunstmann's (1940), that it is a corruption "of *wariangel* (used in FrT III [D].1408), the red-backed shrike" (RI). David prefers the explanation of Whitteridge (1950:35), "who cites 'arcanges' (archangel) in a spurious line in a Fr. MS." written in England in 1323. The relevant passage corresponds to Lc 899–903: "Et si iert tous covers d'oisyaus, / De papegais, de royetiaus; / Il sembloit que ce feust uns anges, / Saint Michiel ou saint Luc l'arcanges, / Qui feust touz droit venus du ciel" ("He was completely covered with birds, with parrots, with wrens; it seemed that he was an angel—Saint Michael or Saint Luke the archangel—who had come straight from heaven"). The fourth line is a corruption of Lc 901 ("de kalendres et de mesanges" "of calander-larks and of titmice"), which appears *before* the third line of this passage, rather than after. Whitteridge also points out the error in making Luke, rather than Michael, the archangel. With the word *arcanges* in the position of *mesanges*, it seems reasonable, as David notes, that "some such variant would have misled the translator into adding a new bird to the language."

923–98 "Swete-Loking is represented as holding two bows, the one ugly and crooked, the other beautiful and straight, to denote the different impressions of love or dislike which looking produces. The arrows belonging to the straight bow, productive of love, are Beauty, Simplicity, Frankness, Company, Faire Semblaunt. The arrows belonging to the ugly bow, and which produce dislike, are Pride, Villainy, or base breeding, Shame, Wanhope, or Despair, New Thought, or Inconstancy" (BE).

923 SK GL RB¹-RI omit the MS phrase *full wel deuysed* because it gives too many syllables and is not in the Fr. (Lc 908–09 "et si gardoit / au dieu d'Amors .II. ars turquois" "and [Sweet Looks] watched over two Turkish bows for the God of Love"). David (RIt) suggests that "the translator perhaps ended the line with *deuysed*, changed his mind about the rhyme, and then forgot to cancel the phrase."

Turke bowes two: BE SK (971n.) Ln Lc (909n.) RB RI find the idea of the two bows and two sets of arrows in Ovid, *Met.* 1.468–71; as RB RI note, Ln (909n.) also cites other examples from medieval literature: e.g., *Eneas* 7976–86 and Huon de Méri's *Tournoiement Antecrist* 1734–37, where the God of Love has a single (Turkish) bow and a quiver. FI, citing *PF* 128, notes that "the motif of the two aspects of love, agony and ecstasy, is a commonplace." GL notes the "bowe Turkeys" in *KnT* A 2895, and David (RI), citing Webster (1932) and Herben (1937:485), observes that "the Turkish bow is a powerful, short, composite, reflexed bow."

928 **ony:** See 212n.

929 **other:** "*r* written above the line" (KA), by MS₁.

932 **Treitys:** TH¹-SP³ FU SU spell *Trectes* (UR *Trectis*), perhaps a learned respelling from Lat. *tractus*; *OED Tretis* a. does not include TH¹'s form. SP glosses "streight." URg (s.v. *Tretes . . . Trectis*) says rather "Well-shaped or Well-proportioned," generally applied to the face or nose but also to other things, as here; "perhaps . . . from Fr. *Trait.*" SKg FI RIg have "graceful."

of ful good fasoun: Omission of *ful* improves the meter and follows the Fr. (Lc 916 "de gente [*var.* bone, MS Bâ; (Ln 916t)] façon" "of fine [*var.* good] workmanship"; noted by GL RBt SU RIt); KA Fr. chooses the var. *bone* from MS Fo, and SU Fr. chooses another var., *droite*, from MS He; see SU Fr. 916n. SU's note to *Rom* 932 ("Skt. and Glo. drop *ful*, but cf. Fr. *trés*) is puzzling, since the word *très* "very" does not appear in the Fr. or in Ln's variants; the error may have arisen from eye-skip to the next line below Ln's variant *bone*, where, in 918t, Ln records the variant "f. trés b."

And it was peynted wel and [thwyten],	18v	Outake the fetheres and the tree.	
And overal diapred and writen		The swiftest of these arowis fyve	
With ladyes and with bacheleris,	935	Out of a bowe for to dryve,	950
Full lyghtsom and glad of cheris.		And best fethered for to flee,	
These bowes two helde Swete-Lokyng,		And fairest eke, was clepid Beaute.	
That semede lyk no gadelyng.		That other arowe, that hurteth lasse,	
And ten brode arowis hilde he there,		Was clepid, as I trowe, Symplesse.	
Of which fyve in his right hond were.	940	The thridde cleped was Fraunchise,	955
But they were shaven wel and dight,		That fethred was in noble wise	
Nokked and fethered right,		With valour and with curtesye.	19r
And all they were with gold bygoon,		The fourthe was cleped Compaigny[e],	
And stronge [poynted] everychoon,		That hevy for to shoten ys;	
And sharp for to kerven well.	945	But whoso shetith right, ywys,	960
But iren was ther noon ne st[e]ell,		May therwith doon grete harme and wo.	
For al was golde, men myght it see,		The fifte of these, and laste also,	

---

933 **thwyten]** twythen MS (MS₂ *corr. first* h) BE-KA   936 **glad]** full g. UR SK   938 **semede]** ne s. UR   940 **right hond]** honde TH³-UR   942 **right]** aryght TH¹-UR SK-FI   944 **poynted]** peynted MS KA   946 **steell]** stell MS (MS₁ *corr.*)   947 **it]** *om.* TH¹-SP³ FU SU   951 **best]** the b. UR   **flee]** flye TH¹-UR FU SU FI   958 **Compaignye]** Compaigny MS (MS₂ *corr.*)

---

933   **thwyten:** KA's suggestion. MS₂d corrects to *thwythen* by inserting an *h*, with caret, above the space between *t* and *w* and by putting an "X" in the margin; see frontispiece. The form *twhitten* in TH¹-SP¹ FU SU FI is a var. sp., not a substantive var. The sense is "shaped by cutting" (*OED Thwite* v.; cf. SPg et al.).   § SK adduces *HF* 1938 "thwite," *RvT* A 3933 "thwitel," and Modern English *whittle.*

936   **glad:** The reading in UR, noted in KA and SK, has no basis in the Fr.

938   **gadelyng:** "stragler" (SP¹g), "stragling" (SP²·³g); "idle fellow that gads and saunters up and down" (URg); "idle vagabond" (TRg et al.); "scoundrel, (knave)" (Davis 1979, RIf).   § SK adduces *Tale of Gamelyn* 102, 106 (SK 4.647).

939–70   On the five arrows, see Dahlberg (1969:575–76). Ln (note to 935ff.) quotes *Carmina Burana* No. 116 on the *quinque modi amoris*, but Lc (924–25n.), citing Curtius (1953:512–13; cf. Robertson 1962:407; Friedman 1965), says that the two series of arrows have nothing to do with this tradition, the *quinque lineae amoris.*

944   **poynted:** David (RIt) suggests that MS *peynted* "results perhaps from attraction to 933."

946   **steell:** "*e* written above the line" (KA) by MS₁. See frontispiece.

949   *Marginalium:* B.p¹ MS₂e (see frontispiece). This mark is probably an instruction to the printer of TH¹. As Blodgett points out (1979:99), "this is probably to be read as the first page of signature B, the one incongruity being that it is the first page of 2B." Blodgett notes that the other indications of signatures are sometimes single, sometimes double, but that TH¹ prints the correct double letters.

951   **flee:** I collate *flye* as a substantive var.; cf. *MED flīen* v., *flēn* v.(1) and lines 2752, 3149, 4697, 4783, 5471, 6268. But *MED* (*flēn*) notes that "OE *fleon* 'flee' differed from *fleogan* 'fly' only in the stem of the present. In some dialects of ME the two verbs seem to have coalesced completely; in others they remained distinct in the present stem."

953   **That:** The scribe supplies a lower case initial *t* in a 9 mm. space, left blank for an initial capital (see frontispiece). Cf. lines 955, 958, 962; in all four of these locations, the scribe leaves space for an illuminated *T.* At lines 955 and 962, the gilt letter was supplied in a rounded form unlike that of the usual line-initial *T,* but more like a copy of the curves of the still larger decorated *T*s throughout MS (ca. 15 mm. by 2 lines high; cf. line 949, frontispiece). At lines 953 and 958, only a small *t* appears; Whatley (1989) notes that at lines 955 and 962, the small *t* has been incorporated within the terminal inside curve of the large *T.*

955   **The:** See 953n.

958   **The:** See 953n.

Compaignye: "*e* added by a later hand" (KA), MS₂d; it converts the flourish on the *y* to a final *-e* by means of two horizontal strokes.

959   **shoten:** SKt RB RIt normalize to *sheten,* "perhaps rightly" (SU). SK SU RI compare line 989, where MS has the inf. form *shete*; see 1453n. For forms, see *MED sheten* v.

960   **right:** KA, following the Fr. (Lc 947 "de pres") suggests *nigh.* SKt RBt SU RIt so note, but none emends.

962   **The:** See 953n.

Faire-Semblaunt men that arowe calle,
The leest grevous of hem alle.
Yit can it make a ful grete wounde. 965
But he may hope his soris sounde,
That hurt is with that arowe, ywys.
His wo the bette bistowed is,
For he may sonner have gladnesse;
[His] langour ought be the lesse. 970
  Five arowis were of other gise,
That ben ful foule to devyse,
For shaft and ende, soth for to telle,
Were also blak as fende in helle.
The first of hem is called Pride. 975
That other arowe next hym biside,
It was cleped Vylanye;
That arowe was [al] with felonye
Envenymed, and with spitous blame.
The thridde of hem was clepe[d] Shame. 980
The fourthe Wanhope cleped is; 19v
The fifte, the Newe-Thought, ywys.
  These arowis that I speke of heere
Were all fyve on oon maneere,
And alle were they resemblable. 985
To hem was wel sittyng and able
The foule croked bowe hidous,
That knotty was and al roynous.

That bowe semede wel to shete
These arowis fyve, that ben unmete 990
And contrarye to that other fyve.
But though I telle not as blyve
Of her power ne of her myght,
Herafter shal I tellen right
The soothe and eke signyfiaunce 995
As fer as I have remembraunce.
All shal be seid, I undirtake,
Er of this book an ende I make.
  Now come I to my tale ageyn.
But aldirfirst I wole you seyn 1000
The fasoun and the countenaunces
Of all the folk that on the daunce is.
The God of Love, jolyf and lyght,
Ladde on his honde a lady bright, 1004
Of high prys and of grete degre. 20r
This lady called was Beaute,
[As] an arowe of which I tolde.
Ful wel thewed was she holde,
Ne she was derk ne broun, but bright,
And clere as the mone lyght, 1010
Ageyn whom all the sterres semen
But smale candels, as we demen.
Hir flesh was tendre as dewe of flour;
Hir chere was symple as byrde in bour,

---

964 **The]** 'Tis the UR   967 **arowe]** arowes ST   970 **His]** Hir MS BE-KA   **ought]** o. to TH² UR BE   972 **to]** for to SP¹ UR   973 **ende]** ends SU   **for to]** to SK   978 **al]** as MS-SP³ BE-SK FU; *om.* UR   980 **cleped]** clepe MS BE KA   982 **the Newe-Thought]** N.-T. GL   984 **on]** of SK   990 **These]** The TH³-UR   991 **And]** *om.* SK   1006 **called was]** w. c. TH²   1007 **As]** And MS-KA FU; A. was SK   1010 **as]** as is UR SK GL FI

---

970 **His:** MS *Hir* is either a scribal error or, possibly, an erroneous reflex of Fr. *sa* (Lc 956 "sa dolor" "his pain"), which takes its fem. gender from the noun that it modifies, rather than from its antecedent.
  ought: SKt erroneously indicates that MS reads "ought to."
978 **al:** This emendation (GL's) is based on the Fr. *tote* (Lc 965; also noted in RBt SU RIt) and on the easy confusion of long *s* for *l*.
980 **cleped:** MS *clepe* is doubtless owing to scribal error.
984 **on:** SK's *of* is mysteriously attributed to "K." (SKt).
989 **shete:** See 1453n.
991 **contrarye:** "Perhaps read *contraire*; cp. 348" (GL); see 348n.
994–98 BE SK RB note that Guillaume de Lorris did not live to fulfill his promise.
1006–07 "This lady's name was Beauty, which was also the name of her arrow of which I have told you" (BE). "The allegory," states SK, "is rather of a mixed kind."
1007 **As:** KA suggests this emendation on the basis of the Fr. *ausi come* (Lc 993 "just as"; noted in RBt-RIt).
  an arowe of which I tolde: See line 952 (SK RB).
1009 Merlo (1981) notes the contrast between "broun" and "bright" in terms of the symbolism of the color brown in Chaucer.
1014 **byrde:** "bride" (TRg et al., citing Fr. *espousee* [Lc 1000]); "lady" (Davis 1979); "young girl" (RIf). SK RB note that *byrde* and *bride* are different words. ME *birde* "a woman of noble birth" is here, as elsewhere, confused with its partial synonym *brīde* "a young woman about to be married, or just married" (*MED birde, bīrde* n.[1]; *brīd(e* n.[1]).

As whyte as lylye or rose in rys,   1015
Hir face gentyl and tretys.
Fetys she was and smale to se;
No [wyndred] browis had she,
Ne popped hir, for it neded nought
To wyndre hir or to peynte hir ought.   1020
Hir tresses yelowe and longe straughten;
Unto hir helys doun they raughten.
Hir nose, hir mouth, and eyhe, and cheke

Wel wrought, and all the remenaunt eke.
A ful grete savour and a swote   1025
Me [toucheth] in myn herte rote,
As helpe me God, whan I remembre
Of the fasoun of every membre.
In world is noon so faire a wight,   20v
For yonge she was, and hewed bright,   1030
Sore plesaunt, and fetys withall,
Gente, and in hir myddill small.

1016 **gentyl]** was g. UR   1018 **wyndred]** wyntred MS-KA GL FU SU   1020 **peynte hir]** p. UR
1026 **toucheth]** thought MS-KA FU; thinketh SK   1031 **Sore]** Wys SK; Sote FI   1032 **Gente]** And gent UR

---

bour: "house" (SP²·³g), to which URg, providing the OE etymon, adds "habitation, . . . chamber"; SK glosses "bower; the usual name for a lady's chamber."

1015   **As:** "*Read* And" (KA).

1018   **wyndred:** SK's emendation accords with *wyndre* in line 1020, which is defined as "to couer, or trim" (SP²·³g), "or adorn" (URg, citing Skinner 1671). TRg (p. 286) simply lists "Winder, Wintred" among "Words . . . not Understood." MOg has "to wind, enshroud." GL cites Coles (1676) for the sense "trim (the hair)." RIf has "embellish." Glosses to the emendation in the present line offer various connotations: "trimmed, artificially embellished" (SK); "trimmed? painted?" (RB); "touched up" (FI); "plucked, painted (?)" (RIf). SK RI note that the Fr. participle *guigniee* (Lc 1004 "painted"; "spelled 'wigniee' in some MSS" [RI]), may have suggested the forms *wyndred*, *wyndre*. SK RB note the two meanings of OF *guignier*, "to wink" and "to trick out." For the former, SK RB cite Cotgrave (1611); for the latter, Godefroy (1881–1902). As an English parallel to the former sense, GL RB note the occurrence of *winrede bruwes* "ogling glances" in *Old English Homilies*, 2nd Ser., ed. Morris, EETS, o.s. 53, 1873, p. 213; GL takes the sense here to be the same as in the OE, but RB thinks this sense "less likely." David (RI) suggests that the translator introduced the word *browis*, not in the Fr., "through misunderstanding 'guignee' as 'plucked.'" Both David and Skeat note another appearance of the word *guigner* in the Fr. (see 2285n.). MS *wyntred*, "aged" (*OED Wintered* a.) is glossed in SP²·³g as "wringled," which URg expands as "Wrinkled, or rather Grey or hoary, as the Winter."

1019   **popped:** UR glosses "over-nicely dressed," and implies an etymology, "dressed up like a puppet"; cf. *MED poppen* v.(2), *popet* n. TRg has "nicely dressed"; GL cites Coles (1676), "drest fine." This word, says SK, "has much the same sense" as *wyndred* in the previous line, "and is evidently allied to F. *popin*, 'spruce, neat, briske, trimme, fine,' in Cotgrave" (1611). FI glosses "Trimmed"; RIf has "adorned . . . , used cosmetics."

hir: "herself" (RIf); T. Thomas (URg, s.v. *Popped*) takes UR's *here* to mean "hair."

1020   Jephson (BE) cites, as parallel, the Fr. line (Lc 1004 "n'estoit fardee ne guigniee" "[she] was neither rouged nor painted") that is instead parallel to line 1018; the parallel to this line is Lc 1006 ("de soi tifer ne afaitier" "to adorn or decorate herself").

wyndre: See 1018n.

1025   **swote:** FI compares his note to *GP* 1; see 128n.

1026   **toucheth:** KA suggests this emendation, which follows the Fr. *touche* (Lc 1010 "touches"; noted in RBt-RIt). As SU reports, SKt misreads KA's suggestion as *thinketh*.

1031   **Sore plesaunt:** "extremely (?) agreeable" (RIf). Comparing line 4305, RB RI seek to validate this reading. "Probably *Sore* is the correct reading and is used merely for emphasis" (RB). RI states: "As an adverb, *sore* qualifies words denoting pain, grief, or intense feeling. Perhaps here it has the force of colloquial modern 'awfully,' 'terribly.'" The emendations of *Sore* are not entirely satisfactory. In the Fr. "sade, plesant" (Lc 1015 "agreeable, pleasant"), *sade* is not an adverbial modifier of *plesant*; it is "simply another of Beauty's traits" (RI). KA's suggestion for *Rom*—"*Perhaps read* Sade" (presumably "sad"; cf. *MED sad* adj., where the closest sense seems to be 4a: "grave; . . . discreet, wise")—assumes that ME *sore* is a scribal error and that it parallels the Fr. in syntax but not in sense. SK's *Wys*, introduced "for want of a better word, . . . answers to one sense of Lat. *sapidus*, whence the F. *sade* is derived. However," SK adds, "Cotgrave [1611] explains *sade* by 'pretty, neat, spruce, fine, compt, minion, quaint.' Perhaps *Queint* or *Fine* would do better." SK's *Wys* (and perhaps KA's *Sad*) corresponds to the Fr. var. *sage*, which appears in MSS Ca Ce Ri (Ln 1015t) and to which RBt RI call attention. SU argues that neither KA's nor SK's emendation "is suitable, for Fr. *Sade* means 'agreeable.' *Sote* is probably the best alternative to *Sore*." FI adopts this suggestion and glosses *Sote* as "sweet (smelling)." The paleographical assumption in this emendation (*r-t* confusion) is slightly more plausible than that in Kaluza's (*or-ad*).

Biside Beaute yede Richesse,
[An high] lady of gret noblesse,
And gret of prys in every place.   1035
But whoso durste to hir trespace,
Or til hir folk, in [word] or dede,
He were full hardy, out of drede,
For bothe she helpe and hyndre may;
And that is nought of yisterday   1040
That riche folk have full gret myght
To helpe and eke to greve a wyght.
The beste and the grettest of valour
Diden Rychesse ful gret honour,
And besy were hir to serve,   1045
For that they wolde hir love deserve;
They cleped hir lady, grete and small.

This wide world hir dredith all;
This world is all in hir daungere.
Hir court hath many a losengere,   1050
And many a traytour envyous,
That ben ful besy and curyous
For to dispreisen and to blame   21r
That best deserven love and name.
Bifore the folk, hem to bigilen,   1055
These losengeris hem preyse and smylen,
And thus the world with word anoynten;
And aftirward they [prikke] and poynten
The folk right to the bare boon,
Bihynde her bak whan they ben goon,   1060
And foule abate the folkis prys.
Ful many a worthy man, ywys

1034 **An high]** And hight MS-ST UR MO KA FU   1037 **word]** werk MS-KA FU   1043 **beste]** leste GL RB[1,2]   **the grettest]** greattest TH[1]-UR SK-FU FI   1055 **Bifore]** To forne TH[1]-UR FU SU FI   1056 **preyse]** prise UR   1058 **And]** But TH[1]-MO SK FU SU FI   **prikke]** prile MS-KA GL FU   1061 **the]** *om.* TH[1]-UR FU SU   1062 **ywys]** and wyse TH[1]-UR SK FU-RI

1034 **An high:** SP[1]'s emendation is noted by KA in BE; in support, SU RIt cite the Fr. (Lc 1018 "de grant hautece" "of great eminence").

1037 **word:** SK's emendation reflects the Fr. "par fez ne par diz" (Lc 1021 "by deed or by word"; noted by GL RBt RIt).

1043 **beste:** The emendation *leste* is based on the Fr. "li plus grant et li menor" (Lc 1027 "the greatest and the least"; noted in GL RBt). But, as SU RIt observe, the variant *meilleur* "best" for *menor* (see Ln 1027t, SU Fr. 1027n.) accounts sufficiently for the MS reading.

1049 **daungere:** URg notes the sense "Power, reach" (cf. TRg); "jurisdiction, authority" (BE), "control" (SK). BE adduces the allegorical character Daunger in *The Court of Love*, a poem no longer attributed to Chaucer (SK 7.lxxii–lxxx). SK adduces *GP* 663 and note and *Rom* 1470. On the word *daunger* see Lewis (1936:364–66), Barron (1965), *MED daunğĕr* n.

1050 **losengere:** "flatterer" (SPg et al.), to which URg et al. add "lyar . . . Deceiver"; "the traditional enemy of lovers in troubadour poetry and romance" (RI). SK adduces *NPT* B[2] 4516, *LGWP* F 352, and compares *Rom* 1056, 1064.

1057–58 SK states: "M. Michel here quotes an O. F. proverb—'Poignez vilain, il vous oindra: Oignez vilain, il vous poindra'" ("stab a churl and he will flatter [oil] you; flatter a churl and he will stab you"). Michel (ed. 1864:1.34) gives no source. Cf. Morawski (1925: nos. 725, 834, 1431–32).

1057 BE and SK emphasize the semantic element "oil" in the word *anoynten*: "They flatter the world with their smooth, oily, unctuous manners" (BE); "And thus anoint the world with (oily) words" (SK).

1058 **prikke:** KA suggests this emendation, which follows the Fr. *poignent* (Lc 1042 "pierce, stab"). Skeat (SK) explains that "as it was usual to write *kk* like *lk*, the word probably looked . . . like *prilke*, out of which *prille* may have evolved"; he cites "*rolke* for *rokke* (a rock) in Gawain Douglas" (cf. *MED priken* v., which records the form *prilke* as an error; see sense 7. [a] for the form). GL, reiterating an idea already proffered in MOg (s.v. *Prile*), suggests a different paleographical confusion (*p-þ*): MS *prile* is "probably the scribe's mistake for *thrill*, pierce; cp. 5556, where *depe* for *dothe*." RBt grants that this explanation is perhaps correct. GL, however, retains the MS reading: "*prille* . . . may be right (cp. sb. *prill*, a top), and mean 'pirouette.'" SP UR gloss *prill* as "gore," but, as SK notes, the word is otherwise unattested in that sense.

poynten: "strike" (SPg and URg, s.v. *prill and pointen*); URg (s.v. *Poincten*) adds, again with reference to this line, "To prick with a point" (cf. TRg); "stab" (SKg et al.).

1062–66 This passage, owing to its elliptical and inverted syntax, has been variously emended. But MS unaltered approximates the French text in Ln (1046–49; cf. KA Fr. and SU Fr.; Lc has only the last 3 lines): "Maint prodomes ont encusez / Li losengier par lor losenges, / Car il font ceus de cort estranges / Qui deüssent estre privé" ("Many good men have the flatterers denounced by their flattery, for they alienate from court those who should be intimate").

1062 **ywys:** Neither this tag nor TH[1]'s formulaic *and wyse*, suggested by KA, has any basis in the French text.

An hundrid, have do to dye
These losengers thorough flaterye,
Have maad folk ful straunge be   1065
There hem ought be pryve.
Wel yvel mote they thryve and thee,
And yvel [aryved] mote they be,
These losengers ful of envye!
No good man loveth her companye.   1070
    Richesse a robe of purpur on hadde;

Ne trowe not that I lye or madde,
For in this world is noon [it] lyche,
Ne by a thousand deell so riche,
Ne noon so faire, for it ful well   1075
With orfrays leyd was everydeell
And portraied in the ribanynges   21v
Of dukes storyes, and of kynges,
And with a bend of gold tasseled,
And knoppis fyne of gold enameled.   1080

1063 **An hundrid have do]** Han hyndred and ydon TH¹-UR FU-FI; A. h. h. they d. BE MO SK RI
1064 **thorough]** with her TH¹-UR FU SU FI   1065 **Have maad]** And maketh TH¹-UR SK FU SU FI;   And make
GL RB¹·²   1066 **There]** There as TH¹-UR SK FU SU FI   **be]** to ben UR   1067 **and thee]** *om.* UR
1068 **aryued]** achyued MS BE-KA   1071 **purpur]** purple TH¹-UR FU SU FI   1073 **it]** hir MS MO KA GL
1080 **fyne]** fyre FU   **enameled]** amyled TH¹-UR SK-RI

1063 **An hundrid, have do to:** David writes (RIt; cf. RBt): "The reading is doubtful and depends on the
syntax of 1063–65. The addition of a subject, as in Skeat, and a full stop after 1064 [*read* 1063] allows G's [= MS's]
lines to stand without further change." BE MO RI all place a full stop after line 1063. David, who remarks that
neither MS nor TH¹ closely matches the Fr., thinks that TH¹'s emendation "looks like an attempt to make sense out of
G (perhaps inspired by *hyndre* in 1039)"; "it is difficult," he adds, "to see how Th's reading could lead to G's." MS
An hundrid, he suggests, "may be a line-filler, translating *Mainz*," and he notes that "Kaluza cites a var., *Mainz
miles d'ommes ont rusez*" ("many thousand men have [flatterers] betrayed"; KA Fr. 1040n. cites MS Fo). One may
also see the emendation as an attempt to solve the problem of the French verb *ont encusez* (denounced, accused),
for which *have do to dye* is not a very close translation.
    do to: FI inaccurately reports MS as reading *to do*.
    1065 **Have maad:** TH¹'s *And maketh,* reported by KA in UR, follows the French change to present tense,
font; but, as RIt notes, the MS reading "is parallel with *have do*" in line 1063. GL reports the Fr. inaccurately as *tout*
(for *font*).
    1066 **pryve:** A term describing "A Confident, a person employed in secret affairs" (URg), "A man entrusted
with private business" (TRg). SKg, making specific reference to this line, has "friendly, intimate."
    1067 **thee:** "To thrive, to prosper" (URg et al.; SKg cites this instance).
    1068 **yvel aryved mote they be:** "may they have an unhappy landing (i.e., bad luck)" (RIf). The gloss in
UR, "A curse, May they be split asunder," wrongly assumes the sense "riven" for *aryved.*
    aryved: TH¹'s emendation—as SK RIt and Blodgett (1984:49) note—follows the French *arivé* (Lc 1048);
SK compares *HF* 1047.
    1071 **purpur:** "purple" (SKg); "purple cloth" (Davis 1979, RIf). For the differing origins of this form and *purple,*
see *MED purpur(e),* n., *purpel* adj. and n. The adjective refers to the color, the nouns to the cloth of that color. § BE
identifies the color as scarlet (crimson? cf. *MED*) and notes that it "is the imperial colour, and denotes magnificence."
    1076 **orfrays:** See 562n.
    1077 **ribanynges:** "borders" (SPg et al., TRg tentatively; MOg adds "welts," SKg "silk trimmings"); "Ribbands,
or Laces, lay'd on robes" (URg); "ribbon-work, silk borders on trim" (Davis 1979, RIf).
    1078 Editions vary as to the use of comma, semicolon, or period at the end of this line.
    1079–82 MSS of *RR* have various readings in the lines that correspond to this passage. KA Fr. 1055–57 prints
the closest correspondence (from MS κω; cf. λο and Fo, in all of which the word *noiax* "buttons, studs" parallels ME
knoppis): "D'une bende d'or neelee / A noiax d'or au col fermee / Fu richement la chevessaille" ("The collar was
richly closed at the neck by a band of gold decorated in black enamel with gold buttons"). SU Fr. 1061–63 gives a
similar version from MS Go; cf. Ln 1062t. BE (1080n.) and SKf print Méon's text, in which only two lines correspond:
"Si estoit au col bien ourlee / D'une bende d'or neelee" ("And it was at the neck well edged," etc.).
    1079 **bend:** "a muffler, kercher, or cawle (SP¹g; SP²·³g omit *kercher*); "A Band, a knot, a fillet; Any thing that
bindeth" (URg, citing this line); heraldic term (SK FI) meaning band, strip, or stripe (TRg SK FI RIf).
    1080–1124 Skeat (1899:66) cites parallels between this passage and *The Kingis Quair* to show the Scottish
King James I's familiarity with Fragment A of *Rom.*
    1080 **knoppis:** "button[s]" (TRg); "knob[s], stud[s]" (Davis 1979); "ornamental buttons, studs" (RIf). MOg SKg
FI have "buds," a sense more appropriate to uses in lines 1675–91; cf. *MED knop(pe* n.(1), senses 1. (b)., 2. (a).

Aboute hir nekke of gentyl entayle
Was shete the riche chevesaile,
In which ther was full gret plente
Of stones clere and bright to see.
 Rychesse a girdell hadde upon;   1085
The bokele of it was of a stoon

Of vertu gret and mochel of myght,
For whoso bare the stoon so bright,
Of venym durst hym nothing doute
While he the stoon hadde hym aboute. 1090
That stoon was gretly for to love,
And tyl a riche man[nes] byhove

1084 **bright]** fayre TH¹-UR FU SU FI 1086 **a]** *om.* TH² ST-BE 1087 **of myght]** might UR
1089 **durst]** thurte SK 1092 **mannes]** man MS BE-KA

---

  fyne: KA recommends omission of this word, presumably to correct meter. It is not in the Fr. (see 1079–82n.).
  enameled: TH¹'s emendation, *amyled* (rhyming with *tassyled*), corrects meter; SK GL RB RI spell *ameled*. BE SK both report that "Speght" reads *ameled*, but in fact SP¹⁻³ have *amiled*. Jephson (BE) thinks that *ameled* "is perhaps right, from the Fr. *email*, enamel." Skeat quotes 16th-century examples of the forms *ammell*, *amelled* from Palsgrave (1530), and he notes that "*enameled* is a lengthened form, with the prefix *en-*." *MED* records more and earlier forms under *enamelen* v. than under *ameled* pa. part., and none for *amelen* v. BE reports that "the word in the original is *néélée*." § Warton (1774–81:1.376–77) has a note on medieval enamelling, quoted in BE, which adduces the Latin forms *amelita, amelitam* in the 1378 will of John de Foxle, knight. BE quotes later additions to this note (Warton 1871;1968:2.322–23), additions that document the flourishing of the art of enameling at Limoges, in France, from 1197 to 1327. SK also refers to Warton.
  1081 **entayle:** "ornamentation" (Davis 1979); for the common gloss, "shape," see 162n. SK states that here the word refers to Richesse's neck, possibly to her collar; FI says "her neck." BE (1082n.) notes the etymological relation to *intaglio* ("cutting"; cf. 140n.). SK reports that "Halliwell [1847] quotes from MS. Douce 291 'the hors of gode entaile,' i.e. of a good shape"; and SK compares *Rom* 609, 3711 (see 3711n.).
  1082 **shete:** "shut" (URg et al.), "i.e. clasped, fastened" (SK).
  chevesaile: "collar" (BE et al.). SK states: "properly, the neckband of the robe, as explained in the New E. Dict. . . . It answers to a Lat. type *capitiale*, from *capitium*, the opening in a tunic through which the head passed; which explains how the word arose." To earlier glosses, Skeat objects that "there seems to be no sufficient reason for explaining it by 'necklace' [URg TRg] or 'gorget' [SPg URg], as if it were a separable article of attire." TRg BE SK say that the word is not in the Fr., but it is absent only in some MSS and in the early editions that are based on them (Méon and Michel). TRg BE SK refer to later occurrences of the word in the Fr. (Lc 1169, 20949).
  1086–90 On the "virtues" (powers) of precious stones, Jephson (BE) refers to the Old English lapidary and to treatises by Marbod of Rennes (died 1123) and Henry of Huntingdon, ca. 1145; see also Isidore of Seville, *Etymol.* 16 (ed. Lindsay 1911). I have not been able to find a treatise *De gemmis* by Huntingdon (see *PL* 195); Jephson probably took his information on Huntingdon from Warton (1774–81:1.378), who cites Tanner (1748:395). For Marbod, see *PL* 171:1737–70; for the Old English lapidary, see Evans and Serjeantson (1933:13–15); for the French and Anglo-Norman lapidaries, and for commentary, see Baisier (1936) and the collections of Pannier (1882) and Studer and Evans (1924). BE RI cite *TC* 2.344; BE cites *HF* 1352. Skeat (SK) notes that "the idea that a gem would repel venom was common," and he cites *Piers Plowman* B 2.14 and his note (1886*b*:2.32).
  1089 **durst:** needed (impersonal); see *MED durren* v. 2. (b). SK's unnecessary emendation has the same sense; GL RB RI point out that "the forms of *durren* and *tharf* were confused" (GL); all three compare line 1324, GL compares line 1360, and RBt compares line 3604.
  1091–92 **love : byhove:** RI calls attention to the Northern rhyme (Mossé 1968:17, 20) and to the discussion in Kaluza (1897 and 1898) and Luick (1898) regarding authorship. Luick (1896) first adduced this Northern rhyme as evidence that Fragment A is not Chaucer's; Koch (1900*a*:67) accepts Luick's argument and (1912:105) notes the same rhyme in Fragment B, at lines 2963–64. Kaluza, however, regards the rhyme as not significantly outweighing other evidence that the fragment is Chaucerian. Koeppel (1898) favors Kaluza's position. Lange, who also supports that position (1911:340–44; 1913:159–60), suggests (1910:317) that the original may have read "That gretly was to love, I leve, / And to a riche man biheve," where he takes *biheve* as the adjective "profitable, fit" (cf. *MED bihēve* adj.); *bihove* would thus have been a bi-form and, presumably, a scribal alteration. See above, "Authorship."
  1092 **mannes:** It is arguable that the Fr. construction favors MS's *man* (Lc 1073–74 "ele vausist a un riche home / plus que . . ." "to a rich man it was worth more than . . .").
  byhove: "Behoof, use, advantage" (URg et al.), "profit" (SK et al.).

Worth all the gold in Rome and Frise.
The mourdaunt wrought in noble wise
Was of a stoon full precious,   1095
That was so fyne and vertuous
That hole a man it koude make
Of palasie and tothe ake.
And yit the stoon hadde such a grace
That he was siker in every place,   1100
All thilk day, not blynde to bene,   22r
That fastyng myght that stoon seene.
The barres were of gold ful fyne
Upon a tyssu of satyne,
Full hevy, gret, and nothyng lyght;   1105

In everiche was a besaunt wight.
  Upon the tresses of Richesse
Was sette a cercle, for noblesse,
Of brend gold, that full lyght shoon;
So faire, trowe I, was never noon.   1110
But [he] were kunnyng, for the nonys,
That koude devyse all the stonys
That in that cercle shewen clere.
It is a wondir thing to here,
For no man koude preyse or gesse   1115
Of hem [the] valewe or richesse.
Rubyes there were, saphires, [jagounces],
And emeraudes more than two ounces;

1094 **wise]** gyse TH¹-UR FU SU FI   1098 **tothe]** of t. TH¹-SP³ SK-FI; of the t. UR   1102 **seene]** have s.
GL   1107 **Richesse]** rychesses TH³ ST   1108 **for]** of TH³ ST SP²-UR   1111 **he]** she MS BE-KA GL
1115 **preyse]** or p. UR   1116 **the]** that MS MO KA   1117 **jagounces]** ragounces MS-UR KA FU

1093 **Frise:** Friesland, Frisia (TRg et al.). RB RI cite Cook (1916a:442) for the suggestion that "it is probably
Phrygia that is meant" rather than Friesland; Jephson (BE) had earlier made the same suggestion: "Perhaps Phrygia,
one of the provinces of Asia Minor, and contiguous to Lydia, the kingdom of Crœsus, may be the country intended."
Cook notes that Friesland did not "abound in gold" and that "Lydia was anciently included in Phrygia." SK RB RI
note that there is no parallel in the Fr. Cook compares *Roman de Thèbes* 6630 (ed. Raynaud de Lage 1966: line 6314
"tot l'or de Frise" "all the gold of *Frise*"; cf. *Thèbes* 1655), where Raynaud de Lage glosses the word *Frise* as "la
Phrygie" (2.159). Robinson feels that "an English parallel would make [Cook's] case stronger," and David (RI) agrees
with Skeat that the word is "merely added for the rhyme" (SK).
  1094 **mourdaunt:** The early glosses (SPg URg TRg, Warton 1774–81:1.377) have "the tongue of a buckle,"
and SK notes that Halliwell (1847) has the same gloss, which, says Skeat, "is probably a guess." He suggests instead
(citing "Fairholt's 'Costume,'") that "it was probably 'the metal chape or tag fixed to the end of a girdle or strap,' viz.
to the end *remote* from the buckle." "Godefroy [1881–1902]," he adds, "explains it in the same way; it terminated the
dependent end of the girdle; and this explains how it could be made of a stone." Further, he quotes from Warton's
note to *Rom* 1103 (1774:1.377), a passage from a wardrobe-roll ("'One hundred garters *cum boucles*, barris, *et
pendentibus de argento*' . . . An. 21, Edw. iii"), that shows a distinction between *boucles* and *pendentibus*. Later eds.
follow SK: "the pendant of the girdle" (GL); "metal trimming, finishing off the end of a belt, in this case set with a
magic jewel" (FI); "a trim (usually metallic) fastened to the end of the girdle and causing it to hang down; here the
material is another precious stone with medicinal properties" (RI).
  1102 **seene:** GL's reading follows KA's recommendation and the Fr. *avoit veüe* (Lc 1080).
  1103 **barres:** "I cannot give the precise meaning of *Barris*, nor of *Cloux* in the French. It seems to be part of
a buckle" (Warton 1774–81:1.377). See further, Andrew (1993), note to *GP* 329. SK states: "bars; fixed transversely to
the satin tissue of the girdle, and perforated to receive the tongue of the buckle." FI has a similar explanation, noting
that "the tongue of the buckle might have pressed against [the bars] to avoid tearing the cloth." The word comes
from OF, but here it parallels Fr. *clou* (Lc 1081 "stud, boss"). For the occurrence of the word with *boucles* and
pendentibus, see 1094n.
  1106 **besaunt wight:** SP¹g's gloss, the "weight" of a "duckett" (gold coin), elicits a lengthy correction from F.
Thynne (1599;1875:31–32), who points out that although "Hollybande, in his french-Englishe dictionarye, make yt
[the bezant] of the valewe of a duckett," the name comes from Byzantium; Thynne quotes the phrase *nummi
Bizantium* "Byzantium coin" from William of Malmesbury. SP²˒³g correct accordingly; URg and TRg cite Skinner
(1671) in support of this sense. SK (cf. GL RB) quotes *OED* as saying that the coin "varied in weight between the
English sovereign and half-sovereign, or less."
  1111 **he:** KA notes *he* in UR. MS *she* probably assumes, in error, the antecedent *Richesse*; as RIt notes, the Fr.
has the masc. *cil* (Lc 1089 "he").
  1112 **devyse:** KA records Skeat's recommendation to add final *-n*; it appears in UR SK FI.
  1113 **that cercle:** "i.e., the headband" (FI).
  1117 **jagounces:** Jephson (BE) corrects the *r* to *j* by the Fr. *jagonces* (Lc 1095); cf. SK. He notes further that
Speght's gloss of MS *ragounces* as "a kind of precious stone" (SPg URg) is misleading since "there is really no such
word," and he defines the *jagonce* as "the jacinthus, or hyacinthus" (so in RB et al.). § Explanations of the color

But all byfore, ful sotilly,
A fyn charboncle sette saugh I.   1120
The stoon so clere was and so bright
That, also soone as it was nyght,
Men myght seen to go, for nede,
A myle or two in lengthe and brede.   1124
Sich lyght sprang oute of the stone   22v
That Richesse wondir bright shone,
Bothe hir heed and all hir face,
And eke aboute hir al the place.

  Dame Richesse on hir honde gan lede
A yong man full of [se]melyhede,   1130
That she best loved of ony thing.
His lust was mych in housholding.
In clothyng was he ful fetys,
And loved [well to have] hors of prys.

He wende to have reproved be   1135
Of theft or moordre if that he
Hadde in his stable ony hakeney.
And therfore he desired ay
To be aqueynted with Richesse,
For all his purpos, as I gesse,   1140
[Was] for to make gret dispense
Withoute wernyng [or] diffense.
And Richesse myght it wel sustene,
And hir dispence well mayntene,
And hym alwey sich plente sende   1145
Of gold and silver for to dispende
Withoute lakke or daunger
As it were poured in a garner.
  And after on the daunce wente   23r
Largesse, that settith al hir entente   1150

1125 **sprang]** tho s. MO SK   1127 **Bothe hir]** B. on h. UR   1128 **the]** her TH²   1130 **semelyhede]** pmelyhede MS KA   1134 **well to have]** t.h. w. MS BE-KA; w. h. SK FI   1137 **ony]** an TH¹-UR SK FU SU FI; on RB¹·²   1141 **Was]** And MS KA   1142 **or]** of MS KA   1144 **dispense]** dispences TH¹-UR SK FU SU FI   1146 **dispende]** spende TH¹-UR SK-RI   1147 **lakke]** lackynge TH¹-UR SK-RI   1150 **settith]** sette TH¹-UR SK-FI

---

vary. SK states: "Godefroy [1881–1902] says that some make it to be a jacinth, but others, a garnet. Warnke explains *iagunce* (in Marie de France, *Le Fraisne*, 130) by 'ruby.'" SK GL RB cite "Lydgate (*Chorl and Bird*, st. 34, Minor Poems, Percy Soc., 1840, p. 188)," who "describes the *jagounce* as 'Cytryne of colour, lyke garnettes of entayle'" (RB). FI explains *iagounces* as "reddish brown zircons," RIf as "precious stones of reddish color."

1120 **charboncle:** "carbuncle" (MOg et al.). SK (*HF* 1363n.) quotes Vincent of Beauvais, *Spec. Nat.* 8.51, "*Carbunculus*, qui et Græcè *anthrax* dicitur, vulgariter *rubith*." FI's "ruby, garnet, or almandine" follows SK's quotation, in the note cited, from "King's Natural History of Precious Stones and Gems."

1131 **ony:** See 212n.

1134 **And loved well to have:** KA notes the emendations in both TH¹ and SK. SU Fr. 1115 has "(E amoit) les cheuaus de pris" "And loved valuable horses"), but SU (Fr. 1115n.) reports that "all MSS have *auoit* [had] for *amoit*" and suggests that "perhaps translator mistook the two."

1135–37 "He would have considered himself amenable to as much blame for having a hackney in his stable as if he had committed a theft or murder" (BE); "he would have expected to be accused of a crime equal to theft or murder, if he had kept in his stable such a horse as a hackney" (SK).

1137 **ony:** See 212n. KA notes *an* in UR.

hakeney: URg contrasts *hakeney*, "a very ordinary horse," and *hors of prys* (line 1134). TRg glosses "An ambling horse, or pad"; SKg, "old horse"; Davis (1979; cf. RIf), "riding horse . . . [prob. from place-name *Hackney*]"; FI, "nag." "The F. text has *roucin* [Lc 1116 'roncin'], whence Chaucer's *rouncy*, in [*GP*] 390" (SK).

1140 **For:** FI reports, in error (see 1141 collation), that MS reads *And*.

1142 **wernyng:** "denial" (SPg), "forbidding" (SKg; cf. URg, s.v. *warne*, MOg); "refusal" (RIf, *OED Warning* vbl. sb.², from OE *wiernung*; cf. TRg), rather than "heed" (FI, *OED Warning* vbl. sb.¹, from OE *war(e)nung*).

diffense: "prohibition" (TRg MOg), "interference, hindrance" (SKg et al.; cf. *MED defense* n. 8. [a]), rather than "care" (FI).

1147 **daunger:** "Frugality, parsimony" (URg), "Coyness, sparingness" (TRg), "difficulty" (MOg, Davis 1979), "sparing, stint" (SKg), "holding back" (RIf), "objection, reservation, or difficulty" (*MED daunǧēr* n. 3); FI's gloss, "aloofness," seems less appropriate in this context. Cf. 1049n.

1148 "As if his wealth had been poured into a garner, like so much wheat" (SK).

garner: "Properly, A Granary. It also signifies any Store-room, or place to lay up Money or other goods" (URg, citing this line). Most glosses specify "granary"; only TRg repeats "store-room"; only BE suggests "garret, where the merchants held their counting houses."

1150 **settith:** KA records a recommendation, "read *set* [W. W. Sk(eat)]"; but SK has *sette*, the spelling of TH¹ SK GL-FI (*set* TH²-UR). Both are contractions of the 3 pres. sing. *settith* (*MED setten* v.).

For to be honourable and free.
Of Alexandres kyn was she.
Hir most joye was, ywys,
Whan that she yaf and seide, "Have this."
Not Avarice, the foule caytyf,   1155
Was half to gripe so ententyf
As Largesse is to yeve and spende.
And God ynough alwey hir sende
So that the more she yaf awey,
The more, ywys, she hadde alwey.   1160
Gret loos hath Largesse, and gret pris,
For bothe [wys] folk and unwys
Were hooly to hir baundon brought,
So wel with yiftes hath she wrought.
And if she hadde an enemy,   1165
I trowe that she coude tristely
Make hym full soone hir freend to be,
So large of yift and free was she.
Therfore she stode in love and grace

Of riche and pover in every place.   1170
A full gret fool is he, ywys,
That bothe riche and nygart is.
A lord may have no maner vice   23v
That greveth more than avarice.
For nygart never with strengthe of honde   1175
May wynne gret lordship or londe,
For freendis all to fewe hath he
To doon his will perfourmed be.
And whoso wole have freendis he[e]re,
He may not holde his tresour deere.   1180
For by ensample I tell this:
Right as an adamaund, iwys,
Can drawen to hym sotylly
The iren that is leid therby,
So drawith folkes hertis, ywis,   1185
Silver and gold that yeven is.
      Largesse hadde on a robe fresh
Of riche purpur Sar[s]ynysh.

1153 **was]** it w. UR   1158 **ynough alwey]** alwaye ynowe TH¹-UR FU SU FI   1162 **wys]** the wise UR; *om.* MS KA   1166 **tristely]** craftely TH¹-UR SK FU-FI   1168 **yift]** yeftes TH¹-UR FU SU FI   **free]** wyse TH¹-UR FU SU   1171 **is he]** h. i. SP²·³   1172 **bothe]** *om.* UR   **riche and]** r. and poore and TH¹-UR FU   1176 **wynne]** w. hym TH¹-UR SK FU-FI   1179 **heere]** here MS (MS₁ *corr.*)   1181 **I tell]** tel I TH¹-UR FU SU FI   1188 **Sarsynysh]** Sarlynysh MS-KA FU

1152 "She was of the race of Alexander" (BE). Alexander the Great was noted for liberality (BE et al.).
1158 **sende:** "sent" (GL RB RIf); "Chaucer's usual preterite is *sente*" (RB), a form that is "avoided for rhyme" (RI).
1163 **baundon:** "custody" (SPg URg); "disposal" (TRg BE SK); "control" (RIf, *MED bandoun* n.). FI's gloss, "feudal service," is perhaps more specialized a sense than the context warrants. Cf. Brusendorff (1925:343–44); 1847–48n.
1166 **tristely:** There is no basis for this word in the Fr. (Lc 1142–43). TH¹'s *craftely* may have been suggested by the Fr. "a devise" (Lc 1144), interpreted as "by plan"; cf. *MED devis* (sense 3).
1168 **yift and free:** RI misrecords FI as reading *yeftes and wyse*.
1172 **riche:** SU suggests that TH¹'s addition of the words *and poore*, "which destroy meter and correspondence to Fr., are probably printer's error" due to repetition of the phrase from line 1170.
1178 **will:** SKt assumes that MS *will* represents an abbreviation for *wille*. It is not certain that, in MS, the crossed -*ll* is a consistent abbreviation, except possibly for -*lles*; see above, "The Manuscript Hands: The Scribe (MS₁)."
1179 **heere:** "second *e* written above the line" (KA) by MS₁.
1182 **adamaund:** "magnet, diamond" (MOg); "lodestone" (SK RB); "magnet" (SKg FI). RB RI refer to notes to *KnT* A 1990 and *PF* 148. RB explains the development of the word (*KnT* 1990n.): "an indestructible substance (from α privative, and δαμαω); finally applied to the diamond. It was also used of the loadstone and incorrectly associated with the Latin 'ad-amare' [fall in love with, be attracted to]." DiMarco's note to *KnT* 1990 (in RI) adduces "Bartolomaeus Anglicus 16.8, tr. Trevisa, 2:833."
1185 **hertis:** "as in v. 76 . . . to be read as one syllable" (GL).
1188 **Sarsynysh:** TRg suggests this emendation: the reading "should perhaps be Sarsinishe, from the Fr. *Sarrasinois*." KA recommends it. SK explains: "the form *sarlynysh* evidently arose from the common mistake of reading a long *s* . . . as an *l.*" The emendation follows the Fr., which RBt RIt cite as follows: "*sarazinesche* (var. *sarradinesche*)" (RIt). Of these alternatives, *sarrazinesche* appears in KA Fr. (1158), SU Fr. (1164); and Lc (1162); *sarradinesche* appears in Ln (1164), which does not report the variant spelling. § SP²·³g URg explain the material as "a kind of silke like Sarcenet," TRg (adducing Du Cange, *saracenicum* and *saracenum*) as "a sort of fine silk, used for veils . . . still called *Sarcenet*." SK explains the sense as "Saracenic, or coloured by an Eastern dye," and compares "mod. E. *sarsnet*, a derivative from the same source."

Wel fourmed was hir face and cleere,
And opened hadde she hir colere,   1190
For she right there hadde, in present,
Unto a lady maad present
Of a gold broche, ful wel wrought.
And certys, it myssatte hir nought,
For thorough hir smokke, wrought
    with silk,   24r
The flesh was seen as white as mylk.   1196
Largesse, that worthy was and wys,
Hilde by the honde a knyght of prys,
Was sibbe to Artour of Britaigne.
And that was he that bare the ensaigne   1200
Of worship and the [gounfanoun].
And yit he is of sich renoun
That men of hym seye faire thynges
Byfore barouns, erles, and kynges.
This knyght was comen all newly   1205
Fro tourne[i]yng faste by.
The[re] hadde he don gret chyvalrie
Thorough his vertu and his maistrie,
And for the love of his lemman

He caste doun many a doughty man.   1210
    And next hym daunced dame Fraunchise,
Arayed in full noble gyse.
She was not broune ne dunne of hewe,
But white as snowe fall[en] newe.
Hir nose was wrought at poynt devys,   1215
For it was gentyl and tretys,
With eyen gladde and browes bente.
Hir here doun to hir helis wente.
And she was symple as dowve [on] tree.   24v
Ful debonaire of herte was she;   1220
She durst never seyn ne do
But that that hir longed to.
And if a man were in distresse,
And for hir love in hevynesse,
Hir herte wolde have full gret pite,   1225
She was so amiable and free.
For were a man for hir bistadde,
She wolde ben right sore adradde
That she dide over-gret outrage
But that she hym holpe his harme to aswage; 1230
Hir thought it elles a vylanye.

1194 **myssate**] myslate TH²   1201 **gounfanoun**] Gousfaucoun MS-SP¹ SP³ BE KA FU; Gousfauuoun SP²; gounfaucoun MO   1204 **erles**] and Erles UR   1206 **tourneiyng**] tourneryng MS KA; t. there UR; a t. GL 1207 **There hadde he]** The h. he MS KA; Where he had UR   1210 **He]** Had SK   1213 **was]** nas TH¹-UR FU SU FI   1214 **fallen]** fall MS KA (*both with crossed -ll*); falle BE MO   1219 **dowve]** downe TH¹,² FU   **on]** of MS MO KA   1221 **never]** neither TH¹-UR GL FU SU   1222 **that that]** t. thing t. SK FI   **longed]** longeth TH¹-SP³ FU SU FI; belongith UR   1231 **elles]** al TH¹-UR FU SU; ell GL

1190–93   SK paraphrases (cf. FI): "Her neck-band was thrown open, because she had given away the brooch, with which she used to fasten it."

1191   **in present:** "just then" (URg; cf. SKg); "now, at present" (*MED present(e* n.[1] 3. [c]).

1194   Following this line, as KA notes, "two lines [are] left blank in MS"; these are the last ruled lines of folio 23v.

1199   BE (cf. SK) explains: "This knight is represented as related (*sibbe*) to the celebrated King Arthur, who was the *beau idéal* of chivalry."

1200–01   "King Arthur is said to be the ensign or banner, and gonfanon of honour, as the office of bearing the gonfanon, or banner of the Church, was the highest dignity of knighthood" (BE).

1201   **gounfanoun:** KA endorses UR's emendation; BE et al. note the Fr. *gonfanon* (Lc 1177). Regarding MS *gousfaucoun*, SK states (cf. FI): "the scribe seems to have thought that it meant a goshawk!" URg and SU compare *gonfenoun* at line 2018. § UR glosses (cf. TRg; and MOg, s.v. *Gownfaucoun*), "The Chief Banner, or Standard"; not necessarily "of the Church," as BE seems to imply (see above, 1200–01n.). SK (cf. FI) specifies "war-banner"; GL and Davis (1979) gloss "pennon."

1206   **tourneiyng:** GL's emendation, based on the Fr. *un* (Lc 1182 "un tornoiement"), amends the meter, but the ME gerund is not exactly parallel to the Fr. noun. KA notes UR's *there*.

1213   **broune:** See Merlo (1981) on the color brown in Chaucer.

1214   **fallen:** The crossed -*ll* of MS may represent an abbreviation for a participial *falle*, see "The Manuscript Hands: The Scribe (MS₁)," but all eds. except BE-KA add a y-prefix, noted in TH¹ by KA.

1215   **at poynt devys:** "with great exactness, with great regularity" (SK); "excellently" (FI). SK adduces *HF* 917. See also 830n.

1216   **tretys:** SK compares lines 932 and 1016 and *GP* 152.

1231   "It seemed to her a base thing" (BE).

     elles: RBt SU FI report MS reading as *ell*; it is rather *ell*, a form which I expand silently (as do BE MO SK) as an abbreviation for *elles*; see above, 300n. and "The Manuscript Hands: The Scribe (MS₁)."

And she hadde on a sukkenye
That not of [hempene] heerdis was;
So fair was noon in all Arras.
Lord, it was ridled fetysly! 1235
Ther nas [nat] a poynt, trewly,
Tha[t] it nas in his right assise.
Full wel clothed was Fraunchise,
For ther is no cloth sittith bet
On damysell than doth roket. 1240
A womman wel more fetys is

In roket than in cote, ywis.
The whyte roket, rydled faire, 25r
Bitokeneth that full debonaire
And swete was she that it bere. 1245
  Bi hir daunced a bachelere;
I can not telle you what he hight,
But faire he was and of good hight,
All hadde he be, I sey no more,
The lord[is] sone of Wyndesore. 1250
  And next that daunced Curtesye,

1233 **hempene]** hempe ne MS BE-KA GL; hempe TH¹-UR FU SU   1236 **nas nat a]** nas a MS BE-KA; nas n. oo SK   1237 **That]** Tha MS KA   1239 **is]** nys TH¹-UR FU SU FI   1244 **Bitokeneth]** Bitokened SK 1250 **lordis]** lord MS (MS₁ *corr.*)

1232 **sukkenye:** SPg URg define as "a white attire like a rotchet" (cf. *roket* in lines 1242–43), TRg as "a loose frock, worn over their other clothes by carters, &c." SK quotes Cotgrave (1611): "a canvas Jacket, frock, or Gaberdine; such a one as our Porters wear." This "loose frock," SK suggests, citing Méon's glossary (1814), probably was made of fine linen; "we are expressly told [line 1233], that it was *not* made of hempen hards." Other glossators variously abridge the features reported above. On the etymology: SK compares Russian *sukno* "cloth," OED *Suckeny* derives it from OF *soucanie* "of Slavonic origin," and MED *sukkenie* n. says that the ultimate origin is Germanic. RR reads *sorquenie* (Lc 1208).

1233 **hempene heerdis:** "Hurds, Tow, the course part of Hemp or Flax when dressed" (URg, s.v. *Herdis*); "coarse parts ('hards') of flax (hemp)" (RIf). Other glosses merely abridge these explanations.

1234 **Arras:** chief city of *Artoys*, in northern France, "early known for its woollen manufacture and production of tapestries" (Magoun 1955:120; 1961:22–23); "famous for its fine cloth (whence 'arras')" (FI).

1235–37 "Every point was in its right place; because it was so evenly gathered ['ridled']." (SK 1235n.)

1235 **ridled:** pleated (SP¹g URg TRg); gathered or pleated as a curtain (SK et al.). As BE et al. note, the Fr. has *cu(e)illie et jointe* (Lc 1211, Ln 1213); both Ln Lc take *cu(e)illie* as pa. part. of *cueillir* "gather." But Ln (1213n.) regards the ME translation ("'ridled' [plissée]") as inaccurate and takes *cuillie* in this context as meaning "ajustée," "fitted"; while Lcg glosses the entire phrase *cueillie et jointe* as *ajustée*. SK (cf. FI) notes "O.F. *ridel* (F. *rideau*), a curtain"; MED *ridel* n.(2) reports "AL *ridellus, redellus* curtain." Adducing lines 1236–37 (see 1235–37n.), SK questions BE's gloss "pierced like a riddle"; this sense—and perhaps the gloss "checkred" (SP²·³g)—arises from a false derivation from *riddle* "sieve"; MED *ridel* n.(1) gives the etymology as "LOE *hriddel*, cp. AL *ridellus* sieve."

1236 **nat a:** Presumably MS *nat* was omitted through eyeskip. KA endorses Skeat's suggestion, for *a* read *oo*, the stressed form which appears in SK, "perhaps correctly" (RBt); GL glosses *a poynt* as "one point."

1239–40 Roscow (1981:111–12) cites these lines as an example of the ellipsis of the relative subject-pronoun when "the antecedent is the subject or complement in an existential clause introduced by *there* or *it*." Roscow says that "Chaucer does not often use [this construction] in its positive form" and that "it occurs more frequently in ME. in negative sentences where the antecedent is a negative pronoun or [as here] a noun premodified by *no*." Roscow also cites *BD* 740–41, *HF* 1044, *TC* 1.203, 3.886, 5.1088, *RvT* A 3932, *FranT* F 854–55. See also 5176n. On omission of the relative object-pronoun, see 2106n.

1240 **roket:** RI notes that the Fr. reads *sorquenie* (Lc 1216), the word translated as *sukkenye* in line 1232. Thus, a *roket* is a short frock (BE et al.). Early glosses are "a linnen garment" (SPg); "a Frock, loose Gaberdine, or Gown of Canvas worn by a Labourer over the rest of his clothes; Also a Prelate's *Rochet*" (URg, quoting Blount 1656); and "a loose upper garment" (TRg). BE SK RB FI also note that the word is used of the bishop's short surplice. GL glosses "linen vest."

1241–42 The roket "is said . . . to be more becoming than a *cote*, a plain dress" (RI 1240n.).

1243 **rydled:** See 1235n. (SKt).

1244 **Bitokeneth:** Even while noting that KA's suggested emendation, followed by SK, is based on the Fr. imperfect *senefioit* (Lc 1220 "signified"), SU maintains that the emendation is unnecessary.

1249 **All hadde he be:** "even if he had been" (SK).

1250 **The lordis sone of Wyndesore:** the son of the lord of Windsor (RB FI RIf). On the order of words, RB compares *ClT* E 1170; see RB's note to this line. David (RI) refers to RI, p. xxxviii, where Davis discusses this idiom.

That preised was of lowe and hye,
For neither proude ne foole was she.
She for to daunce called me—
I pray God yeve hir right good grace— 1255
Whanne I come first into the place.
She was not nyce ne outrageous,
But wys and ware and vertuous,
Of faire speche and of faire answere;
Was never wight mysseid of hire; 1260
She bar rancour to no wight.
Clere broune she was, and therto bright
Of face, of body [avenaunt];
I wot no lady so plesaunt.
She [were] worthy for to bene 1265

An emperesse or crowned quene.
And by hir wente a knyght dauncyng, 25v
That worthy was and wel spekyng,
And ful wel koude he don honour.
The knyght was faire and styf in stour, 1270
And in armure a semely man,
And wel biloved of his lemman.
Faire Idilnesse thanne saugh I,
That alwey was me fast by.
Of hir have I, without fayle, 1275
Told yow the shap and apparayle,
For, as I seide, loo, that was she
That dide to me so gret bounte
That she the gate of the gardyn

1255 **yeve]** give to UR   **right]** om. TH¹-BE FU   1256 **Whanne]** For w. TH¹-UR FU   **into]** to
UR   1257 **was]** nas TH¹-UR FU SU FI   1259 **and of]** and TH¹-UR FU SU FI   1261 **She bar]** S. bare
no TH¹-UR SK FU-FI; S. ne b. MO; Ne she b. GL   1263 **of body]** and body TH¹-UR FU SU   **avenaunt]**
wenaunt MS KA   1265 **were]** om. MS KA   1270 **The]** That FU   1273 **thanne]** than nexte UR
1278 **to]** om. SK   1279 **That she]** She TH¹-SP³ FU; She me UR   **the gardyn]** that g. TH¹-UR FU SU FI

In "Annotations and corrections" (SP¹, sig. 4b6v), Speght asserts that this line is not in the French, "that there was no
lord Winsore in those daies," and that Chaucer added the line "to gratifie Iohn of Gaunt, or some other of the sonnes
of Edward the third." Francis Thynne (1599;1875:65–66) dismisses this theory and corrects two errors made by
Speght. First, the line does appear in the Fr. (Lc 1226), and Thynne explains, apparently assuming that Speght's
French text was not faulty, that in French orthography *qu* is equivalent to English *w*. Second, Thynne notes that
while there may not have been a lord Windsor in Chaucer's day, there was a Sir William Windsor, whom the French,
he asserts, called "seigneure de Windesore" (BE SK), thinks like Speght
that Chaucer added it "as a compliment to some of his patrons" (1774–81:1.370). Tyrwhitt, who identifies the lord of
Windsor as Edward III (TR 3.314), states that *RR* here reads "Il sembloit estre *filz de Roy*." Without a collation of
early *RR* editions, the variation in the Fr. text can only be roughly accounted for. Ln (1227–28t) records one MS—
Ga—that omits the relevant couplet; Ln notes (1.42–43) that the text of *RR* remains substantially the same through
the first 14 editions and that Lenglet du Fresnoy's edition (Amsterdam and Paris, 1735) reproduces the eighth of
these, Vérard's edition of 1499–1500 (Ln 1.45). See 766n.
   Since later editors of *Rom* use Fr. texts where the couplet appears, they look for a lord of Windsor (and a son)
contemporary with Guillaume de Lorris; Henry III, who reigned from 1216 to 1272, and his son Prince Edward, born
1239, are the usual candidates (BE et al.). SK reports that Henry was called "Henry of Windsor" in "the satirical
ballad 'Against the King of Almaigne,' printed in Percy's Ballads, Series II. Book I, and in Wright's 'Political Songs,' p.
69." But, as RB FI RI note, Ln (1228n.) associates the reference with King Arthur: in Chrétien de Troyes's *Cligés*
1237–57 (1227–47, ed. Micha 1965) there is a description of Windsor, which Arthur captures from Count Angrés; and
in *Rigomer* 13188, Arthur is "le roi de Windeskore."
   lordis: "*is* written above the line" (KA) by MS₁.
   1259 **and of:** KA recommends omitting *of*.
   1260 **hire:** All eds. except BE-KA have *here*, for rhyme, and KA recommends *here*. But, as RIt notes (716n),
hir is the consistent MS form for the fem. oblique singular.
   1261 **She bar:** KA, adapting MO's *She ne bar*, recommends *Ne she bar*.
   1262–63 *Rom* follows the Lc version of *RR* here (KA Fr. and SU Fr.), not the Ln version (SK Fr.), which reads
lune (moon) for *brune* and has an extra couplet involving stars and candles. RIt (1263n) quotes, from Ln (1241t), the
Lc version of *Rom* 1263.
   1263 **avenaunt:** Glossing, generally consistent, shows a variety of connotations: "agreeable" (SPg URg; the
French etymology is noted first in SP²g); "comely" (SPg URg SKg GLg), "beautiful" (URg MOg); "pleasant" (MOg,
Davis 1979), "pleasing" (RI); "graceful" (SKg, Davis 1979); "suitable" (GLg); "friendly, convenient" (RBg).
   1264 **plesaunt:** MS₂ adds a second *t* to the end of this word.
   1265 **were:** TH¹'s emendation. KA suggests *was well* (not *well was*, as GL reports) and notes TH¹'s *were*.

Undide and lete me passen in.
    And after daunced, as I gesse,
[Youthe], fulfilled of lustynesse,
That nas not yit twelve yeer of age,
With herte wylde and thought volage.
Nyce she was, but she ne mente   1285
Noon harme ne slight in hir entente,
But oonly lust and jolyte;
For yong folk, [wele] witen ye,
Have lytel thought but on her play.
Hir lemman was biside alway   1290
In sich a gise that he hir kyste   26r
At all tymes that hym lyste,
That all the daunce myght it see;
They make no force of pryvete.
For who spake of hem yvel or well,   1295
They were ashamed never a dell,
But men myght seen hem kisse there,
As it two yonge dowves were.
For yong was thilke bachelere;
Of beaute wot I noon his pere;   1300

And he was right of sich an age   1280
As Youthe his leef, and sich corage.
    The lusty folk [thus] daunced there,
And also other that with hem were,
That weren all of her meyne;   1305
Ful hende folk and wys and free,
And folk of faire port, truly,
There were all comunly.
    Whanne I hadde seen the countenaunces
Of hem that ladden thus these daunces,   1310
Thanne hadde I will to gon and see
The gardyne that so lyked me,
And loken on these faire lore[r]es,
On pyn-trees, cedres, and oliveris.   1314
The daunces thanne eended were,   26v
For many of hem that daunced there
Were with her loves went awey
Undir the trees to have her pley.
    A, Lord, they lyved lustyly!
A gret fool were he, sikirly,   1320
That nolde, his thankes, such lyf lede!

1282 **Youthe]** And she MS-KA FU   1283 **nas]** has SU FI   1288 **wele]** wole MS MO KA   1295 **who]** who so TH¹-SP³ FU SU FI   **yvel]** ill UR   1298 **As]** As though UR   1302 **his]** is MO   1303 **thus]** that MS-KA GL FU   1306 **and wys]** wyse TH¹-SP³ FU SU FI; bothe wise UR   1308 **There]** They GL   1313 **loreres]** loreyes MS MO KA; Laurelles TH¹-SP¹ FU   1314 **and]** *om.* UR   **oliveris]** Olmeres TH¹-SP³ GL-FI   1315 **The]** For SU FI   1317 **Were]** Where TH²   1321 **lede]** to lede UR

1282   **Youthe:** As KA et al. point out, Brink (1870:29–30) suggests this emendation, on the basis of the Fr. *Joinece* (Lc 1258). SU FI also call attention to the Fr., SKt to *Rom* 1302.

1283   **nas:** SU's *has* may be a typographical error, or it may reflect Fr. *avoit*; SU offers no comment.

1284   **volage:** "vnconstant" (SPg); SP²g-UR add that the word is of French origin. TRg, referring also to *ManT* H 239, glosses "Light, giddy" (cf. MOg); SK, "flighty, giddy."

1288   **wele:** TH¹'s emendation (*wel*), as RIt notes, follows the Fr. *bien* (Lc 1265).

1294   "I should like to read—'They ne made force of privetee'; pronounced *They n' mad-e,* &c. But *no fors* is usual" (SK).

1303   **thus:** This emendation, which KA attributes to Skeat, improves the syntax of MS *and,* and, as RBt et al. note, follows the Fr. *Ensi* (Lc 1277); SKt compares *Rom* 1310. FI incorrectly reports MS TH¹ as reading *there.*

1308   **all:** MS has *all,* and here the meter would indicate that the crossed *-ll* is an abbreviation for *-lle;* but no such consistent pattern obtains in MS. See above, "The Manuscript Hands: The Scribe (MS₁)."

1313   **loreres:** KA recommends *loreris,* following UR's *laureris.* KA et al. adduce the Fr. *loriers* (Lc 1287 "laurel trees"). The forms with *-ll-* (TH¹-SP¹ FU) are from Latin, those with *-r-* from French. See *MED laurel* n., *laurer* n. See also 1379n.

1314   **oliveris:** "olive trees." This reading has no basis in the manuscripts that Ln collates; and, although TH¹'s *olmeres* "elm-trees," has slight support in one MS (Da "ormes," Ln 1290t), it is probable that, as RIt notes, the TH¹ "printer has misread the minims in [MS] *iu* as *m.*" Lc 1288 reads *noiers* "walnut-trees," Ln 1290 *moriers* "mulberry-trees." KA Fr. 1282 (from MS Fo) and SU Fr. 1290 (from MS Go) print *moriers,* which, GL suggests, "was perhaps read as ormiers." GL RIt compare *Rom* 1381, where "*olyveris . . .* translates 'oliviers'" (GL).

1315   **The:** SU's error anticipates the first word of line 1316.

    eended: KA and RBt note that SK has *y-ended,* "perhaps correctly" (RBt).

1316   **hem:** RB RI spell *them,* without comment.

1321   **his thankes:** "with his good will" (URg-BE), "willingly" (MOg et al.), rather than "thankfully" (FI); cf. *OED Thank* sb. 2b. TR compares (TRg) French *son gré* and (TR 4.221) Latin *libenter.* BE SK compare *KnT* A 1626; SK adds *KnT* A 2107.

For this dar I seyn, oute of drede,
That whoso myght so wel fare,
For better lyf durst hym not care;
For ther nys so good paradys   1325
As to have a love at his devys.
  Oute of that place wente I thoo,
And in that gardyn gan I goo,
Pleyyng alonge full meryly.
The God of Love full hastely   1330
Unto hym Swete-Lokyng clepte;
No lenger wolde he that [he] kepte
His bowe of gold, that shoon so bright.
He [badde] hym [bend it] anoon ryght;
And he full soone [it] sette an-ende,   1335

And at a braid he gan it bende,
And toke hym of his arowes fyve,
Full sharp and redy for to dryve.
Now God, that sittith in mageste,   27r
Fro deedly woundes he kepe me,   1340
If so be that he hadde me shette!
For if I with his arowe mette,
It hadde me greved sore, iwys.
But I, that nothyng wist of this,
Wente up and doun full many a wey,   1345
And he me folwed fast alwey;
But nowhere wold I reste me
Till I hadde in all the gardyn be.
  The gardyn was, by mesuryng,

1324 **durst]** thurte SK   1326 **to]** *om.* SK   1332 **he kepte]** she k. MS-KA FU   1334 **badde hym bend it]** hadde hym bent MS-KA FU   1335 **it]** *om.* MS-KA GL FU   1340 **he]** *om.* SK   1341 **hadde me shette]** wol m. shete SK   1342 **mette]** mete SK   1343 **hadde me greved]** wol me greven SK   1348 **in all the gardyn]** a. t. yerde in SK

1324 **durst:** needed (impersonal). See 1089n.
1326 **his:** "often indefinite in Middle English" (GL).
1332 **he kepte:** This is KA's suggestion.
1334 **badde hym bend it:** KA suggests this emendation, which follows the Fr. (Lc 1306 "li a lors comandé a tendre"). SK notes that "confusion of *b* and *h* is not uncommon." On *bend*, SK adduces line 1336.
1335 **it:** KA attributes this emendation to Skeat. SU notes that the word "seems necessary."
1336 **at a braid:** In SP *brayd* is glossed "a brunt" (*burnt* in SP³); *OED*, s.v. *Brunt*, defines "at a brunt" as "at one blow, at once, suddenly." Cf. the following glosses of "at a braid": "at a start" (URg TRg BE RBg); "suddenly" (BE RIf); "in a turn, at once" (MOg); "in a moment" (SKg); "immediately" (GL). With FI's gloss, "with a quick movement," cf. *MED breid* n.(1), 1. (a). BE, following TRg, states that "the original is *tantost*," but it is *tot maintenant* (Lc 1308); *tantost* appears three lines down (Lc 1311).
1337 Sweet Looking hands to the God of Love five of his arrows. For *took* in the sense "delivered, handed over, gave" see *OED Take* v., sense 60, and *MED tāken* v., sense 31a (a); in this sense, *toke hym* translates Fr. *li bailla* (Lc 1309 "gave to him"). FI reads *hym of* as "from him," a sense that would require the subject of *toke* to be the God of Love, contrary to the Fr.
1339 **sittith:** SK FI have the contracted form *sit*. KA notes Skeat's preference.
1341–43 KA suggests the emendations adopted in SK—"he wole me shete" (1341n.), "it wol me greue" (1343n.)—and notes TH¹'s form, *mete* (1342n.). SK (1341n.) argues that "*shette* is altogether a false form; the pp. of *sheten*, to shoot, is *shoten*." Koch (1890:10; 1900*a*:66) endorses the emendation as following the Fr., but he notes that the received text infringes no grammatical rule. According to RBt, "it is barely possible that *shete* is a strong past part. from *sheten*, though the normal form is *shote(n)*"; RB suggests (1341n.) that "possibly *shette* is for a past participle *shete(n)*" (cf. RIt: "*shette* may represent a variant form of the pp."). *MED shēten* v. lists *shet(t)(e(n* among the forms of the pa. part.
1341–42 **shette : mette:** See 1341–43n. Although the forms *shete : mete* appear in TH¹-UR SK FU SU FI, I collate them only for SK, where, as RB notes (1341n.), Skeat clearly intends them as the infinitive *shete* and pres. t. *mete*; in other cases, tense sequence shows them to be var. spellings of the pa. part. *shette* and pa. t. *mette*. RB and RIt both note that SK provides correct rhyme but breaks the sequence of tenses.
1341 **hadde:** SK's *wol*, GL and RIt note, has support in the Fr. (Marteau 1364 [= Michel 1324] "Se il fait tant que a moi traie" "if he does so much as to shoot at me"; cf. Lc 1314 "se tant avient qu'il a moi traie").
1342 **For:** GL (1341n.) suggests: "perhaps join [line 1341] with [line 1342] by reading *Or* for *For*."
1343 **hadde me greved:** KA suggests *wol me greue*.
1348 **in all the gardyn:** SK states: "in ll. 1461, 1582, the F. *vergier* is translated by *yerde*. So here, and in l. 1447 (as Dr. Kaluza suggests [KA]) we must read *yerde in*, to make sense. . . . So in l. 1366, *yerde* would be better than *gardin*." The problem may be one of meter rather than sense. The Fr. uses *jardin* as a synonym for *vergier* (Lc 498); our text uses *garden* about four times as often as *yard*; and *MED gardin* n. shows that the word may have the

Right evene and square in compassing;	1350	That baren notes in her sesoun 1360
It as long was as it was large.		Such as men notemygges calle,
Of fruyt hadde every tree his charge,		That swote of savour ben withall.
But it were any hidous tree		And almandres gret plente, 27v
Of which ther were two or three.		Fyges, and many a date-tree
There were, and that wote I full well,	1355	There wexen, if men hadde nede, 1365
Of pome-garnettys a full gret dell;		Thorough the gardyn in length and brede.
That is a fruyt full well to lyke,		Ther was eke wexyng many a spice,
Namely to folk whanne they ben sike.		As clowe-gelofre and lycorice,
And trees there were, of gret foisoun,		Gyngevre and greyn de parys,

---

1350 **in**] by SP¹   1351 **as long was**] w. a. l. SK GL   1356 **dell**] doll RB²   1359 **of**] *om.* TH¹-BE SK FU-RI   1363 **almandres**] of a. UR   1365 **wexen**] weren TH¹-UR SK FU SU FI   **if**] if that UR 1368 **clowe-gelofre**] clowe, gylofre TH² ST-UR   1369 **parys**] paradys SK GL SU FI

---

sense of orchard as well as garden. RBt RIt compare line 1447 and their notes (see 1447n.). On ME *verger* in Fragment B, see 3234n., 3851n. Cf. 481–82n.

1351   **as long was:** SK's reading follows KA's suggestion.

1352–66   RI cites Curtius (1953:194–95) "on the 'mixed forest' as a feature of the *locus amoenus.*"

1352–54   RB RI point out that the translator misunderstood the Fr. (Lc 1324–27 "Nul arbre n'i a, qui fruit charge, / se n'est aucuns arbres hideus, / dont il n'i ait ou trois ou deus / ou vergier, ou plus, se devient" "except for certain hideous trees, there was no fruit-bearing tree of which there were not two or three, or perhaps more, in the orchard"); cf. Ln 1326n. FI's paraphrase—"the orchard had every kind of fruit tree except two or three that were too hideous"—approximates the sense of the Fr. in excluding the hideous trees; but it misreads the ME, which includes them: "Every tree—unless it were some hideous tree, of which there were two or three—had its burden of fruit."

1354   **two or three:** Ln 1328, which RB quotes (1353n.), has *un ou deus* ("one or two"; cf. Lc 1.265); Lc 1326 reads *trois ou deus* ("three or two").

1355–72   These trees, says BE (note to line 1368), "are most of them exotics, and are opposed to the *homly*, or indigenous trees" of lines 1373ff.

1359   **of gret foisoun:** Omitting *of* (noted by KA in UR BE), SK reads the phrase as "a great abundance (of them)," i.e. of trees. While the unemended phrase could have the same sense, it could also mean "of great abundance (in bearing)," a sense that the succeeding lines support.

1361–62   **calle : withall:** MS has *calle : withall*, where *-ll* is a possible abbreviation for *-lle*; see above, "The Manuscript Hands: The Scribe (MS₁)."

1361   **notemygges:** SK finds this spelling in the *Promptorium Parvulorum* and calls attention to the form *notemuges* in Th B² 1953.

1362   *Marginalium:* See above, "Other Marginalia," for the missing-word puzzle "written by a 16th cent. hand" (KA) that appears in the lower margin of fol. 27r, after line 1362.

1363   **almandres:** "almond trees" (URg et al.). SK RB RI have *alemandres*, GL *almanderes*, to repair a metrical deficiency; SK GL RBt adduce the Fr. *alemandiers* (Lc 1335), and SK, citing *OED Almond* (see also *MED alma(u)nde* n., *almaunder* n.), notes that "the O.F. for 'almond' was at first *alemande.*"

1365   **wexen:** TH¹'s *weren* may be a misreading—*r/x* confusion is possible—or it may be a correction from the Fr. "i trovoit" (Lc 1338 "there found"; noted in SU FI).

1366   **Thorough the gardyn:** SKt suggests emendation: "*Throughout the yard?*" See 1348n.

1368–70   TR (4.316) regards this passage as "the most apposite illustration" of Th B² 1951–53. As noted in SK (1361n.), of the six spices listed here, "lycorys," "cetewale," and "clowe-gylofre" appear in Th B² 1951–52; "notemuge" (line 1361) appears in Th B² 1953.

1368   **clowe-gelofre:** T. Thomas (URg) suggests reading *Clove-gilofre* here for UR's *Clowe, Gilofre.* § UR glosses *gilofre* as "A Plant commonly called Clove-Gilli-flower, *Caryophyllus hortensis.*" TRg adduces TR's note to Th B² 1952: "*Clou de girofle.* Fr. *Caryophyllus* Lat. A clove-tree, or the fruit of it." In support TR quotes *Mandeville's Travels*, ch. 26, and adduces the present passage. BE glosses: "the French clou (nail) giroflée, which we call simply clove" (cf. MOg et al.).

1369   **Gyngevre:** TH¹-SP³ spell *Gynger(e)*; UR (followed by TRg) has *Gingiber.*

    greyn de parys: URg reports that Skinner (1671) "thinks it to be contracted from *Grains of Paradise*; The Seed of a Plant brought from *Guinea.*" TRg, repeating the suggested derivation, defines simply as "a sort of

Canell and setewale of prys,   1370
And many a spice delitable
To eten whan men rise fro table.
   And many homly trees ther were
That peches, coynes, and apples beere,
Medlers, plowmes, perys, chesteyns,   1375
Cherys, of which many oon fayne is,
Notes, aleys, and bolas,
That for to seen it was solas.
With many high lore[r] and pyn

Was renged clene all that gardyn,   1380
With cipres and with olyvers,
Of which that nygh no plente heere is.
There were elmes grete and stronge,
Maples, asshe, oke, aspe, planes longe,
Fyne ew, popler, and lyndes faire,   1385
And othere trees full many a payre.
   [What shulde I tel you more of it?   TH¹:135b
There were so many trees yet
That I shulde al encombred be

1377 **aleys]** and a. UR   1379 **lorer]** lorey MS BE-KA   1387 *Lines* 1387-1482 *Out:* MS *(two leaves missing); supplied from* TH¹

Spice" and adduces *MilT* A 3690, where the word *grain* alone appears in the same meaning as the full phrase. SK cites Cotgrave (1611), "*Graine de paradis*, the spice called Grains"; Phillips (1658), "*Paradisi grana* . . . cardamum-seed"; and, from *OED* (s.v. *Cardamom*), Langham (1579), "Cardamom, or Graines of Paradise." RBg FI, Davis (1979), and RIf also gloss as "cardamom." But according to *OED*, *cardamom*, while "occas. applied to the capsules of A. Meleguetta of Western Africa, usually called Grains of Paradise," refers as well to "species of *Amomum* and *Elettaria* . . . natives of the East Indies and China." *MED* defines *greyn de paris* (s.v. *grain* n. 5) as "the seed of Amomum Meleguetta used as spice and in medicines" and (s.v. *parais* n. 1. [b]) as "a spice, prob. cardamom or Amomum cardamon."

       parys: KA recommends *paradys* on the basis of the Fr. *paradis* (KA Fr. 1335), and SK calls the form *parys* "a stupid blunder." But the form *parys* is well attested (*MED parais* n.). RB RI refer to Schöffler (1918), who shows that Lat. *paradisus* gave two forms in OF, the learned *paradis* (as in Lc 1341) and the normal development to *parais* or *pareis*. The latter may have given rise to the form *parevis*, as in Ln (1343), as well as to the folk-etymological *Paris* (see also Pope 1934, sections 267, 660). Thus, as RI notes, "there is no reason to emend to 'paradys.'"

    1370 **Canell:** "Synamon tree" (SPg; from Dutch, according to SP²·³g); "Cinnamon . . . Fr[ench] *Canelle*" (URg et al.).

       setewale: TRg-MOg GLg identify as valerian, but SK et al. gloss as zedoary, "a spice resembling ginger" (Davis 1979), "used as a condiment and stimulant" (RIf); cf. Skeat (SKg, s.v. *Cetewale*), who cites *Promptorium Parvulorum* for this sense, recognizes it as a species of *Curcuma*, and notes that "the name . . . was also given to valerian." *MED setewāle* n. (a) specifies "the root of a plant of the species Curcuma, esp. the long zedoary (Curcuma zedoaria)."

    1372 **whan men rise fro table:** "These spices appear to have been eaten at dessert, as we sometimes see candied orange peel, ginger, or other pungent sweetmeats" (BE).

    1374 **coynes:** "quinches [French]" (SP²·³g); "quinces" (URg et al.); "quins" (RB). The singular *quince* arises as a misunderstanding of this plural (SK RB).

    1375 **chesteyns:** "Chesnuts . . . Fr. *Chastaigne*" (URg et al.).

    1376 **Cherys:** SK adopts the form *Cheryse*, from TH¹ (also in TH²-UR FU SU FI), perhaps as a normalization on the basis of AF *cherise*, a sing. taken as pl.; but *Cherys* is the pl. of the back-formed sing. *cheri* (see *MED cheri* n.).

    1377-78 **bolas : solas:** "the rhyme is only a single one" (SK), i.e. masculine.

    1377 **aleys:** Not "aloes" (URg) or "lote-tree" (TRg MOg) but service-berries; as SK et al. note, the word is adapted from the Fr. *alies* (Lc 1350). SK RB say that no other example is known in English; *MED alīes* n. has one other example, of the sing. *alie*, from a Latin nominale of about 1350.

       bolas: "bullace . . . a sort of wild plum" (URg et al.), or "sloe" (TRg); "Prunus insititia" (*MED*); "damson plum" (FI).

    1379-86 With the tree list SK (1384n.) and RB (1383n.) compare lists in *PF* 176-82 and *KnT* A 2921-23.

    1379 **lorer:** KA recommends this emendation; it follows TH¹'s *laurer*. SK notes MS *loreyes* at line 1313; see 1313n.

    1380 **renged:** "ranged, placed in rows" (SKg et al.), rather than "ringed" (FI).

    1384 **Maples:** KA recommends *maple*, perhaps for meter. The Fr. has the plural *arables* (Lc 1358 "maples").

    1385 **Fyne ew:** "I should read *Pyn, ew* . . . only we have had *pyn* already, in l. 1379" (SK).

    1387-1482 Two leaves are missing from MS, and these lines are supplied from TH¹ (KA SKt RBt SU FI RIt) or "Speght" (BE). See above, "The Missing Leaves."

Er I had rekened every tree. 1390
  These trees were sette, that I devyse,
One from another in assyse
Fyve fadome or sixe, I trowe so;
But they were hye and great also,
And for to kepe out wel the sonne, 1395
The croppes were so thicke yronne,
And every braunche in other knytte,
And ful of grene leves [sette],
That sonne myght there none discende,
Lest [it] the tender grasses shende. 1400
There myght men does and roes yse,
And of squyrels ful great plente
From bowe to bowe alwaye lepynge.
Connes there were also playenge,
That comyn out of her clapers, 1405

Of sondrie colours and maners,
And maden many a tourneyeng
Upon the fresshe grasse spryngyng.
  In places sawe I welles there,
In whiche there no frogges were, 1410
And fayre in shadowe was every wel.
But I ne can the nombre tel
Of stremys smal that by devyse
Myrthe had done come through condyse,
Of whiche the water in rennyng 1415
Gan make a noyse ful lykyng.
  About the brinkes of these welles,
And by the stremes over al elles,
Sprange up the grasse as thicke yset
And softe as any veluet, 1420
On whiche men myght his lemman ley

1398 **sette]** sytte TH¹-KA FU SU FI   1399 **there]** *om.* SK   1400 **Lest it]** L. TH¹-SP³ BE-KA FU; L. that UR   1411 **every]** eche UR   1420 **as]** eke as UR

1391–93 "These trees [that I describe] were set five or six fathoms from one another in situation" (BE). SK observes that these lines are imitated in *BD* 419–20; the spacing—"ten foot or twelve"—is different. Kaluza (1893*a*:140–41) takes the difference as an indication of an earlier date, and freer treatment, in *BD*. See above, "Date of Composition" and cf. 61n.

1396 **yronne:** RI drops the *y-* since MS (which is Out at this point) does not ordinarily use this participial prefix.

1397–98 **knytte : sette:** "The rimed words must needs be *knet, set*, as in the Parl. Foules, 627, 628" (SK). KA so recommends, and SK RB RI so emend; GL has *knette : sette*. The present emendation creates a false rhyme of the sort for which MS offers precedent: cf., in Fragment A, lines 873–74, 953–54, 1489–90; in Fragment B, lines 1785–86, 2005–06, 2371–72, 2759–60; and in Fragment C, lines 6429–30.

1399 **myght there:** KA recommends *myghte* and reports Skeat's recommendation to omit *there*.

1400 **Lest it:** KA's suggested emendation. SK GL RB¹-RI adopt it, partly on the basis of the Fr. (Lc 1370–71 "que li solaus . . . / ne puet" "so that the sun could not"), partly for meter, and partly because an intransitive sense of *shende* is unusual. However, *MED shenden* v. lists the unemended line (as a 16th-century example, since it first appears in TH¹) under sense 1. (f) "to be destroyed, be confounded," where earlier quotations include Layamon's *Brut* 9015 and *Cursor Mundi* 14844.

1401–02 To these lines SK (1391n.) invites comparison with *BD* 429–31.

1403 **bowe:** BE SK prefer *bough*, as in SP²,³ (SKt).

1405 **clapers:** "Rabbet-holes or Burrows," from Fr. *clapier* (URg et al.), "dens, warrens" (RIf). SK quotes Cotgrave (1611) and refers to *OED*.

1407 **tourneyeng:** "The rabbits are prettily represented as making jousts and tournaments, in their play on the grass" (BE).

1411 **shadowe:** "perhaps read *shade*" (GL).

1413–14 **that by devyse . . . condyse:** "which Mirthe had, by contrivance, made to come through conduits" (BE).

1413 **devyse:** perhaps abstract, "contrivance" (BE, Davis 1979) or "ingenuity" (FI *MED dēvīs* n. 6. [b]), rather than concrete, "contrivances" (SK) or "device, contrivance" (RBg RIf); there is no precise parallel in the Fr. (Lc 1385–86).

1414 **condyse:** "conduits" (URg et al.), water pipes (Fr. *conduiz* [Lc 1386]). SK cites Godefroy (1881–1902) for examples of "*conduis* as the pl. of O.F. *conduit*" and *Ayenbite of Inwyt* (ed. Morris 1866*a*:1.91.25) for the ME form *condwys*. On "the loss of *t* in the English plural," RB compares the form *avocas*, "the reading of several MSS.," in *Phy-PardL* C 291.

1420 **softe as any veluet:** Skeat (1896*a*) argues that Lydgate, in *The Complaint of the Black Knight*, line 80 (ed. Skeat 1897:248 "And softe as veluët the yonge gras") follows the ME *Rom* rather than the Fr. (Lc 1391), where

As on a fetherbed to pley,   TH¹:135c
For the erthe was ful softe and swete.
Through moisture of the wel wete
Spronge up the sote grene gras   1425
As fayre, as thicke, as myster was.
But moche amended it the place
That th'erthe was of suche a grace
That it of floures hath plente,
That bothe in somer and wynter be.   1430
  There sprange the vyolet al newe,
And fresshe pervynke, riche of hewe,
And floures yelowe, white, and rede;
Suche plente grewe there never in mede.

Ful gaye was al the grounde, and queynt,   1435
And poudred, as men had it peynt,
With many a fresshe and sondrie floure,
That casten up ful good savour.
  I wol nat longe holde you in fable
Of al this garden dilectable.   1440
I mote my tonge stynten nede,
For I ne maye, withouten drede,
Naught tellen you the beaute al,
Ne halfe the bounte therewithal.
  I went on right honde and on lefte   1445
About the place; it was nat lefte,
Tyl I had [in] al the garden bene,

1429 **hath]** had SK   1440 **dilectable]** delitable SK SU FI   1447 **in al the garden]** a. t. g. TH¹-KA FU
FI; a. t. yerde in SK SU; a. t. g. i. GL

---

the simile "soft as velvet" does not appear; Skeat concludes that Lydgate believed *Rom* "to be Chaucer's work, for otherwise he would have let it alone." Cf. Skeat (1897:xlv; 1899:66).

  softe: KA suggests inserting "*as* before *softe*," but no ed. does so.

  veluet: Trisyllabic, with vocalic *u* (SK GL RIf). SK cites the forms *veluet* from the *Promptorium Parvulorum* and *veluet* from Lydgate (above); he notes further that "the mod. E. *velvet* arose from misreading the *u* as a *v*."

1423 **the erthe:** SK reads *therthe*, for consistency with line 1428 (SKt).

1425 **Spronge:** SU notes that "G. has *Sprang*"; but MS (G.) has a missing leaf at this point, and the text comes only from TH¹.

1426 **as thicke:** KA recommends "*and thicke*" (cf. BE's paraphrase, "as fair and thick as was necessary"), but no ed. so emends.

  myster: The word is a noun, "need" (SPg et al.) or "necessity" (URg et al.), although the sense may be understood adjectivally, as in the paraphrases for *as myster was:* "as was (necessary, needed)" (BE SK FI *MED* 5. [d]), "i.e., 'as could be'" (FI). GL compares lines 6519, 6581, 7324.

1428 **suche:** SKt notes this as TH¹'s form; as elsewhere in Fragment A, Skeat prefers the Chaucerian *swich*; see 26n.

1429 **hath:** SK's emendation, *had*, follows KA's recommendation and the Fr. imperfect *avoit* (Lc 1399). "For a similar change of tense," GL compares line 1652.

1431 **sprange:** See 1425n.

1435 **queynt:** "adorned" (SKg), "pleasing" (RIf). Cf. 65n.

1436 **poudred:** "embrodered" (SPg); "besprinkled" (SKg); "spangled" (*MED poudren* v. 4 [a]); "adorned (with flowers)" (RIf). GL and RB adduce Fr. *piolee* "of varied colors" (Michel 1416) or *pipolee* "adorned" (Lc 1406, with numerous variants [Ln 1408t]).

1439 **holde . . . in fable:** KA recommends that *in* be omitted, but no ed. so emends.

  fable: "discourse" (URg), "idle discourse" (TRg BEg); "story, description" (SKg), "tale; falsehood, deceit" (RBg). *MED fable* n. 3. (c) glosses *holden in fable* as "detain with idle talk," FI as "detain by description." Cf. *MED* on *fable* as (fictitious) narrative (sense 1) and as idle tale or talk (sense 3).

1440 **dilectable:** SK's var. *delitable* represents a different level of borrowing; see *MED delectāble, delītable*.

1441 **nede:** Jephson (BE) thinks that "*nedes* is the proper [genitival] adverbial form," but Skeat (1878c:4.61), notes that "*nede* (dative) is a correct form."

1446 **nat:** KA recommends *nought*, but no ed. so emends.

1447 **in al the garden:** RB's emendation, "for sense" (RBt), is based on the nearly identical line at 1348; GL supplies *in* after *garden*. Either emendation remedies the sense but leaves an extra syllable, as at line 1348. See below.

  garden: KA recommends *yerde in*, an emendation also recommended at line 1348, despite the near identity of the two lines. Eds. compare lines 1348 (KA SK GL RBt RIt), 1366 (SKt), 1461 (SU); see 1348n.

In the [esters] that men myght sene.
   And thus while I wente in my playe,
The God of Love me folowed aye,   1450
Right as an hunter can abyde
The beest, tyl he seeth his tyde
To shoten at good messe to the dere,
Whan that hym nedeth go no nere.
   And so befyl, I rested me   1455
Besydes a wel, under a tree,
Whiche tree in Fraunce men cal a pyne.
But sithe the tyme of Kyng Pepyne,
Ne grewe there tree in mannes syght
So fayre, ne so wel woxe in hight;   1460
In al that yarde so high was none.
And springyng in a marble stone
Had Nature set, the sothe to tel,
Under that pyne tree a wel.
And on the border al without   1465

Was written in the stone about
Letters smal, that sayden thus,
"Here starfe the fayre Narcisus."
   Narcisus was a bachelere
That Love had caught in his dangere,   TH¹:135d
And in his nette gan hym so strayne,   1471
And dyd him so to wepe and playne,
That nede him must his lyfe forgo.
For a fayre lady that hight Echo
Him loved over any creature,   1475
And gan for hym suche payne endure
That on a tyme she him tolde
That if he her loven nolde,
That her behoved nedes dye;
There laye none other remedy.   1480
   But nathelesse for his beaute
So feirs and daungerous was he]
That he nolde graunte hir askyng,   MS:28r

1448 **esters]** efters TH¹-UR KA FU MO   1453 **good messe]** goodnesse TH³-MO   1466 **in]** on BE 1468 **starfe the]** whilome starfe UR   1474 **that]** *om.* UR SK   1478 **loven nolde]** ne lovin wolde UR   1482 *Lines* 1387–1482 *Out:* MS

1448 **esters:** "waies, galleries, entries" (SPg, with some confusion between forms in *ef-* and *es-*); "lodgings, apartments" (URg, with false derivation from Fr. *Hostelerie*); "inward parts of a building" (TRg et al.). Here, "the paths or the recesses of a garden" (*MED estre* n. 3. [e], from OF *estre*, to be, used as noun); "recesses" (Davis 1979). On the sense "inner parts" SK adduces *RvT* A 4295 and note. Magoun (1977) cites *KnT* A 1971, *LGW* 1711 (*sic* for 1715) and *Rom* 3626.

1453 **shoten:** BE RI have *sheten*, the normal Chaucerian form; elsewhere in Fragment A, the root vowel of the inf. is *-o-* (line 959) or *-e-* (line 989), while in Fragment B it is *-e-* (lines 1773, 1798, 1800). SK has *shete*, "perhaps correctly" (RBt).

    at good messe: TH¹·² have *goodmesse* as one word; in SPg *goodmes* is defined as "good time or mood," but SP does not print that word in this line. The TH³-MO variant is glossed as follows: "to good purpose" (URg, s.v. *Godeness*), "at (an) advantage" (TRg BE). The latter sense is close to that of the word *mes(se)*: "an der richtigen Stelle" (Kaluza 1889:529); "to advantage, from a favourable position" (SK et al.); "from a favorable (vantage) point, a good range" (RB et al.). SK explains the word "*Mes* (Lat. *missum*) [as] an old Anglo-French hunting term, answering (nearly) to mod. E. *shot*"; and *MED mes* n.(1) (a,c) glosses the word as "stroke or shot" and the phrase as "in good range or position for a shot." Kaluza (1889:529) et al. note that the phrase translates Fr. *en bon leu* (Lc 1421), and Kaluza (pp. 528–29), SK RB note that it reappears at line 3462, where it translates Fr. *en bon point* (Lc 3198). Skeat adduces line 87 of Marie de France's *Guigemar*, where *mes* means "a good shot," and he refers to "Ducange, ed. 1887, ix. 270, for two more examples."

1458 Corresponds to the var. of MS Ca ("puis le tamps au roi Pepin" "since the time of King Pepin"; see Ln 1428t, KA Fr. 1420n., SU Fr. 1428n.) rather than to the modern texts (Ln 1428, Lc 1426 "puis Charle ne puis Pepin" "since Charles nor since Pepin") or to the principal variant (Ln 1428t: "p. C. le fil P." "since Charles the son of Pepin") in the L family (Lnt) and in MS Go (SU Fr. n.).

    Pepyne: "the son of Charles Martel, the last of the *Maires du Palais*" (BE); "king of France" (SK 6.374) or "of the Franks" (RBg p. 999, RIg p. 1322). SK RB RI RIf report the Fr. var. "puis Charle le fil Pepin" (see above) and note that Pepin (died 768) was the father of Charlemagne (died 814).

1469–1538 BE SK Ln (1439–1506n.) RB Lc (1437–1508n.) RI refer to Ovid, *Met.* 3.356–505 for the story of Narcissus. Lc notes the modifications of Ovid in *RR* and adduces Frappier (1959) and Köhler (1963); see also Goldin (1967) and Fleming (1986a).

1470 **in his dangere:** "within his control" (SK); see 1049n. GL glosses *daungere* as "dominion."

1473 **nede him must:** an impersonal construction in which, as GL notes, *nede* is adverbial. Cf. 1441n.

For wepyng ne for faire praiyng.
And whanne she herd hym werne
   [her] soo,   1485
She hadde in herte so gret woo,
And took it in so gret dispite,
That she, withoute more respite,
Was deed anoon. But er she [deide],
Full pitously to God she preide   1490
That proude-hertid Narcisus,
That was in love so daungerous,
Myght on a day be hampred so
For love, and ben so hoot for woo,
That never he myght to joye atteygne,   1495
And that he shulde feele in eve[r]ly veyne
What sorowe trewe lovers maken,
That ben so velaynesly forsaken.
   This prayer was but resonable;
Therfore God helde it [ferme] and stable. 1500
For Narcisus, shortly to telle,
By aventure come to that welle
To resten hym in that shadowing

A day whanne he come fro huntyng.
This Narcisus hadde suffred paynes   1505
For rennyng alday in the playnes,
And was for thurst in grete distresse   28v
Of heet and of his werynesse
That hadde his breth almost bynomen.
Whanne he was to that wel comen,   1510
That shadowid was with braunches grene,
He thoughte of thilke water shene
To drynke and fresshe hym wel withall;
And doun on knees he gan to fall,
And forth his heed and necke he straught 1515
To drynken of that welle a draught.
And in the water anoon was seen
His nose, his mouth, his yen sheen,
And he therof was all abasshed;
His owne shadowe [had] hym bytrasshed. 1520
For well wende he the forme see
Of a child of gret beaute.
Well kouthe Love hym wreke thoo
Of daunger and of pride also,

1485 **her]** *om.* MS BE-KA GL   1489 **deide]** dide MS BE-KA   1491 **That]** T. the UR   1495 **to]** *om.* SK   1496 **And that he shulde]** Than s. h. TH¹-UR SK FU-FI; Than h. s. GL   **every]** euey MS KA; very SP²˙³   1498 **so]** *om.* UR   1500 **ferme]** forme MS BE-KA   1503 **that]** the TH¹-UR FU-FI   1504 **A day]** O d. UR   1508 **heet]** herte TH¹-UR FU   1515 **heed and necke]** n. a. h. TH¹-UR FU SU FI   **he straught]** out s. TH¹-UR SK-FI   1520 **had]** was MS BE-KA   1521 **see]** to se UR   1522 **gret]** full grete UR   1523 **Well]** Full well UR

1485 **werne:** "denie" (SPg URg RBg), "put aside" (SPg), "forbid" (SP²˙³g RBg), "refuse" (URg et al.), "repulse" (GLg), "reject" (FI). *OED warn* v.² "refuse" shows few such intrans. usages as MS reading might suggest. Cf. 1142n.
     her: KA notes this reading in TH¹.
    1489 **deide:** Although MS *dide* is supported by Chaucer's *dyde* (: homycide, *PardT* C 658) for the pa. t. of "die," all eds. except BE-KA emend to *de(i,y)de*, to rhyme with line 1490 *preide*. KA notes *deide* in UR. Cf. 1397–98n.
    1492 **daungerous:** "disdainful" (SK); see 1049n. and cf. line 1482.
    1495 **to:** KA endorses SK's omission.
    1496 **And that he shulde:** TH¹'s emendation, *Than shulde he*, noted in KA, remedies the meter and conveys roughly the sense of the Fr. *si poroit* (Lc 1462 "thus he could"); GL glosses *than* as "when." With the MS reading, however, the syntax is consistent from line 1489 to line 1498; *that* in line 1491 parallels *that* in line 1496.
    1498 **velaynesly:** SK RB RI normalize to *vilaynsly* on the basis of the Chaucerian forms that SK cites from *ParsT* I 279 (*vileynsly*), 627, 715, 854 (*vileyns*); see *OED Villainsly* adv. obs. The MS form belongs in the development of modern *villainously*.
    1508 **heet:** Fr. *chaut* (Lc 1474), to which TH¹'s *herte* does not correspond (SU FI). RIt mistakenly attributes the TH reading to FI as well.
    1515–16 Skeat (1899:66) finds that Lydgate imitated these lines in *Complaint of the Black Knight* 111–12 (ed. Skeat 1897:249); he adduces this parallel as evidence for Chaucer's authorship of Fragment A.
    1517 *Marginalium:* 7 MS₂ₑ. This mark is an instruction to the printer of TH¹ to begin signature 2B4r (= p. 7 of the signature). Marks for page 6 and its second column were on the missing leaf containing lines 1387–1482; thus the printer's marks show that TH¹ was printed before the leaves were missing from MS (Blodgett 1979:98–99; see above, "The Printer's Marks"). Similar gaps in the sequence of marks coincide with the other missing leaves.
    1520 **had:** TH¹'s emendation, noted in UR by KA, follows the Fr. auxiliary *avoit* (Lc 1484 "had").
    1522 **child:** "young man" (BE RBg).

That Narcisus somtyme hym beere. 1525
He quytte hym well his guerdoun there;
For he musede so in the welle
That, shortly all the sothe to telle,
He lovede his owne shadowe soo
That atte laste he starf for woo. 1530
For whanne he saugh that he his will 29r
Myght in no maner wey fulfill,
And that he was so faste caught
That he hym kouthe comforte nought,
He loste his witte right in that place 1535
And diede withynne a lytel space.
And thus his warisoun he took
For the lady that he forsook.
  Ladyes, I preye ensample takith,
Ye that ageyns youre love mistakith; 1540

For if her deth be yow to wite,
God kan ful well youre while quyte.
  Whanne that this lettre of which I telle
Hadde taught me that it was the welle
Of Narcisus in his beaute, 1545
I gan anoon withdrawe me
Whanne it felle in my remembrance
That hym bitidde such myschaunce.
But at the laste thanne thought I
That scathles, full sykerly, 1550
I myght unto the welle goo.
Wherof shulde I abaisshen soo?
[Unto the welle than went I me], TH¹:136a
And doun I loutede for to see MS:29r
The clere water in the stoon, 29v
And eke the gravell, which that shoon 1556

1527 **musede so]** s. m. SK 1528 **all]** *om.* TH¹-UR FU SU FI 1530 **atte]** at TH¹-SP³ FU SU FI 1538 **For]** Fro GL 1541 **For if]** F. i. of SP²ˑ³; If of UR **be yow]** you be UR 1543 **that]** *om.* UR 1547 **my]** me TH² 1548 **such]** suche a UR 1552 **shulde]** shul TH³ ST SP²-UR 1553 *Out:* MS (*No gap*) KA RI

1525–26 **beere : there:** Skeat (SK) supports final *-e*—as in TH¹-UR SK-FU SU FI—by taking *beere* "bore" as subjunctive (OE *bære*). RB RI, assuming the indicative, have *beer : ther.*
1527 **musede so:** KA endorses SK's change.
1534 **comforte:** ST-UR SK RB FI RI drop *-e*; RBt RIt note that the word is "possibly infinitive, though more probably the noun" (RBt).
1537 **warisoun:** "reward" (SPg et al.); "Cure; Recovery. Fr. *Guerison*" (TRg); "requital" (FI Rif), "payment" (Rif), "'reward,' due punishment" (*OED Warison*, sense 2b.). SK RB RI note the Fr. parallel, *guerredon* (Lc 1504 "reward" or "punishment"). SK states that "'reward' . . . is not the usual sense; it [*warisoun*] commonly means healing, cure, or remedy; see *Guarison* in Cotgrave" (1611); but *OED Warison* lists "wealth, possessions" as the primary meaning, derives the word from the north-eastern form of CF *g(u)arison*, and relates it to the later borrowing of the CF form, mod. Engl. *garrison* (ME *garisoun*; cf. *Rom* 3249, 4279), rather than to OF *guerison* "healing, cure." Thus it is probably unnecessary to conjecture, with Liddell (GL), that the translator confused *guerredon* with *guerison*; David (RI) suggests, however, that "perhaps 'cure' is intended here as an ironic 'requital.'"
1538 **For:** GL's emendation, *Fro*, follows the Fr. *de* (Lc 1502 "from"; noted in GL RBt SU RIt). SU states that the emendation is perhaps correct but that "*For* could have meaning of 'on account of' in this line."
1540 **ageyns:** "in respect to" (GL).
  love: GL, noting that the Fr. is plural (Lc 1506 "vos amis"), suggests "perhaps . . . *loves*" but compares lines 1965–66, where SK FI emend *love* to *lovers*. See 1965n.
1541 **to wite:** "gerundive, i.e. is to be imputed to you" (GL); "to blame" (FI).
1542 **youre while quyte:** literally, "your time repay" (FI), i.e. "repay (wreak revenge on) you" (Rif).
1550 **scathles:** KA reports TH¹'s reading, inaccurately, as *scathelees*; as SKt notes, it is *scathlesse*. § Skeat (SK) observes "a touch of humour here; the poet ran no risk of falling in love with such a face as his own."
1553 BE KA SKt SU FI RIt (but not RB) note that MS omits this line, without a gap; BE supplies it from "Speght," SK RB SU FI from Speght's ultimate source, TH¹; KA gives TH¹'s reading in a note; David (RI) omits it as spurious, shows the omission as a line of dots, and supplies the TH¹ text in a footnote (cf. 892n.). He adduces the Fr. (Lc 1521 "De la fontaine m'apressai" "I drew near the well"), and writes: "A slightly more idiomatic version might be 'To the welle than gan I drawe me.' *Went* is rarely reflexive in Chaucer, but *draw* as a verb of motion is consistently so. Cf. 1546 and 3069–70 [i.e. 3071]." If, however, the line represents Thynne's own adaptation of the Fr., we might not expect a Chaucerian form.
1554–55 A blank line appears at the bottom of MS fol. 29r, following line 1554, but there is no gap in the text; cf. line 1553 (KA).

Down in the botme as silver fyn,
For of the well this is the fyn;
In world is noon so clere of hewe.
The water is evere fresh and newe   1560
That welmeth up with wawis bright
The mountance of two fynger hight.
Aboute it is gras spryngyng,
For moiste so thikke and wel likyng
That it ne may in wynter dye   1565
No more than may the see be drye.
   Downe at the botme sette sawe I
Two cristall stonys craftely
In thilke fresh and faire well.
But o thing sothly dar I tell,   1570
That ye wole holde a gret mervayle
Whanne it is tolde, withouten fayle.

For whanne the sonne, clere in sight,
Cast in that well his bemys bright,
And that the heete descendid is,   1575
Thanne taketh the cristall stoon, ywis,
Agayn the sonne an hundrid hewis,
Blewe, yelowe, and rede that fresh
      and newe is.
Yitt hath the marveilous cristall   30r
Such strengthe that the place overall,   1580
Bothe [flour] and tree and leves grene
And all the yerde in it is seene.
And for to don you to undirstonde,
To make ensample wole I fonde.
Ryght as a myrrour openly   1585
Shewith all thing that stondith therby,
As well the colour as the figure,

1562 **mountance**] mountenaunce TH¹-UR FU SU FI   1563 **gras**] the grasse UR   1564 **so**] for SP¹
1565 **That**] The BE   1567 **at**] atte MS BE-KA   1578 **and rede**] r. UR   1581 **flour**] foule MS-SK FU
1583 **to undirstonde**] u. SK   1587 **the figure**] f. UR

1558 **fyn:** "end" (URg et al.); "(significant objective, the point), i.e., the eyeballs" (FI); "main point" (RIf). Fisher misnumbers his note "1557," where *fyn* means "fine." § On the "eyeballs," see 1568n.

1561 **welmeth:** "riseth" (SPg URg); "springeth" (TRg); "boils . . . bubbles" (SK), "wells" (GLg), "surges" (FI), "swells" (RIf). TRg (cf. BEg MOg GLg), perhaps following URg's derivation from OE *weallan*, takes the form as "put for *welleth*." SK derives the word "from A.S. *wylm*, a spring." *OED* (*Walm* v.) posits "an unrecorded OE derivative *wœlman*," and Davis (1979) suggests derivation from "? O[ld] A[nglian] *welman*."

1562 **mountance:** *MED mountaunce* n. lists the TH¹ var., *mountenaunce*, as an erroneous form.

1563 **Aboute:** SKt has an incomplete entry, "*Both*," presumably for "*Both* [MS TH¹] Aboute"; Skeat's text has *Abouten*, the form that GL RB FI RI also adopt.

1564 **for moiste:** "because it was moist, because of its moisture" (SK). See 276n.

1568–1636 In this passage, there is inconsistency between the plural "two cristall stonys" of line 1568 and the singulars ("the cristall") of lines 1576, 1579, 1589, 1600, 1636. The Fr. MSS also show uncertainty in number, where the corresponding *loci* in Lc are 1536, 1545, 1547, 1558, 1568, 1603 (add +2 for Ln); see Langlois (1910:332–34), Ln 1547n., Lc 1.265–66. Lc summarizes (1.266): "None of the MSS consulted by Langlois [1910:332–34] has a coherent version; they all mix the singular and the plural in the most fantastic and unexpected disorder, all except two, Za and Ha (to which one may add Ca, whose reading is barbarous): Za offers the plural, Ha the singular." The texts of Michel and Langlois are in the plural tradition, from Za, those of SU Fr. and Lecoy in the singular tradition, from Ha. Lecoy (Lc 1541–68n.) believes that the singular may be defended as a name of a material or mass noun. SU Fr. confuses the forms at lines 1549, 1560, where the sing. subject-case should be *cristaus*, from Ha, rather than *cristal*, from Go (SU Fr. 1549n., 1560n.). On the agreement with verbs, cf. 1591n. on *accusith*.

1568 **cristall stonys:** "i.e. the pupils of the eyes" (FI); Fisher's sidenote labels them "her eyes." David (RI) writes: "These have been interpreted as the eyes of the lady (Lewis [1936:]117, 128–29); the dreamer's own eyes (Robertson [1962:]95); and both of these together in the sense that the lady's eyes reflect back the essential self through the mirror of the other (Köhler [1963:]95–100)." See further Hillman (1980:238); Fleming (1986a:213–19); Harley (1986:325). Fleming says that "the well of Narcissus . . . becomes . . . [a] poetic image for the anatomy and physiology of human vision" (pp. 218– 19).

1577 **Agayn:** "i.e., from the reflections of" (FI).

1578 **rede that fresh and newe is:** GL notes that this phrase translates Fr. *vermeil* (Lc 1546).

1581 **flour:** GL's emendation has the support of the Fr. *flors* (Lc 1549 "flowers"; noted by RBt SU FI RIt).

1585 **myrrour:** See 567n.

1586 **stondith:** SK GL FI respell as the contraction *stant* (GL *stont*), for meter; KA endorses SK's *stant*. GL also reads MS *all* as *alle* (modifying neuter pl. *thing*) and scans: "Shew'th alle thing, etc."

Withouten ony coverture,
Right so the cristall stoon shynyng,
Withouten ony disseyvyng, 1590
The [estrees] of the yerde accusith
To hym that in the water musith.
For evere, in which half that [he] be,
[He] may well half the gardyne se,
And if he turne he may right well 1595
Sene the remenaunt everydell.
For ther is noon so litil thyng
So hidde, ne closid with shittyng,
That it ne is sene as though it were
Peyntid in the cristall there. 1600

This is the mirrour perilous
In which the proude Narcisus
Sawe all his face faire and bright, 30v
That made hym [sithe] to ligge upright.
For whoso loketh in that mirrour, 1605
Ther may nothyng ben his socour
That he ne shall there sene somethyng
That shal hym lede into [lovyng].
Full many worthy man hat[h] it
Blent, for folk of grettist wit 1610
Ben soone caught heere and awayted;
Withouten respite ben they baited.
Heere comth to folk of newe rage; 1613

1591 **estrees]** entrees MS-KA FU 1593 **that]** *om.* UR **he]** ye MS-KA GL FU 1594 **He]** Ye MS-KA GL FU 1595 **he turne he]** ye t. ye SP¹ UR 1598 **closid]** closin UR 1600 **in]** is SP³ 1603 **face faire and]** fayre face TH¹-SP³ FU SU FI; fayre face so UR 1604 **sithe]** swithe MS BE-KA GL 1605 **loketh]** loke TH¹ TH³-UR SK FU SU FI 1608 **lovyng]** laughyng MS-KA FU 1609 **many]** many a TH¹-UR SK FU-FI **hath]** hat MS KA 1611 **awayted]** wayted TH¹-SP³ FU SU; ywaited UR

1588, 1590 **ony:** See 212n.
1591 **estrees:** KA's suggested emendation; KA SK compare line 1448. The emendation follows the Fr. *l'estre* (Lc 1559 "situation, surroundings"; noted by SK GL FI RIt). See 1448n.
    accusith: discovers (TRg BEg), discloses (RBg); reveals (RBg RIf). The Fr. has either the pl. (Ln 1560–61 "li cristal . . . encusent" "the crystals . . . reveal") or the sing. (Lc 1558–59 "li cristaus . . . encuse" "the crystal . . . reveals"); Ln (1561t) reports the pl. var. *acusent* in MSS Za Ga L, the sing. *acuse* in He; SU Fr. 1561 adopts the sing. var. *acuse* from MS Go. § For the sense, "reveals, shows," Skeat refers to *OED*; see also *MED ac(c)ūsen* v. 2. (a).
1592 **musith:** "gazes" (TRg MOg SKg FI), rather than "amuses oneself, meditates" (URg).
1593–94 **he . . . He:** KA's suggestion follows the Fr. (Lc 1561–62 "il soit . . . voit" "he may be . . . he sees"; noted by RBt SU RIt). Cf. *hym*, line 1592, *he*, line 1595.
1595 **he:** "the indefinite pronoun, i.e. 'one'" (GL).
1598 **shittyng:** "shutting" (SKg RBg RIf).
1601 **mirrour perilous:** "the well and its crystals" (RIf). RI cites Köhler (1963:98) "on the aspects of hydromancy and crystallomancy in this passage." For bibliographies relating to this passage in the Fr., see Hult (1981:130n.) and Fleming (1986a:206n.).
    mirrour: See 567n.
1603 **Sawe:** TH¹-UR FU SU FI have *Sey*, an alternate form of the pa. t. 3 sg. (see *MED sēn* v.[1]).
1604 "*Upright* signifies Straight (whether lying down, or standing up)" (URg). BE notes that "*Upright* means *resupinus*, with the face upward," and that *to lie upright* "seems . . . to be a sort of euphemism for to die." MO glosses *upright* as "flat on the back." SK paraphrases: "'That made him afterwards lie on his back,' i.e. lie dead (F. *mors*)." GL RB FI RIf gloss similarly, and GL compares *WBP* D 768, "Whan that the corps lay in the floor upright."
    sithe: TH¹'s emendation, noted in KA, follows the Fr. *puis* (Lc 1572 "then, afterward").
    ligge: Skeat (SK), assuming that TH¹'s *lye* was the original form, writes: "The alteration of *lye* to *ligge* in MS . . . is a clear example of the substitution of a Northern form." *Lie* is the usual Chaucerian form and the usual form in MS; but the pres. stem *ligge-* appears in *KnT* A 2205, *Th* B² 2101, and *NPT* B² 4415 (all Hengwrt MS), as well as several times in *TC* (3.660, 669, 685, 1537; 4.626; 5.411).
1605 **mirrour:** See 567n.
1608 **lovyng:** KA's suggestion, as SK RBt SU RIt note, follows the Fr. *d'amors* (Lc 1576 "of love"). Skeat (SK) calls MS *laughyng* "a very queer travesty of *loving*, owing to a similarity in the sound."
1610 **Blent:** All eds. except BE KA RI adopt the prefix *Y-*. Eds. gloss as "blinded (?)" or "deceived (?)" (URg et al.). GL says, "Perhaps we should read *Y-bleint*, deceived," and, with RB, notes the Fr. var. *mis en rage* "put into a frenzy" (from MS λo [KA Fr. 1571n.], also in MS He [Ln 1579t]); SU Fr. 1579, Ln 1579, and Lc 1577 have *mis a glaive* "put to the sword."
1613 **of newe:** According to most eds., an adverbial phrase: "lately" (URg TRg BEg), "newly" (TRg SKg), "again" (SKg), "anew" (GL RBg); thus SK RB hyphenate the two words, *of-newe*. Although the phrase typically

Heere chaungith many wight corage;
Heere lith no rede ne witte therto; 1615
For Venus sone, daun Cupido,
Hath sowne there of love the seed,
That help ne lith there noon, ne rede,
So cerclith it the welle aboute.
His gynnes hath he sett withoute, 1620
Ryght for to cacche in his panters
These damoysels and bachelers.
Love will noon other bridde cacche,
Though he sette [e]ither nette or lacche.
And for the seed that heere was sowen, 1625
This welle is clepid, as well is knowen,
The Welle of Love, of verray right, 31r
Of which ther hath ful many a wight
Spoke in bookis dyversely.
But they shull never so verily 1630

Descripcioun of the welle heere,
Ne eke the sothe of this matere,
As ye shull, whanne I have undo
The craft that hir bilongith too.
    Allway me liked for to dwelle 1635
To sene the cristall in the welle,
That shewide me full openly
A thousand thinges fast by.
But I may say, in sory houre
Stode I to loken or to poure, 1640
For sithen [have] I sore sighede;
That mirrour hath [me] now entriked.
But hadde I first knowen in my wit
The vertu and [the] strenghe of it,
I nolde not have mused there; 1645
Me had bette bene elliswhere,
For in the snare I fell anoon

1614 **many]** many a TH² 1620 **he]** ne UR 1623 **bridde]** birdis UR RB¹,² RI 1624 **either]** oither
MS MO KA RB¹,² 1627 **Welle]** Wells SU 1628 **a]** *om.* TH³-UR 1640 **or]** on MO 1641 **have I sore
sighede]** I sore s. MS-SP³ BE-KA FU; I sore have ysikid UR 1642 **me]** *om.* MS (MS₁ *corr.*) 1644 **vertu]**
vertues MS BE-KA **the strenghe]** strenghes MS-KA FU; t. strenghes SU

---

follows rather than precedes what it modifies, FI takes it to be adjectival here, "sudden"; cf. the Fr. *noveile rage* (Lc 1581 "new madness"). For examples of (postpositive) adjectival use, see *MED neue* n. (d) and *of* prep. 24a. (b) "new, original."

1619 **it:** the seed (1617).
    cerclith: This reading follows the Fr. var. *a ceinte, a chainte* "encircled" (MSS C, Da, L, Za; KA Fr. 1580; see Ln 1590t, Lc 1588t [Lc 1.266]). Lc 1588 has *acuevre* "covers" (MSS H), a reading which SU Fr. prints as *acueure*. Ln 1590 has *a teinte* "colored" (MS Ba and others, including Da, where Lc 1588t reads *a chainte*, c-t confusion is common).

1621 **panters:** "nets" (URg et al.) or "bird snares" (RIf *MED paunter* n.), rather than "pitfalls" or "toiles to take deare" (SPg). SK GL compare *LGWP* F 131.

1623 **bridde:** In support of the pl. *briddes*, RIt compares the Fr. pl. *oisiaus* (Lc 1592).

1624 **either:** I collate MS *oither* as an error for *either*; it may be a var. sp. of *outher*, but *MED* does not record such a form. Cf. 250n.
    lacche: "trap" (SK). Skeat writes: "The usual sense is 'the latch of a door'; but the sense here given is clearly caught from the related verb *lacchen*, which sometimes meant to catch birds. Thus in P. Plowman, B. v. 355, we find 'forto lacche foules,' i.e. to catch birds." Alluding perhaps to earlier glossarists (cf. URg-MOg), Skeat says that "we must not confuse *lacche*, as here used, with *lace*, a snare." See *MED lacche* n., *lacchen* v.(1), *las* n.

1627–29 For suggestions about what authors Guillaume de Lorris had in mind, see Lc 1595–97n. He finds fountains of love in *Floire et Blancheflor* 1800–07 (ed. Pelan 1937 = 2041–48, ed. Leclanche 1980); Andreas Capellanus (ed. Walsh 1982:112–13); and Claudian, *De nuptiis Honorii et Mariae* 69–70 (ed. Platnauer 1922).

1627 **Welle:** FI reports, wrongly, that TH¹ reads *wells*; only SU so reads.

1641–42 **sighede : entriked:** KA suggests *siked* (UR has *ysiked*), and SK GL RB FI RI so respell; SK GL compare *PF* 403–04 (*entriketh : syketh*).

1641 **have:** KA's suggestion. Skeat writes: "as the rime is a double one, the word *have* must be inserted, to fill up the line"; he notes the parallel *ai* in the Fr. (Lc 1606 "have").

1642 **mirrour:** See 567n.
    me: "*me* written above the line" (KA) by MS₁.

1644 **vertu and the strenghe:** KA's suggestion follows the Fr. singulars (Lc 1609 "force . . . vertuz" "strength . . . power"; noted in SU RIt).

That hath bitrisshed many oon.
  In thilk mirrour sawe I tho,
Among a thousand thinges mo,   1650
A roser chargid full of rosis,   31v
That with an hegge about [enclos] is.
Tho had I sich lust and envie
That for Parys ne for Pavie
Nolde I have left to goon [and] see   1655
There grettist hepe of roses be.
Whanne I was with this rage hent,
That caught hath many a man and shent,
Toward the roser gan I go;
And whanne I was not fer therfro,   1660
The savour of the roses swote
Me smote right to the herte rote,

As I hadde all enbawmed [be].
And if I ne hadde endouted me
To have ben hatid or assailed,   1665
[My] thankis, wol[d]e I not have failed
To pulle a rose of all that route
To bere in myn honde aboute,
And smellen to it where I wente;
But ever I dredde me to repente,   1670
And leste it grevede or forthought
The lord that thilk gardyn wrought.
Of roses ther were grete wone;
So faire waxe never in rone.
Of knoppes clos some sawe I there,   32r
And some wel beter woxen were;   1676
And some ther ben of other moysoun

1648 **hath]** had TH¹-UR FU SU   1652 **enclos is]** enclosid is MS UR-KA; enclosis TH¹-SP³ FU   1655 **and]** att MS MO KA   1657 **this]** that SP³   1663 **be]** me MS-UR KA FU   1666 **My]** Me MS BE-KA   **wolde]** wole MS-KA FU SU FI   1673 **ther were]** w. t. SK   1674 **waxe]** ware TH¹-UR FU SU FI   **rone]** Rome SP¹

1648 **bitrisshed:** TH¹ has *bytresshed*, and the -*e*- remains in TH²-UR GL FU SU. KA suggests *bitrasshed*, and RB RI so respell; SK FI have *bitraisshed*, a normalization with -*ai*- from OF (*MED bitraisshen* v.).

1649 **mirrour:** See 567n.

1652 **enclos is:** KA's suggestion follows TH¹'s *enclosis*, which KA notes, and the Fr. *clos* (Lc 1616 "closed"; noted in RIt); SK RB RI note that *enclos* is a Fr. form used for rhyme, and SK compares *Pearl* 2 *clos.* UR's *enclosed* shows disyllabic pronunciation, where -*id* would show the third syllable (Alderson 1970:122).

1654 **Pavie:** Pavia, in northern Italy (FI RIf), "a wealthy town of Lombardy, on the Ticino" (BE).

1655 **Nolde I have left to goon:** "i.e., would I not have gone" (FI).

    and: TH¹'s emendation of MS *att*, "a mere clerical error" (BE). KA notes the emendation in UR BE and compares line 1311 "to gon and see."

1663 **be:** KA notes *be* in BE MO. Jephson (BE), followed by SK RIt, attributes the correction to "Speght," but it does not appear in the texts of SP¹⁻³. In support, SKt RBt adduce Fr. *fusse* (Lc 1627 "had been, would have been").

1666 **My thankis:** "with my goodwill" (SK), "willingly" (RIf), or, as paraphrase, "for my part" (GL). See 1321n.

    wolde: KA's suggestion preserves a tense sequence that corresponds to the Fr. imperfect subjunctives (Lc 1629–30 "cuidasse . . . cueilisse . . . tenisse").

1673 **ther were:** KA endorses SK's reading.

    wone: "store" (SPg URg), "plenty" (SPg URg BEg), "heap . . . assembly" (TRg), "abundance" (BEg GL), "deal" (MOg), "quantity" (MOg SK FI). GL notes: "seems to be plural; cp. Zupitza's *Guy of Warwick*, 10329." See *OED Wone* sb.³, sense 3.

1674 **rone:** bush; see *MED ron* n.(3) (b). URg TRg and Kaluza (1889:528) take *rone* as the city Rouen in Normandy, BE as the Rhone area in Provence, famous for roses. Skeat (SK; cf. GL) first suggested the Northern *rone* "bush," and GL RB RI support this reading by noting the Fr. *soz ciaus* (Lc 1636 "beneath heaven"), a phrase with no specific geographical reference. Koch (1900a:67) notes that the word is not usual in Chaucer. FI's suggestion, "rows," seems less likely; the references in *Promptorium Parvulorum* (*rowe, reenge*) are not to the form *ron(e*, which does not appear in that work. RI suggests that the Northern *rone* is "probably used for rhyme."

1675 **knoppes:** UR, citing this line and line 1683, glosses "Rose-buds . . . From the *AS.* Cnæpa, A button: So the *French* call a bud, *Bouton*" (cf. TRg); "buds" (SKg FI RIf), as at lines 1683, 1685, 1691, 1702. Fisher (FI) writes: "one principal evidence of a different translator for Parts A and B is that instead of *knoppes*, B uses *bothum* (Fr. *bouton*)." See 1721n.

1677 **moysoun:** "size" (SK FI *MED moisoun* n. [b]), rather than "ripeness" (SPg URg), "harvest" (TRg BE MOg RBg RIf), or "crop" (GLg RBg). Lc Ln gloss the parallel Fr. *moison* (Lc 537, 1639) as "dimension." Skeat (SK) quotes Cotgrave (1611)—"*Moyson*, size, bigness, quantity"—and derives the word (via OF) "from Lat. *mensionem*, a measuring" (cf. Wartburg 1922–65, s.v. *mensio*). He adduces Langland, *Piers Plowman* C 12.120 [11.120], "alle þe musons in musyk," and his note (1886b:2.153–54) thereon. He observes further that the word is "not connected with *moisson*, harvest, as suggested in Bell"; *moisson* comes from Lat. *messio* "reaping" (Wartburg 1922–65, s.v. *messio*).

That drowe nygh to her sesoun
And spedde hem fast for to sprede.
I love well sich roses rede, 1680
For brode roses, and open also,
Ben passed in a day or two,
But knoppes will [al] fresh be
Two dayes atte leest or thre.
The knoppes gretly liked me, 1685
For fairer may ther no man se.
Whoso myght have oon of all,
It ought hym ben full lief withall.
Might I [a] gerlond of hem geten,
For no richesse I wolde it leten. 1690
 Among the knoppes I chese oon
So faire that of the remenaunt noon

Ne preise I half so well as it,
Whanne I avise it in my wit.
For it so well was enl[u]myned 1695
With colour reed, [and] as well fyned
As nature couthe it make faire.
And it hath leves wel foure paire,
That Kynde hath sett, thorough
 his knowyng, 32v
Aboute the rede roses spryngyng. 1700
The stalke was as rish right,
And theron stode the knoppe upright,
That it ne bowide upon no side.
The swote smelle spronge so wide
That it dide all the place aboute. 1705

1678 **nygh]** nygth MS KA 1683 **al]** *om.* MS-SK FU 1684 **atte]** at TH¹-UR FU SU FI **or]** or els TH¹-UR FU SU FI 1689 **a]** oon MO; *om.* MS-BE KA GL FU 1694 **it]** *om.* TH¹-BE FU 1695 **For it]** It UR **enlumyned]** enlomyned MS BE-KA 1696 **and]** *om.* MS-SK FU SU FI 1698 **hath]** had SK **wel]** full w. SP¹ 1699 **hath]** had SK 1700 **roses]** rose SK RB¹·² 1705 **dide]** dyed TH¹-UR FU SU FI

1680 Kuhl (1945:33–34) notes that the line is not in the Fr. (cf. Lc 1641–42) and suggests that, in the emphasis on red roses, "Chaucer pays a compliment to the house of Lancaster" (p. 34). On this basis, he argues for a date, for Fragment A, before the death of Blanche, in 1369. See above, "Date of Composition" and 908n. Cf. lines 1696, 1700.

1683 **al:** KA's suggested emendation follows the Fr. *tuit* (Lc 1645 "all, quite"; noted in GL RBt SU RIt).

1688 **lief:** SK FI respell as *leef*. MED *lẽf* adj. and adv. cites the form *lief* as "chiefly SE and sEM"; it appears frequently in Chaucer.

1689 **a:** KA suggests this addition.

1690 **leten:** "give up, relinquish" (*MED lẽten* v. 3. [a]), rather than "hesitate" (FI); the context requires a trans. verb.

1692 **noon:** SU reports TH¹'s reading as "*noue*, a printer's error"; but comparison with the -*un*- combination of the preceding word, *remenaunt*, shows clearly that the reading is *none*.

1694 **it:** Against the omission of this word in TH¹ and others, SU compares the Fr., which has a parallel object, either *l'* (Ln 1658) or *celui* (Lc 1656).

1696 **and:** RIt supports GL's emendation by citing Fr. *e* (Lc 1658).

  fyned: "finished" (GLg), "refined" (RBg), "delicately made" (RBg RIf), "shaped" (FI). *MED finen* v.(3), sense 3. (a), suggests "beautified, embellished"; perhaps sense 1, "purified, refined," would approximate the sense of the Fr. *fine* (Lc 1658).

1697–1700 *Marginalium:* Young and Aitken (1908:330) note that in the lower margin of 32r a 17th-century hand has repeated these lines, the last two of 32r and the first two of 32v. See above, "Other Marginalia."

1698–99 **hath . . . hath:** On SK's emendation to *had . . . had* (suggested by KA), SU supports the first occurence of MS *hath* by citing the Fr. pres. t. *a* in two MSS, Go and Ha (SU Fr. 1662n., Lc 1660). The second case has the simple pa. t. *ot* (SU Fr. 1664, Lc 1662), and the other collated MSS have *ot* in both places (KA Fr. 1652, 1654; Ln 1662, 1664).

1698 **wel:** "*om.* wel?" suggests SKt; the equivalent does not appear in the Fr. (Lc 1660).

1701 **as rish right:** "as upright (straight) as a rush (reed)" (SK RIf). BE noted (1855) that it was "still a proverbial simile."

1705–06 Line 1705 is the last line of Fragment A; see above, "Authorship." SKt GL RBt SU RIt note the imperfect rhyme *aboute : swote*; and BE SKt RBt SU RIt, taking *dide* as the auxiliary "did" (see below), see line 1705 as an incomplete clause without a main verb. Skeat (SK) notes that Kaluza "was the first to observe the change of authorship at this point," but both he and Robinson note that Kaluza "made Chaucer's portion end at l. 1704." This, however, is Kaluza's early position (1890), one that he modified in agreement with Skeat's argument (1891) that "Chaucer's portion is ll. 1–1705" (see Kaluza 1893:13). Skeat (SK) acknowledges further that Kaluza (1890) "remarked, very acutely, that Chaucer translates the F. *bouton* by the word *knoppe*; see ll. 1675, 1683, 1685, 1691, 1702, whereas the other translator merely keeps the word *bouton*; see ll. 1721, 1761, 1770."

[Fragment B]

Whanne I hadde smelled the savour swote,	For mych they distourbled me;
No will hadde I fro thens yit goo,	For sore I dradde to harmed be.
But somdell neer it wente I thoo	The God of Love, with bowe bent, 1715
To take it; but myn hond, for drede,	That all day sette hadde his talent
Ne dorste I to the rose bede, 1710	To pursuen and to spien me,
For thesteles sharpe of many maners,	Was stondyng by a fige tree.
Netles, thornes, and hokede breres;	And whanne he sawe hou that I

Heading: **Fragment B]** *om.* MS-KA GL FU   1713 **For]** Ful SK   1714 **For]** That GL   1718 **stondyng]** stondin UR

As an emendation, Kaluza (KA) proposes *filde* for *dide* (see below). Skeat (SK) suggests that the poem "may have been continued thus (where *dide fulfild* = caused to be filled):—'The swote smelle sprong so wyde, / That it dide al the place aboute / *Fulfild of baume, withouten doute.*' We can easily understand," he continues, "that the original MS. ended here suddenly, the rest being torn away or lost."

Liddell (GL), however, contesting the idea that "the Chaucerian part of the translation ends here," suggests the possibility that "the absence of rhyme is due to a later alteration of a rhyme like *swete*, vb., with *swete*, adj.; or *replete* [vb.] with *swete*." And he argues (1721n.) that the switch from *knoppes* to *botheum* as the translation of Fr. *bouton* is the first sign of a new translator and that "the new part probably begins at v. 1715." See 1715n., 1721n.

Koch (1921:168–69; cf. 1900a:67) agrees that Fragment A continues through line 1714; in his argument that no part of *Rom* is Chaucer's, he contends that the rhyme-pair 1705–06 "is unintelligible because of [faulty] transmission" (1921:168); he thus accepts Kaluza's emendation of *dide* to *filde* (below). Brusendorff (1925:320–22) also thinks the passage corrupt, but feels that Chaucer translated all of *Rom*, and argues "that there is no sharp break at l. 1705, but a gradual transition in lines 1600–1800 from a comparatively close and correct translation to a rather looser and less correct one" (pp. 321–22).

RB RI review previous positions and agree that "in a case of such complete uncertainty it is best to let the MS. reading stand unaltered" (RB).

1705   **dide:** Most eds. (see above) take this word as the auxiliary "did" and conclude, with BE, that "there is a verb wanting to complete the sense"; BE GL RB RI cite the Fr. verb *replenist* (Lc 1668), and KA, on that basis, suggests *filde* (cf. Koch 1921:168). SKt SU accept TH¹'s *dyed* as an alternate spelling for *dide* "did," but early eds. take it as "dyed" (SPg), "perfumed" (URg), or "tinged" (TRg). Reeves (1923:124) argues that MS *dide* and TH¹ *dyed* both mean "dyed," a sense accepted by FI, who glosses *dyed* as "dyed (saturated)" and takes it as a parallel to "Fr. *replenist* (filled)." *MED deien* v. (e) quotes only this line (with the form *dide*) in support of a similar sense: "of an odor: to permeate (a place)."

1706–5810   These lines constitute Fragment B. See above, "Authorship," for discussion of the evidence for dividing *Rom* into three fragments; see also 1705–06n. The notes below record examples of such evidence.

1708   **But:** KA transcribes MS *But*, inaccurately, as *Bot*, a var. spelling that GL RB RI repeat.

1713   **For:** KA suggests *Over* and compares line 3842 *Over-soone*. In support of SK's *Ful*, one might suggest that the translator anticipated Fr. *car* (Lc 1678 "for"), properly translated in the next line; but the Fr. does not support *Ful*, and, as GL notes, "no change is necessary."

mych: Skeat writes: "*muche*, in Sect. B, is usually disyllabic; perhaps the original had *mikel*." RBt also suggests a disyllabic pronuncation, for meter: "perhaps (here and elsewhere) to be read *moch(e)*, as in Th. [TH¹]." Skeat's statement rests largely on meter rather than on MS forms, where, in Fragment B, there are varying spellings of *mych*: without -*e*, with -*e*, and with -*el*. Of those without -*e*, eleven (lines 1713, 1820, 1973, 2258, 2704, 2852, 3282, 3510, 4114, 4951, 5783) need two syllables for meter; of those with -*e*, five (lines 2874, 3263, 3342, 3684, 5555) are metrically monosyllabic; and of those with -*el*, one (line 5625) requires a monosyllable for meter.

1714   **For:** GL's emendation, *That*, is based on a literal reading of the word *Que* (KA Fr. 1670); but most MSS, and the texts of Ln (1680) and Lc (1678), have *Car* "for."

1715   Liddell (GL 1721n.; cf. Koch 1921:169) thinks that Fragment B begins here. Liddell adduces, as evidence, Kaluza's observation of the change at line 1721 from *knoppe* to *botoun* as the translation of Fr. *bouton*. "After this," he writes, "the translation becomes more diffuse, the rhymes have a northern colouring, and the verses more frequently begin with an accented syllable." See 1705n., 1721n.

1718   **fige:** "fig (symbolic of genitalia)" (FI).

Hadde chosen so ententifly 1720
The bot[oun], more unto my paie
Than ony other that I say,
He toke an arowe full sharply whette, 33r
And in his bowe whanne it was sette,
He streight up to his ere drough 1725
The stronge bowe that was so tough,
And shette att me so wondir smert
That thorough [myn eye] unto myn hert
The takel smote, and depe it wente.
And therwithall such colde me hente 1730
That under clothes warme and softe

Sithen that day I have chevered ofte.
    Whanne I was hurt thus, in [a] stounde
I felle doun platte unto the grounde.
Myn herte failed and feynted ay, 1735
And long tyme a-swoone I lay.
But whanne I come out of swonyng,
And hadde witt and my felyng,
I was all maate, and wende full well
Of bloode have loren a full gret dell. 1740
But certes, the arowe that in me stode
Of me ne drewe no drope of blode,
For-why I founde my wounde all drie.

1721 **botoun**] botheum MS BE-KA; bothum TH¹-UR FU SU FI; bothoun GL *(all var. sp.)* **my**] me SP³ 1723 **full**] *om.* UR 1728 **myn eye**] me nye MS KA 1733 **a**] that SK; *om.* MS-BE KA FU SU 1736 **a-swoone**] in swoune TH¹-UR FU SU; ther a-swone SK 1738 **witt**] my w. SP³ UR 1740 **have**] t'have UR **dell**] *om.* ST 1743 **wounde**] woundes TH¹-UR FU SU FI

    1721 **botoun:** In support of *botoun*, suggested by KA and adopted by SK, Kaluza (1893*a*:38) cites the rhymes at lines 3473–74 (*botoun : saluacioun*) and lines 4011–12 (*botouns : sesouns*), where MS has *bothom* and *bothoms*. SK adds lines 4307–08 (*glotouns : botouns*), where MS again has *bothoms*. I regard the variation as non-substantive and do not include it in the counts of variants. Hereafter, I do not collate the variant spellings of this word but give cross-references to this note. Other MS forms are *bothum* (lines 1761, 1790); *bothom* (lines 1770, 1786, 1845, 2960, 2973, 3009, 3013, 3071, 3076, 3078, 3109, 3119, 3364, 3473, 4111); and *bothoms* (lines 3045, 3050, 3064, 4011, 4308). At line 3502, the MS form *bothom* is probably an error for *bothen* "the both" (see note). The usual forms in TH¹-KA SU FI are *bothum* or *bothom*. FI (1721n.) mistakenly reports that MS reads "*botoun* throughout." SK (following KA's recommendation) normalizes throughout to *botoun*, as do RB RI. GL emends somewhat inconsistently to *bothoun(s)* (lines 1721, 1761, 3119, 3473, 4011, 4308), *bothon(s)* (lines 1770, 1786, 1845, 2960, 2973, 3009, 3013, 3045, 3050, 3064, 3071, 3076, 3078, 3109, 4111), or *bothun* (line 1790); he misreads *botheum* as *bothoum* (1721n.), which appears nowhere in the MS readings.
    URg defines *Bothum* as "a bud," (cf. SPg, s.v. *bottom*) citing *Rom* 1721 and adding that "It is the same that is before called a *Knopp*, i.e. A Rose-bud. *Ib.* 1675, 1685, 1691." TRg expressly adduces the Fr. original, *bouton*. MO glosses "cowslip"; GL has "button"; GLg, "bud." RB SU FI RIt, following Kaluza 1893*b*:38, cite the origin of *botoun* as Fr. *bouton*, translated in Fragment A as *knoppe* (URg GL RB SU FI); see, e. g. lines 1675–1702, 1675n. Because *bothom/bouton* appears only in Fragment B of *Rom* and not elsewhere in Chaucer, it is evidence against Chaucer's authorship of Fragment B; see above, "Authorship." Brusendorff, however (1925:346), in arguing for Chaucer as the author of the entire *Rom* (with MS as the descendant of a corrupt memorial reconstruction), suggests that *knoppe(s)* was "the true [i.e. Chaucer's] translation" and *bouton(s)* "a corruption."
    1722 **ony:** See 212n.
    1728 On the concept of love entering the heart through the eye, RB RI adduce *KnT* A 1096; RI cites DiMarco's note to *KnT* A 1077–97 (in RI), a note that adduces *KnT* A 1567, *TC* 2.533–35, *MercB* 1–13, *Compl d'Am* 41–42, and the surveys of the eye-heart topos in Cline (1972) and Donaldson-Evans (1978). The notes of Ln (1693–95) and Lc (1692ff.) give further references.
    myn eye: KA records the correction in BE MO; BE notes MS *me nye* as "a mere clerical error, arising from the similarity in the sound of the two expressions."
    1732 **Sithen:** FI incorrectly reports the MS reading as *Syth.*
    1733 **in a stounde:** "sodainly" (SPg, s.v. *stound*, et al.). TRg (s.v. *Stound*) GL RB note the corresponding Fr. *tantost* (Lc 1698 "straightway").
    a: MO's emendation following the suggestion of TRg (s.v. *Stound*). SK's emendation, *that*, follows KA's suggestion.
    1736 **a-swoone:** As support for the insertion of *ther*, SKt cites the Fr. *ilec* (Lc 1700), "perhaps rightly" (SU).
    1743 **For-why:** BE reads as interrogative (*For why?* "For what reason?"), rather than the relative "On account of which."
    drie: SK GL RB RI, following KA's suggestion, have *dre(y,i)e* (*drey* in TH¹⁻³ SP²,³ FU SU FI).

Thanne toke I with myn hondis tweie
The arowe, and ful fast out it plight,   1745
And in the pullyng sore I sight.
So at the last the shaft of tree   33v
I drough out with the fethers thre,
But [yet] the hokede heed, ywis,
The which [that] Beaute callid is,   1750
Gan so depe in myn herte passe
That I it myght nought arace;
But in myn herte still it stode,
Al bledde I not a drope of blode.
I was bothe anguyssous and trouble   1755
For the perill that I sawe double;
I nyste what to seye or do,
Ne gete a leche my woundis [to];
For neithir thurgh gras ne rote
Ne hadde I helpe of hope ne bote.   1760

But to the bot[oun] evermo
Myn herte drewe; for all my wo,
My thought was in noon other thing.
For hadde it ben in my kepyng,
It wolde have brought my lyf agayn.   1765
For certis evenly, I dar wel seyn,
The sight oonly, and the savour,
Alegged mych of my langour.
    Thanne gan I for to drawe me
Toward the bot[oun] faire to se;   1770
And Love hadde gete hym, in [a] throwe,   34r
Another arowe into his bowe
And for to shete gan hym dresse;
The arowis name was Symplesse.
And whanne that Love gan nyghe
    me nere,   1775
He drowe it up, withouten were,

1745 **out it**] i. o. TH¹ TH³-UR FU SU FI; i. ought TH²   1749 **yet**] atte MS KA   1750 **that**] it MS KA; *om.* TH¹-MO SK FU SU FI   1752 **myght**] ne m. UR   1757 **do**] to do MS BE-KA   1758 **to**] two MS KA   1760 **helpe of hope**] hope o. helpe BE MO   1762 **drewe**] dreme UR   1766 **certis evenly**] certeinly SK RB¹·²   **wel**] *om.* UR   1771 **a**] his MS-SP³ BE-KA FU SU FI; this UR GL   1774 **Symplesse**] Simplenesse UR

1746 "That is, 'I sighed sore in the act of pulling out the arrows'" (BE).

1752 **nought arace:** KA suggests inserting "*out* before *arace*," but no ed. does so.

1753–54 Brusendorff (1925:312) calls attention to the "extraordinary variants" in the text of the Fr. (Lc 1717–18). See Ln 1719n., 1720t; SU Fr. 1719n., 1720n. For the Fr. exemplar of the ME, Brusendorff favors certain MSS of the L family, and SU Fr. favors Ri, with revision from Go. See 1754n.

1754 **drope:** SU Fr. (1720n.) reads *point* "not at all," from Go, for Ri's *onques* (Lc 1718 "ever"). But the closer equivalent, "goute," appears in the L family, as Brusendorff notes (1925:312; cf. Ln 1720t).

1758 **to:** KA notes *to* in UR BE MO; BE terms MS *two* "a mistake of the scrivener." As SU notes, SKt "wrongly ascribes *two* to Th. [= TH¹]."

1759 **gras ne rote:** "i.e., medicinal herbs" (FI).

    rote: KA suggests inserting "*thurgh* before *rote*," but no ed. does so.

1761 **botoun:** See 1721n.

1766 **certis evenly:** SK RB adopt KA's suggestion, *certeinly*; GL glosses *evenly* as "equally," compares line 5280 "And take evenly ech his parte," and notes that "there is no *certes* in Fr."; as RIt notes, Robinson (RBt) thinks that MS may be correct and glosses *certis evenly* as "'certainly in equal measure'?". The line has no parallel in the Fr.

1770 **botoun:** See 1721n.

1771 **a:** KA endorses SK's emendation. The phrase *a throwe* "a moment" (FI) has some support in the Fr. *ja* (Lc 1733–34 "already").

1774 SU notes that, following this line, "there appears to be a break . . . for no attempt is made to render whole Fr. sentence" (Lc 1735–37 "Simpleice ot non, c'est la segonde, / qui maint home par mi le monde / et mainte dame a fet amer" "Its name was Simplicity; it is the second arrow, which has caused many a man and woman all over the world to fall in love"). To account for the break, SU suggests "a damaged R-source translation in this vicinity" (SU Fr. 1736n.).

    Symplesse: the noun "simplicity" (URg TRg SKg₂ RIf), rather than the adjectives "sincere (artless)" (FI).

1775 **gan:** As SU notes, "Kaluza suggests *saw* for *gan* to suit Fr." *vit* (Lc 1738 "saw").

    nyghe: "the verb *to neighe*, to draw near. The construction is, 'When Love began to draw nearer to me'" (BE).

1776 **withouten were:** Eds. gloss *were* as "a maze" (SPg), "doubt" (SPg et al.), "confusion" (TRg BEg, with derivation from Fr. *Guerre*; cf. MOg); and they read the phrase as "without doubt" (URg SKg₂), "without warning" (GL RB RIf), without "hesitation (inward turmoil, Fr. *guerre*)" (FI). GL RB RI note the Fr. parallel *sanz menacier* (Lc

And shette at me with all his myght,
So that this arowe anoon right
Thourghout [myn] eigh, as it was founde,
Into myn herte hath maad a wounde.   1780
Thanne I anoon dide al my crafte
For to drawen out the shafte,
And therwithall I sighede efte.
But in myn herte the heed was lefte,
Which ay encreside my desire   1785
Unto the bot[oun] drawe nere;
And evermo that me was woo,
The more desir hadde I to goo
Unto the roser, where that grewe
The freysshe bot[oun] [so] bright of hewe. 1790
Betir me were to have laten be,
But it bihovede [nedes] me

To done right as myn herte badde.
For evere the body must be ladde
Aftir the herte, in wele and woo;   34v
Of force togidre they must goo.   1796
But never this archer wolde feyne
To shete at me with all his peyne,
And for to make me to hym mete.
The thridde arowe he gan to shete,   1800
Whanne best his tyme he myght espie,
The which was named Curtesie;
Into myn herte it dide avale.
Aswoone I fell bothe deed and pale;
Long tyme I lay and stired nought   1805
Till I abraide out [of] my thought.
And faste thanne I avysede me
To drawe out the shafte of tree;

1777 **with all**] withall ST   1779 **myn**] the SU; *om.* MS-SP³ BE-KA FU   1786 **drawe nere**] drowe I n.
TH¹-UR FU SU FI   1790 **so**] *om.* MS (MS₁ *corr.*)   1791 **to**] *om.* SK   1792 **nedes**] nede MS (MS₁ *corr.*)
TH¹-SP³ GL FU SU FI   1795 **wele**] whele ST   1797 **feyne**] fyne TH¹-UR SK FU-FI   1798 **peyne**] pyne
TH¹-UR SK FU-FI   1803 **it**] he TH³-MO   1806 **of**] on MS BE-KA

1739 "without threatening").   §   RB RI note SK's observation that "Sect. B is strongly marked by the frequent use of
withouten wene, withouten were, withouten drede, and the like tags." RB notes, however, that "in this instance, the
phrase has appropriateness and force."

1779 **myn:** UR's emendation, noted by KA, parallels *myn* in the next line and accords with the idiom of the
Fr. (Lc 1741 "si que par l'ueil ou cuer m'entra" "so that [the point] entered my heart through my eye [lit. entered me
by the eye to the heart]"). SU's emendation, *the,* follows the Fr. literally but neglects the object form *m'* as well as the
parallelism with *myn* in the next line.

    as it was founde: BE, citing the Fr. (above), notes that this phrase "is added merely to fill up the line."

1785–86 **desire : nere:** RB RI note that the rhyme is imperfect and cite other examples: *joynt : queynt* (lines
2037–38); *desyre : nere* (lines 2441–42); *desire : manere* (lines 2779–80); *ademant : foundement* (lines 4181–82);
lere : desire (lines 4685–86).

1786, 1790 **botoun:** See 1721n.

1790 **so:** "written above the line" (KA) by MS₁.

1791 **to:** SK's omission of this word follows KA's suggestion.

1792 **nedes:** "*s* written above the line" (KA), perhaps by MS₁. Thorp (1989) notes that the ink is the same but
the duct of the *s* unusual (on "duct," see Parkes 1969:xxvi).

1794–95   GL RB RI note that these lines are not in the Fr. (GL identifies three lines, 1794–96, but line 1796
corresponds in part to Lc 1759 "m'estovoit aler tot a force" "I had perforce to go wholly") and compare lines
2084–85. BE GL note that the passage "seems to be a quotation"; RB calls it "apparently a proverb or quotation"; and
RI identifies the proverb in Whiting's collection (1968: H302–H303), where the only pre-16th-century quotation
other than the two in *Rom* is *BD* 1152–4.

1797–98 **feyne : peyne:** TH¹-UR SK FU-FI emend to *fyne* (see 1797n.) and *pyne.* ME *peyne* and *pyne* are
parallel in sense; see *MED pein(e* n., sense 7. (f), and *pine* n.(1), sense 4. GL notes: "Either an assonance [?] or *fyne,*
pene; cp. vv. 1785, 1786, *desire, nere.*" RBt grants the possibility of an imperfect rhyme (*fyne : peyne*).

1797 **feyne:** RI takes MS *feyne* as a var. of *fine* "cease," chosen for rhyme. *MED fine(n)* v. (1) does not record
such a spelling, normally a form of the verb *feine(n)* "feign."

1802   **Curtesie:** SK (1820n.) and RB note that, at lines 955–57, the third arrow was named *Fraunchise . . .
fethred . . . With valour and with curtesye.* RI notes that the Fr. has the same inconsistency: (Lc 942–43 "Franchise . . .
empanee / de valor et de cortoisie"; 1765 "Cortoisie").

1804   SU notes that "a break might occur here"; the ME omits a line of the Fr. (Lc 1768 "desoz un oliver ramé"
"beneath a branching [leafy] olive tree") and thus "fails to complete the sentence." On breaks in the ME and SU's
theory of a reviser, see SU xxvi–xxvii.

But evere the heed was left bihynde,
For ought I couthe pulle or wynde. 1810
So sore it stiki[d] whanne I was hit
That by no craft I myght it flit;
But anguyssous and full of thought
I [felte] sich woo my wounde ay wrought,
That somonede me alway to goo 1815
Toward the Rose that plesede me soo,
But I ne durste in no manere,
Bicause the archer was so nere;
For evermore gladly, as I rede, 35r
Brent child of fier hath mych drede. 1820
And, certis yit, for al my peyne,
Though that I sigh yit arwis reyne,
And grounde quarels sharpe of steell,
Ne for no payne that I myght feell,
Yit myght I not mysilf witholde 1825

The faire roser to biholde;
For Love me yaf sich hardement
For to fulfille his comaundement.
Upon my fete I rose up thanne,
Feble as a forwoundid man, 1830
And forth to gon [my] myght I sette,
And for the archer nolde I lette.
Toward the roser fast I drowe,
But thornes sharpe mo than ynowe
Ther were, and also thisteles thikke, 1835
And breres, brymme for to prikke,
That I ne myght gete grace
The rowe thornes for to passe,
To sene the roses fresshe of hewe.
I must abide, though it me rewe, 1840
The hegge aboute so thikke was,
That closide the roses in compas.

1809 **evere**] aye UR   1811 **stikid**] stikith MS BE-KA   1812 **it flit**] flit it MO   1814 **felte**] lefte MS-TH² MO KA FU   1822 **sigh**] syght TH²   1831 **my**] *om.* MS-SP³ KA FU   1838 **The**] Through t. UR   1839 **roses fresshe**] f. r. TH²   1840 **though**] thought TH²

1811–12 **hit : flit**: "The rime *hit* (pp.): *flit* (inf.) is un-Chaucerian. For other cases of the disregard of the final -*e* of the infinitive see lines 1873–74, 1939–40, 1981–82, 2615–16, 2627–28, 2629–30, 2645–46, 2755–56, 3099–3100" (RB; cf. RI). TH¹⁻³ FU SU FI add -*te* to each word.

1812 **flit**: "move" (URg) or "remove" (TRg), rather than "escape" (FI RIf). See *MED*, s.v. *flitten*, for all three senses of the verb.

1813–14 **thought : wrought**: "Another irregular rime in which the final -*e* of the weak preterite, *wroughte*, is clipped"; (RB; cf. RI).

1814 **felte**: GL attributes the correction of MS *lefte* to Skeat, but note TH³-BE.

1816 **plesede me**: SU states: "the translator of Fragment A never uses the first-person form, *plesed me*; consistently he uses *lyked me* (ME 27, 121, 486, 806, 1312, 1635 and 1685). The latter occurs infrequently in the rest of the poem (ME 1843, 1847, 1854, 3075), and is probably the work of the reviser." FI goes farther in saying that "in [Fragments] B [and] C this phrase is regularly used instead of the more Chaucerian *lyked me*, cf. A, l. 27 etc." The phrase is not a "first-person form," as SU alleges, nor is the construction impersonal; the verb is third-person, since the subject *that* has the antecedent *Rose*, and the first-person *me* is object. FI's statement that the phrase *plesede me* is regularly used in Fragments B and C is an inference from SU's argument, for which there is no support as this is the sole example of the phrase in B and C. SU's own evidence shows that the phrase *lyked me* occurs four times as often in Fragments B and C as does *plesede me*; thus,to attribute these four cases to a reviser seems unfounded.

1818 **nere**: RB RI point out that the form is positive here, as at line 1848, but usually comparative in Chaucer; *KnT* A 1439, they note, is an exception.

1819–20 Proverbial in ME and Fr. (Lc 1782 "qu'eschaudez doit eve douter" "he who has been scalded must fear water"). RI cites Whiting (1968: C201), who collects a number of the examples noted in BE SK RB. BE cites related proverbs from "*Lessons in Proverbs*, by R. C. Trench," and Skeat quotes Cotgrave (1611), "'Chien eschaudé craint l'eau froide, the scaulded dog fears even cold water.'" On the Fr. version (Ln 1784n.), RB cites Tobler (1892: 376), and Lc (1782n.) cites Morawski (1925: no. 710).

1820 **mych**: See 1713n.

1822 **reyne**: "rain," rather than "run" or "reign," as in URg.

1831 **my**: UR's emendation, noted by KA in UR BE MO, although probably intended as a metrical improvement, has some basis in the Fr. *m'esforçai* (Lc 1793 "I made an effort [lit. exerted myself]"), and subsequent eds. (except KA FU) have adopted it.

1836 **brymme**: The adjective, "fierce" (URg RIf), "cruel" (FI), rather than the adverb, "fiercely" (SPg).

1842 **closide**: Liddell (GL) reads as "one syllable."

But o thing lyked me right well;
I was so nygh, I myght fele
Of the bot[oun] the swote odour, 1845
And also se the fresshe colour;
And that right gretly liked me,
That I so neer myght it se.
Sich joie anoon therof hadde I
That I forgate my maladie. 1850
To sene I hadde siche delit,
Of sorwe and angre I was al quyte,
And of my woundes that I hadde thore;
For nothing liken me myght more
Than dwellen by the roser ay, 1855
And thens never to passe away.
But whanne a while I hadde be thare,
The God of Love, which al toshar

35v Myn herte with his arwis kene,
Castith hym to yeve me woundis grene. 1860
He shette at me full hastily
An arwe named Company,
The which takell is full able
To make these ladies merciable.
Thanne I anoon gan chaungen hewe 1865
For grevaunce of my wounde newe,
That I agayn fell in swonyng 36r
And sighede sore in compleynyng.
Soore I compleyned that my sore
On me gan greven more and more. 1870
I hadde noon hope of allegeaunce;
So nygh I drowe to desperaunce,
I rought of deth ne of lyf,
Whader that Love wolde me dryf,

1844 **nygh I]** n. that I UR   1848 **myght it]** i. m. MO SK   1851 **I hadde]** it I h. UR; it h. I SK
1852 **sorwe]** woe UR   1860 **Castith]** Caste SK GL RB^{1,2}   1873 **rought]** ne r. UR; r. ne GL   **of lyf]** lyf GL

1843–44 **well : fele:** An imperfect rhyme, short and long *e*. Eds. adjust eye-rhyme in various ways: *wele : fele* (TH^1-UR SK-FU SU FI); *welle : fele* (BE MO); *well : fel* (RB RI).

1845 **botoun:** See 1721n.

1847–48 Brusendorff writes (1925:344): "The translation looks like pure guessing"; and RB also notes the "loose translation" of the Fr. (Lc 1806–07 "et durement m'abelisoit / ce que jou veoie a bandon" "what I could see freely of it greatly pleased me").

1848 **neer:** See 1818n. "Either an adverbial form *nere* . . . or a scribe's mistake for *nerwe*" (GL).

myght it: KA endorses SK's emendation, *it myghte*, which RBt grants may be correct.

1849–50 **I : maladie:** TH^3-UR SK RB RI have *malady*, for rhyme. SK (1.5) RB RI call attention to this un-Chaucerian rhyme [i:]/[i:ə] as a test of authenticity (see above, "Authorship"); they cite, as further examples in Fragment B, lines 1861–62, 2179–80, 2209–10, 2493–94, 2737–38, 3241–42, 4145–46; SK also cites lines 2521–22, 2985–86, 3171–72.

1851 **I hadde:** KA suggests SK's emendation, which GL states "is perhaps right."

1853–54 **thore : more:** As RI notes, Skeat sees these forms as substitutions for the Northern forms *thar : mar*. Hinckley (1906:640) suggests the influence of *Ywaine and Gawin* 235–36 *thare : mare*; but Skeat (1906) points out that this and other such rhymes occur in many Northern writers. GL RB FI also note the un-Chaucerian Northern rhyme, and RB notes that "Chaucer's forms would be *there* and *more*." For the form *thare* in rhyme, SK GL RI adduce line 1857. RI notes the possibility, suggested earlier in URg and TRg, that "the translator simply changed the normal *there* to rhyme with *more*." SP UR had also glossed *thore* as "before," with URg offering two explanations: "It seems to be a contraction of *The yore* . . . or a Corruption of *yore*, the *y*, and the AS. þ, for *th*, being written much alike in the MSS."

1857–58 **thare : toshar:** FI notes the non-Chaucerian rhyme; see 1853–54n.

1860 **Castith:** KA endorses SK's emendation, *Caste* (GL RB *Cast*), for tense consistency; SU, granting that the change may be right, accounts for the pres. t. on the basis of the historical pres. in the Fr. (Lc 1818 "redonne" "makes").

1861–62 **hastily : Company:** FI notes the "non-Chaucerian rhyme *hastely / company(e)*." See 1849–50n. SU takes the "bad rime . . . and lack of close correspondence with Fr." as evidence that the "reviser is probably at work on another break here." The break, SU notes, lies in the omission from MS Go (and, according to Ln 1823–24t, from MSS L Tou) of the couplet at Lc 1821–22 ("si que ou cuer soz la memele / m'a fet une plaie novele" "so that he made a new wound in my heart, under my breast").

1871 **allegeaunce:** "ease," from the Italian (SP^{2,3}g), "Ease, relief; Ceasing; Diminution; Abatement, Release" (URg); "alleviation" (TRg SK FI RIf). SK calls attention to the Fr. *alijance* (Lc 1832); compares line 1890 *aleggement* and the Fr. *aligement* (Lc 1849); and adduces line 1923 *aleggement*.

1874 **Whader:** "whither" (GL). *OED Whither* adv. gives forms with varying medial vowels, but the MS form is the only one listed (with a query) for *whader*. Modern eds. emend to TH^1's *Whether* (FI), to *Wheder* (GL RB RI), or to *Whither* (SK).

Yf me a martir wolde he make;
I myght his power nought forsake.
And while for anger thus I woke,
The God of Love an arowe toke;
Ful sharpe it was and pugnaunt,
And it was callid Faire-Semblaunt,   1880
The which in no wise wole consente
That ony lover hym repente
To serve his love, with herte and all,
For ony perill that may bifall.
But though this arwe was kene grounde   1885
As ony rasour that is founde,
To kutte and kerve, at the poynt
The God of Love it hadde anoynt
With a precious oynement,
Somdell to yeve aleggement   1890
Upon the woundes that he hadde   36v

[Through the body in my herte made] TH¹:137d
To helpe her sores, and to cure,   MS:36v
And that they may the bette endure.
But yit this arwe, without more,   1895
Made in myn herte a large sore,
That in full grete peyne I abode.
But ay the oynement wente abrode—
Thourghoute my woundes large and wide
It spredde aboute in every side—   1900
Thorough whos vertu and whos myght
Myn herte joyfull was and light.
I hadde ben deed and al toshent
But for the precious oynement.
The shaft I drowe out of the arwe,   1905
Rokyng for wo right wondir narwe;
But the heed, which made me smerte,
Lefte bihynde in myn herte

1875

1879 **pugnaunt]** full p. UR SK GL   1881 **no]** *om.* TH³ ST   **wole]** wolde TH³-BE   1884 **bifall]** fall UR   1885 **though this]** thought his SP³   1889 **precious]** full p. UR   1892 **Through the body in my herte made]** That he hadde the body hole made MS₂ KA; T. t. eye i. m. h. m. UR   *Out:* MS RI   1906 **Rokyng]** Looking SP²·³   1907 **which]** whiche that UR   1908 **Lefte]** I left UR

1880 **Faire-Semblaunt:** FI paraphrases as "charm"; lit., Fair-Seeming (Lc 1840 "Biau Samblant").
1882, 1884 **ony:** See 212n.
1885 **though:** BE reports, incorrectly, that "MS. reads *thought.*"
1886 **ony:** See 212n.
1891–92 **hadde : made:** Normally an imperfect rhyme, short and long *a.* TH¹-UR FU SU FI spell *hade : made,* SK RB *had : maad.*
1892 Line printed from TH¹. BE notes that "this line has been scratched out in the MS." and the MS₂ₐ version written over it. But subsequent eds. agree with KA that this version is "written by a later hand on a line originally left blank." The hand is the one that has supplied lines 1984, 2036, 3490; see "The Manuscript Hands: The Corrections." As RIt notes, Brusendorff (1925:296) thinks that this version is "later . . . but in the scribe's hand." If Thynne used MS as printer's copy for TH¹, he must have supplied his own version; there is no equivalent in the French for either line.
   SU states that TH¹'s reading "appears good, but an obvious break occurs here." David (RI) accepts neither version, calling the MS line "nonsensical" and noting that, while TH¹'s substitute "makes a kind of sense," it "has no equivalent in the French, which says that the God of Love made the ointment with his own hands to comfort pure lovers" (Lc 1852–53 "Amors l'avoit fet o ses mains / por les fins amanz conforter"). As SU notes (p. xxvii), "the English omits the first part of this sentence, causing *her* in ME 1893 to have no antecedent." David agrees that "some word like 'lovers' must be the antecedent of *her sores* and *they* (1893–94); therefore, an intervening couplet has perhaps been lost." He proposes "a hypothetical reading (with the emendation 'I' for *he* in 1891): . . . 'Somdell to yeve aleggement Upon the woundes that I had. [To comfort lovers he had it maad].'"
   1906 **Rokyng:** Early glosses relate this form to the verb *rock* (*MED rokken* v.): "rocking, trembling, quaking" (URg); "shaking, trembling" (TRg); "to rock to and fro with pain" (BE). But BE notes that "it is not very apparent how [Lamant] could be said to rock *narrowly* (narwe)." SK, the first to relate *Rokyng* to ME *rouken* "to crouch" (*MED rouken* v. [b]), reads the line as meaning "crouching down very closely on account of the pain" and suggests "*rouking* or *rukking*" as "a better spelling." GL respells as *Roukyng.* RB, like SK, retains the MS form *Rokyng* as "apparently the same word as *rouken,* 'crouch,' 'cower.'" SK RB RI compare *KnT* A 1308. BE SK RB RI all note the absence of any parallel in the Fr. FI relates the form to *rock* but reads the line as "moving it back and forth slightly (to get it out)"; and RI (cf. RIf) presents both alternatives: "Crouching, cowering? Or does the lover 'rock' the shaft to extract the arrow?" The idea of rocking or moving the shaft does not fit the text, where the participle is clearly intransitive. The intransitive sense "rocking to and fro with pain," as in BE's reading above, may reinforce the primary sense, "crouching."

With other foure, I dar wel say,
That never wole be take away. 1910
But the oynement halpe me wele.
And yit sich sorwe dide I fele
That al day I chaunged hewe
Of my woundes fresshe and newe, 1914
As men myght se in my visage. 37r
The arwis were so full of rage,
So variaunt of diversitee,
That men in everiche myght se
Bothe gret anoy and eke swetnesse,
And joie meynt with bittirnesse. 1920
Now were they esy, now were they wode;
In hym I felte bothe harme and goode.
Now sore without aleggement,
Now soft[en]yng with oynement,
It softnede heere and prikkith there; 1925
Thus ese and anger togidre were.
  The God of Love delyverly
Come lepande to me hastily
And seide to me in gret rape,
"Yelde thee, for thou may not escape! 1930
May no defence availe thee heere;

The[r]fore I rede make no daungere.
If thou wolt yelde thee hast[il]ly,
Thou shalt rather have mercy.
He is a foole in sikernesse 1935
That with daunger or stoutenesse
Rebellith there that he shulde plese;
In sich folye is litel ese.
Be meke where thou must nedis bowe; 37v
To stryve ageyn is nought thi prowe. 1940
Come at oones and have ydoo,
For I wole that it be soo.
Thanne yelde thee heere debonairly."
  And I answerid ful hombly,
"Gladly, sir, at youre biddyng 1945
I wole me yelde in al thyng.
To youre servyse I wole me take,
For God defende that I shulde make
Ageyn youre biddyng resistence;
I wole not don so grete offence, 1950
For if I dide, it were no skile.
Ye may do with me what ye wile,
Save or spille, and also sloo;
Fro you in no wise may I goo.

1913 *Lines 1913-14 trans.* RB[1,2]   1914 **fresshe]** so freshe UR   1919 **Bothe]** But ST   1921 **now were they wode]** and n. wode UR   1924 **softenyng]** softyng MS-SP[3] BE KA GL FU SU FI   **with]** w. the UR GL   1925 **softnede]** softed GL   **prikkith]** pricked TH[3]-UR SK GL   1926 **togidre were]** were yfere UR   1929 **rape]** iape TH[1]-BE FU   1932 **Therfore]** Thefore MS KA RB[1]   1933 **hastily]** hastly MS KA   1934 **rather]** the rathir UR SK GL FI   1936 **or]** or with UR   1945 **Gladly]** All gladly UR   1953 **Save]** Or save UR

1909 **other foure:** "That is, the other four love-causing arrows" (BE). SK identifies these as "Beauty (1750), Simplesse (1774), Curtesye (1802, and note to l. 1820), and Companye (1862)" and notes that "the names, even in the F. text, are not exactly the same as in a former passage," at lines 952–63; see 1802n.

1913–14 RB, following a suggestion in SKt, inverts these two lines, "perhaps rightly," states SU, citing the Fr. (Ln 1870–72 "Mais toutesvoies me dolut / La plaie si que la dolor / Me faisoit muer la color" "but nevertheless my wound hurt so much that the pain made me change color"). RIt notes that, although RB's "order is closer to the French, there is no need for the change." FI's "transposed order from Fr." is ambiguous; the text is not transposed.

1922 **hym:** "them." The form appears only in MS KA; all other eds. respell as *hem* (UR *them*), the usual form of the 3 pl. object personal pron.; and KA notes the change in BE MO. I do not collate for *hym* as plural; further examples are at lines 2218, 2221, 4948, 5419–36, 5503–04, 5997, 5999, 6041, 6677, 6925, 7252–53. See also *MED hem* pron. pl. for 14th-15th-century forms in *-i-*. The evidence in *LALME* (4.13; cf. 1.316) shows the main distribution of *him* as pl. in Ely, with secondary distribution in Devon and Sussex, tertiary in Cambridgeshire and Norfolk. Cf. 2854n.

1924 **softenyng:** This emendation of MS *softyng*, for meter, is noted in UR MO by KA and is supported (as SKt notes) by the form *softnede* in line 1925. *MED* lists MS form under *softing(e* ger.; see also *soften* v., *softenen* v.

1925 **softnede:** GL defines as "became less violent"; on GL's form, cf. note above.

  prikkith: SU notes that, since the Fr. has the historical present (Lc 1877 "m'oint . . . cuit" "heals . . . hurts"), the emendation to the pa. t. *pricked* is doubtful. If TH[1] is based on MS, the change is even more doubtful.

1928 **lepande:** RB FI RI note that this is a Northern participle; RI compares line 2263, where *sittande* rhymes with *hande*.

139

My lyf, my deth, is in youre honde; 1955
I may not laste out of youre bonde.
Pleyn at youre lyst I yelde me,
Hopyng in herte that sumtyme ye
Comfort and ese shull me sende;
Or ellis, shortly, this is the eende. 1960
Withouten helthe I mote ay dure
But if ye take me to youre cure.
Comfort or helthe how shuld I have, 38r
Sith ye me hurt, but ye me save?
The helthe of love m[o]t be founde 1965
Where as they token firste her wounde.
And if ye lyst of me to make
Youre prisoner, I wole it take
Of herte and will, fully at gree.
Hoolly and pleyn Y yelde me, 1970
Without feynyng or feyntise,
To be governed by youre emprise.
Of you I here so mych pris,
I wole ben hool at youre devis

For to fulfille youre lykyng, 1975
And repente for nothyng,
Hopyng to have yit in some tide
Mercy of that I abide."
And with that covenaunt yelde I me
Anoon, down knelyng upon my kne, 1980
Proferyng for to kisse his feete.
    But for nothyng he wolde [me] lete,
And seide, "I love thee bothe and preise,
[Sen that thyn aunswar doth me ease],
For thou answerid so curteisly. 1985
For now I wote wel uttirly
That thou art gentyll, by thi speche. 38v
For though a man fer wolde seche,
He shulde not fynden, in certeyn,
No sich answer of no vileyn, 1990
For sich a word ne myght nought
Isse out of a vilayns thought.
Thou shalt not lesen of thi speche,
For [to] thy helpyng wole I eche

1959 **shull**] shul to UR   1965 **love**] lovers SK FI   **mot**] mut MS MO KA   1966 **token**] taken
SP[1]   1969 **will fully**] willefully BE GL   1975 **fulfille**] fulfill all UR   1976 **repente**] to repentin UR-
MO   1977 **have**] haye SU   1978 **Mercy**] The m. GL   **that**] that that UR MO SK   1980 **upon**] on
UR   1982 **me**] *om.* MS MO KA   1984 *Out:* MS (MS₂ *corr.*)   1994 **to**] *om.* MS-KA FU SU

1960   **this is:** "pronounce 'this'" (GL).
1965–66   "'The healing of love must be found where they [the lovers] got their wound'" (RB 1965n.). RI states, "In the French, the God of Love's hand, which gave the wound, must perform the cure" (Lc 1910–11 "se vostre main, qui m'a navré, / ne me done la guerison"). § RI, following RB and comparing *SqT* F 156–65, notes that "the motif of the magic weapon that alone can cure the wound it inflicts (as in the story of Achilles and Telephus) is applied to love."
1965   **love:** KA endorses SK's emendation, *lovers*, and GL, while not adopting the change, suggests support for it with reference to line 1540 (see 1540n.). RB notes GL's suggestion "that *love* is personal (= 'lover') and should perhaps be plural"; RBt grants that SK's emendation may be correct, but the explanatory note (RB) suggests otherwise in its paraphrase of lines 1965–66 (see 1965–66n.). SU RI also grant the possibility of SK's reading, "but the sense implied," notes RI, "may be '[the wound] of love.'" There is no precise parallel in the Fr. (see 1965–66n.).
        mot: According to *MED mōten* v.(2), the form in MS—*mut*—is a var. sp. for "sg. 1 & 3 & subjunctive . . . (by anal. with sg. 2 and p.)."
1973   **mych:** See 1713n.
1976   **repente:** GL cites the Fr. (Lc 1920 "je ne me puis de rien doloir" "I cannot complain of anything") and suggests *me repente* as emendation.
1978   David (RI) suggests "Mercy of that [one] I await"(?); he notes that eds. (except KA GL) punctuate after *Mercy* (TH¹ FU virgule, TH²-MO SK FU-SU comma, FI semicolon) for the sense: "'For which [i.e., Mercy] I am waiting.'" This sense, he writes, is "close to the Fr. [Lc 1922 "la merci que j'atens" "the mercy that I await"]; but *of*," he notes, "is awkward in such a reading." Liddell (GL) cites the Fr. in support of his emendation, *The mercy*.
1983–84   **preise : ease:** Imperfect rhyme.
1983   **bothe:** GL suggests *moche* on the basis of the Fr. *mout* (Lc 1926).
1984   "written by a later hand on a line originally left blank" (KA). The same hand (MS₂ₐ) has supplied lines 1892, 2036, 3490; RBt SU FI RIt agree that the hand is later, but, as RIt notes, Brusendorff (1925:296–97) thinks that the hand is that of the MS scribe. See 1892n.
1992   **Isse:** *MED issuen* v. does not record this form of the inf. but probably should. TH³-MO respell as *Issue*.
1994   **to:** Kaluza's suggested emendation; he compares "vnto thyn helpyng" at line 2126 (KA).

And eke encresen that I may.
But first I wole that thou obaye
Fully, for thyn avauntage,
Anoon to do me heere homage.
And sith kisse thou shalt my mouthe,
Which to no vilayn was never couthe   2000
For to aproche it ne for to touche,
For sauff of cherlis I ne vouche
That they shull never neigh it nere.
For curteys and of faire manere,
Well taught, and full of gentilnesse   2005
He must ben that shal me kysse,
And also of full high fraunchise,
That shal atteyne to that emprise.
And first of o thing warne I thee,
That peyne and gret adversite   2010
He mote endure, and eke travaile,
That shal me serve, without faile.
But ther ageyns, thee to comforte,
And with thi servise to desporte,
Thou mayst full glad and joyfull be   2015

1995   So good a maister to have as me,
And lord of so high renoun.
I bere of love the gonfenoun,
Of curtesie the banere.
For I am of the silf manere,   2020
Gentil, curteys, meke, and fre,
That who ever ententyf be
Me to honoure, doute, and serve,
And also that he hym observe
Fro trespasse and fro vilanye   2025
And hym governe in curtesie
With will and with entencioun.
For whanne he first in my prisoun
Is caught, thanne must he uttirly
Fro thens forth full bisily   2030
Caste hym gentyll for to bee,
39r   If he desire helpe of me."
     Anoon without more delay,
Withouten daunger or affray,   2034
I bicome his man anoon   39v
[And gave hym thankes many a oon]

1997 **thyn]** thine own UR   2003 **neigh]** neyght TH²   2007 **full]** fulle of MO   2019 **Of]** And of UR   2020 **the silf]** selfe the TH³ ST SP² UR   2021 **curteys]** and curteis UR   2022 **who ever]** w. so e. SK   2023 **doute]** re-doute UR   2024 **And also]** Nede is GL   2025 **and]** and and MS KA (*second and underdotted for deletion*) RB¹   2027 **and with]** a. ST-SP³   2029 **he]** be SP¹   2035 **bicome]** b. tho MO   **man]** vassal UR   2036 *Out:* MS (MS₂ *corr.*)

1999   **sith:** KA endorses SK's form *sithen*.

2002–03   "For I do not vouchsafe to churls that they should ever come near it" (BE SK RIf). As RBt RIt note, SK suggests that "for *of* (suggested by *sauf*) we should read *to*," but RIt notes that "the sense seems . . . to be that the God of Love will not vouchsafe that his mouth be touched *of* (i.e., by) churls, nor that they draw near it. The construction," RIt states, "seems mixed." FI has a questionable gloss for *sauff of:* "safely kept from churls." § BE observes that "the kiss was part of the ceremony of doing homage," and refers to the note to line 4681, on that ceremony.

2002   **sauff . . . vouche:** "vo uchsafe" (RB); as BE notes, "the verb *vouche*, and the adverb *sauff*, which, in modern English, make one word, are here disjoined."

2003   **neigh it nere:** "draw any nearer" (RIf).

2006   **kysse:** "*kysse* probably to be read *kesse* (Kentish) for the rime" (RBt). "But with the number of imperfect rhymes in [Fragment] B, one cannot be sure" (RIt). Cf. line 2610.

2016   **to have:** "Read *t' have*" (GL).

2017   **lord:** "*Lord* seems to be dissyllabic; read (perhaps) *laverd*" (SK), from OE *hlaford*.

2018   **gonfenoun:** On the sense, "banner," see 1201n.

2022–27   RI notes that "a verb is required to complete the sense"; see 2024n.

2022   **who ever:** KA endorses SK's reading.

2024   **And also:** GL's *Nede is* resolves the anacoluthon (RB; cf. 2022–27n.). GL RIt quote the Fr. as support (Lc 1950–52 "dedenz li ne puet demorer / vilenie ne mesprison / ne nule mauvese aprison" "in him may dwell no baseness, no wrong or evil instruction").

2028–34   Not in the Fr. RI (2028n.) notes that GL accounts for the prison figure as a misunderstanding of the Fr. *aprison* "instruction" (Lc 1952, above) as *aprisoner* "to make prisoner."

2036   Written by a later hand on a line originally left blank (KA RIt). The hand (MS₂) is the same as that of lines 1892, 1984, 3490. As RIt notes, Brusendorff (1925:296) thinks that this hand is the same as that of the rest of MS. See 1892n.

And knelide doun with hondis joynt
And made it in my port full queynt;
The joye wente to myn herte rote.
Whanne I hadde kissed his mouth
    so swote, 2040
I hadde sich myrthe and sich likyng,
It cured me of langwisshing.
He askide of me thanne hostages.
"I have," he seide, "taken fele homages
Of oon and other, where I have bene 2045
[Disceyved] ofte withouten wene.
These felouns full of falsite
Have many sithes biguyled me
And thorough her falshede her lust achieved,
Wherof I repente and am agreved. 2050
And I hem gete in my daungere,

Her falshede shull they bie full dere.
But for I love thee, I seie thee pleyn,
I wole of thee be more certeyn;
For thee so sore I wole now bynde 2055
That thou away ne shalt not wynde
For to denyen the covenaunt,
Or don that is not avenaunt.
That thou were fals it were gret reuthe, 40r
Sith thou semest so full of treuthe." 2060
    "Sire, if thee lyst to undirstande,
I merveile the askyng this demande.
For why or wherfore shulde ye
Ostages or borwis aske of me,
Or ony other sikirnesse, 2065
Sith ye [wot], in sothfastnesse,
That ye have me susprised so

2044 **he seide]** *om.* UR   2046 **Disceyved]** Disteyned MS-SP¹ BE-KA FU; Distreined SP²-UR 2049 **thorough her]** t. UR SK GL RB¹·² FI RI   2050 **agreved]** greved UR   2055 **so]** *om.* TH³-UR 2057 **the]** thy TH³-UR   2063 **For why]** For-why SK   2064 **Ostages]** Hostage UR **of]** *om.* SP¹   2066 **wot]** wole MS KA   2067 **have me]** me haue TH¹-UR FU SU FI

2037   BE SK RB FI (2038n.) RI note that this is "the posture of the vassal performing homage before his feudal lord" (RI); SK reports that "this is still [in the 1890's] the attitude of one who receives a degree at Cambridge from the Vice-chancellor." Jephson (BE) compares line 4681 (as does SK) and his note; in a note to *The Court of Love* 297 (BE 4.141), he describes a vestige of the ceremony preserved in a nursery game. Cf. 4681n.

2038   **made it in my port full queynt:** GL suggests that *it in* be read "(?) *in it,* i.e. in doing it." But SKg₂ seems to understand the idiom *made it . . . queynt* as "[showed] satisfaction [in my bearing]," RB as "bore myself with due ceremony"; RB adduces the Fr. (Lc 1954 "mout me fis cointes" lit. "I made myself [i.e., I became, I was] very *cointes*"). On Fr. *cointes,* ME *queynt,* see below. RB RI clarify the idiom by reference to *GP* 785 "to make it wys" and the notes thereto, which detail similar idioms. See *MED maken* v.(1) 14b (d). Following RB, Benson suggests (RI *GP* 785n.) that the idiom "is probably derived from French constructions with *faire*" and adduces Prins (1952:203). Andrew (1993:579, *GP* 785n.) cites TR 4.216.

    queynt: As RBt notes, SKt suggests: "perhaps *quoynt.*" Ln Lc gloss Fr. *cointes* as "fier" ("proud") but cf. SKg₁'s glosses ("joli, gentil, agréable, amiable") for this word, citing Godefroy (1881–1902). FI takes ME *queynt* as "curious, artful," *MED maken* v.(1) 14b (d) as "elegant," *MED queint(e* adj. 2 (e) as "gracious, charming." See 65n.

2044–46   "That is, 'I have often received the homage of persons, by whom I have, notwithstanding, without doubt, been often disgraced'" (BE). See 2046n.

2044   **taken:** As RB notes, Skeat (SKt SK) suggests the Northern form *tan,* here and at line 2068.

2046   **Disceyved:** KA suggests this emendation, which SK GL RB-RI have adopted on reasonable paleographical grounds (*t/c* and *n/u* confusions are common) and on the basis of the Fr. *deceüz* (Lc 1960; noted by SKt SU FI). However, *MED disteinen* v. quotes MS *Disteyned* under sense 3. (b) "to dishonor or defame (sb.); defile," from the primary sense, 1. (a), "to color or stain (sth.)." SP²'s *distreined* mistakes the sense (cf. SP²·³g, s.v. *distreineth* "effecteth" and *distraineth* "vexeth"; URg *distrained* "tormented, afflicted"); see *MED distreinen,* sense 4 "oppress, distress."

2051   "'If I get them into my power'" (SK).

    in my daungere: GL compares line 1470; see 1049n.

2063   **For why:** SK takes these two words as a compound interrogative adv., "*For-why,* i.e. why," parallel to the Fr. *por quoi.* However, the syntax of the Fr. is not quite parallel (Lc 1976 "ne sai por quoi vos demandez" "I don't know why you ask"), and other eds. leave the two words uncompounded, with *For* as a conjunction, *why* as the interrogative adv. Cf. 5901n.

2065   **ony:** See 212n.

2066   **wot:** In support of TH¹'s emendation, SKt cites the Fr. *savez* (Lc 1978).

2067   **susprised:** Spelled *surprised* SP¹-BE SK; *suprised* FI. RBt notes that the MS "form occurs, though rarely." SU reports, inaccurately, that GL has *surprised.* All three forms derive from related AF variants of OF; see *MED surprisen* v., *susprisen* v., *supprisen* v. Cf. line 3235 *suspprised.*

And hole myn herte taken me fro
That it wole do for me nothing
But if it be at youre biddyng? 2070
Myn herte is youres, and myn right nought,
As it bihoveth in dede and thought,
Redy in all to worche youre will,
Whether so turne to good or ill.
So sore it lustith you to plese, 2075
No man therof may you desese.
Ye have theron sette sich justice
That it is werreid in many wise;
And if ye doute it nolde obeye,
Ye may therof do make a keye 2080
And holde it with you for ostage."
    "Now certis this is noon outrage,"

Quod Love, "and fully I acorde. 40v
For of the body he is full lord
That hath the herte in his tresour; 2085
Outrage it were to asken more."
    Thanne of his awmener he drough
A litell keye fetys ynowgh,
Which was of gold polisshed clere,
And seide to me, "With this keye heere 2090
Thyn herte to me now wole I shette;
For all my jowelles loke and knette
I bynde undir this litel keye,
That no wight may carie aweye;
This keye is full of gret poeste." 2095
With which anoon he touchide me
Undir the side full softly,

2074 **so turne]** s. it t. SK FI; to t. RB² 2075 **you]** yon TH¹ FU 2079 **ye]** he SU FI 2082 **is]** *om.*
TH³ ST 2083 **I]** *om.* ST SP²,³ 2085 **That]** Than SU FI 2092 **my]** thy UR **jowelles]** iowel TH¹,² SP¹
BE MO GL FU; ioyful TH³ ST SP²-UR

2068 **taken:** See 2044n.
2074 **Whether:** GL reads this word as "monosyllable 'wher'" and compares line 2128 "Where so."
    turne: KA suggests SK's emendation, *it turne*, which RBt states is perhaps correct.
2076 **desese:** "disseize" (URg BE) "dispossess" (URg RB FI), "oust" (BE SK), "rob" (*MED disseisen*, v. 2. [b]).
SKt reports that MS has *disese* and TH¹ *desese*; the reverse is true. SKt RBt RIt note the Fr. *desaisir* (Lc 1986), and SK
RB have *disseise*, for clarity, in the text. § BE states: "*Disese* [*sic*] is put for *desseize*. . . . Siezin is the legal word for
possession." SK notes that "*disseisin* is the opposite of *seisin*, a putting in possession of a thing."
2077–78 RB notes that "the translation is obscure and not quite parallel to" KA Fr. (1979–80 "Tel garnison i
avés mise, / Qui le guerroie a vostre guise" "You have placed there [in my heart] such a garrison as would preserve it
in your manner"). RB also quotes Ln (1989–90 "Tel garnison i avez mise / Qui le garde bien e jostise" ". . . as may
guard and rule it well"); Ln's text is closer to the ME than is Lc's (1987–88 "Tele garde i avez vos mise / qui le garde
bien a devise" "You have placed there such a guard as may guard it quite perfectly"). RI reports a variant of the
second line, from the L family (Ln 1990t "Qui mout le guerroie e jostise" "as would preserve and rule it completely"),
and notes that the translator may have taken *guerroie* as a form of *guerreier* "make war," rather than of *guerir*
"preserve." "Thus," RI states, "the sense of the English is probably that Love has set such enforcers of his law on the
heart that it is in a state of siege." See the notes on lines 2077 *justice* and 2078 *werreid*, below.
2077 **justice:** "right, claim" (SKg₂), "punishment" (GL), "government?" (RB FI), "control(s)?" (RB RI),
"guards?" (RI). The Fr. verb *jostise* "rule" appears in the ME as a noun, parallel to Fr. *garnison* or *garde*; see
2077–78n., above.
2078 **werreid:** "ma[de] war upon, disturb[ed], molest[ed]" (URg, s.v. *Warray*; cf. BEg MOg SKg₂); "perse-
cuted; cf. vv. 3251, 6264, 6926" (GL); "battered (warred upon)" (FI). See 2077–78n., 3251n.
2084–85 GL compares lines 1794–96.
2087 **awmener:** Early eds. gloss as "cubbard" (SPg URg), "store-house," or "store-room" (T. Thomas [URg],
who thinks Lat. *almarium* a corruption of Lat. *armarium*); but TR et al. gloss correctly as "purse" ("for carrying
money to be bestowed in alms" [BE]) on the basis of the Fr. *aumouniere* (Lc 1997; noted by SK).
2088–95 As RB RI note, Ln (1999–2007n.) reports the idea of the key in Chrétien de Troyes, *Yvain* 4632–34
(4626–28, ed. Roques 1965) and *Perceval* 3810–13 (2634–37, ed. Roach 1959).
2092 **jowelles:** "Jewels" (URg TRg SKg₂); BE, however, taking MS *iowell* as an abbreviation for *jowelle*,
regards it as "an adaptation of the old French word *joaille*, jewellery." But KA endorses SK's *iowellis*, and Skeat (SK)
takes the MS form as "the usual (Northern) contraction for *Iowellis*, jewels"; he cites the Fr. pl. *joiau* (Lc 2002 "joal"
"jewels") and says that he "can find no authority for making it a collective noun, as Bell suggests." Cf. 5419n. on
deles. On MS *iowell* as an abbreviation for *iowelles*, see above, "The Manuscript Hands: The Scribe (MS₁)" and cf.
300n.
2095 **poeste:** URg suggests that the word is "contracted from the Lat. Potestas," power; *OED Pouste* n.
confirms the etymology through OF *poesté, pousté*; cf. *MED poustę̄*.

That he myn herte sodeynly
Without anoye hadde spered,
That yit right nought it hath me dered. 2100
    Whanne he hadde don his will al oute,
And I hadde putte hym out of doute,
"Sire," I seide, "I have right gret wille
Youre lust and plesaunce to fulfille.
Loke ye my servise take at gree, 2105
By thilke feith ye owe to me.
I seye nought for recreaundise, 41r
For I nought doute of youre servise;
But the servaunt traveileth in vayne
That for to serven doth his payne 2110
Unto that lord which in no wise
Kan hym no thank for his servyse."
    Love seide, "Dismaie thee nought.
Syn thou for sokour hast me sought,
In thank thi servise wole I take, 2115
And high of degre I wole thee make,
If wikkidnesse ne hyndre thee;
But, as I hope, it shal nought be.
To worshipe no wight by aventure

May come, but if he peyne endure. 2120
Abide and suffre thy distresse
That hurtith now; it shal be lesse.
I wote my silf what may thee save,
What medicyne thou woldist have.
And if thi trouthe to me thou kepe, 2125
I shal unto thyn helpyng eke,
To cure thy woundes and make hem clene
Where so they be olde or grene;
Thou shalt be holpen, at wordis fewe.
For certeynly thou shalt well shewe 2130
Where that thou servest with good wille 41v
For to compleysshen and fulfille
My comaundementis, day and nyght,
Whiche I to lovers yeve of right."
    "A, sire, for goddis love," seide I, 2135
"Er ye passe hens, ententyfly
Youre comaundementis to me ye say,
And I shall kepe hem, if I may,
For hem to kepen is all my thought.
And if so be I wote hem nought, 2140
Thanne may I [erre] unwityngly.

2099 **anoye hadde**] any h. TH³ ST SP²·³; any doute hath so UR; al a. h. SK   2102 **hym**] hem TH²
2104 **plesaunce**] pleasure TH¹-UR FU SU FI   2105 **at**] atte MS BE-KA GL   2108 **of**] or ST   2113 **seide**]
sayid tho UR   2115 **I**] *om.* ST   2116 **degre**] gree SP¹ GL   **I**] *om.* UR BE   2120 **if**] that UR; *om.* TH³-
SP³   2128 **Where so they**] W. s. that t. UR   2132 **compleysshen**] accomplysshen TH¹-UR GL FU SU FI
2141 **may I erre**] m. I MS-SP³ BE-KA FU; m. I sinne   SK

2099 **spered:** "shut (vp)" (SPg GLg), "Lockt up" (URg), "barred" (BEg et al.), "fastened" (MOg et al.), "bolted"
(MOg); SK cites Fr. *ferma* (Lc 2007) and compares line 3320 *sparrede*.
    2106   Roscow (1981:117) cites this line as an example of "the [common] ellipsis of a relative object-pronoun in
constructions of the type 'by the faith I owe to you'"; he also cites *TC* 3.791, 1649. On the ellipsis of the relative
subject-pronoun, see 1239–40n. Cf. 2936n.
    2108   "That is, 'I am not afraid to undertake your service'" (BE).
    2109   **But:** SKt suggests: "om. *But*?"
    2113   **seide:** A later hand—perhaps MS₂ₑ—has added a comma that corresponds to a virgule in TH¹; similar
commas that match virgules appear after *come* in line 2120 and *now* in line 2122. These cases suggest that the
commas, and the parentheses in line 2118, are printer's marks. See above, "The Printer's Marks."
    2116   **degre:** KA notes, as Skeat's suggestion, that we "either omit *And* or read *gre*." RBt's note, "eds. *gree*,"
can apply only to SP¹ GL.
    2118   **as I hope:** A later hand—perhaps MS₂ₑ—has placed parentheses around this clause in MS. The parallel
appearance of parentheses in TH¹ suggests that these are printer's marks. Cf. 2113n.
    2119–20   According to BE, these lines appear "to be an allusion to the proverb, 'Via crucis via lucis'" (the way
of the cross is the way to light).
    2120   **come:** See 2113n.
    2122   **now:** See 2113n.
    2128   **Where so:** "whether" (FI).
    2141   **erre:** UR's emendation follows the sense of the Fr. (Lc 2046 "tost porroie issir hors de voie" "I could go
entirely astray"; noted by SK GL RBt SU RIt). SK has *sinne*, a reading endorsed by KA, but grants that "perhaps the
exact word is *erre*, as suggested by Urry."

Wherfore I pray you enterely,
With all myn herte, me to lere,
That I trespasse in no manere."
The God of Love thanne chargide me 2145
Anoon, as ye shall here and see,
Worde by worde, by right emprise,
So as the Romance shall devise.
The maister lesith his tyme to lere
Whanne that the disciple wole not here. 2150
It is but veyn on hym to swynke,
That on his lernyng wole not thenke.
Who so luste love, late hym entende,
For now the Romance bigynneth
    to amende. 2154

Now is good to here in fay, 42r
If ony be that can it say
And poynte it as the resoun is
Set; for other-gate, ywys,
It shall nought well in all thyng
Be brought to good undirstondyng. 2160
For a reder that poyntith ille
A good sentence may ofte spille.
The book is good at the eendyng,
Maad of newe and lusty thyng;
For who so wole the eendyng here, 2165
The crafte of love he shall mowe lere,
If that ye wole so long abide
Tyl I this Romance may unhide

2143 **me to]** m. for t. UR   2149 **his]** *om.* UR   2150 **that]** *om.* TH¹-BE SK-FI   2151 **is]** was
BE   2154 **bigynneth]** ginneth UR SK   **to]** *om.* SK   2157-58 **is Set; for other]** is. Set forth another
GL   2166 **mowe]** nowe TH¹-BE SK FU   2167 **ye]** he TH¹-UR SK FU-FI

2145–52   At this point, *Rom* omits a further speech of the God of Love (Lc 2049–2054) and moves to indirect discourse that corresponds to Lc 2055ff. ("Li diex d'Amors lors m'encharja . . ." "The God of Love then charged me . . ."). However, four lines from the omitted speech (Lc 2051–54) appear as *Rom* 2149–52, where they serve as the poet's general observation rather than as the direct discourse of the God of Love; see 2149–52n. Sutherland thinks that this shuffling indicates "a break and the hand of the reviser"; see "Partial Acceptance," above, and SU, p. xxvii.

2148   **Romance:** RIt notes that TH¹ (and FI) has *Romaunt* here but "subsequently . . . reads *Romance,* though the running title is *Romaunt.*" See Title note, at the beginning of these notes. Here and at line 2154, the word corresponds to the Fr. *romanz* (Lc 2058, 2060) as a term for a verse narrative in the French (Romance) language (cf. SPg SKg₂); at line 2168, it has the same sense, but at line 2170 the linguistic aspect is primary; at line 3793, it corresponds to Fr. *estoire* (Lc 3487 "story, narrative"). See notes to these lines.

2149–52   GL RB FI RI note that these lines are displaced from their position in the Fr.; RB RI note that in the Fr. "the God of Love speaks these lines to the lover" (RI). See 2145–52n.

2154   **bigynneth to amende:** KA endorses SK's *gynneth amende.* SK suggests the pronunciation "ginn'th," for a monosyllable. "If the reading of the text is retained it must be *gynnith t'amende,*" writes Liddell (GL), but he suggests an alternative emendation, *wole amende,* based on the Fr. (Lc 2060 "des or amende" "from this point on improves"). § With the sense of the line, SK compares line 2168.
    Romance: "by the 14th cent. already a generalized term for a narrative of chivalry and love" (FI). Cf. 2148n.

2156   **ony:** See 212n.

2157–62   SK (2161n.) RB RI note that these lines are not in the Fr.

2158   **other-gate:** "otherwise" (RIf); on Northern *gate* "way," see 5167n.

2161   **poyntith ille:** lit., "punctuates badly" (SK). BE notes that "to *pointe* means, here, to make the proper pauses in reading, to punctuate with the voice." SK RB RI note that MSS were unpunctuated and that the reader had to "construe both syntax and sense" (RI). Brusendorff (1925:379–81) uses this passage in support of his argument for a memorial origin of the Glasgow MS.

2166   **mowe:** be able (to) (SPg et al.); see *MED mouen,* v.(3), sense 2a. *MED* does not list this form of the infinitive but does have *mou(e, mouwe(n; OED may* v.¹ records *mowe(n* from the 14th century.

2167   **ye:** RIt cites the Fr. (Ln 2070 "Por quoi il vueille tant atendre" "provided that he is willing to wait until . . ."), which seems to support TH¹'s *he.* In support of *ye,* RIt accounts for "the confusion of pronouns in the translation" by pointing out that "the French poet is addressing his audience, telling them what a patient reader may expect to learn ([Ln 2068] *Je vos di bien que il porra*—'I tell *you* indeed that *he* can')."

2168   **Romance:** See 2148n. Here, the word corresponds only roughly to the Fr. (which itself has variants (Lc 2069 [MS Ha] has *j'encomance* "I begin," where Ln [2071] has *j'enromance* "I narrate in French").

And undo the signifiance
Of this dreme into Romance. 2170
The sothfastnesse that now is hidde,
Without coverture shall be kidde
Whanne I undon have this dremyng,
Wherynne no word is of lesyng.
   "Velanye, at the bigynnyng, 2175
I wole," say[de] Love, "over all thyng,
Thou leve, if thou wolt [not] be
Fals and trespasse ageyns me.
I curse and blame generaly 42v
All hem that loven vilanye; 2180
For vilanye makith vilayn,
And by his dedis a cherle is seyn.
Thise vilayns arn withouten pitee,
Frendshipe, love, and all bounte.
I nyl resseyve unto my servise 2185

Hem that ben vilayns of emprise.
But undirstonde in thyn entent
That this is not myn entendement,
To clepe no wight in noo ages
Oonly gentill for his lynages. 2190
But who so is vertuous,
And in his port nought outrageous,
Whanne sich oon thou seest thee biforn,
Though he be not gentill born,
Thou maist well seyn, this is in soth, 2195
That he is gentil by cause he doth
As longeth to a gentilman;
Of hem noon other deme I can.
For certeynly, withouten drede,
A cherle is demed by his dede 2200
Of hie or lowe, as ye may see,
Or of what kynrede that he bee.

2175 **at**] atte MS BE-KA   2176 **sayde**] say MS-ST SP²,³ KA FU   2177 **if thou wolt not be**] i. t. w. b. MS-SP³ KA FU; i. that t. w. ybe UR; i. t. w. ne b. BE; i. t. ne w. b. MO   2184 **Frendshipe**] Frendship and UR   2185 **unto**] to UR SK   2188 **is**] om. MO   2189 **ages**] age UR   2190 **lynages**] linage UR   2191 **is**] that is UR SK GL   2195 **is in**] in SP³-BE; is a SK   2198 **deme**] neme SP¹   2201 **ye**] we RB² RI

2170 **Romance:** BE SK RB RIf note that here the word means the Romance language, (Old) French. See 2148n., 2168n., 3793n.

2176 **sayde:** For the emendation to past tense, SU compares "Quod" at line 2083.

2177 **wolt not:** KA recommends "Insert *nought* after *wolt*."

2181–82 RB RI compare *WBT* D 1158.

2185–2202 Brink (1870:28), SK (2190n.) GL RB FI (2191–2202n.) RI note that the passage is not in the Fr. KA Fr. shows no parallel, but SU Fr. 2086 A-F has a parallel to lines 2185–90 in a six-line passage from Guy de Mori's reworking of the *Roman* (see also Sutherland's Introduction, pp. xxx–xxxi). In the note to this passage (p. 184; cf. n. to ME 2185), Sutherland argues that the postulated "reviser" did not adapt these lines from MS He, where Sutherland finds them, since "the ME translator . . . was not following He"; instead, he says, "it appears that the reviser found the six lines in a MS separate from the one he used to assist his revision."

BE SK (2190n.) GL RB FI (2191–2202n.) RI note the parallel to the sermon on *gentilesse* in *WBT* D 1109ff., lines which Skeat thinks may have suggested those in *Rom*. As Kaluza notes (1893a:51–52), Child (1870) and Besant (1871) had pointed out earlier that the idea of true *gentilesse* appears at a later point in Jean de Meun's portion of the French *Roman* (Lc 18577–604); Child credits Tyrwhitt (TR 4.270, on *WBT* D 1159) for noting that the idea derives from Boethius (*De Cons. Phil.* 3p6,3m6); and Child and Besant both note that the idea was widespread by Chaucer's time. RB RI note the work of Brusendorff (1925:399–402), who adduces the similarities to *WBT* as evidence in support of his argument for Chaucer's authorship of the entire *Rom* and who suggests that memorial transmission accounts for the present state of the text (pp. 414–15). Brusendorff writes (p. 401): "When the transmitter had got as far as [line 2186], he was evidently reminded of Jean de Meun's later statement of his democratic views and inserted an imperfectly remembered version of it." FI (2191–2202n.) also cites the parallel to *WBT* D 1109ff., but FI errs somewhat in saying that Skeat argued that the lines "are evidence of Chaucer's authorship of this part of the text"; Skeat (2190n.) argues only that the lines "may have been suggested by Chaucer's Tale," and elsewhere he argues *against* Chaucer's authorship of Fragment B, where these lines appear.

2188 **this is:** "read *this*" (GL).

2191 **is:** KA endorses *that is* in SK.

2195 **is in:** The emendation of SP³-BE, *in*, has a metrical basis in SP³ UR, where the spelling *maiest* (SP³) or *mayist* (UR) shows a disyllable; they construe *this* as the object of *seyn* rather than as subject of *is*. KA endorses SK's *is a*.

2202 **Or of:** "rather than by (before by)" (FI).

"Ne say nought, for noon yvel wille,　43r
Thyng that is to holden stille;
It is no worshipe to mysseye.　2205
Thou maist ensample take of Keye,
That was somtyme, for mysseiyng,
Hated bothe of olde and yong.
As fer as Gaweyn, the worthy,
Was preised for his curtesie,　2210
Kay was hated, for he was fell,
Of word dispitous and cruell.
Wherfore be wise and aqueyntable,
Goodly of word and resonable
Bothe to lesse and eke to m[a]re.　2215
And whanne thou comest there men are,
Loke that thou have in custome ay
First to salue hym, if thou may;
And if it fall that of hem somme
Salue thee first, be not domme,　2220
But quyte hym curteisly anoon,
Without abidyng, er they goon.
　"For nothyng eke thy tunge applye
To speke wordis of rebaudrye.
To vilayne speche in no degre　2225
Late never thi lippe unbounden be;
For I nought holde hym, in good feith,　43v
Curteys, that foule wordis seith.

"And all wymmen serve and preise,
And to thy power her honour reise.　2230
And if that ony myssaiere
Dispise wymmen, that thou maist here,
Blame hym, and bidde hym holde hym stille.
And [set] thy myght and all thy wille
Wymmen and ladies for to please,　2235
And to do thyng that may hem ese,
That they ever speke good of thee,
For so thou maist best preised be.
　"Loke fro pride thou kepe thee wele,
For thou maist bothe perceyve and fele　2240
That pride is bothe foly and synne;
And he that pride hath hym withynne
Ne may his herte in no wise
Meken ne souplen to servyse.
For pride is founde in every part　2245
Contrarie unto loves art.
And he that loveth trewly
Shulde hym contene jolily
Without pride, in sondry wise,
And hym disgysen in queyntise.　2250
For queynte array, without drede,　44r
Is nothyng proude, who takith hede;
For fresh array, as men may see,
Without pride may ofte be.

2204　**that is]** which t. i. UR; t. i. for MO　2215　**mare]** more MS BE-KA　2220　**be not]** b. thou n. UR; b. n. thou MO　2224　**rebaudrye]** rybaudye TH¹ TH³ ST SK FU SU FI　2226　**never]** not UR　2234　**set]** *om.* MS KA　2239　**Loke]** L. that UR

2203–04　SK RB RI cite Ovid (*Ars amatoria* 2.604 "gravis est culpa tacenda loqui" "to utter what should be kept silent is a serious crime"). RI notes that "much of the God of Love's advice is lifted directly from Ovid."
　2206–12　On Kay's ill manners and Gawain's courtesy, BE quotes, without line identification, "*Roman de Merlin* 'Si Keux est felon et dénaturé'"; SK RB cite Malory 7.1; SK RB RI cite *SqT* F 95; and RB RI refer to Ln's examples (2093n.).
　2213　*Marginalium:* "noᵃ bene" appears opposite this line in MS.
　2215–16　**mare : are:** TH¹'s Northern *mare* is supported by the rhyme with *are*, itself a Northern form. Cf. lines 2709–10 and "Authorship," above.
　2218, 2221　**hym:** "them." All except MS BE-KA GL (line 2221 MS TH³ BE-KA GL) respell as *hem*, the usual form of the 3 pl. object personal pron. See 1922n.
　2224　**rebaudrye:** Although the forms in *-drye* and *-dye* differ little in field of meaning, *MED* distinguishes them in terms of OF origin: *ribaudi(e* n. from OF *ribaudie, ribaudri(e* n. from OF *ribauderie.* Cf. 4926n.
　2230　**to:** "according to" (GL FI), "to the extent of" (RB).
　2231　**ony:** See 212n.
　2235　**Wymmen:** As KA notes, an *o* in MS *Wymmen* has been altered to *y.*
　2239–40　**kepe thee wele : perceyve and fele:** On the basis of the Fr. *te garde : entent bien et esgarde* (Lc 2113–14), Brusendorff (1925:416–17) suggests a rather free emendation: "Loke fro pride thou *kepe thee* / For thou maist bothe *here and see.*"
　2250　**queyntise:** Citing this line, UR glosses, "Neatness; Strangeness, oddness."
　2251　**queynte:** "elegant" (SKg₂), although UR, citing this line glosses "strange, odd"; cf. 65n.

"Mayntene thysilf aftir thi rent,　　2255
Of robe and eke of garnement;
For many sithe faire clothyng
A man amendith in mych thyng.
And loke alwey that they be shape—
What garnement that thou shalt make—　2260
Of hym that kan best do,
With all that perteyneth therto.
Poyntis and sleves be well sittande,
Right and streght on the hande.
Of shone and bootes, newe and faire,　2265
Loke at the leest thou have a paire,
And that they sitte so fetisly
That these ruyde may uttirly
Merveyle, sith that they sitte so pleyn,
How they come an or off ageyn.　　2270

Were streit gloves, with awm[en]ere
Of silk; and alwey with good chere
Thou yeve, if thou have richesse;
And if thou have nought, spende the lesse. 2274
Alwey be mery, if thou may,　　44v
But waste not thi good alway.
Have hatte of floures as fresh as May,
Chapelett of roses of Wissonday;
For sich array ne costeth but lite.
Thyn hondis wasshe, thy teeth
　make white,　　　　2280
And lete no filthe upon thee bee.
Thy nailes blak if thou maist see,
Voide it awey delyverly.
And kembe thyn heed right jolily.
[Fard] not thi visage in no wise,　2285

2257　**many sithe]** m. a s. UR　　2260　**shalt make]** s. The m. UR　　2261　**kan best]** k. the b. UR; k. hem b. SK GL　　2264　**Right]** Ful r. UR　　**on]** upon UR SK　　2266　**thou]** you SP²,³　　2268　**ruyde]** rude men UR　　2271　**awmenere]** awmere MS-KA GL FU　　2273　**if]** if that UR　　**richesse]** gret r. GL　　2277　**as fresh]** f. TH³-BE SK　　2279　**ne]** *om.* UR　　**costeth]** costneth MS-KA GL FU SU FI　　2283　**awey]** alwey BE　　2285　**Fard]** Farce MS-KA GL FU SU FI

2255–84　Ln (2135–74n.) RB RI compare Ovid, *Ars amatoria* 1.513–24.

2258　mych: KA recommends adding -*e*, so spelled in TH¹ TH³ ST UR FU-RI. See also 1713n.

2259–60　*Marginalium:* In MS, a fist (hand with pointing finger) appears next to these lines.

2261　**kan best:** KA endorses SK's *can hem beste* and the comparison with line 2259; GL adopts the emendation, "perhaps correctly," says RBt.

2263–64　**sittande : hande:** "*sittand*, the Northern form of the participle, is here established by the rime" (RB). RI also notes the Northern participle and compares line 1928 "lepande." Cf. also lines 2707–08 and "Authorship," above.

2265–70　BE notes the smooth-fitting boots as "a piece of mediæval dandyism" and cites *GP* 203.

2268　**ruyde:** *MED nūde* adj. gives two forms of the OF etymon, *rude* and *ruide*. SKt notes the Fr. parallel, *cil vilain* (Lc 2140).

2270　**an:** "on" (URg et al.). TH² SP BE et al. normalize to *on*; SU regards TH¹'s *an* as "a printer's error," but if MS was the copy for TH¹, as Blodgett thinks (1979:97–101), there was no error.

2271　**awmenere:** KA's suggestion. SK GL note the same form at line 2087; in both places the word translates Fr. *aumouniere* (Lc 1997, 2143). SK RB RIt regard MS *awmere* as a scribal error rather than "a contr. of *awmenere*" (*OED Awmere*, noted in SK). *MED aumenēr* n.(2) lists *aumere* as a var. form, but, like *OED*, supports it only with this quotation. Eds. before SK accepted the MS form without correction.

2273　**yeve:** "The translator seems to be thinking here of alms-giving. The advice in the French is to dress up within one's means" (RI).

　　richesse: GL, quoting the Fr. *grant richece* (Marteau = KA Fr. 2147, Michel 2167), emends to *gret richesse*; the word *grant*, which Ln (2157t) lists as an L-family variant, appears in neither Ln 2157 nor Lc 2145.

2276　**alway:** KA suggests *away*, but no ed. so emends. There is no exact parallel in the Fr.

2278　**of Wissonday:** "suitable for Whitsunday" (SK). Perhaps "of the time, or season, of Whitsunday." BE SK note that Whitsunday (seven weeks after Easter) is a time of great festivity; SK quotes the Fr. parallel (Lc 2150 "Pentecoste").

2279　**costeth:** SK, on KA's suggestion, has *cost*, a contracted form; SK cites Fr. *coste* (Lc 2149).

2280–84　BE SK cite Ovid, *Ars amatoria* 1.515–19.

2285–86　On painting the face, RI notes: "The French explicitly describes such practices as effeminate: 'Ce n'apartient s'as dames non, Ou a ceus de mauvais renon' ([Ln 2171–72] This pertains only to ladies or to men of ill repute)."

2285　**Fard:** In support of this emendation, endorsed by KA, SK quotes the Fr. (Lc 2158 "mes ne te *fardes* ne ne guignes" "but do not rouge or paint yourself") and states: "It is clear that *Fard*, not *Farce*, is the right reading.

148

For that of love is not th'emprise;
For love doth haten, as I fynde,
A beaute that cometh not of kynde.
Alwey in herte I rede thee
Glad and mery for to be, 2290
And be as joyfull as thou can;
Love hath no joye of sorowful man.
That yvell is full of curtesie
That [laughith] in his maladie;
For ever of love the sijknesse 2295
Is meynde with swete and bitternesse.
The sore of love is merveilous,
For now the lover [is] joyous,

Now can he pleyne, now can he grone, 45r
Now can he syngen, now maken mone; 2300
Today he pleyneth for hevynesse,
Tomorowe he [pleyeth] for jolynesse.
The lyf of love is full contrarie,
Which stoundemele can ofte varie.
But if thou canst mirthis make, 2305
That men in gre wole gladly take,
Do it goodly, I comaunde thee.
For men shulde, wheresoevere they be,
Do thing that hem sittyng is,
For therof cometh good loos and pris. 2310
Whereof that thou be vertuous,

2290 **Glad]** Full g. UR   2293 **yvell]** ill UR   2294 **laughith]** knowith MS-KA FU   2298 **the lover is joyous]** t. l. j. MS-TH² SP¹ KA FU; is t. l. j. GL   2302 **pleyeth]** pleyneth MS-KA FU   2305 **mirthis]** som m. SK   2306 **wole]** wolde BE   2309 **that]** t. to GL   **sittyng]** befitting UR; most s. MO; best s. SK SU FI

Farce would mean 'stuff' or 'cram'; see [*GP*] A 233." However, SP UR TR GL FI gloss *farce* as "paint"; GL states that *Farce* is a "variant form of *farde*"; and *MED farsen* v. [OF farcir], cites this line (with *Farce*) and two clear passages from Lydgate for this sense (3. [a]), "to beautify (the face) by applying cosmetics." The same sense is of course primary for SK's emendation, *Fard*, which RB RI adopt, "perhaps rightly" (SU); see *MED farden*, v. [OF farder].

2287–88   The ME again departs from the Fr. (Ln 2173–74), where it is a question of a *love*, rather than beauty, that is contrary to nature.

2288   On natural beauty, BE says: "The poet may, perhaps, have had in his mind the 'simplex munditiis' [simple elegance] of Horace."

2293–94   RB quotes the Fr. (Lc 2167–68 "c'est maladie mout cortoise, / l'en en joe et rit et envoise" "It is a very courtly disease; from it one plays and laughs and has a good time"). See 2294n.

2293   **yvell:** Perhaps "sickness" (see *MED ivel* n. 5. [a]), rather than "sick man (person)" (GL FI). See Fr. *maladie* (Lc 2167, above).

2294   **laughith:** Skeat's emendation (*lauhwith*) for MS *knowith*, which he considers "a strange error." In support, SK GL RB SU FI RIt note the Fr. *rit* (Lc 2168; see above). BE keeps MS *knowith* and reads lines 2293–94 as follows: "That evil [*scil.* love] is full of courtesy, which, even in the height of its malady, does not lose its self-possession." KA suggests "*lowith* (= laughs)," and GL adopts that form; as RIt notes, "some such spelling doubtless accounts for the error." Sutherland probably misreads Skeat's textual note—"G. knowith (!); *so* Th."—when he says that "Skt. wrongly ascribes *laugheth* to Th."; I take Skeat's note to mean that both MS and TH¹ have *know(i,e)th*, as is the case.

2295   **sijknesse:** MS *-ij-* for *-y-* appears also at line 2644 (*sijknesse*) and line 4621 (*wijs*). See above, "The Manuscript Hands: The Scribe."

2296   **meynde:** SK compares *KnT* A 2170.

2297   **sore:** FI glosses as "soreness" and cites the Fr. *maus d'amer* (Lc 2171 "ills of love").

2301–04   Not in the Fr. (SK RB). SU Fr. supplies (as 2188A–D) "the first four lines . . . of a sixteen-line passage probably interpolated by Gui de Mori," a passage which he finds in MS Tou, fol. 24. But the first two and the last of his four lines are not very close to the ME: "Amant sentent le mal d'amer / Vne eure dous et l'autre amer. / Et le amors c'est si contraire / Que tu n'en puisces nul bien traire." See note to SU Fr. 2188A–D and Sutherland's Introduction, pp. xxx–xxxi.

2302   **pleyeth:** SK's emendation; cf. Lounsbury (1892:2.14).

2305–24   On the use of Ovid, see 2311–12n.

2305   **mirthis:** KA endorses SK's reading.

2308–09   See 2315–16n.

2309   **sittyng:** becoming (URg TRg BE SK), suitable (URg SKg₂ FI), (be)fitting (BEg MOg SKg₂ RBg); SK compares *ClT* E 460 "sit." SU FI RIt note the Fr. *mieuz* (Lc 2181 "best") as support for SK's *best sitting*.

2311–12   RB paraphrases: "If you are accomplished in any art, do not be distant and offish about performance." RI quotes the Fr. (Ln 2195–96): "'Se tu es senz viste e legier, Ne fai pas de saillir dangier' (If you feel nimble and light, don't be reluctant to leap)." For the idea, Ln (2189–210n.) RB RI cite Ovid, *Ars amatoria* 1.595–96.

149

Ne be not straunge ne daungerous;
For if that thou good ridere be,
Prike gladly, that men may se.
In armes also if thou konne, 2315
Pursue [tyl] thou a name hast wonne.
And if thi voice be faire and clere,
Thou shalt maken [no] gret daungere
Whanne to synge they goodly prey;

It is thi worship for t'obeye. 2320
Also to you it longith ay
To harpe and gitterne, daunce and play,
For if he can wel foote and daunce, 45v
It may hym greetly do avaunce.
Among eke, for thy lady sake, 2325
Songes and complayntes that thou make,
For that wole meven in hir herte

2313 **that**] *om.* TH² 2314 **se**] The se UR GL 2315 **In**] An SP²·³ 2316 **tyl**] to MS BE-KA
2318 **no**] *om.* MS MO KA 2319 **Whanne**] Whan The UR 2323 **foote**] flute SU FI 2324 **It**] If SU
2326 **that**] se that GL 2327 **meven**] meve hem SK **herte**] hete TH²

2315 "That is, 'If you are skilful in jousting.' *Faire les armes* is the technical phrase for to joust." (BE).
2316 "That is, 'Continue to practice jousting until thou hast won a name'" (BE). BE quotes, as "the original,"
two lines (Lc 2180–81 "Chascuns doit fere en totes places / ce qu'i set qui mieuz li avient" "Everyone in all places
ought to do the things that he knows suit him best") that are parallel rather to lines 2308–09.
2318 **maken no gret daungere:** "Make no great excuse" (SK). As parallel to *daungere*, Skeat notes Fr.
essoine (Lc 2192 "excuse"); and, as source, he cites Ovid, *Ars amatoria* 1.595.
2321–24 On the basis of the Fr. (Lc 2195–98), Brusendorff (1925:417–18) suggests a free emendation: "Also to
you it longith ay / *With* harpe and gittern *to make* play, / For if *ye* can wel *floyte* and daunce / It may *you* gretly do
avaunce." Cf. 2323n.
2321–22 **ay : play:** Brusendorff (1925:418), assuming the infinitive *playe*, alleges a faulty rhyme.
2322 **harpe and gitterne:** As source for this wording, Fleming (1967:49) and Sutherland (SU Fr. 2208n.)
point to the var. *harpper ou chitoler*, from MS. Ra (Ln 2208t), rather than the standard Fr. *vïeler* "to fiddle" (Lc 2196).
gitterne: play the "Giterne" (TRg), a "guitar" (TRg et al.), "cittern" (RBg) "cithern, a guitar-like
instrument" (Rlf). For the Fr. parallel, *chitoler* (above), see *MED*, which defines the *citole* as a plucked stringed
instrument related to the dulcimer or zither.
2323 **he:** GL states that this is the indefinite *he*. As RB Rlt note, Brusendorff (1925:418) suggests *ye*; "the third
person . . . must be wrong," writes Brusendorff, "since the second person is employed throughout the rest of the
passage, both in English and French." In fact, the Fr. has third person at this point (Ln 2207–10, Lc 2195–97).
foote: "dance (formally)" (SKg₂ RBg). KA suggests *floute*, "because *foot* (saltare) is a later word" (GL).
MED fōten v. 1. (a) lists this line and two from Lydgate for the sense "dance." KA's suggestion probably comes,
however, from Fr. *fleüter* (Ln 2209, noted in RB SU FI RI; Lc 2197 has var. *citoler*). FI errs in reporting MS TH¹ as
"*flote*" (for *foote*). § Fleming (1967:49) reasons, from the parallel between the Fr. *fleüter* and the word *floytynge*
"playing the flute" in the description of Chaucer's Squire (*GP* 91), that "the translator of the *Romaunt* was working
from a French text different from that on which Chaucer relied." It is of course the translator of Fragment B that is in
question; cf. 2326n.
2325–28 "Not in the French" (SK 2327n. RB RI). Fleming (1967:49) makes the same observation; cf. 2326n.
2325–26 BE paraphrases: "Remember to make songs mingled with complaints." The reading of GL and others
(see 2325n., 2326n.) would suggest: "From time to time, for your lady's sake, see that you compose songs and
complaints."
2325 **Among:** "adverbial" (RB; cf. URg and 690n.), here meaning "at intervals" (BE), "sometimes" (SKg₂),
"from time to time" (GL RB FI Rlf). See 2325–26n.
2326 Fleming (1967:49) notes that, while *RR* has no reference to composing poetry (see 2325–28n.), this
passage parallels Chaucer's description of the Squire (*GP* 95 "He koude songes make"). Fleming suggests "that the
translator . . . was so familiar with Chaucer's *General Prologue* that . . . he added Chaucer's embellishments"; the
observation suggests a date later than *GP* and a translator (for Fragment B) other than Chaucer (cf. 2323n.). In *RR* the
God of Love does not touch upon *composition* of songs, but he does recommend *performance* of them (Lc 2191–94).
that thou make: "Apparently an independent hortatory subjunctive" (RB), with the sense "(see) that
you compose" (Rlf). On GL's emendation, *se that*, RBt notes that "the hortatory *that*, like Fr. 'que,' is used in Middle
English" and compares *BD* 206, and, in the textual note to that line, *MerT* E 1942. See 2325–26n.
2327–28 Skeat's emendation, *meve hem* "move them" for *meven*, endorsed by KA, implies that Skeat takes
they reden as "they (i.e., ladies) learn," a sense that is probable with or without the emendation. However, there is
no plural antecedent for *they* in the sense of "ladies," and FI thus glosses *they reden* as "they [i.e., songs and
complaints] inform."

150

Whanne they reden of thy smerte.
Loke that no man for scarce thee holde,
For that may greve thee many folde.　　　2330
Resoun wole that a lover be
In his yiftes more large and fre
Than cherles that ben not of lovyng.
For who therof can ony thyng,
He shal be leef ay for to yeve,　　　2335
In [Loves] lore who so wolde leve;
For he that thorough a sodeyn sight,
Or for a kyssyng, anoonright
Yaff hoole his herte in will and thought,
And to hymsilf kepith right nought,　　　2340

Aftir [swich gift] it is good resoun
He yeve his good in ab[a]ndoun.
　"Now [wol] I shortly heere reherce
Of that I have seid in verce,
Al the sentence by and by,　　　2345
In wordis fewe compendiously,
That thou the better mayst on hem thenke,　46r
Whether so it be thou wake or wynke;
For the wordis litel greve
A man to kepe, whanne it is breve.　　　2350
Whoso with Love wole goon or ride,
He mote be curteis and voide of pride,
Mery and full of jolite,

2328　**Whanne]** Whan that UR　　2333　**ben]** kan GL RB[1,2]　　2336　**Loves]** londes MS-KA FU　　**wolde]** woll SP[3]　　2341　**swich gift]** this swiffte MS-SP[3] BE-KA FU; this swift gift UR; so riche gift SU FI　**it is good]** 'tis but UR; is g. SK GL　　2342　**good]** gode too UR; g. al GL　**abandoun]** aboundoun MS MO; a bandon UR; a boundoun KA　　2343　**wol]** woly MS KA　**shortly]** *om.* TH[2]　　2344　**that]** t. that SK　　2345　**the]** thilke MO　　2347　**the better mayst]** m. t. b. TH[2]　　2349　**For the wordis]** F. t. w. do UR; F. that w. BE; F. that the w. MO SK　　2350　**it is]** thei be UR　　2352　**and]** *om.* UR

2329　**scarce:** BE RB RI note the Fr. *aver* (Lc 2199 "miserly").

2333　**ben:** In support of the emendation *kan,* GL cites the next line, and RBt cites the Fr. *sot* (Lc 2204 "knows"). SU RIt also cite the Fr. and grant that the emendation is perhaps correct.

2334　**ony:** See 212n.

2335–36　"Whoso would believe in Love's lore, shall be always ready to give" (BE); "Whoever would live in Love's teaching must be always ready to give" (SK). BE takes *leve* (line 2336) as "believe," SK as "live." The Fr., noted by SK (Lc 2206 "Se nus se veut d'amors pener" "If anyone wants to take pains for love"), might favor the sense "live," and SK's rhyme ("give : live") is commoner than BE's (see lines 2778, 4988, 5448, 5667). For forms, see *MED lę̄ven* v.(4), *liven* v.(1).

2336　**Loves:** BE states that MS "*londes* is evidently a mistake for *Loves,*" the reading suggested by KA, and later eds. (except MO KA FU) so emend on the basis of the Fr. *d'amors* (Lc 2206; noted in SK SU FI RIt). See 2335–36n.

2338　**kyssyng:** RI notes that the Fr. has *ris* (Lc 2209 "smile").

2341　**swich gift:** KA suggests this emendation, in support of which SK GL RBt FI RIt cite the Fr. (Lc 2211 "si riche don" "so rich a gift"); SK also adduces line 2381. UR's emendation, *this swift gift,* was the first to introduce the word *gift.* In a note, Liddell (GL) suggests *so riche gift,* which SU calls "the best emendation"; it follows the Fr. closely but does not account as well as Skeat's does for MS *this swiffte.*

2342　**in abandoun:** Francis Thynne (1599;1875:42) points out that SP[1] glosses "Abandone" as "libertie"; SP[2,3]g retain that gloss but, on the basis of F. Thynne's definition—"relinquere, to forsake and leave a thinge"—they gloss the verb *abandon* as "giue ouer." Other eds. gloss the phrase: "fully" (SKg[2], RBg), "without stint" (SKg[2]), "without check or restraint" (RBg), "freely" (RIf); "at (someone's) disposal" (*MED abandoun* n.). GL cites the Fr. (Ln 2224 "tot a bandon" "without any restraint"). The MS form, *aboundoun* (not *a boundoun,* as KA reads it) shows confusion in meaning and spelling with *aboundaunce.* UR has *a bandon,* which T. Thomas (URg, s.v. *Bandon*), says "should be read *abandon,* in one word."

2345–48　RI notes that the passage is not in the Fr.

2349–50　Ln (2227–28n.) RB compare Horace, *Ars poetica* 335–36.

2349　**wordis:** GL suggests *word is* on the basis of Fr. *la parole* (Lc 2215).

2351–54　BE notes: "These directions answer to the eighteenth statute in *The Court of Love,*" (lines 470–76, ed. Skeat 1897:422).

2352　**He:** KA suggests omitting this word, but no ed. so emends.

And of largesse alosed be.

　　"Firste I joyne thee heere in penaunce　2355
That evere, withoute repentaunce,
Thou sette thy thought in thy lovyng
To laste withoute repentyng;
And thenke upon thi myrthis swete,
That shall folowe aftir, whan ye mete.　2360
　　"And for thou trewe to love shalt be,
I wole and comaunde thee
That in oo place thou sette, all hoole,
Thyn herte, withoute halfen doole
For trecherie and sikernesse;　2365
For I lovede nevere doublenesse.
To many his herte that wole departe,
Everiche shal have but litel parte;
But of hym drede I me right nought

That in oo place settith his thought.　2370
Therfore in oo place it [sette],　46v
And lat it nevere thannys fl[e]tte.
For if thou yevest it in lenyng,
I holde it but a wrecchid thyng;
Therfore yeve it hoole and quyte,　2375
And thou shalt have the more merite.
If it be lent, than aftir soone
The bounte and the thank is doone;
But, in love, fre yeven thing
Requyrith a gret guerdonyng.　2380
Yeve it in yift al quyte fully,
And make thi yift debonairly;
For men that yift holde more dere
That yeven [is] with gladsome chere.
That yift nought to preisen is　2385

2354　**alosed]** a losel BE　　2355　**thee]** t. that MS BE-KA　　2362　**and]** a. eke UR SK　　2365　**For]** Fro
MO; Of GL RB[1,2]　　**and]** in SK　　2369　**hym]** hem ST-SP[3]　　2371　**it]** thou it UR　　**sette]** sitte MS BE-KA
2372　**flette]** flitte MS BE-KA (*var. sp.*)　　2374　**a]** om. TH[3] ST SP[2,3] BE　　2378　**thank]** thankes ST-SP[3]
2379　**fre]** a f. UR　　2383　**holde]** wol h. SK　　2384　**is]** *om.* MS KA

　　2354　**alosed:** "commended" (SP[2,3]g URg RBg), "praised" (URg et al.). BE's emendation, *a losel*, means a
"rogue, rascal" (*MED lōsel* n.), thus, perhaps (?) "profligate"; but the emendation has no basis (Lc 2220 "proisiez"
"esteemed").
　　2355　**joyne:** "enjoin" (URg et al.), "commend" (RIf). GL RB cite Fr. *enjoing* (Ln 2233); Lc (2221) has *doing*
"give."
　　　　　　thee heere: Against the MS reading, *thee that heere*, GL cites the Fr. (KA Fr. 2223–24 "t'enjoing en
penitence / Que" "I order you in penitence that . . ."). To avoid the ambiguous modification structure of the phrase
en penitence, the translator anticipates the noun clause that begins in the next line.
　　2362–65　RB FI RI compare the Fr. (Lc 2228–31 "veil je et comant que tu aies / en un seul leu tot ton cuer mis,
/ si qu'il n'i soit mie demis, / ainz toz entiers sanz tricherie" "I wish and command that you have your whole heart in
a single place so that it be not divided, but whole and without deceit"). RB notes that "the reading and sense are
both doubtful in the translation," and RI agrees that "the meaning of the English, which depends on Liddell's
emendation 'Of' for the MS *For*, is doubtful." See 2365n.
　　2364　**halfen doole:** "half portion" (SKg[2], s.v. *Dool*); i.e., "halfheartedness" (FI); "half-heartedly" (RIf). RB
(note to 2362ff.) states that "the phrase . . . preserves an archaic form of the adjective in -*n* (from AS. 'healfne
dæl')." RI (2363–65n.) notes "the Chaucerian *halvendel*" (*TC* 3.707, 5.335).
　　2365　Skeat takes *For* as "against" and emends *and* to *in*, in order to avoid the two opposed senses of *For*,
"con" and "pro." He thus reads: "'Against treachery, in all security.'" For support he cites the Fr. (Lc 2231 "toz entiers
sanz tricherie" "quite whole, without deceit"), which is parallel in sense but not in construction. MO achieves the
sense "con" by emending *For* to *Fro* "(away) from," but leaves the phrase *and sikernesse* as a seeming contradiction.
GL RB, following KA's suggestion, emend *For* to *Of*; GL takes the phrase *halfen doole / Of trecherie and sikernesse*
as "half treacherous, half faithful." FI paraphrases the unemended phrase, with *For*, as "divided between treachery
and faithfulness." See 2362–65n.
　　2367–68　RI compares *TC* 1.960–61.
　　2367　"For the ellipsis of the subject here cf. line 2416, below" (RB).
　　2371–72　**sette : flette:** RIt notes that "*sette* corresponds to Fr. *metes*" (Lc 2237) and that "*flette* may be a
variant of *flitte*, or *flitte* could be an imperfect rhyme with *sette*." Either rhyming pair has one member that is variant:
sitte for *sette*, a common confusion, or *flette(n)* for *flitte(n)*, a variant spelling (*MED flitten* v.).
　　2383–86　RB RI note the proverbial character of these lines and cite Whiting; see Whiting (1968: G84).

That man yeveth maugre his.

"Whanne thou hast yeven thyn herte, as I
Have seid thee heere openly,
Thanne aventures shull thee fall,
Which harde and hevy ben withall.   2390
For ofte whan thou bithenkist thee
Of thy lovyng, whereso thou be,
Fro folk thou must departe in hie,
That noon perceyve thi maladie.   2394
[But hyde thyne harme thou must alone,   TH¹:
And go forthe sole, and make thy mone.   140c
Thou shalte no whyle be in o state,
But whylom colde and whilom hate,
Nowe reed as rose, nowe yelowe and fade.
Suche sorowe, I trowe, thou never hade; 2400
Cotidien ne quarteyne,
It is nat so ful of peyne.
For often tymes it shal fal
In love, among thy paynes al,
That thou thyselfe, al holy,   2405
Foryeten shalte so utterly
That many tymes thou shalte be
Styl as an ymage of tree,
Domme as a stone, without steryng
Of fote or honde, without spekyng.   2410
Than, soone after al thy payne,

To memorye shalte thou come agayne,
[As] man abasshed wonder sore,
And after syghen more and more.
For wytte thou wele, withouten wene,   2415
In suche astate ful ofte have bene
That have the yvel of love assayde,
Wherthrough thou arte so dismayde.

"After, a thought shal take the so,   TH¹:140d
That thy love is to ferre the fro.   2420
Thou shalte saye, 'God, what may this be,
That I ne maye my lady se?
Myne herte alone is to her go,
And I abyde al sole in wo,
Departed fro myne owne thought,   2425
And with myne eyen se right nought.
Alas, myne eyen [sende] I ne may
My careful hert to convay!
Myne hertes gyde but they be,
I prayse nothyng, whatever they se.   2430
Shul they abyde than? Nay,
But gone and visyten without delay
That myne herte desyreth so.
For certainly, but if they go,
A foole myselfe I maye wel holde,   2435
Whan I ne se what myne hert wolde.
Wherfore I wol gone her to sene,

2386 **man]** a m. UR; men BE   2388 **thee]** to t. GL   **openly]** all o. UR SK   2395 *Lines* 2395-2442
Out: MS (*leaf missing*); *supplied from* TH¹   2401 **ne]** n. the UR; n. yit SK   2402 **nat]** n. half UR   2408 **of]**
made o. UR   2411 **Than]** And t. UR   2413 **As]** A TH¹-UR KA GL FU   2416 **have]** haue I TH²
2427 **sende]** sene TH¹-KA FU   2431 **Shul]** Shulde TH²   **Nay]** why n. UR   2432 **and]** *om.* SK GL
visyten] se UR   2433 **That]** T. whiche UR

2386 **maugre his:** "in spite of him(self)" (URg et al.), "With his ill will; against his will; *Mal gré lui* (TRg; cf.
URg SK). BE states that "*his* agrees with the noun *gré* in maugre," but Skeat (1878c:4.88) corrects this observation by
noting that "*his* is the genitive after *maugre*."

2387–2694 Lecoy (Lc 2253–2566n.) sees the description of the effects of love as an adaptation from Ovid; for
a collection of references, he cites Hilka's Introduction to Aimon de Varennes's *Florimont* (1932:cxx–cxxvii).

2395–2442 A leaf is missing from MS, and these lines are supplied from TH¹ (KA SKt GL RBt SU FI RIt) or
"Speght" (BE). See above, "The Missing Leaves."

2397–98 **state : hate:** FI notes that *hate* is a Northern form; the rhyme is thus Northern.

2398 RI compares *TC* 2.811.

2401 **Cotidien:** "Daily . . . used as a *substantive* for *A quotidian ague*" (TRg SKg₂; cf. URg FI RIf).

quarteyne: "occurring every fourth day; *as s.* Quartan fever or ague" (SKg₂; cf. FI RIf).

2413 **As:** BE's *As*, noted in BE MO by KA, follows the Fr. *ausi come* (Lc 2275; noted by RBt SU FI RIt).

2416 GL notes the omission of the subject, as in line 2367.

2421–25 On the "conceit of the separation of the lover's heart from his body," RB notes that Langlois (Ln
2302–13n.) cites Chrétien de Troyes, *Cligés* 5180ff. (5120–28, ed. Micha 1965). See also Cline (1972).

2427–28 On "the proverb 'Ubi amor, ibi oculus'" (where love is, there is the eye), RB notes that Langlois (Ln
2305n.) gives several versions; RI cites Walther (1963–69: no. 32036) and compares Whiting (1968: L558).

2427 **sende:** In support of KA's suggested emendation, SKt GL RBt SU FI RIt cite Fr. *envoier* (Lc 2293).

2428 **convay:** "convoy, accompany" (SKg₂); "guide (back)" (RIf).

2432 **and:** KA sugggests omitting *and*.

Or eased shal I never bene
But I have some tokenyng.'
  "Than gost thou forthe without
      dwellyng;   2440
But ofte thou faylest of thy desyre,
Er thou mayst come her any nere,]
And wastest in vayn thi passage.   MS:47r
Thanne fallest thou in a newe rage;
For want of sight thou gynnest morne,   2445
And homewarde pensyf thou dost retorne.
In gret myscheef thanne shalt thou bee,
For thanne agayne shall come to thee
Sighes and pleyntes with newe woo,
That no yecchyng prikketh soo.   2450
Who wote it nought, he may go lere
Of hem that bien love so dere.
  "Nothyng thyn herte appesen may,
That ofte thou wolt goon and assay
If thou maist seen, by aventure,   2455
Thi lyves joy, thine hertis cure;
So that, bi grace, if thou myght

Atteyne of hire to have a sight,
Thanne shalt thou done noon other dede,
But with that sight thyne eyen fede.   2460
That faire fresh whanne thou maist see,
Thyne herte shall so ravysshed be
That nevere thou woldest, thi thankis, lete
Ne remove for to see that swete.
The more thou seest in sothfastnesse,   2465
The more thou coveytest of that swetnesse;
The more thine herte brenneth in fier,   47v
The more thine herte is in desire.
For who considreth everydeell,
It may be likned wondir well,   2470
The peyne of love, unto a fere.
For evermore [thou] neighest nere,
[Thou], or whooso that it bee,
For verray sothe I tell it thee,
The hatter evere shall thou brenne,   2475
As experience shall thee kenne.
Whereso comest in ony coost,
Who is next fuyre, he brenneth moost.

2438 **Or]** For GL   2439 **But]** B. that UR   **some]** so SP³   2442 *Lines* 2395-2442 *Out:* MS
2446 **thou]** *om.* UR SK   2450 **soo]** The so UR   2454 **wolt]** wole GL   2457 **if]** if that UR
2466 **of]** *om.* UR   2472 **evermore]** ever the more SK   **thou]** tho MS KA   2473 **Thou]** Thought MS-SP³
BE-SK FU;   In thought UR;   That FI   **whooso]** how so UR   2477 **comest]** thou c. SK RB¹·² RI

2441–42 **desyre : nere:** Cf. 2471–72n.
2450 **yecchyng:** "itching" (RIf). For the form, see *OED Itch* v.¹. The initial consonant (from OE *giccan*) was disappearing in the 14th-15th century.
2453–54 **appesen may : assay:** On the basis of Fr. *apoier : essaier* (Lc 2319–20), Brusendorff (1925:417) suggests *may apaye : assaye.*
2454 **wolt:** "read *nilt?*" (SKt).
2463 "'That thou wouldst never willingly leave off'" (SK; cf. GL).
2466 **of:** "*Om.* of?" (SKt).
2467–68 **fier : desire:** See 2471–72n. Skeat notes (2471n.) that the word for "fire" is "spelt *fyr* in l. 2467," but it is so only in his text (TH¹·² FU SU FI have *fyre*), where he regularly respells with *y* for long *i* [i:].
2471–72 **fere : nere:** "*Fere* for *Fire*," notes TRg. On the rhyme, cf. lines 2441–42 *desyre : nere*, lines 2467–68 *fier : desire*, lines 2779–80 *desire : manere.* Skeat calls attention to lines 2441–42, where, he notes, "*desyr* rimes with *nere.*"
2472–75 BE SK SU note that the English is not very close to the Fr. (Lc 2339–40 "quant il le feu de plus pres sent, / et il s'en vet plus apressant" "when he feels the fire close by, he goes away by approaching closer"). BE notes that line 2473 "appears to be corrupt"; KA suggests reading *Thou* for *Thought* which provides the following translation: "as long as you get closer, you, or anyone else . . . will burn all the hotter." SK states: "The French text . . . means—'whenever thou comest nearer *her.*' Hence *Thought* should be *That swete*, or some such phrase." Literally, of course, the French means "whenever you come nearer *the fire*," and FI's emendation, *That*, maintains the parallel between the fire and the beloved ("As long as you get closer to that [the fire] or to whoever it may be . . . the hotter you will burn").
2477 **comest:** SK's reading follows KA's suggestion.
      ony: See 212n.
2478 RB RI note that the line is proverbial and cite notes to *TC* 1.449, where the reference in RI is to Whiting (1968: F193). Lc (2346n.) cites Morawski (1925: no. 2088).

"And yitt forsothe, for all thine hete,
Though thou for love swelte and swete, 2480
Ne for nothyng thou felen may,
Thou shalt not willen to passen away.
And though thou go, yitt must thee nede
Thenke all day on hir fairhede
Whom thou biheelde with so good will, 2485
And holde thisilf biguyled ill
That thou ne haddest noon hardement
To shewe hir ought of thyne entent.
Thyn herte full sore thou wolt dispise
And eke repreve of cowardise 2490
That thou, so dulle in everything, 48r
Were domme for drede, withoute spekyng.
Thou shalt eke thenke thou didest folye
That thou were hir so fast bye
And durst not auntre thee to say 2495
Somthyng, er thou cam away;
For thou haddist no more wonne,

To speke of hir whanne thou bigonne,
But [yif] she wolde, for thy sake,
In armes goodly thee have take, 2500
It shulde have be more worth to thee
Than of tresour gret plente.
"Thus shalt thou morne and eke compleyne
And gete encheisoun to goone ageyne
Unto thi walke, or to thi place, 2505
Where thou biheelde hir fleshly face.
And never, for fals suspeccioun,
Thou woldest fynde accasioun
For to gone unto hire hous.
So art thou thanne desirous 2510
A sight of hir for to have,
If thou thine honour myghtist save,
Or ony erande myghtist make
Thider for thi loves sake; 2514
Full fayn thou woldist, but for drede 48v
Thou gost not, lest that men take hede.

2483 **thee]** thou SP[2,3]   2484 **fairhede]** fayre hede TH[1]-BE FU SU FI   2487 **noon]** ne SP[2,3]
2495 **auntre]** venture UR   2496 **er]** er that UR   2499 **yif]** yitt MS-SP[3] MO KA GL FU RI; yet if UR BE
2502 **gret]** a grete UR   2504 **gete]** yet SP[3]   2505 **thi . . . thi]** the . . . the GL   2509 **to]** thou TH[2]
unto] in u. UR   2510 **So art thou thanne]** Thou arne than so UR   2511 **for]** but f. UR   2515 **woldist]**
woulde SP[2,3]

2480 **swelte and swete:** RI compares *MilT* A 3703.

2482 **passen away:** "i.e., go from her presence" (FI).

2493–94 **folye : bye:** RIt notes that SK RB drop -*e* and observes that "though doubtless the final -*e* here is not pronounced, it seems best not to adjust the spellings of Fragment B in the interest of rhyme."

2497–2502 RI notes that the meaning is unclear but defends the MS reading, particularly *But yitt* (line 2499), with a period after line 2498, a dash after line 2500, and "the following possible interpretation: The lover did not speak because (at the time) he told himself he would have gained no more than to speak of (to?) her; but yet she would (he thinks now) have greeted him with an embrace, which would have been worth more than a treasure." RI further notes the suggestions in GL (see 2497–99n.) and grants that the emendation in SK RB FI—*But yif* for MS *But yitt* (line 2499)—may be correct.

2497–99 GL RB RI note that these lines correspond only partly to the Fr. (Lc 2362–64 "car se tu n'em peüses treire / fors seulement un bel salu, / si eüst il .c. mars valu" "because if you'd got nothing out of it except a fine salutation [i.e., a kiss of greeting], it would have been worth one hundred marks to you" [trans. RI 2497–2502n.]). KA (2497n.) suggests that we "insert *if* before *thou*." GL notes that "the French suggests that we should supply *though* before *thou* [line 2497] and read *that* for *yitt* in v. 2499." RBt calls the text "apparently corrupt," notes that GL's solution "corresponds pretty well with the Fr." and adduces SK's emendation *But yif* (see above and 2499n.)

2497 **wonne:** "won, obtained" (RIf).

2499 **But yif:** "unless" (FI). SK, followed by RB SU FI, emends on the basis of Fr. *se* (Lc 2362 "if" noted by SU FI). See 2497–2502n., 2497–99n.

2504 **encheisoun:** KA suggests that we read *chesoun*, but no ed. so emends.

2507–09 "For fear of arousing attention, the lover cannot find occasion to visit her house" (RI).

2511 **hir:** KA suggests that we read *hire*, but no ed. so emends.

2513 **ony:** See 212n.

2515 **woldist:** *OED will* v.[1], A. 9. B, explains the 2 pres. sing. ind. form *woulde* without -*st* as "originally subjunctive." But *woulde* may be an error; at line 2533, SP[2,3] have *wouldest*.

Wherfore I rede, in thi goyng
And also in thyne ageyn comyng
Thou be well ware that men ne wite.
Feyne thee other cause than itte 2520
To go that weye, or fast bye;
To hele wel is no folye.
   "And if so be it happe thee
That thou thi love there maist see,
In siker wise thou hir salewe, 2525
Wherewith thi colour wole transmewe,
And eke thy blode shal al toquake,
Thyne hewe eke chaungen for hir sake.
But word and witte, with chere full pale,
Shull wante for to tell thy tale. 2530
And if thou maist so fer forth wynne
That thou resoun d[u]rst bigynne,
And woldist seyn thre thingis or mo,
Thou shalt full scarsly seyn the two.

Though thou bithenke thee never so well, 2535
Thou shalt foryete yit somdell,
But if thou dele with trecherie.
For fals lovers mowe all folye
Seyn, what hem lust, withouten drede, 49r
They be so double in her falshede; 2540
For they in herte cunne thenke [o] thyng
And seyn another in her spekyng.
   "And whanne thi speche is eendid all,
Ryght thus to thee it shall byfall;
If ony word thanne come to mynde, 2545
That thou to seye hast left bihynde,
Thanne thou shalt brenne in gret martire,
For thou shalt brenne as ony fiere.
This is the stryf and eke the affray
And the batell that lastith ay. 2550
This bargeyn eende may never take
But if that she thi pees will make.

2517 **rede]** red the GL   2530 **wante for to]** w. the f. t. GL   2532 **resoun]** to reson UR; thy r. SK GL RB[1,2] **durst]** derst MS BE-KA   2538 **folye]** fouly SP[2,3]; fully UR   2539 **hem]** the TH[2]   2541 **o]** a MS BE-GL RI   2547 **Thanne]** Thau SP[1]   2551 **bargeyn]** batell SU FI

2517–22 "On the importance of secrecy in love, and especially concealment in visiting," RI compares *TC* 2.365–85.

2517 **I rede:** GL compares line 2856 "I rede the."

2522 "This appears to be a proverbial expression," states BE but gives no further evidence. § RB notes that "the observance of secrecy was one of the fundamental principles of courtly love" and cites the note to *NPT* VII 2914ff. (B[2] 4104ff.).

    hele: "cover" (SPg), "to hide, to cover, to conceal" (URg; cf. TRg BE SKg GL RIf). BE SK cite the Fr. (Lc 2378 "de soi celer" "to cover yourself"), and SK expands "to conceal (it) closely."

2530 GL cites the Fr. (Lc 2384 "parole te faudra" "speech will fail you").

2531 **so fer forth wynne** "get so far" (RIf).

2532 **resoun:** KA suggests *thy*, probably on the basis of Fr. *ta* (Lc 2387 "que ta resson comencier oses" "that you dare to begin your speech"; noted in SKt RBt SU RIt). Sutherland retains MS *thou* and has *tu* in his Fr. text (SU Fr. 2399); he writes that "*tu* is in probable source French MS.," presumably Ri, since that MS is his base at this point, and since he has no note to identify any other source; but Langlois, who collates Ri (1914–24:1.50–52), gives no such variant. If the translator had *ta* in his Fr. copy, he may have read *tu* from two lines above or the line below ("Quant tu" in both cases; see Lc 2385, 2388); or he may have been reluctant to suppress the subject as the Fr. does.

    durst: pa. t., parallel with *woldist* in the next line. MS *derst* is pres. t. See *MED durren* v.

2535–37 "Unless you are a deceiver, or if you are really sincere, you will forget half of what you intended to say" (BE).

2538 **mowe:** are able, can (SPg TRg FI).

2541 **o:** I collate the MS form *a* as the indefinite, TH['s] *o* as the definite form, "one." RIt notes the Fr. *un* (Lc 2397). But the definite can appear as the Northern dialectal form *a*. See *MED ō, o* num. "Also . . . (early & N) *ā*."

2545 **ony:** See 212n.

2547–48 **martire : fiere:** On the rhyme, see 2471–72n.

2547 **Thanne:** SP['s] error may be a case of inverted type or an anticipation of the next word, *thou*.

2548 **ony:** See 212n.

2550 **batell:** SKt's note, "G. batell*e*," assumes that MS *batell* is an abbreviation for *batelle*; see above, "The Manuscript Hands: The Scribe."

2551 **bargeyn:** "contention" (TRg), "conflict" (SKg[2]), "strife" (GL), "enterprise" (SKg[2] RIg). *MED bargain(e* n. offers this line under sense 4, "a state of affairs resulting from someone else's actions." KA suggests *batail*, following

"And whanne the nyght is comen, anoon
A thosande angres shall come uppon.
To bedde as fast thou wolt thee dight,   2555
Where thou shalt have but smal delite.
For whanne thou wenest for to slepe,
So full of peyne shalt thou crepe,
Sterte in thi bedde aboute full wide,
And turne full ofte on every side,   2560
Now dounward groff, and now upright,
And walowe in woo the longe nyght;
Thine armys shalt thou sprede abr[e]de   49v

As man in werre were forwerede.
Thanne shall thee come a remembraunce   2565
Of hir shappe and hir semblaunce,
Whereto none other may be pere.
And wite thou wel, withoute were,
That thee shal [seme] somtyme that nyght
That thou hast hir that is so bright   2570
Naked bitwene thyne armes there,
All sothfastnesse as though it were.
Thou shalt make castels thanne in Spayne,
And dreme of joye, all but in vayne,

2554 **uppon]** on UR   2556 **Where]** There SP²,³   2563 **abrede]** abrode MS BE-KA   2564 **for-werede]** forweriede MS BE-KA; forwerreyd   SK RB¹,² RI   2566 **and hir]** a. of h. UR   2569 **seme]** se MS-UR KA FU   2573 **make castels thanne]** t. m. c. TH²   2574 **in]** it TH¹,² FU

Fr. *guere* (Lc 2409 "war"; noted in SU FI RIt). RIt implies that KA actually reads *bataile.* § Fr. *guere* seems to be an over-statement, ME *bargeyn* an understatement.

2561   "'Now groveling on your face, and now on your back'" (SK). URg and BE have similar formulations, and BE quotes the Fr. (Méon 2442 "Une heure envers, autre eure adens"; Lc 2419 "et puis envers et puis adenz" "one hour (now) on your back, another hour (and then) on your stomach"). The ME clearly follows a Fr. MS other than that of Méon's base.

    groff: "Groveling" (URg; cf. SPg, s.v. *growfe*); "flat on the ground" (URg TRg; SPg, s.v. *grofly*); "on thy belly, face downward" (SKg₂ GL). See *MED gruf(fe* (c).

2563–64   **abrede : forwerede:** Normal forms (*abrede : forwered* or *forwerreyd*) give imperfect rhyme. See 2563n., 2564n.

2563   **abrede:** MS *abrode*, based on the adj. *brod*, may give slightly clearer sense than does *abrede*, based on the noun *brede*. See MED *abrōd(e* adv.(1), sense 1. (a) "So as to cover a wide space"; *brēde* n.(2), sense 1a. (a) "*a brede*, in width." See 2563–64n.

2564   **forwerede:** "utterly defeated (lit. utterly warred against)" (SKg₂), "defeated in war" (SK RB), "defeated" (FI RIf), "battled out" (FI). On the possibility of the sense "worn out," suggested in URg et al., see *MED forwēren, -ien* v., sense (a), which quotes *Rom* 235 "And if it were forwered" (Lc 223 "car s'el fust usee"). Here, as GL RB RI note, there is no parallel in the Fr. (Lc 2420 "con home qui a mal es denz" "like a man with toothache"). The emendation is TH¹'s; although it appears to be a var. sp. of MS *forweriede*, lines 2563–64 show Thynne's tendency to maintain at least eye-rhyme (Blodgett 1975:224–25), and if he heard a rhyme with third-syllable stress (for-we-ré-de), he may have had in mind the sense "defeated." But *MED* does not record the form *forwerreyen*, with or without TH¹'s form as a variant; *werreye(n*, of course, existed (*OED Warray* v.). SK RB RI postulate the form in their emendation *forwerreyd*, "to get a rime to *abrede*" (SK); in support, SK cites *Rom* 3251 *to werye* "to make war" (Lc 3009 "guerroier").

2569   **seme:** BE's emendation, noted by KA in BE MO, follows the Fr. (Lc 2425 "tel foiz sera qu'il t'ert avis" "such a time will be that it will seem to you"; noted by SU FI) and completes the impersonal construction with *thee* and the *that*-clause of 2570 ff.

2573   "Thou shalt imagine delightful visions" (SK).

    castels . . . in Spayne: BE cites Lantin de Damerey (see 1799:5.158–59) for the idea "that any chimerical fancy is so called, because all the castles in Spain were destroyed lest they should shelter the Moors." But Spain is not the only location; as BE notes, Lantin de Damerey "quotes an old French poet, Pierre Guingoire, to show that they were also called *châteaux en Asie*." SK states that "the 'castles in Spain' are romantic fictions," and, on the topic of pleasant dreams, compares Gower, *Confessio Amantis* 4.2901–26 (ed. Macaulay 1899–1902: 2.379–80). RB FI RI note that the phrase is still proverbial. RB compares Haeckel (1890: no. 60) and, on the history of the expression, follows Ln (2442n.) in citing Morel-Fatio (1913). RI states: "[the phrase] first appears in Guillaume de Lorris and for the first time in English here. The proverbial meaning had not yet established itself. The reference is to the fantasy of a private retreat for lovers (a castle) in some distant place (Spain). 'Spain' serves for the purpose of rhyme, not from any romantic associations, though Spanish castles placed high on rocks perhaps suggest the exotic (cf. HF 1117); the formula is found with other place names completing other rhymes." RI cites Gallacher (1963); Whiting (1968: C77); and Hassell (1982: C100).

2574   **in:** SU reports TH¹'s reading as *ut*, and FI reports it as *at*; the reading is *it*, an error for *in*.

And thee deliten of right nought,　　　　2575
While thou so slomrest in that thought
That is so swete and delitable,
The which, in soth, nys but fable,
For it ne shall no while laste.
Thanne shalt thou sighe and wepe faste　2580
And say, 'Dere God, what thing is this?
My dreme is turned all amys,
Which was full swete and apparent,
But now I wake, it is al shent!
Now yede this mery thought away.　　　　2585
Twenty tymes upon a day
I wolde this thought wolde come ageyne,　50r
For it aleggith well my peyne.
It makith me full of joyfull thought;
It sleth me that it lastith noght.　　　　2590
A, Lord! Why nyl ye me socoure
The joye, I trowe, that I langoure?
The deth I wolde me shulde sloo
While I lye in hir armes twoo.
Myne harme is harde, withouten wene;　2595
My gret unease full ofte I meene.

"'But wolde Love do so I myght
Have fully joye of hir so bright,
My peyne were quytte me rychely.
Allas, to grete a thing aske I!　　　　　2600
Hit is but foly and wrong wenyng
To aske so outrageous a thyng;
And whoso askith folily,
He mote be warned hastily.
And I ne wote what I may say,　　　　　2605
I am so fer out of the way;
For I wolde have full gret likyng
And full gret joye of lasse thing.
For wolde she, of hir gentylnesse,
Without more, me oonys kysse,　　　　　2610
It were to me a grete guerdoun,　　　　　50v
Relees of all my passioun.
But it is harde to come therto;
All is but folye that I do,
So high I have myne herte sette　　　　　2615
Where I may no comfort gette.
I wote not where I seye well or nought,
But this I wote wel in my thought,

2577　**is]** *om.* TH²　2578　**but fable]** b. a f. TH¹-UR SK FU-FI　2585　**Now]** How GL　2592　**The]** Fro GL RB¹,²　2610　**Without]** W. and RI　2616　**Where]** W. that UR　2617　**wote not]** n'ote UR SK GL RB¹,² FI

2591–92　RI notes, "syntax and meaning are unsatisfactory." There is only a vague parallel with the Fr. (Lc 2445–46 "Diex! verai je ja que je soie / en itel point que je pensoie?" "God! Shall I ever see the day when I may be in the very situation that I imagine?"). To SK's retention of the MS reading, GL objects that Skeat construes *The joye* as object of *languore* but that "'langour' is not used in this sense"; RB agrees that the construction is difficult. David (RI) paraphrases the result of Liddell's emendation *Fro joye* (GL): "Why will you not succor me [parted] from joy?" And he notes that "Robinson adopts the emendation, but divides the sentence differently (Why will you not succor me? From joy, I believe, I languish)." FI keeps the MS reading and glosses *socoure* as "assist me (to attain)" and *langoure* as "languish for." David (RIf) also glosses *langoure* as "languish (for)," and he observes further (RI) that *MED langouren* v. (b) introduces an otherwise unrecorded emendation when it "renders the beginning of the line [as] 'For joy.'" He concludes that, "given the looseness of syntax and the vagueness of the Middle English translation at this point, it seems best to make whatever sense one can of the MS reading." §　The second of the two lines may echo Canticles 2.5 "quia amore langueo" ("because I languish with love").

2609　*Marginalium:* ⁊ col MS₂꜀. The printer's mark "7" is canceled, and the instruction "col," which had been omitted from the sequence, is substituted. Because of the error, the remaining MS instructions for sig. 2C of TH¹ were displaced by one column and were similarly corrected. See above, "The Printer's Marks" and Blodgett (1979:99–100).

2610　**Without:** RI's *Without and* is presumably an error for *Withouten*.

　　　kysse: TH¹ adjusts the rhyme by printing *kesse*, a Kentish form (FI) adopted by all except BE-KA GL RI. But "given the character of [Fragment] B," notes RIt, "the rhyme is doubtless at fault, not the spelling in G [MS]." Cf. line 2006.

2617　**wote not:** SK GL RB FI follow KA's suggestion and adopt UR's emendation, *n'ote*, in the form *no(o)t* (= *ne wot*).

　　　where: "short for 'whether'" (SK). Cf. 2624n.

That it were better of hir alloone,
For to stynte my woo and moone, 2620
A loke on hir I caste goodly,
[Than] for to have al utterly
Of another all hoole the pley.
A, Lord! Where I shall byde the day
That evere she shall my lady be? 2625
He is full cured that may hir see.
A, God! Whanne shal the dawnyng springe?
To liggen thus is an angry thyng;
I have no joye thus heere to lye
Whanne that my love is not me bye. 2630
A man to lyen hath gret disese,
Which may not slepe ne reste in ese.
I wolde it dawed and were now day

And that the nyght were went away; 2634
For were it day, I wolde uprise. 51r
A, slowe sonne, shewe thine enprise!
Spede thee to sprede thy beemys bright,
And chace the derknesse of the nyght,
To putte away the stoundes stronge,
Which in me lasten all to longe.' 2640
   "The nyght shalt thou contene soo
Withoute rest, in peyne and woo.
If evere thou knewe of love distresse,
Thou sha[l]t mowe lerne in that sijknesse,
And thus enduryng shalt thou lye 2645
And ryse on morwe up erly
Out of thy bedde, and harneyse thee
Er evere dawnyng thou maist see.

2621 **on hir I caste]** o. h. i-caste BE MO SU; o. me y-cast SK GL; of h. ycast RB[1,2] FI   2622 **Than]** That MS-SP[3] MO KA FU   2626 **that]** and BE   2628 **liggen]** leggen TH[3] ST SP[2,3]   **is an]** as an SP[2,3]; is UR 2631 **A]** I SP[2,3]   2641 **contene]** contynue TH[1]-UR FU FI   2644 **shalt mowe lerne]** shat m. l. MS KA; m. l. it UR   2645 **enduryng]** endurying RB[1,2]

2619–21   David (RI) reads the unemended text as follows: "'It were better of her alone . . . (that) I should cast a look on her in goodly fashion'(?)." He notes that the emendations (see 2621n.) change *I caste* to *ycast*, but he believes that, "given the rarity of the participle with the prefix *y-* in the MS . . . it seems proper to avoid substituting one poor translation for another. The phrase *of hir alloone*," he adds, "is an embarrassment to either version."

2619   **better:** As KA notes, SK prefers *bet*.
   of hir alloone: "i.e., from her only" (FI). See 2619–21n.

2621   **on hir I caste:** GL adopts SK's emendation, *on me ycast*, endorsed by KA, but suggests "? *of hir*." RB FI so emend on the basis of the Fr. *de li* (Lc 2472 "from her"), although RBt grants that SK's *on me* may be right. RI (2619–21n.) states that "all editors emend . . . to either 'on me ycast' or 'of hir ycast'"; but BE MO SU have a third version, "on hir i-caste," where it is the lover, rather than the lady, who casts the look. Although Sutherland adopts this third version in the text, his note says that GL's suggestion, *of hir*, "seems best," and he compares the Fr. While David (RI) is right in saying that the first two versions make "the translation conform to the French where it is the lady's look that might assuage the lover's woe," the passage that he quotes (Ln 2477–78 [= Lc 2463–64] "se . . . d'un seul baisier / Me deignoit la bele aaisier" "if the fair one deigned to comfort me with a single kiss") is parallel not to this but to lines 2609–10; in his textual note (RIt), David has the correct parallel, *de li* (Lc 2472). See 2619–21n.

2622   **Than:** UR's emendation, noted by KA, follows the structure of the Fr. *que* (Lc 2473 "than").

2624   **Where:** "whether" (BE SK GL). GL notes that the word introduces a direct question, and FI thus paraphrases as "how." Cf. 2617n.

2628   **liggen:** SK GL emend to *ly(e)*, noted in SK by KA, since *liggen* "is a Northern form" and since *ly* "occurs in the next line" (SK); in addition, GL RBt RIt cite rhymes at lines 2629–30 and 2645–46. RI also cites *lyen* at line 2631 but observes that "it is futile . . . to make Fragment B consistent with itself by emending the verb."

2631   **to lyen:** "i.e., in lying down" (GL). RB quotes the Fr. (Lc 2481–82 "Gesirs est aniieuse chose" "to lie down is a vexatious thing").

2641   **contene:** "contain (thyself)" (SK); "remain" (SKg[2] RBg); "continue" (GL); "bear" (RBg RIf), "endure" (RIf). SK GL RB RI note that the Fr. has *contendras* (Lc 2491), which, SK states, "perhaps means 'shalt struggle'"; GL RB also imply a similar meaning in suggesting that *contene* is a mistake for *contende*. However, as RI observes, Ln (s.v. *contient*) glosses *te contendras* as 2 sg. future of *se contenir*, "to comport oneself." RI adduces *MED conteinen* v., which cites this line for sense 5. (a) "To persist (in a certain state or activity)"; the sense is parallel to that of TH[1]'s *contynue*, and the phrase "The night" is adverbial. Cf. line 4923, where the same intransitive sense appears.

2643   RB notes that this line departs from the Fr., which is in first person (Lc 2493 "s'onques le mal d'amer conui" "if ever I knew love's sickness").

2644   **sijknesse:** See 2295n.

159

All pryvyly thanne shal[t] thou goon,
What [weder] it be, thisilf alloon,   2650
For reyne or hayle, for snowe, for slete,
Thider she dwellith that is so swete,
The which may fall aslepe be
And thenkith but lytel upon thee.
Thanne shalt thou goon, ful foule afeerd,   2655
Loke if the gate be unspered,
And waite without in woo and peyne,
Full yvel acoolde, in wynde and reyne.
Thanne shal thou go the dore bifore;   51v
If thou maist fynde ony score,   2660
Or hoole, or reeft, whatevere it were,
Thanne shalt thou stoupe and lay to ere,
If they withynne a slepe be—
I mene all save the lady free,
Whom wakyng if thou maist aspie,   2665
Go putte thisilf in jupartie

To aske grace, and thee bimene,
That she may wite, without wene,
That thou [anyght] no rest hast hadde,
So sore for hir thou were bystadde.   2670
Wommen wel ought pite to take
Of hem that sorwen for her sake.
   "And loke, for love of that relyke,
That thou thenke noon other lyke,
For [whom] thou hast so gret annoy   2675
Shall kysse thee, er thou go away,
And holde that in full gret deynte.
And for that no man shal thee see
Bifore the hous ne in the way,
Loke thou be goone ageyn er day.   2680
Such comyng and such goyng,
Such hevynesse and such [wakyng],
Makith lovers, withouten ony wene,   52r
Under her clothes pale and lene.

2649 **shalt**] shall MS BE KA GL   2650 **weder**] whider MS-SP³ BE-KA FU   2658 **yvel**] ill UR   2660 **score**] shore TH¹-UR FU   2664 **the**] thy TH¹-BE SK FU-FI   2669 **anyght**] nyght MS-SP³ KA FU; all night UR-MO   2675 **whom**] whanne MS-KA GL FU   2682 **wakyng**] walkyng MS-SK FU   2683 **ony**] *om.* SP²-UR SK GL

2649   **shalt:** MS *shall* may be a Northern 2 sg. pres. (*MED shulen* v.), but *shalt* appears elsewhere (lines 2641, 2655); I collate *shall* as an erroneous 1 or 3 sg.

2650   **weder:** UR's *wethre'* anticipates SK's *weder*, endorsed by KA (cf. Lounsbury 1892:2.14). SK notes that *What weder* means "whatever weather it be," and adduces the support of the next line; the two lines convey the sense of the Fr. (Lc 2500 "soit par pluie soit par jelee" "either in rain or in frost").

2660   **score:** "a crack in the wall or door" (BE); "breach" (MOg); "(perhaps) cut, i.e. crack" (SK); "crack" (RB FI Rlf); "hole" (Rlf). BE SK RB *MED* note the Fr. *fendeüre* (Lc 2509). *MED scōr(e* n. cites only this line for sense 1. (a) "A crack, crevice."

2664   **the:** Where most eds. follow TH¹'s *thy*, noted in TH¹ by KA, Rlt defends the MS reading on the basis of the Fr. *la belle* (Lc 2513 "the beautiful one").

2669   "I supply *a*, i.e. by; or we may supply *al*" (SK).

2673–76 SK (2676n.)   RB RI note that the text departs from the Fr. (Lc 2521–24 "Si te dirai que tu doiz faire / por amor dou haut seintuaire / de quoi tu ne puez avoir aise: / au revenir la porte baise" "Now I will tell you what you should do for the love of that high sanctuary whose comfort you cannot possess. On your return, kiss the door"). They note that the text is unclear and perhaps corrupt. See notes below to lines 2673, 2675, 2676.

2673   **relyke:** GL notes that the parallel in the Fr. is *haut seintuaire* (Lc 2522) and compares "the similar use of *relyk* in v. 2907." On the use of this word "as a term of endearment," RB RI compare line 2907 and their notes to *LGW P* F 321, where the word occurs in the passage that has been taken as evidence that Chaucer translated *Rom.*

2675   **whom:** KA's suggestion follows the Fr. (Lc 2523 "de quoi [*var. qui*] tu ne puez avoir aise" lit., "from which [*var. whom*] you cannot have comfort"; noted by SKt RBt SU FI). SKt RBt FI note the var. *qui* for *quoi*; it appears in KA Fr. 2523, based on Michel 2549, as well as in SKt's source, Méon 2548. Ln (2537t) does not record *qui* but does note the reading *dont* (of which, of whom), which SU Fr. 2537 takes from MS Ri.

2676   SKt GL RBt FI Rlt adduce the Fr., which, in a variant version (see Ln 2538t), tells the lover to kiss the door when he leaves (Lc 2524 "au revenir [*var.* departir] la porte baise" "on returning [*var.* leaving] kiss the door"). This variant is the basis for KA's suggestion, noted in GL, "Thou kisse the dore er thou go away," which no ed. adopts.   § On the motif of kissing the door, RI (2673–76n.) compares *TC* 5.551–52.

2682   **wakyng:** GL's emendation follows the Fr. *icil veilliers* (Lc 2530 "these night watches"). Cf. line 4272.

2684–86   BE SK Ln (2548n.) RB RI compare Ovid, *Ars amatoria* 1.729, 733.

For love leveth colour ne cleernesse;
Who loveth trewe hath no fatnesse.
Thou shalt wel by thysilf see
That thou must nedis assaid be.
For men that shape hem other weye 2690
Falsly her ladyes for to bitraye,
It is no wonder though they be fatt;
With false othes her loves they gatt.
For [oft] I see suche losengours
Fatter than abbatis or priours.

 "Yit with o thing I thee charge, 2695
That [is] to seye, that thou be large
Unto the mayde that hir doith serve;
So best hir thanke thou shalt deserve.
Yeve hir yiftes and gete hir g[r]ace,
For so thou may thank purchace, 2700
That she thee worthy holde and free,
Thi lady, and all that may thee see.
Also hir servauntes worshipe ay,
And please as mych as thou may.
Grete good thorough hem may
    come to thee 2705
Bicause with hir they ben pryve;
They shal hir telle hou they thee fande 52v

Curteis, and wys, and well doande, 2685
And she shall preise well [the] m[a]re.
Loke oute of londe thou be not f[a]re; 2710
And if such cause thou have that thee
Bihoveth to gone out of contree,
Leve hoole thin herte in hostage
Till thou ageyn make thi passage.
Thenke longe to see the swete thyng 2715
That hath thine herte in hir kepyng.
 "Now have I tolde thee in what wise
A lovere shall do me servise.
Do it thanne if thou wolt have
The meede that thou aftir crave." 2720
 Whanne Love all this hadde boden me,
I seide hym, "Sire, how may it be
That lovers may in such manere
Endure the peyne ye have seid heere?
I merveyle me wonder faste 2725
How ony man may lyve or laste
In such peyne and such brennyng,
In sorwe and thought and such sighing,
[Ay] unrelesed woo to make,
Whether so it be they slepe or wake, 2730
In such annoy contynuely. 53r

2685 **For love]** Love ne UR   2690 **for]** *om.* UR BE SK GL   2691 **It is no wonder]** No wonder is UR   2693 **oft]** of MS KA   2695 **thee charge]** wolle t. c. UR; c. t. MO   2696 **is]** it MS KA   **be large]** l. b. MO   2699 **grace]** gace MS KA   2700 **thank]** hir t. SK   2709 **well the]** w. thee MS SP²·³ MO KA; The [=thee] w. t. UR BE SK   **mare]** more MS-KA FU SU FI   2710 **fare]** fore MS-KA FU SU FI   2713 **hoole]** wholely UR   2719 **thou]** that t. UR   2720 **aftir]** dost a. UR   2727 **and such]** a. in s. UR GL   2729 **Ay]** A yee MS KA

2695–2709 BE SK RB FI RI compare Ovid, *Ars amatoria* 2.251–260.

2700 **thank:** SK's emendation, *hir thank*, follows KA's suggestion.

2704 **mych:** MO RB adjust meter by using the disyllabic *mychel*. GL suggests that one "read *mychel*, or insert *ever* before *may*." See 1713n.

2707–08 **fande : doande:** On the Northern rhyme, cf. 2263–64n.

2709–10 **mare . . . fare:** On KA's suggestion, SK GL RB RI adopt the Northern *mare*, to rhyme with the emendation *fare*; see 2710n. RIt compares lines 2215–16 and the rhyme *more : sore* at lines 2741–42 and notes that "the B translator appears to use *mare/more* depending on the rhyme."

2709 **well the:** The collation might suggest that SP² made use of MS, but the case is an isolated one and probably an example of editorial activity; cf. Pearsall 1984b.83–91. GL suggests "Perhaps insert *thee* before *well.*"

2710 BE SK RB RI note the parallel in Ovid, *Ars amatoria* 2.357–58; RB RI note the proverb "Out of sight, out of mind" and the parallels in Ln (2569n.); RI adds Whiting (1968: E213).

    fare: "short for *faren*, gone" (SK). The emendation comes from KA's suggestion; see 2709–10n. *MED fāren* v. and *OED Fare* v.¹ record only forms in -*a*- or -*ea*- for the strong past participle (<OE -faren); MS *fore* may reflect either rhyme-attraction (to *more* in the previous line) or simple error. BE gives a false etymology for *fore*, "from the Latin *foris*, abroad," one that SK calls "a cool invention."

2712 **to:** KA notes SKt's suggestion, "perhaps om. *to*"; no ed. adopts it.

2715 **Thenke longe:** FI paraphrases in the future, "it will seem long," but *thenke* may be present subjunctive, "it may seem long."

2726 **ony:** See 212n.

As helpe me God, this merveile I
How man, but he were maad of stele,
Myght lyve a monthe, such peynes to fele."
    The God of Love thanne seide me: 2735
"Freend, by the feith I owe to thee,
May no man have good, but he it bye.
A man loveth more tendirly
The thyng that he hath bought most dere.
For wite thou well, withouten were, 2740
In thanke that thyng is taken more
For which a man hath suffred sore.
Certis, no wo ne may atteyne
Unto the sore of loves peyne;
Noon yvel therto ne may amounte, 2745
No more than a man [may] counte
The dropes that of the water be.
For drye as well the greet see
Thou myghtist as the harmes telle
Of hem that with love dwelle 2750
In servyse, for peyne hem sleeth.
And [yet] ech man wolde fle the deeth,
And trowe thei shulde nevere escape,

Nere that Hope couthe hem make 2754
Glad, as man in prisoun sett, 53v
And may not geten for to ete
But barly breed and watir pure,
And lyeth in vermyn and [in] ordure;
With all this, yitt can he lyve,
Good Hope such comfort hath hym yeve, 2760
Which maketh wene that he shall be
Delyvered and come to liberte.
In fortune is [his] full tr[u]st,
Though he lye in strawe or dust;
In Hoope is all his susteynyng. 2765
And so for lovers, in her wenyng,
Whiche Love hath shitte in his prisoun,
Good Hope is her salvacioun.
Good Hope, how sore that they smerte,
Yeveth hem bothe will and herte 2770
To profre her body to martire;
For Hope so sore doith hem desire
To suffre ech harme that men devise
For joye that aftirward shall aryse.
    "Hope in desire cacche[th] victorie. 2775

    2735 **me]** to me UR   2738 **loveth]** lyveth TH²   2745 **ne]** *om.* UR   2746 **may]** *om.* MS-SP³ BE KA FU   2750 **hem]** all them UR   2752 **yet]** that MS-SK FU   **man]** *om.* TH³ ST SP²-BE   **fle]** flye TH¹˒² SP¹ FU SU FI   2755 **man]** a m. UR   2758 **and in]** and MS (MS₁ *corr.*) UR   2762 **Delyvered]** Relesed UR 2763 **his full]** full MS-SP³ KA FU; fully his UR   **trust]** trist MS BE-KA   2764 **Though]** Although UR 2766 **And so for]** A. s. fare SP²; A. s. faire SP³; So fare UR   2767 **shitte]** set SP³   2768 **is]** in FU   2771 **To profre]** T'offre UR   2772 **sore]** sore sore MS KA   2774 **aftirward]** aftir SK   **aryse]** rise UR 2775 **caccheth]** cacche MS-KA FU; to cacche SK; hathe GL

    2737–39 "Proverbial" (RB RI). RB notes Ln's citation (2601–02n.) of "the Latin line quoted by Rabelais (Pantagruel, iii, 41): 'Dulcior est fructus post multa pericula ductus.'" RI cites Whiting (1968: G356).
    2737 **no man:** KA suggests *noon*, but no ed. so emends.
    2746 **may:** UR's emendation, noted in UR MO by KA, has no parallel in the Fr.
    2752 **yet:** SKt suggests this emendation, as noted by KA, but does not adopt it in his text. GL justifies it on the basis of the Fr. *totes voies* (Lc 2594 "in any case"; noted by RBt SU RIt); the parallel is apt but remote by two lines (Lc 2594–96 "Et totes voies covient vivre / les amanz, qu'il lor est mestiers; / Chascuns fuit la mort volentiers" "And in any case, lovers must live, for life is their occupation. Everyone willingly flees death"). The last of these lines is the parallel to line 2752.
    2753 **trowe:** "i.e. I trowe," notes GL, comparing lines 2756 and 2758.
    2754–55 Ln (2611–17n.) RB compare Ovid, *Ex ponto* 1.6.37.
    2757 **barly breed:** "an inexpensive bread" (RIf). Cf. *WBP* D 144–45.
    2758 **and in:** "Second *in* [i] written above the line" (KA) by MS₁.
    2759–60 **lyve : yeve:** A common rhyme in MS (see lines 2777, 2949, 4987, 5447, 5667, 6655, 6803; cf. 2335–36n.). SK GL RB RI usually adjust to *lyve* and *yive*.
    2763 **trust:** MS *trist* gives an imperfect rhyme, but the sense is the same, and it may be a var. sp.; see *OED Trist* sb.¹. KA suggests "Read *trust*."
    2775 **caccheth:** RB's emendation for the MS subjunctive *cacche* ("may obtain") follows the indicative mood of the Fr. *vaint* (Lc 2613 "Esperance par sofrir vaint" "Hope triumphs through suffering"; noted by GL RB SU RI). SK reads *Hope* as an imperative ("do thou hope") and emends *cacche* to the infinitive *to cacche*. GL emends to the indicative *hathe*. SU notes that RB's version "is closest to Fr." § RB notes that "the French is nearer than the English to the proverb, 'Qui patitur vincit,'" quoted by Ln (2627n.); Lc (2613n.) cites Morawski (1925: no. 1060). RI notes the parallel to the proverb in *TC* 4.1584 "The suffrant overcomith."

162

In Hope, of love is all the glorie,
For Hope is all that love may yeve;
Nere Hope, ther shulde no lover lyve.
Blessid be Hope, which with desire   54r
Avaunceth lovers in such manere!   2780
Good Hope is curteis for to please,
To kepe lovers from all disese.
Hope kepith his [bonde], and wole abide
For ony perill that may betyde;
For Hope to lovers, as most cheef,   2785
Doth hem endure all myscheef.
Hope is her helpe, whanne myster is.
    "And I shall yeve thee eke, iwys,
Three other thingis that gret solas
Doith to hem that be in my las.   2790
    "The first good that may be founde
To hem that in my lace be bounde

Is Swete-Thought, for to recorde
Thing wherwith thou canst accorde
Best in thyne herte, where she be;   2795
Thenkyng in absence is good to thee.
Whanne ony lover doth compleyne,
And lyveth in distresse and in peyne,
Thanne Swete-Thought shal come as blyve
Awey his angre for to dryve.   2800
It makith lovers to have remembraunce
Of comfort and of high plesaunce
That Hope hath hight hym for to wynne. 54v
For Thought anoon thanne shall bygynne,
As ferre, God wote, as he can fynde,   2805
To make a mirrour of his mynde;
For to biholde he wole not lette.
Hir persone he shall afore hym sette,
Hir laughing eyen, persaunt and clere,

2778 **lover**] lenger TH¹-UR FU   2783 **bonde**] londe MS-SK FU   2784 **that**] *om.* UR   2786 **Doth**]
Dother FI   2795 **where**] whethir UR   2796 **Thenkyng**] Thought SK   **is**] *om.* UR   2798 **and in**] and
UR SK   2801 **to**] *om.* UR SK   2808 **afore**] fore UR

2777–78 **yeve : lyve:** See 2759–60n.
2778 "Proverbial," notes RI, citing Whiting (1968: H474).
   lover: In support of this reading over TH¹'s *lenger*, SU FI cite the Fr. *amant* (Lc 2614).
2779–80 **desire : manere:** On the rhyme, cf. 2471–72n.
2783 **bonde:** GL's emendation, for MS *londe*, assumes that the MS scribe omitted the second stroke of a *b*,
the first stroke of which is like an *l*. GL RBt RIt note the similarity in sense between *bonde* and the Fr. *garantira* (Lc
2623–24 "will protect").
2784 **ony:** See 212n.
2787 **myster:** "need" (SPg et al.), "necessity" (URg et al.), rather than "(love) service" (FI).
2790 **be:** KA suggests *ben*, but no ed. so emends.
2793–95 RI notes that "the translator has preserved the rhymes" of the Fr. (Lc 2631–32 "est Douz Pensers, qui
lor recorde / ce ou Esperance s'acorde" "is Sweet Thought, who recalls to them [the lovers] what Hope agrees to")
but has garbled the sense: "Sweet-Thought helps the lover remember whatever thing is most agreeable to his heart,
wherever she (the lady) may be." The ME obscures the relationship, explicit in the Fr., between Sweet-Thought and
Hope.
2793 **Swete-Thought:** "Fr. *Douz Penser*" (FI). BE notes that "this personage is called Privy-Thought in *The
Court of Love*" 1268 (ed. Skeat 1897:443).
2795 **where:** "wherever" (RIf). UR's *whethir* misconstrues his exemplar's *where* as the contracted form of
whether. Thus Urry reads the following line and a half ("whethir she be / Thinking in absence gode to The") as a
single clause. See 2793–95n.
2796 **Thenkyng:** KA suggests *Thought*, which only SK adopts. KA SKt compare line 2804 "Thought," but GL
adduces line 2815 "Swete-Thenkyng."
2797 **ony:** See 212n.
2806 **a mirrour of his mynde:** BE RI compare *TC* 1.365–66, in the note to which, BE observes that the
metaphor of the mirror is not in Boccaccio's *Il Filostrato* (1, st. 34) or in the Fr. at this point, although it amplifies the
idea there (Lc 2640–41 "au devant li met / les ieuz rianz, le nés tretiz . . ." "[Sweet Thought] presents him [the Lover]
with [images] of laughing eyes, a well-formed nose . . ."). On the figure of the *speculum mentis*, see Bennett
(1982:159–60).
2808 **he shall:** Liddell (GL) compares his note to line 2945, where he observes that "two unaccented
syllables, one of which is *shall*, are not uncommon in the poem; cp. vv. 2808, 2813."
2809 **eyen:** "one syllable; cp. vv. 2913, 2814" (GL).

Hir shappe, hir fourme, hir goodly chere, 2810
Hir mouth, that is so gracious,
So swete and eke so saverous.
Of all hir fetures he shall take heede,
His eyen with all hir lymes fede.
   "Thus Swete-Thenkyng shall aswage 2815
The peyne of lovers and her rage.
Thi joye shall double, withoute gesse,
Whanne thou thenkist on hir semlynesse,
Or of hir laughing, or of hir chere,
That to thee made thi lady dere. 2820
This comfort wole I that thou take;
And if the next thou wolt forsake,
Which is not lesse saverous,
Thou shuldist ben to daungerous.
   "The secounde shal be Swete-Speche, 2825
That hath to many oon be leche,

To bringe hem out of woo and were, 55r
And h[o]lpe many a bachilere,
And many a lady sent socoure,
That have loved paramour, 2830
Thorough spekyng whanne they myght heere
Of her lovers, to hem so dere.
To [hem] it voidith all her smerte,
The which is closed in her herte.
In herte it makith hem glad and light, 2835
Speche, whanne they [ne] mowe have sight.
And therfore now it cometh to mynde,
In olde dawes, as I fynde,
That clerkis writen that hir knewe,
Ther was a lady fresh of hwe, 2840
Which of hir love made a songe
On hym for to remembre amonge,
In which she seide, 'Whanne that I here

2813 **he]** *om.* UR   2814 **His]** Her TH²   2816 **peyne]** paynes TH²   2817 **Thi]** The SU FI 2819 **of hir chere]** h. c. UR   2823 **lesse]** the l. BE   2824 **ben]** not b. MS-KA FU   2828 **holpe]** helpe MS-SK FU SU FI   2830 **have]** hath UR   2833 **hem]** me MS-KA FU   2836 **ne mowe have]** m. h. MS-SP³ BE-SK FU; m. not h. UR; m. h. no GL

2813   **hir:** KA attributes to SK the suggestion that this word be omitted, but neither SK nor any other ed. so emends.
     he shall: See 2808n.
2814   **eyen:** See 2809n.
2822–24   "i.e., and if you don't accept the next comfort (also), which is no less pleasing, you are too disdainful" (FI).
2824   **Thou shuldist ben:** KA's suggested omisssion follows the Fr. *tu seroies* "you would be" (Lc 2656; noted by SKt GL RBt SU RIt). SK points out "*not ben* ruins sense and metre."
2826–29   With KA's emendation (see 2828n.) the construction corresponds approximately to the Fr. (Lc 2658–59 "qui a fet a mainz bachelers / et a maintes dame secors").
2828   **holpe:** KA's suggested emendation ("*Read* holpen") construes *holpe(n* as a past participle parallel with *be* in line 2826. Without the emendation, *helpe* is an infinitive parallel to *bringe* in line 2827.
2833–36   "Not in the Fr." (RB RI).
2833   **hem:** KA's suggested emendation. RBt explains MS *me* as "apparently an error anticipating l. 2845"; noted also by SKt RIt.
2836   **ne:** "The negative . . . seems necessary to the sense" (RB).
2837–50   Cook (1919:24–25) argues, on the basis of rhymes and certain phrases, for "Chaucer's probable translatorship" (p. 25) of this passage, even though Fragment B is generally denied to him.
2840–50   BE suggests, with little certainty, that the lady "may possibly be Sappho." Lc (2664n.) states that the song is unknown. Ln (2677n.) quotes Gaston Paris's identification of "la dame de Faiel" (1881:373n.) but feels that the allusion is not certain, particularly because (in the Fr.) Guillaume seems to recall the exact words of the song. RB RI summarize Ln's remarks, and both note that "the translator has made a free and expanded version of the song, which is only four lines long in the French" (RI). It is the God of Love who quotes the song (Lc 2665–68 "'Mout sui, fet ele, a bone escole, / qui de mon ami me parole. Si m'aïst Dex! i m'a garie / qui m'en parle, que qu'il m'en die'" "'I am in a very good school,' she said, 'when anyone discusses my lover with me. God help me, anyone who speaks to me about him, no matter what he may say, has given me relief'"). RB notes that "the lady's words, in the original, refer only to hearing speech about her lover. In the English, they include speaking about him herself, and this of course is involved, in both versions, in the advice which follows about selecting a confidant."
2840   **hwe:** hue, color. For the form, see *MED heu* n.
2842   **amonge:** Citing this line and adducing lines 3771 and 3881 and *BD* 298, URg defines as "often times, every now and then" (cf. TRg). FI here provides "constantly," RIf "always."

Speken of hym that is so dere,
To me it voidith all smerte,					2845
Iwys, he sittith so nere myne herte.
To speke of hym, at eve or morwe,
It cureth me of all my sorwe.
To me is noon so high plesaunce
As of his persone dalyaunce.'					2850
She wist full well that Swete-Spekyng			55v
Comfortith in full mych thyng.
Hir love she hadde full well assaid;
Of hem she was full well apaied;
To speke of hym hir joye was sett.				2855
   "Therfore I rede thee that thou gett
A felowe that can well concele,
And kepe thi counsell, and well hele,
To whom go shewe hoolly thine herte,
Bothe well and woo, joye and smerte.			2860
To gete comfort to hym thou goo,
And pryvyly, bitwene yow twoo,
Yee shall speke of that goodly thyng
That hath thyne herte in hir kepyng,
Of hir beaute and hir semblaunce,				2865
And of hir goodly countenaunce.

Of all thi state thou shalt hym seye,
And aske hym counseill how thou may
Do ony thyng that may hir plese;
For it to thee shall do gret ese				2870
That he may wite thou trust hym soo,
Bothe of thi wele and of thi woo.
And if his herte to love be sett,
His companye is myche the bett,				2874
For resoun wole he shewe to thee				56r
All uttirly his pryvyte;
And what she is he loveth so,
To thee pleynly he shal undo,
Withoute drede of ony shame,
Bothe tell hir renoun and hir name.			2880
Thanne shall he forther, ferre and nere,
And namely to thi lady dere,
In syker wise. Yee, every other
Shall helpen as his owne brother,
In trouthe withoute doublenesse,				2885
And kepen cloos in sikernesse.
For it is noble thing, in fay,
To have a man thou darst say
Thy pryve counsell every deell;

2845 **smerte]** my s. SK RB[1,2]   2853 **love]** *om.* SP[2,3]   2860 **joye]** and j. UR   2873 **herte]** het TH[2]
2880 **renoun]** renome TH[1]-UR FU SU   2881 **forther]** farther TH[2]

2845 **smerte:** RIt grants that SK's emendation, following KA's suggestion, may be correct. KA compares lines 2833, 2848.
2846 **sittith:** As KA notes, SK has the contracted form, *sit,*
2852 **mych:** See 1713n.
2853 **Hir:** KA suggests *His,* but no ed. so emends.
2854 **hem:** "him." BE-KA retain this MS form, but all other eds. respell as *him,* the usual form of the 3 sg. object masculine personal pron. I do not collate for *hem* as sing. (cf. lines 4267, 4498, 5107. See *MED him* pron. for sg. forms in *-e-*. LALME (4.198) shows the primary distribution of *hem* as sing. in Cambridge and East Anglia, with tertiary distribution in Ely, Lincoln, and the West Riding of Yorkshire. See above, "The Manuscript Hands: The Scribe (MS₁)" and 1922n.
2860 **joye:** KA suggests UR's addition but does not credit UR with the reading.
2869 **ony:** See 212n.
2874 **myche:** See 1713n.
2875 **For resoun:** "i.e., reasonably (in return for your confidence)" (FI).
2879 **ony:** See 212n.
2880 **renoun:** SU, using TH[1] as base, suggests that "perhaps [TH[1]'s] *renome* should be *renoune,*" the MS form. *Renome* may be only a spelling variant, but it has a separate history (*MED renomē* n. < OF *renomee; renoun* n. < AF *renoun,* OF *renom*).
2881 **Thanne shall he forther:** SKg₂ takes *forther* as a trans. verb ("further, advance, help [?]") with "*thee . . .* understood" (cf. RIg); *MED* takes *forther* as an intrans. verb and cites this line under *furtheren, -ien* v. 4. (a) "to go forth, proceed." Others seem to suggest that it is adverbial in an elliptical construction: "Then shall he [go] further" (GL RB); "he goes farther (in your behalf)" (FI).
2883-86 On the duty of sworn brothers to help each other, BE SK RB adduce *KnT* A 1132 (Palamon and Arcite).
2888 **thou:** GL suggests "(?) supply *that* before *thou*"; no ed. so emends.
   darst: "The trilled *r . . .* perhaps constitutes a syllable" (SK).

For that wole comforte thee right well, 2890
And thou shalt holde thee well apayed
Whanne such a freend thou hast assayed.
  "The thridde [good] of gret comforte,
That yeveth to lovers most disporte,
Comyth of sight and of biholdyng, 2895
That clepid is Swete-Lokyng,
The which may noon ese do
Whanne thou art fer thy lady fro;
Wherfore thou prese alwey to be 56v
In place where thou maist hir see. 2900
For it is thyng most amerous,
Most delytable and [saverous]
For to aswage a mannes sorwe,
To sene his lady by the morwe;
For it is a full noble thing 2905
Whanne thyne eyen have metyng

With that relike precious,
Wherof they be so desirous.
But al day after, soth it is,
They have no drede to faren amysse; 2910
They dreden neither wynde ne reyne,
Ne noon other maner peyne.
For whanne thyne eyen were thus in blisse,
Yit of hir curtesie, ywysse,
Alloone they can not have her joye, 2915
But to the herte they [it] conveye;
Parte of her blisse to hym [they] sende
Of all this harme to make an ende.
The eye is a good messangere,
Which can to the herte in such manere 2920
Tidyngis sende that [he] hath sene,
To voide hym of his peynes clene.
Wherof the herte rejoiseth soo 57r

2893 **good]** god MS (MS$_1$ *corr.*)   2894 **to]** *om.* UR   2895 **of biholdyng]** b. TH¹-UR SK FU-FI 2896 **That clepid is]** The c. i. SP³; T. i. yclepid UR; T. c. in SU   2897 **noon]** thee n. GL   2902 **delytable]** delectable SP²·³   **saverous]** fauerous MS-ST SP²-UR MO KA FU   2905 **a]** *om.* BE   2906 **Whanne]** Whan that UR   2907 **precious]** so p. UR   2912 **Ne]** N. yit SK   **maner]** m. of UR   2916 **it]** *om.* MS-KA FU   2917 **they]** thou MS-KA FU   2918 **this]** his TH²   **an ende]** amende UR   2921 **he]** *om.* MS-SP³ KA GL FU

2893 **good:** "*o* written above the line" (KA); it is the second *o*, inserted by MS$_1$.

2895 **of biholdyng:** Without *of*, the line is headless, with eight syllables and a weak ending; with it, nine syllables and a weak ending, a normal octosyllabic line; if *Comyth* be scanned as a monosyllable, the *of* is necessary even for the headless line. If TH¹ derives from MS, it has no independent authority (Blodgett 1975:221; on TH¹'s prosodic changes, see pp. 221–28).

2896 **Swete-Lokyng:** BE FI note the Fr. *Douz Regart* (Lc 2702).

2902 **saverous:** The same error occurs at lines 84 and 3767; cf. lines 2812, 2823, where MS has the correct form, with *s*; cf. 84n. As RIt notes, "the scribe of [MS] misread long *s* for *f*, perhaps not understanding the word. Thynne emends [line 84] but not here nor in 3767. His editing has grown very casual." URg reads unemended *favirous* as "favourable," and *MED fáverous* adj. glosses the word as "favorable, pleasant," with a derivation from *favour*, but the sole examples are *Rom* 84 and 2902. § In all three cases with the *f*- reading, the contexts emphasize sensory appeal and seem to support the *saverous* reading. At line 84, where the adjectives describe the weather, *savoureus* appears in the Fr. as a var. in MSS Ca and κω (Ln 80t, KA Fr. 80n.). At line 2902 the Fr. has *savoreus* (Ln 2724, Lc 2708) in reference to the sight of one's lady. And at line 3767 the adjectives refer to the flower and its odor (Ln 3487, Lc 3469 "si sade et bien olenz" "so pleasant, so very fragrant").

2907 **relike:** BE calls attention to the Fr., where, as at line 2673, the parallel word is *saintuaire* (Lc 2711). § "The [ME] poet calls the lady a relic because relics were at that time held the most precious of all things" (BE).

2913 **eyen:** See 2809n.

2916–18 The ME does not follow the Fr. very closely (Lc 2720–21 "ainz veulent que li cuers s'esjoie / et font ses maus rasoagier" "but [the eyes] want the heart to enjoy itself, and they alleviate its woes"). SK emends by inserting *it* in line 2916 and reading *they* for *thou* in line 2917, endorsed by KA. BE MO keep MS readings, with punctuation as follows: "But to the herte they conveye, / Part of her blisse; to hym thou sende / Of all this harme to make an ende."

2920 "The verse is made smoother by placing *can* after the first word of the next line" (GL).

2921 **he:** KA notes *he* in UR BE MO. SU FI adduce the Fr. *il* (Lc 2724 "noveles de ce qui il voient" "reports of what they see"); but there the antecedent of *il* is the plural *li oel* "the eyes" (line 2722), while the ME antecedent is singular, "The eye" (line 2919).

166

That a gret partye of his woo
Is voided and putte awey to flight.　　2925
Right as the derknesse of the nyght
Is chased with clerenesse of the mone,
Right so is al his woo full soone
Devoided clene, whanne that the sight
Biholden·may that fresh wight　　2930
That the herte desireth soo,
That al his derknesse is agoo;
For thanne the herte is all at ese,
Whanne [the eyen] sene that may hem plese.
　　"Now have I declared thee all oute　　2935
Of that thou were in drede and doute;
For I have tolde thee feithfully
What thee may curen utterly,
And all lovers that wole be
Feithfull and full of stabilite.　　2940
Good-Hope alwey kepe bi thi side,

And Swete-Thought make eke abide,
Swete-Lokyng and Swete-Speche—
Of all thyne harmes thei shall be leche;
Of every thou shalt have gret plesaunce.　　2945
If thou canst bide in suffraunce,
And serve wel withoute feyntise,　　57v
Thou shalt be quyte of thyne emprise
With more guerdoun, if that thou lyve;
But [at] this tyme this I thee yeve."　　2950
　　The God of Love whanne al the day
Had taught me, as ye have herd say,
And enfourmed compendiously,
He vanyshide awey all sodeynly,
And I alloone lefte, all soole,　　2955
So full of compleynt and of doole,
For I sawe no man there me by.
My woundes me greved wondirly;
Me for to curen nothyng I knewe,

2931　**That]** Whiche t. UR　　2934　**the eyen sene that may]** they s. t. m. MS TH¹ TH³-SP³ BE-KA FU; they s. t. they TH²; thei s. that that m. UR SK　　2935　**declared thee]** t. d. SK　　2940　**full]** *om.* UR　　2942　**make]** may SP¹　　2945　**every]** bale UR　　2950　**at]** all MS-SK FU SU　　2952　**Had]** He' had UR　　2953　**enfourmed]** e. me TH²　　2954　**awey]** *om.* UR　　2958　**wondirly]** wondersly TH¹-UR FU SU FI

2925　**voided:** GL suggests "(?) *void*."

2934　**the eyen sene that:** GL's emendation follows the Fr. (Lc 2734 "quant *li oil* voient ce qu'il viaut" "when the eyes see what it [the heart] wishes"; noted by GL RBt SU FI RIt). The UR SK emendation leaves MS *they* without a clear referent.

　　hem: The antecedent is *the eyen*, and the sense departs from the Fr. (above).

2936　**that:** "that of which." Roscow (1981:117–18) explains the construction as one "which, though it has the appearance of ellipsis, may be accounted for by the use of *that* as a demonstrative-relative particle representing a phonetically reduced form of OE. *þæt þe* 'that which' . . . . The demonstrative-relative in sentences of this kind acts as an object to the verb in each of two clauses" (p. 117). Cf. 2106n., 3041n.

2945　**Of every:** "i.e., from each of them" (GL; cf. RIf)

　　thou shalt have gret: KA suggests omitting *gret*, but no ed. so emends. GL counters KA's suggestion by noting that "two unaccented syllables, one of which is *shall*, are not uncommon in the poem," and comparing lines 2808, 2813. See 2808n.

2946　**suffraunce:** Although TH¹ TH³ ST-SP² UR SK FU-RI have *sufferaunce*, the MS form is the normal one, from AF, OF *suf(f)rance, soffrance*; it existed beside the form with medial *-e-*, influenced by *suffer*. See *OED Sufferance*.

2947　**feyntise:** Either "feigning" (URg GLg); "hypocrisy, dissimulation" (URg); "deceit, guile" (SKg, RBg)— or "faint-heartedness" (RIf). FI spells as *fayntise* and paraphrases as "growing faint." See *OED*, s.v. *faintise*, for both senses.

2949–50　**lyve : yeve:** See 2759–60n.

2950　**at:** GL's emendation, based on the Fr. *des ore* (Michel 2777 "from now"). Ln (2764) and Lc (2748) have "a ja" "for the moment"; Ln records the variants *des ja* (MS Ri), *des ore* (MSS Bâ Ga), and others; SU has *des ia*, from MS Ri, and FI notes it as "*des ia (déja)*"; RIt notes the Lc reading and the two variants.

2951–52　"When the God of Love had (all day) taught (me) . . ." (BE SK RB); RB notes that "the inversion is unusual."

2953　**enfourmed:** TH² anticipates GL's later suggestion "Perhaps supply *me* before *enfourmed*."

　　compendiously: "briefly" (URg); spelled without *i* in TH¹-UR and without *s* in ST UR.

2954　**awey:** "does not seem to belong to the verse" (GL); it is redundant to meter and sense.

2958　**wondirly:** *OED Wonders*, a. and adv., identifies TH¹'s variant *wondersly* as a parallel derivation from the "gen. of *wonder sb.*; a·Scand. idiom"; *wondrous* is an "alteration of *wonders . . .* by substitution of suffix *-ous*" (*OED Wondrous* a.).

Save the bot[oun] bright of hewe,
Wheron was sett hoolly my thought.
Of other comfort knewe I nought,
But it were thorugh the God of Love;
I knewe not elles to my bihove
That myght me ease or comfort gete,
But if he wolde hym entermete.
   The roser was, withoute doute,
Closed with an hegge withoute,
As ye toforn have herd me seyne;
And fast I bisiede, and wolde fayne
Have passed the hay, if I myght
Have geten ynne by ony slight
Unto the bot[oun] so faire to see.
But evere I dradde blamed to be,
If men wolde have suspeccioun
That I wolde of entencioun
Have stole the roses that there were;
Therfore to entre I was in fere.

2960

2965

2970
58r

2975

But at the last, as I bithought
Whether I shulde passe or nought,
I sawe come with a glad chere
To me, a lusty bachelere,
Of good stature and of good hight,
And Bialacoil forsothe he hight.
Sone he was to Curtesie;
And he me grauntide full gladly
The passage of the outter hay,
And seide, "Sir, how that yee may
Passe, if youre will be
The fresh roser for to see,
And yee the swete savour fele.
Youre warran[t] may [I be] right wele;
So thou thee kepe fro folye,
Shall no man do thee vylanye.
If I may helpe you in ought,
I shall not feyne, dredeth nought,
For I am bounde to youre servise,

2980

2985

2990

2994
58v

   2960 **bright]** so b. UR   2964 **elles]** ele TH¹-SP¹ FU   2968 **hegge]** haye GL   2970 **And]** As MO
2971 **if]** i. that GL   2973 **Unto]** To UR   2977 **there were]** w. t. SP¹   2985 **to]** unto MO   2988 **how]**
nowe SU FI   2989 **if]** i. that it UR; i. it SK; i. that GL   2992 **Youre warrant may I be]** Y. warrans m. MS-SP³
BE KA FU; Y. w. I m. b. UR; You w. m. I GL SU FI   2996 **nought]** right n. UR

   2960 **botoun:** See 1721n.
   2964 **elles:** See above, "The Manuscript Hands: The Scribe (MS₁)" and 300n.
   2968 **hegge:** As RBt notes, GL emends to *haye* because this form occurs later (lines 2971, 2987, 3007, and eight other *loci*). See 2971n., 3398n.
   2971 **hay:** TH¹˒² SP²˒³ SK FU SU FI normalize by adding *-e* but SK, citing line 2987, notes that the form may not be a disyllable. FI notes that *haye* is "the usual form for 'hedge' in the B part of the *Romaunt*; seldom used elsewhere in *Romaunt* or Chaucer's poems." In fact, both forms occur in both fragments, with *hay* predominant in Fragment B—eleven times to three for *hegge* (lines 1841, 2968, 3398). In Fragment A, we have *hay* once (line 54) and *hegge* twice (lines 481, 1652).
   if: GL's emendation follows KA's suggestion.
   2972 **ony:** See 212n.
   2973 **botoun:** See 1721n.
   2984 **Bialacoil:** "Fair Welcome" (RIf). TRg BE SKt RI note that the Fr. is *Bel Acueil* (Lc 2776), and TRg SU RI note that this character is called *Fair-Welcoming* in Fragment C (e.g., lines 5856, 7522); see 5856n. BE SK explain the characteristic as "graceful address," useful, as a quality of the lover, in propitiating the lady in a first approach; but TRg sees the quality as the lady's "courteous reception," and RI, adducing Lewis (1936:122–23), sees it as "the lady's disposition to be open . . . to the lover's presence." Fleming (1969:43–46) sees this "lusty bacheler" as an abstract idea with gender that is grammatical only.
   2988 **how:** GL suggests "(?) *now*" and compares line 2585. SU FI have *nowe*; SU cites the Fr., but there is no exact parallel (Lc 2781–82 "se il vos plest, / pasez la haie sanz arest" "if it pleases you, pass through the hedge without hindrance").
   2989 **if:** KA endorses Sk's reading.
   2992 **Youre warrant may I be:** MO's emendation, noted in KA, adapts UR's *I may be*. BE also suggests *I may be* on the basis of the Fr. (Lc 2784 "Je vos i puis bien garantir" "I can well assure you"; noted by SKt RBt RIt). GL SU FI adduce the Fr. in support of the emendation *You warrante may I*, one which takes *warrant* as a verb, glossed by FI as "protect." Neither the noun nor the finite verb is an exact syntactic parallel to the Fr. infinitive. GL's emendation is perhaps closer to the Fr., but it requires greater change from the MS.

Fully devoide of feyntise."
Thanne unto Bialacoil saide I,
"I thanke you, sir, full hertly,　　　　　　3000
And youre biheest take at gre,
That ye so goodly profer me;
To you it cometh of gret fraunchise,
That ye me profer youre servise."
Thanne aftir, full delyverly,　　　　　　3005
Thorough the breres anoon wente I,
Wherof encombred was the hay.
I was wel plesed, the soth to say,
To se the bot[oun] faire and swote
So fresh spr[o]nge out of the rote.　　　3010
And Bialacoil me served well,
Whanne I so nygh me myght fele
Of the bot[oun] the swete odour,
And so lusty hwed of colour.
But thanne a cherle—foule hym bityde—　3015

Biside the roses gan hym hyde,
To kepe the roses of that roser,
Of whom the name was Daunger.
This cherle was hid there in the greves,　59r
Kovered with gras and with leves,　　3020
To spie and take whom that he fonde
Unto that roser putte an honde.
He was not soole, for ther was moo;
For with hym were other twoo
Of wikkid maners and yvel fame.　　3025
That oon was clepid, by his name,
Wykked-Tonge—God yeve hym sorwe!—
For neither at eve ne at morwe
He can of no man good speke;
On many a just man doth he wreke.　3030
Ther was a womman eke that hight
Shame, that, who can reken right,
Trespace was hir fadir name,

2998 **feyntise]** all f. UR　　3001 **take]** I t. UR SK　　3005 **full]** fully MS MO KA　　3008 **the]** and BE　　3010 **spronge]** sprange MS BE-KA　　3013 **the]** thilke MO　　3019 **This cherle was]** The c. way FU　　3020 **with leves]** leves UR　　3025 **yvel]** ill UR　　3026 **That]** Than TH²　　3029 **good]** no g. SK RB¹²; good ne GL　　3030 **On]** Of FU　　3031 **eke that]** t. e. TH³ ST SP²-UR

2998　**devoide:** "Possibly *devoided*; but cp. v. 3723" (GL).

3001　**biheest:** TH¹ MO GL-RI add -*e*, the form noted by KA in MO, and justified by GL as an "inorganic -*e* as in Chaucer." *MED bihēst(e* n. ("promise; what is promised") gives the origin as OE *behās* with "-*t* of the synonym *hight*"; see *MED hight* n. (a) "hope, expectation."

　　　take: KA endorses *I take* in SK.

3009, 3013　**botoun:** See 1721n.

3014　**hwed:** For the pa. part. form *hwed*, see *MED heuen* v.(2). Cf. 2840n.

3018　**Daunger:** RI, noting that the character is "the personification of something like disdain, standoffishness," quotes Lewis's analysis of elements in the personification (1936:124): "the rebuff direct, the lady's 'snub' launched from the height of her ladyhood . . . and perhaps her anger and comtempt," and cites Barron (1965) "on the literary uses of 'luf-daungere.'" For the analysis of Daunger as "a moral category which manifests itself in psychological restraint," see Fleming (1969:188–89). See also Dahlberg (1977) on the relationship between Daunger as resistance and Daunger as restraint. Cf. 490n., 3130–37n.

3024–32　Brusendorff (1925:309–10) notes that this passage corresponds to the variants in the MS families K, L, M, N, of Ln's group II to which Sutherland (SU, pp. xxiii–xxiv) adds MS Ri, his base MS for Fragment B (cf. Ln 2835t). But where Brusendorff takes this fact as an argument for a corrupt French MS as the original of the ME translation by Chaucer alone, Sutherland takes it as evidence that different parts of the ME *Rom* were by different authors. RI explains: "The best French MSS name four guardians of the Rose at this point: 'Daunger,' 'Male Bouche' (*Wykked-Tonge*), 'Honte' (*Shame*), and 'Peor' (*Drede*). The English translation comes from one of the great majority of French MSS designated by Langlois [1910:241–43] as Class II, which omit 'Peor' and speak of only three guardians. Cf. 3060, 3066." The translation, like the Fr., includes "Drede" from line 3958 forward, and the four guardians occupy the four gates of Jealousy's tower (lines 4203–36).

3030　**wreke:** Probably a noun, "vengeance" (RIf *OED Wreak* sb.), construed as object of *doth*; *OED* identifies *wreak* as a Northern form. If *doth* is construed as an auxiliary, *wreke* would have to be intrans., "take vengeance" (*OED Wreak* v., sense 10), rather than trans., "mistreat (avenge)" (FI).

3033–34　**fadir . . . moder:** both gen. sg., from the OE uninflected gen. sg. in nouns of relationship (Campbell 1959:255–56). TH¹-UR FU SU FI emend to *fathers* but not to *mothers*, and the probable parallel construction, "Trespass was her father's name, her mother's Reason" becomes imparallel and elliptical: "Trespass was her father's name, Reason [was] her mother."

Hir moder Resoun; and thus was Shame
Brought of these ilk twoo. 3035
And yitt hadde Trespasse never adoo
With Resoun, ne never ley hir bye,
He was so hidous and so oughlye—
I mene this that Trespas hight;
But Resoun conceyveth of a sight 3040
Shame, of that I spake aforne.
And whanne that Shame was thus borne,
It was ordeyned that Chastite 59v
Shulde of the roser lady be,
Which, of the bot[oun]s more and lasse, 3045
W[ith] sondre folk assailed was,
That she ne wist what to doo.

For Venus hir assailith soo
That nyght and day from hir she stale
Bot[oun]s and roses overall. 3050
To Resoun thanne praieth Chastite,
Whom Venus hath flemed over the see,
That she hir doughter wolde hir lene
To kepe the roser fresh and grene.
Anoon Resoun to Chastite 3055
Is fully assented that it be,
And grauntide hir, at hir request,
That Shame, by cause she [is] honest,
Shall keper of the roser be.
    And thus to kepe it ther were three, 3060
That noon shulde hardy be ne bolde—

3034 **and thus was**] a. t. TH²; t. w. UR   3035 **Brought of**] Ybrought forth o. UR; On lyve b. o. SK
3038 **so hidous and so**] h. a. s. TH³-UR; s. h. a. SK   3040 **conceyveth**] conceyved GL RB¹·²   3041 **Shame
of that**] That s. o. which UR   **spake**] speake ST SP¹   3042 **thus**] this TH²   3046 **With**] W MS (MS₂
corr.)   **folk**] folkes SP²·³   3052 **hath**] om. SK   3058 **is**] om. MS KA

3035 **ilk:** This is a rare case in which Skeat does not normalize, by adding -*e*, perhaps because his emendation had already adjusted meter; he glosses his phrase *On lyve* as "to life" (SKt). As RIt notes, RBt "calls the line 'defective' but does not emend it." RBt notes SK's emendation but states, "perhaps read *Y-brought forth* (Urry)"; KA notes UR's reading.

3038 **so hidous and so:** KA suggests omission of the second *so*, but GL and SU cite the Fr. (Lc 2826 "si hideus et si lez" "so hideous and so ugly") in support of MS as it stands.

3040 **conceyveth:** The emendation *conceyved* (GL RB) follows KA's suggestion.

3041 **of that:** "of whom." Roscow (1981:120) notes the unusual construction: "A restriction on the placing of prepositions in relative clauses introduced by *that* or *as* is that they cannot generally precede the relative pronoun, except . . . when *that* is used as a demonstrative-relative equivalent to 'that which.'" Since the latter is not the case here (cf. 2936n.), Roscow takes "this exceptional usage . . . as further evidence that Fragment B of the translation . . . is not by Chaucer."

spake: ST SP¹ have *speake*, probably not the pr. t. but a var. of the pa. t.; see Dobson (1968:626 n.3): "the rhyme of *speak* with *make* may depend on the analogical infinitive *spake* . . . which is due to the variation in eModE in the p[ast] t. between *spake* (the normal form) and *speak* (from the OE and ME plural)." *OED speak* v. does not record the form *speak* as a 15th-century δ-form of the pa. sg. At line 7517, ST-SP³ have the same var., but not at lines 4042, 5286, 5838, 7606.

3043–47 RB quotes the Fr. (Lc 2830-33 "Chasteez, qui dame doit estre / et des roses et des boutons, / ert asaillie de glotons / si qu'ele avoit mestier d'aïe" "Chastity, who should be the lady of roses and buds, was attacked by scoundrels so that she had need of help") and notes that "the English translation departs from the original, perhaps through some confusion." See 3045n.

3045 **Which, of:** "which because of" (FI). The antecedent of *which* may be "roser" or—if one follows the Fr.—"lady." See 3043-47n.

botouns: See 1721n.

3046 **With:** Thorp and Whatley (1989) call attention to the fact that the full correction is *ith*, with the "*h* written above the line" (KA). The three letters are in a light brown ink and a later hand, MS₂d. See above, "The Manuscript Hands: The Corrections."

3050 **Botouns:** See 1721n. UR glosses as "bottoms" rather than "buds."

3052 **hath flemed:** KA suggests *flemed hath*; no ed. so emends, although SK omits *hath*.

3054 **kepe:** There is no parallel in the Fr., but the context supports the sense "protect" (FI) the fresh, green Roser, rather than "keep" the Roser fresh and green.

3057–58 **request : honest:** KA suggests *requestis : honest is* and adduces lines 6039-40, 6977-78; no ed. so emends, but all except KA insert *is* before *honest*.

3060 Here again, as at lines 3024-32, there are three guardians rather than the four of the best French MSS and of the ME translation from line 3958 onward, where the missing fourth guardian "Drede" (Fr. *Peor*) appears for the first time. See 3024-32n.; Ln 2863t; Brusendorff (1925:310); SU, p. xxiv.

Were he yong or were he olde—
Ageyn hir will awey to bere
Bot[oun]s ne roses that there were.
I hadde wel spedde, hadde I not bene   3065
Awayted with these three and sene.
For Bialacoil, that was so faire,   60r
So gracious and debonaire,
Quytt hym to me full curteislye,
And, me to please, bade that I   3070
Shulde drawe me to the bot[oun] nere;
Prese in, to touche the rosere
Which bare the roses, he yaf me leve;
This graunte ne myght but lytel greve.
And for he sawe it liked me,   3075
Ryght nygh the bot[oun] pullede he
A leef all grene, and yaff me that,
The whiche full nygh the bot[oun] sat,
I made [me] of that leef full queynte,
And whanne I felte I was aqueynte   3080
With Bialacoil, and so pryve,
I wende all at my will hadde be.
Thanne waxe I hardy for to telle
To Bialacoil hou me bifelle
Of Love, that toke and wounded me,   3085
And seide, "Sir, so mote I thee,

I may no joye have in no wise,
Uppon no side, but it rise;
For sithe (if I shall not feyne)
In herte I have hadde so gret peyne,   3090
So gret annoy and such affray,   60v
That I ne wote what I shall say;
I drede youre wrath to disserve.
Lever me were that knyves kerve
My body shulde in pecys small,   3095
Than in any wise it shulde fall
That ye wratthed shulde ben with me."
   "Sey boldely thi will," quod he,
"I nyl be wroth, if that I may,
For nought that thou shalt to me say."   3100
   Thanne seide I, "Sir, not you displease
To knowen of myn gret unnese,
In which oonly Love hath me brought;
For peynes gret, disese, and thought,
Fro day to day he doth me drye;   3105
Supposeth not, sir, that I lye.
In me fyve woundes dide he make,
The soore of whiche shall nevere slake
But ye the bot[oun] graunte me,
Which is moost passaunt of beaute,   3110
My lyf, my deth, and my martire,

3068 **and]** a. so MO   3071 **me]** *om.* TH³-BE   3073 **roses]** Rose UR   3079 **me]** *om.* MS-KA
FU   3082 **at]** *om.* TH³-BE   3083 **Thanne]** That TH³-SP¹   **waxe]** wext TH¹-UR FU SU FI   3088 **rise]**
aryse TH³-UR   3096 **in any wise]** any weyes GL   3105 **he]** it TH³-UR

3064   **Botouns:** See 1721n.
3066   **Awayted with:** "waylaid by" (RIf; cf. URg), "spied upon by" (*MED awaiten* v. 2 [b]), or "watched for by," rather than merely "watched by" (SKg₂ FI).
3071   **botoun:** See 1721n.
3073   **roses:** UR's reading, noted by KA, may be based on the Fr. (KA Fr. 2851–53 [= Lc 2855–57] "Sovent me semont d'aprochier / Vers le bouton et d'atouchier / Au rosier qui l'avoit chargié" "He often urges me to approach the rosebud and to touch the bush which bore it").
3076, 3078   **botoun:** See 1721n.
3079   **made me . . . full queynte:** TR glosses *queynt* in this line as "strange"; however, SKg₂ reads as "pleased" and FI as "happy (strange)." URg, s. v. *Queint*, paraphrases the unemended line: "I made very much of that leaf, put a great value upon it." RIf provides "took great pleasure." See also 65n.
   me: KA's suggested emendation; in support, SKt RIt cite the Fr. me fis (Lc 2863 "made myself").
3088   **but it rise:** "unless it happen (?)," suggests Robinson (RB), who compares line 3115, "where *arise* translates Fr. 'avenir'" (Lc 2893); similarly, David (RIf) suggests "unless it comes to pass (?)" and notes (RI) that there is no Fr. parallel to this line, comparing line 3115 and Lc 2893. FI's paraphrase, "unless I recover," suggests the sense.
3089   **sithe:** KA suggests *sithen,* but only GL adopts the derivative form, *sithens.*
3096   **in any wise:** KA suggests ("perhaps") *any weyes* and compares line 3249 ("Other weyes"). GL so emends; see 3240n.
3101   **Sir:** See 800n.
3105   **doth me drye:** "makes me suffer; Scotch 'gars me dree'" (SK); however, SKg₂ defines *drye* at this line as "endure" and at line 4390 as "suffer." See 4390n.
3109   **botoun:** See 1721n.

171

And tresour that I moost desire."
  Thanne Bialacoil, affrayed all,
Seyde, "Sir, it may not fall;   3114
That ye desire, it may not arise.   61r
What? Wolde ye shende me in this wise?
A mochel foole thanne I were,
If I suffride you awey to bere
The fresh bot[oun] so faire of sight.
For it were neither skile ne right,   3120
Of the roser ye broke the rynde,
Or take the rose aforn his kynde;
Ye are not curteys to aske it.
Late it still on the roser sitt
And growe til it amended be,   3125

And parfytly come to beaute.
I nolde not that it pulled were
Fro the roser that it bere,
To me it is so leef and deere."
  With that sterte oute anoon Daungere,   3130
Out of the place were he was hidde.
His malice in his chere was kidde;
Full grete he was and blak of hewe,
Sturdy and hidous, whoso hym knewe;
Like sharp urchouns his here was growe,   3135
[His eyes reed sparclyng as the
    fyre glowe];   TH¹:144c
His nose frounced, full kirked stoode.   MS:61r
He come criande as he were woode,

3114 **fall]** befall UR   3115 **arise]** rise UR SK   3125 **And growe]** A. late it g. MS-SP³ BE-KA FU; Let it g. UR   3127 **not]** *om.* SP¹   3128 **the]** thilke MO   **that]** t. doth UR   3130 **sterte oute anoon]** a. s. o. TH¹-UR FU SU FI   3133 **and]** the SU FI   3136 **sparclyng]** *om.* SK GL   **the]** *om.* UR   *Out:* MS (*blank line*) KA RI

3115 **arise:** "happen" (FI). KA notes UR's *rise* and compares line 3088. GL also compares line 3088 and suggests that the word may originally have been *arive*, with assonance. See 3088n.

3118 **awey:** GL notes that "the verse would be smoother without *awey*." See 2954n.

3119 **botoun:** See 1721n.

3122 **aforn his kynde:** lit., before its nature, thus "before its natural time (maturity)" (FI).

3125 **And growe:** The omission of MS *late it* is KA's suggestion. RBt SU note that the words *late it* are probably repeated from line 3124.

3127–28 **were : bere:** SK drops *-e* from each word, and RBt RIt note that, although the rhyme should probably be so read, the subjunctive *bere* is possible.

3130–37 RB RI note that "the description of *Daunger* is characteristic of the 'vilain,' or peasant, as he appears in mediæval literature" (RB); RI notes the "grotesque, animalistic features." Both refer to Ln (2922–23n.) for examples; RI emphasizes "the ugly herdsman in Chrétien's Yvain and the peasant in Aucassin et Nicolette." RB refers to "G. M. Vogt, The Peasant in Mid. Eng. Lit., unpublished Harv. diss., 1923," and RI adduces Colby (1965:72–88, 170–73). On the quality that Daunger represents, see 3018n.; on Daunger's nose, see 3137n.

3136 BE notes the omission of the line in MS; KA notes that TH¹ inserts the line and that SK suggests omission of *sparclyng*; SK GL adduce the Fr. (Lc 2907 "s'ot les ieuz roges come feus" "and he had eyes as red as fire"). GL reports inaccurately that TH¹ has *sparklingly*. RBt calls the line "doubtless corrupt," and FI notes the absence of any Fr. equivalent for *sparclyng*. Blodgett (1984:49–50; cf. 1975:215–16) takes the line as partial evidence for his contention that TH¹ supplied omissions in MS by consulting the Fr. text. "The metrical awkwardness," he says (1984:50), ". . . at least hints at editorial fabrication." RI omits the line as spurious, adduces the Fr., and notes TH¹'s use of the form "*eyes* in place of the usual *eyen*"; cf. 892n.

3137 On the iconography of Daunger's "wrinkled and crooked" nose, see David (1985:81–84), who sees such a nose as a stereotypical feature, with sexual valence, of characters like the ugly herdsman in Chrétien de Troyes's *Yvain*, the ugly peasant in *Aucassin et Nicolette*, and Chaucer's Miller (*GP* 554–57), and as a contrast to the well-formed, "tretis" noses of characters like the Prioress (*GP* 152) or Fraunchise (*Rom* 1215–16). Cf. 3130–37n.

        kirked: Skeat endorses the sense "'crooked,' as Morris suggests" (see MOg), saying, "It may be a mere dialectal form of 'crooked,' or it may be miswritten for *kroked*, the usual old spelling." Skeat traces the false sense "turned upwards" from Halliwell (1847) back to Skinner (1671), who, Skeat notes, derived it "from A. S. *cerran*, to turn, which is out of the question." The same gloss appears in SPg and in URg, where URg cites Skinner; but TRg has the laudable notation "not understood." Later eds., and *MED crǒked* ppl. 1. (d) accept the suggestion "crooked." RB calls the "form unexplained," and RIt suggests that it may be "an error for *kroked*"; both RBt and RIt cite the Fr. parallel, *froncié* (Lc 2908 "wrinkled"), which appears separately in this line as *frounced* and again, as GL notes, at line 7259 as *frouncen*.

3138 **criande:** Northern present participle, as FI notes.

And seide, "Bialacoil, telle me why
Thou bryngest hider so booldly 3140
Hym that so nygh [is] the roser;
Thou worchist in a wrong maner.
He thenkith to dishonoure thee;
Thou art wel worthy to have maugree
To late hym of the roser wite. 3145
Who serveth a feloun is yvel quitte.
Thou woldist have doon gret bounte,
And he with shame wolde quyte thee.
Fle hennes, felowe! I rede thee goo!
It wanteth litel [I] wole thee sloo. 3150
For Bialacoil ne knewe thee nought,
Whanne thee to serve he sette his thought;
For thou wolt shame him, if thou myght,
Bothe ageyns resoun and right.
I wole no more in thee affye, 3155
That comest so slyghly for t'espye;
For it preveth wonder well,
Thy slight and tresoun, every deell."
    I durst no more there make abode,
For the cherl he was so wode, 3160

So gan he threte and manace,
And thurgh the haye he dide me chace.
For feer of hym I tremblyde and quoke, 62r
So cherlishly his heed it shoke,
And seide, if eft he myght me take, 3165
I shulde not from his hondis scape.
    Thanne Bialacoil is fledde and mate,
And I, all soole, disconsolate,
Was left aloone in peyne and thought;
For shame to deth I was nygh brought. 3170
Thanne thought I on myn high foly,
How that my body utterly
Was yeve to peyne and to martire;
And therto hadde I so gret ire
That I ne durst the hayes passe; 3175
There was noon hope, there was no grace.
I trowe nevere man wiste of peyne,
But he were laced in loves cheyne;
Ne no man [wot], and sooth it is,
But if he love, what anger is. 3180
Love holdith his heest to me right wele,
Whanne peyne he seide I shulde fele.

61v (line 3139 marker)

3141 **so nygh is]** s. n. MS-SP³ BE KA FU; s. n. to UR; s. n. cam MO; is s. n. GL   3146 **a]** *om.* UR GL
yvel] ill UR   3149 **Fle]** Flye TH¹-UR FU SU FI   3150 **I]** it MS KA; he TH¹-UR FU   3154 **and right]** a.
'gainst r. UR   3156 **slyghly]** slightly ST-BE   3157 **wonder]** wondirly UR   3159 **there make]** m. t. TH¹-
UR FU SU FI   3160 **the]** thilke MO   3164 **So]** For SU FI   **cherlishly]** chorlishe ST SP²·³   **it]** he TH¹-BE
SK FU-FI   3166 **hondis]** hones SU   3168 **soole]** s. and TH³ ST SP²·³   3170 **For]** Fro TH³ ST SP²-BE
3171 **I]** *om.* TH³ ST SP²·³   3174 **ire]** desire SP²·³   3175 **hayes]** haye GL RB¹·²   3179 **wot]** wist UR MO;
not GL; *om.* MS-SP³ BE KA FU   3181 **his]** this SP¹

3140 **booldly:** TH¹ TH³ ST UR MO GL-RI have *boldely*, the usual Chaucerian form, particularly in rhyme, but
the form with *-e-* is not necessarily a historical normalization; cf. OE *bealdlice*, from the adj. *beald* + the adverb-
forming suffix *lice*. See *MED bōldelī(che* adv.

3141 **is:** SK's emendation. BE, noting that "the line appears to be corrupt" and lacks a verb, suggests that
"perhaps we ought to read *than*" for *that*. KA notes the readings of both MO and SK.

3144 **maugree:** "ill will" (URg SK GL RIf), "disfavour" (BE SK), "reproach" (SKg₂ RIf), "displeasure" (FI). In
citing the French etymon *malgré*, FI may seem to suggest that it appears at this point in the Fr. text; such is not the
case.

3146 Proverbial; RB cites Haeckel (1890: no. 139), and RI cites Whiting (1968: F118).

3150 **I:** BE so emends MS *it*, without annotation, presumably on the basis of the Fr. *je* (Lc 2920 "Par poi que je
ne vos oci" "for little would I kill you"; noted by SKt GL RBt SU FI RIt). KA notes the change in BE MO.

3156 **slyghly:** The variant *slightly* differs from *slyghly* in its formation from the nominal base, *sleight*, rather
than from the cognate adjectival base, *sleigh*. See *MED sleightlī* adv., *sleighlī* adv.; the meaning, "craftily," is the
same.

3164 **it:** TH's emendation *he*, noted in UR BE by KA, is perhaps closer to the Fr. (Lc 2932 "et li vilain crolle la
teste" "and the churl shook his head") and would support Blodgett's argument that TH¹ used the Fr. (1975:139,
210–220; 1984:49–50). However, as RIt points out, "no emendation is needed; it is the head that shakes."

3175 **hayes:** GL's emendation follows the Fr. singular *la haie* (Lc 2943; noted in GL RBt RIt).

3179 **wot:** SK's emendation, anticipated by the preterite form *wist(e* in UR MO, follows the Fr. *conoisse* (Lc
2945 "ne cuidez pas que nus conoisse" "don't believe that anyone could know").

Noon herte may thenke, ne tunge seyne,
A quarter of [my] woo and peyne.
I myght not with the anger laste; 3185
Myn herte in poynt was for to b[ra]ste
Whanne I thought on the rose, that soo 62v
Was thurgh Daunger cast me froo.
    A long while stode I in that state,
Til that me saugh, so madde and mate, 3190
The lady of the high warde,
Which from hir tour lokide thiderward.
Resoun men clepe that lady,
Which from hir tour delyverly
Come doun to me, without more. 3195
But she was neither yong ne hoore,
Ne high ne lowe, ne fat ne lene,
But best as it were in a mene.
Hir eyen twoo were cleer and light

As ony candell that brenneth bright; 3200
And [on] hir heed she hadde a crowne.
Hir semede wel an high persoune,
For rounde enviroun, hir crownet
Was full of riche stonys frett.
Hir goodly semblaunt, by devys, 3205
I trowe were maad in paradys,
For Nature hadde nevere such a grace
To forge a werk of such compace.
For certeyn, but if the letter lye,
God hymsilf, that is so high, 3210
Made hir aftir his ymage, 63r
And yaff hir sith sich avauntage
That she hath myght and seignurie
To kepe men from all folye.
Whoso wole trowe hir lore 3215
Ne may offenden nevermore.

3183   **ne**] no ST SP²-UR SU FI   3184   **my**] *om.* MS (MS₁ *corr.*)   3186   **braste**] barste MS MO KA
3188   **Was**] That w. MS MO KA   3200   **ony**] a UR   3201   **on**] in MS KA GL   3202   **an**] and UR
3204   **frett**] afret UR   3206   **were**] was TH¹-UR FU SU FI   3207   **For**] *om.* SK   **a**] *om.* UR   3209   **if**]
om. SK   3210   **God**] Grete G. UR   3211   **Made**] Formid UR   3215   **trowe**] t. wele UR

3183–85   Lc (2949–51n.) calls the parallel passage in the Fr. a banal hyperbole of classical rhetoric and compares Virgil *Aeneid* 6.625. But he also cites the Biblical parallel of 2 Cor. 2.9 (*sic* in error for 1 Cor. 2.9, noted earlier by Paré 1947:78); the passage in turn echoes Isa. 64.4. Koeppel (1892:262) adduces *RR* (Lc) 20345–46; *MerT* E 1341; *TC* 5.445, 1321. Cf. also *ParsT* I 949.

3183   **ne:** ST's variant shows an adjectival parallelism (no . . . no) rather than the adverbial connective *ne*.

3184   **my:** "written above the line" (KA), probably by MS₁, possibly by a later hand.

3185   **with the anger:** "against the pain" (SK RB). Not in the Fr. (RB RI).

3186   **braste:** TH¹'s emendation, noted by KA. MS *barste* is a var. sp.—see *MED bresten* v.—but the rhyme with *laste* supports the emendation.

3191–216   Jephson (BE) sees in this passage on Reason "an allusion to Prov. viii." On "Reason's divine lineage" and the sources in Prov. 7–8 and Wisdom 6–8, see Fleming (1984:26–38). David (RI 3191n.) writes: "Reason belongs to the class of allegorical mentors who appear to the protagonist in distress as Philosophy does to Boethius, or Holy Church to Will in Piers Plowman."

3198   BE states: "This description of Reason appears to be formed on the ancient philosophical maxim, Ne quid nimis" (nothing to excess). FI glosses *mene* as "the golden mean."

3200   **ony:** See 212n.

3204   **full of . . . frett:** "thickly set with" (RIf; cf. SKg₂'s "adorned"; *MED frēten* v.[2] 1. [b]), rather than URg's suggestion for *afret* "looking like fret-work." See also 4705n., 7257n.

3205–11   RB RI cite Langlois's references (Ln 2985–90n.) to similar passages in Chrétien de Troyes' *Yvain* 1496–1503 (ed. Roques 1965) and in a poem edited by P. Meyer (1874–77:2.372; also ed. Faral 1912a:268–269; cf. Faral 1912b:412). RB adduces the passage on Nature in *PhysT* C 9ff. and note. On Nature as the creator of beauty—"a common topos in descriptive portraits in Latin and Romance literature"—RI cites Curtius (1953:181–82). See Fleming (1984:32–33 and 1986a:208–09), on God as the creator of Reason and on the relevance of Gen. 1.26 to the terms *semblaunt* "likeness" (line 3205) and *ymage* (line 3211).

3207–08   **grace : compace:** RIt notes that RB (alone) has *gras : compas*. Since the OF forms are *grace*, *compas*, either rhyming pair has one abnormal member.

3207   **For . . . a:** According to KA's note—"omit *a* [Sk]"—Skeat had this emendation in mind; but SK retains *a* and omits *For*.

3209   **if:** In omitting this word, SK follows KA's suggestion.

And while I stode thus derk and pale,
Resoun bigan to me hir tale.
She seide, "Al hayle, my swete freende!
Foly and childhoode wole thee sheende, 3220
Which [the] have putt in gret affray.
Thou hast bought deere the tyme of May,
That made thyn herte mery to be.
In yvell tyme thou wentist to see
The gardyne, wherof Ydilnesse 3225
Bare the keye and was maistresse,
Whanne thou [yedest] in the daunce
With hir, and hadde[st] aqueyntaunce.
Hir aqueyntaunce is perilous,
First softe, and aftir noious; 3230
She hath [thee] trasshed, withoute wene.
The God of Love hadde the not sene,
Ne hadde Ydilnesse thee conveyed
In the verger where Myrthe hym pleyed. 3234

If foly have supprised thee, 63v
Do so that it recovered be,
And be wel ware to take no more
Counsel that greveth aftir sore.
He is wise that wole hymsilf chastise.
And though a yong man in ony wise 3240
Trespace amonge, and do foly,
Late hym not tarye, but hastily
Late hym amende what so be mys.
And eke I counseile thee, iwys,
The God of Love hoolly foryete, 3245
That hath thee in sich peyne sette,
And thee in herte tourmented soo.
I can [not] sene how thou maist goo
Other weyes to garisoun;
For Daunger, that is so feloun, 3250
Felly purposith thee to [werreye],
Which is ful cruel, the soth to seye.

3217 **thus]** this TH¹-SP³ FU   3221 **the]** ye MS MO KA   3222 **the]** om. TH³ ST SP²·³   3227 **Whanne]** W. that UR   **yedest]** didest MS KA   3228 **haddest]** hadde MS-KA FU SU FI   3230 **aftir]** a. full UR; aftirward SK   3231 **thee]** om. MS-SP¹ KA FU   3234 **In]** Within UR   **verger]** verge TH³ ST SP²-UR   3240 **And though]** Though UR   3242 **tarye]** dwelle UR   3247 **tourmented]** tormenteth SP²·³   3248 **not]** om. MS KA   **maist]** must TH²   3249 **to]** thee t. SP²-BE   3251 **werreye]** werye MS BE-KA   3252 **the]** om. UR

3219–20 **freende : sheende:** On the basis of Fr. (Lc 2983 "t'ont mis em poine et en esmoi" "have brought you to suffering and dismay"), Brusendorff (1925:417) suggests *have thee shend* for *wole thee shende*, to provide a pa. part. without -e to rhyme with *freend*.
3228 **haddest:** KA's suggested emendation, for agreement with the verb in the previous line.
3231 **trasshed:** "betrayed" (URg TRg SK). SK notes the Fr. *traï* (Lc 2991) and gives the stem as (Fr.) *traiss-*; see *OED Traise, traishe* v.
3232–34 "That is, 'The God of Love would not have seen thee, had not Idleness conveyed thee into the *verger*, or orchard, where Mirth was playing'" (BE).
3233 "If Idleness had not led thee" (RB).
3234 **verger:** "orchard" (SK GLg RBg FI); URg provides this definition for the Fr. word and SK cites Fr. *vergier* (Lc 2994) and Lat. *uiridiarium* [*sic* for *uiridiarium?*] as well as the further occurrences at lines 3618, 3831. Fragment A translates Fr. *vergier* as *garden*, the definition provided by SPg URg TRg MOg; Fragment B as *verger* (lines 3234, 4528) or *gardyne* (line 3225). I report *verge* as a variant ("margin, bound"; *OED verge* sb.¹, senses 10–14) even though SPg records it as meaning "a garden." *OED* shows no spelling of *verger* without -r and no form *verge* as meaning "garden." At line 3851, MS has *verge* for Fr. *porprise* (Lc 3533 "enclosure"), but at line 4094 uses *verger* for the same word. Cf. 481–82n., 1348n., 3851n.
3235 **supprised:** "seized" (RIf). SP1-UR spell *surprised*; See 2067n.
3240 **a . . . in:** KA suggests "omit *a* or *in*," but no ed. so emends.
in ony wise: Liddell (GL) compares his note to line 3096, where, following Kaluza's suggestion, he emends the same phrase to *any weyes*.
ony: See 212n.
3241 **amonge:** "sometimes" (SKg₂), "from time to time" (FI); "therewith" (RIf). Cf. 690n., 2325n., 2842n.
3249 **to garisoun:** "to defend" (SP²·³g URg); "Seems to be used as a *v.* to heal. The Orig. has *Garison*, a *n.* Healing, recovery" (TRg); "to protection" (SK FI), "to safety; here, to your cure" (SK). In support, SK quotes the Fr. (Lc 3006–07 "Je ne voi mie ta santé / ne ta garison autrement" "I cannot otherwise envision your health or your cure").
3251 **werreye:** "destroy" (SPg), "war against" (TRg SK), "make war on" (URg SKg₂ FI). Cf. the Fr. *guerroier* (Lc 3008–09 "car mout te bee durement / Dangier le fel a guerroier" "for cruel Dangier intends to make violent war

"And yitt of Daunger cometh no blame,
In rewarde of my doughter Shame,
Which hath the roses in hir warde,   3255
As she that may be no musarde.
And Wikked-Tunge is with these two,
That suffrith no man thider goo;
For er a thing be do, he shall,   64r
Where that he cometh, overall,   3260
In fourty places, if it be sought,
Seye thyng that nevere was don ne wrought;
So moche tresoun is in his male
Of falsnesse, for to seyne a tale.
Thou delest with angry folk, ywis,   3265
Wherfore to thee bettir is
From these folk awey to fare,
For they wole make thee lyve in care.
This is the yvell that love they calle,
Wherynne ther is but foly alle,   3270

For love is foly everydell.
Who loveth in no wise may do well,
Ne sette his thought on no good werk.
His scole he lesith, if he be a clerk;
Of other craft eke if he be,   3275
He shal not thryve therynne, for he
In love shal have more passioun
Than monke, hermyte, or chanoun.
The peyne is hard, out [of] mesure;
The joye may eke no while endure;   3280
And in the possessioun
Is mych tribulacioun.
The joye it is so short lastyng,   64v
And but in happe is the getyng;
For I see there many in travaill,   3285
That atte laste foule fayle.
I was nothyng thi counseler,
Whanne thou were maad the omager

3264 **seyne]** faine SP²-BE SK   3266 **thee bettir]** The the b. UR; t. b. it MO; t. it b. SK   3267 **these]** thilke MO   3269 **yvell]** ill UR   3273 **sette his thought]** setteth h. though TH²   3274 **a]** *om.* TH² UR SK GL   3275 **Of]** Or TH¹-MO FU SU FI   **eke]** *om.* UR   **if]** i. that TH¹-UR FU SU FI   3279 **The]** This TH¹-BE FU SU FI   **of]** *om.* MS KA   3280 **eke]** *om.* UR   3281 **And]** A. eke UR   3283 **it]** *om.* BE   **short lastyng]** s. and l. SP²˒³   3285 **For]** *om.* UR   3286 **atte laste foule]** at l. f. TH¹-SP³ FU SU FI; at the l. shall fouly UR

---

on you"). MS *werye* may be a var. sp.; see *OED Warray* v. MS has the forms *werreid* (line 2078), *werieth* (line 3699), *werried* (line 3917), *werrey* (line 6926), *werrien* (line 7018); see SKg₂.

3253–54 BE reads the passage literally: "Reason says that of Danger comes no blame in comparison of that which comes of Shame." The translator had difficulty with the Fr., which RB RI quote (Ln 3027–28 [= Lc 3011–12] "E de Dangier neient ne monte / Envers que de ma fille Honte" "And Dangier counts for nothing compared to my daughter Shame").

3254 **In rewarde of:** "in comparison with" (TRg), "compared to" (RIf). UR glosses *rewarde* literally, as "regard," as does FI. BE notes, "*reward* and *regard* were originally the same"; *reward* is the earlier borrowing, from AF, *regard* the later, from CF (*MED*).

3256 "Like one who is no sluggard" (RB). RB quotes the Fr. (Lc 3014 "con cele qui n'est pas musarde") and, for the idiom, compares line 4235 and the note to *MLTB¹* 1090, where RB attributes the ME *As (she, he) that* "as one who" to the parallel Fr. construction, as here; RI also quotes the Fr. and compares line 4235. SK, noting *musarde* at line 4034, refers back to this line.

3263 **moche:** See 1713n.

3264 **seyne:** SP²-UR, perhaps misreading a long *s*-, emend to *faine*, noted in UR BE by KA, and BE SK prefer this reading (in the form *feyne*), "perhaps correctly" (RBt). As SK notes, the line is not in the Fr.

3269–94 "Such references to the folly of love were commonplace in medieval literature," notes Robinson (RB), who cites Theseus's speech in *KnT* A 1785–1814 and his note thereto. There he cites *Rom* 878 ff. and sees the influence of *RR* (Ln) 4229 ff. (*Rom* 4629 ff.) on Theseus's speech.

3274 **a:** KA notes UR's omission of this word. In support of omission, GL RBt cite the Fr. (Lc 3030 "s'il est clers" "if he is clerk").

3277 **passioun:** "suffering, trouble" (BE SK FI). SK notes the Fr. *poine* "pain" (Lc 3033).

3282 **mych:** See 1713n.

3284 **but in happe:** "only in chance, i.e. a matter of chance" (SK); "only by chance" (FI RIf).

3285 **in:** KA suggests omitting *in*, which leaves *travaill* as a verb, as in the Fr. (Lc 3039 "maint s'en travaillent" " many strive for it"); no ed. so emends.

     travaill: MS has *travaill*, where *-ll* may be an abbreviation for *-lle*; see above, "The Manuscript Hands: The Scribe (MS₁)."

Of God of Love to hastily;
Ther was no wisdom, but foly. 3290
Thyne herte was joly but not sage,
Whanne thou were brought in sich [a rage]
To yelde thee so redily,
And to [leve] of [is] gret maistrie.
   "I rede thee Love awey [to] dryve, 3295
That makith thee recche not of thi lyve.
The foly more fro day to day
Shal growe, but thou it putte away.
Take with thy teeth the bridel faste,
To daunte thyne herte; and eke thee caste, 3300
If that thou maist, to gete thee defence
For to redresse thi first offence.
Whoso his herte alwey wole leve,
Shal fynde amonge that shal hym greve."
   Whanne I hir herd thus me chastise, 3305

I answerd in ful angry wise.
I prayed hir ceessen of hir speche, 65r
Outher to chastise me or teche,
To bidde me my thought refreyne,
Which Love hath caught in his demeyne: 3310
"What? Wene ye Love wole consente,
That me assailith with bowe bente,
To drawe myne herte out of his honde,
Which is so qwikly in his bonde?
That ye counseyle may nevere be; 3315
For whanne he firste arestide me,
He took myne herte so hoole hym tille
That it is nothyng at my wille.
He [taught] it so hym for to obey
That he it sparrede with a key. 3320
I pray yow late me be all stille,
For ye may well, if that ye wille,

3289 **to]** so SP²·³ 3290 **Ther]** Where ST-UR 3292 **a rage]** arrage MS MO KA 3293 **thee]** t. up UR 3294 **And to]** To UR **leve of is]** loue of his MS-SK FU SU FI; l. o. his GL 3295 **to]** do MS (MS₁ *corr.*) 3296 **thee]** that ST 3297 **The]** Thy SP¹ 3301 **to]** *om.* GL **thee]** *om.* UR SK 3308 **Outher]** Eyther TH¹-UR FU SU FI 3312 **assailith]** assaieth ST-UR 3317 **hoole]** sore TH¹-UR FU SU FI 3319 **taught]** thought MS-SP¹ MO KA FU 3320 **he]** *om.* TH²

3292 **a rage:** The MS form *arrage* is undoubtedly an error for *arage* or *a rage*. The Fr. (Lc 3044 "te fist entrer en tel folage" "made you enter into such folly") supports this reading in the variant *en ceste rage*, which Langlois (3060t) cites from the L family, SU (Fr. 3060n.) from Lb. SK compares line 3400 "in his rage."

3294 "And to leave off is a masterly course" (RB). See below.

   leve of is: KA suggests this emendation; RB RI adopt it fully, GL partially (see below). RB SU RI cite the Fr., particularly the var. *au laissier* (Lc 3045–46 "La folie fu tost emprise, / mes a l'issir [*var.* au laissier] a grant mestrise" "Folly was undertaken quickly, but to get out of it [*var.* to leave off] requires great skill"). Langlois (Ln 3062n.) locates the var. in many MSS: Be C He Ri Ra Tou; of these, Ri Ra have "au laissier (est, ert) la mestrise." RB reads the emended line as "And to leave off is a masterly course." SU errs in quoting RB's *leve* as *love*; he thinks that "none of these emendations is satisfactory" and that "the line is best left alone." But he reads the Fr. (SU Fr. 3062 "Mès a lessier [a grant] mestrise") as follows: "But to leave yourself to great domination (by Love)." David's translation (RI) is closer (Lc 3045–46 "although it is easy to fall in love, it requires great mastery to extricate oneself again"); and he notes (RIt) that KA's emendation "is closest to the French; *leue* is easily misread as *loue*, especially with the anticipation of *loue* in the next line."

   On Liddell's variant and punctuation, RI quotes GL lines 3294–95 ("And to leve of his gret maistrie, / I rede thee Love awey to dryve") and notes that "in the MS *I* (3295) is a large initial beginning a new paragraph."

   leve of: "leave off" (RB RIf).

3295 **to:** "*do* altered to *to*" (KA) by MS₁.

3299 BE notes the origin of the metaphor in "the habit which runaway horses have, of taking the bit in their teeth."

3303 **leve:** "believe" (SK RB RIf), on the basis of Fr. *croit* (Lc 3055 "believe"; noted by SK RB), rather than "allow to leave" (FI).

3304 **amonge:** "sometimes" (SKg₂), "from time to time" (FI). See 690n.

3308 **Outher:** See 250n., 5168n.

3315 **counseyle:** SKt errs in reporting MS reading as *counsele*.

3319 **taught:** SP²·³ BE spell *tought*, which Jephson (BE) identifies as the pa. t. of *teche*; Skeat (1878c:4.115) corrects it to *taughte*, and KA recommends the emendation. The Fr. (Lc 3069 "il le *justice* si forment" "he rules it so firmly") has a structural but not a verbal parallel.

177

Youre wordis waste in idilnesse;
For utterly, withouten gesse,
All that ye seyn is but in veyne.　　3325
Me were lever dye in the peyne,
Than Love to me-ward shulde arette
Falsheed, or tresoun on me sette.
I wole me gete prys or blame,
And love trewe, to save my name;　　3330
Who that me chastisith, I hym hate."　　65v
　　With that word Resoun wente hir gate,
Whanne she saugh for no sermonynge
She myght me fro my foly brynge.
Thanne dismaied, I lefte all sool,　　3335
Forwery, forwandred as a fool,
For I ne knewe no che[v]isaunce.
Thanne fell into my remembraunce
How Love bade me to purveye

A felowe to whom I myght seye　　3340
My counsell and my pryvete,
For that shulde moche availe me.
With that bithought I me that I
Hadde a felowe fast by,
Trewe and siker, curteys and hende,　　3345
And he was called by name a Freende;
A trewer felowe was nowher noon.
In haste to hym I wente anoon,
And to hym all my woo I tolde;
Fro hym right nought I wold witholde.　　3350
I tolde hym all, withoute were,
And made my compleynt on Daungere,
How for to see he was hidous,
And to me-ward contrarious,　　3354
The which thurgh his cruelte　　66r
Was in poynt to [have] meygned me.

3327 **Than]** That SP^{2,3}　　3330 **to]** for to UR　　3331 **that]** *om.* UR SK　　**chastisith]** chastith GL
3337 **chevisaunce]** cherisaunce MS-KA FU SU　　3338 **Thanne]** Than I FI　　3346 **was called]** c. w. TH^3-UR
3347 **trewer]** true SP^3　　3353 **How]** Nowe TH^2　　**see]** say SP^1　　3356 **have]** *om.* MS KA

　　3326 **dye in the peyne:** "to die under (by) torture" (SK RB RIf). BE adduces *TC* 1.674 and, in the note to that passage, *KnT* A 1133, noted also by SK RB RI. As RI observes, the phrase *in the peyne* is not in the Fr.
　　3329 **prys:** Perhaps "esteem," "praise," "value" (URg TRg SKg$_2$), rather than "reward (prize)" (FI). See 446n.
　　3331 **chastisith:** GL's emendation represents a variant form of the same root. See *MED chāsten* v., *chastien* v., *chastisen* v.
　　3332 **gate:** "way" (URg TRg SKg$_2$ FI); SKg$_2$ FI identify the word as Northern; see 5167n.
　　3336 **Forwery, forwandred:** URg suggests that the phrase "should be read, *Forwerie for wandred*, i.e. Very weary with wandring"; but the pa. part. *wandred* can hardly be so construed. See below.
　　Forwery: "very weary" (TRg RB), "tired out" (SKg$_2$), "exhausted" (RIf). RB compares *KnT* A 2142. In the note to that line RB discusses constructions with *for* as prep. before substantival adjective (cf. 276n., 356n.) and also instances where, as FI notes here, "*for* is an intensifier."
　　forwandred: "exhausted from wandering" (GL RIf; cf. SKg$_2$). See above.
　　3337 **chevisaunce:** KA's suggested emendation follows the Fr. *chevisance* (Lc 3085; noted by SKt FI RIt). SU retains *cherysaunce* but grants that the emendation is perhaps right. The sense is "resource" (SK) or "remedy" (SK RIf; cf. *MED chevisaunce* n., sense 2), rather than "trading for profit" (FI; cf. URg and *MED*, sense 3). As SK notes, the early editors understood MS *cherisaunce*, otherwise unrecorded, to mean "comfort" (SPg TRg), presumably as a nominal derivative of *cherishen*; SK remarks that *cherisaunce* "is fictitious" and that, as a result, "Kersey, by a misprint, gives '*cherisaunei*, comfort'; which Chatterton adopted" (on Kersey and Chatterton, see Starnes and Noyes 1946:255–56).
　　3342 **moche:** See 1713n.
　　3346 **a Freende:** SK cites the Fr. (Lc 3093 "Amis a non" "has the name Friend") in support of the proper name. RB notes that, although it is a proper name in the Fr., "it is apparently not to be so taken in the English," presumably because of the indefinite article; RI notes that "it is unclear whether the translator intended a proper name."
　　3356 **meygned:** "maimed" (BE SK GL RIf), "wounded" (BE), "injured" (RIf). BE notes the form *meimed* in "Speght"; KA notes *meymed* in TH^1; it appears in all eds. except BE-GL RI. As SK observes, "this word takes numerous forms both in M. E. and in Anglo-French." *MED maimen* v. lists *meygned* as a past participial form but, as RIt notes, "cites *meygned* in this line without *have*, taking it as a form of the infin. (from OF *mahaigner*). Perhaps read *meygne*," an inf. parallel in structure, but not sense, to the Fr. *mengier* (Lc 3100 "qui par pou ne me vout mengier" "who was about to eat me"; noted in RI).

With Bialacoil whanne he me sey
Withynne the gardeyn walke and pley,
Fro me he made hym for to go;
And I, bilefte aloone in woo,　　　　　　3360
I durst no lenger with hym speke,
For Daunger seide he wolde be wreke,
Whanne that he sawe how I wente
The fresh bot[oun] for to hente,
If I were hardy to come neer　　　　　　3365
Bitwene the hay and the roser.
　　This freend, whanne he wiste of my thought,
He discomforted me right nought,
But seide, "Felowe, be not so madde,
Ne so abaysshed nor bystadde.　　　　　3370
Mysilf I knowe full well Daungere,
And how he is feers of his cheere
At prime temps, love to manace;
Ful ofte I have ben in his caas.
A feloun firste though that he be,　　　3375
Aftir thou shalt hym souple se.
Of longe passed I knewe hym well;
Ungoodly first though men hym feele,
He wole m[e]ke aftir in his beryng　　　66v

Been, for service and obeysshyng.　　　3380
I shal thee telle what thou shalt doo.
Mekely I rede thou go hym to;
Of herte pray hym specialy
Of thy trespace to have mercy,
And hote hym well, here to plese,　　　3385
That thou shalt nevermore hym displese.
Who can best serve of flaterie,
Shall please Daunger most uttirly."
　　Mi freend hath seid to me so wel
That he me esid hath somdell,　　　　　3390
And eke allegged of my torment;
For thurgh hym had I hardement
Agayn to Daunger for to go,
To preve if I myght meke hym soo.
　　To Daunger came I all ashamed,　　　3395
The which aforn me hadde blamed,
Desiryng for to pese my woo;
But over hegge durst I not goo,
For he forbede me the passage.
I fonde hym cruel in his rage,　　　　　3400
And in his honde a gret burdoun.
To hym I knelide lowe adoun,

3359 **made**] had BE　　3362 **seide**] says SU FI　　3363 **that**] than MO　　**how**] h. that UR　　3367 **my**] *om.* SP[3]　　3372 **how**] h. that UR　　**his**] *om.* TH[1]-UR FU　　3379 **meke**] make MS BE KA　　3385 **hym well**] him w., him SK; well, hym GL RB[1,2]　　3394 **meke**] make UR　　3397 **pese**] please SP[1]; apese UR 3399 **he**] h. for SP[2]

3364 **botoun:** See 1721n.
3373–74 **manace : caas:** RB notes that "the rime *manace* (with silent -e): *caas* is un-Chaucerian." TH[1]-UR FU SU FI have *case*, for eye-rhyme.
3373 **At prime temps:** "the first time, at first" (URg), "at the first time" (TRg SKg[2]; cf. RIf), "first off" (FI).
3377–78 **well : feele:** RB RI adjust rhyme by dropping *-e* from *feele*, but *feel* is an unusual form for the pres. pl. (or sing., if *men* be so construed).
3377 As RB notes, the line "departs from the French, which has the comparison (still proverbial): 'Je le conois come un denier'" (Lc 3118 "I know him like a penny").
Of longe passed: "of old" (SKg[2]), "since long ago" (RIf), rather than "a long time ago" (URg).
3379 **meke:** TH[1]'s emendation follows the Fr. *amoloier* (Lc 3119 "become mild"; noted by GL). Jephson (BE) keeps MS *make* but understands it as "be meek"; Skeat (1878c:4.117) notes the incorrect spelling. KA notes the form in TH[1] UR MO, and compares the form *meke* at line 3403, where, however, it is an adj.; for the verb, see lines 2244, 3394, 3541.
3383 **Of herte:** GL compares line 3902.
3385 **hym well:** Liddell (GL) reports SK's emendation as "*well hym* . . . for *hym well* of MSS." It is *him well*, *him*; see collation.
here to plese: GL suggests: "(?) *his ire to pese* (*pese* aphetic form of *appese*); cp. v. 3397."
3394 **meke:** FI notes the Fr. *soploier* (SU Fr. 3150 "entreat, supplicate"); Ln Lc have *apaier* (Lc 3134 "se Dangier porroie apaier" "if I might placate Dangier").
3398 **hegge:** GL comments that this form is probably a mistake for *haye*, but does not emend. See 2968n., 2971n.
3401 **burdoun:** "staff" (SPg URg TRg SKg[2]), "cudgel" (GL SKg[2] FI), "stick, club" (RIf); RB cites the Fr. *baston d'espine* (Lc 3141 "club of thorn"). On the iconography of the club, see Dahlberg (1977:46–47). Cf. 4092n., 7401n.

179

Ful meke of port and symple of chere,   67r
And seide, "Sir, I am comen heere
Oonly to aske of you mercy.   3405
That greveth me full gretly
That evere my lyf I wratthed you.
But for to amenden I am come now,
With all my myght, bothe loude and stille,
To doon right at youre owne wille.   3410
For Love made me for to doo
That I have trespassed hidirto,
Fro whom I ne may withdrawe myne herte.
Yit shall [I] never, for joy ne smerte,
What so bifall, good or ille,   3415
Offende more ageyn youre wille;
Lever I have endure disese
Than do that you shulde displese.
   "I you require and pray that ye
Of me have mercy and pitee,   3420

To stynte your ire that greveth soo,
That I wole swere for ever mo
To be redressid at youre likyng,
If I trespasse in ony thyng.
Save that I pray thee graunte me   3425
A thyng that may not warned be,
That I may love, all oonly;   67v
Noon other thyng of you aske I.
I shall doon elles well, iwys,
If of youre grace ye graunte me this.   3430
And ye may not letten me,
For wel wot ye that love is free,
And I shall loven, [sithen] that I wille,
Who evere like it well or ille;
And yit ne wold I, for all Fraunce,   3435
Do thyng to do you displesaunce."
   Thanne Daunger fille in his entent
For to foryeve his male talent;

3406 **That]** It SP²-BE GL   **me]** me, sir SK   3407 **my lyf I]** I have UR   3413 **withdrawe]** drawe UR
3414 **I]** om. MS KA GL   3415 **bifall]** b. me UR   3418 **that]** t. whiche UR   **you shulde]** s. y. TH¹-UR SK
FU-FI   3429 **elles well]** al wel TH¹⁻³ UR FU SU FI; all ST-SP³; al your wyl RB¹·²; om. BE   3431 **And ye may]**
A. that y. m. UR; A. y. ne m. MO SK   3433 **sithen]** sichen MS BE-KA; suche TH¹-UR FU   3435 **I]** I not SP²·³

3407 **evere my lyf:** GL suggests "(?) *ever in my lyf.*"
3418 **do that:** KA suggests *do thing that*, and compares line 3436 "do thing to do"; no ed. so emends.
3422 **That:** Lounsbury (1895:22) GL RB RI suggest *And*, on the basis of Fr. *et* (Lc 3158).
3424 **ony:** See 212n.
3427 **all oonly:** KA attributes to SK the suggestion "Read *al anerly*," but SK has *al only*, with no annotation.
3429 **elles well:** In a note, BE suggests the reading *al your wil* and adduces the Fr. (Lc 3165 "Totes vos autres volentez" "all your other wishes"); KA GL RBt SU RIt note Bell's reading, while SKt GL RBt SU RIt adduce or quote the Fr. Only RB actually incorporates the emendation in the text. TH¹ (*al wel*) appears to have made a partial emendation of the MS (*elles well*) by consulting the Fr. (*Totes*). See also above, "The Manuscript Hands: The Scribe (MS₁)" and 300n.
3432 RB calls the idea that love is free "a commonplace sentiment," and David (RI) calls it "proverbial." Both compare *KnT* A 1606, where RB's note calls the idea proverbial, cites Haeckel (1890: nos. 3–5), and compares *TC* 4.618; but DiMarco (RI *KnT* A 1606n.) notes that the idea is "proverbial after Chaucer"; he refers to Whiting (1968: L516) and *FranT* F 767.
3433 **sithen:** SK RB¹-FI emend MS *sichen* to *sith* on the basis of the Fr. (Lc 3169 "puisqu'il me siet" "since it suits me"; noted by SKt RBt) as well as on paleographical and metrical grounds. KA endorses the form in SK. RIt states: "The scribe confused *t* and *c* and may actually have intended to write *t*; Thynne or his printer, however, interpreted the word as a form of *such*."
3435–36 KA Fr. (3167–68) and SU Fr. (3187–88) have "por finance / Qu'il fust a vostre desplaisance" ("for money That it should be displeasing to you"), a reading that accounts roughly for the ME; but they take this variant from printed eds., KA from the Jean Du Pré facsimile ed. (1493;1878), SU from the Marteau ed. (1878–79). As SU notes, Ln "records no similar reading. Source MS is not indicated." The standard text differs (Ln 3187–88 [= Lc 3171–72] "por mon pois / D'argent, qu'il fust sor vostre pois" "for my weight in silver, that it should be a burden to you"); RI (3435n.) quotes the first phrase, "por mon pois D'argent."
3437–38 GL RB RI quote the Fr. (Lc 3173–74 "Mout trovai Dangier dur e lent / de pardoner son mautalant" "I found Dangier very difficult and slow to give over his ill humor"). The ME translation departs from the Fr.; see 3437n.
3437 **fille in his entent:** GL RB RI (3437–38n.) find the meaning of *fille* obscure. SKg₂ has "condescended"; but GL queries "has *fall* such a meaning?" and *MED fallen* v. does not include this among its many senses. GL suggests "(?) failed." RIf glosses the phrase as "decided," presumably from the literal sense "fell into his intention," i.e. "made up his mind."

But all his wratthe yit at laste
He hath relesed, I preyde so faste.   3440
Shortly he seide, "Thy request
Is not to mochel dishonest,
Ne I wole not werne it thee,
For yit nothyng engreveth me.
For though thou love thus evermore,   3445
To me is neither softe ne soore.
Love where that the list; what recchith me,
So [thou] fer fro my roses be?
Trust not on me, for noon assay,
[If] ony tyme [thou] passe the hay."   3450
    Thus hath he graunted my praiere.   68r
Thanne wente I forth, withouten were,
Unto my freend, and tolde hym all,
Which was right joyfull of my tall.
He seide, "Now goth wel thyn affere.   3455
He shall to thee be debonaire.
Though he aforn was dispitous,

He shall heere aftir be gracious.
If he were touchid on somme good veyne,
He shuld yit rewen on thi peyne.   3460
Suffre, I rede, and no boost make,
Till thou at good mes maist hym take.
By suffraunce and wordis softe
A man may overcome ofte
Hym that aforn he hadde in drede,   3465
In bookis sothly as I rede."
    Thus hath my freend with gret comfort
Avaunced [me] with high disport,
Which wolde me good as mych as I.
And thanne anoon full sodeynly   3470
I toke my leve, and streight I wente
Unto the hay, for gret talent
I hadde to sene the fresh bot[oun]
Wherynne lay my salvacioun.   3474
And Daunger toke kepe if that I   68v
Kepe hym covenaunt trewly.

3439 **at**] at the UR MO GL   3447 **that**] *om.* UR SK GL   3448 **So thou fer**] S. f. MS-SP³ KA FU; S. f. t. UR   3450 **If ony tyme thou**] I o. t. to MS KA; In o. t. to TH¹-MO SK FU   3462 **good mes**] goodnes BE MO   3463 **and**] a. by SP²-BE SK   3468 **me**] *om.* MS KA   3475 **toke**] to TH²

3448 **thou:** BE's emendation, noted in BE MO by KA, is an adaptation of UR's *So ferre thou*, and follows the Fr. *tu* (Lc 3183–84 "mes que tu soies / loing de mes roses totes voies" "as long as you always stay far from my roses"; noted in BE SKt).

3450 **If ony tyme thou:** GL's emendation follows the Fr. (Lc 3186 "*se tu ja mes* passes la haie" "if you ever pass through the hedge"; noted in GL RBt SU RIt).

    ony: See 212n.

3454 **tall:** MS has *tall*, rhyming with *all* line 3453; TH¹-UR SK-FU SU FI respell as *tale*. BE MO take -*ll* as an abbreviation and have *talle*, and SKt notes MS reading as "talle." RB RI (as here) do not assume the abbreviation and thus have *tall*; they note that it is an unusual spelling, "with final -*e* apocopated for rhyme" (RBt RIt). See also above, "The Manuscript Hands: The Scribe (MS₁)."

3455–56 **affere : debonaire:** TH¹-UR SK-RI respell *affa(y,i)re*, for eye-rhyme; KA so recommends.

3459 BE notes that the line translates the Fr. literally (Lc 3195 "S'il iere pris en bone vaine" "if he were caught in good vein [humor]") and suggests that "it appears to be a metaphor taken from surgery."

3462 **at good mes:** "at a favourable time (opportunity)" (SK RB FI); "from a favorable vantage point" (RIf); lit., at a good (position for a) shot. See 1453n. T. Thomas (URg) misreads as "in good humour," and Kaluza (1889:529) suggests a similar sense, "in a good state, in a good mood," but he notes that *mes* translates Fr. *en bon point*. Tyrwhitt (TRg, s.v. *Mes*) thought that the phrase should be "at godeness," although (s.v. *Godeness*) he understands the correct sense as "at advantage"; and Lounsbury (1892:2.14) also regards *at good mes* as "a blunder for *at goodnes*, that is, 'at advantage.'" Jephson (BE) again, as in line 1453, emends to *at goodnes* and calls the MS reading "a mere clerical error"; he regards his emendation as supported by the Fr. *en bon point* (Lc 3198 "in a favorable situation"), which SKt RB RI cite as support for their readings, all of which recognize MS *mes* (shot) as correct and a better parallel to the Fr.; SK RB RI refer to line 1453.

3463 RB RI compare Prov. 15.1; RB cites Ln's note to Ln 2627 (= *Rom* 2775).

3468 **me:** TH¹'s emendation, noted in TH¹ UR BE by KA, is based perhaps on the Fr. (Lc 3202–3 "Amis, qui *mon avancement* / vousist" "Friend, who wanted my advancement").

3473 **botoun:** MS *bothom* gives an imperfect rhyme with *saluacioun*; cf. lines 4011, 4308. This situation gives warrant, here and elsewhere, to the respelling of the various MS forms to *botoun*, as in SK RB RI and, at times, GL. KA recommends it here. Cf. 1721n.

So sore I dradde his manasyng,
I durst not breke his biddyng;
For, lest that I were of hym shent,
I brake not his comaundement, 3480
For to purchase his good wille.
It was [hard] for to come ther-tille;
His mercy was to ferre bihynde.
I wepte, for I ne myght it fynde.
I compleyned and sighed sore, 3485
And langwisshed evermore,
For I durst not over goo
Unto the rose I loved soo.

Thurgh my [demenyng] outerly
[Tha(n) he had knowlege certanly] 3490
[That] Love me ladde in sich a wise
That in me ther was no feyntise,
Falsheed, ne no trecherie.
And yit he, full of vylanye,
Of disdeyne, and cruelte, 3495
On me ne wolde have pite,
His cruel will for to refreyne,
[Though] I wepe alwey, and me compleyne.
     And while I was in this torment, 69r
Were come of grace, by God sent, 3500

3482 **hard]** nat GL RB[1,2] RI; *om.* MS-BE KA FU   3484 **I wepte]** I kepte TH[1]-SP[3] FU; Ykept UR 3486 **evermore]** evir the more UR   3487 **durst]** ne d. UR   3489 **Thurgh my demenyng]** Thurgh out m. demyng MS-SK FU-FI   3490 **Than he had knowlege certanly]** That h. h. k. c. MS[2]-KA FU; T. had he k. c. SK; Tyl h. h. k. c. SU FI   *Out:* MS   3491 **That]** Thanne MS-KA FU SU   **a]** *om.* TH[3]-UR   3493 **Falsheed]** Ne f. UR   **no]** mo SU FI   3495 **Of]** And o. UR   **and]** a. of MO   3496 **have]** h. no UR   3498 **Though]** Thou MS KA; Tho TH[1]-BE FU SU FI (*var. sp.*)   **wepe]** wepte TH[1]-UR FU SU FI   **me]** *om.* SK

3479–83   See 3482n.

3481 **good:** KA suggests the normalization *goode*, but later eds. do not adopt it; earlier, UR had *gode*, presumably with silent *-e*, since *purchase* appears as the trisyllabic *purchasin*.

3482 **hard:** MO's emendation, noted by KA, is followed by SK SU FI. BE notes that "this passage appears to be corrupt," that "the true reading is probably 'It was *fer* to come thertille,'" and that "*o* and *e* are scarcely distinguishable in MSS." The passage is a loose translation in more than this line. With lines 3479–83 cf. the Fr. (Lc 3213–17): "ainz me sui penez longuement / de fere son comandement / por lui acointier et atraire. / Mes ce me torne a grant contraire / que sa merci trop m'i demeure" ("To get acquainted with him and win him over, I took pains for a long time to perform his command, but it hindered me greatly that he withheld his grace for so long"). SU thinks that MO's *hard* "seems closer to the Fr." than is GL's *nat*. RBt queries "something omitted?" and supplies *nat*. RIt quotes the Fr. (Lc 3216) in support of *nat*.

3484 **wepte:** SU FI cite the Fr. *pleure* (Lc 3218 "weep") in support of MS *wepte* over TH[1]'s *kepte*.

3489–91   For the various emendations, see notes to the separate lines. BE GL RBt RIt quote the Fr. (Lc 3223–25 "et tant qu'il a certainement / veü en mon contenement / qu'Amors malement me jostice" "and he certainly saw, by my behavior, that Love ruled me harshly").

3489 **Thurgh my demenyng:** GL's emendation follows the Fr. (Lc 3224 "en mon contenement" "by my behavior"); see 3489–91n. RBt states that the emendation is "perhaps" correct. RI adopts it because it "makes sense of the passage: Daunger perceives the Lover's plight through his comportment." All other eds. retain the MS reading, *Thurghout my demyng* "to my judgment" (FI). RIf has the same gloss, "judgment," for *demenyng*, but the note (RIt) implies "comportment, behavior."

3490   KA notes that the reading in MS is "written by a later hand on a line originally left blank"; the hand is the one that has supplied lines 1892, 1984, and 2036; see above, "The Manuscript Hands: The Corrections" and 1892n. KA suggests "*Thanne* for *that*," and SK GL RB RI adopt the emendation. SU FI emend to *Tyl* on the basis of the Fr. *tant qu'*; see 3489–91n. RIt notes that "the emendation *tyl* (from Sutherland), though closer to the French, does not fit the syntax"; that "the first words of 3490–91 have been reversed"; and that "the entire line . . . may be spurious."

3491 **That:** BE's suggested emendation, noted by KA, follows the Fr. *qu'* (Lc 3225; see 3489–91n.). SU notes that it completes the sense, but does not emend the text.

3498 **Though:** MS *Thou* could be an obsolete form of *though* (see *OED Though*, adv. and conj., γ-forms); but, as RIt states, "the normal form in both G. [MS] and Th. [TH[1]] is *though*. Th's exceptional *tho* indicates that it is a correction of the scribal error in G."

    wepe: str. pa. t. TH[1] and its followers have the wk. *wepte*.

    me: SK's omission follows KA's suggestion.

Fraunchise, and with hir Pite,
Fulfild the [bothen] of bounte.
They go to Daunger anoon-right
To forther me with all her myght,
And helpe in worde and in dede, 3505
For well they saugh that it was nede.
First, of hir grace, dame Fraunchise
Hath taken [word] of this emprise.
She seide, "Daunger, gret wrong ye do
To worche this man so mych woo, 3510
Or pynen hym so angerly;
It is to you gret villanye.
I can not see why ne how
That he hath trespassed ageyn you,
Save that he loveth, wherfore ye shulde 3515

The more in cherete of hym holde.
The force of love makith hym do this;
Who wolde hym blame he dide amys?
He [leseth] more than ye may do;
His peyne is harde, ye may see, lo! 3520
And Love in no wise wolde consente
That [he] have power to repente;
For though that quyk ye wolde hym sloo, 69v
Fro love his herte may not goo.
Now, swete sir, [is it] youre ese 3525
Hym for to angre or disese?
Allas, what may it you avaunce
To done to hym so gret grevaunce?
What worship is it agayn hym take,
Or on youre man a werre make, 3530

3501 **Fraunchise**] Dame F. UR 3502 **bothen**] bothom MS-KA FU SU; botoun SK 3505 **helpe**] h. me UR **and in**] a. ek i. MO 3508 **Hath taken word**] H. t. MS-SP³ BE-KA FU; Ytakin hath UR 3513 **why**] ne w. UR GL 3519 **leseth**] lefeth MS-BE FU **ye**] he TH³-UR 3522 **he**] ye MS-SP³ KA FU 3524 **may**] ne m. UR 3525 **is it**] it is MS-ST SP²-UR KA FU

3501–02 SK, taking *botoun* as "rosebud" and *of* as "with," reads: "And Pity, (coming) with her, filled the Rosebud with gracious favour." Jephson (BE), noting the obscurity of line 3502, thinks it corrupt, and states that "the original throws no light upon it"; however, the line BE quotes as the original (Lc 3234 "N'i ot onques plus respitié" "without any further delay") does not appear in the ME, except perhaps in line 3503 (*anoon right*). The difficulty lies in the fact that MS *bothom* (SK *botoun* "rosebud") does not appear in the Fr. (RBt). GL therefore emends to *bothen* and, on the basis of the Fr. "l'une et l'autre," paraphrases "both, full of kindness, visit Daunger immediately." RB RIt also quote the Fr. and adopt the emendation, "perhaps rightly," grants SU. Cf. Lc 3233–37: "Franchise, et avec li Pitié. / N'i ot onques plus respitié, / a Dangier vont endeus tot droit, / car l'une et l'autre me voudroit / aidier, s'eus peueent, volontiers" ("with no further delay, Franchise, and Pity with her, go straight to Dangier, for the one and the other wanted to help me if they could").

3502 **bothen:** "both" (GL). For the phrase *the bothen*, *MED bōthe* num., 1a. (b), gives only one quotation, from Mannyng's *Chronicle.*

3505 **in dede:** GL suggests "(?) omit *in*" but no ed. so emends.

3508 **word:** KA's suggested emendation. SK SU FI RIt call attention to the basis in the Fr. *parole* (Ln 3255–56 (= Lc 3239–40) "La parole a premiere prise [Lc a. p. mise], / Seue merci, dame Franchise" "Lady Franchise—thanks be—spoke first").

3510 **mych:** See 1713n.

3516 **cherete of hym holde:** The sense of *cherete* is not strictly "charity," as in FI's paraphrase, "be charitable to him," but rather "affection" (URg), "fondness" (URg SKg₂ RIf; cf. *MED charitē* n. 3. [a]), "kindness" (SKg₂), "dearness" (GLg).

3519 **leseth:** While *f* and long *s* have very similar forms, here MS clearly has *lefeth*, a reading that persists in early eds. UR glosses *leveth* as "loves." TRg, however, notes the misprint in the eds. and adduces the evidence of the Fr. *pert* (Lc 3249 "Plus i piart il que vos ne fetes" "He loses more thereby than you do") for the correct reading. Eds. that read *leseth* do not indicate any correction of MS.

3522 **he:** UR's emendation, noted in UR BE MO by KA. BE SKt RBt-FI adduce the Fr. *il* (Lc 3252 "que il s'en puise repentir" "that he might repent of it"). GL calls *ye* for *he* "a common scribal error."

3525 **is it:** BE (following SP¹?) so emends, but says that "there is nothing in the original answering to this couplet." There is, however, a parallel question (Lc 3255–56 "Mes, biau sire, que vos avance / de li fere anui ne grevance?" "But, fair sir, how does inflicting pain and torment on him help you?") that the ME translates in lines 3527–28. KA notes the change in BE MO.

3526 **angre:** KA suggests *angren*, but no ed. so emends.

3529–30 "That is, 'What honour is it to you to take part against him, or to make war on your own vassal?'" (BE).

Sith he so lowly, every wise,
Is redy, as ye lust devise?
If Love hath caught hym in his lace,
You for t'obeye in every caas,
And ben youre suget at youre will,   3535
Shuld ye therfore willen hym ill?
Ye shulde hym spare more, all oute,
Than hym that is bothe proude and stoute.
Curtesie wole that ye socour
Hem that ben meke undir youre cure.   3540
His herte is hard that wole not meke,
Whanne men of mekenesse hym biseke."
    "That is certeyn," seide Pite.
"We se ofte that humilite
Bothe ire and also felonye   3545
Venquyssheth, and also malencolye.
To stonde forth in such duresse,   70r
This cruelte and wikkidnesse.
Wherfore I pray you, Sir Daungere,
For to mayntene no lenger heere   3550
Such cruel werre agayn youre man,
As hoolly youres as ever [he] can;
Nor that ye worchen no more woo
Upon this caytif, that langwisshith soo,
Which wole no more to you trespasse,   3555
But putte hym hoolly in youre grace.

His offense ne was but lite;
The God of Love it was to wite
That he youre thrall so gretly is,
And if ye harme hym, ye done amys.   3560
For he hath hadde full hard penaunce,
Sith that ye refte hym th'aqueyntaunce
Of Bialacoil, his most joye,
Which alle hise peynes myght acoye.
He was biforn anoyed sore,   3565
But thanne ye doubled hym well more;
For he of blis hath ben full bare
Sith Bialacoil was fro hym fare.
Love hath to hym do gret distresse;
He hath no nede of more duresse.   3570
Voideth from hym youre ire, I rede;   70v
Ye may not wynnen in this dede.
Makith Bialacoil repeire ageyn,
And haveth pite upon his peyne;
For Fraunchise wole, and I, Pite,   3575
That mercyful to hym ye be.
And sith that she and I accorde,
Have upon hym misericorde.
For I you pray and eke moneste
Nought to refusen oure requeste,   3580
For he is hard and fell of thought
That for us twoo wole do right nought."

3533 **hath]** have TH¹-UR FU   3539 **wole]** wolde TH³-UR   3543 **That]** This TH¹-UR FU SU FI 3548 **This]** Is BE MO   3552 **he]** ye MS KA   3554 **Upon]** On UR SK GL   **that langwisshith]** languishing UR   3555 **you]** your FI   3557 **His]** And his UR   3560 **And if ye harme hym]** If y. him harme UR   3566 **hym]** hem GL   3569 **do]** *om.* TH¹-SP³ BE FU   3571 **Voideth]** Voided ST-SP³ 3574 **upon]** on UR   3579 **eke]** *om.* SP¹

3534   **t'obeye:** As SKt SU RIt note, MS has *to beye*, TH¹ *to bey*.

3539–40   SK RB Ln (3281–82n.) cite Ovid, *Ex ponto* 2.9.11.

3546   **Venquyssheth:** "two syllables; cp. 3554" (GL).

3548   **This:** KA SKt GL RB RIf note that *This* is a contraction for "This is"; SK compares *PF* 411 "This is oure usage alwey, fro yer to yeere," where meter requires monosyllabic pronunciation of *This is*. SU FI punctuate *Th'is*. BE, however, calls MS *This* "nonsense," and notes that the context requires the verb *is* and that the Fr. has the parallel verb *est* (Lc 3272). Cf. lines 6057, 6452.

3558–59   BE paraphrases: "It was proper to blame the God of Love for it"; literally, "It was the God of Love to blame that he . . ."

3560   **amys:** KA SKt both recommend the noun form *m(y,i)s*, but SK does not emend. Cf. *MED amis* adv., *mis* n.

3566   **hym:** GL emends to *hem* on the basis of the Fr. *ses anuis*, which, however, is singular (Lc 3284 "mes or est ses anuis doublez" "but now his grief is doubled"); in the subject case, *ses* is the 3d sing. possessive form (Raynaud de Lage 1962:58). The translation, which does not parallel the Fr. in this phrase, takes "this caytif" (line 3554) as antecedent of *hym*.

3579   **moneste:** "admonish" (SPg URg TRg GLg); "advise" (URg). SK calls this form "short for *amoneste*, i.e. admonish"; but *monesten* and *amonesten* existed side by side in ME as well as in OF., with related ranges of meaning. Here, the sense is "urge" (*MED monesten* v. [d]).

Daunger ne myght no more endure;
He mekede hym unto mesure.
　"I wole in no wise," seith Daungere,　3585
"Denye that ye have asked heere;
It were to gret uncurtesie.
I wole [he] have the companye
Of Bialacoil, as ye devise;
I wole hym lette in no wise."　3590
　To Bialacoil thanne wente in high
Fraunchise, and seide full curteislye,
"Ye have to longe be deignous
Unto this lover, and daungerous,　3594
[Fro him to withdrawe your presence,　TH¹:
Whiche hath do to him great offence,　146d
That ye not wolde upon him se;
Wherfore a sorouful man is he.　TH¹:147a
Shape ye to paye him, and to please,
Of my love if ye wol have ease.　3600
Fulfyl his wyl, sithe that ye knowe
Daunger is daunted and brought lowe
Through helpe of me and of Pyte;
You dare no more aferde be."
　"I shal do right as ye wyl,"　3605
Saith Bialacoil, "for it is skyl,
Sithe Daunger wol that it so be."
Than Fraunchise hath him sent to me.

Byalacoil at the begynnyng
Salued me in his commyng;　3610
No straungenesse was in him sene,
No more than he ne had wrathed bene.
As fayre semblaunt than shewed he me,
And goodly, as aforne dyd he;
And by the honde, without dout,　3615
Within the haye, right al about
He ladde me, with right good chere,
Al envyron the vergere,
That Daunger hadde me chased fro.
Nowe have I leave overal to go;　3620
Nowe am I raysed, at my devyse,
Fro hel unto paradyse.
Thus Bialacoil, of gentylnesse,
With al his payne and besynesse,
Hath shewed me, onely of grace,　3625
The [estres] of the swote place.
　I sawe the rose, whan I was nygh,
Was greatter woxen and more high,
Fresshe, roddy, and fayre of hewe,
Of coloure ever yliche newe.　3630
And whan I hadde it longe sene,
I sawe that through the leves grene
The rose spredde to spaunysshinge;
To sene it was a goodly thynge.

3588　**he]** ye MS-SK FU-RB²　3595　**Fro]** For ST SP²·³　*Lines 3595-3690　Out:* MS (*two leaves missing*);
supplied from TH¹　3602　*Out:* MS FU　3604　**dare]** thar SK　**be]** to b. UR　3612　**ne]** *om.* BE
3617　**right]** a r. UR　3618　**envyron the]** e. on t. UR; e. thilke MO　3622　**unto]** up u. UR　3626　**estres]**
eftres TH¹-UR FU　3629　**roddy]** and r. UR

3588　**he:** GL emends, adducing no evidence, but SU FI RIt note that *he* follows the Fr. *il* (Lc 3306 "Je veil qu'il
ait la compaignie" "I wish that he may have the company").
　3591　**high:** "haste" (FI); cf. lines 2393, 4021.
　3595–3690　Two leaves are missing from MS, as noted in KA, and these lines are supplied from TH¹ (BE SKt
GL RBt SU FI RIt). See above, "The Missing Leaves."
　3602　FU, in a note after line 3608, states, "l. 3602 'Daunger is daunted & brought lowe' is left out." Skeat (FU,
p. xi) remarks that this note "is due to some oversight. For *Thynne* really has this line. . . . It is [MS] that omits it."
　3604　**dare:** need (impersonal). Skeat (SK) holds that TH¹ turned *thar* into *dare*; he emends to *thar*, in the
same sense, and adduces line 3761 "Thar" and his note to line 1089. However, GL RB, in their notes to line 1089, call
attention to the confusion of forms between *durren* and *thurven*. See *MED durren* v. 2 (b), *OED Dare* v.¹, *Tharf,
thar* v. Cf. 1089n., line 1324.
　3622　**hel:** GL attributes the form *hell* to TH¹; but TH¹ has *hel*, TH² *hell*.
　3626　**estres:** See 1448n.
　3633　**spaunysshinge:** For the sense, eds. have "expanding" (BE RIf), "expansion" (SK FI), "full bloom" (FI).
URg has "full breadth" from SPg and cites Skinner (1671) for the sense "a span broad," which suggests a false
etymology from OE *spann*. TRg notes the correct origin in "Fr. *Espanouissement*, the full blow of a flower," and BE,
concurring, distinguishes modern English *expanding* as a later borrowing from the Latin etymon. SK cites the Fr.
espanie, "pp. fem. of *espanie*, which Cotgrave [1611] explains by 'To grow or spread, as a blooming rose.'" The
textual parallel to *spaunysshinge*, however, is not *espanie* but *s'eslargissoit* (Lc 3343 "enlarged"); *espanie* (Lc 3354) is
parallel textually to *Rom* 3643 "spradde."

But it ne was so sprede on brede 3635
That men within myght knowe the sede;
For it covert was and close,
Bothe with the leves and with the rose.
The stalke was even and grene upright;
It was theron a goodly syght, 3640
And wel the better, without wene,
For the seed was nat sene.
Ful fayre it spradde, God [it] blesse,
For suche another, as I gesse, 3644
Aforne ne was, ne more vermayle.   TH¹:147b
I was abawed for marveyle,
For ever the fayrer that it was,
The more I am bounden in Loves laas.
    Longe I abode there, sothe to saye,
Tyl Bialacoil I ganne to praye, 3650
Whan that I sawe him in no wyse
To me warnen his servyce,
That he me wolde graunt a thynge,
Whiche to remembre is wel syttynge:
This is to sayne, that of his grace 3655
He wolde me yeve leysar and space,
To me that was so desyrous,
To have a kyssynge precious
Of the goodly fresshe rose,
That so swetely smelleth in my nose. 3660

"For if it you displeased nought,
I wolde gladly, as I have sought,
Have a cosse therof freely
Of your yefte; for certainly
I wol none have but by your leve, 3665
So lothe me were you for to greve."
    He sayd, "Frende, so God me spede,
Of Chastite I have suche drede;
Thou shuldest nat warned be for me,
But I dare nat, for Chastyte. 3670
Agayne her dare I nat mysdo,
For alway byddeth she me so
To yeve no lover leave to kysse.
For who therto maye wynnen, ywisse,
He of the surplus of the praye 3675
[May lyve] in hoope to gette some daye.
For whoso kyssynge maye attayne
Of loves payne hath, sothe to sayne,
The best and most avenaunt,
And ernest of the remenaunt." 3680
    Of his answere I sighed sore;
I durst assaye him tho no more,
I hadde suche drede to greve him aye.
A man shulde nat to moche assaye
To chafe his frende out of measure, 3685
Nor putte his lyfe in aventure;

3637 **close]** enclose SK   3642 **For]** F. that UR   3643 **God it]** the god of TH¹-KA FU   3652 **warnen]** to w. UR   3653 **me]** to m. UR   3654 **syttynge]** fyttyng BE   3659 **the goodly]** t. so g. UR; thilke g. MO   3660 **so]** *om.* SK   3661 **it]** *om.* TH²   3662 **wolde]** woll ST-BE   3676 **May lyve]** My lyfe TH¹-SP¹ KA FU   3679 **most]** the m. UR GL   3685 **chafe]** chase UR

3637   **close:** KA suggests *enclose* and cites line 1652.
3643   **God it blesse:** BE suggests "May God it blesse" on the basis of the Fr. (Lc 3353 "Diex la beneïe"; noted by SKt RBt SU FI RIt), and KA endorses SK's reading, adopted here.
3646   **abawed:** "abashed, daunted" (SPg), "astonished, confounded" (URg; cf. FI), "dismayed" (SK), "disconcerted" (RIf). TRg cites the Fr. *esbahi* (Lc 3356 "astonished"). SK notes that the form is a var. of *abaved*, BD 614, to which URg also refers, and compares line 4041 below. Cf. *MED abāven* v. (b).
3656   **wolde me:** "(?) omit *me*" (GL).
3660   **so:** KA suggests omission.
3675   **surplus:** FI glosses as "remainder" and cites the Fr. *atant remaindre*, but the Fr. text is not exactly parallel to the ME (Lc 3385–86 "car qui au bessier puet ateindre, / a poine puet a tant remaindre" "for he who can attain to the kiss can scarcely remain at that point").
        praye: FI glosses as "suit (with perhaps a *double entendre* of prey, 'victim')."
3676   **May lyve:** SP²'s emendation. KA notes its presence in MO. There is no parallel in the Fr.
3677–80 RB² calls the idea "a commonplace" and cites Whiting (1934: 28); RI calls it proverbial and cites Whiting (1968: K69).
3680   **ernest:** "pledge" (SKg, RIf). KA suggests *ernes*, but no ed. so emends. See *MED ernes* n., from OF *erres*, L *arra* (cf. Modern Fr. *arrhes*); *MED ernest* n., "seriousness of intention," is from OE *eornust, -est*. But identical forms, encouraged by semantic overlap, exist even in ME. Cf. 4838n.
3684   **moche:** See 1713n.
3686   **his lyfe in aventure:** "i.e., his friend's life in jeopardy" (FI).

186

For no man at the first stroke
Ne maye nat fel downe an oke,
Nor of the reysyns have the wyne
Tyl grapes be rype, and wel afyne]   3690
Be sore empressid, I you ensure,   MS:71r
And drawen out of the pressure.
But I, forpeyned wonder stronge,
[Thought] that I aboode right longe
Aftir the kis, in peyne and woo,   3695
Sith I to kis desired soo;
Till that, [rewyng] on my distresse,
Ther [to me] Venus the goddesse,
Which ay [werreyeth] Chastite,

Came of hir grace to socoure me,   3700
Whos myght is knowe ferre and wide,
For she is modir of Cupide,
The God of Love, blynde as stoon,
That helpith lovers many oon.
This lady brought in hir right honde   3705
Of brennyng fyre a blasyng bronde,
Wherof the flawme and hoote fire
Hath many a lady in desire
Of love brought, and sore hette,
And in hir servise her [hertes] sette.   3710
This lady was of good entaile,
Right wondirfull of apparayle;

3688 **downe**] adoune UR   3690 **be**] *om.* SK   *Lines* 3595–3690 *Out:* MS   3694 **Thought**]
Though MS-SP³ BE-KA GL FU   3695 **Aftir**] And a. ST SP²,³   3697 **rewyng**] rennyng MS-SP³ KA FU
3698 **to me**] come MS-KA GL FU   3699 **werreyeth**] werieth MS BE-KA   3703 **blynde**] as b. UR
3710 **hertes**] herte is MS-SP³ KA FU SU; herte UR-MO

3687–88   "Proverbial," note RB RI. RB calls attention to Ln's parallels (3414–15n.) from Latin and French and
compares Haeckel (1890: no. 44). RI cites Whiting (1968: T471). Lc (3396n.) cites Morawski (1925, nos. 189, 1474).

3689–92   Jephson (BE) quotes the Fr. (Lc 3398–99 "ne l'en n'a pas le vin de l'ene / tant que li presors soit
estroiz" "nor does one get the wine from the wine-grapes before the press be squeezed") in support of (a) his idea
that *be* is redundant in the ME, and (b) his paraphrase of the ME: "We cannot have the wine until the grapes be ripe,
and finally (afyne) well and sore pressed, and drawn out of the pressure"; but the paraphrase does not seem to
support the idea that *be* is redundant (see 3690n., 3692n.).

3690   **be:** Jephson (BE) thinks that *be* is redundant and spoils the sense; but only SK, endorsed by KA, so
emends, "unnecessarily," states GL.

afyne: "finally" (GL), "completely" (FI), "thoroughly" (RIf); see 3689–92n. The word is adverbial, from
OF *a fin* "to the end" (*MED afin(e* adv.), but SPg and URg read it as an adjective, SPg as "fined" (i.e., refined), and
URg as a mistake for *and fine*.

3691   MS resumes here (BE SKt).

3692   **pressure:** "wine press" (SKg₂ FI RIf); see 3689–92n.

3694–95   **aboode . . . Aftir:** "waited for" (FI)

3694   **Thought:** UR's emendation makes *forpeyned* (line 3693) a participle and somewhat clarifies the sense.
MS *Though* would require that *forpeyned* be construed as an intransitive pa. t. "was overcome by suffering," a usage
not otherwise recorded (*MED forpeined*). The Fr. provides no parallel (Lc 3400–01).

3697   **rewyng:** "having pity" (SKg₂ FI). UR's emendation is noted by KA in MO. Although there is no parallel
in the Fr., the emendation is reasonable on paleographical grounds.

3698   **to me:** SK's suggestion, endorsed by KA and noted in GL, is reasonable paleographically (*c/t* confusion
and anticipation of *Came*, line 3700), and follows the Fr. (Lc 3402–03 "Venus . . . *me vint* au secours" "Venus came to
my help [lit., came to me to the help]"; noted in SU); cf. *Rom* 3700 "Came . . . to socoure me."

3699   **werreyeth:** TH¹'s emendation (*werryeth*), endorsed in SK by KA. Cf. the Fr. *guerroie* (Lc 3402).   § For
the sense, "makes war upon" (URg et al.), SK compares *KnT* A 2236 "And holden werre alwey with chastitee,"
where the parallel is not with the verb form but with the idea of making war on chastity. SK considers the
emendation "necessary to the sense," but MS *werieth* may be a var. sp. See 3251n., 3917n. and SKg₂.

3700   **Came:** GL suggests *come*, if the word be a pa. part.; but does not so emend.

3705–10   These six lines expand three of the Fr., quoted by BE (Lc 3406–08 "Ele tint un brandon flanbant / en
sa main destre, dont la flame / a eschaufee mainte dame" "In her right hand she held a flaming torch, whose flame
has warmed many a lady").

3707   **flawme:** SKt notes TH¹'s *flame*, which appears also in TH²-UR FU SU FI; the forms in -*a(u,w)*- are from
AF, those in -*a*- from CF (*MED flaume* n.).

3710   **hertes sette:** SK's emendation, endorsed by KA, is adopted, "perhaps rightly" (SU). BE considers MS
[herte] is sette "a mistake for *[herte] ysette*."

3711   **of good entaile:** There is no parallel in the Fr., although URg and BE cite the Fr. phrase: "*De belle taille,*
Proper, handsome" (URg); "d'une belle taille, of a fine figure" (BE). On *entaile* "shape," see 162n.

Bi hir atyre so bright and shene
Men myght perceyve well and sene 3714
She was not of religioun. 71v
Nor I nell make mencioun
Nor of robe, nor of tres[s]our,
Of broche, neithir of hir riche attour,
Ne of hir girdill aboute hir side,
For that I nyll not longe abide; 3720
But knowith wel that certeynly
She was araied richely.
Devoyde of pruyde certeyn she was.
To Bialacoil she wente apas,
And to hym shortly, in a clause, 3725
She seide, "Sir, what is the cause
Ye ben of port so daungerous
Unto this lover, and deynous,
To graunte hym nothyng but a kisse?
To worne it hym ye done amysse, 3730

Sith well ye wote how that he
Is Loves servaunt, as ye may see,
And hath beaute, wherthrough [he] is
Worthy of love to have the blis.
How he is semely, biholde and see, 3735
How he is faire, how he is free,
How he is swoote and debonaire,
Of age yonge, lusty, and faire.
Ther is no lady so hawteyne, 72r
Duchesse, ne countesse, ne chasteleyne, 3740
That I nolde holde hir ungoodly
For to refuse hym outterly.
His breth is also good and swete,
And eke his lippis rody, and mete
Oonly to [pleyen] and to kisse. 3745
Graunte hym a kis, of gentilnysse!
His teth arn also white and clene.
Me thenkith wrong, withouten wene,

3717 **robe]** her r. UR SK   **tressour]** tresour MS-RI   3718 **neithir]** ne UR; nor SK GL   3719 **hir girdill]** g. FU   3733 **he]** *om.* MS-SP³ KA GL FU   3740 **ne countesse]** c. TH¹-BE SK FU SU FI   3744 **eke]** *om.* UR   **and mete]** are thei m. UR   3745 **pleyen]** pleyne MS-KA FU SU FI   **to kisse]** not to kisse? UR   3748 **thenkith]** t. it GL

3715 **religioun:** "a religious order" (BE SK RB FI RIf).

3716 **nell:** BE MO SKt take MS *nell* as an abbreviation for *nelle*, and SK normalizes to *nil.* TH¹-UR FU SU FI have *n(y,i)l(l).* See above, "The Manuscript Hands: The Scribe (MS₁)."

3717 **tressour:** "head band"; cf. the Fr. (Lc 3416 "et de son treçoër doré" "and of her golden tressour") and 568n., where MS *tresour,* as here, is perhaps a var. sp., although I collate it as an error ("treasure") in both places. No ed. emends here, but at line 568, TH¹ SK FU-RI have *tressour.*

3718 **attour:** BE and SK cite the Fr. as *ator;* but that word (Lc 3411) is parallel rather to ME *atyre,* line 3713. The parallel here is *corroie* (Lc 3417 "belt"), although ME *attour* undoubtedly means "attire" (SPg BE GLg), "array" (SK *MED*). SU finds the var. *atour* (for Lc 3415 *oré* "face veil") in MS Ga (SU Fr. 3433–34n.). § TR glosses *attour* as "head-dress."

    neithir: KA recommends SK's reading.

3723 **pruyde:** *MED prīde* n.(2) lists this form as chiefly West Midland and Southwest.

3730 **worne:** "denie" (SP²·³g URg), "refuse" (URg TRg), "withhold" (FI). See *OED Warn* v.².

3733 **beaute:** "Here and in line 3796 Liddell [GL] would give *beaute* three syllables. But this seems unlikely. The same question arises in the *KnT,* I [A], 2385" (RB).

    he: UR's emendation, noted in UR MO by KA. MS's omission of the pronoun may be due to the Fr. exemplar; Ln 3449 reads "Par quoi est digne d'estre amez" ("for which [he] is worthy to be loved"), and his variants show three MSS (Ha Da Ra) that include the pronoun *il.* Ha is Lc's base (Lc 3431 "por qu'il est dignes d'estre amez"). SU does not note this variant, but it would provide negative evidence for his conclusion (1968:xxxiv) that the translator of Fragments B and C "worked from a *Roman* R MS." If so, it may well *not* have been Ra; SU favors Ri (xxiii, xxviii).

3740 **chasteleyne:** "a gentlewoman of a great house" (SPg), "in general, any Lady of Quality under the Degree of a Countess" (URg), "the wife of a *Chastelain,* or lord of a castle" (TRg), "mistress of a castle; F. chastelaine" (SK).

3741 **ungoodly:** TRg quotes the Fr. parallel *vilaine* (Lc 3438 "boorish").

3745–46 **kisse : gentilnysse:** RB's forms *kesse : gentilnesse,* noted by RIt, provide a Kentish rhyme.

3745 **pleyen:** "play." KA suggests the emendation; the early eds., with the spelling *pla(y,i)ne,* presumably read MS *pleyne* as "complain (of love)" (FI; cf. URg, s.v. *pleyne*). There is no parallel in the Fr.

    to kisse: Since the line is not in the Fr., UR's emendation, *not to kisse?,* has no support.

If ye now worne hym, trustith me,
To graunte that a kis have he. 3750
The lasse [to] helpe hym that ye haste,
The more tyme shul ye waste."
    Whanne the flawme of the verry bronde
That Venus brought in hir right honde
Hadde Bialacoil with hete smete, 3755
Anoon he bade, withouten lette,
Graunte to me the rose kisse.
Thanne of my peyne I gan to lysse,
And to the rose anoon wente I,
And kisside it full feithfully. 3760
Thar no man aske if I was blithe,
Whanne the savour soft and lythe

Stroke to myn herte withoute more, 72v
And me alegged of my sore,
So was I full of joye and blisse. 3765
It is faire sich a flour to kisse,
It was so swoote and [saverous].
I myght not be so angwisshous
That I mote glad and joly be,
Whanne that I remembre me. 3770
Yit ever among, sothly to seyne,
I suffre noye and moche peyne.
    The see may never be so stille
That with a litel wynde it wille
Overwhelme and turne also, 3775
As it were woode, in wawis goo.

3751 **to]** ye MS-KA FU   3752 **The]** And the TH¹-BE FU   3755 **hete]** his h. TH¹-UR FU   3756 **bade]** b. me MS-KA GL FU   3757 **Graunte to]** Grauntede t. MS BE-KA GL; And grauntid UR   **kisse]** to k. UR   3761 **Thar]** There nede TH¹-SP³ FU; Nede UR; There SU FI (*var. sp.*)   3762 **soft]** so s. UR   3767 **saverous]** fauerous MS TH¹ MO KA FU   3769 **mote]** ne m. GL RB¹-RI   3770 **remembre]** do r. UR   3774 **That with]** But w. UR; T. SU FI   **it wille]** at w. TH¹-UR FU; it nil SK GL RB¹·² SU RI   3775 **Overwhelme]** May o. UR

3749   **worne:** deny, refuse, "withhold" (FI); cf. 3730n.

3751   **to:** BE, as KA notes, suggests this emendation in a note. SK adduces the Fr. (Lc 3453–54 "car tant con vos plus atendroiz, / tant, ce sachiez, de tens pardroiz" "for the longer you wait, you know, the more time you will lose"), which has only an implied parallel to the verb phrase *to helpe*.

3752   **The:** BE apparently lapsed here from his announced intent to reproduce MS and instead follows "Speght's edition" (BE 7.12), which has *And the*. See above, "Descriptions of the Printed Editions."

3756–57   "Immediately, without delay, he ordered to grant me [i.e., that I be granted the right] to kiss the rose." Cf. the Fr. (Lc 3456–57 "sanz plus deloer, / m'otroia un bessier en dons" "without delaying longer, he granted me the gift of a kiss").

3756   **bade:** KA endorses SK's omission of *me* and adduces line 3757, where *me* appears.

3761   **Thar:** Need (impersonal); see *OED Tharf* v., 3 sing. β-forms. TH¹'s *There nede* seems to indicate that the verb was already obsolete in the 16th century; as RIt notes, "Thynne misunderstood *Thar* = 'it needs.'" SU FI's *There* is a variant form of the 3 sing. verb, not the adverb. Cf. 3604n.

3762   **lythe:** URg, s.v. *lithe*, citing this line and *HF* 119 [sic for 118], provides "Gentle, tractable; Smooth, plain; Softe." See also GLg who adds "easy," and SKg FI "delicate." Cf. *MED lith(e* adj.

3767   **saverous:** See 2902n.

3769   **That I mote:** The absence of the negative particle *ne* in MS and early eds.—here and in lines 3774, 4764, 5068–9—leads one to suspect that the force of the negative in the main clause (lines 3768, 3773, 4757–63, 5067–68) carried over to the following dependent clause and that, as a result, the conj. *That* had the same adversative sense, "but that, but what," that it has when the negative particle is present. See *OED That*, conj. 5, for examples where both clauses are negative. RB calls attention to the possibility of such an idiom; see 3774n., 4764n. KA indicates that SK recommends insertion of *ne*; SK does not so emend.

3771   **ever among:** "Oftentimes; every now and then" (URg), "ever at the same time" (TRg), "now and again" (FI); see also 690n.

3773–86   With this passage, which expands five lines of the Fr. (Lc 3476–80), BE compares *KnT* A 1531–39, and GL *Bo* 253 ff. (= 1m7). Neither parallel is close. RI notes that lines 3776–84 are not in the Fr. and that "the translator has elaborated a commonplace about the vicissitudes of love." On this same "common topic" RB (3779–86n.) compares *KnT* A 1785–1814.

3773   RB² adduces Whiting (1934: 24).

3774   **wille:** In support of the emendation *nil*, endorsed in SK by KA, SK adduces the Fr. (Lc 3477 "qu'el ne soit troble" "that it may not be troubled"). Robinson (RBt) thinks that the MS reading is "perhaps" correct and notes that "the emendation *nille . . .* may be unnecessary" (RB). He refers to the note on *MLH* (B¹ 49n.) where he says that "the illogical construction is probably to be regarded as an idiom" and adduces *TC* 1.456–57 and *Rom* 4764 as well as this line; RI makes the same observations. See also 3769n., 4764n., 5069n.

Aftir the calme the trouble soune
Mote folowe and chaunge as the moone.
Right so farith Love, that [selde] in oon
Holdith [his] anker; for right anoon   3780
Whanne they in ese wene beste to lyve,
They ben with tempest all fordryve.
Who serveth Love can telle of woo;
The stoundemele joie mote overgoo.
Now he hurteth, and now he cureth;   3785
For [selde] in oo poynt Love endureth.
　Now is it right me to procede,   73r
How Shame gan medle and take hede,
Thurgh whom fele angres I have hadde,
And how the strong wall was maad,   3790
And the castell of brede and lengthe,
The God of Love wanne with his strengthe.
All this in romance will I sette,
And for nothyng ne will I lette,

So that it lykyng to hir be,   3795
That is the flour of beaute;
For she may best my labour quyte,
That I for hir love shal endite.
　Wikkid-Tunge, that th[e] covyne
Of every lover can devyne   3800
Worste, and addith more somdell—
For Wikkid-Tunge seith never well—
To me-ward bare he right gret hate,
Espiyng me erly and late,
Till he hath sene the gret chere   3805
Of Bialacoil and me ifeere.
He myght not his tunge withstonde
Worse to report than he fonde,
He was so full of cursed rage;
It satte hym well of his lynage,   3810
For hym an Irish womman bare.   73v
His tunge was fyled sharpe and square,

3777 **soune**] sonne TH[1,2] FU SU FI　　3779 **selde**] yelde MS KA　　3780 **his**] *om.* MS (MS, *corr.*)　　3786 **selde**] elde MS KA　　3793 **in**] *om.* SP[2,3]　　3796 **of**] o. all UR　　3799 **that**] whiche t. UR　　**the**] th MS KA　　3801 **and**] a. aie UR　　3807 **myght**] ne m. UR　　3811 **Irish**] irous SP[2,3]

3777　**trouble soune:** "disturbance soon"; *OED* identifies *soune* as a Northern form (*Soon* adv., Forms, 2 γ), but *MED sǫne* adv. does not. FI, glossing *trouble* as "troubled (bringing trouble)" (see *OED Trouble* adj.), would presumably understand *soune* as "sun," a reading fostered by TH['s] *sonne*; such a reading creates difficulties in sense and rhyme.

3778　"Proverbial," notes RI, citing Whiting (1968: M655).

　　chaunge: KA attributes to SK the suggestion *chaungen*, but no ed. so emends.

3779–86　See 3773–86n.

3779　**selde:** GL suggests that MS *yelde* may have arisen from an earlier *zelde* (ʒelde).

3780　**his:** "written above the line" (KA), perhaps by MS₁, perhaps by a later hand. Thorp (1989) notes that the ink is similar to that of MS but that the duct is unusual (cf. 1792n.). Whatley (1989) also questions the letter *s*.

3784　**The stoundemele:** As RB notes, Brusendorff (1925:376) would emend *The* to *That*; he would also take *stoundemele* as an adv., as at line 2304, rather than an adj. "momentary" (FI RIf); presumably, his sense would be "(woe) which from time to time must overcome joy" rather than the usual reading "the momentary joy must pass away."

3789　**fele:** "painful" (SKg₂) or "cruel" (FI), not "many."

3793　**romance:** "the language of romance" (SKg₂), "French (verse)" (FI). At 2154n., Fisher makes clear that narrative is involved, and in fact, as BE notes, the Fr. word here is *estoire* (Lc 3487). See 2148n.

3795　**hir:** Cf. 42–48n.

3796　**beaute:** See 3733n.

3799　**Wikkid-Tunge:** Fr. *Male Bouche* (Lc 3493), as BE notes.

3811　**Irish:** The capital *I* appears in MS and indicates at least the scribe's understanding of locality. BE, following Méon, takes Fr. *irese* (Lc 3499) as "given to ire." SK objects that the OF for "full of ire" is *irous* and that Michel prints *Irese* in upper case and explains it by "Irlandaise"; "besides," Skeat writes, "there is no point in speaking of 'an angry old woman'; whereas G. de Lorris clearly meant something disrespectful in speaking of 'an old Irishwoman.'" As he notes, "Michel explains [4126n.] that the Irish character was formerly much detested in France." Cook (1916*b*:181–82) notes Godefroy's understanding of *ires(s)e* as "heretic" [Godefroy 1881–1902] and considers the B-translator's "Irish" an error. Ln had earlier suggested (1.192n.) that MS. Ha's form *irese* stands for *iraise* (rhyming with *punese*) and that it involves a pun on *irais* "angry" and *Irois* "Irish." RB presents both senses and cites Ln; FI accepts the probability of such a pun. David, on the basis of the Fr., leans toward the sense "angry woman (?)" (RIf), although he notes (RI) Ln's suggestion of the pun. On the reputation of the "Wild Irish" in the Middle Ages, RB RI cite Snyder (1920), who quotes this passage (pp. 172–73).

Poignaunt and right kervyng,
And wonder bitter in spekyng.
For whanne that he me gan espie,　3815
He swoore, affermyng sikirlye,
Bitwene Bialacoil and me
Was yvel aquayntaunce and pryve.
He spake therof so folilye
That he awakide Jelousye,　3820
Which, all afrayed in his risyng,
Whanne that he herd janglyng,
He ran anoon, as he were woode,
To Bialacoil, there that he stode,
Which hadde lever in this caas　3825
Have ben at Reynes or Amyas;
For foot-hoot, in his felonye,
To hym thus seide Jelousie:
"Why hast thou ben so necligent
To kepen, whanne I was absent,　3830
This verger heere left in thi warde?
To me thou haddist no rewarde,

To truste—to thy confusioun—
Hym [thus], to whom suspeccioun　3834
I have right gret, for it is nede;　74r
It is well shewed by the dede.
Grete faute in thee now have I founde.
By God, anoon thou shalt be bounde,
And fast loken in a tour,
Withoute refuyt or socour.　3840
For Shame to longe hath be thee froo;
Over-soone she was agoo.
Whanne thou hast lost bothe drede and feere,
It semede wel she was not heere.
She was bisy in no wyse　3845
To kepe thee and chastise,
And for to helpen Chastite
To kepe the roser, as thenkith me.
For thanne this boy-knave so booldely
Ne shulde not have be hardy,　3850
[Ne] in this verge[r] hadde such game,
Which now me turneth to gret shame."

3813 **Poignaunt**] And right p. UR　3818 **yvel**] ill UR　3822 **janglyng**] the j. UR; him j. SK GL
3834 **thus**] this MS BE-KA　3845 **She was**] For s. w. UR; S. ne w. MO; S. w. not SK　3846 **chastise**] to c.
UR SK GL RB¹-FI　3851 **Ne**] *om.* MS-SP³ BE-KA FU-SU　**verger**] verge MS-SP³ BE-KA FU　**hadde**] and SP³

3820 **Jelousye:** "'le jalous' in the allegories of love," notes FI, "was typically the husband." See *RR* (Lc)
8425–9412. In the Fr., this character (Lc 3510 "Jalousie") is the grammatically feminine abstraction rather than the
grammatically masculine "jealous one." In his exploration of the evidence for authorship of the ME translation,
Schoch (1906:345) notes that ME *jelousye* takes masc. pronouns (line 3821 etc.) and that all the cases except one are
in Fragment B; that case (line 7563) has no indication of gender. Cf. 3958n. on the parallel abstraction "Drede."

3822 **herd:** KA suggests *herde him.*

3826 **Reynes or Amyas:** *Reynes* is usually identified as Rennes, in Brittany (TRg SK GL RB FI RIf); SK cites
his note to *BD* 255 "cloth of Reynes." "Amiens" (URg TRg) is a guess for *Amyas;* "Where *Amyas* is," states SK, "is of
no consequence; for the name is wrongly given"; GL says that it "corresponds to Fr. 'a Miaus'"; RB notes that it "is
apparently only a mistake for Meaux"; FI notes that it "has not been identified," and RIf glosses it simply as "Meaux."
The Fr., as BE SK GL RB FI RI note, has *Estampes ou a Miauz* (Ln 3534 "Etampes or Meaux," near Paris). But there
are variants (Ln 3534t): MS Ga *encore en son lit* ("still in his bed"); MS He *en Baiviere* ("in Bavaria"); and Lc
(3515–16; MS Ha) has no place names.

3827 **foot-hoot:** "straightway" (SP¹g), "forthwith" (SP²·³g), "immediately" (SK). Skeat compares his note to
MLT B¹ 438, where he cites examples.

3832 **rewarde:** "regard" (SK RB RIf); SK cites *PF* 426. Cf. 3254n.

3845 **was:** MO's *ne was* anticipates SK's *was not,* noted by KA; SK cites the Fr. *Si ne s'est mie* (Méon 3555 =
Lc 3528 "si ne s'est pas").

3851 **Ne in this verger hadde:** UR's emendation. KA attributes to Skeat the suggestion "*Nor in this verger
had.*" RI notes, "Robinson does not add the negative and translates *hadde,* '(that he) had'"; Robinson (RB) calls this
"a difficult ellipsis, but not impossible," and compares *MLT* B¹ 1091 "Sente" ("as to send") and his note thereto,
where he adduces "Owl and Nightingale 1093ff."; here, he grants that those who supply *Ne* or *Nor* may be correct.

verger: SPg defines *verge* as "a garden." In support of *verger,* SKt adduces line 3234, where *verger*
adapts Fr. *vergier* (Lc 2994); here the Fr. is *porprise* "enclosure" (Lc 3533), translated again by *verger* at line 4094. Cf.
3234n.

hadde: SK has *had.* SKt attributes *had* to "Th." (TH¹), but it appears first in TH³. On the sense of *hadde,*
see 3851n.

191

Bialacoil nyst what to sey;
Full fayn he wolde have fled awey,
For feere han hidde, nere that he   3855
All sodeynly toke hym with me.
And whanne I saugh he hadde soo,
This Jelousie, take us twoo,
I was astoned and knewe no rede,   74v
But fledde awey for verrey drede.   3860
    Thanne Shame cam forth full symply—
She wente have trespaced full gretly—
Humble of hir port, and made it symple,
Weryng a [vayle] in stide of wymple,
As nonnys don in her abbey.   3865
Bycause hir herte was in affray,
She gan to speke withynne a throwe
To Jelousie right wonder lowe.
First of his grace she bysoughte,
And seide, "Sire, ne leveth noughte   3870
Wikkid-Tunge, that fals espie,
Which is so glad to feyne and lye.

He hath you maad, thurgh flateryng,
On Bialacoil a fals lesyng.
His falsnesse is not now anewe;   3875
It is to long that he hym knewe.
This is not the first day;
For Wikkid-Tunge hath custome ay
Yonge folkis to bewreye
And fals lesynges on hem [leye].   3880
    "Yit nevertheles I see amonge
That the loigne it is so longe
Of Bialacoil, hertis to lure,   75r
In Loves servyse for to endure,
Drawyng such folk hym too,   3885
That he hath nothyng with to doo.
But in sothnesse I trowe nought
That Bialacoil hadde ever in thought
To do trespace or vylonye,
But for his modir Curtesie   3890
Hath taught hym ever to be
Good of aqueyntaunce and pryve.

3853 **nyst]** n'is UR   3857 **he]** that he UR   3864 **vayle]** bayle MS KA; fayle MO   3869 **his]** the SP³
bysoughte] him b. UR   3877 **is]** ne i. UR   3879 **Yonge]** The y. UR   3880 **leye]** lye MS-KA FU SU FI
3882 **loigne]** soigne SP²-UR   3886 **hath]** had BE SK   3891 **taught]** thaught ST SP¹   **to]** for t. UR MO SK

3855 **hidde:** "We should probably insert *him* after *hid*" (SK).
      he: "Jealousy" (FI RIf).
3856 **toke:** "caught" (SK FI); "see l. 3858" (SK); BE glosses as "detected."
3862 **wente:** SPg, s.v. *wend*, provides "thought"; cf. URg, s.v. *Wene*, citing OE *wenan*, et al. Eds. except BE-KA respell to *wend(e*, but *OED Ween* v. records MS *wente* as a pa. t. spelling variant, commoner, perhaps, in the North. *Wente* translates Fr. *cuide* (*cuidoit*), which appears as a variant of *crient*, "feared," in MSS Be and Ri (Ln 3562t). See lines 4322, 4352.
3863 **made it symple:** "behaved with simplicity" (RB RIf); on the idiom, see 2038n.
3864 **vayle ... wymple:** FI distinguishes the two as "the nun's veil" and the "secular lady's wimple (pleated headdress)."
3878–80 "Langlois [3574–76n.] compares Pamphilus de Amore, l. 417: 'Sepius immeritas incusat fama puellas' (ed. Baudouin, Paris, 1874)" (RB) which Garbáty (1967:122) translates as "gossip often accuses an innocent maiden."
3880 **leye:** KA notes that this is SK's emendation, "both for rime and sense" (SK). On the *lie-lay* confusion, cf. 4143n.
3881 **amonge:** "together, at the same time; at the same place" (TRg), "constantly" (FI). See 690n. and cf. 3771n.
3882 **loigne:** "a line" (URg), "tether" (BEg et al.), "leash for a hawk" (SK FI), "leash" (RIf). SP-TR gloss the erroneous *soigne* (SP²-UR) as "care, diligence," and URg relates it to Fr. *soin*. BE notes that Speght's reading is nonsense, defines *loigne* as "line, or tether; metaphorically, liberty," and quotes the Fr. *longe* (Lc 3560 "leash"). Skeat (SK) quotes Cotgrave (1611) ("*Longe*, . . . a hawks lune or leash'") and suggests that Cotgrave's *lune* is a variant; he derives ME *loigne* from OF *loigne*, Low Lat. *longia*, a tether, from *longus*, long. See *MED loine* n.(2).
3885–86 "i.e., Fair Welcome inspires love in folk of whom he is not even aware" (FI). Both the ME and the Fr. (Lc 3561–62 "l'en li a sosfert a atraire / tel gent dont il n'avoit que fere" [Bel Acueil] has been allowed to attract people of a kind he has no business with") suggest that Fair-Welcoming is or at least becomes aware of those whom he attracts.
3885 GL notes that "this verse, like 3895, has but three accented syllables."
3890 **for:** "because" (BE).

For he loveth noon hevynesse,
But mirthe and pley and all gladnesse.
He hateth all [trecherous],   3895
Soleyn folk, and envyous;
For ye witen how that he
Wole ever glad and joyfull be
Honestly with folk to pleye.
I have be negligent, in good feye,   3900
To chastise hym; therfore now I
Of herte crye you heere mercy,
That I have been so recheles
To tamen hym, withouten lees.
Of my foly I me repente;   3905
Now wole I hoole sette myn entente
To kepe, bothe [lowde] and stille,   75v
Bialacoil to do youre wille."
    "Shame, Shame," seyde Jelousie,
"To be bytrasshed gret drede have I.   3910
Leccherie hath clombe so hye
That almoost blered is myn yhe;

No wonder is, if that drede have I.
Overall regnyth Lecchery,
Whos myght growith nyght and day   3915
Bothe in cloistre and in abbey;
Chastite is werried overall.
Therfore I wole with siker wall
Close bothe roses and roser.
I have to longe in this maner   3920
Left hem unclosid wilfully;
Wherfore I am right inwardly
Sorowfull, and repente me.
But now they shall no lenger be
Unclosid; and yit I drede sore,   3925
I shall repente ferthermore,
For the game goth all amys.
Counsell I must newe, ywys.
I have to longe tristed thee,
But now it shal no lenger be;   3930
For he may best, in every cost,   76r
Disceyve, that men tristen most.

3895 **hateth]** h. eke UR   **trecherous]** trechours MS-SP² UR BE KA GL FU; trechous SP³   3896 **Soleyn]**
And s. UR   **envyous]** envyours GL   3897 **ye witen]** y. wele w. UR; wel y. w. SK   3900 **good]** *om.* UR
3902 **crye]** I c. MS-SP³ KA GL FU FI; ycrie UR   3907 **lowde]** lowe MS-KA FU   3909 **Shame Shame]** O S.
O S. UR   3913 **that]** *om.* UR   3915 **growith]** yit g. SK   3919 **roses]** the r. UR   3928 **must]** mot
take SK

3895–96 **trecherous : envyous:** BE states that "*trecherous*" is "probably the true reading"; KA endorses it,
and Skeat (SK) adopts it "for the sake of the metre and the rime," although he recognizes that "*Trechours* means
'traitors'" (See *OED Treacher*, Obs. "deceiver, cheat").
     3896 **Soleyn:** "onely" (SP²·³g), "alone" (BEg), "solitary" (URg GLg FI RBg RIf), as well as "sullen" (URg TRg
BEg SKg₂ RBg RIf).
     3904 **withouten lees:** "truly" (URg TRg BEg SKg₂ [all s.v. *lees*], FI). Eds. gloss *lees* as "leasing" (SPg), i.e. "lies"
(URg et al.). But *lees* may mean "leash" (TRg et al.), a possibility that FI recognizes; for forms, see *OED Leash* sb.,
MED les(se n.(1).
     3907 **lowde:** KA's suggestion. Skeat (SK) points out that "*loude and stille* is an old phrase" that means
"'whether loudly or silently,' i. e. under all circumstances," and he adduces "Barbour's Bruce, iii. 745." See *MED
loude* adv. 1 (c) for many other examples, including *Rom* 7530. There is no parallel phrase in the Fr.
     3912 **blered is myn yhe:** "My sight is grown dim" (URg); TRg (cf. BEg) explains the literal sense of *blered* as
describing "a particular disorder of the eye, attended with soreness, and dimness of sight" and notes that "more
commonly, in Chaucer, a man's *eye* is said to be *blered* metaphorically, when he is in any way *imposed upon*." Thus
eds. gloss the phrase as "I am made a fool of" (SK); "I have been (beguiled, deceived)" (RB RIf). FI calls the idiom
"the familiar Chaucerian image for cuckolding." Eds. cite *RvT* A 3865 (FI RI), *RvT* A 4049 (RB), *CYT* G 730 (SK RB),
ManT H 252 (FI).
     3917 BE states: "This is one of the reflections on the state of ecclesiastical institutions which accounts for the
hostility of the clergy to this poem." The voice here is that of Jealousy. Cf. Jean Gerson's "Traité contre le Roman de
la Rose" (ed. Hicks 1977:58–87), where Chastity is the complainant against the poem in the court of Christianity
before the judge called Canonical Justice.
          werried: "warred against" (SK), "warred upon" (FI). See 3251n., 3699n., and SKg₂.
     3928 **must:** KA endorses SK's *mot take*. SK's reading for the emended version, "I must (have) fresh counsel"
is substantially the same as those of RB FI for the unemended version, "I must (have) new (advice, counsel)."
     3931–32 "Proverbial," note RB RI; RB compares *TC* 5.1266–67, and RI cites Whiting (1968: E97).

I see wel that I am nygh shent,
But if I sette my full entent
Remedye to purveye.   3935
Therfore close I shall the weye
Fro hem that wole the rose espie,
And come to wayte me vilonye.
For, in good feith and in trouthe,
I wole not lette, for no slouthe,   3940
To lyve the more in sikirnesse,
Do make anoon a fortresse
[T'enclose] the roses of good savour.
In myddis shall I make a tour
To putte Bialacoil in prisoun,   3945
For evere I drede me of tresoun.
I trowe I shal hym kepe soo
That he shal have no myght to goo
Aboute to make companye
To hem that thenke of vylanye;   3950
Ne to no such as hath ben heere
Aforn, and founde in hym good chere,

Which han assailed hym to shende,
And with her trowandyse to blynde.   3954
A foole is eyth to bigyle;   76v
But may [I] lyve a litel while,
He shal forthenke his fair semblaunt."
    And with [that] word came Drede avaunt,
Which was abasshed and in gret fere
Whanne he wiste Jelousie was there.   3960
He was for drede in sich affray
That not a word durst he say,
But quakyng stode full still aloone,
Til Jelousie his weye was gone,
Save Shame, that [him] not forsoke.   3965
Bothe Drede and she ful sore quoke,
That at last Drede abreyde,
And to his cosyn Shame seide:
"Shame," he seide, "in sothfastnesse,
To me it is gret hevynesse   3970
That the noyse so ferre is go,
And the sclaundre of us twoo.

3934   **sette**] shette TH² 3935   **Remedye**] Some r. for UR 3936   **Therfore**] Wherfore TH¹-UR FU SU
FI 3939   **For**] F. now UR 3942   **Do**] To SK GL RB¹-RI 3943   **T'enclose**] Thanne close MS-KA
FU 3955   **to**] for t. SK 3956   **I**] *om*. MS (MS, *corr*.) 3958   **that**] *om*. MS (MS, *corr*.) 3962   **durst he**]
he durste MO 3965   **him**] hin MS, KA; *om*. MS 3967   **That at last**] T. at the l. UR MO RB¹,² RI; Til t. a. l. SK;
Than atte l. Gl 3971   **so ferre is go**] i. s. f. ygo UR 3972   **And the**] A. eke t. UR; A. thilke MO

3938   "come to lie in wait to do me a shame" (BE); "come to watch how to cause me shame" (SK). BE quotes
the Fr. (Lc 3603–04 "a ceus qui por moi conchier / vienent mes roses espier" "to those who, in order to dupe me,
come to spy out my roses").
    wayte: "to beset (me) with, to plot" (SKg₂), "waylay (ambush)" (FI). Cf. 3066n.
    3940–43   SK quotes the Fr. (Lc 3605–07 "Il ne me sera ja parece / que ne face une forterece / qui les rosiers
clora entor" "I shall never be idle in building a fortress that will enclose the roses all around"). See 3942n., 3943n.
    3942   **Do:** Although KA's suggestion, *To*, simplifies the sense, BE's analysis of lines 3940–42 supports MS *Do*:
"'In order to live in greater security, I will not, for any sloth, delay [lete] to cause a fortress to be made.'" The ME has
an awkward translation of the Fr. negative subjunctive *que ne face* (Lc 3606).
    3943   **T'enclose:** BE (3942n.) notes that this "line appears to be corrupt," and SK GL RB¹-FI adopt KA's
suggestion (*To enclose*); GL FI RIt note the Fr. (Lc 3607, above). It may be possible to construe MS *Thanne close* as a
parallel to *do make* in the previous line: "to cause to build a fortress, then (= consequently, so as) to enclose the
roses."
    of good savour: Not in the Fr. (Lc 3607, above).
    3953   **assailed:** "attempted" (FI *MED assail(l)en* v., sense 5); *MED* notes that this sense "may be from
assaien," and Davis (1979, s.v. *assaille*) notes that the sense "test" (*CITE* 1180) is influenced by *assaye(n*.
    3954   "And to blind him with their imposture" (SK).
    3956   **I:** "written above the line" (KA) by MS₁.
    3958   **that:** "*that* written above the line" (KA), in the form *þ*, perhaps by MS₂d. Thorp (1989) notes that both
ink and duct are different from those of MS₁.
    Drede: Schoch (1906:345) notes that the Fr. *Peor* (Lc 3620) is grammatically feminine; that the ME takes
it as both masc. (lines 3960–69) and fem. (lines 4216–26); and that the only occurence outside of Fragment B (line
5861) has no indication of gender.
    3962   **durst he:** "Perhaps read *he durste*" (SK); the suggestion comes from MO's emendation.
    3965   **Save:** "refers to *alone* in the line next but one before" (BE).
    him: "*hin* written above the line" (KA) by MS₁.

194

But sith that [it] is byfall,
We may it not ageyn call,
Whanne onys sprongen is a fame.   3975
For many a yeer withouten blame
We han ben, and many a day;
For many an April and many a May
We han passed, not shamed,   77r
Till Jelousie hath us blamed   3980
Of mystrust and suspecioun,
Causeles, withoute enchesoun.
Go we to Daunger hastily,
And late us shewe hym openly
That [he] hath not aright wrought   3985
Whanne that [he] sette nought his thought
To kepe better the purprise;
In his doyng he is not wise.
He hath to us do gret wronge,
That hath suffred now so longe   3990
Bialacoil to have his wille,
All his lustes to fulfille.

He must amende it utterly,
Or ellys shall he vilaynesly
Exiled be out of this londe,   3995
For he the werre may not withstonde
Of Jelousie, nor the greef,
Sith Bialacoil is at myscheef."
    To Daunger, Shame and Drede anoon
The right weye ben goon.   4000
The cherle thei founden hem aforn,
Liggyng undir an hawethorn;
Undir his heed no pilowe was,   77v
But in the stede a trusse of gras.
He slombred, and a nappe he toke,   4005
Tyll Shame pitously hym shoke
And grete manace on hym gan make.
"Why slepist thou whanne thou shulde wake?"
Quod Shame; "Thou doist us vylanye!
Who tristith thee, he doth folye,   4010
To kepe roses or bot[oun]s,
Whanne thei ben faire in her sesouns.

3973 **it]** *om.* MS (MS₁ *corr.*)   **is]** is so SK   3974 **call]** do c. SK   3977 **ben and many a day]** passed not ashamed RB²   3978 **and]** *om.* UR   3979 **not shamed]** n. ashamed SP³ BE SK GL RB¹·²; nothing s. UR   3985 **he]** *om.* MS KA   3986 **he]** *om.* MS KA   3995 **this]** his FI   3997 **nor the]** n. bere t. UR   4000 **weye]** weyes MO   **goon]** both ygon UR; agoon MO RB¹·²; bothe a-goon SK

3973   **sith:** KA transcribes erroneously as *sithe*, the form adopted in GL RB¹·².
    it is: "*it* written above the line" (KA) by MS₁. KA also endorses SK's insertion of *so* after *is.*
3974   **call:** KA endorses SK's insertion of *do* before *call.*
3977   **han:** As SKt SU note, TH¹ has *haue*; so do TH²-UR FU SU FI.
    ben ... day: As RIt notes, RB²'s error anticipates line 3979.
3978–79   **many an April and many a May / We han passed:** RB RI note that the expression is proverbial in French and that Ln (3652n.) cites examples (from Rutebeuf); Lc (3634n.) cites Chrétien's *Perceval* 6220–21 (ed. Roach 1959).
3987   **the purprise:** As SK notes, the Fr. parallel in this case is fem., *ceste porprise* (Lc 3642; cf. Lc 3533, 12370); but the word also appears in *RR* as a masc., *porpris*, with the same meaning, "enclosure" (Lc 3332, 10264, 12491). SK notes that Cotgrave (1611) has *pourpris*, masc., and he (SK) compares *Rom* 4171 "this purprise," where Lc (3815) has the fem., *la porprise.*
3994   **vilaynesly:** As at line 1498, Skeat (SK) emends to *vilaynsly*; he thus scans *ellys* as a disyllable. Liddell (GL), however, reads *vilaynesly* as four syllables, with stress on the second "as in v. 178"; he thus takes *ellys* as "one syllable as usual" (but cf. lines 300, 3429, 4429). RB RI follow SK's *vilaynsly* at line 1498 but not here. See 1498n.
3995–96   **londe : withstonde:** "Possibly the -*e* of the inf. *withstonde* should be kept, and *londe* allowed an (irregular) dat. -*e*; so also in the case of *stonde : bond*, ll. 4091 f." (RB). As RI notes, Robinson's "practice is to normalize rhymes."
3998   As RBt notes, GL suggests that the translator may have misread the Fr. (Lc 3650 "s'ele le cuilloit en haïne" "if she conceived a hatred for him") as "Se belacueil l'ait en haïne" ("if Belacueil hate her").
4001   **cherle:** BE notes that the original is *le paisan* (Lc 3653 "le peïsant").
4011–13   RB calls attention to Brusendorff's "very free emendation" (1925:331) of these lines: "Roses or knoppe forto kepe, / More than he doth a shepe. / Thou art to sluggy and coward here." The basis is the Fr. (Ln 3680–83 [= Lc 3662–65] "Fos est qui en vos s'asseüre / De garder rose ne bouton / Ne qu'en la queue d'un mouton. / Trop estes recreanz e lasches" "Anyone is a fool to trust in you, any more than in a sheep's tail, to guard a rose or a rosebud. You are too lazy and idle").
4011–12   **botouns : sesouns:** The imperfect rhyme of MS *bothoms : sesouns* gives warrant, as elsewhere, to the normalization. See 1721n., lines 3473, 4308.

Thou art woxe to familiere,
Where thou shulde be straunge of chere,
Stoute of thi porte, redy to greve.   4015
Thou doist gret folye for to leve
Bialacoil hereinne to calle
The yonder man to shenden us alle.
Though that thou slepe, we may here
Of Jelousie gret noyse heere.   4020
Art thou now late? Rise up [in] high
And stoppe sone and delyverly
All the gappis of the hay.
Do no favour, I thee pray.
It fallith nothyng to thy name   4025
To make faire semblaunt where
    thou maist blame.
Yf Bialacoil be sweete and free,   78r
Dogged and fell thou shuldist be,

Froward and outerageous, ywis;
A cherl chaungeth that curteis is.   4030
This have I herd ofte in seiyng,
That man [ne] may, for no dauntyng,
Make a sperhauke of a bosarde.
Alle men wole holde thee for musarde,
That debonair have founden thee;   4035
It sittith thee nought curteis to be.
To do men plesaunce or servise,
In thee it is recreaundise.
Lete thi werkis fer and nere
Be like thi name, which is Daungere."   4040
    Thanne, all abawid in shewing,
Anoon spake Drede, right thus seiyng,
And seide, "Daunger, I drede me
That thou ne wolt bisy be
To kepe that thou hast to kepe;   4045

4018 **yonder]** yonger TH³ ST SP²-UR   4021 **in]** an MS-KA GL FU   4024 **thee]** do t. UR   4026 **To make]** Make SK   4032 **man ne]** m. MS-SP³ BE KA GL FU; man[ne] RB¹   4034 **wole]** *om.* SP²·³   4041 **abawid]** abashed TH³ ST SP²-UR   4044 **ne wolt]** me w. FU; n. w. not SK

4015 **Stoute:** "strong" (MOg FI); "stubborn, arrogant" (SKg₂); "proud" (RIf). The latter sense, while reasonable, is perhaps more appropriate at line 6158 than here (see SKg₂).

4018 **shenden:** KA attributes to SK the spelling *shende*; SK does not so spell, but GL does.

4021–22 **in high / And:** Brusendorff (1925:416) suggests *and by / To*, with *by* as an imperative ("hasten") parallel to *Rise*. See 4021n. below.

4021 **in high:** "in haste" (URg TRg SK RBg FI). T. Thomas suggests the emendation (URg, s.v. *Hie*); KA records the same suggestion in SK who notes that the phrase is common and adduces line 3591; see *MED hi(e* n.(2) (var. *high*), (b). GL quotes part of the Fr., "'Esties vous ore couchies?'"; RB quotes both parts (Lc 3673–74 "Estiez vos ore couchiez? / Levez tost sus . . ." "Have you been lying down now? Get up immediately . . ."). Eds. with *in high* take it as a translation of Fr. *tost*, but SU suggests that "Fr. *sus* (= en haut) perhaps explains ME," and RIt suggests "perhaps read *on hye*." If so, MS *an high* would mean "on high, upright"; see *MED heigh* adj. 8b (as noun in adv. phrases). See 4021–22n. above.

4026 **To:** SK's omission of this word follows KA's suggestion.

    where: "as extra syllable after caesura" (GL).

4030 "'A churl changes his nature, ceases to play his part, when he is courteous'" (RB). RB RI quote the Fr. (Lc 3682 "Vilains qui est cortois enrage"), and RI translates: "a churl who is courteous has lost his wits."

4032–33 "'No man, by taming it, can make a sparrow-hawk of a buzzard'" (SK). BE SK FI note that a buzzard is unfit for falconry, a sparrow-hawk excellent. BE SK RB RI note that the saying is a proverb in the Fr. (Lc 3684–85); SK refers to two similar proverbs in Cotgrave (1611), s.v. *Esparvier.*; RB RI refer to parallels in Ln (3702–03n.); RB refers to "Li Proverbe au Vilain, 41 (ed. Tobler, Leipzig, 1895, p. 19)" and to Haeckel (1890: no. 117). Lc (3684–85n.) adduces Morawski (1925: nos. 96, 965, 914). BE observes that "the corresponding proverb in English is not so refined:—'You cannot make a silk purse out of a sow's ear.'"

4032 **ne:** UR's emendation, noted in UR MO by KA, adjusts meter, clarifies sense, and follows the Fr. *ne puet* (Lc 3684 "can not").

    dauntyng: "taming" (SK SKg₂), "threatening" (FI), "taming (by threats)" (RIf).

4034 **musarde:** "lingerer" (SPg), "that amuses himself with trifles" (URg); "A muser" (TRg-SKg₂ RBg), "dreamer" (TRg-GLg); "a sluggish, and hence a useless person" (SK); "sluggard" (SKg₂ RBg FI RIf). See 3256n.

4036 **sittith:** KA reports SK's use of the contraction *sit*.

4038 **recreaundise:** SK notes the Fr. *recreantise* (Lc 3690 "cowardice").

4041 **abawid:** "abashed" (FI); "disconcerted" (RIf). See *MED abaven* v., where a quotation from "*Trivet Constance* p. 242" has the phrase "'Full sore abasshed and a-baude.'" There is no parallel in the Fr. See 3646n.

Whanne thou shuldist wake, thou art aslepe.
Thou shalt be greved, certeynly,
If the aspie Jelousie,
Or if he fynde thee in blame.
He hath today assailed Shame,   4050
And chased awey with gret manace   78v
Bialacoil oute of this place,
And swereth shortly that he shall
Enclose hym in a sturdy wall;
And all is for thi wikkednesse,   4055
For that thee faileth straungenesse.
Thyne herte, I trowe, be failed all;
Thou shalt repente in speciall,
If Jelousie the sooth kn[e]we;
Thou shalt forthenke and sore rewe."   4060
　　With that the cherl his clubbe gan shake,
Frounyng his eyen gan to make,
And hidous chere, [as] man in rage.
For ire he brente in his visage,
Whanne that [he] herd hym blamed soo.   4065
He seide, "Oute of my witte I goo!
To be discomfyt I have gret wronge.

Certis, I have now lyved to longe,
Sith I may not this closer kepe.
All quykke I wolde be dolven deepe,   4070
If ony man shal more repeire
Into this gardyne, for foule or faire.
Myne herte for ire goth a-fere,
That I lete ony entre heere.   4074
I have do folie, now I see,   79r
But now it shall amended bee.
Who settith foot heere ony more,
Truly he shall repente it sore;
For no man moo into this place
Of me to entre shal have grace.   4080
Lever I hadde with swerdis tweyne
Thurghoute myne herte in every veyne
Perced to be with many a wounde,
Thanne slouthe shulde in me be founde.
From hennes forth, by nyght or day,   4085
I shall defende it, if I may,
Withouten ony excepcioun
Of ech maner condicioun;
And if I it eny man graunte,

4046　**shuldist]** shuldeth TH²　　4049　**in]** to GL　　4050　**today]** to do ST SP²·³　　4056　**thee]** he TH²
4059　**knewe]** knowe MS KA　　4063　**as]** a MS KA　　4065　**he]** *om.* MS KA　　4069　**closer]** roser GL
4070　**wolde]** woll TH²　　4072　**Into]** To UR　　4075-84　*Lines* 4081-84 *precede line* 4075 *in* SU FI　　4089　**it
eny man]** e. m. i. MO SK

4046　**shuldist:** KA notes that Skeat suggests *shulde* on the basis of line 4008; but no ed. so emends.

4059　**knewe:** TH¹'s emendation parallels the Fr., which has the simple past *conui* (Lc 3712 "knew"); MS *knowe*, as a pres. subj., is syntactically possible. KA notes *knewe* in UR BE MO.

4063–65　The punctuation follows FI. Most eds. have a semicolon after *chere*, a period after *visage*, and a comma after *so* (BE SK GL RB SU); RI has a semicolon after *chere*, comma after *visage*, and period after *so*. Although the punctuation of the Fr. is no reliable guide, the modern eds. (Ln 3731–35, Lc 3713–17) would support FI and RI, both of which take the *when*-clause as depending on *brente* rather than on *seide*.

4065　**he:** *om.* MS, through eyeskip to *herd.*

4069　**closer:** enclosure (*MED clōsĕr(e* n. 1. [a]). This reading follows the Fr. *porpris* (Lc 3721 "enclosure"), which does not support GL's emendation, *roser.*

4070–71　"That is, 'Would that I might be buried alive, if any man,' &c" (BE). For *dolven* "buried," BE adduces *BD* 222.

4071　**ony:** See 212n.

4073　**a-fere:** "on fire" (SK FI RIg *MED fīr* 1b. [c]); "Kentish form of *A-fyre*, afire" (RBg). UR glosses inaccurately as "In fear, afraid," and TRg lists the phrase among those "not understood." Jephson's reading (BE), "my heart beats for anger," omits the phrase.

4074, 4077　**ony:** See 212n.

4081–84　KA notes the displacement of lines 4081–83 in comparison with the French; SU and FI transpose lines 4081–84 and renumber accordingly (4075–84 = SU FI 4081–84, 4075–80). "It is probable," states SU, "that they were misplaced by the reviser; cf. Fr. In this instance, no Fr. MS explains the misplacement, and it is impossible to adjust the Fr. text by moving a couplet." There are other problems of displacement; the entire passage from line 4075 to line 4090 is a free translation of the Fr. (Lc 3726–36). On the SU-FI shift, David (RIt) observes that "although 4081–83 thus fit the French sequence more closely, 4084, which corresponds to the end of Daunger's speech, is displaced by the shift"; David concludes that "the translator has not followed the loose logic of Daunger closely, and the MS should stand."

4087　**ony:** See 212n.

197

Holdeth me for recreaunte." 4090
 Thanne Daunger on his feet gan stonde,
And hente a burdoun in his honde.
Wroth in his ire, ne lefte he nought,
But thurgh the verger he hath sought.
If he myght fynde hole or trace, 4095
Wherethurgh that me mote forth-by pace,
Or ony gappe, he dide it close,
That no man myght touche a rose
Of the roser all aboute; 79v
He shitteth every man withoute. 4100
 Thus day by day Daunger is wers,
More wondirfull and more dyvers,
And feller eke than evere he was.
For hym full ofte I synge "Allas!"
For I ne may nought, thurgh his ire, 4105
Recovere that I moost desire.
Myne herte, allas, wole brest a-twoo,
For Bialacoil I wratthed soo.
For certeynly, in every membre
I qu[a]ke, whanne I me remembre 4110
Of the bot[oun], which I wolde
Full ofte a day sene and biholde.

And whanne I thenke upon the kisse,
And how mych joye and blisse
I hadde thurgh the savour swete, 4115
For wante of it I grone and grete.
Me thenkith I fele yit in my nose
The swete savour of the rose.
And now I woot that I mote goo
So fer the fresh floures froo, 4120
To me full welcome were the deth.
Absens therof, allas, me sleeth.
For whilom with this rose, allas, 80r
I touched nose, mouth, and face;
But now the deth I must abide. 4125
But Love consente another tyde
That onys I touche may and kisse,
I trowe my peyne shall never lisse.
Theron is all my coveitise,
Which brent myn herte in many wise. 4130
Now shal repaire agayn sighinge,
Long wacche on nyghtis, and no slepinge,
Thought in wisshing, torment and woo,
With many a turnyng to and froo,
That half my peyne I can not telle, 4135

4090 **Holdeth]** There h. UR 4096 **me]** men SK SU FI 4099 **the]** thilke MO 4110 **quake]** quoke MS BE-KA **whanne]** w. that UR **me]** *om.* TH² 4111 **which]** w. that UR SK 4114 **and blisse]** a. how much b. UR 4124 **mouth]** and m. UR

4092 **burdoun:** "a staff" (SPg URg TRg SKg₂), "burden" (URg), "cudgel" (SKg₂ GLg FI), "stick, club" (RIf). See 3401n.

4093 BE paraphrases—"'In his ire he did not cease to be wroth'"—and says that *wrath* "may imply the outward manifestation of rage (courroux), which does not necessarily accompany" *ire*. As parallel in the Fr., he cites the line "Semblant fit d'estre correcies" (= Lc 3738 "he put on the appearance of being enraged").

4096 **me:** "one" (SK GL RB *MED me* pron.[1]); "one (impersonal)" (RIf); "*me* miswritten for *men* [Sk.]" (KA). SK notes that "*me* sometimes occurs in M. E. as a shorter form of *men*, in the sense of 'one'; but it is better to read *men* at once, as it receives the accent. If written '*mē*,' it might easily be copied as 'me.'" RB does not emend but agrees that *men* "is perhaps more natural under the accent."

4097 **ony:** See 212n.

4111 **botoun:** See 1721n. As KA notes, the last two strokes of MS *bothom* are erased.

4114 **mych:** See 1713n.

4116 **grete:** "lament" (FI RIf). On the confusions between *grete* and *grede*, cf. the glosses of SPg et al. See *MED grēten* v.(3) "weep, cry, lament", *grēden* v. "cry out . . . shout, call out".

4117 Jephson (BE) contrasts this line with the Fr. (Lc 3759–60), where the sweet taste of the rose is enclosed in the heart rather than felt in the nose. Assuming Chaucerian authorship, he observes that "Chaucer has not rendered this passage with his usual happiness of expression."

4123–24 **allas : face:** RB notes the un-Chaucerian rhyme with silent *-e* in *face*.

4126 "Unless Love consent, at another time" (SK); as BE notes, *But* means "unless."

4135–40 The punctuation shown here is FI's ("so that I cannot tell half my pain, for I am fallen into hell from paradise and wealth. The more my torment grieves, [the] more and more the bitterness now annoys, that [because] I have felt sweetness before"). BE MO SK RB¹·² SU RI have a period after line 4135 ("so that I cannot tell half my pain."); GL FI have commas. For further punctuation, see 4136–38n.

198

For I am fallen into helle
From paradys and welthe. The more
My turment greveth, more and more
Anoieth now the bittirnesse,
That I toforn have felt swetnesse.   4140
And Wikkid-Tunge, thurgh his falshede,
Causeth all my woo and drede.
On me he leieth a pitous charge,
Bicause his tunge was to large.
    Now it is tyme, shortly, that I   4145
Telle you som thyng of Jelousie,
That was in gret suspecioun.   80v
Aboute hym lefte he no masoun
That stoon coude leye, ne querrour;
He hirede hem to make a tour.   4150
And first, the roses for to kepe,
Aboute hem made he a diche deepe,
Right wondir large, and also broode;

Upon the whiche also stode
Of squared stoon a sturdy wall,   4155
Which on a cragge was founded all,
And right grete thikkenesse eke it bare.
Aboute, it was founded square,
An hundred fademe on every side;
It was all liche longe and wide.   4160
Lest ony tyme it were assayled,
Ful wel aboute it was batayled,
And rounde enviroun eke were sette
Ful many a riche and faire tourette.
At every corner of this wall   4165
Was sette a tour full pryncipall;
And everich hadde, withoute fable,
A porte-colys defensable
To kepe of enemyes, and to greve,
That there her force wolde preve.   4170
And eke amydde this purprise   81r

4137 **welthe]** wel GL RB¹˒² RI   4142 **my]** me TH²   4143 **leieth]** lieth ST SP²-UR   4145 **it is]** is it
UR   4149 **ne]** n. no UR   4160 **all liche]** aliche GL   **longe]** both l. UR   4164 **tourette]** tournet TH³
ST SP²-UR   4170 **That]** And MO

4136–38 "That is, 'inasmuch as I am fallen into hell from paradise and wealth, so much the more my torment grieveth me'" (BE, with a semicolon after *greveth*). MO SK follow BE. GL RB¹˒² RI emend MS *welthe* to *wel* in line 4137; GL punctuates to read "For I am fallen into hell from paradise, and well the more my torment grieves more and more." RB¹˒² RI punctuate to read "For I am fallen into hell from paradise, and well the more my torment grieves; more and more . . .". See 4135–40n. for FI's punctuation.

4137–40 BE RB RI note that the "comparison between former happiness and present misery is not in the original" (BE). RB cites the parallels in *TC* 3.1625 ff., *Bo* 2p4, Dante *Inf.* 5.121 ff.; RI cites *TC* 3.1625–28n., where Barney (RI) gives additional references to Latin proverbs (Walther 1963–69: nos. 6534, 31586), to "Thomas Aquinas, Summa theol. 2–2.36.1," and to Augustine *Confessions* 10.14. See also Augustine *Confessions* 10.21.30.

4137 **welthe:** See 4136–38n.

4143 **leieth:** *lieth* may show *lie-lay* confusion. T. Thomas (URg) correctly interprets UR's *lieth* as *layeth.* Cf. 3880n.

4145–300 RB notes that "the English translation here shows a number of omissions and insertions, as compared with the Fr. ([Ln] 3797–936 [= Lc 3779–3908j])."

4148 **Aboute hym:** Brusendorff (1925:416) suggests *In londe,* on the basis of Fr. *Ou païs* (Lc 3782), and accounts for *Aboute hym* as eyeskip to line 4152 *Aboute hem.*

4149 **querrour:** SPg et al. identify as a stone-digger, stone-miner, stone-cutter, or quarry-worker; SK cites Cotgrave (1611), s.v. *quarrieur.*

4152 **he . . . diche:** "Possibly *he* is to be omitted. For *diche* cp. 4205" (GL).

4160 **all liche:** GL emends to *aliche* and suggests "(?) all aliche."

4161 **ony:** See 212n.

4162 **batayled:** "(walled with, made with, provided with) battlements" (SPg FI), "battlemented" (SKg, GLg RBg), "indented" (GLg), or "notched with (indentations, crenellations)" (RBg RIf); "embattled" (URg-MOg) has the same sense (*OED Embattled* ppl. a.²).

4164 **tourette:** The variant *tournet* may be a mixed form from *tourette* and *tournelle.* See *OED Turret,* sb.¹; *Tournelle* Obs. TRg notes that *Tournet* "should be written *Tourette,* as in MS. Hunter."

4166 **tour:** GL notes the discrepancy from the Fr. *portaus* (Lc 3805 "gates") and suggests "(?) *port* or some such word." Up to a point, however, the ME represents the Fr. correctly (Lc 3803 "au quatre coingnet en a .IIII." "there are four [turrets] at the four corners"); but it omits any mention of the gates at this point, with the result that the portcullises (line 4168) are associated not with the gates, as in the Fr. (Lc 3805–14), but with the turrets.

4171 **this purprise:** See 3987n.

Was maad a tour of gret maistrise;
A fairer saugh no man with sight,
Large and wide and of gret myght.
They dredde noon assaut   4175
Of gynne, gunne, nor skaffaut.
The temprure of the mortere
Was maad of lycour wonder dere:
Of quykke lyme, persant and egre,
The which was tempred with vynegre.   4180

The stoon was hard, of ademant,
Wherof they made the foundement.
The tour was rounde, maad in compas;
In all this world no riccher was,
Ne better ordeigned therwithall.   4185
Aboute the tour was maad a wall,
So that bitwixt that and the tour
Rose[r]s were sette of swete savour
With many roses that thei bere.

4174 **myght]** hyght SU FI   4175 **dredde]** d. nought UR; ne d. MO SK RB[1,2]   4176 **gunne nor]** or g. n. of UR   4177 **The]** For t. SK SU FI   4180 **The which was tempred]** Which temprid was UR   4181 **of]** as SK SU FI   4188 **Rosers]** Roses MS-KA FU

4172 **maistrise:** "masterly workmanship" (URg et al.), "strength, dominion" (SKg[2]), or "skill, expertise; magical art" (*MED maistrise* n. [c]), rather than simply "strength" (FI), a gloss which could imply a quality of the tower rather than of the builders. GL says that *maistrise* does "not seem to be an English word"; *MED* lists over 15 examples of the borrowing, starting ca. 1390.

4174 **myght:** SU's *hyght* follows the Fr. *haute* (Lc 3819 "tall"; noted in SU FI RIt).

4176 **gynne:** In general, "contrivance . . . engine" (URg et al.); here, "war-engine" (BE SK FI RIf; cf. RBg), "catapult" (FI RIf). Jephson (BE) notes that "there were several kinds, some called petrariæ, others mangonels," and in his note to *HF* 1934, he writes that "these engines, called by the ancients *ballistæ* and *catapultæ*, were constructed on the principle of a crossbow." Other kinds of *gynnes* are springolds (line 4191), arbalests (see 4196n.), and trepegets and mangonels (line 6279).

    gunne: Glosses, s.v. *gunne* or *gonne*: "gun" (URg et al.), "cannon" (RBg RIf). BE cites *HF* 1643–44 to show that gunnery, in the form of powder-impelled missiles, was known in Chaucer's time. Cf. 4191n.

    skaffaut: "an engin of warre" (SPg), "perhaps what is in Lat. called *Testudo*, A Scaffold or Fence made of boards, covered with raw hides, under which the Besiegers of Towns approached the Walls" (URg). BE explains it as "a kind of engine which was wheeled to the walls, and by means of which the soldier could fight on an equality with the besieged, or under cover of which they worked the battering ram"; SK RB RIf define it as "a shed on wheels" for the protection of besiegers (SK RB) or of the approach of a battering ram (RIf). TRg takes it for the other kind of scaffold, "a wooden tower," as does FI's gloss, "scaffold (for scaling walls)"; cf. *OED Scaffold* sb., sense 2 "a military engine for *assailing* a wall," and *MED scaffold* n. 3. "some kind of movable wooden structure used in siege warfare." SK refers to "the description of [a scaffold], called 'a sow,' employed at the siege of Berwick in 1319, in Barbour's Bruce, xvii. 597–600."

4177 **The:** KA suggests *For the* on the basis of Fr. *car* (Ln 3840 "for"; noted by SKt RBt SU FI RIt; Lc 3822 has *que* [Ln 3840t]).

    temprure: "tempering" (SKg[2] GLg RBg), "mixing" (SKg[2] RBg RIf); "tempering liquid" (*OED Temperure*); "the mixing of mortar with other materials for proper consistency" (*MED temperure* n. 5. [b]). Skeat apparently intended to have *temperure*, since he notes (SKt) the form *temprure* as a variant in MS and TH[1], but the emended form does not appear in the text.

4179 **persant and egre:** "sharp" and "active," notes FI, adding that "unslaked lime can burn badly."

    persant: "piercing" (URg et al.), "sharp" (SKg[2] RBg).

    egre: "sharp" (URg et al.), "biting" (BEg), "acid" (SKg[2] RBg).

4180 **vynegre:** Jephson (BE) speculates on the possibility that vinegar accounted for the superior hardness of the mortar in medieval churches and castles. Robinson (RB) writes: "Langlois cites [3840–41n.], for mediæval recipes for mortar, G. Anelier, Hist. de la Guerre de Navarre, ed. F. Michel in Collection de Documents Inédits sur l'Hist. de France, Paris, 1856. p. 602, n. In none of them," he notes, "is vinegar mentioned." FI (4178n.) notes that "vinegar is not a common additive."

4181–82 **ademant : foundement:** RB notes that the rhyme is imperfect.

4181 **of:** SK's *as* follows the suggestion of KA, who compares line 4385. SU FI cite Fr. *come* (Lc 3826 "as").

4188 **Rosers:** KA's suggestion follows the Fr. *li rosier* (Lc 3833 "the rosebushes"; noted in SKt RBt FI RIt).

And eke withynne the castell were   4190
Spryngoldes, gunnes, [bows, and] archers;
And eke above, atte corners,
Men seyn over the wall stonde
Grete engynes, who were nygh honde.   4194
And in the kernels, heere and there,   81v
Of arblasters grete plente were;
Noon armure myght her stroke withstonde;
It were foly to prece to honde.
Withoute the diche were lystes maade,

With wall batayled large and brade,   4200
For men and hors shulde not atteyne
To neighe the dyche over the pleyne.
      Thus Jelousie hath enviroun
Sette aboute his garnysoun
With walles rounde and diche depe   4205
Oonly the roser for to kepe.
And Daunger [bereth], erly and late,
The keyes of the utter gate,
The which openeth toward the eest.

4191 **bows and]** a. bow MS; a. b. MS₁ MO KA; b. BE SK   4192 **above]** about TH¹-UR FU   **atte]** at TH¹-SP³ FU SU FI   4194 **who]** which UR SK   **nygh honde]** nerehonde TH¹-UR FU SU FI   4200 **wall]** walles SK   **brade]** drade UR   4207 **bereth]** bothe UR MO; eek SK; bere GL; *om.* MS-SP³ BE KA FU-RI   4208 **keyes]** k. kepte TH¹-MO SK FU-RI   4209 **openeth]** opened TH⁵-UR

4190–98 BE quotes the parallel Fr. passage on the implements of war (Lc 3835–41): "Dedenz le chastel a perrieres / et engins de maintes manieres. / Vos peüsiez les mangoniaus / veoir par desus les creniaus, / et es archieres tot entor / sont les arbelestes a tor / qu'armeüre ne puet tenir" ("Within the castle were catapults and machines of many sorts. You could have seen the mangonels above the crenels, and at the apertures all around were screw-jack arbalests that no armor could withstand"). On the individual implements, see notes below.

4191 **Spryngoldes:** "warlike engines" (URg, citing Skinner 1671), "machines for casting stones and arrows" (TRg, citing Du Cange, s.v. *Muschetta*; cf. MOg SKg₂), "machines of war for casting stones" (BEg; cf. SK GLg), "catapults" (SKg₂ RB FI RIf); see 4176n. on *gynne.* BE SK RB note the Fr. parallel, *perrieres* (Lc 3835, above), which BE SK derive from Lat. *petrariae.* SK, following TRg, derives *springold* "from O.F. *espringale,* a catapult; from G. *springen,* to spring"; and notes the Northern spelling "*spryngaldis* in Barbour's *Bruce,* xvii. 247." SPg have the fanciful gloss, "yong men."

      gunnes: "machines for casting stones" (SKg₂). Cf. 4176n.

      bows: "*s* written above the line" (KA) by MS₁.

4192 **above:** In support of MS, SU and FI quote the Fr. *par desus* (Lc 3838, above).

4194 **who:** UR SK emend to *which* and take *engynes* as the antecedent. RB construes the (remote) antecedent as *men* (line 4193): "i. e., the men 'who might be close at hand' (?)." RIf notes that "the reference could be to the men or the engines." There is no true parallel in the Fr. (above).

4195 **kernels:** "corners, or holes in batilments" (SPg); "battlements" (URg et al.). SK adduces the Fr. parallel, *creniaus* (Lc 3838, above), as well as *Piers Plowman* C 8.235 [7.235], and B 5.597 [5.588].

4196 **arblasters:** "crossebowes" (SPg BEg MOg); "engines to cast darts, &c." (TRg MOg); "large crossbows" (FI). Skeat (SK) writes: "*arblasters* (answering to Lat. *arcuballistra*), a variant form of *arblasts* or *arbalests* (answering to Lat. *arcuballista*), huge cross-bows, for discharging missiles." But SKg₂, following URg ("Engineers, such as use *Arblasts*"), takes the word as the operator rather than the weapon: "men with cross-bows"; and GLg RBg RIf also gloss as "crossbowmen." The former definition belongs to *MED arblast, -blaster* n., the latter to *MED arblastēr, -rēr* n., where the distinction lies in the long *ē* of the final syllable. While the meter might favor the latter sense, "crossbow-men," the Fr. *arbelestes* (Lc 3840, above) favors the former. The arbalest is a specific kind of *gynne*; see 4176n.

4198 **to honde:** "close" (FI RIf), "(within range)" (RIf).

4199–200 **maade : brade:** "a Northern rime" (RB).

4200 **wall:** Following KA's suggestion, Skeat transcribes as *walles.* Although MS has *wall,* I do not in this case regard *-lles* as an appropriate expansion of the crossed *-ll,* since *wall* appears consistently for the singular throughout MS, often in rhyme with forms like *all, shall, withal.* See above, "The Manuscript Hands: The Scribe (MS₁)."

      brade: URg, s.v. *Drad,* defines UR's *drade* here as meaning "Dreadfull, terrible. . . . unless it should be. . . read, *brade.*"

.   4207 **bereth:** KA's emendation follows the Fr. *porte* (Lc 3851 "carries, bears"). GL inserts *bere* (subjunctive?) without comment.

4208 **keyes:** If, as Blodgett (1975:221) argues, TH¹ used MS as copy-text, his emendation *keyes kepte* has no greater authority than that of any other editor.

And he hadde with hym atte leest 4210
Thritty servauntes, echon by name.
  That other gate kepte Shame,
Which openede, as it was couth,
Toward the parte of the south.
Sergeauntes assigned were hir too 4215
Ful many, hir will for to doo.
  Thanne Drede hadde in hir baillie
The kepyng of the conestablerye
Toward the north, I undirstonde,
That openyde upon the lyfte honde; 4220
The which for nothyng may be sure,
But if she do bisy cure,
Erly on morowe and also late,
Strongly to shette and barre the gate.
Of every thing that she may see 4225
Drede is aferd, wher so she be;
For with a puff of litell wynde
Drede is astonyed in hir mynde.

Therfore, for stelyng of the rose, 4210
I rede hir nought the yate unclose. 4230
A foulis flight wole make hir flee,
And eke a shadowe, if she it see.
  Thanne Wikked-Tunge, full of envye,
With soudiours of Normandye, 82r
As he that causeth all the bate, 4235
Was keper of the fourthe gate;
And also to the tother three
He wente full ofte for to see.
Whanne his lotte was to wake anyght,
His instrumentis wolde he dight, 4240
For to blowe and make sowne
Ofte thanne he hath enchesoun,
And walken oft upon the wall, 82v
Corners and wikettis overall
Full narwe serchen and espie; 4245
Though he nought fonde, yit wol[d]e he lye.
Discordaunt ever fro armonye,

4210 **atte]** at TH¹-SP³ FU SU FI   4212 **kepte]** was kept by UR   4222 **bisy]** her b. UR MO SK
4231 **wole]** wolde TH³-BE   4235 **the bate]** debate TH³-UR   4239 **wake]** walke TH³-UR   4240 **he]** be
UR   4241 **make]** maketh SP¹   4242 **Ofte]** Ofter TH¹ TH³-UR MO SK FU SU FI; After TH²   4246 **wolde]**
wole MS KA GL

4218 **conestablerye:** "Apartment of the Constable or Governor of a Castle, The Keeper" (URg; cf. *MED constablerīe* n.), "ward (or division) of a castle" (TRg RB RIf). As Brusendorff (1925:342) and RB note, the Fr. has *conestablie* (Lc 3861 "troop").
4219–20 RI (4220n.) cites the Fr. (Lc 3863–64 "l'autre porte, qui est asise / a main senetre devers bise" "the other gate, which is situated on the left facing north") and notes that "the omission of 'gate' in the English spoils the sense."
4220 **lyfte:** SKt reports, inaccurately, that MS has *lyft.*
4229 **for stelyng of the rose:** "for fear that the rose should be stolen" (BE); "to prevent stealing" of the rose (SK RB FI RIf). As parallel, BE cites "Percy's ballad of Syr Cauline," in which "a lady is carried 'for fyling of her feet,' i.e., for fear her feet should be defiled." For further examples, see *MED for* prep., sense 8. (b).
4234 BE cites Méon's text (3899 "Qui ne pense fors a boidié" "who thinks only of treachery") and notes that Méon was aware that most MSS read "ot soudoiers de Normandie" (Lc 3872 "had Norman soldiers"), as in the ME. Méon's text is based on MS Za, the only one in Ln's collation that has that reading (Ln 3890t, 3891n.). § Jephson (BE) suggests that "the Norman soldiers, alternately subjects of France and England, were probably regarded by the French with all the virulence of hatred which distinguishes civil discord."
     soudiours: "mercenary soldiers" (RIf).
4235 RB reads "As being the one that causes all the strife" and compares line 3256.
     bate: "strife" (SKg₂ GL FI RIf). TH³'s variant shows the origin: "from *debāte*, prob. by taking *debāte* as *the bate*" (*MED bate* n.[1]).
4239 **lotte:** "turn (i.e., when he was officer of the day)" (FI).
4242 **Ofte:** TH¹'s *Ofter* (no parallel in the Fr.), makes *thanne* a conj. of comparison. MS *Ofte* raises the possibility that *thanne* is a conjunctive adv. of time (= "when"), an un-Chaucerian usage that, at this date, may contribute to the Northern character of Fragment B. See *OED Then* adv. 6.
4247–50 BE quotes the Fr. (from Méon 3908–10: "Une hore dit lés et descors, / Et sonnez dous de controvaille / As estives de Cornoaille" "at one time he played *lais* and *descorts* and composed sweet airs on Cornish pipes"). This text comes from MS Za; Lc 3880 has *chanz* "songs" for *lés,* and Ln 3899 has *sons noviaus* "original airs" for *sonnez douz.* For details of variants, see Ln's textual notes and Ln 3893n. For details of the ME, see the notes below.
4247–48 RB RI, following Brusendorff (1925:341) note that the word *discordaunt* comes from a misunderstanding of Fr. *descorz* (Lc 3880), a type of song; in fact, the entire two lines appear to be an expansion of the single word. According to Reese (1940:225–26), the *descors* was a form of *lai*; Reese defines the *lai* as "a secular piece

And distoned from melodie,
Controve he wolde, and foule fayle,
With hornepipes of Cornewaile.   4250
In floytes made he discordaunce,
And in his musyk, with myschaunce,
He wolde seyn, with notes newe,
That he fonde no womman trewe,
Ne that he saugh never in his lyf   4255
Unto hir husbonde a trewe wyf,
Ne noon so ful of honeste
That she nyl laughe and mery be
Whanne that she hereth, or may espie,
A man speken of leccherie.   4260

Everiche of hem hath somme vice;
Oon is dishonest, another is nyce;
If oon be full of vylanye,
Another hath a likerous ighe;
If oon be full of wantonesse,   4265
Another is a chideresse.
    Thus Wikked-Tunge—God yeve
        hem shame!—   83r
Can putt hem everychone in blame
Withoute [dissert] and causeles;
He lieth, though they ben giltles.   4270
I have pite to sene the sorwe
That [waketh] bothe eve and morwe,

4248 **distoned**] dissoned SP²-UR   4254 **fonde**] ne f. UR MO SK   4262 **another is**] t'othir UR
4269 **dissert**] disseit MS KA   4272 **waketh**] walketh MS-TH² MO KA FU

---

constructed on the plan of the ecclesiastical sequence" and the *descort* as one of "three ways in which a *lai* might deviate from the standard sequence." Reese reports a hypothesis that the discordance consisted in a rhythmic variation in the repetition of a series of notes. Fallows (1980:365) writes that "*descort* was the standard Provençal word for lai and was carried into Old French." The discordance, he says, may be in form—lais in general had a different form in each stanza (p. 364) and, in one case, a different language in each stanza—or in content, when the term *descort* may refer to "a poem whose subject matter is discordance, disagreement or most characteristically severe disappointment in love" (p. 365).

4248 **distoned:** "Dissonant" (SPg URg TRg, all s.v. *dissoned*; SKg₂); "disagreeing" (URg), "out of tune (with)" (SK RIf); "untuned" (FI); "deviating (from a tune)" (*MED distōned* ppl., quoting this passage as its sole example). SK quotes Cotgrave (1611): "'*Destonner*, to change or alter a tune, to take it higher or lower.'" See 4247–48n.

4249 **Controve:** "feign" (SP²·³g URg), "devise" (SPg URg), "invent" (URg TRg SKg₂); "compose (poetry, music)" (BE SK FI RIf).

foule fayle: "fail miserably (in his musical inventions)" (SK FI RIf). The phrase seems to be a further elaboration of the misunderstanding of Fr. *descors*; see 4247–48n.

fayle: "make mistakes" (GL RB). GL states that "it may be an error for *fall* (rhyming with Cornewall), in which case the meaning is to make mistakes in counterpoint," a suggestion that RB calls "unlikely."

4250 **hornepipes of Cornewaile:** FI, on the basis of SU's text, *estriuuenz de Cornouaille*, glosses as "Cornish horns" (see below). The form *estriuuenz* comes from SU Fr. 3900, but Ln (3900t) reports the reading of SU's base, MS Ri, as *estrumenz*; SU must have misread the five minims of *um* as *iuu*.

hornepipes: "pipes made of horn" (BE SK RB RIf). BE SK GL RB RI note the Fr. (Lc 3882, above), which has *estives* "pipes made of straw, straw pipes" (SK RB RI). BE cites Méon's gloss on *estives* ("trompettes") and notes that Warton (1774–81:I.369) had a text with *chalemaux* ("straw-pipes, reed-pipes"); "it seems not unlikely," states BE "that this was the reading of Chaucer's original, and that he wrote *corn*-pipes, which would be the proper translation of *chalemeaux*." Ln (3900t, 3893n.) places the *chalumiaus* reading in MSS Be Da Ra Za.

Cornewaile: "probably a town in Brittany" (RB RIf; cf. SK) "rather than Cornwall" (RIf; cf. SK). SK cites a note in Méon's edition (1814:3.300) which "suggests 'la ville de *Cornouaille*, aujourd'hui *Quimper-Corentin*, qui est en basse Bretagne.'" BE notes that Warton (1774–81:I.369) assumes the English Cornwall.

4254–66 GL states: "This seems to be the part of the Romaunce that Chaucer refers to in [*LGWP* G 431]." RB observes that "since the abuse of women is here ascribed to *Wikked Tunge*, it is not probable that the blame of Chaucer in *LGW Prol F*, 322 ff., *G*, 248 ff. rests especially on this passage."

4256 **Unto:** KA suggests *To*, but no ed. so emends.

4267 **hem:** "him." KA GL retain this MS form, but all other eds. respell as *him* (TH² BE *hym*), the usual form of the 3 sg. object masculine personal pron., noted by KA in UR-MO. See 2854n.

4269 **dissert:** TH¹'s emendation, in the form *deserte*, is noted in various spellings in UR BE MO by KA. OF has forms with and without -*e* (*MED desert* n.[1]). Jephson (BE) reports MS reading as *dissait*; it is *disseit*.

4272 **waketh:** TH³'s emendation, noted by KA in UR BE, is without any parallel in the Fr. GL RBt compare line 2682, where a similar emendation, *wakyng* for MS *walkyng*, has the support of the Fr. text.

To innocentis doith such grevaunce.
I pray God yeve hem evel chaunce,
That he ever so bisie is   4275
Of ony womman to seyn amys!
  Eke Jelousie God confounde,
That hath maad a tour so rounde,
And made aboute a garisoun
To sette Bealacoil in prisoun,   4280
The which is shette there in the tour,
Ful longe to holde there sojour,
There for to lyve in penaunce.
And for to do hym more grevaunce,
[Ther] hath ordeyned Jelousie   4285
An olde vekke for to espye

The maner of his governaunce;
The which devel, in hir enfaunce,
Hadde lerned of loves arte,
And of his pleyes toke hir parte;   4290
She was except in his servise.   83v
She knewe eche wrenche and every gise
Of love, and every wile;
It was [the] harder hir to gile.
Of Bealacoil she toke ay hede,   4295
That evere he lyveth in woo and drede.
He kepte hym koy and eke pryve,
Lest in hym she hadde see
Ony foly countenaunce,
For she knewe all the olde daunce.   4300

4273 **doith]** doe SP¹   4277 **God confounde]** may G. c. UR   4280 **To]** So BE MO   4283 **to]** *om.*
TH³ ST SP²·³   4285 **Ther]** Which MS-KA FU   4286 **espye]** spie SP³   4289 **of loves]** o. lovers SP¹; all o. l.
UR; muche o. l. SK   4291 **except]** expert SP¹ UR SK GL RB¹·² RI; so expert SU FI   4293 **wile]** secret w. UR;
loveres w. SK   4294 **the harder]** harder MS BE-KA; harde TH¹-SP³ FU SU FI; right harde UR   **gile]** begyle
TH¹-UR FU SU FI   4298 **in]** that i. UR   **hadde]** had h. TH³-SP¹   4299 **foly]** lite f. UR

4274 **hem:** See 4267n.; in this case, GL joins other eds. in emending to *hym.* KA notes *him* in UR MO.

4276 **ony:** See 212n.

4279 **garisoun:** Brusendorff (1925:342) notes that "French *garnison* [Lc 3897] is evidently taken to mean some sort of entrenchment"; RB also notes the "mistaken rendering of Fr. 'garnison'" (defense troop). Cf. *MED garisoun* n., sense (d), and *garnisoun* n., sense (a).

4285 **Ther:** SK's emendation, endorsed by KA, has no parallel in the Fr. BE notes the lack of antecedent for MS *Which* and suggests that "*Which* may mean . . . *what*" in the construction "'Which [*what*] an olde vekke hath Jelousie ordained!' &c." BE also adduces *KnT* A 2675 ("Which a miracle ther bifel anon"), but the constructions are not parallel.

4286–4300 RI notes that the character of the *vekke*, "greatly developed by Jean de Meun, becomes a prototype for the Wife of Bath." RB RI note that "with the description of La Vieille Langlois [Ln 3925–30n.] compares *Pamphilus*, ll. 281–82, 425" (RB); see Garbáty (1967:118,123). RI adds that "the figure has a long literary ancestry, including the bawd Dipsas in Ovid, *Amores* 1.8." Cf. Robertson (1962:199).

4286 **vekke:** "old woman" (SPg et al.), "old trot" (URg), "hag" (URg SKg₂ RIf), "as in l. 4495" (SK). URg SK compare Italian *vecchia*, but SK notes that "it is difficult to see how we came by the Ital. form"; *OED Vecke* suggests the possibility "that the word existed in OF. colloquial use."

4291 **except:** BE notes that "the printed editions [*sic* for SP¹ and UR] read *expert*, but *except* is probably right, meaning accepted." There is no parallel in the Fr., except in the general sense of the passage. GL states that MS *except,* "even in the sense of 'acceptable,' is not very clear"; and SK says that "*expert* . . . is clearly right; *except* gives no sense." However, *MED excepten* v. 4 supports the sense "accepted" with three examples (including this line) from the 15th century. The emendation is possible on paleographical grounds: *p-c* metathesis (except-expect) and *r-c* confusion. SK suggests that "*Expt,* with a stroke through the *p,* may have been read as *except.*"

4292 **wrenche:** "trick" (RIf), rather than "twist" (FI); cf. *OED Wrench* sb.¹, sb.². Early eds. provide support for RIf's definition, s.v. *wrenches:* "trappes" (SPg), "wiles or cunning sleights, snares, traps" (URg), "frauds, stratagems" (TRg). SKg₂ provides both senses for this line: "turn, trick."

4294 **the harder:** KA's suggested emendation.

4299 **ony:** See 212n.

4300 As BE SK note, the expression comes directly from the Fr. (Lc 3908j "qu'el set toute la vielle dance"). TR glosses *the olde daunce* as "the old game" and cites Cotgrave (1611) for the French formula. SK RB RI all cite the appearance of the phrase in the description of the Wife of Bath, *GP* 476, and RB RI note that the phrase became proverbial. "According to Langlois [3936n.], the expression has a general sense of 'to be cunning, shrewd' before it acquires its special application to the 'dance of lovers'" (RI). Hilary notes (RI *GP* 476n.) that "Chaucer was apparently the first to use it in English (Whiting [1968] L535), and he always applies it to matters of love or sex." RB (*GP* 476n.) cites *PhysT* C 79, *TC* 3.694–95; Hilary adds *HF* 639–40, *TC* 1.517, 2. 1106.

And aftir this, whanne Jelousie
Hadde Bealacoil in his baillie,
And shette hym up that was so fre,
For seure of hym he wolde be,
He trusteth sore in his castell; 4305
The stronge werk hym liketh well.
He dradde not that no glotouns
Shulde stele his roses or bot[oun]s;
The roses weren assured all,
Defenced with the stronge wall. 4310
Now Jelousie full wel may be
Of drede devoide in liberte,
Whether that he slepe or wake,
For of his roses may noon be take. 4314

But I, allas, now morne shall; 84r
Bicause I was withoute the wall,
Full moche doole and moone I made.
Who hadde wist what woo I hadde,
I trowe he wolde have had pite.

Love to deere hadde soolde to me 4320
The good that of his love hadde I.
I wente [ha bought] it all queyntly;
But now, thurgh doublyng of my peyne,
I see he wolde it selle ageyne,
And me a newe bargeyn leere, 4325
The which all-oute the more is deere,
For the solace that I have lorn,
Thanne I hadde it never aforn.
Certayn, I am ful like, in deede,
To hym that caste in erthe his seede, 4330
And hath joie of the newe spryng,
Whanne it greneth in the gynny[n]g,
And is also faire and fresh of flour,
Lusty to seen, swoote of odour;
But er he it in sheves shere, 4335
May falle a weder that shal it dere,
And make it to fade and falle,
The stalke, the greyne, and floures alle,

4313 **slepe]** or s. UR   4314 **For of]** For MO KA GL RI; Of UR   4318 **hadde]** so h. UR   4320 **to deere]** all t. d. UR   **to me]** me TH¹-UR FU SU FI   4322 **wente ha bought]** wente aboute MS-KA   4324 **I see]** If so FI   **wolde]** wol TH³-UR   4331 **spryng]** springing ST-UR   4332 **gynnyng]** gynnyg MS KA   4333 **also]** so UR   4335 **sheves]** his s. ST-SP³ BE MO   4336 **a]** om. UR

4305 **sore:** "extremely" (RIf). On *sore* as an intensifying adverb, RB RI refer to line 1031; see n. Here again, the Fr. is only loosely parallel (Lc 3913–14 "Son chastel qu'ele vit si fort / li a doné mout bon confort" "Her castle, which she saw was very strong, gave her great comfort"). *Jelousie*, grammatically feminine in the Fr., takes the masc. pronouns in the ME. See 3820n.

4307 **glotouns:** "gluttons (used as a general term of abuse)" (RIf).

4308 **botouns:** The imperfect rhyme of MS *bothoms* (: *glotouns*) gives warrant, as elsewhere, to the normalization. See 1721n., lines 3473, 4011.

4313–14 "We get the best rhythm by reading *wher* and stressing *For* in the next line. *roses* is often thus followed by an unaccented syllable" (GL).

4314 **of:** Apparently following KA's text, SKt mistakenly reports that MS omits *of*; cf. RIt, "*of his roses* Th Skt Rob Fsh."

4320–28 "In the complicated syntax of ll. 4320–28, the Lover is complaining that he had already paid too dearly for love, but now sees that Love would sell it to him again at double the price, i.e., double the pain for the solace he had lost" (FI).

4322 **wente ha bought:** "thought to have bought" (FI RIf). Emendation is made on three bases: KA's suggestion, "I wende a (= *have*) bought it all queyntly"; the Fr. (Lc 3926) "Jes cuidoie avoir achetez" "I thought that I had bought them [the benefits of Love]" (noted by SK GL RB FI RI); and MS's typical spelling of *bought* (see lines 237, 2739, 3222, 5048, 5235, 5906, 5922, 7373) and in particular "have bought" (line 5569). SK states that the "old reading gives no sense" and credits KA with the emendation which SK translates as "'I weened to have bought it very knowingly.'" GL states that KA's correction "is justified by the Fr. original"; SK GL cite line 4352. For the form *wente*, see *OED Ween* v. and cf. 3862n., 4352n., 4320–28n.

4328 Following Lounsbury's suggestion (1895:22), RB cites the Fr. (Lc 3930 "que s'onques ne l'eüse eue" "than if I had never had it"), noting that in the ME "there is an ellipsis of *if* after *Thanne*."

4332 **gynnyng:** TH's emendation; KA notes the change in MO.

4333 **also:** KA notes UR's *so*, and SK notes that perhaps one should "read *als*, or *so*."

4335–36 On the image of the storm that destroys the grain in the ear, RB notes that Langlois (Ln 3966n.) compares Ovid, *Met.* 1.269–73 and Virgil, *Georgics* 1.226.

That to the tylyer is fordone 84v
The hope that he hadde to soone. 4340
I drede, certeyn, that so fare I,
For hope and travaile sikerlye
Ben me byraft all with a storme;
The floure nel seeden of my corne.
For Love hath so avaunced me, 4345
Whanne I bigan my pryvite
To Bialacoil all for to telle,
Whom I ne fonde froward ne felle,
But toke a-gree all hool my play.
But Love is of so hard assay 4350
That all at oonys he reved me,
Whanne I wente best aboven to have be.
It is of Love, as of Fortune,
That chaungeth ofte, and nyl contune,

Which whilom wole on folk smyle 4355
And glowmbe on hem another while;
Now freend, now foo, [thou] shalt hir feele;
For a twynklyng turne hir wheele;
She can writhe hir heed awey;
This is the concours of hir pley. 4360
She canne ar[e]ise that doth morne,
And whirle adown, and overturne
Who sittith hieghst, but as hir lust. 85r
A foole is he that wole hir trust;
For it is I that am come down 4365
Thurgh [change] and revoluc[i]oun!
Sith Bealacoil mote fro me twynne,
Shette in the prisoun yonde withynne,
His absence at myn herte I fele;
For all my joye and all myne hele 4370

4339 **tylyer]** tylyers MS-SP³ BE-KA FU SU FI   4340 **that he hadde]** he had conceved UR
4348 **froward]** ne f. MO   4352 **to]** *om.* SK GL   4355 **on folk]** of f. ST-SP³; o. folkes GL   4357 **thou shalt]** shalt MS-SP³ BE KA FU; shaltow GL FI   4358 **For a]** F. in a SK GL RB¹-RI   **turne]** tourneth TH¹-UR SK FU-RI   4361 **areise]** arise MS BE-KA GL   4363 **but]** al SK   4365 **is]** am SK   4366 **change]** charge MS-UR MO KA FU   **revolucioun]** reuolucoun MS KA   4367 **me]** my TH²   4368 **the]** her ST-BE

4339 **tylyer:** "husbandman" (SKg₂), "tiller, farmer" (RIf). UR's emendation to singular (*tiller*) is noted by KA. RBt RIt cite the Fr. *vilain* (Lc 3941 "churl, rustic").

4352 **wente:** weened, thought, supposed (BE SK FI). SK calls attention to the Fr. *cuidai* (Lc 3952 "believed, thought"). KA suggests that we read *wende to*, and omit *to*, and compares line 4322. As at lines 4322 and 3862, eds. here respell *wente* as *wened* (UR), *wend* (SK), or *wende* (RB¹-RI). See 3862n., 4322n.

4353–63 RB RI call this passage a typical complaint against Fortune. RB cites *KnT* A 925–26; RI adds *BD* 618–49, *TC* 4.2–7, and compares Whiting (1968: L502).

4354 **contune:** "continue" (URg et al.). *MED continūen* v. notes that the form *contūnen* occurs "chiefly in rime" and that its "origin . . . is obscure." Cf. lines 5205, 5332; all three cases are in rhyme. TRg calls the form a licence for the sake of rhyme and notes its absence in *CT*, its presence in Lydgate; BE also calls the form "a violent poetical licence."

4356 **glowmbe:** "frowne" (SPg URg SKg₂), "look gloomy" (URg TRg), "look glum" (SKg₂). SK normalizes to *gloumbe*, see *MED gloumen* v.

4357 **thou:** UR's emendation; KA suggests the same change. BE notes that "*thou* is understood, and is probably omitted by mistake." GL's *shaltow* supplies the pronoun. FI reports MS reading, inaccurately, as *shalte*.

4358–59 "The reading *turne*," writes RB, "would have to be taken as a protasis in the subjunctive"; (presumably, "For in a twinkling, if her wheel turn, she can twist her head away"). Without emendation, the MS might be read as two main clauses, with *turne* as a subjunctive of possibility ("Her wheel may turn for a twinkling; she can twist her head away"). See 4358n.

4358 KA credits SK with the suggestion: "insert *in* before *a*." See 4358–59n.

4361 **areise:** TH¹'s emendation (*areyse*), is noted by KA.

4363–64 **lust : trust:** SK has *list : trist*. *List* is the usual Chaucerian form for the verb and the normal development from OE *lystan*; at line 3532, SK does not so emend.

4363 "Liddell [GL] prints the line as a rhetorical question" (RIt).

hieghst: SKt reports the reading of "Th." as *hyest*; this is the reading of TH³; TH¹,² have *hyghest*.

but: SK's *al*, which KA endorses, has no near parallel in the Fr. Cf. the phrase *quant ele veut* "when she wishes," a few lines earlier (Lc 3959).

4365 **is:** SK's *am* follows the suggestion of Lounsbury (1892:2.13), who sees *is* as a trace of modernization.

4366 **change:** URg KA both suggest this emendation, first adopted by BE.

revolucioun: KA notes this spelling in UR BE; I do not count the MS form as a variant.

Was in hym and in the rose,
That but yon w[a]l, which hym doth close,
Opene, that I may hym see,
Love nyl not that I cured be
Of the peynes that I endure, 4375
Nor of my cruel aventure.

A, Bialacoil, myn owne deere,
Though thou be now a prisonere,
Kepe atte leste thyne herte to me,
And suffre not that it daunted be, 4380
Ne late not Jelousie in his rage
Putten thine herte in no servage.
Although he chastice thee withoute,
And make thy body unto hym loute,
Have herte as hard as dyamaunt, 4385
Stedefast, and nought pliaunt.
In prisoun though thi body be, 85v
At large kepe thyne herte free;
A trewe herte wole not plie
For no manace that it may drye. 4390
If Jelousie doth thee payne,
Quyte hym his while thus agayne,

To venge thee, atte leest in thought,
If other way thou maist nought;
And in this wise sotilly 4395
Worche, and wynne the maistrie.
But yit I am in gret affray
Lest thou do not as I say;
I drede thou canst me gret maugre,
That thou enprisoned art for me. 4400
But that [is] not for my trespas,
For thurgh me never discovred was
Yit thyng that ought be secree.
Wel more anoy is in me
Than is in thee, of this myschaunce, 4405
For I endure more harde penaunce
Than ony can seyn or thynke,
That for the sorwe almost I synke.
Whanne I remembre me of my woo,
Full nygh out of my witt I goo. 4410
Inward myn herte I feele blede, 86r
For comfortles the deth I drede.
Owe I not wel to have distresse,
Whanne fals, thurgh hir wikkednesse,

4372 **yon wal**] yone wole MS KA; you wol TH¹-BE FU; thoue wole MO   4373 **I**] so I UR   4374 **nyl**] wol TH¹-SP³ FU SU FI   **not**] *om.* BE   4379 **Kepe**] Kepith UR   **atte**] at TH¹-UR FU SU FI   4380 **And suffre**] Suffir UR   4384 **unto**] to UR   4386 **and nought**] and stout, and naught UR   4388 **kepe**] kept SU FI   4389 **wole**] ne w. UR   4393 **atte**] at TH¹-UR FU SU FI   4395 **sotilly**] full s. UR   4396 **the**] thy BE   4398 **do not**] sholdest nat doe UR   4401 **that is not**] that not MS-SP³ BE-KA FU; yet right nought UR   4403 **Yit**] That GL   **be**] by TH²; to b. UR   4404 **is**] ther is SK   4407 **ony**] o. man UR SK GL *Out:* SP¹

4372   **yon wal:** SK's emendation, endorsed by KA. SK quotes the Fr. (Lc 3970 "qui est entre les murs enclose" "that is enclosed within the walls"; noted in SU FI).

4377–4432   BE (4432n.) states: "The sorrow and lamentation of l'Amant for the loss of Bialacoil are intended to represent the misery which the lover suffers, when deprived of the conversation of his mistress."

4377–88   BE suggests that "this passage will remind the reader of the beautiful verses in Percy's *Reliques*, entitled *Loyalty Confined*."

4389–90   BE SK RB call attention to the Latin proverb, quoted by Méon (4025n.): "Qui plus castigat, plus amore ligat" ("the more one chastises, the more he binds in love"). RI notes the proverbial nature of the ME and refers to Whiting (1968: H298).

4390   **drye:** "suffer" (SPg et al.), "endure" (URg GLg), "undergo" (SKg₂). Cf. 3105n.

4399   **canst me . . . maugre:** "Thou takest it unkindly of me" (URg); "bear me . . . ill will" (RIf). URg TRg BE note the Fr. original of the idiom (Lc 3999–4000 ". . . vos me savez / mau gré"). *Maugre* here is a substantive meaning "ill will" (URg SKg₂; cf. FI RIf). See also 7643n.

4401   **that is not:** SK's emendation, endorsed by KA.

4404   **is:** KA endorses SK's insertion of *ther* before *is.*

4407   **ony:** See 212n. KA notes UR's insertion of *man* after *ony.*

4411   **feele:** FI glosses as the adverb "greatly," rather than the verb "feel." Although there is no exact parallel in the Fr., the phrase *ai poor et desconfort* (Lc 4013 "I am frightened and troubled") favors the verbal sense "feel."

4413   **Owe:** "ought" (SKg₂ FI), a present form.

4414   **fals:** i.e., false persons (BE FI).

And traitours, that arn envyous,
To noyen me be so corious?
A, Bialacoil, full wel I see
That they hem shape to disceyve thee,
To make thee buxom to her lawe,
And with her corde thee to drawe   4420
Where so hem lust, right at her wille;
I drede they have thee brought thertille.
Withoute comfort, thought me sleeth;
This game wole brynge me to my deeth.
For if youre good wille I leese,   4425
I mote be deed; I may not chese.
And if that thou foryete me,
Myne herte shal nevere in likyng be,
Nor elleswhere fynde solace
If I be putt out of youre grace,   4430
As it shal never been, I hope;

4415   Thanne shulde I falle in wanhope.
     Allas, in wanhope? Nay, pardee!
For I wole never dispeired be.   4434
If hope me faile, thanne am I   86v
Ungracious and unworthy.
In hope I wole comforted be,
For Love, whanne he bitaught hir me,
Seide that Hope, whereso I goo,
Shulde ay be reles to my woo.   4440
But what and she my baalis beete,
And be to me curteis and sweete?
She is in nothyng full certeyne.
Lovers she putt in full gret peyne,
And makith hem with woo to deele.   4445
Hir faire biheeste disceyveth feele,
For she wole byhote, sikirly,
And failen aftir outrely.

4416 **corious]** coraious MS-SK FU-RB² RI   4423 **thought]** the t. BE   4424 **wole]** would ST-UR
4425 **youre good wille I]** I y. g. w. TH²; that I y. g. w. UR   *Heading before line* 4431: JEAN DE MEUN'S
CONTINUATION SU FI   4435 **thanne]** t. alle UR   4439 **Seide]** Says SU FI   4445 **with]** that MO

4416 **corious:** curious, "eager" (FI). KA's suggestion, *curious* follows the Fr. (Lc 4018 "sont de moi nuire curieus" "are eager to injure me"; noted in SU FI RIt); GL SU FI so emend. For the form adopted here, see *MED cūrious* adj.

4425 **good:** KA endorses "goode or gode [Sk]."

4429–33   These lines correspond roughly to the last two lines of Guillaume de Lorris's portion and the first line of Jean de Meun's, according to the division in the eds. of Ln (4057–58 / 4059) and Lc (4027–28 / 4029 "se je pert vostre bienveillance, / car je n'ai mes aillors fiance. / Et si l'ai je perdue, espoir" "if I lose your good will, for I have no trust elsewhere. And perhaps I have lost it"). Accordingly, SU FI identify the ME break with the heading "JEAN DE MEUN'S CONTINUATION" above line 4431. RB RI take line 4429 as corresponding to the last line of Guillaume's portion, but do not identify any correspondence between the ME and the first line of Jean's portion; as RI states, "the looseness of the translation . . . makes it difficult to fix the exact dividing point between Guillaume and Jean." BE and SK identify a different point of division between Guillaume and Jean, following the text of Méon, who places the division two lines later in the Fr., between Méon's 4069 and 4070 (=Lc 4030 / 4031 "a poi que ne m'en desespoir. / Desespoir! Las! je non feré" "I am ready to despair of it. Despair! Alas! I shall not do so"); BE and SK therefore place the division in the ME between lines 4432 and 4433, where the "wanhope . . . wanhope" echo follows the assumed "desespoir . . . desespoir" echo between Guillaume and Jean. BE notes that, for the location of the division in the Fr., Méon relies on a six-line rubric that "he justly . . . attributes to the later copyists"; BE quotes it as follows: "Cy endroit trespassa Guillaume / De Lorris, et n'en fist plus pseaulme; / Mais, aprés plus de quarante ans, / Maistre Jehan de Meung ce Romans / Parfist, ainsi comme je treuve; / Et ici commence son œuvre" ("At this point Guillaume de Lorris died and composed no more verse; but, after more than forty years, master Jean de Meung finished this Romance, as I find; and here his work begins"). Presumably this rubric comes from Méon's base, MS Za (Ln 1.46).

4429 **elleswhere:** MS has *ell where*. I treat -ll here as an abbreviation for -*lles*. KA notes MO's *elles*. See above, "The Manuscript Hands: The Scribe (MS₁)," and also 300n.

4441 **my baalis beete:** "remedy my misfortune" (BE), "(my) sorrows cure" (FI), "amend my sufferings" (RIf). See also URg SKg₂.

4443–45   On the uncertainty of hope, RB notes that Ln (4071n. = Lc 4041) adduces Ovid, *Epitres* 18.234 (= *Heroides* 17.234), as well as "the beginning, 'Spes fallax.' of the Elegia de Spe, Anthologia veterum Latinorum . . . Poematum, ed. Meyer, Leipzig, 1835, no. 932" (RB).

4444 **putt:** KA endorses SK's form *put* (contraction); it appears earlier in TH²-UR. Cf. line 4460.

4446–48   "Proverbial; Whiting [1968] H470" (RI).

A, that is a full noyous thyng!
For many a lover, in lovyng,   4450
Hangeth upon hir, and trusteth fast,
Whiche leese her travel at the last.
Of thyng to comen she woot right nought;
Therfore, if it be wysely sought,
Hir counseill foly is to take.   4455
For many tymes, whanne she wole make
A full good silogisme, I dreede
That aftirward ther shal in deede
Folwe an evell conclusioun.   87r
This putte me in confusioun;   4460
For many tymes I have it seen

That many have bigyled been
For trust that they have sette in Hope,
Which felle hem aftirward aslope.
    But nevertheles, yit gladly she wolde   4465
That he, that wole hym with hir holde,
Hadde all tymes [his] purpos clere,
Withoute deceyte or ony were;
That she desireth sikirly.
Whanne I hir blame[d], I dide foly.   4470
But what avayleth hir good wille,
Whanne she [ne] may staunche my
        stounde ille?
That helpith litel that she may doo,

4449 **a full]** fulle BE   4459 **evell]** ill UR   4465 **nevertheles]** nathelesse TH¹-UR SK FU SU FI
4467 **his]** her MS-UR KA FU   4468 **or ony were]** any where TH³ ST SP²-BE; or any where SP¹
4470 **blamed]** blame MS (MS₁ *corr.*)   4472 **ne]** no MS MO KA

4455   "The direct construction is, 'To take hir counseille is foly'" (BE).

4456–69   A somewhat confused passage. RI (4457–59n.) adduces Paré (1947:35–36), who analyzes the scholastic terminology in the Fr., early in Jean de Meun's continuation (Lc 4054–61): "car quant el [Esperance] fet bon sillogime, / si doit l'en avoir grant peeur / qu'el ne conclue le peeur, / qu'aucune foiz l'a l'en veü, / s'en ont maint esté deceü. / Et ne porquant si voudroit ele / que le meilleur de la querele / eüst cil qui la tient o soi" ("For when she [Hope] constructs a good syllogism, one must be in great fear lest she draw the worse conclusion; we have sometimes seen many who have been deceived by her. At the same time, she would want him who takes her side to have the better conclusion to the disputation"). Paré shows that *le peeur* "the worse" conclusion is one that is necessarily particular or negative; *le meilleur* "the better" conclusion would then be universal or affirmative. In support, he cites one of the laws of logic, the conclusion always follows the worse [i.e. more restricted] part; that is, says Paré, if one of the premises is negative or particular, the conclusion cannot be affirmative or universal (p. 35). In the text, Jean's Lover fears that Hope's conclusion will be negative—that he will not possess the rose (p. 36)—and thus "worse" for him; but then, he reasons, Hope may stick by a partisan and come to an affirmative, or "better" conclusion in the scholastic disputation—better in the sense that it would bring the realization of his hopes (p. 36).

Huppé (1948:334–35) finds that the translator (B) has produced an incomplete and inexact translation in three respects. Understandably, he neglects the *rime riche* play on *peeur* "fear" and *peeur* "worse." More importantly, he misses the technical significance of the phrase *conclue le peeur* (see above); "he contrasts the *good silogisme* with the *evell conclusion*, which may *in deede folwe*, that is, in actuality come to pass. Thus *evell conclusioun* simply retains the literal meaning of the French, that the event may be unpleasant for the lover" (p. 335). Finally, he has not only failed to translate the phrase *meilleur de la querele* but has changed its meaning.

The contrast with the quite exact handling of similar terms at lines 7465–72 (see note) would support the view that the translators of Fragments B and C are different.

4457–59   FI notes that "a scholastic syllogism has a major premise, a minor premise, and a conclusion," and cites the use of these terms as evidence of Jean de Meun's association with the University of Paris; RI also notes Jean's "university background" and cites Paré (1947). See 4456–69n., 7465–72n.

4457   **silogisme:** "read 'silogim'" (GL).

4460   **putte:** Again, as at line 4444, KA endorses SK's form *put* (contraction); it appears earlier in TH²-UR, and RB RI also normalize to *put.* Cf. 4486n.

4464   **aslope:** "contrary to expectation" (URg), "aside, awry" (SKg₂). BE and SK take the image to be that of a sloping, therefore insecure, surface; FI RIf gloss as "askew"; cf. *MED aslōp(e* adv., sense (a), where the idiom *fallen aslope* is defined as "go wrong, miscarry."

4467   **his purpos clere:** BE explains as "what he proposes or wishes, perfectly." RI quotes the Fr. (Lc 4060 "le meilleur de la querele" "the better of the argument"); but see 4456–69n.

        his: BE cites the Fr. masc. *cil* (Lc 4061 above) in support of the reading *his*, noted in BE MO by KA.

4468   **ony:** See 212n.

4470   **blamed:** "*d* written above the line" (KA) by MS₁.

4472   **stounde ille:** UR glosses *stounde* as "vicissitude or change, turn, hap"; and paraphrases the line: "She cannot stop or help my misfortune." Cf. "bad time" (FI), "evil time" (RIf). BE SK GL RBt SU RI all suggest that *stounde*

Outake biheest unto my woo.
And heeste certeyn, in no wise, 4475
Withoute yift, is not to [prise].
Whanne heest and deede asundry varie,
They doon a gret contrarie.
Thus am I possed up and doun
With dool, thought, and confusioun; 4480
Of my disese ther is no noumbre.
Daunger and Shame me encumbre,
Dre[de] also, and Jelousie, 87v
And Wikked-Tunge, full of envie,
Of whiche the sharpe and cruel ire 4485
Full ofte me putte in gret martire.
They han my joye fully lette,
Sith Bialacoil they have bishette
Fro me in prisoun wikkidly,
Whom I love so entierly 4490
That it wole my bane bee

But I the sonner may hym see.
And yit moreover, wurst of all,
Ther is sette to kepe—foule hir bifall—
A rympled vekke, ferre ronne in age, 4495
Frownyng and yelowe in hir visage,
Which in awayte lyth day and nyght,
That noon of hem may have a sight.
    Now mote my sorwe enforced be;
Full soth it is that Love yaf me 4500
Three wonder yiftes of his grace,
Whiche I have lorn now in this place,
Sith they ne may, withoute drede,
Helpen but lytel, who taketh heede.
For here availeth no Swete-Thought, 4505
And Sweete-Speche helpith right nought.
The thridde was called Swete-Lokyng, 88r
That now is lorn, without lesyng.
    Yiftes were faire, but not forthy

4474 **Outake]** Or take SP²,³   4476 **yift]** yfete TH³ ST SP²-UR   **prise]** preise MS-KA FU SU   4478 **doon]** d. me have SK RB¹-FI   4479 **possed]** posted SP²,³   4483 **Drede]** Dre MS KA   4495 **age]** rage TH¹-SP³ FU   4509 **Yiftes]** The y. SK

---

may be a mistake for *wounde*; SK suggests that the mistake "arose from repeating the *st* in *staunche*'; and BE SK quote the Fr. (Lc 4064 "puis qu'el ne me fet desdouloir" "since she doesn't relieve my suffering") which is only roughly parallel to *wounde*.

4474 **Outake biheest:** "except promise" (FI RIf).

4475–76 RB notes that this passage "sounds proverbial" and cites Ln (4097n.), who compares Huon de Méri, *Tornoiement Antecrist* 1662–63. RI also notes the proverbial quality and refers to Whiting (1968: H371).

4476 **yift:** "(tangible) gift" (FI). SPg URg used texts with TH's error, *yfete*, and thus err in the gloss, "effect."

  prise: SK's emendation, endorsed by KA, aids in rhyme but not necessarily in sense, since *MED preisen* v., 3. "value" overlaps the sense of *MED prisen* v.(1), sense (c) "to value . . . highly, . . . praise." The Fr. (Lc 4067 "Promesse sanz don ne *vaut* gueres" "promise without gift is worth little") confirms the sense. FI offers a less likely sense for *prise*: "take (accept)"; see *MED prisen* v. (2) "to seize (sth.), capture."

4478 **doon:** KA endorses SK's insertion of *me haue* after *doon*, which, while not strictly necessary for sense, does help meter and roughly follows the Fr. (Lc 4068 "Avoir me let tant de contreres" "She [Promesse] lets me have so many reverses"; noted in SKt RBt SU FI RI). But, as RI observes, "the translator seems to have turned [the Fr.] into a general observation about the harm done when promise and deed fail to accord."

4486 **putte:** KA endorses SK's form *put* (contraction); *put* appears earlier in TH² ST-UR, but RB RI do not, as at line 4460, adopt SK's form. Cf. 4460n.

4492 **the sonner may hym see:** For syntax, GL compares line 4515 [*sic* for 4514].

4493 **And yit moreover:** RB RI cite the Fr. *Enseurquetout* (Lc 4079 "above all, especially") and the notes to the same phrase in *KnT* A 2801, glossed there as "and still further"; note its correspondence to *Teseida* 10.3 "ed ancor"; and compare *Bo* 2p6.79 [RI], where the phrase translates *ad haec*.

4494 **Ther is:** "one syllable" (GL).

4495 **ronne in age:** "advanced in age" (RB RIf). RB RI compare *NPT* B² 4011 "stape in age," literally "stepped" in age; see their note to *NPT* VII 2821.

4498 **hem:** "him" (i.e., Bialacoil). SP²-UR GL RB RI respell as *him* or *hym*, the usual form of the 3 sg. object masculine personal pron.; only RIt calls attention to the basis in the Fr. (Lc 4082 "qu'il n'ose nullui regarder" "That he dares see no one"). See 2854n.

4499 **enforced:** RB RI note the literal adaptation of Fr. *enforcera* (Lc 4083 "will strengthen," "will increase"). Eds. gloss variously as "increased in force" (BE), "made stronger, i.e. increased" (SK RIf), "enhanced" (RB), "reinforced" (FI).

4509 **Yiftes:** KA endorses SK's reading, *The yiftes*.

They helpe me but symply,   4510
But Bialacoil loosed be,
To gon at large and to be free.
For hym my lyf lyth all in doute,
But if he come the rather oute.
Allas, I trowe it wole not bene,   4515
For how shult I evermore hym sene?
He may not oute, and that is wronge,
Bycause the tour is so stronge.
How shulde he oute? By whos prowesse,
Oute of so stronge a forteresse?   4520
By me, certeyn, it nyl be doo;
God woot, I have no witte therto!
But wel I woot I was in rage,
Whonne I to Love dide homage.
Who was in cause, in sothfastnesse,   4525
But hirsilf, Dame Idelnesse,
Which me conveied, thurgh [my] praiere,

To entre into that faire verger?
She was to blame me to leve,
The which now doth me soore greve.   4530
A foolis word is nought to trowe,   88v
Ne worth an appel for to lowe;
Men shulde hym snybbe bittirly,
At pryme temps of his foly.
I was a fool, and she me leevede,   4535
Thurgh whom I am right nought releeved;
Sheo accomplisshid all my wille,
That now me greveth wondir ille.
Resoun me seide what shulde falle.
A fool mysilf I may well calle,   4540
That love [asyde] I hadde [not] leyde
And trowed that Dame Resoun seide.
Resoun hadde bothe skile and ryght,
Whanne she me blamed with all hir myght
To medle of love, that hath me shent;   4545

4511 **loosed]** may l. SK   4519 **By]** or b. TH¹-UR FU SU FI   4520 **Oute of]** Of TH¹-SP³ FU SU FI
4524 **homage]** my h. UR   4525 **in cause]** the c. TH³-UR GL   4527 **my]** faire MS-SK FU   4532 **lowe]**
love GL   4540 **I may well]** I m. w. I m. w. MS KA   4541 **asyde I hadde not]** assayde I h. MS KA

4510   RI notes the Fr. (Lc 4092 "il ne me vaudront riens ja mes" "they will never be worth anything to me").
   symply: KA endorses SK's suggestion *simpilly*, the form UR has. Although Skeat (SK) does not emend,
he observes that the form is Northern, "occuring in Barbour's Bruce, i. 331, xvii. 134," and compares line 3861. GL
has the more historical *symplely*, here and in line 3861. Cf. 3861n.
   4511   **Bialacoil loosed:** KA endorses SK's insertion of *may* before *loosed.* GL suggests: "(?) Add *all* after
Bialacoil."
   4514   **rather:** "quicker" (URg), "sooner" (URg BE SKg₂ FI); "the comparative degree of *rathe*, soon, early"
(BE).
   4516   **shult:** = *shuld.* For pa. t. 3 sg. (but not 1 sg.) forms in *-te*, see *OED Shall* v.
   4520   **Oute:** SU FI inaccurately attribute the form *Out*, without *-e*, to MS.
   4525   **in cause:** "in blame" (BE), "to blame" (SK). SK compares line 4529.
   4527   **my:** GL RB RIt note that MS *faire* comes from the next line; GL RBt SU FI RIt cite the Fr. *ma* (Lc 4106).
   4532   **lowe:** "praise" (URg), "value" (FI). BE notes that "*lowe* appears to be written for *allowe*, approve." SK
reads "*for to lowe*, to appraise; hence, to be valued at"; refers to *OED Allow*; and quotes the Fr. (Lc 4110 "de la value
d'une pome" "for the value of an apple"). GL emends to *love*, in the same sense, noting that "medial *v* and *w* were
sometimes rhymed together in Northern poems," and comparing line 4709 "wode," where MS has *vode*, TH¹ *voyde*,
see 4709n. RB, following SK, reads "appraise" and quotes the Fr. For *lowe* as a "shortened form of *allowen*," see
MED louen v.(4), which quotes this passage under sense (c) "to esteem . . . value" and notes that this verb is "often
hard to distinguish from *loven* v.(2)" (from OE *lofian* "praise"), the verb to which GL refers.
   4534   **pryme temps:** "first beginning" (SKg₂), "at first" (RIf), "first time" (FI), but not "springtime" (FI), as at
line 4747. See also 3373n.
   4537   **Sheo:** TH¹-UR SK-RI respell as *She*. Jephson (BE) suggests that the origin of the form was OE *heo* "she,"
3 sg. nom. fem. personal pronoun. Skeat (1878c:4.154) identifies it as "a Northern form" and gives the origin as OE
seo, 3 sg. nom. fem. demonstrative pronoun; *OED She* favors this view. *MED shē* pron. (citing *LALME* 4.7–8) returns
to Jephson's idea and gives the origin as "prob. from OE *hīo*, (A) *hīu*, (Merc.) *hīe*, (Nhb.) *hīæ*, vars. of *hēo*, with LOE
stress shift in the diphthongs." *LALME* 4.7 locates the form *sheo* in SW and SWM; cf. *LALME* 1.307–09; 2.9–14. See
Brunner (1963:59), Mossé (1968:56–57), Jones (1972:127–30). Cf. 5051n.
   4541   **asyde I hadde not:** TH¹'s emendation, noted by KA, follows the Fr. (Lc 4119 "quant des lors d'amer ne
recrui" "when from that time I did not renounce love") and improves meter as well as sense.

But certeyn now I wole repente.
   And shulde I repente? Nay, parde!
A fals traitour thanne shulde I be.
The develles engynnes wolde me take
If I my [lorde] wolde forsake,   4550
Or Bialacoil falsly bitraye.
Shulde I at myscheef hate hym? Nay,
Sith he now, for his curtesie,
Is in prisoun of Jelousie.   4554
Curtesie certeyn dide he me,   89r
So mych that may not yolden be,
Whanne he the hay passen me lete,
To kisse the rose, faire and swete.
Shulde I therfore cunne hym mawgre?
Nay, certeynly, it shal not be;   4560

For Love shall nevere, [yef God] wille,
Here of me, thurgh word or wille,
Offence or complaynt, more or lesse,
Neither of Hope nor Idilnesse.
For certis, it were wrong that I   4565
Hated hem for her curtesie.
Ther is not ellys but suffre and thenke,
And waken whanne I shulde wynke,
Abide in hope, til Love, thurgh chaunce,
Sende me socour or allegeaunce,   4570
Expectant ay till I may mete
To geten mercy of that swete.
   Whilom I thenke how Love to me
Seide he wolde take att gree
My servise, if unpacience   4575

4550 **If]** I. evir UR   **my lorde]** m. loue MS-TH³ SP¹ BE-KA FU; love ST SP²-UR   4554 **Jelousie]** Telousie MO   4556 **that]** t. it TH¹-SP³ BE FU SU FI; it UR SK   4561 **yef God]** yeve good MS-SP¹ BE-KA FU; yeue G. SP²·³; save gode UR   4562 **thurgh]** ne t. UR   4574 **he]** that he UR   **att]** atte BE MO SK

4546 **certeyn:** Brusendorff (1925:310) takes this word as parallel to the Fr. *Par foi* in the var. of the L family (Ln 4154t "Par foi je m'en vueil repentir" "Indeed I shall repent"). SU Fr. has the standard reading, from Ri (= Lc 4124 "Je m'en veill, ce croi, repentir").

4547–48 Diekstra (1981:224) notes the relevance of this passage to the ambiguous concept of "shryfte wythoute repentaunce," *BD* 1114. Cf. lines 4608–09.

4549 **develles engynnes:** "the contrivances of the devil" (SK), rather than "the *ingenium*, or mind proper to" the devil (BE), although BE's etymology is appropriate; see *MED* en*ğ̄in* n., senses 1. (a-b), 2. (b).

    develles: Rlt reports MS as *devell*; it is *devell*, which I take as an abbreviation for *develles*; see above, "The Manuscript Hands: The Scribe (MS₁)." § BE cites the Fr. *Maufez* (Lc 4127) and quotes—from Lantin de Damerey (1799:5.255–56)—a note on this term in Du Cange's *Observations sur l'Histoire de S. Louis*; the term arose from *mauffez* "evil do(er)" and served as a euphemism for "diable," a word which, according to Du Cange, people avoided. BE notes that the word *Maufez* as a term for "devil" did not penetrate into England and that Chaucer, Langland, and their contemporaries did not hesitate to use the word *devil*.

4550 **lorde:** KA's suggested emendation; in support, RBt Rlt note the Fr. *mon seigneur* (Lc 4128).

4556 **that:** KA endorses *it* in SK.

    yolden: "yeelded" (SPg), "paid" (URg), "repaid" (TRg); "requited" (URg BE SK); "returned" (FI). SK compares *SumT* D 2177. BE notes the phrase "God yield" as common in Shakespeare "in the mouths of the clowns and peasants" (*OED* Yield v., sense 7, dates it ca. 1400–1600). *OED* also notes that "this verb has had a remarkable sense-development in English owing to its having been used as an equivalent of L. *reddere* and F. *rendre.*"

4557 **lete:** SKt notes that *lete* = *leet*.

4559 **cunne hym mawgre:** "take it ill of him" (URg), "to be displeased" (TRg, s.v. *conne*), but "show him ill will" (SK FI), "show him spite, ingratitude" (RIf). URg, s.v. *Maugre*; TRg, s.v. *Conne*; and RB RI note the Fr. idiom, *mau gré savoir* (Lc 4137), of which the ME is a translation; RB RI also compare *KnT* A 1808 ("kan hem . . . thank") "for a similar use of *cunne*" (RI).

4561 **yef God:** KA's suggested emendation, anticipated perhaps by *yeue God* in SP²·³. BE, with *yeve Good* in the text, notes the sense as "if God." In support, SKt RBt FI Rlt note the Fr. (Lc 4139 "se Dieu plest").

4562 **of me:** Brusendorff (1925:311) notes that this phrase corresponds to the Fr. var. *de moi*, of the K family, where the standard text has *de lui* (Lc 4140 "of him"); SU Fr. 4170 takes the reading *de moi* from MS Ke. Ln 4170t does not show this var.

4568 "lie awake at night" (BE), "lie awake when I ought to sleep" (SK).

    wynke: "close the eyes (in sleep)" (RB). RB compares *NPT* B² 4621.

4571 **expectant:** TRg notes that the form is that of a Fr. present part. with the sense "waiting." It translates the Fr. *Atendre* (Lc 4149).

4574 **att gree:** "with favour" (BE SK FI; cf. URg).

[Ne] caused me to done offence.
He seide, "In thank I shal it take,
And high maister eke thee make,
If wikkednesse ne reve it thee;   89v
But sone, I trowe, that shall not be." 4580
These were his wordis, by and by;
It semede he lovede me trewly.
Now is ther not but serve hym wele,
If that I thenke his thanke to fele.
My good, myne harme, lyth hool in me; 4585
In Love may no defaute be.
For trewe Love ne failide never man;
Sothly, the faute mote nedys than—
As God forbede—be founde in me,
And how it cometh, I can not see. 4590
Now late it goon as it may goo;
Whether Love wole socoure me or sloo,
He may do hool on me his wille.
I am so sore bounde hym tille,
From his servise I may not fleen; 4595
For lyf and deth, withouten wene,

Is in his hande; I may not chese;
He may me doo bothe wynne and leese.
And sith so sore he doth me greve,
Yit if my lust he wolde acheve, 4600
To Bialacoil goodly to be,
I yeve no force what felle on me.
For though I dye, as I mote nede, 90r
I praye Love, of his goodlyhede,
To Bialacoil do gentylnesse, 4605
For whom I lyve in such distresse
That I mote deyen for penaunce.
But first, withoute repentaunce,
I wole me confesse in good entent
And make in haste my testament, 4610
As lovers doon that feelen smerte:
To Bialacoil leve I myne herte
All hool, withoute departyng,
Doublenesse of repentyng.
  Coment Raisoun vient a lamant
Thus as I made my passage 4615
In compleynt and in cruel rage,

4576 **Ne]** *om.* MS-SU 4614 **Doublenesse]** Or d. TH¹-MO SK-FI **of]** or UR *Rubric:* **Coment Raison vient a lamant]** *Out:* GL

4575–76 RI notes that the passage is not in the Fr., states that FI's insertion of *Ne* before *caused* "seems essential to the sense," and compares lines 2117, 4579, where the negative appears in both ME and Fr. (Lc 2025, 4153).

4576 **Ne:** FI's emendation. See 4575–76n.

4577–80 RI compares lines 2115–18 and notes that (in the original) "Jean de Meun is quoting Guillaume."

4580 **But sone, I trowe, that:** GL's punctuation ("But, sone, I trowe that . . .") may suggest reading *sone* as "son," a noun of address, rather than as the adverb "soon"; the latter reading follows the Fr. (Lc 4154 "'Mes, espoir, ce n'iert mie tost'" "But, perhaps, that will not be soon").

4581 **by and by:** BE, quoting the Fr. *mot à mot* (Lc 4155 "word for word"), offers "one after another, word by word." On the basis of the *Promptorium Parvulorum*, TR glosses the phrase as *Sigillatim*, "i.e. 'Severally, distinctly.'" See *MED bi and bi*, phrase, sense (c).

4587 "Proverbial; Whiting [1968] L556" (RI).

 ne: KA endorses as Skeat's suggestion the omission of *ne*, but no ed. so emends; SKt only queries the suggestion: "*Om. ne?*"

4592 **Whether:** "Read *Wher*" (GL). UR respells as *Wher*.

4608–09 Cf. 4547–48n.

4612–14 RI quotes the Fr. (Lc 4189–90 "au departir mon queur li les, / ja ne seront autre mi les" "at my death I leave him my heart. I shall make no other legacy"); and notes as follows: "At 4614, Thynne and editors read 'Or doublenesse,' perhaps correctly. The translator seems to have taken Fr. 'departir' (referring to the lover's death) in the sense of 'division (of the heart).' Possibly his original read 'Sans departir,' though no such variant survives. *Doublenesse of repentyng* is then in apposition with *departyng*: repenting of love is a falsehood or division of the heart. The passage echoes 2361–68."

4614 **Doublenesse:** KA notes *Or doublenesse* in TH¹ UR BE MO; see 4612–14n.

Rubric: "How Reason comes to the Lover" (RIf); SKt SU FI note the presence of the rubric in both MS and TH¹. In our text, italics show the presence in MS of these headings in red ink. They occur from lines 4614 to 5201, on fols. 90r to 102v, and are used principally for speech-headings in the dialogue between Reason and the Lover; written in

And I not where to fynde a leche
That couthe unto myne helpyng eche,
Sodeynly agayn comen doun
Out of hir tour I saugh Resoun, 4620
Discrete and wijs and full plesaunt,
And of hir porte full avenaunt.
The right weye she tooke to me,
Which stode in gret perplexite, 4624
That was posshed in every side, 90v
That I nyst where I myght abide,
Till she, demurely sad of chere,
Seide to me, as she come nere,
"Myne owne freend, art thou yit greved?
How is this quarell yit acheved 4630
Of Loves side? Anoon me telle.
Hast thou not yit of love thi fille?
Art thou not wery of thy servise,
That the hath [greved] in sich wise?
What joye hast thou in thy lovyng? 4635
Is it swete or bitter thyng?
Canst thou yit chese, late me see,

What best thi socour myght be?
"Thou servest a full noble lorde,
That maketh thee thrall for thi rewarde, 4640
Which ay renewith thy turment,
With foly so he hath thee blent.
Thou fell in my[s]cheef thilke day
Whanne thou didist, the sothe to say,
Obeysaunce and eke homage; 4645
Thou wroughtest nothyng as the sage.
Whanne thou bicam his liege man,
Thou didist a gret foly than;
Thou wistest not what fell therto, 91r
With what lord thou haddist to do. 4650
If thou haddist hym wel knowe,
Thou haddist nought be brought so lowe;
For if thou wistest what it were,
Thou noldist serve hym half a yeer,
Not a weke, nor half a day, 4655
Ne yit an hour, withoute delay,
Ne never [ilovede] paramours,
His lordshipp is so full of shoures.

4629 **yit**] *om.* TH¹-UR FU   **greved**] agreved UR   4631 **me telle**] t. m. TH¹-SP¹ FU   4634 **greved**] pyned SK FI; *om.* MS-SP³ BE-KA GL FU   4636 **swete**] a s. UR   4641 **renewith**] returneth TH²   **thy**] thy thi MS KA   4643 **myscheef**] mycheef MS KA   4645 **Obeysaunce and eke**] To him o. a. UR   4651 **If**] I. that UR   4653 **if**] i. that UR   4654 **noldist**] woldest TH²   4655 **Not**] No n. UR   4657 **ilovede**] I lovede MS-SP¹ UR KA FU; han loved SK GL RI

French, they follow a common tradition of the MSS of the Fr. *Roman.* § BE notes that "in Méon's edition [4231–32] the following short argument is here inserted: "Cy est la très-belle Raison, / Qui est preste en toute saison / De donner bon conseil à ceulx / Qui d'eulx saulver sont paresceux" ("Here is Reason, the very beautiful, who is ready at all times to give good counsel to those who are slow to save themselves"). Presumably it comes from MS Za (Ln 1.46).

4617 **not:** SK glosses as "know not" (pres. t.), suggests that the pa. t., "*nist*, would suit better," and compares line 4626; RBt agrees ("perhaps to be emended to *niste*"), but no ed. so emends.

4618 **eche:** "eke" (URg SK GLg), "add" (URg TRg), "contribute" (URg), "assist" (SK), "help, aid" (SKg₂ RI).

4621 **wijs:** See 2295n.

4634 **greved:** In support of the emendation, *pyned* "punished," SK quotes the Fr. (Lc 4202 "N'as tu pas eü mal assez?" "Haven't you had enough suffering?"), but UR's *grevid*—noted by KA—serves as well; RIt compares line 4530 "greve" and line 4538 "greveth." GL suggests "some word like *harmed* after *hath*." As RBt notes, "some such word appears necessary." The unemended MS reading, while remotely possible, is metrically deficient.

4639 **noble:** See 4668n.

4646 "'Thou didst act not at all like a wise man'" (SK).

4657 **ilovede:** This adaptation of MS *I lovede* follows SP²'s (inadvertent?) setting, which was repeated in SP³ BE MO and (respelled *yloved*) in RB¹-FI. SU prints "[y] loued" but indicates (p. 165) an intended agreement with RB. KA endorses SK's emendation, *han loved* (cf. GL and RI), a reading perhaps closer to the Fr. (Lc 4222 "ne ja mes par amor n'amasses" "you would never have loved *par amour*") than is SP²'s *iloued;* but the latter presents a clearer paleographical case.

4658 "Reason says that the service of love is as liable to reverses, as a fine day is to be obscured with showers" (BE).

lordshipp: "kingdom" (BE)

shoures: "hardships (literally, showers, storms, or battles)" (RIf). For the latter sense, URg, s.v. *Stoure,* suggests that "perhaps *shoures . . .* should be *stoures,*" i.e. skirmishes, battles.

Knowest hym ought?"
   Lamaunt. "Yhe, Dame, parde!"   4659
   Raisoun. "Nay, nay."
   Lamaunt. "Yhis, I."
   Raisoun. "Wherof? Late se."   4660
   Lamaunt. "Of that he seide I shulde be
Glad to have sich lord as he,
And maister of sich seignorie."   4663
   Raisoun. "Knowist hym no more?"
   Lamaunt. "Nay, certis, I,
Save that he yaf me rewles there,   4665
And wente his wey, I nyste where,
And I aboode, bounde in balaunce."
   Raisoun. "Lo, there a noble conisaunce!
But I wille that thou knowe hym now,
Gynnyng and eende, sith that thou   4670
Art so anguisshous and mate,   91v

Di[s]figured oute of [astate];
Ther may no wrecche have more of woo,
Ne caityfe noon enduren soo.
It were to every man sittyng   4675
Of his lord have knowleching;
For if thou knewe hym, oute of doute,
Lightly thou shulde escapen oute
Of the prisoun that marreth thee."
   Lamant. "Yhe, dame, [sith]
     my lord is he,   4680
And I his man, maad with myn honde,
I wolde right fayne undirstonde
To knowe of what kynde he be,
If ony wolde enforme me."   4684
   Raisoun. "I wolde," seide Resoun,
    "thee lere,
Sith thou to lerne hast sich desire,

4660 **Wherof]** Wherfore TH¹-UR FU SU FI   4662 **lord]** a l. UR   4665 **Save]** Saie ST SP¹   **he]** ye TH²   4671 **mate]** so m. UR   4672 **Disfigured]** Diffigured MS MO KA   **astate]** a state MS KA   4674 **caityfe]** cautyfe TH²   4676 **have]** to h. UR   4678 **escapen]** scapen TH³-UR   4679 **the]** thy TH¹-UR FU SU FI   4680 **Yhe]** He SP¹   **sith]** *om.* MS (MS₁ *corr.*)   4683 **be]** by MO

4659–64   KA provides these lines as they appear in MS, showing its odd disposition of rubrics.

4659–60   **Yhe . . . Yhis:** MS consistently (13 times) spells these two words with *-h-*; one exception is at line 2883 *Yee*. Here and elsewhere, eds. except BE-KA respell without *-h-*. *OED Yea* adv. lists the forms with *-h-* as 14th–15th century (ʒhe) and 15th century (yhe).

4659   As SKt SU note, the line ends with *parde*. SKt notes that MO misnumbers this line as 4660; see above, "Descriptions of the Printed Editions" for a schedule of the misnumberings in MO.

4660   *Raisoun.* **"Nay, nay.":** In MS, the rubric appears at the end of the previous line.

4661   **Of that:** "on the basis of what" (FI); perhaps rather "on the basis that, in that."

4664   *Raisoun:* In MS, the rubric appears at the end of the previous line.

    Nay, certis, I: BE cites the Fr. *Je non* (Lc 4228) and notes that "the *I*, and six lines before, is emphatic."

4667   Misnumbered 4670 in MO (SKt); see above, "Descriptions of the Printed Editions."

4668   *Raisoun:* As KA notes, the rubric appears at the end of the line in MS. TH¹, using MS as copy-text, assumed from other positions of the rubric (see 4660n., 4664n., 4685n.) that this one belonged with the following line, 4669, instead of at line 4668; as SU notes, TH¹ so placed it, and the error persisted through TH²-UR FU.

    noble: BE notes the irony and the lack of it in the Fr. *povre* (Lc 4232 "Certes, c'est povre connoissance" "Certainly, it's a poor acquaintance"). SK also notes the irony, here and at line 4639.

4674   **caityfe:** KA mistranscribes as *caytyfe*, the form found in TH¹ and most other editions.

4680   *Lamant:* As KA notes, the rubric appears at the end of the previous line in MS.

    Yhe: See 4659–60n.

    sith: "written above the line" (KA) by MS₁.

4681   On "the ceremony of doing homage, in which the man put his hands between those of his lord," BE quotes a description from "Fauchet, *Des fiefs, selon l'usage du Châtelet de Paris.*" SK RB compare line 2037; see 2037n.

4684   **ony:** See 212n.

4685–4784   The introduction to and the oxymoronic description of love come, as RB Lc (4249–4328n.) RI note, from the character Nature in Alanus de Insulis, *De planctu naturae* (see *PL* 210:455–56). Ln (4279–358n.) prints the text from *PL*.

4685   *Raisoun:* In MS, the rubric appears at the end of the previous line.

And shewe thee, withouten fable,
A thyng that is not demonstrable.
Thou shalt [wite] withouten science,
And knowe withouten experience,   4690
The thyng that may not knowen be,
Ne wist, ne shewid, in no degre.
Thou maist the sothe of it not witen,
Though in thee it were writen.   4694
Thou shalt not knowe therof more,   92r
While thou art reuled by his lore;
But unto hym that love wole flee
The knotte may unclosed bee,

Which hath to thee, as it is founde,
So long be knette and not unbounde.   4700
Now sette wel thyne entencioun,
To here of love discripcioun.
   "Love, it is an hatefull pees,
A free acquitaunce withoute relees,
[A trouthe] frette full of falsheede,   4705
A sikernesse all sette in drede.
In herte is a dispeiryng hope,
And full of hope, it is wanhope;
Wise woodnesse, and [w]ode resoun,
A swete perell [in to] droune;   4710

4689 **wite]** knowe UR; here lerne SK; *om.* MS-SP³ BE-KA FU   4690 **knowe]** *om.* UR   4692 **ne shewid]** n. s. n. s. MS KA (*second set underdotted for deletion*)   4694 **Though]** Although UR   4697 **flee]** flye TH¹-UR FU SU FI   4698 **unclosed]** vnlosed SP²³   4700 **be knette]** to knytte TH¹-UR FU   4702 **discripcioun]** the d. UR BE   4704 **acquitaunce]** acquaintaunce TH²   4705 **A trouthe]** And thurgh the MS-UR KA FU   4707 **herte is]** hertis GL   4709 **Wise]** A w. UR   **wode]** vode MS KA; voyde TH¹-UR FU   4710 **in to]** into MS KA

4687   **withouten:** "perhaps disyllabic" (GL). Perhaps the note should be numbered 4690; cf. 4690n.
4689   **wite:** KA suggests emendation, comparing line 4692 *wist*. BE SK RBt RIt note the Fr. *savras* (Lc 4251 "si savras tantost sanz sciance" "you will know immediately without knowledge").
    withouten: To compensate metrically for his emendation, *here lerne*, SK drops *-en* from *withouten*.
4690   **withouten:** SK drops *-n*, for meter. Cf. 4687n.
4693–94   GL RB RI note that these lines are not in the Fr. "Perhaps we should connect v. 4693 with v. 4692 (reading *now witen* for *not witen*), and v. 4694 with v. 4695" (GL).
4697–4700   "To him who flees love, its nature is explicable; to you, who are still under its influence, it remains a riddle" (SK). BE also notes the sense that "no lover can understand the true nature of love, as long as he is under its influence."
4697   **flee:** TH¹'s emendation, *flye*, creates an imperfect rhyme with *be* for all who adopt it.
4703–84   FI notes the "series of conventional troubadour-like oxymora"; as RB RI note (see 4685–4784n.), Alanus de Insulis is the source of the Fr.
4703–05   *Marginalium:* In MS, in the right margin opposite these lines from Alanus, there is a hand resting on a decorative device that may be a capital "A."
4705   **A trouthe:** BE SK RIt note that this is Tyrwhitt's suggested emendation (TRg, s.v. *Fret*); BE SK SU note the Fr. *leautez* (Lc 4265 "c'est leautez la desleaus" "it is disloyal loyalty"). KA notes the change in BE MO.
    frette full of: "set thickly with (as an ornament)" (RIf).
    frette full: "adorned or furnished, so as to be full" (SK); "fully furnished" (RB). As RB notes, SK "mentions and rejects the emendation *bret ful* (= brim full)." SK compares line 7259 (= 7257) "fretted full," and SK GL RI compare *LGW* 1117 "fretted ful." SK cites the origin of *frette* as OE *frætwian*, "to adorn," but *MED* quotes this line under *freten* v.(4), sense (b) "loaded or fraught with"; for the origin, *MED* compares OF *fret* "transportation, cargo (from MDu. *vrecht*)"; thus, *MED* supports TRg, s.v. *Fret* ("Fraught, filled"), and RB. The sense "adorned" (SK FI) appears in *MED freten* v.(2), from OF pa. part. *freté*. See also 3204n., 7257n.
4709   **wode:** crazy. BE notes incorrectly that MS "reads *voide* . . . a mistake for *woode*' and quotes the Fr. (Lc 4269–70 "c'est reson toute forsenable / c'est forcenerie resnable" "it is totally mad reason, it is reasonable madness"). *OED Wood* adj. lists *vode* as a 14th-century Scottish form; and GL (4532n.) notes that "medial *v* and *w* were sometimes rhymed together in northern poems." RIt notes that MS *vode*, a sp. var., accounts for the substantive variant *voyde* ("empty, vacant") in TH¹ and the early printed eds. This observation reinforces Blodgett's argument that MS was TH¹'s copy-text (1975, 1979); see above, "The Printer's Marks."
4710   **perell:** SKt records MS *perell* as "perelle," i.e. as an abbreviation for *perelle*. See above, "The Manuscript Hands: The Scribe (MS₁)."
    in to: TH¹'s emendation is noted by KA in TH¹ MO.

An hevy birthen, lyght to bere,
A wikked wawe awey to were.
It is Karibdous perilous,
Disagreable and gracious.
It is discordaunce that can accorde, 4715
And accordaunce to discorde.
It is kunnyng withoute science,
Wisdome withoute sapience,

Witte withoute discrecioun, 92v
Havoire withoute possessioun. 4720
It is [sike] hele and hool sekenesse,
A [thrust] drowned [in] dronknesse,
And helth full of maladie,
And charite full of envie,
And [hunger] full of habundaunce, 4725
And a gredy suffisaunce;

4712 **wawe]** vawe TH² **awey to were]** alwey t. ware GL 4716 **to]** unto UR 4718 **wisdome]** And w. UR 4719 **Witte]** om. TH² 4720 **Havoire]** Havior RB² 4721 **sike]** like MS-UR KA FU 4722 **thrust]** trust MS-BE KA FU **in]** and MS-UR KA FU 4723 **And]** An SK GL SU FI **full]** all f. UR 4725 **And hunger]** A. anger MS-KA FU; An h. SK GL SU FI 4726 **gredy]** full g. UR

4712 BE SK GL RI note that the Fr. has no corresponding line. SK reads "a wave, harmful in wearing away the shore." GL emends (*alwey to ware*) and reads "a dangerous sea always to be avoided." FI does not emend but reads *awaye to weare* as "(?) always to beware," a reading that would seem to favor GL's emendation. However, GL's *ware* creates an unnecessarily imperfect rhyme.

4713 **Karibdous:** "Charybdis, the whirlpool" (SK), "the dangerous whirlpool near Italy" (RIf). SK compares Horace, *Carmina* (*Odes*) 1.27.19, and RI compares *TC* 5.644 and the note (RI), where Barney compares Virgil, *Aeneid* 3.420, 558, and Ovid, *Met.* 14.75. As David (RI) notes, eds. except BE-KA GL follow "Thynne's learned spelling, 'Carybdes' (or 'Caribdis')." He adds that "something is lost in changing the MS form, which may well originate with the translator," and cites Blodgett (1984:48) "on Thynne's corrections of the spellings of classical names."

4715–20 Ln (4304t), Brusendorff (1925:317–18), SU (note to SU Fr. 4304a-b), and RI all note that this passage is an interpolation that appears only in certain MSS of the Fr.: "B C He Eb" (Ln): "Be, Ba, and other B MSS . . . but not Bu" (SU). The six lines do not appear in KA's French text nor in Lc (between line 4274 and 4275), since Lc bases his text on Ha. SU Fr. takes the six lines from MS Ba and numbers them 4304a-f: "C'est descordance qui s'accorde / Acordance qui se descorde. / C'est sapience sans science, / C'est science sans sapience; / C'est sen que nus ne puet savoir, / C'est possessions sans avoir" ("It is discord that agrees, accord that disagrees. It is wisdom without knowledge, it is knowledge without wisdom; it is sense that none can know, it is possession without having"). See 4722n.

4717–18 RB RI quote the Fr. (above, 4304c-d) and cite Brusendorff (1925:318), who recommends that *kunnyng* and *wisdom* be interchanged; although RB seems to favor this view, he does not so emend, and RI observes that "the MS also makes sense."

4720 **Havoire:** FI reads this word in the verbal sense "to have (Fr. *avoir*)," but others take it in the substantive sense—"riches" (URg, s.v. *Aver*, citing Skinner 1671), "wealth" (TRg), "property" (SK), "possession" (RIf)—parallel with the other noun sets.

4721 **sike:** BE's emendation; KA notes it in BE MO. MS *like* shows the easy misreading of long *s* as *l*. BE notes, "the copyist . . . did not understand the paradoxes . . . in every line"; and quotes the Fr. (Lc 4275–76 "c'est langueur toute santeïve, / c'est santé toute maladive" "it is a healthful languor, it is diseased health").

4722 SU, noting "that this line corresponds to Fr. line three couplets below," observes that "its position and state seem to indicate change and misplacement when reviser incorporated ME 4715–20, probably missing in the original translation." See 4715–20n.

thrust: URg TRg note the sense "thirst" and the form *thurst* (recommended here by KA and present in RB RI) at line 5713. BE also notes this metathetic form of *thurst* "thirst," a form that, according to *OED Thirst* sb., was "in use from [about] 1200 to 1590." BE SK RBt SU RIt cite the Fr. *soif* (Lc 4279–80 "c'est la soif qui toujors est ivre, / ivrece qui de soif s'enivre" "it is the thirst that is always drunk, a drunkenness intoxicated by its own thirst").

in: Considering MS *and* a clerical error, BE reads *in*, noted in BE MO by KA.

4723 **And:** KA suggests *An*, an emendation made "perhaps correctly," (RBt) here and before *hunger* in line 4725.

4725 **hunger:** KA's suggested emendation follows the Fr. *fain* (Lc 4277 "hunger"; noted by RBt SU FI RIt).

Delite right full of hevynesse,
And dreried full of gladnesse;
Bitter swetnesse and swete errour,
Right evell savoured good savour;   4730
Sen that pardoun hath withynne,
And pardoun spotted withoute [with] synne.
A peyne also it is, joious,
And felonye right pitous;
Also pley that selde is stable,   4735
And stedefast [stat], right mevable;
A strengthe, weyked to stonde upright,
And feblenesse full of myght;
Witte unavised, sage folie,
And joie full of turmentrie;   4740

A laughter it is, weping ay,
Reste that traveyleth nyght and day.
Also a swete helle it is,   93r
And a soroufull paradys;
A plesaunt gayl and esy prisoun,   4745
And, full of froste, somer sesoun;
Pryme temps full of frostes white,
And May devoide of al delite,
With seer braunches, blossoms ungrene;
And newe fruyt, fillid with wynter tene.   4750
It is a slowe, may not forbere
Ragges ribaned with gold to were;
For also well wole love be sette
Under ragges as riche rochette;

4728 **dreried]** drerinesse UR   4731 **Sen]** A sin UR   4732 **withoute with]** withoute MS-UR KA FU; oute with GL SU   4735 **pley]** a p. UR   4736 **stedefast]** stedfastness UR   **stat]** *om.* MS-KA FU   4738 **feblenesse]** a f. UR   4745 **esy]** *om.* TH²   4746 **froste]** frostis UR   **somer]** a s. GL   4753 **be]** he SU FI

4728 **dreried:** "That is, *Drerihed*, dreariness" (BE); URg (s.v. *drerie*) defines the UR form here as "sorrow, saddness" and cites "AS. Dryrmian, *Tristitia afficere.*" For the sense, "sadness," SK adduces the Fr. *tristeur* (Lc 4281) and compares German *Traurigkeit*. *MED drērihēd* n. quotes this single example of the spelling *dreried*.

4731 **Sen:** Sin. KA suggests *Sinne*. MS *Sen* may be a Southeastern variant (Mossé 1968:25), but, if so, we might expect *zen(ne* (Mossé 1968:39), as in Dan Michel's *Ayenbite of Inwyt* (ed. Morris 1866a:1.6 and throughout).

4732 **withoute with synne:** "on the outside" (SK RB RIf) with sin. BE notes that the MS reading, *withoute synne*, "makes nonsense" and that *with* may have been accidentally "omitted by the copyist." BE SK RI cite the Fr. in support of the emendation (Lc 4285–86 "entechiez de pardon pechiez, / de pechiez pardon entechiez" "sin stained with pardon, pardon spotted with sin"). KA notes the insertion of *with* in BE MO. The GL SU reading *oute with synne* has the same sense.

4736 **stedefast stat:** KA suggests the UR reading *stedefastnesse*; SK first supplies *stat*, in support of which SKt RBt SU FI RIt quote the Fr. *estaz* (Lc 4290 "estaz trop fers et trop muables" "a state too fixed and too movable").

4737 **weyked:** "(too) weak" (BE SKg₂ FI), "(too) weakened" (RIf). BE quotes the Fr. (Lc 4291–92 "force enferme, enfermeté fors / qui tout esmeut par ses efors" "a weak power, a strong weakness, that moves all by its efforts").

4747 **Pryme temps:** here "spring" (URg FI RIf), "spring-time" (SK); URg SK cite the Fr. "printemps." Cf. 3373n., 4534n.

4751 **slowe:** There is a variety of glosses: "slough" (URg) does not fit the context; "moth" (TRg BE SK) has the support of the standard Fr. *taigne* (Lc 4301 "c'est taigne qui riens ne refuse, / les porpres et les buriaus use" "it is the moth that refuses nothing, that consumes both purple robes and homespun"). TRg BE SK GL RB SU RI cite the Fr. *taigne*. SK notes the origin in Latin *tinea* and admits that he knows of no other example of *slowe* in the sense "moth." GL first suggests that the Fr. *taigne* ("moth") . . . is probably a mistake for *caigne* ["bitch, bad dog"]. . . . At least that seems to be the word here translated *slowe*, 'a vagabond.'" Ln (4331t) records the var. *kaigne* in MS Ca, and SU, pointing out the form *caigne* in MS Ri, confirms GL's conjecture; cf. Brusendorff (1925:308). *OED Slow* sb. "sluggard" doubts that the word here means "moth," "and, like SK, RB notes that "no other occurrence of the word in this sense ["moth"] seems to be known." RI states: "The translation is doubtless based on the var. 'caigne' (bitch) for 'teigne.' . . . Probably the word is to be taken as a general term of abuse." Thus recent glosses follow GL in suggesting "vagabond" (SU), "sluggard" (SU FI RIf *MED slou* adj. 1. [c]), or "loafer" (FI).

4752 **were:** BE SK, taking *slowe* as "moth," read *were* as "fret, wear away"; Skeat (SK) compares his note to line 4712, where he takes *awey to were* as "in wearing away the shore." RB objects that SK's reading does not suit the context, which requires the wearing of rags (cf. the Fr. above). See 4751n.

4753–54 "Proverbial; Whiting [1968] L539" (RI).

And eke as wel [be] amourettes 4755
In mournyng blak, as bright burnettes.
For noon is of so mochel pris,
Ne no man founden so wys,
Ne noon so high is of parage,
Ne no man founde of witt so sage, 4760
No man so hardy ne so wight,

Ne no man of so mychel myght, 4755
Noon so fulfilled of bounte,
That he with love may daunted be.
All the world holdith this wey; 4765
Love makith all to goon myswey,
But it be they of yvel lyf, 93v
Whom Genius cursith, man and wyf,

4755 **be]** by MS-UR KA GL FU   4758 **founden]** f. is UR MO SK GL   4759 **noon]** no man UR   **is]** *om.* TH³ ST SP²-UR   4764 **That he with love may]** But h. w. l. m. SK; T. h. w. l. ne m. GL RI; T. ne w. l. m. SU FI   4768 **cursith]** cursed TH¹-UR FU SU FI

4755–56   "'Amourettes [sweethearts] are as agreeable when clothed in black mourning as when arrayed in the most splendid garments'" (BE); SK FI offer parallel readings, and BE quotes the Fr. (Lc 4303–04 "car ausint bien sunt amoretes / souz bureaus conme souz brunetes" "for lovers are as good beneath coarse clothing as in fine"). SK RB RI note the proverbial nature of the couplet. SK RB cite Cotgrave (1611), s. v. *Amourette*, from whom SK quotes the proverb: "'Aussi bien sont amourettes / Soubs bureau, que soubs brunettes.'" RI cites Whiting (1968: A119), who reads "Amorets (*love-knots*) (may) be as well in black mourning as in bright burnet (*cloth*)"; notes that "the interpretation of *amourettes* as 'love-knots' rests on a misreading of the French in a line probably interpolated by Thynne for one [892] missing in the MS"; and recognizes that FI's translation—"sweethearts are as good in black mourning as in bright robes"—is closer to the Fr. RB cites *Romania* 13:533 (= Meyer 1884:533) from Ln (4333–34n.); there the two lines appear in a collection of proverbs from the 14th century, but Ln notes that the lack of a syllable in the first line of the "proverb" argues for the belief that it is a borrowing from *RR*, minus the opening word *car* (Lc 4303–04 above). On the sense of the supposed proverb, RI notes that Ln quotes a later formulation from La Fontaine's *Joconde*: "Sous les cotillons des grisettes / Peut loger autant de beauté / Que sous les jupes des coquettes" ("Beneath working girls' petticoats there can dwell as much beauty as beneath the skirts of coquettes").

4755   **be:** MS *by* may be a spelling variant of *be* (see *MED bēn* v.) rather than an error, and therefore GL keeps the form; but KA recommends *ben*. (At line 4683, MO's 19th-century *by* for *be* can hardly be a spelling variant; see the collation). BE RBt SU RIt quote the Fr. *sont* (Lc 4303–04, quoted above). See 4755–56n.

amourettes: "amorous" women (TRg), "lovers, pretty girls" (RIf), rather than "louers fauours" (SP²·³g) or "love-stories" (URg); see 4755–56n.

4756   **burnettes:** Specifically, "hoodes, or attire for the head" (SP²·³) or "dresses" (SKg, RIf). More generally, "rich stuff worn by Persons of Quality" (URg), "cloth died of a brown colour" (TRg), or "cloth of a superior quality" (SK). TRg cites Du Cange, s.v. *Burnetum*. Skeat refers back to his note on line 226. See 226n., 227–29n., 4755–56n.

4758   **founden:** KA notes the insertion of *is* after *founden* in UR MO.

4762   **mychel:** SKt refers to line 4757 in support of his selection of the form *mochel*.

4764   As at lines 3769 and 3774 (see notes and cf. 5069n.), the unemended text probably implies the negative sense in the subordinate clause. KA endorses SK's emendation, *But for that*. GL compares the "similar mistake" at line 3774. RB suggests that emendation may not be necessary, citing "for a similarly inconsequent construction," *Rom* 3774 and *MLH* B¹ 49, the note to which adduces *TC* 1.456–57. In support of emendation, SK SU FI RIt cite the Fr. *ne* (Lc 4310 "qui par Amors ne soit dontez" "who may not be overcome by the God of Love"). RIt notes that at line 3774 Robinson defends the "inconsequent construction" but nevertheless "follows Skeat and Liddell in changing *wille* to *nille*"; RIt adopts GL's emendation "as the simplest." The resulting line has an extra syllable.

4766   **goon myswey:** KA notes that in MS "there is an erasure" between these two words. The space is 12 mm. long, large enough for the word *this*, which may have been repeated by error from the previous line.

4767–68   **they of yvel lyf, / Whom Genius cursith:** "homosexuals" (RIf). Ln (4343–44n.) RB (4768n.) FI (4769n.) RI identify the source in Alanus de Insulis, *De planctu naturae*, prose 9 (see *PL* 210:482A; cf. 432A). RI states: "The reference is to the excommunication pronounced against homosexuality at the end of De planctu naturae by Nature's priest Genius against 'omnis qui legitimum Veneris obliquat incessum' (whoever turns awry the lawful course of love), or 'Qui a regula Veneris exceptionem facit anormalam' (who makes an irregular exception to the rule of love)." FI notes that the *De planctu* greatly influenced *RR* and Chaucer's *PF*. On Genius, see 4768n.

4768   **Genius:** SK RB FI RI (4767–68n.) observe that Genius appears in a later part of *RR* (Lc 16242–20673) as Nature's priest, and as Venus's priest in Gower's *Confessio amantis* 1.193ff. (ed. Macaulay 1899–1902:2.40ff.). "In both cases, as in the philosophy of the 'Chartrian' school, Genius serves as priest of the fundamental sexual drive for procreation" (FI). On the history of Genius as an allegorical figure, RB cites Knowlton (1924; see also 1920), and RI cites Nitzsche (1975).

219

That wrongly werke ageyn nature.
Noon such I love, ne have no cure   4770
Of sich as Loves servauntes bene,
And wole not by my counsel flene.
For I ne preise that lovyng
Wherthurgh men, at the laste eendyng,
Shall calle hem wrecchis full of woo,   4775
Love greveth hem and shendith soo.
But if thou wolt wel Love eschewe,
For to escape out of his mewe,
And make al hool thi sorwe to slake,
No bettir counsel maist thou take   4780
Than thynke to fleen wel, iwis;
May nought helpe elles, for wite thou this:
If thou fle it, it shal flee thee;
Folowe it, and folowen shal it thee."   4784
    Lamant. Whanne I hadde herde
    all Resoun seyne,
Which hadde spilt hir speche in veyne,
"Dame," seide I, "I dar wel sey,

Of this avaunt me wel I may
That from youre scole so devyaunt
I am, that never the more avaunt   4790
Right nought am I thurgh youre doctrine. 94r
I dulle under youre discipline;
I wote no more than [I] wist [er],
To me so contrarie and so fer
Is every thing that ye me lere,   4795
And yit I can it all [par cuere].
Myne herte foryetith therof right nought,
It is so writen in my thought;
And depe greven it is so tendir
That all by herte I can it rendre,   4800
And rede it over comunely;
But to mysilf lewedist am I.
But sith ye love discreven so,
And lak and preise it, bothe twoo,
Defyneth it into this letter,   4805
That I may thenke on it the better;
For I herde never [diffyne it ere],

4771 **Loves]** loue TH²   4774 **men]** man TH³ ST SP²-BE   4779 **thi]** the ST SP²-UR   **to]** *om.* UR   4783 **fle . . . flee]** flye . . . flye TH¹-UR FU SU FI   4785 **all]** *om.* TH³ ST SP²-UR   4793 **I wist]** w. MS-SP³ KA FU; w. I GL SU FI   **er]** euer MS-KA GL FU   4796 **par cuere]** by partuere MS-SP³ KA FU; by partivere UR; by parcuere MO GL   4800 **by]** myne TH¹-SP¹ UR FU   4802 **mysilf]** my fele FU 4807 **diffyne it ere]** diffyned heere MS-KA FU

4772 **flene:** "flee away, escape" (SKg₂), "flee (from love)" (FI).

4778 **mewe:** URg and TRg both state that a mew was originally a cage for hawks, while "they *mue,* or change their feathers," hence "cage in general, or any sort of confinement."

4783–84 Proverbial; RB cites Haeckel (1890: no. 12), and RI cites Whiting (1968: L487). RI, following Ln (4357–58n.), notes that the Fr. (Lc 4327–28) follows Alanus's Latin (see *PL* 210: 456B), and compares *TC* 1.747–48.

4783 **fle . . . flee:** See 951n.

4785 **Lamant:** In MS, the rubric appears at the end of the previous line.

4790 "I am never the further advanced" (BE); however, BE's text, like all others, has a comma after *I am* (TH¹ FU have virgules), and such punctuation would place *I am* in the clause that begins in the previous line. Probably the BE note refers to the next clause, "never the more avaunt / Right nought am I," and the footnote number is misplaced.

    avaunt: "forward" (SPg URg TRg SK FI), "ahead, advanced" (RB), "successful" (FI). SK quotes the Fr. (Lc 4332 "je n'en sai pas plus que devant" "I know no more of it than before").

4793–94 **er : fer:** On KA's recommendation, SK RB-RI emend MS *ever* to *er,* for rhyme and sense ("before"). In support of the sense, RBt RIt cite the Fr. *devant* (Lc 4332, above). Perhaps MS *euer* was pronounced *er,* homonymous with *er* "before" (*MED er* conj.[1]).

4793 **I:** UR's emendation. KA endorses the insertion in UR BE MO.

4796 **par cuere:** BE's emendation; MS has *ptuere,* with crossed *p.* KA notes the change in BE MO. SK SU RBt cite the Fr. *par queur* (Lc 4336 "by heart"). URg accepts Skinner's suggestion (1671) that SP's *partuere* (UR *partivere*) is a corruption of *parcuere*; TRg also suggests *par cuere.*

4797 **foryetith:** KA attributes to SK the suggestion *forget,* but no ed. so emends.

4800–02 "I know all your lesson by heart; but yet, so impossible do I find it to apply my learning to myself, that, as regards my own conduct, I am the most unlearned of men" (BE).

4800 **by:** URg (s.v. *Partivere*) states that UR's *mine* is wrong and should read *by.*

4807 **diffyne it ere:** KA's suggested emendation follows the Fr. (Lc 4345 "quar ne l'oï defenir onques" "for I never heard it defined"; noted by RBt SU FI RIt).

And wilfully I wolde it lere."
  "If love be serched wel and sought,
It is [a] sykenesse of the thought   4810
Annexed and kne[t] bitwixt tweyne,
[Which] male and female with oo cheyne
So frely byndith that they nyll twynne,
Whether so therof they leese or wynne. 4814
The roote springith thurgh
      hoote brenny[n]g   94v
Into disordinat desiryng
For to kissen and enbrace,
And at her lust them to solace.
Of other thyng love recchith nought,

But setteth her herte and all her thought 4820
More for delectacioun
Than ony procreacioun
Of other fruyt by engendr[ing],
Which love to God is not plesyng;
For of her body fruyt to gete   4825
They yeve no force, they are so sette
Upon delite to pley in-feere.
And somme have also this manere,
To feynen hem for love seke;
Sich love I preise not at a leke.   4830
For paramours they do but feyne;
To love truly they disdeyne.

4810 **a]** *om.* MS (MS₁ *corr.*)   4811 **knet]** kned MS-KA FU SU FI   4812 **Which]** With MS-SP³ BE-KA FU   4813 **byndith]** that b. MS-SP³ BE-KA FU   4814 **so]** *om.* UR   4815 **brennyng]** brennyg MS KA   4821 **for]** f. ther UR   4823 **engendring]** engendrure MS-KA GL FU SU FI   4824 **plesyng]** pleasure TH¹-BE GL FU SU FI

4809–27 Ln (4377–88n.) Lc (4347–58n.) RB RI call attention to the source in Andreas Capellanus, *De amore* 1.1–1.2 (ed. and trans. Walsh 1982:32–37).

4809 UR-MO SK GL RB RI supply the speech-heading *Raisoun* at the beginning of this line. KA notes the presence of the heading in BE MO.

4810 **a:** "written above the line" (KA) by MS₁.

4812 **Which:** UR's emendation; KA suggests it as well. MS *With* shows erroneous anticipation of *with*, three words later.

4813 **byndith:** UR's emendation; KA also suggests it. MS *that byndith* shows erroneous anticipation of *that*, two words later. KA attributes to SK the suggestion *bint* (contraction of *byndith*), but no ed. so emends.

    nyll: SKt reports MS *nyll* as *nylle*. See above, "The Manuscript Hands: The Scribe (MS₁)."

4814 **Whether:** "*Whether* for *wher*" (GL).

4815 **brennyng:** TH¹'s emendation (*brennynge*); KA notes it in UR MO.

4820 **setteth:** KA attributes to SK the suggestion *set* (as a contraction for meter), but no ed. so emends. Contracted pronunciation is probable.

4821–24 RB RI note that these lines are not in the Fr., and both compare *NPT* B² 4534–35. RI points out, however, that "the lines elaborate the idea in 4825–27, which corresponds to [Ln 4387–88 = Lc 4357–58] 'De fruit aveir ne fait il force; Au deliter senz plus s'efforce' (He cares not to have fruit; he takes pains for pleasure and nothing else)."

4822 **ony:** See 212n.

4823 **engendring:** KA's suggested emendation. KA SKt compare line 6114 ("They made a full good engendryng").

4826 **They yeve no force:** "They do not mind" (URg, s.v. *Force*), "they care not" (TRg, s.v. *Force*). TRg cites the Fr. (Lc 4357 "De fruit avoir ne fet il force" "he makes no effort to have fruit")

4830 **I preise not a leke:** one of several figures of worthlessness (cf. 6191n.). For further examples, Lounsbury (1892:2.137) cites lines 5374, 5730 (leek); line 6464 (bean); lines 5762, 7550 (mite); line 6856 (hen). Since these all have parallels in Chaucer's genuine works, Lounsbury argues, they support the position that Chaucer wrote *Rom*. Kittredge (1892:40–42) cites numerous examples from ME to show that such figures are so common that parallels between Chaucer and *Rom* do not prove that Chaucer wrote *Rom*; he grants (p. 41) that he has no example of *not worth an hen* beyond the parallel between *Rom* 6856 and *WBT* D 1112.

    at: As SU notes, SKt errs in saying that MS omits *at*.

4831–32 Compare the Fr. (Lc 4361–62 "toutevois fins amanz se faignent, / mes par amors amer ne daignent" "but while they pretend to be pure lovers, they do not deign to love *par amour*"). In KA Fr. and SU Fr. these lines are probably misplaced as parallels to lines 4830–31, and SK RB RI so take them in their notes to line 4831. See 4831n.

·   4831 **paramours:** Skeat (SK) takes this word as a noun (cf. SPg URg) in his paraphrase, "For paramours only feign," but notes the adverbial sense in the French line that he takes as the parallel (Lc 4362, above), a line that he translates as "'but they do not deign to love like true lovers'; unless," he continues, "it is a mere exclamation, 'I swear by love.'" RB RI take *paramours* adverbially, "with passionate love," and both assume the same parallel line in the

They falsen ladies traitoursly,
And swerne hem othes utterly,
With many a lesyng and many a fable,   4835
And all they fynden deceyvable;
And whanne they han her lust geten,
The hoote ernes they al foryeten.
Wymmen, the harme they bien full sore;   95r
But men this thenken evermore,   4840
That lasse harme is, so mote I the,
Deceyve them than deceyved be;
And namely where they ne may
Fynde none other mene wey.

For I wote wel, in sothfastnesse,   4845
That [who] doth now his bisynesse
With ony womman for to dele,
For ony lust that he may fele,
But if it be for engendrure,
He doth trespasse, I you ensure.   4850
For he shulde setten all his wille
To geten a likly thyng hym tille,
And to sustene, if he myght,
And kepe forth, by kyndes right,
His owne lyknesse and semblable,   4855
[For bycause al is corrumpable];   TH¹:153c

4835 **and]** *om.* UR   4837 **han her lust]** her lust han SK   4839 **they]** *om.* TH¹-UR FU SU FI
4840 **this]** thus SP²·³   4841 **That]** The ST SP²-UR   4842 **than]** that SU FI   4844 **wey]** ne w.
UR   4846 **That who]** T. what MS TH¹ TH³-SP¹ KA FU; What wight GL; What man RB¹·² RI   4849 **for]** so f.
TH²   4853 **if]** i. that UR   4856 *Out:* MS (*blank line*) KA RI

Fr. (Lc 4362). FI's nominal gloss, "sexual love," obscures the construction. It is possible that Skeat was correct in his nominal reading of *paramours* but chose the wrong parallel in the Fr.; the previous line (Lc 4361, above) has the nominal phrase *fins amanz* in the line that seems the closer parallel; and while the Fr. phrase *par amors* is generally adverbial, the translator here may have chosen it, possibly through anticipation of the next line, to translate *fins amanz*. RB cites *KnT* A 1155 for the adverbial sense of *paramours*; cf. A 2112 and Skeat's note (SK 5.84). For the nominal sense, see *NPT* B² 4057, *FrT* D 1372.

4835   KA's suggestion, "Omit *a*," does not specify which *a* (both?), and no ed. so emends; the omission(s)? would not remedy the meter.

4837   **han her lust:** KA suggests the SK reading.

4838   **ernes:** The sense "promise" (SPg) is appropriate to the form without final *-t-* (from OF *erres*; see *MED ernes* n.). But the sense here—"desire" (URg RB), "passion" (RB RIf), "ardor" (FI)—clearly relates the word to the OE etymon *eornust*; see *MED ernest* n. 4 (b); cf. 3680n. RB RI compare *LGW* 1287.

4841–42   Proverbial; RB compares "Haeckel [1890], p. 54"; RI compares Whiting (1968: H137).

4842   After the corresponding line in the Fr. (Méon 4413, Ln 4400, Lc 4370), as BE notes, Méon (1814:2.19–22) prints as a footnote a passage of 106 lines that he rejects as an interpolation; presumably he found the passage in his MS, Za (Ln 1.46). Langlois (1910:425) finds that this passage, which falls between lines 4400 and 4401 of his ed., is characteristic of the families K M N of Group II in his classification. It constitutes an extended definition of charity; cf. Dahlberg (1971:374–75 n. 4400–01).

them: On the basis of the Fr. (Lc 4370 "decevoir que deceüz estre" "to deceive than to be deceived"), Lounsbury (1895:22) suggests that we "omit 'them,' which of course should itself be 'hem.'"

than: *that* has no basis in the Fr. (above).

4846   **That who:** TH²'s emendation, *who* for MS *what*; the latter may well be an echoic scribal error after *That*. *Who* is perhaps simpler and closer to the Fr. (Lc 4376 "quiconques a fame geüst" "whoever lay with a woman") than either KA's suggestion *What man* or GL's *What wight*.

4847, 4848   **ony:** See 212n.

4852   FI (cf. URg) paraphrases, "beget a thing like himself," and adds that "this is the 'natural' justification for sex in Chartrian philosophy." URg compares line 4855 *His owne lyknesse.*

4856   BE SKt SU FI RI note that MS omits this line; KA RI also omit it; cf. 892n. Jephson (BE) says that he supplies it from "Speght"; SK and later eds. use Speght's ultimate source, TH¹. BE RI quote TH¹'s source, the Fr. (Lc 4378 "pour ce qu'il sunt tuit corrunpable" "because they are all corruptible"). RIt explains the problems in the relation between ME and Fr.: "TH¹'s line closely renders the French except for *For*, which causes difficult syntax. Skeat and Fisher place a comma after 4855; Liddell [GL, following BE MO], a period; Robinson, a semicolon. Although the clause should complete the thought as it does in the French (man should beget his likeness because all is corruptible), *For* seems to start a new period to which the *bycause* clause is subordinate." Such a period could not conclude before the end of line 4864 and would distort the sense of the Fr. The punctuation here adapts that of SK, FI, and the Fr., and it assumes, as RI observes, that "'For' seems redundant with 'bycause.'"   § RB RI note the proverbial nature of the idea; RB cites Haeckel (1890: no. 146), and RI cites Whiting (1968: A93).

corrumpable: "corruptible" (URg et al.), "destructible" (FI),

And faile shulde successioun,   MS:95r
Ne were ther generacioun
Oure sectis strene for to save.
Whanne fader or moder arn in grave,   4860
Her children shulde, whanne they ben deede,
Full diligent ben, in her steede,
To use that werke on such a wise   95v
That oon may thurgh another rise.
Therfore sette Kynde therynne delite,   4865
For men therynne shulde hem delite,
And of that deede be not erke,
But ofte sithes haunt that werke;
For noon wolde drawe therof a draught

Ne were delite, which hath hym kaught.   4870
    "[Thus hath sotilled] Dame Nature;
For noon goth right, I thee ensure,
Ne hath entent hool ne parfight;
For her desir is for delyte,
The which fortened crece and eke   4875
The pley of love for-ofte seke,
And thrall hemsilf, they be so nyce,
Unto the prince of every [vice].
For of ech synne it is the rote,
Unlefull lust, though it be sote,   4880
And of all yvell the racyne,
As Tulius can determyne,

4858 **ther]** their MS-SP¹ MO KA FU SU FI   4859 **strene]** sterne TH¹-SP³ FU SU FI   4861 **they]** then
UR   **deede]** bede TH¹-ST FU   4866 **hem]** haue TH²   4868 **sithes]** sythens TH²   4871 **Thus hath**
sotilled] This hadde sotille MS-SK FU   4875 **fortened crece]** for tene crece GL   4876 **seke]** thei s.
UR   4878 **Unto]** Onto SU FI   **vice]** wise MS KA   4881 **all]** a SU FI

4858   **ther:** SP²'s emendation (*there*) is suggested by KA (*ther*). Of those who retain MS *their*, FI, at least, assumes the adverbial sense in paraphrasing the line as "were there not procreation." In support of Blodgett's thesis that MS was copy-text for TH¹, RIt states: "The form in G [MS] is unique (the adv. is normally *ther*, the pro. *hir*); its occurrence in Th [TH¹] would be a remarkable coincidence if it had not been taken over directly."

4859   **Oure sectis strene:** "the seed, or race, of our species" (BE); "the progeny (or strain) of our species" (SK).

    Oure sectis: "of our species, race" (RB).

    strene: TH¹'s variant, *sterne*, is perhaps an error, rather than a metathetic spelling variant, but it was not changed until UR's ed. SU FI keep the form *sterne*, and FI accepts it as a spelling variant: "*sectis sterne*, species' strain." SK compares *CIT* E 157.

4865   **sette:** Present tense. KA endorses SK's contraction *set*, the form in TH²-UR, here and at line 4889. RB RI retain *sette* at line 4865, but have *set* at line 4889.

4867   **erke:** "weary" (SP²·³g URg TRg SKg₂ FI RIf *MED irk(e* adj. 1. [a]); but for the phrase *erke of*, the sense "averse to" (*MED* 1. [b]) is perhaps closer to the context.

4871   **Thus hath sotilled:** GL's emendation follows the Fr. (Lc 4391 "Ainsinc Nature i sotiva" "thus hath Nature subtly reasoned"; noted by RBt SU FI RIt).

    sotilled: perhaps "subtly arranged" (RIf) rather than "figured out" (FI).

4875–76   BE states that the couplet is "evidently corrupt and unintelligible" and quotes the Fr. to show that the lines, as SK RB RI note, are not in the original. SK says that the couplet "seems to mean—'who very often seek after destroyed increase (abortion) and the play of love.'" RB FI accept SK's reading (RB with a query), but RI, taking *fortened crece* as "stimulated procreation," argues as follows: "Skeat's guess that the phrase refers to abortion is mistaken. The antecedent of *which* is *desir*. The desire for sexual pleasure caused by a kind of irritation (*fortened*) results in human reproduction." See 4875n.

4875   **fortened crece:** SK (4875–76n.) gives only tentative support for his reading (see above): "Cf. *tenen*, to harm. But no other instance of *for-tened* is known, nor yet of *crece* as short for *increes*. However, the verb *cresen*, to increase, is used by Wyclif." GL reads *for tene crece*, taking *tene* as a noun and *crece*, presumably, as verb ("who increase to offset harm"?). RB ("destroyed increase, i.e., abortion?") and FI ("obstructed increase") follow SK. *MED*, however, takes *fortened* as "excited, stimulated" and adduces—from the ME translation of Palladius's *De re rustica*—a quotation unknown to Skeat that clearly supports the sense; see *MED fortēnen* v., *crēse* n. RI follows *MED* with the gloss "stimulated procreation." See 4875–76n.

4876   **for-ofte:** "very often ('for' is an intensifier)" (FI).

4878   **vice:** TH¹'s emendation for MS *wise*, noted by KA in UR BE MO, follows the Fr. (Lc 4398 "au prince de trestouz les vices"). MS *wise* may be a 15th-century (Northern) spelling of *vice*, see *OED Vice* sb.¹ and cf. line 5946, 4709n. At lines 5379–80, MS rhymes *vice* with *wys*; see n.

4880   **Unlefull lust:** "unlawful pleasure (i.e., sexual pleasure not with the intention of procreation)" (FI).

4882–84   Ln (4430–32n.) BE SK RB RIf note the reference to Cicero's *De senectute*, particularly Chapter 12, from which Ln quotes material on the liberation from *voluptas* in old age.

Which in his tyme was full sage,

In a boke he made *Of Age*,

Where that more he preyseth eelde, 4885

Though he be croked and unweelde,

And more of commendacioun, 96r

Than youthe in his discripcioun.

For youthe sette bothe man and wyf

In all perell of soule and lyf; 4890

And perell is, but men have grace,

The perell of yougth for to pace

Withoute ony deth or distresse,

It is so full of wyldenesse;

So ofte it doth shame or damage 4895

To hym or to his lynage.

It ledith man now up, now doun,

In mochel dissolucioun,

And makith hym love yvell companye,

And lede his lyf disrewlilye, 4900

And halt hym payed with noon estate.

Withynne hymsilf is such debate,

He chaungith purpos and entente,

And yalte [him] into somme covente

To lyven aftir her emprise, 4905

And lesith fredom and fraunchise

That Nature in hym hadde sette,

The which ageyne he may not gette,

If he there make his mansioun

For to abide professioun. 4910

Though for a tyme his herte absente, 96v

It may not fayle, he shal repente

And eke abide thilke day

To leve his abite, and gone his way,

And lesith his worshipp and his name, 4915

And dar not come ageyn for shame;

4884 **he]** whiche h. UR   4891 **And]** The FU   4892 **The]** And FU   **perell]** tyme SK RB¹-RI
4895 **or]** and TH³-BE   4896 **to his]** unto h. UR   4899 **yvell]** well TH²; ill UR   4903 **chaungith]**
chaunged ST SP¹   4904 **him]** *om.* MS-KA FU   4909 **he there]** t. h. UR

4887 **of commendacioun:** "to be praised" (FI).
4889 **sette:** See 4865n.
4892 **perell:** Although the repetition is awkward, the Fr. (Lc 4405 "et trop est fort chose a passer" "and [youth] is too great a force to live through") gives little support to SK's emendation *tyme*, endorsed by KA; it remains possible that *perell* appears for *tyme* through dittography.
4893 **ony:** See 212n.
4899 **yvell:** KA attributes to Skeat the suggestion *ill* here and at lines 4936 and 4959; no later ed., including SK, adopts the emendation, although UR used it earlier.
4901 "Holdeth himself content with no situation in which he may be placed" (BE); "and considers himself satisfied with no situation" (SK FI RIf).
4904–24 BE notes that "the danger of taking religious vows, which may afterwards be repented of, forms the subject of one of the colloquies of Erasmus, called *Virgo mempsigamos.*"
4904 "The English omits the reason for joining a religious order: 'E cuide prendre au ciel la grue' ([Lc 4417] (And thinks to grab the crane in the sky, i.e., to make a good bargain, to enjoy 'pie in the sky')" (RI).
  him: KA's suggestion. SK adduces the Fr. *se rant* (Lc 4414 "Or se rant an aucun couvent" "or he may go [lit., give himself up] into some convent"; noted also in TRg RIt).
4910 **abide professioun:** RIf's gloss, "live under vows," is not exactly accurate, since to abide (await) profession (of vows) refers to the probationary period before taking final vows (BE SK FI); cf. the Fr. (Lc 4419 "et remaint tant qu'il soit profés" "and remains until he is professed").
4914–16 BE quotes the Fr. (Lc 4420–25 "ou, s'il resent trop grief le fes / si s'en repent et puis s'en ist; / ou sa vie, espoir, i fenist, / qu'il ne s'en ose revenir / pour honte qui l'i fet tenir, / et contre son queur i demeure" "or if he feels the burden too heavy, he may repent [of his vows] and leave the convent, or perhaps—since he dares not go back, on account of the shame that makes him stay—he may finish out his life and remain there against his heart's desire"). Jephson (BE) makes no comment, but his point is presumably the one that RI makes: "The English here conflates two choices confronting the man who has entered monastic life: he may leave the monastery ('s'en ist'), or he may stay because he is ashamed to leave ('Pour Honte qui l'i fait tenir'). The conflation results in a further contradiction; in the Fr., the man is ashamed to return to secular life; in the ME, he is ashamed to return to the convent after leaving it.
4914 **leve his abite:** "give up his friar's dress" (SK).
  gone his way: KA suggests *go way*, but no ed. so emends.
4915 **worshipp:** Here and at line 5296 the scribe puts a macron over the final *-pp*. MS spells *worship* at lines 1201, 2320, 3529, 6173 and *worshipe* at lines 180, 2119, 2205, 2703, 5886. See also 5251n.

But al his lyf he doth so morne,
Bycause he dar not hom retourne.
Fredom of kynde so lost hath he
That never may recured be,   4920
But [if that] God hym graunte grace
That he may, er he hennes pace,
Conteyne undir obedience
Thurgh the vertu of pacience.
For Youthe sett man in all folye,   4925
In unthrift and in ribaudie,
In leccherie and in outrage,
So ofte it chaungith of corage.
Youthe gynneth ofte sich bargeyne,
That may not eende withouten peyne.   4930

In gret perell is sett youthede,
Delite so doth his bridil leede.
Delite [thus] hangith, drede thee nought,
Bothe mannys body and his thought,   4934
Oonly thurgh [Youthe, his chamberere],   97r
That to done yvell is custommere,
And of nought elles taketh hede
But oonly folkes for to lede
Into disporte and wyldenesse,
So is [she] frowarde from sadnesse.   4940
   "But Eelde drawith hem therfro.
Who wote it nought, he may wel goo
[Demande] of hem that now arn olde,
That whilom Youthe hadde in holde,

4921 **if that]** that if MS-BE KA GL FU   4926 **and in]** and KA RB[1,2]   **ribaudie]** rybandrie TH[1] FU;
rybaudrye TH[2]-UR   4929 **bargeyne]** a b. UR   4933 **thus]** this MS-UR KA FU   4935 **Youthe his
chamberere]** youthes chambre MS-UR KA FU; youthes chamberere MO   4936 **yvell]** ill UR   4940 **is she
frowarde]** i. f. MS-SP[3] KA FU; f. i. it UR; i. he f. BE MO; s. i. f. GL   4943 **Demande]** And moo MS-KA GL
FU   4944 **Youthe]** youthhed GL

4917 **doth:** "here apparently not causative, but used as in modern English" (RB).

4921 **if that:** MO's emendation for MS *that if,* noted by KA.

4923 **conteyne:** "contain or keep himself" (SK), "contain his dissatisfaction" (RIf), rather than "continue" (FI).
SK RI adduce the Fr. *le tiegne* "keep him," but the subject of *tiegne* is *qui,* with the antecedent *Dex* "God" (Lc
4429–32 "se n'est que Dex grace li face, / qui sa mesese li efface / et le tiegne en obedience / par la vertu de
pacience" "unless God grant him grace—(God) who may relieve his discomfort and keep him in obedience through
the virtue of pacience").

4926 **and in:** RIt reports KA's erroneous omission of *in* and its presence in UR BE. RB seems to have been
following KA rather than MS. SKt also errs in saying "G om.," and GL, following KA SK, inserts *in* in square brackets.

   ribaudie: Although the forms in *-drye* and *-dye* differ little in field of meaning, *MED* distinguishes them
in terms of OF origin. See 2224n.

4933–35 BE first emended this passage, on the basis of the Fr. (Lc 4441–43 "Ainsint Delit enlace et maine / le
cors et la pensee humaine / par Jennece, sa chamberiere" "Delight thus ensnares and directs both body and mind of
man by means of his servant Youth"). See 4933n., 4935n. Ln (4471–72n.) adduces Cicero, *De senectute* 12.42.

4933 **thus:** BE's emendation (see 4933–35n.) follows the Fr. *Ainsint* (Lc 4441, above; noted by GL SU FI RIt).
KA notes the change in BE MO.

   hangith: RI quotes the Fr. *enlace et maine* (Lc 4441 "ties up and leads").

   drede thee nought: "i.e. you may be sure" (GL).

4935 **Youthe, his chamberere:** BE's emendation, noted by KA, remedies both sense and meter, and follows
the Fr. (Lc 4443 "Jennece, sa chamberiere"; noted in SKt RBt SU FI RIt). See 4933–35n.

4936 **yvell:** See 4899n.

   custommere: "accustomed" (TRg RIf *MED custumḗre* adj.). MS has *-ōm-,* the usual abbreviation for
-omm-.

4940 BE paraphrases somewhat freely: "So far does he wander wilfully from seriousness." FI takes *frowarde
from sadnesse* as "obstinate against sobriety." On BE's pronoun *he,* see below.

   she: As GL notes, MS lacks a subject pronoun. KA suggests "insert *she* (cf. l. 4988) or *it* (cf. l. 4894)."
The Fr. is not parallel, but the antecedent is *Youthe* (line 4935), which translates the grammatically feminine *Jennece*
(Lc 4443).

4943 **Demande:** SK's emendation, as endorsed by KA. The sense is clearly "ask," and the change follows the
Fr. (Lc 4449 "ou le demant aus anciens" "or ask it of the old"; noted by SK RBt SU FI RIt). Liddell (GL) retains MS
And moo, taking *moo* as "either verb meaning *to ask* or mistake for some such word"; he compares line 5290 "The
more," which, he feels, may be "either a subst. meaning *request,* or a similar mistake to that in v. 4943." However,
neither the exact form nor the nature of the mistake is clear. *MED mḗven* v. 6a. (b) ". . . put a (question) to (sb.)"
might suggest that *moo* may be a form of *meven, move(n* v.; but the idiom *move of* is not recorded in such a sense.

Which yit remembre of tendir age 4945
Hou it hem brought in many a rage
And many a foly therynne wrought.
But now that Eelde hath hym thurgh sought,
They repente hem of her folye,
That Youthe hem putte in jupardye, 4950
In perell, and in mych woo,
And made hem ofte amys [to do],
And suen yvell companye,
Riot and avoutrie.

   "But Eelde [can] ageyn restreyne 4955
From sich foly, and refreyne,
And sette men by her ordinaunce
In good reule and in governaunce.
But yvell she spendith hir servise, 97v
For no man wole hir love neither [prise]; 4960
She is hated, this wote I welle.
Hir acqueyntaunce wolde no man fele,
Ne han of Elde companye;
Men hate to be of hir alye.
For no man wolde bicomen olde, 4965
Ne dye whanne he is yong and bolde.
And Eelde merveilith right gretlye,
Whanne thei remembre hem inwardly
Of many a perelous emprise,
Whiche that they wrought in sondry wise, 4970
Houevere they myght, withoute blame,

Escape awey withoute shame,
In youthe, withoute damage
Or repreef of her lynage,
Losse of membre, shedyng of blode, 4975
Perell of deth, or losse of good.
Woste thou nought where Youthe abit,
That men so preisen in her witt?
With Delite she halt sojour,
For bothe they dwellen in oo tour. 4980
As longe as Youthe is in sesoun,
They dwellen in oon mansioun.
Delite of Youthe wole have servise 98r
To do what so he wole devise;
And Youthe is redy evermore 4985
For to obey, for smerte of sore,
Unto Delite, and hym to yeve
Hir servise, while that she may lyve.
   "Where Elde abit I wole thee telle
Shortly, and no while dwelle, 4990
For thidir byhoveth thee to goo.
If Deth in youthe thee not sloo,
Of this journey thou maist not faile.
With hir Labour and Travaile
Logged ben, with Sorwe and Woo, 4995
That never out of hir court goo.
Peyne and Distresse, Syknesse and Ire,
And Malencoly, that angry sire,

4945 **remembre**] remembreth MS-SP³ BE-KA FU   4952 **to do**] d. t. MS KA   4954 **Riot**] And r. UR
4955 **can**] gan MS TH¹ TH³-KA FU   4958 **and in**] and TH³-SP³ MO   4959 **yvell**] ill UR   4960 **neither**]
ne UR SK GL FI   **prise**] preise MS-KA GL FU SU FI   4973 **damage**] any d. UR   4974 **Or**] Without
UR   4986 **of**] or SP²-BE   4992 **thee**] hath t. GL   4994 **and**] a. eke UR

4945   **remembre:** KA suggests the emendation UR makes.
4948   **hym:** "them." See 1922n. UR SK GL RB¹-RI respell as *hem*, the usual form of the 3 pl. object personal pron. KA notes *hem* in UR.
4951   **mych:** See 1713n.
4954   **avoutrie:** UR SK GL RB RI respell with a medial *-e-*; KA suggests the change. Although the medial *-e-* is present in Latin *adulterium*, it is not usual in the OF etymon. The resulting line is headless except in UR, where the variant *And riot* supplies an extra syllable.
4955–5026   As at lines 349–68 (see n.), BE compares the portrait of Old Age in Sackville's Induction.
4955   **can:** TH³'s emendation; KA endorses the change in SK.
4959   "i.e., her efforts are unprofitable" (FI).
      yvell: See 4899n.
4960   **neither:** UR emends to *ne*; KA suggests the same change. Liddell (GL) compares line 3718, where he has *nor* for MS *neithir*. RBt RIt grant that the change may be correct.
      prise: KA's suggested emendation follows the Fr. *prise* (Lc 4462 "car nus ne l'aime ne ne prise" "for no one loves or values her") and improves the rhyme. Cf. 4476n.
4973   **damage:** KA attributes to Skeat the suggestion *any damage*, but the change appears only in UR.
4987–88   **yeve : lyve:** See 2759–60n.
4995–5000   RI notes that there is no parallel in the Fr. for these lines. See 5000–04n.
4998   **sire:** "A respectful title . . . sometimes put for *personage*" (TRg).

Ben of hir paleys senatours;
Gronyng and Grucchyng, hir herbejours, 5000
The day and nyght, hir to turment,
With cruell Deth they hir present
And tellen hir, erliche and late,
That Deth stondith armed at hir gate.
Thanne brynge they to her
    remembraunce 5005
The foly dedis of hir infaunce,
Whiche causen hir to mourne in woo 98v
That Youthe hath hir bigiled so,
Which sodeynly awey is hasted.
She wepe[th] the tyme that she
    hath wasted, 5010
Compleynyng of the preterit,
And the present, that not abit,

And of hir olde vanite,
That, but aforn hir she may see
In the future somme socour, 5015
To leggen hir of hir dolour,
To graunte hir tyme of repentaunce,
For her synnes to do penaunce,
And at the laste so hir governe
To wynne the joy that is eterne, 5020
Fro which go bakward Youthe [her] made,
In vanite to droune and wade.
For present tyme abidith nought;
It is more swift than any thought.
So litel while it doth endure 5025
That ther nys compte ne mesure.
  "But hou that evere the game go,
Who list to [have] joie and mirth also

4999 **paleys]** pale is SP³ 5010 **wepeth]** weped MS TH¹ TH³-UR KA FU 5015 **socour]** smale s. UR 5019 **at]** atte MS BE-KA 5021 **her]** he MS-SP³ MO KA FU 5028 **to have]** t. love MS-SP³ BE-KA FU; love UR; have SK

5000–04 BE presents as parallel to this passage the following lines from the Fr. (Lc 4493–96): "Travaill et Douleur la herbergent, / mes il la lient et l'enfergent / et tant la batent et tourmentent / que mort proichaine li presentent" ("Labor and Suffering provide her with lodging, but they put her in chains and irons and so beat and torment her that they present her with the prospect of approaching death"). This passage, however, is parallel rather to the loosely translated block from lines 4994 to 5004. See 4995–5000n. BE notes the image in the ME where Gronyng and Grucchyng "continually inform" Elde "that Death is standing armed at the gate, desiring admittance. This grand image is Chaucer's own conception; the original is comparatively tame." There is question about Chaucer's authorship of Fragment B; and there may be some question too about the quality of the translation, although the image of Death standing armed at the gate is certainly not present in the Fr.

5000 **herbejours:** "chamberlains" (URg); "*maîtres d'hôtel*, the officers who announce and provide lodgings for the guests" (BE; cf. *MED herberǧ(e)our* n. 1. [a]); thus "harbingers (who go before to arrange lodging)" (RIf; cf. *MED* 1. [b]), rather than simply "hosts (as in an inn)" (FI). SKg notes that this word develops to "modern *harbinger*, with excrescent (inserted) *n*." KA endorses SK's spelling *herbergeours* (as in OF), and RB adopts the same form.

5004 **stondith:** KA endorses SK's contraction *stant* (GL RB have *stont*).

5010–26 The passage involves an incomplete sentence—see 5014–15n.—and has been variously punctuated. BE MO SK RB RI place periods after lines 5022 and 5026, and either semicolon (BE MO SK) or period (RB RI) after line 5024; only RB RI have a semicolon after line 5023. GL has a semicolon after line 5013, a comma and dash after line 5022, and a period after line 5026. FI has periods after lines 5020 and 5023, semicolon after line 5024, and period after line 5026.

5010 **wepeth:** TH²'s emendation, noted by KA in MO.

5014–15 SK notes that the incomplete sentence (lines 5010–22) arises from the translator's partial omission of the first line of the parallel Fr. couplet (Lc 4505–06 "et qu'el a sa vie perdue / se du futur n'est secourue" "and that she has wasted her life if she is not saved by the future"). SK states that "by the time [the translator] came to 'wade' at the end of l. 5022, where this line should have come in, he had lost the thread of the sentence, and so left it out!" GL RB RI, in their notes to line 5022, agree that the translator seems to have forgotten the conclusion of the *but*-clause that begins here, and they quote the Fr. As RB RI note, GL suggests that after line 5022, we might supply the line "Al her lyf she hath forlorn." This line might appear as easily at line 5014—"That al her lyf she hath forlorn"—where it would follow the construction of the Fr.

5021 **her:** KA notes *her* in UR BE.

5022 On the incomplete sentence (lines 5010–22), see 5014–15n.

5028–29 GL's emendation, based on KA SK, takes *to have* as a single syllable, "t'have." KA suggests *have* for MS *to love*, and SK so emends; SK also quotes the Fr. (Lc 4516 "qui veust d'amors joïr sanz faille" "whoever wants to enjoy love without fail"). TRg, following UR's text, "Who list love joye," and the Fr., takes *joye* as a verb, "to enjoy"; if so, *love* would be a noun and the syntax of the phrase *Of love* would be unclear.

227

Of love, be it he or she,
High or lowe, who it be, 5030
In fruyt they shulde hem delyte; 99r
Her part they may not elles quyte,
To save hemsilf in honeste.
And yit full many one I se
Of wymmen, sothly for to seyne, 5035
That desire and wolde fayne
The pley of love, they be so wilde,
And not coveite to go with childe,
And if with child they be, perchaunce,
They wole it holde a gret myschaunce; 5040
But whatsomever woo they fele,
They wole not pleyne, but concele,
But if it be ony fool or nyce,
In whom that Shame hath no justice.
For to delyte echone they drawe, 5045
That haunte this werke, bothe high and lawe,
Save sich that arn worth right nought,
That for money wole be bought.

Such love I preise in no wise,
Whanne it is goven for coveitise. 5050
I preise no womman, though [sho] be wood,
That yeveth hirsilf for ony good.
For litel shulde a man telle
Of hir, that wole hir body selle, 5054
Be she mayde, be she wyf, 99v
That quyk wole selle hir bi hir lyf.
Hou faire chere that evere she make,
He is a wrecche, I undirtake,
That love[th] such one, for swete or soure,
Though she hym calle hir paramoure 5060
And laugheth on hym, and makith hym feeste.
For certeynly no such beeste
To be loved is not worthy,
Or bere the name of drurie.
Noon shulde hir please, but he
    were woode, 5065
That wole dispoile hym of his goode.
Yit nevertheles, I wole not sey

5029 **he]** or he UR   5030 **High]** Or h. UR   **who]** w. so UR SK   5036 **That]** T. ay SK   5043 **if]** *om.* UR   5051 **sho]** so MS-SP¹ BE KA FU; she SP²-UR SK GL RB¹-RI   **be]** is UR   5054 **wole]** wel TH¹ FU   5055 **mayde be]** a m. or b. UR   5059 **loveth]** loved MS-SP³ BE-KA GL FU; love UR   5060 **calle]** called TH¹-UR FU SU FI   **hir]** *om.* SP¹   5062 **For]** And SP¹   **beeste]** a b. SK   5067 **nevertheles]** nathelesse TH¹-UR FU SU FI

5043 **ony:** See 212n.
    nyce: "foolish (woman)" (FI).
    5047 **arn:** "with the trilled *r*, is dissyllabic; see l. 5484" (SK). At line 5484, RB notes that *arn* is "the Northern form, for which Chaucer almost invariably has *ben*."
    5050 **goven:** "given" (FI); see *OED Give*, A. 8. γ.
    5051 **though sho be wood:** Following Lounsbury (1895:22), GL suggests *to be good* and quotes the Fr. (Lc 4533 "Mes ja certes n'iert fame bone" "certainly there would never be a good woman").
    sho: MO's emendation, noted by KA. BE states that MS *so* "is the Anglo-Saxon *heo*, she, with a hissing aspirate"; cf. 4537n., where we see that Skeat favors OE *seo* as the origin and that more recent thought favors *heo*. Skeat (1878c:4.172) holds that "*so* is for *sho*, Northern form of *she*." In his own ed., Skeat writes that *so* is "clearly an error for *sho*" and suggests (SKt) that we "read *she* (or *sho*)." Of these alternatives, RB prints *she* but suggests (RBt) that "perhaps we should read *sho* (a Northern form)," while RIt supports *she* as "the, normal form throughout G. [MS]." MS *so* may be a var. sp.; *MED shē* lists the form *so* as "chiefly Northern" and quotes it (l. d.) from the Northern prose version of the Benedictine Rule (before 1425); and *LALME* (4.8; 2.9,11) shows two locations for the MS form *so*—one in East Lothian and a questionable one in North Lincolnshire.
    5054 **wole:** TH¹'s form *wel* is probably an error. *OED Will* v.¹ A. 2. δ records 13th-15th-century dialectal forms in *-e*.
    5059 **loveth:** KA's suggestion. Although the Fr. parallel is not exact (Lc 4541 "qu'il cuide que tel fame l'aime" "that he believes that such a woman loves him"), the present tense (*aime*) favors the change.
    5064 **drurie:** BE, in accord with TRg, notes that the word "means sometimes courtship, gallantry. . . . Here it means a mistress." BE SK cite the Fr. *amie* (Lc 4545); Skeat (SK) thinks this sense of *druerie* improper, but *MED drūerie* n. 2. (a) gives nine examples from as early as Gower's *Confessio amantis* (ante 1393), cited in URg. SKg₂ (cf. GLg) offers "loyal affection," and FI glosses as "chivalric love service," the sense at line 844, but RIf glosses as "lover," the sense appropriate to this context. See 844n.

That she, for solace and for pley,
May a jewel or other thyng
Take of her loves fre yevyng—   5070
But that she aske it in no wise,
For drede of shame of coveitise.
And she of hirs may hym, certeyn,
Withoute sclaundre yeven ageyn
And joyne her hertes togidre so   5075
In love, and take and yeve also.
Trowe not that I wolde hem twynne,
Whanne in her love there is no synne;
I wole that they togedre go,   100r
And don al that they han ado,   5080
As curteis shulde and debonaire,
And in her love beren hem faire,
Withoute vice, bothe he and she,
So that alwey, in honeste,
Fro foly love [they] kepe hem clere,   5085
That brenneth hertis with his fere;
And that her love, in ony wise,
Be devoide of coveitise.
      "Good love shulde engendrid be
Of trewe herte, just, and secre,   5090

And not of such as sette her thought
To have her lust and ellis nought;
So are they caught in Loves lace,   5070
Truly, for bodily solace.
Fleshly delite is so present   5095
With thee, that sette all thyne entent
Withoute more (what shulde I glose?)
For to gete and have the rose,
Which makith [thee] so mate and woode
That thou desirest noon other goode.   5100
But thou art not an inche the nerre,
But evere abidist in sorwe and werre,
As in thi face it is sene.   100v
It makith thee bothe pale and lene;
Thy myght, thi vertu goth away.   5105
A sory geste, in goode fay,
Thou herberest hem in thyne inne,
The God of Love whanne thou let inne!
Wherfore I rede thou shette hym oute,
Or he shall greve thee, oute of doute;   5110
[For to] thi profight it wole turne,
Iff he nomore with thee sojourne.
In gret myscheef and sorwe sonken

5068 **That]** But SK RB[1,2] FI   5069 **May]** Ne m. GL RI   5070 **loves]** lovers TH[2]   5071 **it]** *om.* SP[2,3]
5072 **of coveitise]** or c. TH[1]-MO FU SU FI   5077 **wolde]** wol TH[1]-UR FU SU FI   5081 **curteis]** certeis
MO   5085 **they]** to MS-KA FU   5088 **coveitise]** all c. UR   5099 **thee]** *om.* MS KA   5103 **sene]** to
s. TH[2]   5107 **herberest hem]** herborest TH[1]-SP[3] FU; h. than UR BE GL SU RI; herberedest than SK RB[1,2]

5068   **That:** For the negative sense, KA endorses SK's *But.* GL RI supply the negative particle *Ne* in the next
line; RIt (line 5069) regards GL's emendation "as preferable to Skeat's." See 5069n.
5069   **May:** On the emendation *Ne may* (GL RI), see 5068n. On the possibility that emendation may not be
necessary, see notes to lines 3769, 3774, 4764.
5080   **han ado:** "have to do" (URg TRg SK); SK explains that *ado* is "short for *at do,* i.e. to do," and that "*at* =
to, is Northern."
5085   **they:** KA's suggestion. SK RIt quote the Fr. (Lc 4563 "mes de la fole amor *se gardent*" "but [that they]
keep themselves from the foolish love"). "But," states RBt, "the anacoluthon" with MS *to* "is possible."
         foly: "foolish (unnatural)" (FI).
5087   **ony:** See 212n.
5099   **thee:** KA notes the insertion of *thee* in UR-MO.
5107   **herberest hem:** MS *hem* may be a 3 sg. object masculine pronoun (see 2854n.), referring to "geste" in
the preceding line and "The God of Love" in the next; but the syntax is awkward, and only MO FI retain this
reading. Perhaps on the basis of the Fr. (Lc 4578–79 "Mout receüs doulereus hoste / quant onques Amor hostelas"
"You received a very burdensome guest when you took in the God of Love"), TH[1] omitted MS *hem* and thus
improved the sense, if not the meter; SK RBt note the Fr. Early eds. all follow TH[1], and RIt says that "perhaps Th is
correct." RIt supports UR's *herborist than* by noting that "*Than* is suggested by *whanne* in 5108," but grants that "it is
difficult to see how [MS] *hem* originates." KA endorses SK's pa. t. *herberedest,* which SK reads as a trisyllable,
"herb'redest." SK RB combine these two changes (*herberedest than*), and SK cites Lounsbury (1892:2.14), who
thought that "*herberedest* should take the place of *herberest hem.*" While Lounsbury's is the clearest reading in terms
of sense and syntax, it does not sufficiently account for MS *hem.*
5111   **profight:** MS *p̄fiȝt,* for forms, see *MED profit(e* n.(1).

229

Ben hertis that of love arn dronken,
As thou peraventure knowen shall, 5115
Whanne thou hast lost [thy] tyme all,
And spent [thy youth] in ydilnesse,
In waste and wofull lustynesse.
If tho[w] maist lyve the tyme to se
Of love for to delyvered be, 5120
Thy tyme thou shalt biwepe sore,
The whiche never thou maist restore;
For tyme lost, as men may see,
For nothyng may recured be.
And if thou scape yit, atte laste, 5125
Fro Love, that hath thee so faste
Knytt and bounden in his lace, 101r
Certeyn I holde it but a grace.
For many oon, as it is seyne,
Have lost and spent also in veyne, 5130

In his servise, withoute socour,
Body and soule, good and tresour, 5115
Witte and strengthe and eke richesse,
Of which they hadde never redresse." 5134
    Lamant.   Thus taught and preched
        hath Resoun,
But Love spilte hir sermoun,
That was so ymped in my thought,
That hir doctrine I sette at nought.
And yitt ne seide she never a dele
That I ne undirstode it wele, 5140
Word by word, the mater all;
But unto Love I was so thrall,
Which callith overall his pray,
He chasith so my thought [alway],
And holdith myne herte undir his sele 5145
As trust and trew as ony stele,

5116 **thy]** the MS-SP³ BE-KA FU   5117 **thy youth]** by thought MS-ST KA FU; thy thought SP¹-MO   5119 **thow]** thou MS (MS₁ corr.)   5124 **recured]** recouered TH¹-UR FU-FI   5125 **atte]** at TH¹-SP³ FU SU FI   5133 **Witte]** And w. UR   5136 **hir]** hath h. UR   5144 **He]** And MO   **thought alway]** t. ay MS-SP³ BE-KA FU SU FI; thoughtis ay UR; t. al day GL

5115 **peraventure:** KA, adducing line 5192, attributes to Skeat the suggestion *peraunter*, but only GL adopts the form.

5116 **thy:** KA notes UR's emendation; SKt GL SU-RIt cite the Fr. *ton tens* (Lc 4588 "your time").

5117 **thy youth:** KA's suggestion follows the Fr. *ta jovente* (Lc 4589 "your youth"; noted by SK GL RB¹-RI).

5119 **thow:** "*thou* altered to *thow*" (KA); MS₁ has added three strokes to the *u*.

5123–24 SK RB RI suggest that these lines, which are not in the Fr., are perhaps from *HF* 1257–58. "The converse," writes Skeat (SK), "seems to me unlikely; however," he adds, "they are not remarkable for their originality." RB FI compare *MLH* B¹ 20ff.; in the note to those lines, RB calls attention to the "commonplace or even proverbial" nature of the passage and adduces Chaucerian (*ClT* E 118–19, *Rom* 369ff.) as well as classical parallels. RI also notes the proverbial character and cites *TC* 4.1283n., where Barney (RI) refers to Whiting (1968: T307) and (for a parallel Latin proverb) Walther (1963–69: no. 4893). FI also notes that these lines are a commonplace found in *HF* 1257 and *MLH* B¹ 20 ff.

5124 **recured:** SU FI support TH¹'s *recouered*, noted by KA, on the basis of the Fr. *recouvrer* (Lc 4594). For the form *recured*, SK refers to examples in Halliwell (1847), RIt to *OED recured*; see *MED recoveren* v.(2), *recūren* v. RIt compares line 4920.

5135 **Lamant:** In MS, the rubric appears at the end of the previous line. RIt notes that SK GL RB omit this heading, "though they print an identical rubric with 4785."

5136–37 "Love that was so grafted in my thought, destroyed Reason's teaching" (RB). SK notes that "*That* refers to *love*, not to the *sermon*; and *hir* refers to Reason."

5137 **ymped:** "(en)grafted" (SPg et al.), "(im)planted" (TRg FI RIf). BE explains the metaphor as one from falconry: "When the wing or tail feather of a hawk is accidentally broken, so that her flight might be impeded, it is spliced with another of the same sort by means of a needle, one end of which is driven into the stump, and the other into the new feather. This is called *imping*." But *MED impen* v. takes the basic senses as (a) planting or (b) grafting, with the splicing of the falcon's broken feather as a specialized sense (g).

5144 **thought alway:** KA, noting that in MS there is "an erasure between *thought* and *ay*," endorses Skeat's suggestion, "*alway* or *al day* (5174) for *ay*." GL notes the "alday" at line 5174 and RIt notes the erasure. The erased space (8 mm.) leaves room for a word-space and two letters, which, under ultra-violet examination, appear to have been *aw*, presumably an error for *alw*; the erasure of these two letters—leaving *ay*—restored the sense but not the meter.

5145 **holdith:** KA attributes to Skeat the suggestion *halt*, but only GL so emends.

5146 **trew as ony stele:** RI notes the proverbial phrase and compares *MerT* E 2426, where Tavormina's note (RI) cites Whiting (1968: S709) as well as *PF* 395, *LGW* F 334, 2582, *TC* 5.831.

    ony: See 212n.

So that no devocioun
Ne hadde I in the sermoun
Of Dame Resoun, ne of [hir] rede;
It toke no sojour in myne hede,   5150
For all yede oute at oon ere   101v
That in that other she dide lere.
Fully on me she lost hir lore;
Hir speche me greved wondir sore.
   [Than] unto hir for ire I seide,   5155
For anger as I dide abraide:

"Dame, and is it youre wille algate
That I not love, but that I hate
Alle men, as ye me teche?
For if I do aftir youre speche,   5160
Sith that ye seyne love is not good,
Thanne must I nedis [ay] with mood,
If I it leve, in hatrede ay
Lyven, and voide love away
From me, [and been] a synfull wrecche, 5165
Hated of all [that love] that tecche.

5147 **that**] t. I UR 5148 **I in the**] in the wise UR 5149 **hir**] *om.* MS (MS₁ *corr.*) 5150 **It**] I ST-MO FU 5151 **oon**] that o. GL 5155 **Than**] That MS-KA FU 5159 **teche**] now do t. UR 5162 **ay**] say MS-FI 5164 **Lyven**] To l. GL **away**] alwaye TH² 5165 **From me and been**] F. m. MS-SP³ BE-KA FU; Ferre f. m. UR; F. m. wole I SU FI 5166 **that love that tecche**] that tecche MS-KA FU; that vertu tetche SU FI

5149 **hir:** "written above the line" (KA) by MS₁.

5151–52 RB RI note that the expression "in one ear and out the other" is still proverbial and compare *TC* 4.432–34, where RB's note cites Haeckel (1890: no. 4) and where Barney's note (RI) cites Whiting (1968: E4) and observes further that the "'deaf ears' of a lover are known in antiquity (Propertius 2.16.35; Walther [1963–69, no.] 31975)." Both Robinson and Barney cite the Fr. (Lc 4610–11 "par l'une des oreilles giete / quan que Reson en l'autre boute" "[The God of Love] throws out of one of my ears all that Reason pushes into the other").

5155 **Than:** KA's suggestion; SKt SU FI RIt note the basis in the Fr. *Lors* (Lc 4614 "Then"). As RIt notes, "a large initial in both G and Th indicates a new paragraph."

5156 **abraide:** Perhaps "speak" or "start to speak" (RIf *MED abreiden* v.[1], sense 3 [c]), rather than "vp-start" (SP²,³g); "start (up)" (URg et al.; cf. *MED* 2 [a]).

5162–66 SK notes that "the sense is doubtful" and that "ll. 5165, 6 are both deficient, and require filling up." With two emendations (see lines 5165–66), SK proposes the following reading: "'Then must I needs, if I leave it (i. e. Love), boldly essay to live always in hatred, and put away love from me, and be a sinful wretch, hated by all who love that fault.'" The reading takes *say* (line 5162) as a form of *assay* (see below) and *tecche* (line 5166) as "spot, fault" (*OED Tache* sb.¹).

David (RI) notes that the passage is "obscure" and follows SK in all but the first line, where he adopts *ay* for MS *say* (see 5162n.). He quotes the Fr. lines that form a rough parallel to lines 5162–66 (Ln 4650–52 [= Lc 4620–22] "Ainz vivrai toujourz en haïnes, / Lors si serai morteus pechierres, / Veire, par Deu, pires que lierres" "thus I should live ever in hatred; then I would be in mortal sin, truly, by God, worse than a thief"). The Lecoy text has a question mark instead of a semicolon after the first line; see 5162n.

SU FI's emendations suggest another reading: "Then I must needs, if I leave it, try with anger to live always in hatred; and I will put away love from me, a sinful wretch, hated by all who teach virtue." In this reading, *tecche* (line 5166) is taken as "teach." For details, see the collations and the notes below.

5162 **ay:** In support of his emendation, David (RIt) quotes the Fr. (Ln 4648–50 [= Lc 4618–20, where the passage closes with a question mark rather than a semicolon] "Puis qu'amours ne sont mie bones, / Jamais n'amerai d'amours fines, / Ainz vivrai toujourz en haïnes" "Since love is not good, I would never love according to 'fine amour,' thus I would live perpetually in hatred"). "The verb *say*," argues David, "corresponds to nothing in the French and lacks an object. The *s* may be repeated from the final letter of *nedis*. Dropping it, *ay with mood* becomes parallel with *in hatrede ay* in 5163." Others accept MS *say* as "assay?" (SKt), "an apheticform of *assay*, to attempt" (GL); "attempt" (*MED saien* v. [e]).

    with mood: "boldly" (SK; see 5162–66n.); "with anger" (FI RIf).

5165–66 Sutherland (SU 5164–66n.) notes that the "text is corrupt," reviews the emendations of SK GL RB, and says that he bases his emendations "on the Fr. ('But I will always live in hate. . . .')"; see 5162–66n., 5165n., 5166n.

5165 **me, and been a:** KA endorses SK's emendation. SK GL RB RI take the statement "I must nedis . . . be a sinful wretch" as a parallel to the Fr. (Lc 4621 "Lors si seré mortex pechierres" "I would be a mortal sinner").

5166 Jephson (BE) thinks this line "evidently corrupt" (he is silent about line 5165), and he compares it with a couplet in the Fr. (Lc 4621–22, above) that is only loosely related to the ME. KA endorses SK's insertion of *that love* after *all*, for the sense "hated by all who love that fault." GL observes that the inserted words "seem necessary to the

I may not go noon other gate,
For other must I love or hate.
And if I hate men of-newe,
More than love, it wole me rewe,   5170
As by youre preching semeth me,
For Love nothing ne preisith thee.
Ye yeve good counsel, sikirly,
That prechith me alday that I   5174
Shulde not Loves lore alowe.   102r
He were a foole, wolde you not trowe!
In speche also ye han me taught
Another love, that knowen is naught,
Which I have herd you not repreve,
To love ech other. By youre leve,   5180

If ye wolde diffyne it me,
I wolde gladly here, to se,
At the leest, if I may lere
Of sondry loves the manere."   5184
    Raisoun. "Certis, freend, a fool art thou,
Whan that thou nothyng wolt allowe
That I for thi profit say.
Yit wole I sey [thee] more in fay,
For I am redy, at the leste,
To accomplisshe thi requeste.   5190
But I not where it wole avayle;
In veyn, perauntre, I shal travayle.
    "Love ther is in sondry wise,
As I shal thee heere devise.

5168 **other**] eyther TH¹-UR SK FU SU FI   5172 **ne**] *om.* BE   5175 **Shulde**] Ne s. UR   5179 **have**] *om.* TH²   5181 **wolde**] I w. TH²   5183 **At**] Atte MS BE-KA   **may**] mowin UR   5184 **loves**] Loue SP²˒³ 5185 **fool**] grete f. UR   5187 **That I**] Which t. I UR; T. I thee SK   5188 **thee**] the MS (MS₁ *corr.*)   5190 **thi**] they FU   5192 **perauntre**] pareuenture SU FI   **shal**] *om.* UR   5194 **As**] Right a. UR; And FU

---

sense." RIt notes that they are "not in the French" and that "the whole passage is probably corrupt." SU FI insert *vertu* before *tetche*, to read "hated by all who teach virtue." See 5162–66n., 5165–66n.

    tecche: "fault, bad habit" (SKg₂ SK 5162n.), "quality" (RIf). With emendation, SU FI read as "teach."

    5167 **gate:** "way" (URg et al.), "manner" (URg FI), "wise" (SKg₂ RBg). *MED gate* n.(2) is a northern word of Old Norse origin that appears also at lines 2158, 3332, 5230, and 5722; all five occurrences are in Fragment B and support KA's theory that the B-translator is different from that of A and C.

    5168 **other:** Distinct in origin (*OE ōþer*) from *outher* (*OE āhwæþer*). On *outher* and *eyther*, see 250n. *MED ōþer* conj. notes that "there is a tendency, esp. in correl. constructions, to substitute *ōþer* for *outher*."

    5169–72 "L'Amant means that just as Reason blames Love, Love blames Reason; and that, therefore, he would probably suffer just as much by following one as the other" (BE). RB (5169–71n.) and RI call this passage "obscure" and quote the Fr. (Lc 4626–28 "Mes espoir que je conparré / plus la haïne au dasrenier, / tout ne vaille amors un denier" "But maybe I would in the end pay more for hatred, even though love be not worth a penny"); RI notes that "lines 5171–72 are either not in the Fr. or stem from a misreading." A literal reading might be: "And if again I hate men more than love [them], I'll be sorry, as it seems to me from your preaching, for Love doesn't value you at all."

    5172 **ne preisith thee:** GL quotes the Fr. from Michel, "Tout me vaille Amors un denier" (= Lc 4628, above); as RB notes (5169–71n.), "Michel reads 'me' for 'ne.'"

    5173–74 As KA notes, these two lines appear at the bottom of 101v; at the top of 102r, they "are repeated . . . but afterwards cancelled."

    5176 Jephson (BE) writes: "Sir Harris Nicolas places a note of interrogation at the end of this line, which makes it unintelligible"; he refers to the Aldine ed. (1845; MO [a revision of the Aldine] has an exclamation point). The question mark appears first in SP³ and then in later eds. like the Chiswick of 1822, the basis of the 1845 *Romaunt* (Hammond 1908:137, 140). § BE SK note that the line ("He who would not believe you would be a fool") is ironic, and SK compares lines 5185–87. Both BE and SK note that the omission of the relative pronoun is common, and SK notes that the relative *qui* appears in the Fr. (Lc 4632). Cf. 1239n. for another example of the omission of relative subject-pronoun; Roscow (1981:110–15) omits the example here.

    5185 *Raisoun:* In MS, the rubric appears at the end of the previous line.

    5186 "When that thou wilt approve of nothing" (SK). TRg BE SKg₂ GLg all provide "approve" for *allowe*, and SKg₂ cites the Fr. *prises* (Ln 4674). BE quotes "the English translation of the Psalms. 'The Lord *alloweth* the righteous,'" giving no reference; but *OED allow* v., sense 2 "approve," cites the Coverdale Bible (1535), Ps. 1.6 "the Lord aloweth yᵉ way of the rightuous," where the Authorized Version has *knoweth the way.* Neither the AV nor the Douai has a similar passage, with *alloweth*, in Psalms.

    5187 **That I:** KA, noting lines 5188 and 5194, endorses SK's *That I thee.*

    5188 **thee:** "second *e* written above the line" (KA) by MS₁.

    5191 "But I know not whether it will profit" (SK). BE FI note that *where* means "whether."

For somme love leful is and good;   5195
I mene not that which makith thee wood,
And bringith thee in many a fitte,   102v
And ravysshith fro thee al thi witte,
It is so merveilouse and queynte;
With such love be no more aqueynte.   5200
   Comment Raisoun diffinist a[mi]sete
Love of freendshipp also ther is,
Which makith no man done amys,
Of wille knytt bitwixe two,
That wole not breke for wele ne woo;
Which long is likly to contune,   5205
Whanne wille and goodis ben in comune;
Grounded by Goddis ordinaunce,
Hoole, withoute discordaunce;

With hem holdyng comunte
Of all her goode in charite,   5210
That ther be noon excepcioun
Thurgh chaungyng of entencioun;
That ech helpe other at her neede,
And wisely hele bothe word and dede;
Trewe of menyng, devoide of slouthe,   5215
For witt is nought without trouthe;
So that the ton dar all his thought
Seyn to his freend, and spare nought,
As to hymsilf, without dredyng
To be discovered by wreying.   5220
For glad is that conjunccioun,   103r
Whanne ther is noon susspecioun
[Of blame in hem], whom they wolde prove

5200 **no]** *om.* BE   *Rubric:* **amisete]** aunsete MS-KA FU   *Out:* GL   5207 **Goddis]** Goodes SU FI
5208 **Hoole]** All whole UR   5209 **comunte]** commaunce TH³ ST SP²-UR   5210 **in]** *om.* SU FI   5223 **Of blame in hem]** Betwixtin 'hem UR; Ne lak in hem SK GL RB¹-FI; *om.* MS-SP³ BE-KA FU

5199 **queynte:** "strange" (SKg₂); cf. 65n.
Rubric: "How Reason defines friendship" (RIf). In MS, the rubric appears in the right margin, the first two words at the end of line 5200, the last two at the end of line 5201.
     amisete: KA's suggested emendation, "*amisete* (*amisté, amistiē*) for *aunsete.*" The reading *aunsete*, in TH¹-KA FU, may be an accurate transcription of MS or, alternatively, a misreading of *amisete*. There are four minims that may be read *un* or *mi*; if Kaluza was right in reading *un* (cf. line 5205 *contune*, line 5206 *comune*), then it is "the MS copyist's misreading . . . for *amisete*" (Kaluza 1889:529). Eds. respell as *amistie* (SK), *amiste* (RB RI), or *amitie* (SU FI).
5201–5310 On the definition of friendship, RB RI note that Ln compares Cicero, *De amicitia*, chaps. 5, 6, 13, 17. Lc (4655–732n.) notes the use of Cicero, and Ln quotes passages in notes to specific lines from *RR* 4685 to 4774 (= Lc 4655–4744). On Aelred of Rievaulx's *De spiritali amicitia* as Jean de Meun's source, see Friedman (1962) and Fleming (1984:76–82).
5201 **Love of freendshipp:** "friendly love" (RB), "love between friends" (RIf). RB RI compare *TC* 2.371, 962. For a similar construction, they compare *KnT* A 1912 *Dyane of chastitee* "the chaste Diana." In notes to the latter passage, RB points out that "the phrase with *of* is equivalent to an adjective," and DiMarco (RI), citing Mustanoja (1960:80–81), calls the construction "the genitive of description or quality"; RB compares *MkT* B² 3327.
5205 **contune:** continue. See 4354n.
5206–10 This passage reflects the Fr. (Lc 4659–60 "et soit entr'els conmunité / de touz leur biens en charité" "and among them there is community of all their goods in charity"), which, as Fleming points out (1984:78–79), derives from Acts 4.32, a passage that Aelred of Rievaulx connects with the Ciceronian definition of friendship. Ln (4689–92n.) quotes Cicero, *De amicitia* 17.61.
5209 **holdyng comunte:** UR has *yholding commaunce*, and URg suggests *commanaunce*, "to compleat the Verse, which wants a Syllable."
5213 Ln (4693n.) quotes Cicero, *De amicitia* 13.44.
5215–16 Ln (4695–96n.) quotes Cicero, *De amicitia* 5.18, 6.20
5217–20 Ln (4697–700n.) quotes Cicero, *De amicitia* 6.22.
5222–24 Eds. call the unemended passage "corrupt" (BE SU) or "obscure" (RI). On the missing first half of line 5223, see 5222–23n. With David's emendation, "the sense of the English is that the ones true and perfect in love suspect no blame in those (i.e., their friends) they would prove" (RI). § RI notes that "the idea of testing friendship is proverbial," and compares Whiting (1968: F656) "One true Friend should prove another."
5222–23 The words *Of blame in hem* are not in MS. The emendation adopted is that of RI, the first to identify the correct parallel in the Fr. (Lc 4670 "sanz soupeçon d'ancusemant" "without fear of denunciation" [RIt: "without suspicion of blame"]). Other eds. have neglected this line and taken the next two lines of the Fr. as the parallel (Lc

That trewe and parfit weren in love.
For no man may be amyable,   5225
But if he be so ferme and stable
That fortune chaunge hym not, ne blynde,
But that his freend allwey hym fynde,
Bothe pore and riche, in oo state.
For if his freend, thurgh ony gate,   5230
Wole compleyne of his poverte,
He shulde not bide so long til he
Of his helpyng hym requere;
For goode dede, done thurgh praiere,
Is sold and bought to deere, iwys,   5235
To hert that of grete valour is.
For hert fulfilled of gentilnesse
Can yvel demene his distresse;
And man that worthy is of name
To asken often hath gret shame.   5240
A good man brenneth in his thought
For shame, whanne he axeth ought.
He hath gret thought and dredeth ay
For his disese, whanne he shal pray   5244
His freend, lest that he warned be,   103v

Til that he preve his stabilte.
But whanne that he hath founden oon
That trusty is and trewe as stone,
And assaied hym at alle,
And founde hym stedefast as a walle,   5250
And of his freendshipp be certeyne,
He shal hym shewe bothe joye and peyne,
And all that [he] dar thynke or sey,
Withoute shame, as he wel may.
For how shulde he ashamed be   5255
Of sich one as I tolde thee?
For whanne he woot his secre thought,
The thridde shal knowe therof right nought;
For tweyne of noumbre is bet than thre
In every counsell and secre.   5260
Repreve he drede[th] never a deele,
Who that bisett his wordis wele,
For every wise man, out of drede,
Can kepe his tunge til he se nede.
And fooles cannot holde her tunge;   5265
A fooles belle is soone runge.
Yit shal a trewe freend do more

5233 **hym]** doth h. UR   5234 **thurgh]** but t. SK   5236 **valour]** value FI   5238 **demene]** demeaue TH[1,2] FU   5242 **whanne]** w. that UR   5246 **that]** *om.* UR   5249 **assaied]** hath a. UR SK GL   5253 **he]** *om.* MS-SP[3] KA FU   5254 **wel]** *om.* SP[2,3]   5256 **one]** an o. UR   5257 **secre]** secrete TH[2] ST-UR   5259 **of]** in TH[1]-BE SK FU SU FI   5261 **dredeth]** dreded MS BE-KA

4671–72 "Tels meurs avoir doivent et seulent / qui parfetement amer veulent" "Those who wish to love perfectly ought to have such customs as habitual practices"). Jephson (BE) thinks that this couplet does not "enable us to suggest the true reading." The statement is true of the lines that he quotes, where only the second ("those who wish to love perfectly") appears in approximate form (line 5224 "That trewe and parfit weren in love"); the first ("ought to have such customs as habitual practices") does not appear at all. KA Fr. places these two lines opposite ME 5223–24, and GL RB quote the same Fr. couplet. Skeat (SK) also neglects the previous line (Lc 4670); thus he notes that "the F. text does not help here" and that, in the ME, "half the line is lost; the rest means—'whom they, that ought to be true and perfect in love, would wish to prove.'" KA endorses SK's *Ne lak in hem.* In this emendation, SK glosses *lak* as "defect"; FI glosses it as "shortcoming (failure of friendship)."

5225–27 Ln (4703–05n.) quotes Cicero, *De amicitia* 17.62.

5230 **thurgh ony gate:** in any "occasion" (SP[2,3]g), "manner, wise" (URg), "circumstance" (FI RIf); "way" (*MED gate* n.[2] 5. [a]). See 5167n.

ony: See 212n.

5234–35 "Proverbial" (RB RI). RB quotes the Latin "satis emit qui petit," and notes that "Langlois [4712–14n.] cites parallels from Latin and French." RI cites Whiting (1968: D130).

5236 **valour:** "value" (TRg), "worth" (SKg[2]). FI's *value*, in the same sense of "worth," seems an unnecessary emendation and may be an error for *valure*, the form in TH[1], FI's base text.

5238 **demene:** Probably "express, show" (*MED dēmeinen* v. 3. [c]), rather than "endure" (SKg, Glg FI) or "control" (RIf), either of which senses would contradict the notion of concealing distress. Not in the Fr.

5249 **assaied:** KA suggests *hath assaied.*

5251 **freendshipp:** MS has a macron over the final *-pp.* MS spells *freendshipp,* line 5201; *frendshipp,* lines 5536, 5540; *frendshipe,* line 2184; and *frendship,* line 7056. Cf. 4915n.

5253 **he:** UR's emendation; KA notes it in UR BE MO.

5259–60 "a commonplace sentiment, if not exactly proverbial" (RB). Not in the Fr. (RB RI).

5266 Proverbial (BE SK RB RI). BE compares the expression "A fool's bolt is soon shot"; RB compares Haeckel (1890: no. 61), and RI cites Whiting (1968: F407). Not in the Fr. (SK RB RI).

To helpe his felowe of his sore,
And socoure hym, whanne he hath neede, 104r
In all that he may done in deede, 5270
And gladder [be] that he hym plesith
Than his felowe that he esith.
And if he do not his requeste,
He shal as mochel hym moleste
As his felow, for that he 5275
May not fulfille his volunte
Fully, as he hath requered.
If bothe the hertis Love hath fered,
Joy and woo they shull departe,

And take evenly ech his parte. 5280
Half his anoy he shal have ay,
And comfort [him] what that he may;
And of [his] blisse parte shal he,
If love [wel] departed be.
    "And whilom of this [amyte] 5285
Spake Tulius in a ditee:
'[Man] shulde maken his requeste
Unto his freend, that is honeste;
And he goodly shulde it fulfille,
But it the more were out of skile, 5290
And otherwise not graunte therto

5271 **be]** *om.* MS-UR MO KA FU   5272 **Than]** T. is SK   5275 **for]** bicause UR   5276 **not]** noe
SP²·³   5277 **Fully]** All f. UR; As f. SK   5279 **Joy]** Bothe j. UR   5282 **him]** *om.* MS-SP³ BE-KA
FU   5283 **his]** this MS-ST SP²·³ BE-KA FU   5284 **wel]** wole MS-SK FU   5285 **amyte]** vnyte MS-KA GL
FU   5287 **Man]** And MS-SP³ BE-KA FU; A man UR SK SU FI   5290 **it]** if GL

5271 **be:** BE's emendation, noted by KA.
5274–75 "That is, 'He shall vex himself as much as his friend is vexed, because he cannot grant his friend's request'" (BE); "He will be troubled as much as his fellow" (RIf). SK notes that *him* is reflexive, meaning "himself," but GL, as RB RI note, suggests that for *He* (line 5274) "perhaps read *that* or *it*, as a reflexive verb *molest* is unusual."
5277–78 **requered : fered:** RB RI (5278n.) note that *fered* is a Kentish form that Chaucer and others use occasionally for rhyme.
5277 **Fully:** KA endorses SK's *As fully*.
5278 **the:** SKt suggests, "perhaps om. *the*," and KA endorses the suggestion; but neither SK nor any other ed. so emends.
    fered: "fired" (SK RB), "inflamed" (SK RIf).
5280 **take:** KA attributes to SK the suggestion *taken*, but no ed. so emends.
5281 Ln (4743–46n.) RB compare Cicero, *De amicitia* 6.22.
5282 **him:** KA notes UR's insertion of *him*, as a result of which, *comfort* becomes a verb, as in the Fr. (Lc 4714 "et de quan qu'il peut le conforte" "and he comforts him as much as he can"; noted in GL).
5283 **his:** SP¹'s *his*, suggested in KA, follows the Fr. *sa* (Lc 4715 "et de sa joie a sa partie" "and has his share of his [i.e., the friend's] joy"; noted by SU).
5284 **wel:** GL's emendation follows the Fr. *a droit* (Lc 4716 "rightly"; noted by GL RBt SU RIt).
5285 **amyte:** SK's emendation (*amitee*) follows the Fr. *amistié* (Lc 4717 "friendship"; noted by SK SU FI RIt).
5286 **Tulius:** BE SK RB RI note the direct reference to Cicero's *De amicitia* (12, 13, 17). Cf. 5201–5310n. Ln (in notes from 4747 to 4762) quotes the passages.
5287–5300 "A friend is bound to assist his friend in any just and reasonable cause, except only in two cases, and then he is bound to assist him even though his cause be unjust; and these two cases are, when his life or his good name are in danger" (BE). SK gives a similar summary and includes Cicero's statement of the two cases: "in quibus eorum aut caput agatur aut fama" (*De amicitia* 17.61 "in which either life or reputation is concerned").
5287 **Man:** GL's emendation is based on the Fr. *devons* (Lc 4719 "we should, one should"; noted in RIt). UR anticipated this change with *A man*, suggested by KA. The form *man* is perhaps slightly closer to the Fr. and produces a headless line.
5290 RB RI call the line obscure. RB suggests: "perhaps: 'Unless it were too unreasonable.'" FI RIf also take *out of skile* as "unreasonable." RI quotes the Fr. (Lc 4722 "s'ele contient droit et reson" "If it [the request] is just and reasonable").
    But it: "Unless it," where the antecedent of *it*, as in line 5289, is *requeste* (line 5287). As RBt RIt note, GL emends to *But if* ("unless") and says that "*more* is either a subst. meaning *request*, or a similar mistake to that in v. 4943." See 4943n.
5291 RI quotes the Fr. (Lc 4723 "Ne doit pas estre autrement fete"), translating, "'It must not be done differently,' i.e., the request must be performed if it is reasonable," and commenting that "this is perhaps the intended meaning of the English also, but the actual meaning is just the opposite, for if the request were other than unreasonable, it should be granted."

Except oonly in cause[s] twoo:
If men his freend to deth wolde drife, 104v
Late hym be bisy to save his lyve;
Also if men wolen hym assayle, 5295
Of his wurshipp to make hym faile,
And hyndren hym of his renoun,
Late hym, with full entencioun,
His dever done in eche degre
That his freend ne shamed be. 5300
In [thise] two caas with his myght,
Taking no kepe to skile nor right,
As ferre as love may hym excuse,
This ought no man to refuse.'
This love that I have tolde to thee 5305
Is nothing contrarie to me;
This wole I that thou folowe wele,
And leve the tother everydele.
This love to vertu all entendith,

The tothir fooles blent and shendith. 5310
"Another love also there is,
That is contrarie unto this,
Which desire is so constreyned
That [it] is but wille feyned.
Awey fro trouthe it doth so varie 5315
That to good love it is contrarie;
For it maymeth, in many wise, 105r
Sike hertis with coveitise.
All in wynnyng and in profit
Sich love settith his delite. 5320
This love so hangeth in balaunce
That, if it lese his hope, perchaunce,
Of lucre, that he is sett upon,
It wole faile and quenche anoon;
For no man may be amerous, 5325
Ne in his lyvyng vertuous,
But he love more, in moode,

5292 **causes**] cause MS BE-KA; cases SK SU FI   5301 **thise**] this MS-SP³ BE-FU SU FI   **caas**] casis UR SK SU FI; causes GL   5304 **to**] for t. UR   5305 **to**] *om.* TH²   5308 **tother**] other SP²·³ 5309 **entendith**] attendeth SP²·³ BE SK SU FI   5314 **it**] i. ne UR; *om.* MS-SP³ KA FU   5317 **many**] any SP²·³   5326 **lyvyng**] loving SP¹   5327 **But**] But if UR SK

5292 **causes twoo:** See 5287–5300n.

causes: TH¹ corrects MS's singular form, perhaps by reference to the Fr. (Lc 4724 "fors an .II. cas" "save in two cases"; noted by SK SU FI). KA attributes to Skeat the plural form *casis* and compares line 5301; SK compares line 5523 as well. Here UR has *causis*; SK SU FI *cases*. *MED cause* n. notes that "ME *cause* overlaps *cas* 'case' in meaning" and quotes this line under sense 8 (c) "a situation or case." See 5301n.

5296 **wurshipp:** See 4915n., and cf. 5251n.

5301 **thise:** RB's spelling; RI adopts it also. UR emends MS *this* to *these*. *Thise* is an East Midland-Northern plural (see *OED These* A. ϵ; Mossé 1968:61) that appears elsewhere in *Rom* (lines 102, 2183, 6860–66) as well as throughout Chaucer. *This* may also appear as a plural form, as GL notes at line 6759 (see *OED These* dem. pron. and adj.: "A frequent form of *þes* from the 12th to the 16th c. was *þis*, identical with the sing.: see γ[- forms] below"). The two forms, with and without final -*e*, may thus be spelling variants, as at lines 5791, 6759, although I collate them as substantive (singular/plural) variants.

two: FI notes, in error, that MS omits *two*.

caas: See 5292n. Here, however, MS *caas* appears—as a plural—in all except those collated. As at line 5292, SK SU FI have *cases*; UR here has *casis*. KA endorses SK's *cases*.

5309 **entendith:** SU FI base the emendation *attendith* on the Fr. *s'amort* (Lc 4737 "attaches itself, is attached"). RIt also cites the Fr. but retains *entendith* and, in support, cites *Sq-FranL* F 689 "For he to vertu listeth nat entende."

5310 **blent and shendith:** Jephson (BE) notes the combination of the contracted form, *blent*, with the uncontracted form, *shendith*; however, the two forms are not "used indifferently," as he says, since meter and rhyme dictate the choices.

5311–30 and ff.   With the section on the contrast between love from friendship and the love that comes from Fortune, Ln (4769–74n.) and RB compare Cicero, *De amicitia* 14.51.

5313 **desire:** KA suggests, "perhaps insert *with* before *desire*," but no ed. so emends.

5314–20   BE quotes the Fr. (Lc 4742–44 "c'est fainte volenté d'amer / en queurs malades du mahaing / de couvoitise de gaaing" "it is the simulated desire of loving in hearts sick with the disease of coveting profit"). The ME is a loose and expanded translation; line 5314 omits "of loving," and the last two lines of the Fr. relate loosely to ME 5317–20.

5314 **it:** KA notes insertion of *it* in BE MO and *it ne* in UR.

5327 **But:** KA endorses SK's *But if*, which appears first in UR; GL suggests "perhaps insert *if* after *But*."

Men for hemsilf than for her goode.
For love that profit doth abide
Is fals, and bit not in no tyde. 5330
    "[This] love cometh of Dame Fortune,
That litel while wole contune;
For it shal chaungen wonder soone,
And take eclips, right as the moone,
Whanne [she] is from us lett 5335
Thurgh erthe, that bitwixe is sett
The sonne and hir, as it may falle,
Be it in partie or in all.
The shadowe maketh her bemys merke,
And hir hornes to shewe derke, 5340
That part where she hath lost hir lyght 105v
Of Phebus fully, and the sight,
Til, whanne the shadowe is overpaste,

She is enlumyned ageyn as faste,
Thurgh the brightnesse of the
    sonne bemes, 5345
That yeveth to hir ageyne hir lemes.
That love is right of sich nature;
Now is faire and now obscure,
Now bright, now clipsi of manere,
And whilom dymme and whilom clere. 5350
As soone as Poverte gynneth take,
With mantel and wedis blake
Hidith of love the light awey,
That into nyght it turneth day.
It may not see Richesse shyne 5355
Till the blak shadowes fyne.
For, whanne Richesse shyneth bright,
Love recovereth ageyn his light;

5330 **bit]** byddeth FU   **in]** *om.* UR   5331 **This]** Soche UR; *om.* MS-SP³ BE-KA FU   5333 **wonder]** wonders TH³-SP³   5334 **right]** *om.* TH³-UR   **as]** a. doth UR   5335 **she]** he MS-SP³ BE-KA GL FU; that s. UR   5345 **the brightnesse]** b. SK   5346 **to hir]** t. hem SP²·³   5348 **is]** is it UR SK   5352 **and]** a. with UR MO SK GL   5353 **Hidith]** It h. SK SU FI   5356 **Till]** T. that UR   5357 **whanne]** w. that UR

5328 **Men:** "here means man or woman, like *homo*, in Latin" (BE).
5330 **bit not in no tyde:** "abides not, at any time" (SK).
    bit: "lasts, abides" (SKg₂; cf.RB FI), a contraction of *bideth* (BE SK SU RIf). SKt RIt note TH¹'s *bydeth*, also in TH²-UR SU FI.
5331 **This love:** KA suggests the emendation, comparing lines 5305, 5321. SU FI cite the Fr. *ceste*, apparently from SU's French text (4783 "Ceste amour si vient de Fortune" "This love comes from Fortune") which differs from Ln (4783, cited by RIt) and Lc (4753), both of which have "C'est l'amour qui vient de Fortune" ("It is the love which comes from Fortune"). Neither Ln's collations nor SU's textual notes offer a rationale for the form *Ceste* rather than *C'est*; the punctuation, of course, is modern, but the absence of final -*e* seems to favor the texts of Ln and Lc.
5332 **contune:** continue. See 4354n.
5333 **wonder:** On the var. *wonders*, see 2958n.
5335 **she:** Citing lines 5339–46, KA notes UR's *she*, based perhaps on the Fr., where *la lune* (Lc 4754–62) is feminine. BE notes that MS *he* shows "some confusion in the gender attributed to the moon," since feminine pronouns appear at lines 5337–46; "in Old English," BE states, "the moon is always masculine." SKt RIt note lines 5337, 5341.
    lett: "prevented (hidden)" (FI).
5338 "That is, 'Whether the eclipse be partial or total'" (BE).
    all: BE MO SK assume that MS *all* is an abbreviation for *alle* and thus spell *alle*. See above, "The Manuscript Hands: The Scribe (MS₁)."
5341 **hir:** BE states that "*hir* appears to be a mistake of the copyist for *the*," and SK suggests *the* in a note but does not so emend.
5342 **and the sight:** GL notes that "such displacements as this of *and* were common in 15th century verse."
5345 **Thurgh the:** KA notes, incorrectly, that UR "omits former *the*"; it is SK that so omits.
5348 **is:** KA notes *is it* in UR but not in SK.
5351 **take:** GL RB RI quote the Fr. *l'afuble* (Lc 4765 "muffles it"). RI explains that "Poverty cloaks love with a dark mantle."
5352 **and:** KA notes *and with* in UR MO
5353 **Hidith:** KA endorses *It hit*, which he attributes to SK. SK has *It bidith* in the text, but explains in a note that "the original reading would be *It hit*, i.e. it hideth; then *It* was dropped, and *hit* became *hidith*." GL errs slightly in stating that "Skeat reads *It hit*, and perhaps rightly," and RBt records SK's ambiguity as "Skeat *It hit* (or *hidith*)." SU FI adopt SK's *It*, which, states SU, "seems to improve the sense."

237

And whanne it failith he wole flit,
And as she gr[ow]eth, so gr[ow]eth it.　5360
Of this love—here what I sey—
The riche men are loved ay,
And namely tho that sparand bene,
That wole not wasshe her hertes clene　5364
Of the filthe nor of the vice　　　106r
Of gredy brennyng avarice.
The riche man full fonned is, ywys,
That weneth that he loved is.
If that his herte it undirstode,
It is not he, it is his goode;　5370
He may wel witen in his thought,
His good is loved, and he right nought.
For if he be a nygard eke,
Men wole not sette by hym a leke,
But haten hym; this is the sothe.　5375

Lo, what profit his catell doth!
Of every man that may hym see
It geteth hym nought but enmyte.
But he amende hym of that vice,
And knowe hymsilf, he is not wys.　5380
　"Certys, he shulde ay freendly be,
To gete hym love also been free,
Or ellis he is not wise ne sage
Nomore than is a gote ramage.
That he not loveth, his dede proveth,　5385
Whan he his richesse so wel loveth
That he wole hide it ay and spare,
His pore freendis sene forfare,
To kepen ay his purpose,　　　106v
Til for drede his iyen close,　5390
And til a wikked deth hym take.
Hym hadde lever asondre shake

5360 **groweth so groweth]** greueth s. greueth MS-KA FU　　5361 **here]** herith UR　　5369 **it]** is SU
5374 **wole]** would SP[2,3]　　5376 **his]** this MO KA　　5379 **hym]** hym silf MS-SP[3] BE-KA FU SU　　5389 **ay]**
it a. is SK; alway GL　　**purpose]** ill p. UR　　5390 **Til]** T. that UR

5360 **groweth, so groweth:** KA suggests the emendation. SU FI note the Fr. (Lc 4772 "et saut si toust conme el resaillent" "and shoots up when they reappear"). RBt RIt note that MS *greueth* may represent *grewith*.
5363 **sparand:** FI notes the Northern present participle.
5367–68 See 5384n.
5367 **fonned:** KA endorses SK's *fond*.
5369 **it:** FI attributes the reading *is* to MS TH[1]; the error appears only in FI's source, SU.
5374 **leke:** See 4830n.
5376 **his:** As RIt notes, "Kaluza, Skeat [SKt], and Fisher mistakenly show [MS] reading as *this*." KA notes *his* as the reading in TH[1] UR BE.
5379–80 In his study of the medieval and modern interpretations of the theme "nosce te ipsum" ("know thyself"), Bennett (1982:153) notes that at this point in the Fr. (Lc 4771–84) Lady Reason follows "the lines laid down in Boethius's *Consolatio* II.pr.viii. But the English lines," he observes, "have no equivalent in the Latin or in the *Roman*."
　vice : wys: RB notes that "*vice*, with silent -*e*," makes "an un-Chaucerian rime with *wys*." Cf. lines 4878, 5946, where MS has *wise* for *vice*.
5379 **hym:** KA notes UR's emendation; MS *hym silf* may have been an anticipation, through eyeskip, of *hym silf* in the next line.
5382 FI's paraphrase of *love . . . free*—"i.e., love that is sincere"—seems to take *love* as the subject of *been*, a violation of concord. *Been* is probably rather an inf. with *shulde* in the previous line; read "in order to get love for himself, [he should] also be generous." There is no parallel in the Fr.
5384 **gote ramage:** "wild goat" (BE SK FI); "horned goat" (RIf). As BE SK RB FI RI note, the Fr. has *cers ramages* (Lc 4786 "branched stag"). The senses "branched, horned" are correct etymologically and in the Fr., but *MED* does not record them. § Jephson (BE) questions "the propriety of this simile," because, he says, "a wild goat (gote ramage) is rather a cunning animal." The contrast, however, is between wisdom in humans and lack of it in animals. The Fr. introduces the implicit contrast a few lines earlier (Lc 4779–80 "s'est plus cornairs q'uns cers ramez / riches hom qui cuide estre amez" "a rich man who thinks himself loved is more horned than a branched stag"), where the idea of the foolish cuckold is present as well; the ME parallel (lines 5367–68) does not use the simile from the Fr.
5389 **kepen ay:** KA endorses SK's *kepe it ay is*; SKt adduces line 5387 in support. GL adduces line 5144 in support of *alway* for MS *ay*; see 5144n. RBt calls the line "doubtful," and RIt quotes the Fr. (Lc 4793 "et toujurs garder la propose" "and always intends to keep it"), which reveals another case of loose translation.

And late all hise lymes asondre ryve,
Than leve his richesse in his lyve.
He thenkith parte it with no man; 5395
Certayn, no love is in hym than.
How shulde love withynne hym be,
Whanne in his herte is no pite?
That he trespasseth, wel I wote,
For ech man knowith his estate; 5400
For wel hym ought to be reproved
That loveth nought, ne is not loved.
    "But [sen] we arn to Fortune comen,
And ha[n] oure sermoun of hir nomen,
A wondir will Y telle thee nowe; 5405
Thou herdist never sich oon, I trowe.

I note where thou me leven shall,
Though sothfastnesse it be all,
As it is writen, and is soth,
That unto men more profit doth 5410
The froward Fortune and contraire
Than the swote and debonaire.
And if thee thynke it is doutable, 107r
It is thurgh argument provable,
For the debonaire and softe 5415
Falsith and bigilith ofte.
For lyche a moder she can cherishe
And mylken as doth a norys,
And of hir goode to hym deles,
And yeveth hym parte of her joweles, 5420

5393 **all]** *om.* SK GL   **asondre]** *om.* RB[1,2]   5395 **thenkith]** t. to TH[1]-UR FU   5397 **How]** For h. UR
5401 **For]** Ful SU FI   **to]** *om.* SK   5403 **sen]** se MS KA; sithe TH[1]-BE SK FU-RI   5404 **han]** hath MS-KA
GL FU   5408 **Though]** Although UR   **all]** it a. MS KA; in a. MO SK; at a. GL   5412 **Than]** T. doth UR
5413 **thee thynke]** they thinke SP[2,3]   5415 **the]** fortune UR   5418 **mylken]** m. hem GL   5420 **of
her]** *om.* SP[3]

5393   KA suggests that we "omit *all* or *asondre.*" RIt suggests that the RB omission may have occurred as "an error in 1st ed."
5399–5400   **wote : estate:** Eds. except BE-KA adjust the rhyme by using the Northern form *wat(e).* RB notes that the rhyme *wat : estat* is Northern.
5401   **For:** GL suggests *Full,* on the basis of Fr. *mout* (Lc 4805; noted in RBt SU FI RIt).
    ought to: KA endorses SK's normalized *oughte,* without *to.*
5403   **sen:** MO's emendation. KA notes TH[1]'s *sithe,* based, perhaps, on the Fr. (Lc 4807 "Et puis qu'a Fortune venons" "and now that we come to Fortune"). MO GL prefer *sen,* a form closer to MS. *Sithe* and *sen* are shortened forms of *sithen,* from OE *siððan; sen* is "chiefly Sc. and north." (*OED Sen* adv., prep., and conj.). Cf. *MED sin* conj., *sitthen* conj.; *MED sitthe* conj. cites *LALME* 4.70–73 for other spellings.
5404   **han:** SK's emendation, for pl. concord; KA suggests *have,* the form that SU FI adopt.
5408   **all:** TH[1]'s emendation of MS *it all* is noted by KA. The sense is adverbial ("entirely"), as is the case for *in all* (MO SK) and *at all* "altogether" (GL). There is no exact parallel in the Fr. (Lc 4812 "toutevois est ce chose voire" "nevertheless it is a fact"), although the element *tout-* in the word *toutevois* may have influenced the selection of *all.*
5409–5560   GL (5405n.) adduces *Bo* 2p8; RB RI, following Ln (4837–974n.) and Lc (4813n.), note that the argument "is a greatly expanded version of Boethius 2.pr8" (RI).
5410   **doth:** See 5556n.
5411   **froward:** "Averse" (URg-BEg); "unfavorable" (*MED frōward* adj. 2. [c]); rather than "obstinate" (FI).
5413   "'If it seems to thee doubtful'" (BE).
    thee thynke: BE notes that "*thynke* is the Anglo-Saxon *thinkan,* to seem." Unless SP[2,3]'s variant, *they thinke,* is a simple error, it shows the loss of the impersonal sense of *thynke,* with the consequent confusion of OE *þyncan* "to seem" and *þencean* "to think."
5417–18   **cherishe : norys:** RB notes that, even without final *-e,* the rhyme is irregular.
5419   **hym:** them. Although absent in the ME, the plural antecedent appears in the Fr. *genz* (Lc 4814 "people") and governs a series of plural pronouns (*leur, les,* Lc 4820 ff.) that parallel those in the ME. KA suggests *hem,* the usual plural form, and SK GL RB[1]-RI so respell. Sutherland (SU) thinks that "since *hem* is used elsewhere, *hym* appears to be an error," and he makes the same observation for lines 5420, 5425, 5427, and 5436. But *hym* appears about fifteen times for the pl.; cf. 1922n.
    deles: GL suggests but does not adopt an emendation: "(?) *dele* infinitive construed with *can* and rhyming with *jowele,* cf. v. 2092. If so, read *yeve* in v. 5420." But, as RB RI note, *deles* is a Northern 3 sg. form, and no emendation is necessary. At line 2092, MS reads *iowell,* which I transcribe as *jowelles* (see above, "The Manuscript Hands: The Scribe [MS,]"), and offers only ambiguous support for the emendation in line 5420 to *jowele.*
5420   **hym:** them. See 1922n., 5419n. KA suggests *hem,* as in UR SK GL RB[1]-RI.
    yeveth . . . joweles: See 5419n.

With grete richesse and dignite.
And hem she hoteth stabilite
In a state that is not stable,
But chaungynge ay and variable;
And fedith hym with glorie veyne 5425
And worldly blisse noncerteyne.
Whanne she hym settith on hir whele,
Thanne wene they to be right wele,
And in so stable state withall,
That never they wene for to falle. 5430
And whanne they sette so high be,
They wene to have in certeynte
Of hertly freendis [so] grete noumbre
That nothyng mygght her state encombre.
They trust hem so on every side, 5435
Wenyng with hym they wolde abide
In every perell and myschaunce, 107v
Withoute chaunge or variaunce,
Bothe of catell and of goode;
And also for to spende her bloode 5440

And all her membris for to spille
Oonly to fulfille her wille.
They maken it hole in many wise,
And hoten hem her full servise,
How sore that it do hem smerte, 5445
Into her naked sherte!
Herte and all so hole they yeve
For the tyme that they may lyve
So that with her flaterie
They maken foolis glorifie 5450
Of her wordis spekyng
And han [therof] a rejoysyng,
And trowe hem as the Evangile;
And it is all falsheede and gile,
As they shal aftirward se, 5455
Whanne they arn falle in poverte
And ben of good and catell bare;
Thanne shulde they sene who freendis ware.
For of an hundred, certeynly,
Nor of a thousande full scarsly, 5460

5421 **richesse]** richesses RB[1,2] RI   5423 **a]** *om.* TH[3] ST SP[2,3]   **not]** nothing UR   5425 **veyne]** and v. MS MO KA   5426 **And]** In GL   **noncerteyne]** none certeyne TH[3]-SP[3]; nothing certeine UR   5431 **be]** to b. TH[3]-UR   5433 **so]** to MS-UR KA FU   5438 **chaunge]** chaunce TH[3] ST UR   5440 **for]** f. hem BE 5442 **to]** for to. TH[2]   5445 **that]** so t. UR   5446 **naked]** very n. TH[1]-MO SK FU-FI   5447 **and]** a. hande UR   **all so]** also TH[2] ST SP[2]-UR   5448 **For]** F. all UR   5449 **her]** this ther UR   5451 **Of]** Onely of UR   **spekyng]** greet s. SK   5452 **therof]** cheer of MS-SP[2] UR-KA FU   5456 **falle]** full SP[2,3] 5458 **shulde]** shul TH[1,2] SP[1] FU SU FI

5421 **richesse:** Either a singular ("wealth") or a plural ("riches"); *MED riches* n. pl. lists *richesse* as a var. sp. RB RI's *riches(s)es* is clearly pl.
   5425 **hym:** them. See 1922n., 5419n. KA notes UR's *bem*, as in SK RB[1]-RI.
      glorie veyne: BE notes MS *and* as a clerical error, and KA notes the correction in TH[1] UR BE.
   5426 **And:** In support of *In*, GL cites Fr. *en* (Lc 4830).
   5427 **hym:** them. See 1922n., 5419n. KA notes UR's *bem*, as in SK GL RB[1]-RI.
   5433 **so:** KA notes the change in BE MO. In support, GL cites Fr. *tant* (Lc 4837 "so many").
   5436 **hym:** them. See 1922n., 5419n. KA suggests *hem*, as in SP[2]-UR SK GL RB[1]-RI.
   5443 **maken it hole:** "Obscure. . . . perhaps it means 'perform it (their will) wholly'; see l. 5447" (SK); "i.e., promise their whole service" (FI); "perform their all (?) (cf. 5447)" (RI). BE SK quote from the Fr. a line that is not really parallel to the ME (Lc 4840 "et que por seignors ne les tiegnent" "and consider them lords"); and on the basis of this line BE suggests the emendation *maken hem lordes.*
      maken: KA suggests *make.*
   5446 **Into her naked sherte:** Although the Fr. (Lc 4842 "jusqu'au despendre les chemises" "up to the point of giving away their shirts"; noted in RB) does not support TH[1]'s *very*, subsequent eds. (except KA GL RI) have adopted the emendation, which KA notes in TH[1] UR BE MO.
   5447–48 **yeve : lyve:** See 2759–60n.
   5450 **foolis glorifie:** FI paraphrases: "fools to be glorified." This reading, in passive voice, would take ME *foolis* as object (not subject) of the active infinitive *glorifie* and would leave the phrase *Of her wordis spekyng* without a clear structure. SK[g2], citing the Fr. *s'englorefient* (Lc 4848), glosses *glorifye* as "boast (themselves), feel glory," and *MED glōrifīen* v. 1. (b) takes the phrase *glorifien of* as "be proud of (sth.), boast of."
   5451 **spekyng:** KA endorses SK's insertion of *greet* before *spekyng.* There is no parallel in the Fr.
   5452 **therof:** SP[3]'s emendation (as *there of*), suggested independently by KA, has no parallel in the Fr. SK notes "the common mistake of *c* for *t*."
   5455–58 "A commonplace," observes RB[2], who cites Whiting (1934:31) and compares line 5551, below.
   5458–62 BE notes the same theme in *Timon of Athens.*

Ne shal they fynde unnethis oon,
Whanne poverte is comen upon.
For [this] Fortune that I of telle,
With men whanne hir lust to dwelle,
Maketh [hem] to leese her conisaunce,   5465
And norishith hem in ignoraunce.
    "But froward Fortune and perverse,
Whanne high estatis she doth reverse,
And maketh hem to tumble doune
[Of] hir whele, with sodeyn tourne,   5470
And from her richesse doth hem fle,
And plongeth hem in poverte,
As a stepmoder envyous,

108r And leieth a plastre dolorous
      Unto her hertis, wounded egre,   5475
      Which is not tempred with vynegre,
      But with poverte and indigence,
      For to shewe, by experience,
      That she is Fortune verelye,
      In whom no man shulde affye,   5480
      Nor in hir yeftis have fiaunce,
      She is so full of variaunce.
      Thus kan she maken high and lowe,
      Whanne they from richesse arn throwe,   5484
      Fully to knowen, without were,   108v
      Freend of affect and freend of chere,

5463 **this]** thus MS-KA FU   5464 **whanne]** w. that UR   5465 **hem]** men MS BE-KA   5470 **Of]**
Or with MS KA; Of with MO   **sodeyn]** a s. UR   5471 **fle]** flye TH¹-ST SP²·³ FU SU FI   5480 **shulde]** ne
s. UR   5486 **affect]** effect SP²·³ SK RB¹·²

5463 **this:** KA's suggestion; GL SU FI call attention to the Fr. *Ceste* (Lc 4859 "This").
5465 **hem:** KA notes this reading in TH¹.
5467–82 As RB notes, "the sentence is not completed." It corresponds to a 12-line period in the Fr. (Lc 4863–74), and SKt's suggested emendation at line 5478 ("She sheweth, by experience") would remedy the basic structure and correspond, roughly, to the original. See 5470n., 5473–74n., 5478n.
5467 **froward:** See 5411n.
5470 **Of hir whele:** KA notes the emendation in TH¹ UR BE. Jephson (BE) notes that MS *Or with hir whele* "makes the passage nonsense"; he adopts "the reading of Speght" (*Off hir whele*), which stems from TH¹, and notes that it corresponds to the Fr. (Lc 4865–66 "et les tumble, au tor de la roe, / du sonmet envers an la boe" "and tumbles them around the wheel from summit toward the mud").
    Of: "off, off from" (SK), "off" (SKg₂ GL FI).
5471–72 Not in the Fr. SU Fr. offers as parallel text (4896A-D) a four-line passage from MS Tou, fol. 38, a passage "presumably composed by Gui de Mori" (note to SU Fr. 4896A-D): "Quant de trés grant prosperité / Les met en grant adversité, / E en grant poureté les tume / Si com fait couuent par coustume ("When from very great prosperity she puts them into adversity and tumbles them into great poverty, just as is her custom"). Of these four lines, only the third offers a real parallel.
    fle : poverte: TH¹'s *flye* creates an imperfect rhyme with *poverte*. SP²·³ respell to *povertie*. On *fle, flye*, see 951n.
5473–74 Although no ed. emends, GL notes that *And* (line 5474) "seems to belong before *As* [line 5473], else v. 5474 precedes v. 5473"; and RB RI agree that "perhaps *And* should be shifted to the head of 5473" (RI). All three quote the Fr. (Lc 4867–68 "et leur assiet, conme marrastre, / au queur un douleurus emplastre" "and, like a stepmother, lays a painful plaster on the heart").
5474 **And:** See 5473–74n.
5476 **tempred with vynegre:** FI notes that "vinegar was used to soothe irritations."
5478 Skeat suggests (SKt), "read *She sheweth by experience*," but he does not adopt the change in his text. It would remedy the sentence structure and correspond, roughly, to the Fr. (Lc 4871 "ceste moustre qu'el est veroie" "this shows that she is sincere"), but it is hardly accountable in terms of the ME text as it stands. See 5467–82n.
5480 **In whom no:** KA attributes to Skeat the suggestion *In whom that no*, but no ed., including SK, adopts the emendation.
5484 **arn:** Skeat (SK) notes that "*arn*, with trilled *r*, is disyllabic; as in l. 5047," and in the text he respells it as *aren*. RB notes that *arn* is "the Northern form, for which Chaucer almost invariably has *ben*."
5486 "A truly affectionate or sincere friend, and one that is so only in countenance or appearance" (URg, s.v. *Affecte*); "'Friend in reality, and friend in appearance only'" (BE). KA endorses SK's *effect*, found earlier in SP²·³; SU reports incorrectly that GL has *effect*. Skeat (SK) reads the unemended line as "'Friend from affection (*affect*), and friend in appearance,'" but emends to *effect* on the basis of *For* 34: "'Frend of *effect* [i. e. in reality], and frend of countenance'"; he notes that "as the passage is not in the French, but is probably borrowed from Chaucer, we see that *effect* . . . is the right reading here"; and he compares line 5549 "freend in existence." Liddell (GL) keeps MS

241

And which in love weren trewe and stable,
And whiche also weren variable,
After Fortune, her goddes,
In poverte outher in richesse,   5490
For all [she] yeveth here, out of drede,
Unhappe bereveth it in dede;
For [Infortune] late not oon
Of freendis, whanne Fortune is gone;
I mene tho freendis that wole fle   5495
Anoon as entreth poverte.
And yit they wole not leve hem so,
But in ech place where they go

They calle hem 'wrecche,' scorne, and blame,
And of her myshappe hem diffame;   5500
And namely siche as in richesse
Pretendith moost of stablenesse,
Whanne that [they] sawe hym sett on lofte,
And weren of hym socoured ofte,
And most [iholpe] in all her neede.   5505
But now they take no maner heede,
But seyn in voice of flaterie
That now apperith her folye
Overall where so they fare,   109r
And synge, 'Go, farewel, feldfare.'   5510

5490 **outher]** either TH¹-UR FU SU FI   5491 **she yeveth here]** that y. h. MS-UR MO KA FU; that
bereveth BE; s. y. SK   5492 **bereveth]** beareth TH³ ST SP²-UR   5493 **Infortune]** in fortune MS-SP¹ KA FU
5498 **where]** w. that UR   5502 **Pretendith]** Pretendid GL RB¹·²   5503 **they]** the MS KA   5505 **iholpe]**
I hope MS KA   5509 **so]** s. that UR

---

affect and cites *OED affect*, where this line appears (under I. 1. b.) as an example of the sense "intention . . . reality";
he also compares *For* 34 as well as *Bo* 590ff. (= 2p8.32–39 [RI]). RB emends to *effect* on the same basis as SK and
refers to Brusendorff (1925:404ff.) "for full discussion of the *Fortune* passages." SU FI keep *affect*; SU refers to SK's
note, and FI glosses *affect . . . chere* as "true . . . false." David (RI) notes that *MED affect* n. 1. b. cites the phrase
frend of affect for the sense "a friend by inclination, a loving friend"; that the line is not in the Fr.; and that the
emendation to *effect* on the basis of *For* 34 would give the sense "'a friend in deed, a true friend,' as in 5549." "The
phrases," David notes, "may well have been confused," and *MED affect* n. has quotations from the 15th century
(under sense 2. "result, effect") that show confusion between the two forms, *affect* and *effect*. On Brusendorff's
parallels between *For* and *Rom* (1925:404–07), David writes: "The conclusion, however, need not be that Fragment
B is a garbled version of Chaucer's translation, but that the translator was familiar with Chaucer's poetry and used it
in appropriate places."

5490 **outher:** See 250n., 5168n.

5491 **all she yeveth here:** KA recommends *she yeueth* for MS *yeueth here*. Skeat (SK) glosses *al she* as "all
that she"; "the F[r]. text," he says, "helps but little." Liddell (GL), however, quotes it as support for his emendation,
adopted here (Lc 4879 "car cels que beneürtez done" "for those [friends] that good fortune gives"); the word *que*
may account for MS *that*.

5493 GL reads *oon* as "the subject of *late*, 'remains,'" and suggests emending *late* to *leveth* on the basis of the
Fr. *remaint* (Lc 4882 "remains"). RB reads *oon* as object of *late*, "'misfortune leaves not one (remaining),'" but notes
GL's alternative, "perhaps emend *lat* to *leveth*, Fr. 'remaint.'"

Infortune: KA notes *In-fortune* in UR BE MO.

5503–04 **hym . . . hym:** Some eds. have *hem:* UR SU FI (line 5503); TH³-UR SU FI (line 5504). SU compares
the Fr. pl. (SU Fr. 4920 "Quant en leur grant estaz les virent" "when they saw them in their high estate"; Ln 4920 Lc
4890 have *se virent* "saw themselves"). On *him* as a pl., see 1922n.

5503 **they:** KA notes *they* in TH¹ UR BE MO.

5505 **iholpe:** KA notes the reading in TH¹ UR BE MO.

5507 **flaterie:** Lounsbury (1892:2.14) thinks that, on the basis of the Fr., "some such word as *jolitee* should be
substituted for *flaterye*" (Lc 4891 "a voiz jolie" "in gleeful voice"). SK notes the Fr. and states "*flaterye* is very
inappropriate; we should expect *taperye*, i.e. mockery."

5510 **farewel, feldfare:** URg BE note the parallel to *TC* 3.861; see below. TRg (TR 5.285) lists the phrase
among those "not understood." SK RB FI RI also note the *TC* parallel; Skeat (SK) thinks that the phrase is "probably
borrowed from Chaucer" and glosses it as "'Begone, and let us be rid of you.'" GL refers to *OED Farewell* (int. 2. b
"*Farewell fieldfare*; said to one of whom the speaker wishes to see no more, with allusion to the fieldfare's
departure northward at the end of winter"). See also *MED fären* v. 10b. (c) "*farewel feldefare!*, good riddance"; *MED
feld(e-fāre* n. (b) "*farewel feldefare!*, goodbye!, all is lost!"; Whiting (1968: F130). BE RB RI note that the proverb is
not in the Fr.

feldfare: "Feldfare, called *Frosty* [*PF*] 364. because they come in hard weather" (URg). Citing "*Ms. Sp.*"
i.e. Devonshire MS of *TC* (Alderson 1970:110–11), Thomas (URg) reads *TC* 3.861 as two words, "*Feld yfare . . . *The

All suche freendis I beshrewe,
For of trewe ther be to fewe.
But sothfast freendis, what so bitide,
In every fortune wolen abide;
Thei han her hertis in suche noblesse   5515
That they nyl love for no richesse,
Nor for that Fortune may hem sende
Thei wolen hem socoure and defende,
And chaunge for softe ne for sore,
For who is freend loveth evermore.   5520
Though men drawe swerde his freend to slo,
He may not hewe her love a-two.
But, in case that I shall sey,
For pride and ire lese it he may,
And for reprove by nycete,   5525
And discovering of privite,
With tonge woundyng, as feloun,

Thurgh venemous detraccioun.
Frende in this case wole gone his way,
For nothyng greve hym more ne may;   5530
And for nought ellis wole he fle,
If that he love in stabilite.
And certeyn, he is wel bigone,   109v
Among a thousand that fyndith oon.
For ther may be no richesse   5535
Ageyns frendshipp, of worthynesse;
For it ne may so high atteigne
As may the valoure, soth to seyne,
Of hym that loveth trew and well.
Frendshipp is more than is catell.   5540
For freend in court ay better is
Than peny in purs, certis;
And Fortune, myshappyng
Whanne upon men she is [fallyng],

5512 **trewe]** the t. SK   5520 **is]** hys TH³-MO   5521 **drawe swerde his freend]** drewe s. h. f. TH²; d. s. h. TH³-SP¹; d. s. him SP²³; d. swerdis him UR   5522 **He]** Thei UR   5523 **But]** B. if UR   **case]** the c. SK   5532 **that]** om. UR   5535 **may]** ne m. UR MO   5542 **in purs]** is in p. UR; in his p. SK   5543 **And]** A. than is UR   5544 **fallyng]** fablyng MS-KA FU

Field is gone, or the Battle is lost"; "it seems," he writes, "to be the Beginning or Burden of some known Song in *Chaucer*'s time." Jephson (BE *TC* 3.861n., noting URg and TRg) identifies *feldefare* as one word, *fieldfare*, "a kind of thrush" that "suddenly appear[s] with the advent of cold weather, and as suddenly depart[s]." Others gloss as "name of a bird" (MOg), "field-fare" (SKg₂ GLg RBg), "a kind of large thrush (Turdus pilaris), the fieldfare" (*MED fẹ̄ld(e-fāre* n. [a]). KA notes TH¹'s form *feldefare.*

5513–14 SK RB compare Prov. 17.17, but RI notes that "the parallel is very general" and that "the tenor of the entire passage is proverbial." He compares lines 5520, 5523, 5534, 5540; see 5534n., 5540n.

5519 **And:** GL suggests that "*Ne* with semicolon after *sende* [line 5517] would make better sense," but no ed. so emends. There is no parallel in the Fr. for this line.

5520 "Proverbial," notes RB, citing Haeckel (1890: no. 13).

5521–29 BE (5523–32n.) quotes the parallel in Ecclus. 22.26–27 (Douai): "To a friend, if thou hast opened a sad mouth, fear not, for there may be a reconciliation: except upbraiding, and reproach, and pride, and disclosing of secrets, or a treacherous wound; for in all these cases a friend will flee away." SK RB RI give the reference to the Authorized Version (Ecclus. 22.22); SK RB restrict the parallel to lines 5523–29; SK notes the further parallel between lines 5521–22 and verse 26 (AV 21): "Although thou hast drawn a sword at a friend, despair not: for there may be a returning." RI combines the two verses 26–27 (AV 21–22) as the parallel to lines 5521–29.

5523 **in case:** KA attributes to Skeat the suggestion *in this case* and compares line 5529; but SK has *in the case*, and no other ed. emends.

    case: See 5292n.

5524 **lese it:** "i.e., lose true friendship" (FI).

5534 BE SK RB RI compare Eccles. 7.28.

    fyndith: KA attributes to Skeat the suggestion *fint*, but SK neither so emends nor so notes.

5535–36 "For there is no wealth which may be compared to friendship, in respect to worthiness" (RB).

5536 **Ageyns:** "in comparison with" (SKg₂ RBg RIg *MED ayẹ̄n(e)s* prep. 7. [b]); cf. 6875.

5538 **valoure:** BE SK RB note the sense, "value," SK RB compare the Fr. *valor* (Lc 4916), and SK adduces line 5556. BE notes that "Valour is still used in this, its primary sense, by the vulgar in Norfolk."

5540 Proverbial; RB compares Haeckel (1890: no. 15), and RI cites Whiting (1968: F670).

5541–42 Proverbial; RI cites Whiting (1968: F633). BE SK cite *2 Henry IV* 5.1.34 "a friend i' the court is better than a penny in purse," and SK cites Michel's quotation (ed. 1864:1.165) of the Latin proverb "Verus amicus omni praestantior auro." Ln (4947n.) quotes other parallels; Lc (4917–18n.) cites Morawski (1925: no. 1241). Cf. 5683n.

5542 **in purs:** RBt notes that UR's *is in purs* (noted by KA) or SK's *in his purs* may be correct.

5544 **fallyng:** KA's suggestion follows the Fr. *cheanz* (Lc 4920 "falling"; noted by GL RBt SU FI RIt).

243

Thurgh mysturnyng of hir chaunce,   5545
And caste[th] hem oute of balaunce,
She makith, thurgh hir adversite,
Men full clerly for to se
Hym that is freend in existence
From hym that is by apparence.   5550
For [Ynfortune] makith anoon
To knowe thy freendis fro thy foon,
By experience, right as it is;
The which is more to preise, ywis,
Than [is] myche richesse and tresour.   5555
For more [doth] profit and valour
Poverte and such adversite   110r
Bifore, than doth prosperite;
For the toon yeveth conysaunce,
And the tother ignoraunce.   5560
   "And thus in poverte is in dede
Trouthe declared fro falsheed;
For feynte frendis it wole declare,
And trewe also, what wey they fare.

For whanne he was in his richesse,   5565
These freendis, ful of doublenesse,
Offrid hym in many wise
Hert and body and servise.
What wolde he thanne ha [yove] to ha bought
To knowen openly her thought,   5570
That he now hath so clerly seen?
The lasse bigiled he shulde have bene,
And he hadde thanne perceyved it,
But richesse nold not late hym witte.
Wel more avauntage doth hym thanne,   5575
Sith that it makith hym a wise man,
The gret myscheef that he [receyveth],
Than doth richesse that hym deceyveth.
   "Richesse riche ne makith nought
Hym that on tresour sette his thought;   5580
For richesse stonte in suffisaunce   110v
And nothyng in habundaunce;
For suffisaunce all oonly
Makith men to lyve richely.

5546 **casteth]** caste MS-SP³ BE-KA FU FI   5548 **full]** f. and UR   5551 **Ynfortune]** yn fortune MS-SP¹ KA FU   5555 **is]** in MS TH¹ TH³-KA FU   5556 **doth]** depe MS-KA FU   5558 **Bifore]** Bi fer GL   5559 **the toon]** that one TH¹-UR FU SU FI   5560 **the tother]** t'othir grevith UR   5561 **thus in]** thys TH²   5563 **feynte]** feyne BE   5568 **Hert]** Ther h. UR   5569 **yove]** yow MS-UR KA FU   5572 **he]** she MO   5576 **it]** *om.* TH²   5577 **receyveth]** perceyueth MS-KA FU   5582 **in]** stonte i. UR

5546 **casteth:** UR's emendation (*castith*), endorsed in SK by KA. Among recent eds., FI alone keeps MS *caste*, presumably as a subjunctive. There is no parallel in the Fr.

5549–50 See 5486n.

5551–53 RI notes the proverbial nature of the passage and cites Whiting (1968: F634).

5551 **Ynfortune:** KA notes *yn-fortune* in MO. Cf. line 5493 and n.

5552 RI compares *For* 10.

5555 **is:** TH²'s emendation; KA makes the same suggestion. There is no parallel in the Fr.
     myche: See 1713n.

5556–58 FI paraphrases *doth profit* as follows: "i.e., do poverty and adversity profit and enhance [true friendship]." Perhaps "For poverty and such adversity bring about surpassingly greater profit and value than prosperity does."

5556 **doth:** Comparing line 5410, KA suggests *doth* for MS *depe*. SKt suggests the possibility that the form *doþ* was the source of MS's *depe*. Cf. the parallel *doth*, line 5558.
     valour: "worth" (SKg₂).

5569 KA records as Skeat's suggestion the reading "*What wolde he than ha yeve, ha bought*"; but SK retains *to* before *ha bought*. GL recommends "Read *to ha* as one word." § GL notes that "the thought is borrowed from Boethius; see Chaucer's *Boece*, 590" (2p8.41–45 [RI]).
     yove: BE emends MS *yow* to *yeve* on the basis of the Fr. (Lc 4937–38 "que vosist il acheter lores / qu'il en seüst ce qu'il set ores?" "[wouldn't he] have wanted to buy then the knowledge that he now has?"; noted in SK). Most eds. have adopted the emendation, either in the o-form (*yove* MO GL RB¹-RI) or the e-form (*yeve* SK).

5577 **receyveth:** KA's suggestion for MS *perceyveth* follows the Fr. *receit* (Lc 4943 "receives"; noted by GL RBt SU FI RIt).

5581–84 and ff. BE (5600n.) cites Boethius 3 as a source for the passage on riches and sufficiency and quotes Chaucer's *Bo* (3p3.52–53 [RI]).

5581–82 "The meaning is, that true riches consists in having enough, and not more than enough" (BE).

5583–84 Proverbial. RB compares Haeckel (1890: no. 36), and RI cites Whiting (1968: S867).

[For] he that [at] mycches tweyne 5585
Ne [valued is] in his demeigne,
Lyveth more at ese, and more is riche,
Than doth he that is chiche
And in his berne hath, soth to seyn,
An hundred m[u]is of whete greyne, 5590
Though he be chapman or marchaunte,
And have of golde many besaunte.
For in the getyng he hath such woo,
And in the kepyng drede also,
And sette evermore his bisynesse 5595
For to encrese, and not to lesse,

For to aument and multiplie.
And though on hepis [it] lye hym bye,
Yit never shal make his richesse
Asseth unto his gredynesse. 5600
But the povre that recchith nought,
Save of his lyflode, in his thought,
Which that he getith with his travaile,
He dredith nought that it shall faile, 5604
Though he have lytel worldis goode, 111r
Mete and drynke and esy foode,
Upon his travel and lyvyng,
And also suffisaunt clothyng.

5585 **For**] Lor MS KA **at**] hath MS-SP³ BE-KA FU; hath but UR SK 5586 **valued is**] value MS-KA FU; more value SK **his**] h. whole UR 5588 **that**] whiche t. UR **chiche**] so c. SK 5590 **muis**] mavis MS-KA FU SU FI; muwis SK; mowis GL RB¹·² RI 5592 **besaunte**] a b. GL 5593 **the**] *om.* SP²·³ BE 5598 **it**] that MS-KA GL FU 5601 **povre**] p. man UR

5585–90 BE notes the Fr. (Lc 4949–51 "car tex n'a pas vaillant .II. miches / qui est plus a ese e plus riches / que tex a .C. muis de forment" "for the man in easier circumstances and richer than one with a hundred barrels of grain still possesses nothing worth two fine loaves"). RIt (5586n.) translates the first line as "For someone not worth two loaves." See also 5585n., 5590n.
5585–86 "I fill up the lines so as to make sense" (SK).
5585 **at:** GL's *at* (for MS *hath*) follows the Fr. (see 5585–90n.). KA endorses SK's emendation, *hath but,* present already in UR.
mycches: SPg-BE gloss as "manchet," which TRg BE gloss further as "loaf of fine bread." SK, citing Cotgrave (1611, s.v. *Miche*), also has "a loaf of fine manchet bread," and *MED* (*miche* n.) has "a loaf of white bread." GL has "small loaves," FI RIf "loaves of bread." For *manchet,* see *MED main-chẹt* n.: "the finest kind of wheat bread."
5586 **Ne valued is:** GL's emendation follows the Fr. (see 5585–90n.). KA endorses SK's *Ne more value.*
5588 **is:** KA endorses SK's *is so.*
5590 **muis:** SP UR gloss *mavis* as "bushel." TRg (cf. BE) notes that *mavis* "is probably a mistake for *muis*" and that "the Paris *muid* contains something more than five quarters English." Five quarters are about 40 gallons at "approximately eight bushels" to the quarter (*MED quartẹr(e* n. 3. [e]). KA records the form *mowis* as Skeat's suggestion, and GL RB RI so emend; but there is disagreement on the sense of *mowis,* which GLg glosses (presumably through inadvertence) as "grimaces" (see *MED moue* n.[2]), RB as "bushels" (see *MED mui* n.), and RIf as "stacks" (see *MED moue* n.[3]). Moreover, Skeat (SK) does not adopt the suggestion that KA attributes to him, for his text has *muwis,* and his explanatory note says that "*mauis* (as in G. and Th.) is clearly an error for *muwis,* or, *muis,* bushels." SK also notes that "the A. F. form *muy* occurs in the Liber Custumarum, ed. Riley, i. 62." SK's forms are close to *muys,* the only other form that appears in *MED mui* n. SK GL RB FI all quote the Fr. *muis* (GL misspells as *mius,* and FI gives the Latin origin as *medius* rather than *modius*). SK RB FI give the size as a bushel; but, as TRg implies (see above), it was probably closer to our barrel than our bushel. The Roman *modius* was around "a 'peck'" (*Oxford Latin Dictionary* 1982), but, by the later Middle Ages, the word *muiee* designated a plot of ground that could be seeded with a *muie* of grain, a plot of "environ six arpents" (Godefroy 1881–1902, s.v. *moiee*) or about nine acres, far more than could be seeded with a bushel; and *MED mui* n. gives the size as "prob. the equivalent of four bushels," i.e., 32 gallons.
5592 **besaunte:** FI RIf note that the gold coin was "Byzantine" (RIf) or "originally of Byzantium" (FI); cf. 1106n.
5598 **it:** KA endorses SK's *it* (for MS *that*) and notes that it refers to *richesse.* Skeat (SK) implies that the word *that* might be a demonstrative: "perhaps 'that gold'; see l. 5592," but he favors the change; Liddell (GL) also takes *that* as "the gold," but he considers emending to "*they,* referring to the *besauntes.*"
5599–5600 "He shall never make his riches satisfy (*asseth*) his greed" (GL; cf. RIf). GL thus reads *Asseth* as a verb, but it translates the Fr. adv. *assez* (Lc 4959 "enough"). See 5600n.
5600 **Asseth:** Cf. 5599–5600n. SP UR gloss incorrectly as "assent," and URg has a false etymology from "AS. Aseðian, *Affirmare.*" TRg has the right sense, "sufficient, enough," and cites the Fr. *assez.* For the nominal sense, "sufficiency," BE SK cite *Piers Plowman* C 20.203 [19.202], "yf hit sufficeth nat for asseth"; MO glosses as "satisfaction, sufficiency"; and SK further adduces *Catholicon Anglicum* (ed. Herrtage and Wheatley 1881:13 n. 6). *MED as(s)ẹth* adv. and adj. notes that "it is possible to take *asseth . . .* as a noun meaning 'sufficiency.'"
5607 **Upon his travel:** "i.e., which he himself earns" (FI).

Or if in syknesse that he fall,
And lothe mete and drynke withall,   5610
Though he have no[gh]t his mete to bye,
He shal bithynke hym hast[i]ly,
To putte hym oute of all daunger,
That he of mete hath no myster;
Or that he may with lytel eke   5615
Be founden, while that he is seke;
Or that men shull hym berne in haste,
To lyve til his syknesse be paste,
To somme maysondewe biside;
He cast nought what shal hym bitide.   5620
He thenkith nought that evere he shall
Into ony syknesse fall.
  "And though it fall, as it may be,
[That all betyme spare shall he]

As mochel as shal to hym suffice,   5625
While he is sike in ony wise,
He doth for that he wole be
Contente with his poverte
Withoute nede of ony man.   111v
So myche in litel have he can,   5630
He is apaied with his fortune;
And for he nyl be importune
Unto no [wight], ne honerous,
Nor of her goodes coveitous,
Therfore he spareth, it may wel bene,   5635
His pore estate for to sustene.
  "Or if hym lust not for to spare,
But suffrith forth, as no[ugh]t ne ware,
Atte last it hapneth, as it may,
Right unto his last day,   5640

5611 **noght**] not MS-KA GL FU SU FI   5612 **hastily**] hastly MS BE KA   5613 **all**] *om.* SP2,3
5619 **To**] Unto UR   5620 **He**] Or he GL   **cast**] caste MS-ST UR-KA GL FU SU FI   5624 *Out:* MS (MS2
corr.)   5627 **doth**] d. it SK RB1-SU RI; d. that GL   5628 **Contente**] Contentid UR   5633 **wyght**] witte
MS KA   5634 **goodes**] goodnesse SP2,3; godesse UR   5638 **forth as nought ne**] f. a. not n. MS-TH2 SP1 BE-
KA GL FU; f. a. nat ye TH3 ST; f. a. not yet SP2-UR; frost a. hot ne SU FI   5640 **Right**] All r. UR

5611 **noght:** KA endorses SK's emendation (*nought*) for MS *not*; cf. 5638n. *Not, no(u)ght* are interchangeable as adverbs, but here the sense requires the pronominal form; see *MED nought* pron. BE's text retains *not* as adv., but Jephson (BE) notes that "*wherewithal* is understood; thus, 'Though he have not wherewithal to buy his meat.'"
5614 **myster:** "need" (SPg et al.); "necessity (i.e., fasting is the best cure)" (FI).
5617 **berne:** bear, "take" (FI). KA suggests *bere*, and SK so respells; RB RI have *beren*. On *berne* for *beren*, GL compares line 6496 *myxnes*.
5619 **maysondewe:** "hospital" (SPg et al.), from *Maison-Dieu*, "house of God" (SK); the word is parallel to the Fr. *ostel Dieu* (Lc 4979; noted in FI). BE cites Matt. 25.40 as background.
5620 **He:** GL emends to *Or he* on the basis of the Fr. *ou* (Lc 4981 "or"; noted in GL RBt).
  cast: "think, contrive, foresee" (URg), "considers" (SKg2), "contemplates" (FI). Cf. *MED casten* v. 21 and 22 [a]. KA endorses SK's *cast*, a present tense form. MS *caste* may be a var. sp. of the present, but it is the usual form of the past.
5622 **ony:** See 212n.
5624 BE states that the "line has been erased in the MS., and filled up by a later hand"; but KA RIt note only that the line is "written by a later hand on a line originally left blank." RIt adds that the hand is "probably fifteenth-century." I classify as MS2b; see "The Manuscript Hands: The Corrections."
5625 **mochel:** See 1713n.
5626 **ony:** See 212n.
5627 **doth:** KA endorses SK's *doth it*; GL supplies *that* instead of *it*. But the intransitive sense, "acts" (*MED dōn* 9a. [a]), may exist without emendation.
5629 **ony:** See 212n.
5633 **honerous:** "burthensom" (URg et al., s.v. *onerous* or *honerous*; *MED onerous* adj.).
5634 **goodes:** T. Thomas (URg) glosses UR's form *godesse* as "goods" and notes that "it were better to read it *Godes*."
5638–39 On the basis of the Fr. (Lc 4988–89 "ainz viegne li froit et li chaut / ou la faim qui morir le face" "before cold and heat come, or hunger that may cause death"), GL suggests that we "perhaps read 'But suffrith frost as hot ne ware / He lat it hapne as it may.'" RIt (5638n.) states that GL's suggestion "is not really parallel" to the Fr.
5638 **forth as nought ne:** RBt notes GL's suggestion, *frost as hot ne* (see above). SU FI adopt the change on the basis of SU Fr. 5018 "le froit que le chaut"; the source of the var. *que* is MS Bu (SU Fr. 4881–5178n.), not collated by Ln.
  nought: KA's suggestion for MS *not*; cf. 5611n.

246

And take[th] the world as it wolde be;
For evere in herte thenkith he,
The sonner that deth hym slo,
To paradys the sonner go
He shal, there for to lyve in blisse, 5645
Where that he shal noo good misse.
Thider he hopith God shal hym sende
Aftir his wrecchid lyves ende.
Pictigoras hymsilf reherses
In a book that 'The Golden Verses' 5650
Is clepid, for the nobilite
Of the honourable ditee:
'Thanne, whanne thou goste thy body fro, 112r
Fre in the eir thou shalt up go,
And leven al humanite, 5655

And purely lyve in deite.'
He is a foole, withouten were,
That trowith have his countre heere.
'In erthe is not oure countre,'
That may these clerkis seyn and see 5660
In Boice 'Of Consolacioun,'
Where it is maked mencioun
Of oure countre pleyn at the eye,
By teching of Philosophie,
Where lewid men myght lere witte, 5665
Whoso that wolde translaten it.
If he be sich that can wel lyve
Aftir his rent may hym yeve,
And not desireth more to have
Than may fro poverte hym save, 5670

5641 **taketh**] take MS-KA FU FI   5643 **deth**] the d. SK GL   5646 **good**] godis UR   5648 **his**] thys TH³ ST SP²-UR   5653 **Thanne**] That GL   5670 **Than**] That BE SK SU FI

5641 **taketh:** KA endorses SK's *taketh*. FI retains MS *take*, presumably as a subjunctive. There is no parallel in the Fr.

5643 **deth:** RBt notes that *the deth* (SK GL) may be correct.

hym: KA suggests *shall hym*, but no ed. so emends.

5649 **Pictigoras:** TH¹-UR FU SU FI respell as *Pythagoras*, the form that KA notes in TH¹; SK GL RB have *Pictagoras*, "the usual form, as in Book Duch. 1167" (SK). David (RIt) refers to 4713n. "on the spelling of classical names in Th [TH¹]"; see 4713n. § SK notes that Pythagoras was a Greek philosopher who died about 510 B.C.; he "taught the doctrine of the transmigration of souls, and he is here said to have taught the principle of the absorption of the soul into the supreme divinity. None of his works are extant. Hierocles of Alexandria, in the fifth century, wrote a commentary on the Golden Verses, which professed to give a summary of the views of Pythagoras." As RB RI note, "Langlois suggests that the source of Jean de Meun's information was the commentary of Chalcidius on the Timaeus" (RB). Ln (5025–32n.) quotes Chalcidius, chapter 125: "Pythagoras etiam in suis Aureis versibus: 'Corpore deposito cum liber ad aethera perges, / Evades hominem factus deus aetheris almi'"; RB gives the reference as chapter 136, "ed. Wrobel, Leipzig, 1876, p. 198," and Lc (4997n.) quotes the same passage from Waszink's ed. (1962:177).

5650 **The Golden Verses:** GL suggests: "(?) Omit *the*; there is no article in the Fr." (Lc 4997 "*Vers dorez*"). § See 5649n. BE notes that the Golden Verses (line 5650) "are seventy-one in number, and are said to have been composed, as a summary of his doctrines, by Lysis, one of his disciples." Like SK (5649n.), BE notes the commentary of Hierocles. GL states that "the book referred to is the *Aurea Carmina*, extant in the Middle Ages as a work of Pythagoras."

5653–56 See 5649n.

5659 SK (5661n.) RB RI cite *Bo* 1p5.8–25 [RI]; 5p1.12–15 [RI]; *Truth* 17, 19. GL (5661n.) also cites Boethius (*De Cons. Phil.* 1p5. FI (5663n.) cites *Bo* 3p5 (*sic* for 1p5?), 5p1. Although the idea is clearly present in these *loci*, the literal statement does not appear there or in Boethius's Latin. Jephson's quotation (BE 5661n.) of 4m1.1–2 is less apt.

5661 **Boice:** Boethius. All eds. except BE-KA GL respell as *Boece*, the usual form in Chaucer and the Fr.

5662–64 Lounsbury (1892:2.120) notes that these lines do not appear in the original but that the emphasis on "oure countre" appears also in Chaucer's *Truth*; he argues that this common feature is evidence for Chaucer's authorship of the entire *Rom*. Kittredge (1892:23) notes that knowledge of Boethius was widespread.

5666 RB RI note that "both Jean de Meun and Chaucer translated Boethius." For Jean's translation, see Dedeck-Héry (1952).

5667–68 "That is, 'If he be such a one as can live according to what his income will admit of'" (BE); for line 5668, SK has "According as his income may afford him means," and FI has "live according to what his income allows."

lyve : yeve: On the rhyme, see 2759–60n.

247

A wise man seide, as we may seen,
Is no man wrecched but he it wene,
Be he kyng, knyght, or ribaude.
And many a ribaude is mery and baude, 5674
That [swynkith] and berith, bothe
    day and nyght,
Many a burthen of gret myght,
The whiche doth hym lasse offense 112v
For he suffrith in pacience.
They laugh and daunce, trippe and synge,
And ley not up for [her] lyvyng, 5680
But in the taverne all dispendith
The wynnyng that God hem sendith.
Thanne goth he fardeles for to bere
With as good chere as he dide ere.
To swynke and traveile he not feynith, 5685

For for to robben he disdeynith;
But right anoon aftir his swynke
He goth to taverne for to drynke.
All these ar riche in abundaunce
That can thus have suffisaunce 5690
Wel more than can an usurere,
As God wel knowith, withoute were.
For an usurer, so God me se,
Shal nevere for richesse riche be,
But evermore pore and indigent, 5695
Scarce and gredy in his entent.
    "For soth it is, whom it displese,
Ther may no marchaunt lyve at ese;
His herte in sich a were is sett
That it quyk brenneth [more] to gete, 5700
Ne never shal [ynough have] geten, 113r

5672 **wrecched]** wrecche GL 5673 **kyng]** a k. UR 5674 **And many]** Many UR 5675 **swynkith]** wynkith MS KA **bothe]** *om.* UR 5678 **For]** F. that UR 5679 **trippe]** thei t. UR 5680 **not]** nought TH¹-UR FU SU FI **her]** he MS (MS₁ *corr.*) 5682 **that]** whiche t. UR 5685 **feynith]** feyntith MS BE-KA 5686 **For for]** For TH¹-UR FU SU FI **disdeynith]** disdeyntith MS BE-KA 5688 **taverne]** the t. TH² 5699 **were]** where MS-UR KA FU 5700 **quyk brenneth more to]** q. b. t. MS-SP³ BE KA FU; q. b. for t. UR; b. q. t. MO 5701 **ynough have]** though he hath MS-KA FU

5672 **wrecched:** In support of the noun *wrecche*, GL cites *Bo* 394 (2p4.111–13 [RI] "ne no wyght . . . nis a wrecche but whanne he weneth hymself a wrechche"); however, the adj. appears immediately before (2p4.109–10 "nothyng [is] wrecchid but whan thow wenest it"). RB RI compare *For* 25, where the adj. appears.

5673 **ribaude:** SP glosses as "baud" and cites the Lat. *leno* (a procurer, seducer, panderer); URg offers "Idle persons attending Courts and Camps . . . Lewd persons, Ruffians, Pimps, Bawds, Whores, &c." Compare "poor labourer" (TRg); "here means simply a poor man" (BE); "a profligate character"(MOg); "labouring man" (SK); "churl" (FI); and "laborer, churl" (RIf). SK notes that in the Fr. (Lc 5019) the *ribaut* "is spoken of as carrying 'sas de charbon,' i.e. sacks of coal." The senses in URg and MOg reflect Fr. *ribaud*; see 6068n.

5675–76 See 5683n.

5675 **swynkith:** KA notes the emendation in TH¹ UR BE MO.

5680 **her:** "*r* written above the line" (KA) by MS₁.

5682 **that:** KA notes UR's *whiche that*.

5683 **fardeles for to bere:** BE SK both recall Shakespeare, *Hamlet* 3.1.76 "Who would fardels bear," and SK considers the possibility that "Shakespeare caught up the phrase . . . from this line in a black-letter edition of Chaucer. His next line—'to grunt and sweat under a weary life'—resembles ll. 5675–6 and 'The undiscovered country' may be from ll. 5658–5664. And see note to l. 5541." SK adds that "Shakespearian scholars in general do not accept this as a possibility." Cf. 5541–42n.

5685 "He does not *feign*, or *pretend, only* to labour; i.e. he labours seriously" (TRg, s.v. *Faine*).
    feynith: TH¹'s emendation (*fayneth*) for MS *feyntith*. Jephson (BE) thinks that in "Speght" it "was probably an emendation of the copyist, to accommodate the rhyme, without introducing a *t* into *disdeyneth*" and that "the original does not give us any help in choosing between them." KA notes TH¹'s *fayneth* and compares line 4831 "For paramours they do but feyne."

5686 **disdeynith:** KA notes TH¹'s *disdayneth* and compares line 4832 "To love truly they disdeyne."

5693 **an:** KA suggests omitting this word, but no ed. so emends.

5699 **were:** TRg suggests the emendation, glossing *were* as "confusion" and citing the Fr. *guerre* (Lc 5043 "conflict"). Jephson (BE) takes MS *where* as "a mistake of the copyist for *were*"; he and SK cite the Fr. KA notes *were* in BE MO.

5700 **more to:** KA endorses SK's insertion of *more*. SK RBt SU FI RIt note the basis in Fr. *plus* (Lc 5044 "more").

5701 **ynough have:** KA's suggestion follows the Fr. *assez acquis* (Lc 5045 "gotten enough"; noted by RBt RIt).

Though he have gold in gerners yeten,
For to be nedy he dredith sore.
Wherfore to geten more and more
He sette his herte and his desire;   5705
So hote he brennyth in the fire
Of coveitise, that makith hym woode
To purchace other mennes goode.
He undirfongith a gret peyne
That undirtakith to drynke up Seyne;   5710
For the more he drynkith, ay
The more he leveth, the soth to say.
Thus is thurst of fals getyng,
That laste ever in coveityng,
And the angwisshe and distresse   5715
With the fire of gredynesse.
She fightith with hym ay and stryveth,
That his herte asondre ryveth.
Such gredynesse hym assaylith
That whanne he most hath, most
    he failith.   5720

"Phiciciens and advocates
Gone right by the same yates;
They selle her science for wynnyng
And haunte her crafte for gret getyng.   5724
Her wynnyng is of such swetnesse   113v
That if a man falle in sikenesse
They are full glad for ther encrese;
For by her wille, withoute lees,
Everiche man shulde be seke,
And though they die, they sette not
    a leke.   5730
After, whanne they the gold have take,
Full litel care for hem they make.
They wolde that fourty were seke at onys,
Yhe, two hundred, in flesh and bonys,
And yit two thousand, as I gesse,   5735
For to encrecen her richesse.
They wole not worchen, in no wise,
But for lucre and coveitise.
For fysic gynneth first by *fy*—

5702 **have**] hath TH²   5711 **he**] that h. UR   5712 **the soth**] s. TH² UR   5713 **Thus is**] T. i. the UR; This i. the SK   5715 **distresse**] the d. UR   5718 **That**] So t. UR   5720 **he failith**] be f. SU 5723 **wynnyng**] wenyng TH²   5725 **wynnyng**] wenyng TH²   5730 **And though**] Though UR 5732 **for**] of SP²³ BE   5733 **that**] *om.* UR

5702 **yeten:** SP²-BE gloss as the pa. part. "gotten" (cf. SP¹g GLg), but SK notes the right sense, "poured," and calls it "a false form; correctly, *yoten*, pp. of *yeten*, to pour (A. S. *gēotan*, pp. *goten*)." However, *OED Yet* v. *Obs.*, lists *yeten* as a β-form of the pa. part. from the 14th century, perhaps a transition toward the weak pa. part. ʒetted (γ-form), which appears in the 15th century.

5706–07   GL RB RI compare *Bo* 2m2. 20–21 [RI].

5710   **to drynke up Seyne:** Proverbial (RB RI). RB cites Haeckel (1890: no. 58); RI cites Whiting (1968: S140).   **Seyne:** SK et al. identify as the river Seine.

5713   **Thus:** KA suggests *This*.   **thurst:** TH³ UR have the metathetic form *thrust*; see 4722n. KA notes *the* before *thurst* in UR, but not in SK.

5722   **yates:** "ways" (*MED gate* n.[2] 5. [a]); "routes" (FI). See 5167n.

5727   **ther:** SKt SU FI RIt note this MS reading, the Northern 3 pl. possessive pron. Eds. except UR-KA GL have *h(e,i)r*.

5728   **lees:** The sense of *lees*, which FI gives as "doubt (loss)," is probably rather "lies," as at *Rom* 3904, *HF* 1464. See 3904n.

5730   KA suggests omitting the second *they*, but no ed. so emends.   **leke:** See 4830n.

5733   **that:** KA notes UR's omission of *that*.

5734   **Yhe:** See 4659–60n.

5739–44   Not in the Fr. (BE SK RB FI RI). T. Thomas (URg, s.v. *Phi*) notes that "the Poet plays upon the first syllable of *Phisicke*, and *Phisicien*, both beginning with *Phi*, a Note of Abhorrence; and from thence pleasantly infers the folly of trusting in them." Sandras (1859:39) suggests an indebtedness to Guiot de Provins; as a parallel to lines 5739–41, he quotes, without documentation, Guiot's lines "Fisiciens sont appelés, / Sans *fi* ne sont-ils point nommés" (see below). Brink (1870:28) suggests that a parallel might eventually be found in one of the many MSS of the Fr., but he offers no candidate. Lounsbury (1892:2.222–23) refers to Sandras, cites "Guiot's *Bible*, lines 2581–2593," and, like Thomas, takes the syllable *fi* as "the interjectional expression of contempt [fie!] . . . precisely indicative of [the physicians'] profession and practice" (p. 223). He notes that "the further statement in the English version . . . that the word *phicien* goes from *fy* to *sy*—a not very brilliant play upon the word *sigh*—is found

The phicicien also sothely—   5740

But aboven all, specialy,   5750

And sithen it goth fro *fy* to [s]*y*,

Sich as prechen [for] veynglorie

To truste on hem is foly,

And toward God have no memorie,

For they nyl, in no maner gre,

But forth as ypocrites trace,

Do right nought for charite.

And to her soules deth purchace,

"Eke in the same secte ar sette   5745

And outward shew[en] holynesse,   5755

All tho that prechen for to gete

Though they be full of cursidnesse.

Worshipes, honour, and richesse.

Not liche to the apostles twelve,

Her hertis arn in grete distresse

They deceyve other and hemselve;

That folk lyve not holily.   114r

Bigiled is the giler thanne.

5740 **sothely]** sorthely MS KA   5741 **fy to sy]** fy to fy MS-ST SP²-UR KA FU; sie to sie SP¹   5742 **is]** it is TH¹-UR SK-FI   5747 **honour]** and h. UR   5749 **lyve]** ne l. SK GL   5751 **for]** in GL; *om.* MS-KA FU   5753 **as]** *om.* BE   5755 **And]** An GL   **shewen]** shewing MS-KA GL FU

---

neither in the original nor in Guiot's *Bible*'; RB FI RI make the same point. SK RB SU (p. xxix) RI all cite Lounsbury; SK RB RI give the reference to *La Bible Guiot de Provins*, l. 2582, in *Fabliaux et Contes*, ed. Barbazan and Méon (1808:2.390). SK accepts the Thomas-Lounsbury reading of *fy* as "fie!" and explains the "mild joke" of lines 5739–41 as follows: "These words begin with *fy*, which (like E. *fie!*) means 'out upon it'; and go on with *sy* (=si), which means 'if,' and expresses the precariousness of trusting to doctors." Liddell (GL), however, finds "the key of the pun in v. 5742," and he reads lines 5739–41 as follows: "'Physyc' goes from 'fying' = trusting, to 'sying' = sighing and groaning"; he adds that "the joke was probably an old one in our author's time, for it depends for its fullest point on the earlier form of 'sien,' viz. '*sicen*,' still used by Chaucer, and by the translator of the 'A' part of the Romaunt (cp. v. 1641)." RB also takes *fy* as "fier'?" (trust) and *sy* as "English *syen* or *syken*"; FI gives much the same reading. This reading is more accurate than Lounsbury's, who writes that "the word *phicicien* goes from *fy* to *sy*," while the text states that it is the word *fysic* (like the word *phicicien*, of course) that does so.

As RI notes, SU (p. xxix) quotes Guiot from the ed. of Mary (1951:288) and gives a longer passage as the parallel to lines 5739–44, one that supports both readings, the idea of "fi" as "trust" and as an expression of disgust. A fuller text appears in the ed. of Orr (1915:90, lines 2578–90), who notes (2580n.) that the syllable "fi" was an expression of disgust in OF as well as Latin.

David (RI) summarizes the previous positions as follows: "The Fr. puns on *fi* ('fi' = 'fie!' 'fier' = 'trust,' 'defie' = 'defy'). The Engl. carries over the play on *fy* (= 'fie,' 'trust') and adds a play on *sy* = 'sigh' (Lounsbury) or on Fr. *si* ('if'), i.e., 'the precariousness of trusting doctors' (Skeat)." In a footnote to line 5739, RI glosses *fy* as "trusting."

5740 **sothely:** KA notes *sothely* in TH¹ BE MO.

phicicien: SK prefers the spelling *fysycien*, to accord with the contextual emphasis on *fy*, but other eds. retain variants of the *ph-* spelling.

5741 **sy:** KA notes "*sy* for second *fy*" in MO.

5742 **is:** KA notes TH¹'s emendation.

5743 **in no maner gre:** "Not in the least degree" (URg), "in no kind of way" (SKg₂).

gre: "degree" (URg et al.), rather than "pleasure" (FI). See 42n.

5747 **richesse:** As KA notes, the capital *R* is faded in MS.

5748–49 BE SK note that the sentence is ironic. Skeat (SK) reads line 5749 as "Because people do not live in a holy manner." He explains: "the word 'Her' [line 5748] refers to 'tho that prechen' [line 5746], i.e. the clergy; F. 'devins' [Lc 5071]. But the F. text has—'*Cil* [i.e. the preachers] ne vivent pas loiaument.' See ll. 5750–51."

5749 **lyve:** KA endorses SK's *ne live.*

5751 **for:** KA suggests the insertion of *for*, in support of which SU FI note Fr. *por* (Lc 5077 "for").

5755 **outward:** "outwardly" (BE).

shewen: KA's suggestion. There is no parallel in the Fr.

5759 Proverbial (SK RB RI); SK quotes the Fr. (Lc 5079 "Deceüz est tex decevierres" "such a deceiver is deceived"). SK RB RI cite *RvT* A 4320–21. In notes to that passage, SK compares Ps. 7.16, 9.15 (= Douai 7.17, 9.16); SK RB compare Gower's *Confessio amantis* 6.1379–81 (ed. Macaulay 1899–1902:3.204); RB compares *RR* (Lc 7312–13, 7357, 11521–22); and Gray (RI) adduces Whiting (1968: G491). SK also adduces *Piers Plowman* C 21.166 [20.163–65]. In notes to that passage, Skeat (1886*b*:2.255) and Pearsall (1979:326) observe that at C 21.166a [20.165a], Langland quotes the phrase "Ars ut artem falleret" (trans. Pearsall, "one cunning stratagem in order to deceive another") from the Latin hymn *Pange, lingua* of Venantius Fortunatus (ed. Raby 1953:90–91); Skeat cites as well Ovid, *Ars amatoria* 1.645 "Fallite fallentes" "deceive deceivers."

For prechyng of a cursed man,
Though [it] to other may profite,
Hymsilf it availeth not a myte;
For ofte goode predicacioun
Cometh of evel entencioun.
To hym not vailith his preching, 5765
All helpe he other with his teching;
For where they good ensaumple take,
There is he with veynglorie shake.
  "But late us leven these prechoures,
And speke of hem that in her toures 5770
Hepe up her gold, and fast shette,
And sore theron her herte sette.
They neither love God ne drede;
They kepe more than it is nede,
And in her bagges sore it bynde, 5775
Out of the sonne and of the wynde;
They putte up more than nede were,
Whanne they seen pore folk forfare,
For hunger die, and for cold quake;
God can wel vengeaunce therof take. 5780
[Thre] gret myscheves hem assailith,

And thus in gadring ay travaylith: 5760
With mych peyne they wynne richesse;
And drede hem holdith in distresse,
To kepe that they gadre faste; 5785
With sorwe they leve it at the laste.
With sorwe they bothe dye and lyve
That unto richesse her hertis yive;
And in defaute of love it is,
As it shewith ful wel, iwys. 5790
For if [thise] gredy, the sothe to seyn,
Loveden and were loved ageyn,
And goode love regned overall,
Such wikkidnesse ne shulde fall;
But he shulde yeve that most
  good hadde 5795
To hem that weren in nede bistadde, 115r
And lyve withoute false usure,
For charite full clene and pure.
If they hem yeve to goodnesse,
Defendyng hem from ydelnesse, 5800
In all this world thanne pore noon
We shulde fynde, I trowe, not oon.

114v (line 5773)

5761 **it]** *om.* MS-SP³ BE-KA FU   5762 **it]** *om.* SK SU FI   **availeth]** vaileth GL   5765 **vailith]** availith UR   5767 **ensaumple]** example TH³-UR   5770 **that]** which SP²,³   5772 **herte]** hertis UR   5781 **Thre]** The MS-UR KA FU   5786 **the]** *om.* UR   5788 **unto]** to SK   5791 **thise]** this MS BE-KA GL   **the]** *om.* UR   5799 **to]** unto UR

5761 **it:** UR's emendation, noted by KA, follows the Fr. *ele* (Lc 5086). Skeat (SKt) also suggests "supply *it*," and notes the presence of the word *it* in the next line, where he omits it.
5762 **it:** KA endorses SK's omission of *it*.
       availeth: GL supports *vaileth* by reference to line 5765.
       myte: See 4830n.
5763–64 RB RI compare *PardP*, passim (especially C 407–08).
5765 **To hym:** Between these two words in MS, the scribe left a 5.5 mm space in which there appears a wavy line, (∼), probably to indicate "run on" or "close up." A similar mark appears at line 5858.
5772 **herte:** KA notes UR's *hertis*.
5774–80 "The poet contrasts the manner in which misers lay up their gold in places defended from the sun and wind, with their conduct in leaving their fellow-creatures to starve in the cold" (BE).
5781–86 BE compares the Latin proverb "Dives divitias non congregat absque labore, / Non tenet absque metu, non desinit absque dolore" ("The rich man does not amass riches without labor, does not keep them without anxiety, does not abandon them without sorrow"); RB notes that Ln (5127–32n.) compares the same couplet, and gives the reference as Werner (1912;1966: no. 123). Lc (5097–102n.) cites Walther (1963–69: nos. 6059, 6125). RI cites Whiting (1968: R113).
5781 **Thre:** BE's *Thre*, noted in BE MO by KA, follows the Fr. *Trois* (Lc 5097 "three"; noted by BE SKt SU FI).
5783 **mych:** See 1713n.
5788 **unto:** KA suggests *to*.
       yive: RIt notes the form *yeue* in TH¹; it persists through TH²-UR FU SU FI.
5791 **thise:** TH¹'s emendation (*these*), noted by KA, is based presumably on both Fr. and ME plural contexts (Lc 5107 "cil qui richeces amassent"). RB first uses the form *thise*. MS *this* may be a plural, and the two forms may be spelling variants here, as at lines 5301, 6759; see 5301n.
5799 **yeve:** "gave, i.e. were to give; past pl. subjunctive" (SK).
5801 **pore:** UR has *povir*, GL *pover*, both disyllables; GL cites line 6489 *pover* in support.

But chaunged is this world unstable,
For love is overall vendable.
We se that no man loveth nowe, 5805
But for wynnyng and for prowe;
And love is thralled in servage

Whanne it is sold for avauntage.
Yit wommen wole her bodyes selle;
Suche soules goth to the devel of helle." 5810
[Fragment C]
Whanne Love hadde told hem his entent,

5803 **is]** in SU FI 5806 **wynnyng]** his w. UR 5810 **to]** *om.* TH² *Heading:* **Fragment C]**
om. MS-KA GL FU

5804 For the proverb, RI cites Whiting (1968: L525).

5811–7692 These lines constitute Fragment C. Tyrwhitt (1775:3.314) BE SK GL RB SU (Fr. 5154n.) FI RI note that the translation leaves a large gap, from Lc 5124 (*Rom* 5810) to Lc 10651 (*Rom* 5811); the remainder of the translation, from line 5811, has come to be known as Fragment C, and SK RB refer to the bearing of this fragment on the question of authorship; see above, "Authorship."

BE GL RB SU (Fr. 5154n.) RI summarize the content of the omitted material; KA (Fr. 5137–10694n.) quotes Jephson's summary (BE), and GL condenses it. David's summary (RI), a close adaptation of RB, is representative:

> In the omitted passage Reason continues her discourse, but fails to persuade the Lover to abandon the service of the god of Love. The Lover then consults L'Ami (Friend), who advises him to approach Belacueil's prison by a road called "Trop Doner" (i.e., large expenditure of money), constructed by Largesse. Ami also tells the Lover at length about the Golden Age, the corruption of society, and the proper treatment of one's mistress or wife. The Lover then approaches the castle, but Richesse bars his entrance. The god of Love now comes to his assistance, first calling a council of his barons. Among them are two new characters, False-Seeming and his female companion Constrained Abstinence. The god of Love opens the assembly with a speech in which he declares that his servant Guillaume de Lorris had begun and left unfinished the romance to be completed more than forty years after his death by Jean de Meun. He asks the barons' advice on how to conquer the castle. At this point Fragment C begins.

In addition to these details, Jephson's summary (BE) calls attention to the "satire on women," i.e., the diatribe of the Jealous Husband (Le Jaloux, Lc 8437–9330), which forms part of Ami's contrast between love now and in the Golden Age (Lc 8325–9510); to the relation between the end of the Golden Age and the rise of kingdoms; to Ovid's *Ars amatoria* as a source for the passage on the proper conduct toward one's mistress or wife (Lc 9649–928; cf. *Ars* 2.121–642); to the list of the God of Love's barons (Lc 10419–62); and to the God of Love's evocation of Ovid, Tibullus, and Gallus as fore-runners of Guillaume de Lorris (Lc 10477–500).

In their summaries, Jephson (BE), Liddell (GL), and SU (Fr. 5154n.) mislead somewhat in saying that Reason shows the vanity of natural love; in fact, Reason says that natural love (Lc 5733 "amor naturel"), the impulse to engender and nurture offspring, is common to men and beasts and deserves neither praise nor blame (Lc 5733–58). It is not, she tells the Lover, the foolish love that interests him (Lc 5759–64).

On the continuity of this section, Dahlberg (1988:116–20) sees Ami (Friend) as an ironic reflection of Reason's discourse on friendship (Lc 4650–4738) and Fals-Semblant as a development of Ami's emphasis on the use of deception in the Lover's pursuit of the rosebud. Jean de Meun here amplifies Guillaume de Lorris's earlier introduction of the characters Reason and Friend (Lc 3091–3203, *Rom* 3343–3469), but Fals-Semblant is a new development in Jean de Meun.

In his theory of the composition of *Rom*, Kaluza (1893a:245–48) regards Fragment C as Chaucer's translation of an independent section that attracted him, the Fals-Semblant passage. He presents two pieces of evidence: the heading *Falssemblant* which appears on each page from 115v onward (see note prior to 5821n.) and the fact that line 5811 reads "Whanne *Love* hadde told hem his entent" rather than "Whanne *he* hadde told hem . . ." as it would be if it formed part of a continuing translation. For the Fr. has "Quant *il* ot sa reson fenie" (Lc 10651), where *il* has as its antecedent the word *Amor* two lines above; if those two previous lines had formed part of the translation, there would have been no need to supply the word *Love*. See below for text of Fr.

Heading: **Fragment C:** Although Liddell (GL) does not use this heading, he shows the discontinuity by a line of dots.

5811–12 SK quotes the Fr. (Lc 10649–53): "Ainsinc Amors a ceus parole / qui bien reçurent sa parole. / Quant il ot sa reson fenie, / conseilla soi la baronie" ("Thus Love spoke to them, and they received his speech well. When he had finished his reasoning, the barons consulted among themselves"). As SK notes, the English corresponds to the last two of these lines.

The baronage to councel went.
In many sentences they fille,
And dyversely they seide hir [wille];
But aftir discorde they accorded,   5815
And her accord to Love recorded.
"Sir," seiden they, "we ben at one,
Bi evene accorde of everichone,
Outake Richesse al oonly,
That sworne hath ful hauteynly   5820
[That] she the castell nyl not assaile,   115v
Ne smyte a stroke in this bataile
With darte ne mace, spere ne knyf,
For man that spekith or berith the lyf,
And blameth youre emprise, iwys,   5825
And from oure hoost departed is,
Atte lest way, as in this plyte,

So hath she this man in dispite.
For she seith he ne loved hir never,
And therfore she wole hate hym evere.   5830
For he wole gadre no tresoure,
He hath hir wrath for evermore.
He agylte hir never in other caas;
Lo, heere all hoolly his trespas!
She seith wel that this other day   5835
He axide hir leve to gone the way
That is clepid To-Moche-Yevyng,
And spak full faire in his praiyng.
But whanne he praiede hir, pore was he;
Therfore she warned hym the entre.   5840
Ne yit is he not thryven so
That he hath geten a peny or two
That quytely is his owne in holde.

5814   **wille**] tille MS MO KA   5821   **That**] The MS KA   **not**] *om.* UR SK   5823   **spere**] ne s. UR
5824   **or**] and SP²·³ BE   **the**] *om.* UR   5827   **Atte**] At TH¹-UR SK FU SU FI   5843   **quytely**] quietly ST-UR

5812   **baronage:** "nobility" (URg; cf. *MED barnāǧe* n.[1]), "the assembly of barons" (SKg₂). BE notes that "baron was at this period a generic name given to all the noblesse."

5814   In opposing Chaucer's authorship of *Rom* 5811–7692 (= our Fragment C), Lindner (1887:172) considers this line as a somewhat feeble translation of the Fr. (Lc 10654 "Divers diverses choses distrent" "different ones said different things") in comparison with *SqT* F 202 ("Diverse folk diversely they demed"). Kaluza (1893a:138–40), in sustaining Chaucer's authorship of this fragment, regards this line as a more accurate *translation* of the Fr., given the constraints of the octosyllabic line, because *seyde* corresponds more closely to *distrent* than does *demed*; and he compares two parallel lines in *CT*, *RvP* A 3857 ("Diverse folk diversely they seyde") and *MerT* E 1469 ("Diverse men diversely hym tolde"), where *seyde* and *tolde* are closer to the *Rom* version than is *demed*.

wille: TH¹'s emendation (*wyll*) for MS *tille*; KA endorses the change in TH¹ UR BE. There is only a loose parallel in the Fr. (Lc 10654, above).

5815–16   **discorde . . . accorded . . . accord . . . recorded:** BE regards "this playing upon the words" as "a sort of onomatopeia, representing the differences of opinion and final agreement of the barons."

5820   **hauteynly:** "haughtily" (URg SKg₂), "arrogantly" (FI RIf) "(or loudly)" (RIf).

Page heading: ¶ **Falssemblant.** So MS. KA RIt note that this heading appears at the top of each page from 115v to the end of the MS, 150r. The heading is centered and underlined in red; the ¶-sign is not always present.

5821   **That:** KA notes *That* in TH¹ UR BE MO.

5824   RI quotes the Fr. (Lc 10664–65 "por home qui parler en sache, / ne de nule autre arme qui soit" "Notwithstanding anyone who might have something to say about it, nor with any other kind of weapon"), and notes that "Richesse refuses to fight in any way, no matter what anyone might say." See below, on *lyf*.

lyf: SK notes that the word answers to Fr. *âme* but that the Fr. has *arme*, a weapon. RI notes that "the English is probably based on a variant for the second line: 'Ne pour ame qu'el monde seit' (Nor for any soul on earth)"; Ln (10695t) collates the var. in MS Eb.

5827   "The meaning is, 'As far as this quarrel is concerned.' The feudal nobility could generally check the inordinate power of the crown, by refusing, under some pretext, to join the sovereign in the wars" (BE).

5835   "Written twice in the MS.; but the first line struck out" (KA).

5837   **To-Moche-Yevyng:** SK RB RI note the Fr. *Trop Doner* (Lc 10679).

5839   **praiede:** KA endorses SK's *prayde*, which appears only there and in GL's *praide*.

5843   **quytely:** "quite, entirely" (SKg₂), "without obligation" (FI), "freely" (RIf; cf. TRg). KA endorses SK's normalization *quitly*, adopted also by GL RB RI. I collate *quietly* as an error, but it may be a sp. var.; *MED quiet(e)lī* adv. ("freely") notes the var. at *KnT* A 1792 in the Petworth MS (Hengwrt *quitly*), and in the 15th-century *Godstow Register*.

Thus hath Richesse us all tolde;	5844	They shull assailen that ilke gate.	5860
And whanne Richesse us this recorded,	116r	Agayns Drede shall Hardynesse	
Withouten hir we ben accorded.		Assayle, and also Sikernesse,	
"And we fynde in oure accordaunce		With all the folk of her ledyng,	
That False-Semblant and Abstinaunce,		That never wist what was fleyng.	
With all the folk of her bataille,		"Fraunchise shall fight, and eke Pite,	5865
Shull at the hyndre gate assayle,	5850	With Daunger, full of cruelte.	
That Wikkid-Tunge hath in kepyng,		Thus is youre hoost ordeyned wele.	
With his Normans full of janglyng.		Doune shall the castell every dele,	
And with hem Curtesie and Largesse,		If everiche do his entent,	116v
That shull shewe her hardynesse		So that Venus be present,	5870
To the olde wyf that kepte so harde	5855	Youre modir, full of vesselage,	
Fair-Welcomyng withynne her warde.		That can ynough of such usage.	
Thanne shal Delite and Wel-Heelynge		Withouten hir may no wight spede	
Fonde Shame adowne to brynge;		This werk, neithir for word ne deede.	
With all her oost, erly and late,		Therfore is good ye for hir sende,	5875

5855 **kepte]** kepeth SK   5860 **that ilke]** thilke SK   5864 **was]** wast BE   **fleyng]** sleyng TH³ ST
SP²-UR   5867 **Thus]** This ST UR

5852 *Marginalium:* In MS, right margin, is a "nō" (nota) opposite this line.

Normans: See 4234n. Jephson (BE) claims that Méon, in an addition to the note on his line 3899, writes that in some MSS one reads *Flamans*, in others *Picards*; Jephson suggests that "these MSS. were probably written by Norman scriveners." Ln (10724t) records the var. *Francheis* "French."

5855 **To:** "i.e. against; F. 'Contre'" (SK; see below for the Fr.).

kepte: KA suggests *kepeth*, in support of which SKt cites Fr. present tense *mestrie* (Lc 10697 "contre la Vielle qui mestrie" "against the Old Woman, who rules"); RBt grants that the change may be correct.

5856 **Fair-Welcomyng:** TRg (s.v. *Bialacoil*) BE SK GL RB RI note that this character, Fr. *Bel Acueill* (Lc 10698), is called Bialacoil earlier in the poem (in Fragment B); Child (1870:721) and Lindner (1887:170) suggest that this difference shows that there were two different translators, and Kaluza (1890; 1893a:5, 8, 37) uses the distinction as one means of showing separate translators in Fragments B and C. Cf. Lounsbury (1892:2.12–13); Kittredge (1892:11); Kaluza (1893a:37 n.1). RI also notes that this is "one of the indications that a new translator is at work." Brusendorff (1925:344–46), arguing for Chaucer's authorship of the entire *Rom*, believes that the *Bialacoil*-forms are "due to later corruption of the text, and that the original . . . was the true ME. form *Fair-Welcomyng*."

5857 **Wel-Heelynge:** BE SK RB FI RI note that this name is a translation of Fr. *Bien-Celer* (Lc 10699); the glosses (BE SK FI RIf) follow the basic sense of "well-concealing." BE gives the source as *hille*, but it is ME *bēlen*, OE *helan* (*MED bēlen* v.[2] "cover").

5858 **Fonde Shame:** Between these two words in MS, the scribe left a 6.5 mm space in which there appears a wavy line (∼), probably to indicate "run on" or "close up." A similar mark appears at line 5765.

Fonde: "try" (TRg), "attempt" (SKg₂; see also URg RIf *MED fonden, -ien* v. 7 [a]), rather than "manage" (FI).

5860 **that ilke:** KA endorses SK's *thilke*.

5869–70 **entent : present:** KA suggests adding -*e* to each word, but only SK so emends. RB RI point out that the rhyme is un-Chaucerian, since Chaucer regularly has *entente*; both point out two other instances of dropping of Chaucerian -*e* in rhyme—lines 6105–06 (*atte last[e]* : *agast*) and lines 6565–66 (*wrought* [pl.] : *nought*)—and "six instances of *I* or words ending in -*y*, rhyming with words in which Chaucer regularly has a final -*e*, at 6111–12, 6301–02, 6339–40, 6373–74, 6875–76, 7317–18" (RI). See above, "Authorship."

5870 **So that:** Perhaps "provided that" (Fr. *por quoi* [Lc 10712]), rather than "if that" (FI).

5871 **vesselage:** "valour, courage" (TRg); "worthiness, courage, that which becomes a good vassal" (BE); "prowess" (RIf). KA endorses *vasselage* and attributes the spelling to Skeat; but SK has *vassalage*; RB RI adopt KA's *vasselage*. BE notes the Fr. (Lc 10713 "vostre mere, qui mout est sage" "your mother,' who is very wise"), which is without a clear parallel.

For thurgh hir may this werk amende."
  "Lordynges, my modir, the goddesse,
That is my lady and my maistresse,
Nis not [at] all at my willyng,
Ne doth not all my desiryng.   5880
Yit can she some tyme done labour,
Whanne that hir lust, in my socour,
[Al] my [nedis] for to acheve,
But now I thenke hir not to greve.
My modir is she, and of childehede   5885
I bothe worshipe hir and eke drede;
For who that dredith sire ne dame
Shal it abye in body or name.
And, netheles, yit kunne we
Sende aftir hir, if nede be;   5890
And were she nygh, she comen wolde;
I trowe that nothyng myght hir holde.

  "Mi modir is of gret prowesse;   117r
She hath tan many a fortresse,
That cost hath many a pounde, er this,   5895
There I nas not present, ywis.
And yit men seide it was my dede;
But I come never in that stede,
Ne me ne likith, so mote I the,
That such toures ben take withoute me. 5900
For-why me thenkith that in no wise
It may bene clepid but marchandise.
  "Go bye a courser, blak or white,
And pay therfore; than art thou quyte.
The marchaunt owith thee right nought, 5905
Ne thou hym, whanne thou it bought.
I wole not sellyng clepe yevyng,
For sellyng axeth no guerdonyng;
Here lith no thank ne no merite;

5878 **and my]** and UR   5879 **at all]** all MS-KA FU   5880 **not]** *om.* SP²·³   5883 **Al my nedis]** As m. nede is MS-KA GL FU   5886 **eke]** *om.* GL   5889 **netheles]** natheles TH¹-BE SK FU-RI   5900 **That such toures ben take]** Such t. take SK   **without]** with TH¹-UR FU   5901 **me]** My TH²   5902 **but]** by SU FI   5906 **thou it bought]** t. hast i. b. UR SK RB¹·²; t. i. hast b. MO; t. is b. SU

5876 **amende:** Perhaps "improve" (*MED amenden* v. 7 [a]), rather than "be helped" (FI).

5877–80 TH¹-ST supply a question mark after line 5879; TH² has another question mark after line 5880.

5877 BE MO SK supply speech-heading *Amour.*

5879 **at all:** KA's suggestion for MS *all.* RBt RIt note the basis in the Fr. *du tout* (Lc 10721 "n'est pas du tout a mon desir" "is not at all subject to my wish").

5883 **Al my nedis:** KA's suggestion for MS *As my nede is,* adopted on two bases: the confusion between *l* and long *s* (*As/Al*); and the Fr. (Lc 10725 "a mes besoignes achever" "to finish my tasks"; noted by GL RBt SU FI RIt). GL retains the MS reading but states that KA's is perhaps correct. GL RB RI note the confusion in translating the Fr. *besoignes* ("affairs") as *besoinges* ("needs"), and GL compares a "similar translation in *Boece,* 147" (1p4.174–78 [RI] "nedes"; Jean de Meun 1p4.93, ed. Dedeck-Héry 1952:179 "besoingnes"). The feminine (Modern Fr. *besogne*) and masculine (Modern Fr. *besoin*) forms probably had a common origin and were distinguished also in older Fr., but the semantic fields of each contained both senses. See Bloch-Wartburg (1968:68–69, s.v. *besogne*); Tobler-Lommatzsch (1925– :1.944–48, s.v. *besoigne, besoing*); Wartburg (1922–1965:17.275–82, s.v. **sunni* II).

5886 **eke:** KA endorses SKt's suggestion, "omit *eke,*" but only GL so emends.

5889 **netheles:** KA endorses *natheles.* Although not substantive in sense, this variant is substantive in the form of the first element, *nō, nā* rather than *ne.* See *MED nō-the-les(se* adv., *ne-the-les* adv. Cf. lines 6073, 6195.

5894 **tan:** taken. SK RB FI note that the contracted pa. part. is a Northern form; SK suggests that perhaps *take* in line 5900 should be *tan.*

5900 KA suggests omitting *That* and *ben*; the meter is improved, but the MS version is perhaps closer to the Fr. construction (Lc 10741–42 "ne ne me plust onques tel prise / de forterece *sanz moi prise*" "nor did such a capture of a fortress, *taken without me*, ever please me").

       take: See 5894n.

       withoute: SU errs in saying that G. [MS] has *oute.*

5901 **For-why:** TH¹-BE FU place a question mark after these words, and thus take them as the compound interrogative adv. "why?" rather than as the pronominal conj. "wherefore, therefore" (see *MED for-whī* 1, 6); the latter sense more nearly follows that of the Fr. conj. *car* (Lc 10743). Cf. 1743n., 2063n.

5902 **but:** The variant *by,* first appearing in SU with no sign of emendation or note, gives rise to FI's reading and FI's gloss on *cleped by marchaundyse,* "called buying (love)"; the sense is clear in the unemended version.

5906 **thou it bought:** KA notes MO's *thou it hast bought.*

That oon goth from that other [al] quyte. 5910
But this sellyng is not semblable;
For whanne his hors is in the stable,
He may it selle ageyn, parde,
And wynnen on it, such happe may be;
All may the man not leese, iwys, 5915
For at the leest the skynne is his.
Or ellis, if it so bitide 117v
That he wole kepe his hors to ride,
Yit is he lord ay of his hors.
But thilk chaffare is wel wors 5920
There Venus entremetith ought;
For whoso such chaffare hath bought,
He shal not worchen so wisely
That he ne shal leese al outerly
Bothe his money and his chaffare. 5925
But the seller of the ware
The prys and profit have shall.
Certeyn, the bier shal leese all;
For he ne can so dere it bye
To have lordship and full maistrie, 5930
Ne have power to make lettyng,

Neithir for yift ne for prechyng,
That of his chaffare, maugre his,
Another shal have as moche, iwis,
If he wole yeve as myche as he, 5935
Of what contrey so that he be;
Or for right nought, so happe may,
If he can flater hir to hir pay.
Ben thanne siche marchauntz wise?
No, but fooles in every wise, 5940
Whanne they bye sich thyng wilfully, 118r
There as they leese her good [fully].
But natheles, this dar I say,
My modir is not wont to pay,
For she is neither so fool ne nyce 5945
To entremete hir of sich [vice].
But trust wel, he shal pay all,
That repent of his bargeyn shall,
Whanne poverte putte hym in distresse,
All were he scoler to Richesse, 5950
That is for me in gret yernyng,
Whanne she assentith to my willyng.
    "But [by] my modir, Seint Venus,

5910 **al]** *om.* MS (MS, *corr.*)   5921 **ought]** nought BE SK   5924 **al]** *om.* SP²-UR   5926 **the ware]** thilke w. UR   5939 **Ben]** And b. UR   5942 **as]** *om.* UR   **fully]** folyly MS-KA FU   5946 **vice]** wise MS KA   5947 **trust]** trustith UR GL   5950 **he]** the TH²   5953 **by]** om. MS-SP³ KA FU

5910 **al:** "written above the line" (KA) by MS₁.

5915 **All:** "*All* is object of *leese*" (GL).

5919–20 **hors : wors:** SK (1.6–7) RB RI note the un-Chaucerian rhyme. RI, following SK and RB, states: "Chaucer rhymes *wors* with *curs* [*CkP* A 4349] and *pervers* (BD, 813). Other irregular rhymes in Fragment C are *force : croce*, 6469–70; *pacience : vengeaunce*, 6429–30; *Abstynaunce : penaunce*, 7481–82 (Chaucer's form is *Abstinence*); *science : ignorence*, 6717–18. The last three instances, however, are taken directly from the Fr." Cf. 6429–30n.

5921 **ought:** SU notes that SK "has *nought* for *ought*, perhaps unintentionally."

5931 **to make lettyng:** "to let or hinder" (BE), to "put hindrance in his way" (GL). SK FI gloss *lettyng* as "hindrance" and explain that the buyer does not have the power to stop "another from having what he has himself paid for." BE SK quote the Fr. *puisse enpeeschier* (Lc 10773 "ne que ja puisse enpeeschier" "nor can he ever prevent").

5933 **maugre his:** "in spite of him(self)," "against his will." See 2386n.

5935 **myche:** Eds. except BE-KA GL RB RI have *m(o,u)ch(e)*; cf. line 5934, where MS has *moche*. See 1713n.

5939 **marchauntz:** The *-z* is the yogh-like "ȝ." SKt notes this MS form and TH¹'s *marchauntes*; SK respells as *marchaunts*, for a disyllable. Cf. 6175–76n.

5942 **fully:** KA suggests *fully* for MS *folyly*. GL SU FI RIt note the basis in the Fr. *ou tout* (Lc 10784 "ou tout perdent" "or lose everything"), but GL misquotes *tout* as *tant*.

5946 **vice:** TH¹'s emendation (*vyce*) for MS *wise* follows the Fr. *vice* (Lc 10790 "vice"); KA notes the correction in TH¹ UR MO. BE states that MS *wise* was "a mere clerical error"; but cf. 4878n., 4709n., 5379–80n.

5947 **trust:** KA notes *truste* in TH¹ MO and *trustith* in UR.

5949 **putte:** "the contracted form of *putteth*" (BE). The normal contraction, however, would be *put*, as in TH³-UR SK; see Mossé (1968:79).

5953 **by:** UR's emendation, noted by KA in BE MO, follows the Fr. *par* (Lc 10797 "Mes par sainte Venus, ma mere" "but by my mother Saint Venus").

And by hir fader Saturnus,
That hir engendride by his lyf—   5955
But not upon his weddid wyf—
Yit wole I more unto you swere,
To make this thyng the seurere.
Now by that feith and that [leaute]
That I owe to all my britheren fre,   5960
Of which ther nys wight undir heven
That kan her fadris names neven,
So dyverse and so many ther be
That with my modir have be prive!   5964
Yit wolde I swere, for sikirnesse,   118v
The pole of helle to my witnesse,

Now drynke I not this yeere clarre,
If that I lye or forsworne be!
(For of the goddes the usage is
That whoso hym forswereth amys   5970
Shal that yeer drynke no clarre.)
Now have I sworn ynough, pardee;
If I forswere me, thanne am I lorne,
But I wole never be forsworne.
Syth Richesse hath me failed heere,   5975
She shal abye that trespas ful dere,
Atte leest wey, but [she] hir arme
With swerd, or sparth, or gysarme.
For certis, sith she loveth not me,

5959 **leaute**] beaute MS-UR KA FU   5960 **That I**] I SK   5963 **so many**] m. UR   5965 **wolde**]
wol TH³ ST SP²-UR FU   5973 **me**] om. UR   5976 **ful**] om. UR BE SK GL   5977 **Atte**] At TH²-UR SK
wey] ways SU FI   **she**] I UR BE; om. MS-SP³ KA GL FU   **arme**] harme TH³ ST SP²-UR   5978 **or**
gysarme] o. with g. UR GL

5954–56 "According to one account, Aphrodite was the daughter of Cronos and Euonyme; and the Romans identified Aphrodite with Venus, and Cronos with Saturnus. The wife of Cronos was Rhea" (SK 5953n.). RB gives much the same account, and RI adds that "the Fr. text is probably alluding to a famous story told by Reason in the *Roman* [Lc 5506–12] after the point where Fragment B breaks off, how Venus was born from Saturn's genitals when Jupiter cut them off and cast them into the sea. A spurious passage interpolated in several Fr. MSS at this point (printed in Langlois's notes to 10830–31) refers the reader to the story ('Car maintes foiz oï avez'—For you've heard it many times) and proceeds to tell how Jupiter begot Cupid on Venus." On the origins of the story, see Dahlberg (1971:379 n.5537–42).

5958 **seurere:** KA suggests *sikerere* and compares lines 6147, 7308. GL FI so spell, RB has *sikerer* (: *swer*). SKt notes TH¹'s *surere*, adopted by TH²-UR FU SU.

5959 **leaute:** BE's emendation for MS *beaute* is reasonable on paleographical grounds. KA notes the change in BE MO, and KA GL compare line 6006, where "the same error occurs" (GL). SU notes that "eds. emend from the Fr.," but no actual parallel to *leaute* is present (Lc 10803 "par la foi que doi touz mes freres" "by the faith that I owe to all my brothers").

5960 **That:** KA suggests omitting this word; only SK so emends.

5962 "Two of the fathers were Mars and Anchises; and there are several other legends about the loves of Venus" (SK).

5966 **pole of helle:** The river Styx (Ln 10838n., Lc 10809–13n., RIf); from the Fr. (Lc 10808 "la palu d'enfer" "the marsh of hell"; noted in BE SK RB).

pole: "pool" (BE SK RB); BE notes that Méon glosses Fr. *palu* as "marais" (marsh).

5967 **clarre:** wine mixed with honey and spices (TRg BE), and clarified by straining (*MED clarę* n.[1]); "spiced and sweetened wine" (RIf). It is not "claret wine" (FI), except in the obsolete sense (*OED Claret* sb.¹); in modern English usage (*OED* sb.²), *claret* means the red wine of Bordeaux, which is neither spiced nor sweetened. TRg BE note that the Fr. parallel is *piment* (Lc 10809), and TRg quotes—from "the *Medulla Cirurgiæ Rolandi*, MS. *Bod.* 761. fol. 86"—a recipe for "*Claretum* bonum, sive *pigmentum*," that specifies spices and honey. Cf. 6027n.

5976 **ful:** KA notes the omission of *ful* in UR BE. GL bases the omission on the Fr. *cher* (Lc 10818 "dear, at high cost"), which has no qualifier; RBt grants that the omission may be correct.

she: MO's *she*, noted by KA, follows the Fr. *el* (Lc 10819).

5978 **sparth, or gysarme:** KA attributes UR's emendation to Skeat, who does not adopt the change but notes (SK), as a metrical alternative, that "*sparth*, with trilled *r*, appears to be disyllabic," and compares lines 3962, 5047, 5484, 6025. § Eds. gloss *sparth* as "speare" (SP¹g), "*bipennis*, double ax" (SPg URg), "ax, or halberd" (TRg), "battle-ax" (FI RIf). *Gysarme* presents a greater variety of interpretation. SPg give "a certaine weapon" and URg has a long explanation of the term: "A military weapon, supposed by some to be a Pike with Two points, or a Staff with Two pikes within it, which with a Thrust forward came forth, and thought by *Spelm[an]* to be the same which in

257

Fro thilk tyme that she may se 5980
The castell and the tour toshake,
In sory tyme she shal awake.
If I may [grype] a riche man,
I shal so pulle hym, if I can,
That he shal in a fewe stoundes 5985
Lese all his markis and his poundis.
I shal hym make his pens outslynge,
But they in his gerner sprynge.
Oure maydens shal eke pluk hym so 119r
That hym shal neden fetheres mo, 5990
And make hym selle his londe to spende,
But he the bet kunne hym defende.
  "Pore men han maad her lord of me;
Although they not so myghty be
That they may fede me in delite, 5995
I wole not have hem in despite.
No good man hateth hym, as I gesse,
For chynche and feloun is Richesse,
That so can chase hym and dispise,
And hem defoule in sondry wise. 6000
They loven full bet, so God me spede,

Than doth the riche, chynchy g[n]ede,
And ben, in good feith, more stable
And trewer and more serviable;
And therfore it suffisith me 6005
Her good herte and her [leaute].
They han on me sette all her thought,
And therfore I forgete hem nought.
I wole hem bringe in grete noblesse,
If that I were god of richesse, 6010
As I am god of love, sothely,
Sich routhe upon her pleynt have I.
Therfore I must his socour be, 119v
That peyneth hym to serven me,
For if he deide for love of this, 6015
Thanne semeth in me no love ther is."
  "Sir," seide they, "soth is every deel
That ye reherce, and we wote wel
T[h]ilk oth to holde is resonable;
For it is good and covenable 6020
That ye on riche men han sworne.
For, sir, this wote we wel biforne:
If riche men done you homage,

5983 **grype]** grepe MS BE-KA   5988 **But]** B. that UR; But-if SK   5990 **shal]** shel SU FI
5991 **selle]** selfe FU   6002 **gnede]** grede MS-SK FU   6006 **herte]** hertis UR   **leaute]** beaute MS-KA
FU   6007 **thought]** though MO   6009 **wole]** wolde SK GL RB[1,2]   6010 **If]** I TH[1] FU   6011 **As I am]**
If that I were SP[2,3]   6019 **Thilk]** Tilk MS KA

Spanish is called *Bifarma* or *Vifarma*; but in the Statute of *Winton*, he thinks it signifies a Bille, in Lat. *Bipennis*, a
Battle-ax, a Hand-ax with Two edges. See *Fr. Gl.* in *Gisarme.*" Other eds. gloss as "battle-ax" (TRg), "battle scythe"
(FI), "long-shafted battle-axe, halberd" (RIf). TRg cites Du Cange, s.v. *Sparth, Securis Danica, Gisarma.*
    5981 **toshake:** KA suggests *to-shake.*
    5983 **grype:** KA notes TH[1]'s *grype.*
    5984 **pulle:** "pluck" (SK FI); TRg (s.v. *Finch*) BE SK adduce *GP* 652, and TRg cites *Rom* 6820. BE cites the Fr.
(Lc 10826 "vos le me verrez si taillier" "you will see me so trim him").
    5988 **But they:** KA endorses SK's *But if they.*
        sprynge: "continue to increase" (SK); "increase" (RB); "grow voluntarily" (FI); "spring up, grow" (RIf).
SK GL RB cite Fr. *sordent* (Lc 10830 "spring, gush, well")
    5989 BE quotes the Fr. (Lc 10831 "si le plumeront nos puceles"), of which the ME is a literal translation.
    5997, 5999 **hym:** them; see 1922n. All eds. except KA (and GL in line 5999) respell as *hem.* KA notes *hem* in
TH[1] UR BE MO.
    6002 **gnede:** KA endorses SKt's suggestion, "read *gnede.*" Eds. gloss as "stingy (person)" (SK RIf), from "A. S.
gneð" (SK); "stingy" (FI). MS *grede* is difficult to justify in this sense; *gredy* (as in line 5791) would give a false rhyme;
and *grede* (= "greed," as a nominal back-formation from *gredy*) is unknown in this sense, or even in its modern
abstract sense at this period (*OED Greed* sb.). See *MED gnēde* adj. 1. (b)., where this quotation is the sole entry.
    6006 **leaute:** KA's suggestion. BE does not emend MS *beaute*, as at line 5959, but Jephson (BE) says that
"*beaute* was probably written by the scrivener by mistake for *bounte*," and he quotes the Fr. (Lc 10846 "leur bons
queurs et leur volonté" "their good heart and their good will"). SK cites Fr. *volonté* in support of *leaute*, and KA SK
RBt SU compare line 5959.
    6009 **wole:** KA suggests *wolde*; in support, SK cites the Fr. imperfect subjunctive *meïsse* (Lc 10849 "would
set").
    6017 **they:** "i.e. a number of barons; see l. 5812" (SK).

258

That is as fooles done outrage;
But ye shull not forsworne be,   6025
Ne lette therfore to drynke clarre,
Or pyment makid fresh and newe.
Ladies shull hem such pepir brewe,
If that they fall into her laas,
That they for woo mowe seyn 'Allas!'   6030
Ladyes shullen evere so curteis be
That they shal quyte youre oth all free.
Ne sekith never othir vicaire,

For they shal speke with hem so faire
That ye shal holde you paied full wele   6035
Though ye you medle never a dele.
Late ladies [worche] with her thyngis,   120r
They shal hem telle so fele tidynges,
And moeve hem eke so many requestis
Bi flateri, that not honest is,   6040
And therto yeve hym such thankynges,
What with kissyng and with talkynges,
That, certis, if they trowed be,

6026 **lette]** let TH²-UR SK   6029 **they]** he SP²·³   6035 **you]** ye TH¹·² FU SU FI   6037 **worche]** worthe MS BE-KA   6039 **hem eke]** *om.* UR   6042 **kissyng]** kissings SP¹   **talkynges]** thalkynges TH²

6024 Jephson (BE) finds this line corrupt and quotes the Fr. (Lc 10864 "il ne feront mie que sage" "they do not act wisely"; noted in SK RI). Skeat (SK) reads the ME as "they act like fools who are outrageous," and he thinks that the Fr. "seems to mean just the contrary." However, the sense is parallel; the Fr. expresses it negatively, the ME affirmatively and with some loss of irony.

6025 **shull:** In reporting MS reading as *shulle*, SKt interprets MS *-ll* as *-lle*; see above, "The Manuscript Hands: The Scribe (MS₁)."

forsworne: SK, normalizing to *forsworen*, states: "*forsworn*, with trilled [second] *r*, seems to be trisyllabic. . . . But it is better to read *forsworen*"; see 5978n.

6026 **lette:** "cease. Cf. l. 5967. But read *let*, pp. prevented" (SK). In the former reading, *lette* (inf.) would parallel *be*, cf. *MED letten* v. 11. (e), where the eds. note an overlapping with *lēten* v. 11. In the latter reading, *let* (contracted pa. part.) would parallel *forsworne*; cf. *MED letten* v. 5. (c). I collate on the basis of this distinction, although it is not certain that the forms in TH²-UR are anything more than sp. variants. Cf. 5335n.

clarre: See 5967n.

6027 **piment:** "drink of wine and honie" (SPg URg), "spiced wine" (TRg; cf. RIf); "same as *clarree*" (SK FI); "in fact, in l. 5967, where the E. has *clarree*, the F. text has *piment*" (SK). In support, SK notes that TRg, s.v. *clarre*, quotes a recipe for "Claretum bonum, sive Pigmentum"; see 5967n. Both URg TRg adduce *Bo* 2m5.

6028–30 RB compares *KnT* A 1951–52.

6028 **such pepir brewe:** BE notes the Fr. (Méon 10933 "braceront tel poivre" "shall brew such pepper"); cf. Lc 10868 "braieront tel poivre" "shall grind such pepper." Ln 10898t collates the var. *braceront* in MSS Ce L but at this point in his collation does not include Méon's probable source, Za (Ln 1.46, 52–55). In his glossary, Méon does not define *bracer* as "brasser" (brew) but as "piler, broyer" (crush, grind), the sense of *braieront* in other MSS.

6033 "i.e., Love need seek no agents but women to subdue rich men" (FI). *Sekith* is an imperative.

vicaire: SK notes that Méon (10938) has *victaires*; Ln 10903t reports the var. *victoires* in MS He but at this point does not report the readings of Za, Méon's probable source.

6035 **you:** TH¹'s *ye* is probably a spelling variant, either as the unstressed objective form (cf. *TC* 1.5 "or that I parte fro ye") or as TH¹'s normal objective; see *OED Ye* pers. pron.: "when *you* had usurped the place of *ye* as a nom., *ye* came to be used (in the 15th c.), vice versa, as an objective sing. and pl." If, however, TH¹ misread the line as "you shall consider that you paid very well," then the variant would be substantive. For the traditional syntax of *ye/you*, see the next line.

6037 BEg reads the unemended line, with *worthe*, as "let ladies be, or, let ladies alone, with their tricks." SKg₂, with *worche*, reads: let ladies "deal (with what they have to do)."

worche: "deal" (SK FI). The basis of TH¹'s emendation, noted by KA, is paleographical (*c/t* confusion); there is no parallel in the Fr.

6041–42 **thankynges . . . talkynges:** KA suggests *thwakkynges* for *thankynges*; GL RB RI note the basis in the Fr. *colees*, "blows" (Lc 10881–82 "et leur douront [*sic for* donront] si granz colees / de beseries, d'acolees" "and will give them such great blows of kisses, of embraces"), and SU says that KA's suggestion is perhaps right. As an alternative, Liddell (GL) suggests "(?) read *wakynges*" for *talkynges*, on the basis of the Fr. *acolees* "embraces" (above), and he compares lines 2682, 4272; RB also notes the Fr. Through a misreading of GL's note, SU (6042n.) says that it was KA who suggested *wakynges*, "perhaps rightly." § As RI observes, "the rhyme words *thankynges* and *talkynges* do not convey the sense that the ladies' flatteries are in reality 'blows' dealt to their rich lovers. . . . The translator has simply used rhymes to suggest flattering words that might accompany the 'baiseries.'"

6041 **hym:** them. See 1922n. All eds. except KA GL respell as *hem*. KA notes *hem* in TH¹ UR BE MO.

Shal never leve hem londe ne fee
That it nyl as the moeble fare,   6045
Of which they first delyverid are.
Now may ye telle us all youre wille,
And we youre heestes shal fulfille.
    "But Fals-Semblant dar not, for drede
Of you, sir, medle hym of this dede,   6050
For he seith that ye ben his foo;
He note if ye wole worche hym woo.
Wherfore we pray you alle, beau sire,
That ye forgyve hym now your ire,
And that he may dwelle, as your man,   6055
With Abstinence, his dere lemman;

This oure accord and oure wille nowe."
    "Parfay," seide Love, "I graunte it yowe.
I wole wel holde hym for my man;
Now late hym come." And he forth ran.   6060
    "Fals-Semblant," quod Love,
        "in this wise   120v
I take thee heere to my servise,
That thou oure freendis helpe [alway],
And hyndre hem neithir nyght ne day,
But do thy myght hem to releve,   6065
And eke oure enemyes that thou greve.
Thyne be this myght, I graunte it thee:
My kyng of harlotes shalt thou be;

6044 **fee**] se UR   6054 **ye**] we FI   6063 **alway**] away MS KA GL   6064 **hyndre**] hyndreth MS-SP³ BE-KA GL FU   6068 **harlotes**] haroltes SP¹

6044–46 "After the rich lover has first been stripped of his liquid assets (*moeble*) he will give up land and rents" (RI 6045–46n.).

6044 **shal never leve hem:** "Shall there never remain to them" (SK); RB RIf agree that *leve* has the sense "remain," and SK RB RI cite Fr. *leur demorra* (Lc 10884 "ne leur demorra tenement" "there will not remain to them a property-holding"). RI notes that "the Fr. construction is impersonal, but possibly *ladies* is to be understood as the subject."

    fee: URg (s.v. *Fe, Se*) notes the incorrect reading *se* in UR and observes that it should be *fe*. URg takes *fee* as "Land of Inheritance, in opposition to *Moeble*, Moveables, in the following Verse"; TRg makes the same distinction, between "inheritable possessions" and "money, or moveables"; others gloss *fee* as "land held in fee simple" (BEg), "property, fief" (SKg, RBg). RI (6045–46n.) takes *fee* as rents, i.e. income from real property; cf. 6044–46n.

6045–46 **fare : are:** Skeat (SK 1.7) notes that "Chaucer never uses *are* at the end of a line" and takes the rhyme as evidence that Fragment C is not Chaucer's. But Feng (1990:52) cites lines 505–06 in Fragment A as evidence that "in Chaucer's genuine works, Northern forms ARE occasionally employed for rime." Cf. Feng 1990:31–35.

6045 **moeble:** "houshold stuffe" (SPg URg), "Moveables" (URg, noting derivation from French), "personal (estate, property)" (URg RIf), "moveable (property, belongings)" (SKg, FI).

6049 **Fals-Semblant:** KA transcribes MS *falssēblant* as *falsseblant*, without the italicized *m* to indicate the nasal-stroke over the *e*; accordingly, KA notes *Fals-semblant* in UR BE MO. Although KA's transcription may be correct, the mark over -*e*- seems more than a horizontal extension of the top stroke of the long *s*; there is a slight but perceptible thickening of the line that shows the presence of two overlapping strokes.

6057 **This:** "This is" (KA SKt GL); SK notes that *This* is "a common contraction for *This is*" and compares modern English '*tis* as well as line 3548; see 3548n. and cf. line 6452.

6063 **alway:** TH¹'s *alway*, noted by KA in TH¹ UR BE MO, for MS *away*, although it has no direct parallel in the Fr., is a reasonable inference from the negative *ja . . . n'* of the following line (Lc 10903–04 "que touz noz amis aideras / et que ja nul n'en greveras" "that you will help our friends and never give them any trouble").

6064 **hyndre:** KA notes UR's emendation of MS *hyndreth*; as 2 sg. subj., it remedies meter and concord.

6068 **kyng of harlotes:** F. Thynne (1599;1875:71–73) points out the typographical error in SP¹'s *haroltes* and, in a long note on the phrase, refers to Johannes Tyllius and Vincentius Luparius on the French office of *rex ribaldorum* and to Thomas of Brotherton on the office of the English Marshall. F. Thynne takes *harlots* as "evill or wicked persons" (p. 72) or, more specifically, "meretric[es]" (p. 73); and he notes (p. 71) the equivalent French phrase "'Roye des Ribauldez'" in Molinet's moralization (=Lc 10908 "Tu me seras rois des ribauz" "you will be my king of ribalds"). SP² corrects the misprint and, in the glossary, inserts a note on the correction and on the phrase *Roi des Ribaulds* (SP²g, s.v. *Harrolds*); the note is based on F. Thynne. URg cites Du Cange, s.v. *Ribaldi*, on the office of the *Rex ribaldorum*. BE also notes the Fr. phrase and states that "Lantin de Damerey [1737, ed. 1799:5.284–87] quotes the *Philippide* of Guillaume le Bréton, and Froissart, to show that the word *ribauds* sometimes meant merely common soldiers, and that the chief of the body-guard of Philip Augustus was called *Le roi des ribauds*." SK RIf take

We wole that thou have such honour.
Certeyne, thou art a fals traitour, 6070
And eke a theef; sith thou were borne,
A thousand tyme thou art forsworne.
But netheles, in oure heryng,
To putte oure folk out of doutyng,
I bidde thee teche hem, wostowe howe, 6075
Bi somme general signe nowe,
In what place thou shalt founden be,
If that men had myster of thee,
And how men shal thee best espye,
For thee to knowe is gret maistrie. 6080
Telle in what place is thyn hauntyng."
   "Sir, I have fele dyverse wonyng,
That I kepe not rehersed be,
So that ye wolde respiten me. 6084
For if that I telle you the sothe, 121r
I may have harme and shame bothe.

If that my felowes wisten it,
My talis shulden me be quytt;
For certeyne, they wolde hate me,
If ever I knewe her cruelte, 6090
For they wolde overall holde hem stille
Of trouthe that is ageyne her wille;
Suche tales kepen they not here.
I myght eftsoone bye it full deere,
If I seide of hem ony thing 6095
That ought displesith to her heryng.
For what word that hem prikke or biteth,
In that word noon of hem deliteth,
Al were it gospel, the evangile,
That wolde reprove hem of her gile, 6100
For they are cruel and hauteyne.
And this thyng wote I well, certeyne,
If I speke ought to peire her loos,
Your court shal not so well be cloos

6072 **tyme]** tymes TH¹-UR FU SU FI   6073   **netheles]** nathelesse TH¹-UR SK FU-RI   6082 **fele]** ful TH¹-SP³ FU SU FI; fully UR   6096 **ought]** *om.* UR   6097 **prikke]** pricketh TH³-UR GL   6103 **her]** or ST-UR

---

the sense as "'king of rascals.'" SK refers to Méon's note (1814:2.321–24), which comes from Lantin de Damerey; Skeat misrepresents Méon when he says that he "quotes Fauchet, Origine des Dignités, who says that the *roi des ribauds* was an officer of the king's palace, whose duty it was to clear out of it . . . men of bad character"; Méon is quoting Lantin de Damerey, who quotes Fauchet. Skeat notes further that "Méon quotes an extract from an order of the household of King Philippe, A. D. 1290," one that provides payment for "'*Le Roy des Ribaus*.'" Skeat adds that "the title of *Roi des ribaus* was often jocularly conferred on any conspicuous vagabond." GL RB FI RI all note the French phrase; RB FI note its origin as "the actual title of an officer of the court" (RB); GL RB interpret it as "provost marshal." As RI notes, Lecoy (Lcg, s.v. *ribaut*) defines the phrase as "a petty official of the king's retinue with jurisdiction over gaming places and houses of prostitution" (RI). RI also observes that "Skeat's notion (derived from Méon's edition) that this functionary's duties were 'to clear out . . . men of bad character' doubtless misinterprets his role and hardly accords with Skeat's further observation that the title was applied humorously to any notorious vagabond." Cf. FI, who repeats "Skeat's notion." Since Fals-Semblant is in effect given a command of troops, the word *harlots* (*ribauz*) has the two senses, "soldiers" and "rascals." See Godefroy (1881–1902) and Tobler-Lommatzsch (1925– :8.1253–57, s.v. *ribaut*).

6073   **netheles:** KA notes *nathelesse* here in TH¹. See 5889n. and cf. line 6195.

6078   **myster:** "need" (SPg et al.), "use" (SK); BE SK cite Fr. *mestier* (Lc 10918 "need").

6082   BE MO SK supply speech-heading *F. Sem.*

6083   "Which I do not wish to be divulged" (BE); "Which I do not care should be mentioned" (SK). SK compares line 6093; see 6093n.

kepe: "care" (SPg et al.), "wish" (SKg₂), "desire" (RB, comparing line 6093).

6090   RI quotes the Fr. (Lc 10930 "s'onques leur cruiauté quennui"), of which the ME is a literal translation. BE notes that "*knewe*, like *beknewe*, means here *disclosed*"; SKg₂ RBg define similarly; cf. *MED knouen* v. 7. (a) "make known; . . . reveal."

6091   **wolde overall:** "i.e., would rather" (FI).

6093   "They do not care to hear such tales" (BE SK 6083n.).

6094   **full:** KA suggests omitting this word, but no ed. so emends.

6095   **ony:** See 212n.

6097   **prikke:** Although KA notes *prikith* in UR, TH³ is the first to emend, for parallelism with *biteth*.

6103   **peire her loos:** "impair their credit or reputation" (TRg, s.v. *Paire*); "impair (or lessen) their fame" (SK FI); "injure her [*sic* for *their*] reputation" (RIf). UR et al. gloss *(a)p(a,e)ire* as "impair, (damage, disparage, injure)"; SKg₂ *MED* note that *peire(n* is short for *apeire(n* or *(MED) empeire(n.*

That they ne shall wite it atte last.   6105
Of good men am I nought agast,
For they wole taken on hem nothyng,
Whanne that they knowe al my menyng;
But he that wole it on hym take,   121v
He wole hymsilf suspecious make,   6110
That he his lyf let covertly
In Gile and in Ipocrisie
That me engendred and yaf fostryng."
     "They made a full good engendryng,"
Quod Love, "for whoso sothly telle,   6115
They engendred the devel of helle.
But nedely, howsoevere it be,"
Quod Love, "I wole and charge thee
To telle anoon thy wonyng places,
Heryng ech wight that in this place is;   6120
And what lyf that thou lyvest also,
Hide it no lenger now; wherto?
Thou most discovere all thi wurchyng,

How thou servest, and of what thyng,
Though that thou shuldist for
     thi sothesawe   6125
Ben al tobeten and todrawe;
And yit art thou not wont, pardee.
But natheles, though thou beten be,
Thou shalt not be the first that so
Hath for sothsawe suffred woo."   6130
     "Sir, sith that it may liken you,
Though that I shulde be slayne right now,
I shal done youre comaundement,   122r
For therto have I gret talent."
     Withouten wordis mo, right thanne,   6135
Fals-Semblant his sermon biganne,
And seide hem thus in audience:
"Barouns, take heede of my sentence.
That wight that list to have knowing
Of Fals-Semblant, full of flatering,   6140
He must in worldly folk hym seke,

6105 **atte**] at TH¹-UR FU SU FI   6111 **his**] is ST   6112 **gile**] gyse FU   6121 **that**] *om.* TH²-UR

     6105–06 **atte last : agast:** Skeat (SK 1.7) notes the un-Chaucerian rhyme ("*laste* . . . is never monosyllabic"). Feng (1990:52) cites lines 53–54, *RvT* A 4117–18, and *FranT* F 1273–74, to show that "omission of final -*e* in rime words is not entirely inadmissible for Chaucer." Cf. Feng (1990:36–38).
     6111–12 **covertly : ipocrisie:** The first of a group of seven loose rhymes in -*y* : -*ye* that Kaluza (1893*a*:106, 136) identifies in Fragment C; the others are at lines 6301, 6339, 6373, 6875, 7317, 7571 (the last of these does not occur in MS). Like this one, they all rhyme native and Romance elements. Since such rhymes argue against Chaucer's authorship (SK 1.6), Kaluza justifies them as liberties in a close translation (1893*a*:136); cf. Feng (1990:58–67). TH¹·³ SK FU-RI have -*y* on each word, for apparent rhyme.
     6111 "That he leads his life secretly" (SK); URg et al. note that *let*—as contraction of *ledeth*—means "leads."
     6112 RI quotes the Fr. (Lc 10952 "de Barat et d'Ypocrisie" "Of Fraud and Hypocrisy") and notes that "the vices practiced by Fals-Semblant and his kind are represented allegorically by his parents."
     6120 "Whilst every one here hears" (SK).
          Heryng: "in the hearing of" (FI RIf).
     6122 **wherto:** "What would be the use?" (BE).
     6127 **wont:** "accustomed (to telling the truth)" (RIf), rather than "accustomed (to be punished)" (FI); cf. lines 6125, 6130 *sothesawe* "truth-telling" (FI), "speaking the truth" (RIf).
     6135–7334 RB notes Ln's suggestion (note to 11007ff.) "that the description of Fals-Semblant may owe something to John of Salisbury, Policraticus, vii, ch. 21." Lc (note to 10976ff.) gives the same reference (ed. Webb 1909:2.191–201; trans. Dickinson 1927:312–22) and relates the charge of hypocrisy to the anti-mendicant positions of Jean de Meun and Rutebeuf. RI states: "The self-portrait, . . . though drawing generally on anticlerical satire common throughout the thirteenth century, has as its special target the mendicant friars. Specifically it echoes the attacks of the secular faculty at the University of Paris who were engaged in bitter controversy during 1250–59 to deny the friars chairs of public instruction that the secular clergy wished to keep under their exclusive control." The leader of the seculars was William of Saint-Amour (lines 6763–96); as RI notes, Dufeil (1972) has "a detailed discussion of the parties, personalities, and issues" in the controversy; see also Szittya (1986:11–61). For further references, see Dahlberg (1971:395–97). RB RI note that the self-portrait of Fals-Semblant served as a model for Chaucer's Pardoner; RI adds that it served "as well . . . for certain touches in the Friar's portrait." Cf. 6390–97n.
     6141–42 **in worldly folk . . . in the cloistres eke:** RB, following Ln (11008n.), interprets *worldly folk* as the secular clergy, but RI, taking the phrase to mean "the laity as opposed to the clergy," argues that "in 6149–50, *Religiouse folk* and *Seculer folk* may refer to the regular (cloistered) as opposed to the secular clergy; nevertheless, the secular clergy, though living more in the world, are also 'religious folk.' Cf. 6232ff., where *seculer* definitely

And, certes, in the cloistres eke.
I wone nowhere but in hem twey,
But not lyk even, soth to sey.
Shortly, I wole herberwe me 6145
There I hope best to hulstred be;
And certeynly, sikerest hidyng
Is undirnethe humblest clothing.
Religiouse folk ben full covert;
Seculer folk ben more appert. 6150
But natheles, I wole not blame
Religious folk, ne hem diffame,
In what habit that ever they go.
Religioun umble and trewe also
Wole I not blame ne dispise; 6155
But I nyl love it in no wise.
I mene of fals religious,
That stoute ben and malicious,
That wolen in an abit goo,
And setten not her herte therto. 6160
    "Religious folk ben al pitous;

Thou shalt not seen oon dispitous.
They loven no pride ne no strif,
But humbely they wole lede her lyf;
With [swich] folk wole I never be, 6165
And if I dwelle, I feyne me.
I may wel in her abit go;
But me were lever my nekke a-two,
Than lete a purpose that I take,
What covenaunt that ever I make. 6170
    "I dwelle with hem that proude be,
And full of wiles and subtilite,
That worship of this world coveiten,
And grete [nedes] kunnen espleiten,
And gone and gadren gret pitaunc[es], 6175
And purchace hem the acqueyntaunc[es]
Of men that myghty lyf may leden;
And feyne hem pore, and hemsilf feden
With gode morcels delicious,
And drinken [good] wyne precious, 6180
And preche us povert and distresse,

122v

123r

6158 **stoute**] dout SP³   6159 **an**] her SP³   6165 **swich**] which MS-KA GL FU   6169 **lete**] lette MS-TH³ BE-KA FU SU FI; let ST-UR   6174 **nedes**] nede MS-KA FU SU FI   6175 **pitaunces**] pitauncȝ MS KA 6176 **acqueyntaunces**] acqueyntauncȝ MS KA   6179 **morcels**] morcets SU FI   6180 **good**] *om.* MS (MS₂ *corr.*)

---

refers to layfolk. The issue here and below is that good and evil cannot be judged on the basis of one's estate or outward appearance." Cf. note to *RR* 11008 (Dahlberg 1971:392).

6143 **nowhere but in hem twey:** "That is, 'Everywhere'" (BE).

6146 **hulstred:** "hidden" (SPg et al.), "concealed" (SK et al.). URg TRg postulate an OE derivation, and SK compares "A. S. *beolstor*, a hiding place"; *MED bulstred* ppl. also gives the OE noun as the etymon but lists no other forms of the verb.

6149–50 See 6141–42n. SPg URg take *Seculer folk* as laymen, although URg suggests the possibility that they may be secular clergy as contrasted with the regular, the *Religiouse folk.*

6149 "Remember that the speaker is Fals-Semblant, who often speaks ironically; he explains that he has nothing to do with *truly* religious people, but he dotes upon hypocrites. See l. 6171" (SK).

6165 **swich folk:** "These are they who are really imbued with the spirit of their profession, and who not only wear the habit of religion, but also conform to its precepts: with these False-Semblant says he does not consort" (BE).

        swich: KA's suggestion for MS *which.* SKt RBt RIt note the basis in Fr. *tex* (Lc 11001 "such").

6169 **lete:** KA endorses SK's emendation. I collate as substantive the distinction between *lete* and *lette*—see *MED lēten* v. 3. (b) "relinquish" and *letten* v. 2. (a) "hinder"—even though the forms of the two verbs were confused and, in this case, may well be sp. variants. SK's observation, "*lette* makes no sense," should be understood in terms of the formal distinction. On the sense, SK has "*lete*, let alone, abandon," and FI has "*lette*, turn from." Cf. 5335n.

6172 **subtilite:** KA endorses the trisyllabic form *sotelte*, which he attributes to SK. In fact, SK adopts TH's *subtelte.*

6174 **nedes:** KA endorses SK's plural, which agrees in number with the Fr. *besoignes* (Lc 11010 "et les granz besoignes esploitent" "and carry out big deals"; noted in SKt GL RBt RIt). GL RB RI compare line 5883, where, as here, the translator chose the wrong sense for *besoignes,* "need(s)" rather than "affairs"; see 5883n.

6175–76 **pitaunces . . . acqueyntaunces:** TH's spellings; all eds. except KA adopt them, and KA notes them in UR BE. In MS final *z* (the character "ȝ" [like "yogh"]) serves as a sign of the plural inflection (cf. line 5939 "marchauntz"). I do not count the forms as variants.

6180 **good:** "written above the line" (KA) by a later hand, MS₂ₔ. Thorp (1989) notes that ink and duct differ from those of the scribe; ·Whatley (1989) notes that the ink is lighter and the hand different. See above, "The Manuscript Hands: The Corrections."

And fisshen hemsilf gret richesse
With wily nettis that they cast.
It wole come foule out at the last.
They ben fro clene riligioun went;
They make the world an argument
That [hath] a foule conclusioun.
'I have a robe of religioun,
Thanne am I all religious.'
[This argument is all roignous];

It is not worth a croked brere.
Abit ne makith neithir monk ne frere,
But clene lyf and devocioun
Makith gode men of religioun.   6185
Netheles, ther kan noon answere,   6195
How high that evere his heed he shere
With resoun whetted never so kene,
That gile in braunches kut thrittene;
Ther can no wight distincte it so,   6190

6184   **out]** *om.* BE   6187   **hath]** *om.* MS KA   6190   *Out:* MS (MS₁ *corr.*)   6192   **neithir]** *om.* UR
SK   6194   **gode men of]** m. o. g. SP²·³   6195   **Netheles]** Nathelesse TH¹-UR SK FU-RI   6197   **resoun]**
rasour TH¹-MO SK-FI   6199   **Ther]** That FU

6182   **fisshen:** "fish for (accumulate)" (FI).

6186–87   "That is, 'They try to convince the world by an argument which has a false conclusion'" (BE). In support, BE quotes the Fr. (Lc 11022–23 "il font un argument au monde / ou conclusion a honteuse" "to the world they present an argument in which there is a discreditable conclusion"). For the first line SK reads: "They offer the world an argument."

6187   **hath:** TH¹'s *hath*, noted by KA in TH¹ UR BE MO, follows the Fr. *a* (above).

6190   "Written in the margin by the same hand" (KA), MS₁; see above, "The Manuscript Hands: The Corrections." Cf. lines 6609, 7035, 7592.

roignous: "scabby" (URg TRg MOg), "(scurvy), rotten" (SKg₂ GLg RBg RIf); from OF *roignos, roigneus* (*MED roinous(e* adj.). The sense "ruinous" (SPg URg FI) belongs to *MED ruinous* adj., from OF *rüinos, runeus*, but the forms were to some extent confused.

6191   **a croked brere:** RB RI note that this is one of the many figures of worthlessness; they compare *GP* 177 ("a pulled hen"), where RB adduces *GP* 182 ("an oystre") and "Haeckel [1890], pp. 60ff." and Cavanaugh (RI) adds *WBT* D 1112 and *TC* 3.1167 and the index to Whiting (1968, s.v. *not worth*). For the Fr. influence on the construction, both notes (following Fansler 1914:74) cite Sykes (1899:24–39). Fansler calls the figure "picturesque negation" and (1914:74–77) lists examples in Chaucer and in *RR*, as well as in French and ME generally. RB RI note that, in *Rom*, the ME image of a croked briar is different from that in the Fr. (Lc 11027 "un coustel troine" "a knife of privet"). On other figures of worthlessness, cf. 4830n.

6192   Proverbial. SK RB cite the Latin form, "Cucullus non facit monachum" "the cowl does not make the monk"; SK quotes Alexander Neckham from Michel (ed. 1864:2.5): "Non tonsura facit monachum, nec horrida vestis, / Sed virtus animi, perpetuusque rigor" "The tonsure does not make a monk, nor rough clothing, but strength of spirit, and unceasing strictness." RB cites Haeckel (1890: no. 133) and RI cites Whiting (1968: H2); for the Fr. form, Lc cites Morawski (1925: no. 1053).

neithir: KA notes only UR's omission of this word.

6195   **Netheles:** KA notes *Nathelesse* here in TH¹; see 5889n. and cf. line 6073.

6197–98   David (RI) restores the MS reading *resoun* in line 6197 (see n. below), in spite of the fact that Fr. *rasoer* might seem to support emendation. He quotes the Fr. (Lc 11031–32 "voire rere au rasoer d'Elanches, / qui barat tremche en .xiii. branches" "Even though [he] shave with the razor of De elenchis, which divides fraud into thirteen branches"). Following Paré (1947:36–37), Lc (11031–32n.) identifies the *Elanches* as Aristotle's *De sophisticis elenchis*, in which he divides the means of sophistical reasoning into thirteen categories. David (RI) argues that "Thynne and editors emend *resoun* to 'rasour,' taking the reference to be a literal razor by which a cleric is tonsured. The Fr. plays upon the literal tonsure and the metaphorical razor of Aristotle, but the translator has reduced the complicated figure of the 'razor of reason' to plain English."

6197   **resoun:** KA notes *rasour* in TH¹ UR BE MO. BE calls MS *resoun* "a mere clerical error" and quotes the Fr. (Lc 11031, above). For David's restoration (RI) of *resoun*, see 6197–98n.

6198   **That:** Following the Fr. (above), *That* should refer back to *resoun* in the previous line ("reason . . . that cuts guile into thirteen branches"); BE seems to read the word in this way: "Guile, or *Barat*, cut into thirteen branches." SK reads *Guile* as subject rather than object of *kut*: "'whom Guile cuts into thirteen branches.' I.e. Guile makes thirteen tonsured men at once." GL specifies that "*That* has *noon* [line 6195] for its antecedent."

braunches . . . thrittene: "thirteen types of sophistical reasoning; see [6197–98]n." (RIf). BE SK GL RB FI suggest "an allusion to the fact that thirteen friars made a . . . convent" (BE), or "the allusion . . . to the twelve monks and prior who made up a convent" (GL). Jephson (BE) refers to *SumT* D 2259,· where he notes the tradition that the number reflects that of Christ and the twelve apostles.

That he dare sey a word therto. 6200
"But what herberwe that ever I take,
Or what semblant that evere I make,
I mene but gile, and folowe that;
For right no mo than Gibbe oure cat, 6204
[That awayteth myce and rattes
  to kyllen], TH¹:160d
Ne entende I but to bigilyng. MS:123v
Ne no wight may by my clothing
Wite with what folk is my dwellyng,
Ne by my wordis yit, parde,
So softe and so plesaunt they be. 6210
Biholde the dedis that I do;
But thou be blynde, thou oughtest so.
For, varie her wordis fro her deede,
They thenke on gile, without dreede,
What maner clothing that they were, 6215
Or what estate that evere they bere,
Lered or lewde, lord or lady,

Knyght, squyer, burgeis, or bayly."
    Right thus while Fals-Semblant sermoneth,
Eftsones Love hym aresoneth, 6220
And brake his tale in his spekyng,
As though he had hym tolde lesyng,
And seide, "What, devel, is that I here?
What folk hast thou us nempned heere?
May men fynde religioun 6225
In worldly habitacioun?"
    "Yhe, sir; it folowith not that they
Shulde lede a wikked lyf, parfey,
Ne not therfore her soules leese 124r
That hem to worldly clothes chese; 6230
For, certis, it were gret pitee.
Men may in seculer clothes see
Florishen hooly religioun.
Full many a seynt in feeld and toune,
With many a virgine glorious, 6235
Devoute, and full religious,

6205 **That awayteth myce and rattes to kyllen]** Fro m. a. r. went his wyle SK *Out:* MS (*blank line*) KA
RI 6206 **Ne]** Me BE **but to bigilyng]** b. t. begylen TH¹-UR GL-FI; not b. t. begyle SK 6221 **in his]** i.
the BE SK 6233 **religioun]** religiouns SP³

---

braunches: KA suggests, "perhaps read *trenches* for *braunches*." Cf. Fr. (above).

kut: SK RB note that the form is a contraction of *cutteth*, "cuts" and compare Fr. *tremche* "cuts" (above).

6204 **Gibbe:** A common English name for a tom-cat (BE SK GL RB RI). BE adduces "Skelton, *Death of Philip Sparrow* . . . 'Whom Gib our cat hath slain'"; and BE SK adduce Shakespeare, *1 Henry IV* 1.2.83 "as melancholy as a gib-cat." BE SK RB RI note that the name in the Fr. is *Tiberz* (Lc 11038), which SK notes as the origin of English *Tibert, Tybalt*; BE Ln (11068n.) RB RI note that the cat in the *Roman de Renard* is named *Tiberz*.

6205–06 **kyllen : bigilyng:** On the imperfect rhyme, see 6205n., 6206n.

6205 BE KA-GL SU-RIt note that MS leaves the line blank; as KA SK GL SU note, TH¹ supplies the line, which GL notes is "found in Fr." Kaluza (1893*b*:110) thinks that (with lines 6318, 6786) this is one of the lines that Thynne restored with the help of the French original (Lc 11039 "n'entent qu'a soriz et a raz" "has his mind on nothing but mice and rats"). If so, TH¹ may have used a Fr. text with a verb, other than *entent* (?*atent*), that justified the translation "awayteth . . . to kyllen"; or the phrase could be a loose translation. KA Fr. uses Michel's reading, *Ne tent qu'a* "strives only for" rather than *N'entent qu'a*, and SK quotes the same text from Méon. SK objects to TH¹'s line that it "will not rime, and is spurious"; in his emendation, "*went his wyle* means 'turns aside his wiliness.'" He achieves rhyme, however, only by further emendation of the next line; and his version does not correspond to the Fr.; see 6206n. David (RI) omits the line, as spurious, quotes it in a footnote, and retains MS *bigilyng* in the next line; cf. 892n. In his explanatory note, he quotes the Fr. and suggests that "another solution, not necessitating an emendation for rhyme, would be 'But [= "except"] to mys and rattes n'entendeth nothyng.'"

6206 **bigilyng:** SK's *begyle*, a spelling variant of TH¹'s inf. *begylen*, noted in KA, is occasioned by his need for a rhyme with *wyle*. RI retains the MS reading. See 6205n.

6213–14 "That is, 'For if men's words vary from their deeds, their intention is to deceive'" (BE).

6223 **What, devel:** "i.e. what the devil" (SK).

6226 "In secular dwellings" (RIf); RI quotes the Fr. (Lc 11060 "en seculere mansion"). RB RI note that lines 6234–46 show that the reference is "to the laity, not to the secular clergy" (RB). Cf. 6141–42n.

6227 **Yhe:** See 4659–60n.

6227 BE MO SK supply speech-heading *F. Sem.*

6228 After this line in MS, as KA notes, there is "a line left blank . . . at the bottom of leaf 123, back." There is no break in the text.

6232–33 See 6141–42n.

Han deied, that comyn cloth ay beeren,
Yit seyntes nevere the lesse they weren.
I cowde reken you many a ten;
Yhe, wel nygh [al] these hooly wymmen,   6240
That men in chirchis herie and seke,
Bothe maydens and these wyves eke,
That baren full many a faire child heere,
Wered alwey clothis seculere,
And in the same dieden they,   6245
That seyntes weren, and ben alwey.
The eleven thousand maydens deere
That beren in heven her ciergis clere,
Of whiche men rede in chirche and synge,
Were take in seculer clothing   6250
Whanne they resseyved martirdome,
And wonnen hevene unto her home.
Good hert makith the good thought;   124v

The clothing yeveth ne reveth nought.
The good thought and the worching   6255
That makith the religioun flowryng—
Ther lyth the good religioun,
Aftir the right entencioun.
    "Whoso took a wethers skynne,
And wrapped a gredy wolf therynne,   6260
For he shulde go with lambis whyte,
Wenest thou not he wolde hem bite?
Yhis, neverthelasse, as he were woode,
He wolde hem wery and drinke the bloode,
And wel the rather hem disceyve;   6265
For, sith they cowde not perceyve
His treget and his cruelte,
They wolde hym folowe, al wolde he fle.
    "If ther be wolves of sich hewe
Amonges these apostlis newe,   6270

6237 **Han]** Had SK   6240 **al]** *om.* MS KA   6243 **full]** *om.* SK   6245 **same]** s. clothes UR
dieden] dydden TH²   6247 **eleven]** ix TH³ ST SP²-UR   6255 **the worching]** t. gode w. UR   6256 **the]**
om. SK   6264 **the]** ther GL   6268 **al wolde]** al tho TH¹-SP³ FU SU FI; tho UR   **fle]** flye TH¹-UR FU SU FI

6240 **Yhe:** See 4659–60n.
     al: TH¹'s *al*, noted by KA, is based, presumably, on the Fr. *trestoutes* (Lc 11074 "all").
6241 **herie:** "praise" (URg et al. RIf), rather than "harass" (FI). Cf. *MED herien* v.(1) "praise" and v.(2) "pillage."
6243 **full:** KA GL suggest omitting this word, and SK does so.
6245 **in the same dieden:** probably "died in the same (worldly clothes)" rather than "died in the same way
as saints" (FI).
     dieden: I collate TH²'s *dydden* as a substantive var.— as the pa. t. of *dǫn*—but it may be a var. sp.
6247 **eleven thousand maydens:** BE SK FI RIf note the reference to the legend of St. Ursula and the eleven
thousand virgins martyred by the Huns at Cologne in the fifth century (in 352, says BE). BE SK cite the source as the
Legenda Aurea (*Golden Legend*), and SK cites Butler's *Lives of the Saints.* See Butler (1963:2.165–68); *Legenda
Aurea* (ed. Graesse 1890:701–05; trans. Ryan and Ripperger 1941:627–31).
6248 **ciergis:** "wax (candles, tapers)" (SPg et al.). "The *cierge*, or lighted candle, symbolizes faith.—Rev. ii. 5.
Hence a lighted candle is placed in the hands of the expiring Catholic, to denote that he dies in the faith" (BE).
6255 **good:** SK (6256n.) specifies disyllabic pronunciation of the weak adj., "*the god-e.*"
6256 **makith the:** SK omits *the* and pronounces "*mak'th.*"
6259–60 RB RI note that for *a wether* the Fr. has "dam Belin" and for *wolf* "sire Isengrin" (Lc 11093–95),
characters from the *Roman de Renard*; BE SK make the observation for *wolf* and "sire Isengrin" only.
6259 **took:** KA endorses SK's spelling *toke*, presumably as a 3 sg. pa. subjunctive.
6263 **Yhis:** See 4659–60n.
6264 **wery:** "worry" (URg, s.v. *Wirry*, et al.) in the specific sense "to seize by the throat with the teeth and
tear or lacerate" (*OED Worry* v. 3); "strangle" (MOg et al.). GL (2078n.) considers *wery*, in this line, a form of *werreye*
"make war upon"; and the Tatlock-Kennedy *Concordance* (1927) places this line under *Weary. OED Worry* analyzes
forms in -*i*-, -*y*- (α), -*e*- (β), and -*o*-, -*u*- (γ); the α- and β-forms come from OE *wyrgan*, while the γ-forms, which
survive in Modern English, "apparently represent a late WS. **wurgan*, with later graphic substitution of *wo*- for *wu*-"
(*OED*). SK cites examples of the α- and β-forms and variants from *Piers Plowman*, C 10.226; Pearsall's text
(1979:9.226) has the γ-form *woryeth*.
     the bloode: As RBt RIt note, GL cites the Fr. *leur sanc* (Lc 11099) for his emendation *ther bloode*.
6267–68 **cruelte : fle:** TH¹'s *flye* creates an imperfect rhyme; SP¹⁻³ have *crueltie.* See 951n.
6267 **treget:** "deceit" (SPg GLg); "Imposture, tricking, cheating" (URg); "guile, craft" (MOg); "trickery" (MOg
et al.); SK compares *FranT* F 1141, 1143.
6270 **apostlis newe:** "The friars are here called new apostles, because their chief mission was to supply the
deficiencies of the secular priests and monks, by their learning and skill in preaching" (BE). Lc (11104n.) also
identifies them as the mendicant orders and notes that the image of the wolf comes from Matt. 7.15, a text

Thou, Hooly Chirche, thou maist [be wailed]!
Sith that thy citee is assayled
[Thourgh] knyghtis of thyn owne table,
God wote thi lordship is doutable!
If thei enforce [hem] it to wynne 6275
That shulde defende it fro withynne,
Who myght defense ayens hem make? 125r
Without stroke it mote be take
Of trepeget or mangonel,
Without displaiyng of pensel. 6280
And if God nyl done [it] socour,
But lat [hem] renne in this colour,

Thou most thyn heestis laten be.
Thanne is ther nought but yelde thee,
Or yeve hem tribute, doutlees, 6285
And holde it of hem to have pees,
But gretter harme bitide thee,
That they al maister of it be.
Wel konne they scorne thee withal;
By day stuffen they the wall, 6290
And al the nyght they mynen there.
Nay, thou planten most elleswhere
Thyn ympes, if thou wolt fruyt have;
Abide not there thisilf to save.

6271 **be wailed]** biwailed MS KA   6273 **Thourgh]** Though MS (MS₁ *corr.*)   6275 **hem]** *om.* MS-KA
FU   6281 **it]** *om.* MS (MS₁ *corr.*)   6282 **hem]** *om.* MS-KA FU; it GL   6287 **bitide]** betidith UR GL
6292 **planten most]** m. p. SK

---

traditionally used against religious hypocrites, specifically by Guillaume de Saint-Amour, *De periculis* 3, 7 (1632:28, 36). On Guillaume, see 6763n. Cf. Szittya (1986:41–54, 207–12, 231–46); Dahlberg (1971:393 n.11134).

6271 **be wailed:** KA notes this correction of MS *biwailed* in UR BE MO.

6273 "Not only the knights of Arthur's Court, but all orders of knighthood were founded on the plan of a religious brotherhood, living in equality, and eating at a common table" (BE).

Thourgh: "*r* written above the line" (KA) by MS₁.

6275 **hem:** "Insert *hem* after *enforce*, see l. 6407 [Sk.]" (KA); the basis is presumably the Fr. s' of *s'efforcent* (Lc 11109 "exert themselves").

6279 **trepeget or mangonel:** SP¹ glosses *Magonell* (*sic*) as "an instrument to cast stones" and *trepeget* as "a Ram to batter walls." F. Thynne (1599;1875:41) objects that "the trepegete was the same [as] the mangonell," and SP²·³ accordingly gloss each word as "an instrument to cast stones." Although BEg MOg are vague (defining both as engines of war and specifying only that the mangonel was used to batter walls), most later glosses agree that they were "two kinds of catapults" (FI; cf. RIf and *MED*). URg TRg adduce Du Cange, s.v. *Trebuchetum*, for Latin quotations to that effect. In his note (1886*b*:2.165) to *Piers Plowman* A 12.91, SK quotes Cotgrave (1611) on Fr. *Trebuchet* as a catapult and cites Halliwell (1847) for the sp. *trepeget*. See also 4176n.

6280 **displaiyng of pensel:** "showing the banner, giving the signal to attack" (RIf).

pensel: "(small) banner" (SPg et al.), "Pendant" (URg), "small (pennon or) streamer" (TRg RBg), "standard, ensign" (SKg₂); "lady's token borne by a knight" (RBg). "A Dim. of *Penon*," says URg, and SK calls it "short for *penoncel*"; cf. *MED pencel* n.(1). SK compares *Piers Plowman* C 19.189 [18.188] "Thre persones in o pensel."

6281–83 RB notes the "mistranslation of the Fr." (Lc 11115–17 "et se d'eus ne la veuz rescorre, / ainceis les lesses par tout corre, / lesses? mes se tu leur conmandes" "And if you [Holy Church] won't rescue it [your city] from them [the knights of your own table], then you let them run everywhere. Let them! But if you command them . . ."). See 6281n.

6281 **God:** GL RB RI note that "the translator misread . . . *d'eus* [from them] . . . as *deus* [God] and failed to see that the Church (in the second person) is subject of the whole passage" (RB). See 6281–83n.

it: "written above the line" (KA) by MS₁.

6282 **lat hem:** KA endorses SK's emendation. The omission of *hem* may be due to the confused translation; see 6281–83n.

in this colour: "in this (way, manner)" (SKg₂, s.v. *colour*, RB FI). The Fr. has *par tout* "everywhere"; see 6281–83n.

6283 **heestis:** Perhaps "commands" (SKg₂) rather than "promises" (FI); the Fr. has "conmandes." The entire line departs from the Fr.; see 6281–83n.

6286 **holde it of:** "hold as a subject of" (FI).

6290–91 "The author insinuates that the friars, while they pretended to repair the breaches in the defences of the church, were really sapping them in secret" (BE).

6290 **stuffen:** "furnish . . . with defenders" (SK); KA GL attribute to SK the reading *wel stuffen*, but it does not appear in SK's text or notes. RI notes the Fr. parallel *garnir* "fortify, strengthen" (Lc 11124).

6292 **planten most:** KA endorses SK's *most planten*.

"But now pees! Heere I turne ageyne. 6295
I wole nomore of this thing [seyne]
If I may passen me herby;
I myght maken you wery.
But I wole heten you alway
To helpe youre freendis what I may, 6300
So they wollen my company; 125v
For they be shent al outerly
But if so falle that I be
Ofte with hem and they with me.
And eke my lemman mote they serve, 6305
Or they shull not my love deserve.
Forsothe, I am a fals traitour;
God jugged me for a theef trichour.
Forsworne I am, but wel nygh none
Wote of my gile til it be done. 6310

"Though me hath many oon deth
    resseyved,
That my treget nevere aperceyved;
And yit resseyveth, and shal resseyve,
That my falsnesse shal nevere aperceyve.
But whoso doth, if he wise be, 6315
Hym is right good be warre of me.
But so sligh is the [deceyvyng]
[That to hard is the aperceyvyng];
For Protheus, that cowde hym chaunge
In every shap, homely and straunge, 6320
Cowde nevere sich gile ne tresoune
As I; for I come never in toune
There as I myght knowen be,
Though men me bothe myght here
    and see. 6324

6296 **seyne**] feyne MS TH¹ TH³-SP³ KA FU   6297 *Out:* SP²³   6298 **I**] If I SP²³; For I UR-MO
6314 **shal**] *om.* SK   **aperceyve**] perceve UR   6317 **deceyvyng**] aperceyvyng MS-SP³ BE-KA FU; perceiving
UR   6318 **That to hard is the aperceyvyng**] T. al to late cometh knowynge TH¹-MO FU   *Out:* MS (*blank
line*) KA RI   6324 **and see**] *om.* TH³ ST

6296 **seyne:** KA suggests *seyn*, the normalized form of TH²'s emendation (*sayne* for MS *feyne*); it follows the
Fr. *dire* (Lc 11130 "say").
6297 **may passen me herby:** omitted in SP²³ through eyeskip to the next line.
6298 **I:** SP²³ skip from the *I* (or the *If*) of line 6297 to the *myght* (or the *I*) of this line.
6301–02 **company : outerly:** See 6111–12n.
6305 **lemman:** "mistress" (URg TRg), "lover" (TRg FI), "sweetheart" (SK). BE and SK note that the reference
is to "Dame Abstinence-Streyned"; cf. line 6341, as noted by SK.
6314 **shal:** KA endorses SK's omission of this word. GL notes that "*shal* often thus makes an extra
unaccented syllable."
6317–18 KA's emendation (see below). The MS scribe presumably skipped from the last word of line 6317
(*deceyvyng?*) to the last word of line 6318, *aperceyvyng*; left a blank line when he saw the error; and continued with
line 6319 in its correct place. Blodgett (1984:50) notes that line 6318 is omitted in MS and suggests that the "line that
Thynne [TH¹] supplies, . . . *That al to late cometh knowyng*, could translate a French source that reads *tart* for *fort* in
Que trop est (fort) l'aperceuance; unfortunately," Blodgett grants, "Ernest Langlois records no such variant." Ln, of
course, does not collate all MSS (Ln 1.50–55). If TH¹ was indeed working with MS as copy-text and with a copy of
the French text, as Blodgett argues (cf. Kaluza 1893*b*:110), his version of line 6318 accords loosely with the sense of
the Fr. (Lc 11149–50 "Mes tant est forz la decevance / que trop est grief l'aperceuance" "But the deception is so
strong that it is very difficult to recognize it"). Faced with MS's already corrupt line 6317 ("But the *per*ception is so
skillfull") and the blank line 6318, TH¹ concentrated on the blank line rather than on the corruption; he did not want
to repeat *aperceyvyng* and instead used the synonym *knowynge* for the Fr. *aperceuance*; and he made more specific
the sense of Fr. *trop . . . grief* in the phrase *al to late*.
   BE notes the omission of line 6318 and quotes the Fr. parallel (Lc 11150, above). KA, recognizing the
corruption of MS 6317, suggests, on the basis of the Fr., that we "read *But so sligh is the deceyvyng That to hard is
the aperceyuyng*," and SK GL RB¹-FI adopt the emendation; RI adopts the first of the two lines but omits the second,
as spurious, and records it in a footnote. SK GL RBt SU FI RIt note the omission, the Fr. text, TH¹'s version, and KA's
emendation; on SU's Fr. text, see 6317n.
6317 **sligh:** "skillful"; see 6317–18n. SU's Fr. text (11179) is based here on MS Be, which reads *gries* "difficult"
instead of *fors* "strong"; but the usual reading, *fors*, seems closer to the sense "skillful" than does *gries*; see Ln
11179–80t.
6318 KA's suggestion; see 6317–18n. MS leaves the line blank (KA).
6319 **Protheus:** "the sea god, whose power of transformation has given its meaning to the adjective
'Protean'" (RB; cf. FI RI). Proverbial; RI adduces Whiting (1968: P425).

Full wel I can my clothis chaunge,   126r
Take oon, and make another straunge.
Now am I knyght, now chasteleyne,
Now prelat, [and] now chapeleyne,
Now prest, now clerk, and now forstere;
Now am I maister, now scolere,   6330
Now monke, now chanoun, now baily;
Whatever myster man am I.
Now am I prince, now am I page,

And kan by herte every langage.
Somme tyme am I hore and olde;   6335
Now am I yonge, stoute, and bolde.
Now am I Robert, now Robyn,
Now Frere Menour, now Jacobyn.
And with me folwith my loteby,
To done me s[o]las and company,   6340
That hight Dame Abstinence-[Streyned],
In many a queynte array feyned.

6328 **and]** *om.* MS (MS₁ *corr.*)   6329 **and]** *om.* TH³ ST SP²·³ BE   **forstere]** fostere TH¹-UR FU
6335 **Somme tyme]** Somtimis UR   6336 **stoute]** and s. UR SK GL   6340 **solas]** salas MS KA
6341 **Streyned]** and reyned MS-KA FU

6328 **and:** "*and* [sic for *&*] written above the line" (KA) by MS₁.

6329 **forstere:** TH¹'s *fostere* may be a sp. var.; *MED foster* n.(2) lists the form as a "var. of *forster*" and gives a dozen quotations for the sense "a forest officer."

6332 SK paraphrases: "I am a man of every trade."

    Whatever myster: "of every kind of (any) occupation" (Skg₂ FI). SKg₂ cites the Fr. (Lc 11164 "je sui de touz mestiers").

    myster man: "(kind, sort) of man" (URg RIf). TRg refers to a similar phrase "myster men" ("kind of men") in *KnT* A 1710.

    myster: "trade, service, occupation" (SPg et al.)

6336 **yonge:** KA endorses SK's *yong and.*

6337 **Robert . . . Robyn:** BE SK GL RB FI RI note variously that *Robert* is the name of a knight, or gentleman, and that *Robin* is the name of a person of mean estate, a common man, clown, shepherd, or farm boy. BE states: "In the story *Flores d'Ausi*, published by M. F. Michel in his *Theat. Franc. du Moyen Age*, the esquire is called *Robin*, but as soon as he is knighted he becomes *Messire Robiers.*" Ln (11199n.) makes a similar observation and, as RB RI note, adds that in the *Jeu de Robin et Marion* the knight is called Robert and the shepherd Robin. See also 7453n.

6338 **Frere Menour:** Franciscan (or Gray) friar (BE SK GL RB FI RIf), "the title minor, or lesser, being adopted from humility" (BE; cf. FI).

    Jacobyn: TRg errs in glossing *Jacobyn* as "grey-frier"; this is the Dominican (or Black) friar (URg et al.). Eds. give the origin of the name as Saint Jacques, the name of the Dominicans' first convent, from the church (FI), hospital (URg), or street (URg BE) of that name in Paris; Knowles (1948–59:1.164) writes that Philip Augustus presented the hospital of Saint Jacques to the Dominicans in 1218; cf. Dufeil (1972:30–32).

6339–40 **loteby : company:** See 6111–12n.

6339 **loteby:** "companion or love" (SPg URg), "wench" (SK), "paramour" (SKg₂ GLg). TRg cites the Fr. *compaigne*, "A private companion, or bedfellow" (cf. RB). Skeat (SK) adduces *Piers Plowman* B 3.150 [151] (cited also in URg TRg) and his note to it (1886b:2.47), which states that the word, "meaning paramour or concubine, was used of both sexes." TRg suggests that the word may be derived from OE "*loute,* to lurk."

6340 **solas:** KA notes *solace* in TH¹ UR and *solas* in BE MO.

6341 **Streyned:** KA's suggestion for MS *and reyned.* KA SK compare lines 7323, 7364, and KA compares line 7481. SK RBt RIt note the Fr. *Contrainte* (Lc 11173 "Constrained"). Brusendorff (1925:301–02) reasons that "in the ancestor of the Thynne-Glasgow parent MS. the initial long *s* [of *streyned*] must have been joined to the *t*, as often happens, and separated a little from the continuation *reyned* in such a way that the copyist mistook it for a common ME abbreviation of *and.*" § RI notes: "She is portrayed as a nun. Her name indicates that her chastity is not natural; nor, since she is the *lemman* of Fals-Semblant, is it real."

6341–44 Most modern eds. punctuate as here, but GL has period after *Streyned* (line 6341), commas after *feyned* (line 6342) and *lykyng* (line 6343), and semicolon after *desiryng* (line 6343). In a note, GL suggests that "*To fulfille* [line 6344], with comma after *streyned* and full stop after *desiryng*, would better translate Fr." See Lc 11171–76: "si pregn por sivre ma compaigne, / qui me solace et m'acompaigne / (c'est dame Attenance Contrainte), / autre desguiseüre mainte, / si com il li vient a plesir, / por acomplir li son desir" ("And in order to follow my companion, Lady Constrained Abstinence, who comforts me and goes along with me, I take on many another disguise, just as it strikes her pleasure, to fulfill her desire").

6342 **queynte:** "curious, fanciful" (SKg₂); cf. 65n.

    feyned: SK has *yfeyned,* "perhaps correctly," says RBt.

Ryght as it cometh to hir lykyng,
I fulfille al hir desiryng.
Somtyme a wommans cloth take I; 6345
Now am I a mayde, now lady.
Somtyme I am religious;
Now lyk an anker in an hous.
Somtyme am I prioresse, 126v
And now a nonne, and now abbesse; 6350
And go thurgh all regiouns,

Sekyng all religiouns.
But to what ordre that I am sworne,
I take the strawe and [lete] the corne.
To [gyle] folk I enhabite; 6355
I axe nomore but her abite.
What wole ye more? In every wise,
Right as me lyst, I me disgise.
Wel can I [wre] me undir wede;
Unlyk is my word to my dede. 6360

6346 **a]** *om.* BE SK-FU   6349 **prioresse]** a p. UR MO   6351 **regiouns]** religiouns ST   6354 **lete]** bete MS-KA FU   6355 **gyle folk]** Ioly folk MS-KA GL FU; blynde f. ther SK RB[1,2]   6359 **wre]** were MS BE-KA; beare TH[1]-UR SK FU SU FI

6345 "I.e. 'Sometimes I wear women's clothes'" (SK).

6346 **a:** KA suggests omitting this word. FU's omission is an erroneous transcription of TH[1].

6348 **anker:** "An anchorite, or hermite" (TRg, citing the OE as proximate etymon), "an anchorite, or anachorite, one who retires (ἀναχωρέω) from the world into the desert" (BE); "anchoress" (SKg[2] Glg RBg), "a female recluse shut up either in a cell attached to a church, or living under a religious rule in her own house" (SKg[2]). Cf. *MED ancre* n.

6349 **prioresse:** "A prioresse was the principal of a female priory, that is, a religious house subject to an abbey, which directed its discipline, and appointed its officers" (BE).

6352 **all religiouns:** all religious orders (BE RB RIf).

6354 As RB RI note, some Fr. MSS transpose the two verbs, *lais* "leave," and *pregn* "take." As a result, BE (following Méon's text; see SK's note, below) says that "we ought to read:—'I lete the strawe and take the corne.'" Lounsbury (1892:2.14), not recognizing the irony, also thinks that "the words *take* and *lete* have been transposed with the result of giving the passage a meaning exactly opposite to its real one." SK notes that "Méon's edition [11256] has 'G'en pren le grain et laiz la paille'"—"I take its kernel and leave the husk." The standard text (Lc 11186) has "j'en lés le grain et pregn la paille" "I leave its kernel and take the husk"; see Ln 11216t and KA Fr. 11232n. § Proverbial. As RB notes, Ln (11216n.) says that the expression occurs often in medieval French; it signifies "take the less good and leave the better." RI cites Whiting (1968: S824).

lete: "leave" (SK FI). BE's suggestion, noted by KA; in support, GL compares lines 5544, 5959, 6006 (for the *l-b* confusion), and RBt SU FI RIt cite the Fr. *lais* "leave" (above).

6355 **gyle:** "deceive." SU's *gyle* follows the Fr. (Lc 11187, Ln 11217 "Por genz embacler i abit" "I dwell there in order to trick (?) people"). SK's *blynde*—"hoodwink" (SK)—follows the Fr. var. *avugler* (for *embacler*) in Méon (11256), the reading also of KA Fr. (11233), based on Michel. Neither Ln nor Lc records the variant *avugler*, and Ln (11217t) records only *embrachier* "embrace" (?). Liddell (GL) retains *joly* and notes that "the French texts vary here" but believes that "the verse should run: *To blynde folk ther I enhabit*, and be taken with 6356." He suggests that "*Ioly* is perhaps a mistake for *sely*, translating 'por gens avugler' misread as 'por gens avugles.'" RB notes Ln's reading *embacler* but follows KA's *avugler* and keeps the emendation *blynde*. Sutherland's French text reads *enbascler* (error?) "deceive," and he records no variants. We are thus left with *enbacler* (Lc) as the best reading, but the word is unique (Lcg) and may well lie behind the easier *avugler*. Ln and Lc gloss the word as "tromper (?)," and Tobler-Lommatzsch (1925– :3.34, s.v. *embacler*) records only this definition and quotation. Thus SU's emendation, *gyle*, seems as close as we may expect; cf. lines 6112, 6198, 6203, 6206, 6214, 6310, 6321.

folk: About the insertion of *ther* after *folk*, SK comments "i. e. where; for sense and metre."

6356 Jephson (BE), misled by the rich rhyme (*abit : abit*) misquotes the Fr. "Por gens aveugler i abit," the line that parallels line 6355. The true parallel is "je n'en quier sanz plus que l'abit" "I seek only the habit [of religion], no more" (Lc 11188).

6359 **wre:** "cover, conceal"; see *OED Wry* v.[1]. GL RBt RIt quote the Fr., which is not parallel (Lc 11191 "Mout est en moi muez li vers" "the tune is very much changed in me"). KA notes *beare/bere* in TH[1]/UR. SK, with FI, reads *bere me* as "behave" and takes the MS phrase *were me* as "defend myself." RIt misreports SK as reading *were*.

"[I] make into my trappis falle,
Thurgh my pryveleges, alle
That ben in Cristendome alyve.
I may assoile and I may shryve—
That no prelat may lette me—   6365
All folk, where evere thei founde be.

I note no prelate may done so,
But it the pope be, and no mo,
That made thilk establisshing.
Now is not this a propre thing?   6370
But, were my sleightis aperceyved,
[Ne shulde I more ben receyved]

6361   **I make]** Make MS KA; Thus make I TH¹-MO SK FU-FI   **into]** in SK   6362   **Thurgh]** The people t.
TH¹-SP³ FU SU FI; The folke t. UR   6368   **it the pope be]** I onlye TH²   6371   **were my sleightis**
aperceyved] where m. sleight is a. GL   6372   **Ne shulde I more ben receyved]** Of hem I am nomore r. GL; N.
s. I ben so r. SU FI   *Out:* MS (*blank line*) TH¹-BE KA FU RI

6361–6472   As RI notes, these lines correspond to portions of a passage that Ln and Lc regard as an interpolation and that appears as a composite text, from several MSS, in Ln's note (11222–23n.). Brusendorff (1925:311) records the correspondences between *Rom* and Ln's composite text. RB (6371–72n.) observes that KA Fr. has 110 lines, corresponding to *Rom.* 6361–6472, which Langlois does not include in his text but which appear in Ln 11222n. KA bases his French text on Michel, who includes the passage in his text (based on MS Za); SU Fr., starting from Ln's note, supplements MS Ri from Ke and κω; and Lc, based on MS Ha, does not include the passage. Line references to the Fr. will be to Ln 11222.x, where *x* is the line number in Langlois's note. SU (note to Fr. 11222) observes that this "apocryphal chapter" appears "in several *Roman* MSS, including Ga, Jo, Li, Ri, Ke, Eg [κω], and Za. The order of lines in none of MSS, however, corresponds to the ME." On SU's textual theory, see above, "Partial Acceptance" and "Theories of the Manuscript's Original." §   On the content, see Dahlberg's suggestion (1971: 394–95) that, in the Fr., the interpolation belongs to the period of the 1280s. See Dufeil (1972:358–59).

6361   **I make:** KA, following Michel (KA Fr. 11239 "Si fais" "Thus I make") notes *Thus make I* in TH¹ UR BE MO. But the texts of Ln and SU read "Je faz" ("I make") (Ln 11222.1). Jephson (BE) thinks the connective *Thus* "necessary for sense and metre," but GL's *I make* is closer to the best Fr. texts and gives satisfactory sense as well as meter.

    into: KA endorses SK's *in*.

6362   **Thurgh:** TH¹'s phrase, "the people through," follows the Fr. *Le monde par* (Ln 11222.2); MS translates *le monde* in line 6363.

6364–65   BE SK RI note that the friars' power of confession and absolution, held independently of bishops and priests, was a "bitter grievance" (SK) and "a major point of contention" (RI) between the secular clergy and the friars. BE quotes a passage from *Jack Upland* (ed. Skeat 1897:191): "And all men knowen wel, that they [i.e. Antichrist and his disciples the friars] ben not obedient to bishoppes, ne lege men to kinges." In a later note (to lines 6385–86), BE adds: "The licences granted by the Pope to the Mendicant Orders, to administer the sacrament of Penance within the jurisdiction of the secular clergy, gave rise to frequent disputes, which arrived at such a height in the 13th century, that Martin IV and Boniface VIII were obliged to modify them." This statement is perhaps truer of Boniface (1294–1303) than of Martin (1281–85); cf. 6361–6472n. and Dufeil (1972:358–59). RI compares *GP* 218–20 and *SumT* D 2093–98. The strictures against the friars reflect the writings of Guillaume de Saint-Amour; see 6544–7692n.

6365   **That:** GL notes the Fr. parallel *ce* (Ln 11222.4) as support for the demonstrative sense.

6368–69   Perhaps a reference—in the Fr. (Ln 11222.7–8 "Fors l'apostoile seulement [var. MS Ca 'Fors le pape tant seulement'], / Qui fist cest establissement" "except the pope alone, who established that rule")—to papal support of the mendicants, as in Martin IV's bull *Ad fructus uberes* (1281; ed. Denifle and Chatelain 1889–97:1.592); see Dufeil (1972:358–59).

6371–73   As basis for his analysis of the emendations in lines 6371–72 (see below), David (RI) quotes and translates the Fr. (Ln 11222.8.5–7 "Mais mes traiz ont aperceüz, / Si n'en sui mais si receüz / Envers eus si con je souloie" "But they [the prelates] have detected my treachery, and I am no longer received by them as I used to be"). "It is noteworthy," he adds, "that the only blank line in the MS not filled in by Thynne is from a spurious passage unlikely to have been in Thynne's Fr. MS"; see 6361–6472n.

6371   **were my sleightis:** Liddell (GL) emends to *where my sleight is* on the basis of the Fr. (Ln 11222.8.5–7, above), which, as he observes, is not conditional.

6372   MO's emendation, noted by KA, for MS's blank line follows the Fr. and BE's suggestion (in note) "I shulde no lenger ben received" (also noted by KA). David (RI) omits the line, as spurious, and supplies MO's reading in a footnote. MS leaves the line blank at the bottom of a page, where TH¹ either overlooked the lacuna or could not supply it from his Fr. copy (see 6371–73n.). UR supplies a line of dots (BE, asterisks) to show the lacuna.

As I was wont; and wostow whye?   127r
For I dide hem a t[r]egetrie.
But therof yeve I lytel tale;   6375
I have the silver and the male.
So have I prechid and eke shreven,
So have I take, so have [me] yeven,
Thurgh her foly, husbonde and wyf,
That I lede right a joly lyf,   6380
Thurgh symplesse of the prelacye;
They knowe not al my tregettrie.
    "But forasmoche as man and wyf
Shulde shewe her paroch-prest her lyf
Onys a yeer, as seith the book,   6385
Er ony wight his housel took,

Thanne have I pryvylegis large,
That may of mych thing discharge.
For he may seie right thus, parde:
'Sir Preest, in shrift I telle it thee,   6390
That he to whom that I am shryven
Hath me [assoiled] and me yeven
Penaunce, sothly, for my synne,
Which that I fonde me gilty ynne;
Ne I ne have nevere entencioun   6395
To make double confessioun,
Ne reherce efte my shrift to thee;   127v
O shrift is right ynough to me.
This ought thee suffice wele;
Ne be not rebel never a dele.   6400

6374 **tregetrie**] tegetrie MS BE KA   6375 **lytel**] a l. MS-KA FU   6377 **So**] Lo FU   6378 **So**] Lo FU   **me**] I MS-KA FU   6381 **symplesse**] symplnesse FU   6383 **man**] a m. TH²   6392 **assoiled**] assailed MS KA   6393 **Penaunce**] For p. MS BE-KA GL   **my**] alle m. UR   6398 **to**] for SP¹   6399 **suffice**] to s. UR

Liddell (GL) emends to *Of hem I am nomore receyved* on the basis of the Fr. (above), and he objects to the readings of BE and MO that the Fr. is not conditional. SU FI's emendation translates the second *si* of the Fr. but omits the phrase *n' . . . mais.*

6373–74 **whye : tregetrie:** See 6111–12n.

6374 **tregetrie:** "a piece of trickery; see l. 6267" (SK).

6375 **lytel:** KA's suggestion for MS *a lytel*; it clarifies the sense of *tale* "account" (FI); cf. the Fr. (Ln 11222.8.9 "Mais ne me chaut coment qu'il aille" "but it doesn't matter to me in any case"). GL compares line 6346.

6377–78 **shreven : yeven:** Cf. 2759–60n.

6378 **me:** KA's suggestion, for MS *I*, follows the Fr. *m'* (Ln 11222.8.12 "tant m'a l'en doné" "so much have people given me"). The subject of "have . . . yeven" would be "husbonde and wyf" in the next line.

6379 "Through their folly, whether man or woman" (SK).

6381 "The gullibility of the prelates who fail to detect the friars' sharp practices" (RI).

6384 "make confession" (RIf).

    paroch: For the form, see *MED parish(e* n. MS has a stroke over the body of the *h* in this word here and in lines 6442 and 6874; cf. 7167n.

6385 **Onys a yeer:** BE FI RI note, as RI puts it, that "annual confession to one's parish priest, generally at Easter, was made mandatory by Innocent III at the Fourth Lateran Council in 1215." SK RB FI also specify Easter as the time, SK refers to *Rom* 6435, and SK RB FI RI adduce *ParsT* I 1027. In a note at line 6403, BE states: "Those who did not communicate at Easter, were liable, both before and after the Reformation, to be presented to the Ordinary, and incurred the penalty of the lesser excommunication, which subjected them to civil penalties at common law."

    the book: BE suggests "the Bible," and adduces Matt. 18.16 and John 20.23. These passages support the idea of confession, but not that of annual confession to the parish priest, as does the conciliar statute. BE notes further that "the practice of confession to a priest may be traced to the first three centuries."

6386 **ony:** See 212n.

6388 **mych:** Cf. 1713n.

6389 **he:** "the parishioner making his annual confession to his curate" (RIf).

6390–97 FI (6397n.) observes: "Like Chaucer's Pardoner, False-Semblant sets himself up in competition with the parish priest, taking offerings due the priest and giving lighter penance." He compares *GP* 221ff., *PardP* C 387ff. Cf. 6135–7334n.

6390–91 "Note that the penitent is here supposed to address his own parish-priest. Thus *he* in l. 6391 means the friar" (SK).

6391–92 **shryven : yeven:** Cf. 2759–60n.

6393 **Penaunce:** KA notes TH¹'s emendation.

6398 BE SK compare Thomas's argument in *SumT* D 2094–98.

For certis, though thou haddist it sworne,
I wote no prest ne prelat borne
That may to shrift efte me constreyne;
And if they done, I wole me pleyne,
For I wote where to pleyne wele.   6405
Thou shalt not streyne me a dele,
Ne enforce me, ne not me trouble,
To make my confessioun double.
Ne I have none affeccioun
To have double absolucioun.   6410
The firste is right ynough to me;
This latter assoilyng quyte I thee.
I am unbounde; what maist thou fynde
More of my synnes me to unbynde?
For he that myght hath in his honde   6415
Of all my synnes me unbonde.
And if thou wolt me thus constreyne,
That me mote nedis on thee pleyne,

There shall no jugge imperial,
Ne bisshop, ne official,   6420
Done jugement on me; for I   128r
Shal gone and pleyne me openly
Unto my shriftfadir newe—
That hight not Frere Wolf untrewe—
And he shal cheveys hym for me,   6425
For I trowe he can hampre thee.
But, Lord, he wolde be wrooth withall,
If men hym wolde Frere Wolf call!
For he wolde have no pacience,
But done al cruel vengeaunce.   6430
He wolde his myght done at the leest,
Nothing spare for Goddis heest.
And, God so wys be my socour,
But thou yeve me my Savyour
At Ester, whanne it likith me,   6435
Withoute presyng more on thee,

6405 **pleyne**] plaining UR   6407 **not**] yit SK   6412 **This**] The FU   6423 **Unto**] Anon to UR   6424 **That**] Whiche t. UR   **not**] *om.* TH¹-MO FU   6425 **cheveys**] chuse TH¹-UR FU   6428 **hym wolde**] w. h. TH³ ST SP²-UR   6432 **Nothing**] Than n. UR; Ne n. SK

6412 **quyte:** "release" (SKg₂), "excuse" (*MED quiten* v. 4. [d]), rather than "reject" (FI), although the ironic excusing amounts to a rejection.

6413–16 **unbounde . . . unbynde . . . unbonde:** "To unbind means to absolve from ecclesiastical censures, in allusion to our Lord's commission to the Apostles.—John xx.28" (BE). Cf. Matt. 16.19; *Piers Plowman* B Prol. 100–01.

6418 **me:** SK, adducing the reflexive *m'* in the Fr. idiom *je m'aille* (Ln 11222.44 "Si que je m'aille de vous plaindre" "then I may go lodge a complaint against you"), notes "*I . . .* would be better grammar. As it stands, *me* is governed by *pleyne*, and *I* is understood."

6422–23 "That is, the penitent will again apply to the friar" (SK).

6424 **That hight not Frere Wolf:** "Whose name is not Friar Wolf" (SK RB). SK explains: "Such is his right name, but he does not answer to it; see l. 6428." RB FI also point out the irony; RI comments that the name is "ironically appropriate." RB adduces the Fr. "frere Louvel" (Ln 11222.50). TH¹-MO FU, not recognizing the irony, omit *not*.

Frere Wolf: BE adduces John 10.12.

6425 "He will help me against you" (BE). "'He will occupy himself for me.' i. e. he will take my part; see *Chevise* in the New E. Dict., sect. 4 b" (SK; cf. SKg₂ RBg, s.v. *Chevise*). FI glosses *chevyse* as "justify" (cf. *MED* 1. [b]), a reading that might apply to the phrase "cheveys hym for." RIf takes *cheveys hym* as "sustain himself," *MED* (s.v. *chevishen* v. 1 [a]) as "exert (himself)." See below for the Fr.

cheveys: BE's restoration of MS *cheveys* follows Fr. *chevir* (Ln 11222.58 "Se savroit bien de vous chevir" "he would know well how to deal with you"; noted in BE SKt RBt SU).

6429–30 **pacience : vengeaunce:** "dreadful rhyme," says Skeat (1887:vii). But it follows the Fr. (Ln 11222.53–54 "pacience : venjance"), where the nasalized vowels may rhyme (cf. Pope 1934, sec. 441). Kaluza (1893a:44–45; cf. 136) lists such rhymes at lines 5847, 6429, 6567, 6717, 7075, 7323, 7353, 7435, 7481, 7667. Cf. Feng (1990:52–54).

6431–32 "At the least, he would exert his power to spare nothing because of any command of God" (Ln 11222.55–56 "Son pouoir au meins en feroit, / Que ja pour Dieu nou laisseroit" "at least, he would exercise his power so that he would never, for God, leave it"). See 6432n.

6432 **Nothing:** KA suggests insertion of *Ne* before *Nothing*. See 6431–32n.

6434 "Unless you admit me to communion" (BE SK RB FI RIf). RI explains that "the priest might withhold Communion from someone who had not been to confession."

273

I wole forth, and to hym gone,
And he shal housel me anoon.
For I am out of thi grucchyng;
I kepe not dele with thee nothing.' 6440
    "Thus may he shryve hym that forsaketh
His paroch prest, and to me takith.
And if the prest wole hym refuse,
I am full redy hym to accuse, 6444
And hym punysshe and hampre so 128v
That he his chirche shal forgo.
    "But whoso hath in his felyng
The consequence of such shryvyng
Shal sene that prest may never have myght
To knowe the conscience aright 6450
Of hym that is undir his cure.
And this ageyns holy scripture,
That biddith every heerde honeste
Have verry knowing of his beeste.

But pore folk that gone by strete, 6455
That have no gold, ne sommes grete,
Hem wolde I lete to her prelates,
Or lete her prestis knowe her states,
For to me right nought yeve they.
And why? It is for they ne may; 6460
They ben so bare, I take no kepe.
But I wole have the fat sheepe;
Lat parish prestis have the lene.
I yeve not of her harme a bene!
And if that prelates grucche it, 6465
That oughten w[r]oth be in her witt,
To leese her fat beestes so,
I shal yeve hem a stroke or two,
That they shal leesen with force, 129r
Yhe, bothe her mytre and her croce. 6470
Thus jape I hem, and have do longe,
My pryveleges ben so stronge."

6452 **this**] t. is TH¹-BE FU SU FI   6460 **And why? It is**] "A. w. is it?" MO SK   6466 **wroth**] woth
MS-ST KA FU   6469 **That**] So that UR   **force**] her f. SP¹ GL; the f. MO SK   6478 **that**] tha TH²

6440   "I.e. I don't care to deal with you in any way" (GL); RB FI RIf gloss similarly. Cf. 6083n.
6442   **paroch:** See 6384n.
6449   **may never have myght:** "will never be able," notes SK, and explains: "If the priest is not confessed to,
he will not understand the sins of his flock."
6452–54 BE SK RB RI adduce Prov. 27.23; SK RB RI also adduce John 10.14.
6452   **this:** "this is" (KA SK GL RB RIf). SK compares lines 3548, 6057; cf. notes.
6460   **And why? It is:** BE MO SK give these words as a separate speech to the God of Love ("'And why it is
[is it MO SK]?'"); KA notes *is it* in MO. BE SK supply the speech-headings *Amour* and (for the following words) *F.
Sem.* GL RB give only the words "And why" to the God of Love, with "It is" as the beginning of Fals-Semblant's
reply. The basis for the separation of the speeches lies in the texts of Méon (11401) and Michel (12131), who
separate by means of speech-headings, and of KA, who punctuates accordingly (KA Fr. 11336 "'Porquoi?' 'Pour ce
qu'il ne porroient'"). Ln does not separate the two speeches (11222.86 "Pour quoi? Par foi, qu'il ne porroient" "Why?
Faith, because they could not"); nor do SU-RI; as RIt observes, "*Pour quoi?* sounds like a rhetorical question and is
treated as part of Faux Semblant's speech in Langlois." Possibly TH¹'s virgule after *is* (comma in TH²-UR) may also
have influenced the tradition of speech separation; but MS has no such punctuation.
6464   "I care not a bean for (all) the harm they can do (to) me" (BE SK). On *bean* as a figure of worthlessness,
see 4830n.
6466   **wroth:** KA notes SP¹'s correction in UR BE MO.
6469–70 **force : croce:** "The rime is a bad one" (SK); "the passage is obviously corrupt" (Kaluza 1893*a*:44).
Feng (1990:54–55) defends the assonance as one dictated by the translator's desire to retain Fr. *croce*, which has few
rhymes in English. See 6469n.
6469   **with force:** "(by, with) the force of the blow" (SK FI). KA, comparing *WBP* D 483, suggests: "perhaps
read *by seint Joce.*" In support of the emendation *her force* for *force*, GL quotes the Fr. parallel to lines 6468–70 (Ln
11222.95–96 "Que lever i ferai teus boces / Qu'il en perdront mitres et croces" "that I shall raise such bumps there
[i.e. on their heads] that they will lose mitres and croziers"). Cf. 6469–70n.
6470   **Yhe:** See 4659–60n.
    croce: "crozier(s)" (SKg₂ RIf) or "symbols of prelacy" (FI), rather than "cross" (TRg FI; cf. GLg RBg) in
the modern sense; the word follows the Fr. *croces* "croziers" (Ln 11222.96, above), distinct from OF *crois* "cross."
6472   **pryveleges:** "By privileges is meant the extraordinary jurisdiction granted to the Mendicants by various
Bulls" (BE); see Dufeil (1972).

Fals-Semblant wolde have stynted heere,
But Love ne made hym no such cheere
That he was wery of his sawe;   6475
But for to make hym glad and fawe,
He seide, "Telle on more specialy
Hou that thou servest untrewly.
Telle forth, and shame thee never a dele,
For, as thyn abit shewith wele,   6480
Thou [semest] an hooly heremyte."
    "Sothe is, but I am but an ypocrite."
    "Thou goste and prechest poverte."
    "Yhe, sir, but richesse hath pouste."
    "Thou prechest abstinence also."   6485
    "Sir, I wole fillen, so mote I go,
My paunche of good mete and wyne,
As shulde a maister of dyvyne;
For how that I me pover feyne,

Yit all pore folk I disdeyne.   6490
    "I love bettir [th'a]queyntaunce
Ten tyme of the kyng of Fraunce
Than of a pore man of mylde mode,   129v
Though that his soule be also gode.
For whanne I see beggers quakyng,   6495
Naked on myxnes al stynkyng,
For hungre crie, and eke for care,
I entremete not of her fare.
They ben so pore and ful of pyne,
They myght not oonys yeve me a dyne,   6500
For they have nothing but her lyf.
What shulde he yeve that likketh his knyf?
It is but foly to entremete,
To seke in houndes nest fat mete.
Lete bere hem to the spitel anoon,   6505
But, for me, comfort gete they noon.

6481 **semest]** seruest MS-KA FU   6482 **am but]** am SK GL RB¹·² RI   6487 **wyne]** gode w. UR GL
6489 **how]** thowe TH²   6491 **th'aqueyntaunce]** that queyntaunce MS MO KA; the queyntaunce BE
6492 **tyme]** tymes TH¹-UR SK FU-FI   6493 **a]** *om.* SK   6500 **a]** *om.* SK RB¹·² FI RI

6473 Here the ME text resumes its correspondence to the Ln-Lc text after the interpolated passage; see 6361–6472n.

6481 **semest:** Brink (1870:29), followed by KA, recommends this change; it is based on the Fr. *sembles* (Lc 11201 "seem"; noted by SKt SU FI RIt).

6482–86 BE SK supply speech-headings *F. Sem.* and *Amour* for the alternate lines of this dialogue.

6482 **but an:** KA suggests omitting both of these words. No ed. omits both, but SK GL RB RI omit the first of them (i.e., the second *but* of the line), and SU FI note the Fr., which has only the first *but* (Lc 11202 "mes je suis ypocrites" "but I am a hypocrite").

6484 **Yhe:** See 4659–60n.

6486 **so mote I go:** FI paraphrases, "whatever happens." Cf. *MED m̄ōten* v.(2), sense 11. (c) "so may I go (live), as sure as I hope to live."

6490 BE notes that the disdain of the poor "was a favorite topic of censure on the Mendicants" and adduces *GP* 243–48. See also *SumT* D 1904–67, 2074–78. For background, see Dufeil (1972:174–80).

6491 **th'aqueyntaunce:** KA suggests this emendation and compares line 3562. SK notes the Fr. *l'acointance* (Lc 11211 "the acquaintance").

6492 **Ten tyme:** GL notes the Fr. (Lc 11212 ".c. mile tanz" "a hundred thousand times").

6493 **mylde:** KA suggests omitting this word, but no ed. so emends. GL, however, favors KA's suggestion and compares the Fr. (Lc 11213 "que d'un povre, par Nostre Dame" "than of a poor [man], by Our Lady"), adding that "*pover*... is more frequent than *pore* in [*Rom*]."

6500 **a dyne:** KA suggests omitting *a*. SK's reading—"*yeve me dyne*, give me something to dine off"—takes *dyne* as the verb, as does RI's gloss, "something to eat." *MED dine* n.(2) takes *a dyne* as the noun "dinner" and cites this passage as one of two.

6502 Proverbial. As RB notes, Ln (11254n.), citing "*Recueil Rawlinson*, II, 191," compares "Mal done a sun vassal qui son coutel leche" ("He who licks his knife treats his vassal badly"). Lc (11224n.) cites Morawski (1925: no. 1707); RI cites Whiting (1968: K92).

6504 **fat mete:** BE states that fat-mete appears to mean *par excellence*, black pudding: the original is *saing*, blood." The argument is tenuous, since BE's original is Méon's ed., where the word *saing* occurs in a couplet (11446–47) that comes, presumably, from MS Za (Ln 1.46) and that appears in Ln Lc only as a var.; since Ln does not collate Za (Ln 1.52), the word *saing* does not appear in his var. (Ln 11254t), which has *oint* "animal fat" from the B family (Be *oing*). SU has *oint* (SU Fr. 11254.B²), from MSS Bu κω Ri (SU Fr. 11249–50n.), a reading that parallels the ME.

6505 "let them be taken to the hospital" (FI).

6506 **for me:** "as far as I am concerned" (BE).

275

But a riche sike usurere
Wolde I visite and drawe nere;
Hym wole I comforte and rehete,
For I hope of his gold to gete. 6510
And if that wikkid deth hym have,
I wole go with hym to his grave.
And if ther ony reprove me,
Why that I lete the pore be,
Wostow how I [mot] ascape? 6515
I sey, and swere hym ful rape,
That riche men han more tecches 130r
Of synne than han pore wrecches,
And han of counsel more mister;
And therfore I wole drawe hem ner. 6520
  "But as grete hurt, it may so be,
Hath a soule in right grete poverte

As soule in grete richesse, forsothe,
Al be it that they hurten bothe.
For richesse and mendicitees 6525
Ben clepid two extremytees;
The mene is cleped suffisaunce;
Ther lyth of vertu the aboundaunce.
For Salamon, full wel I wote,
In his Parablis us wrote, 6530
As it is knowe to many a wight,
In his thrittene chapitre right,
'God thou me kepe, for thi pouste,
Fro richesse and mendicite.'
For if a riche man hym dresse 6535
To thenke to myche on richesse,
His herte on that so fer is sett
That [he] his creatour foryett.

6507 **riche**] full r. UR   6509 **wole**] wolde TH³-BE   6512 **to**] in TH³ ST SP²-BE   6513 **if**] *om.* SP³
6515 **mot**] not MS-SP³ BE-KA FU; know how to UR   6518 **pore**] these p. UR   6520 **wole**] wolde TH¹-UR
FU SU FI   6522 **a**] *om.* UR SK GL   6523 **in**] is BE MO   6528 **Ther**] The t. TH³ ST   6530 **Parablis**]
wise P. UR   6531 **to**] of TH¹-BE SK FU SU FI   6532 **thrittene**] thirtieth UR; thrittethe SK RB¹,²
6536 **richesse**] his r. SK GL   6538 **he**] *om.* MS (MS₁ *corr.*)   **foryett**] dothe f. TH¹-UR FU SU FI

6507 **usurere:** "seems to be dissyllabic here, like *seculer* in v. 6263 [*sic for* 6232?]" (GL).

6513 **ony:** Cf. 212n.

6515 **mot ascape:** "i. e., must excuse myself" (FI). The Fr.(Lc 11233 "savez vos conment j'en eschape?" "do you know how I escape from him?") may support a reading with the auxiliary *may*: "*may* escape, *may* excuse myself"; see *MED mōten* v.(2), senses 1a, 2a.

  mot: KA's suggestion for MS *not*.

6519 **mister:** "need" (URg SKg₂ FI). At line 1426, GL adduces this line.

6522 **a:** KA notes the omission of this word in UR and compares line 6523.

6527–28 FI calls attention to the "golden mean," RB to "the Aristotelian doctrine of the mean." RB compares *LGWP* F 165.

6531 **to:** KA notes TH¹'s *of.*

6532 **thrittene:** "thirteen," an error for "thirtieth" that may be due to the Fr. exemplar. KA notes UR's correction to *thirtieth*, based, presumably, on the Biblical text, Prov. 30.8. BE SK GL RB RI RI note the Biblical reference as Prov. 30.8–9, and GL quotes the Fr. *trentiesne* (Lc 11250 "tout droit ou treintiesme chaspistre" "right in the thirtieth chapter"). The source of the error, as SU points out (Fr. 11281n.), may be a MS like Be, which reads *tresime* (cf. Ln 11280t); FI RIt also note the erroneous Fr. form.

6533–42 SK and later eds. (except FU) have punctuated this passage as a quotation from Prov. 30.8–9. Lc (11251–60) punctuates similarly except that he ends the quotation after the first two words of the last line ("et parjurs"), words that correspond to the single word "Forsworne" of the ME (line 6542); Ln (11281–90) has no quotation marks, but his note (11277–90n.) assumes that the passage goes back to Prov. 30, 8–9. The punctuation of SK and later eds. may come from KA Fr. (11409–18), which follows the punctuation of Michel (12204–13; for the differences between KA's Fr. text and those of Ln and Lc, see 6541–43n.). Here, I take the quotation as two lines long, 6533–34, where the first-person voice is the same as that of the Fr. and of Prov. 30.8 ("Give me neither beggary nor riches"); in the next four lines (6535–38) the first-person voice of Prov. 30.9 ("Lest perhaps being filled, I should be tempted to deny, and say: Who is the Lord?") shifts in both the Fr. and the ME to third-person, indirect discourse about the rich man whose heart is so set on riches that he forgets his creator. In lines 6539–40, the first-person *I* is that of Fals-Semblant, not of the speaker in Prov. 30, and this voice continues thereafter.

6536 **myche:** Cf. 1713n.

  richesse: KA suggests *his richesse*. GL notes the Fr. *sa richece* (Lc 11254 "his wealth").

6538 **he:** "written in the margin" (KA), perhaps by MS₁. Thorp (1989) questions the ink, and Whatley (1989) thinks that the hand could be later.

And hym that beggi[ng] wole ay greve,
How shulde I bi his word hym leve?　6540
Unnethe that he nys a mycher　130v
Forsworne, or ellis [God is] lyer.
Thus seith Salamon[es] sawes.

Ne we fynde writen in no lawis,
And namely in oure Cristen lay—　6545
Whoso seith 'yhe,' I dar sey 'nay'—
That Crist, ne his apostlis dere,
While that they walkide in erthe heere,

6539　**hym]** he BE　　**begging]** beggith MS-KA FU　　6541　**that]** is t. GL　　6542　**God is]** goddis MS-KA FU　　6543　**Salamones]** Salamon MS-SP³ BE KA FU SU FI　　6546　**Whoso]** Who TH³-SP³ BE SK

6539　**begging:** KA compares line 6787 in support of this change, which follows the Fr. *mendicitez* (Lc 11257 "Cil que mendicitez guerroie" "him whom beggary attacks"). GL quotes the Fr. "mendicité guerroie" as the parallel to "wole greve," where the full phrase in ME should be "begging wole . . . greve."

6541–43　The translator has misread the French and omitted a line; moreover, KA's Fr. text, based on Michel's, may have misled modern editors (KA Fr. 11417–20; cf. Michel 12212–15):

"Envis avient qu'il ne soit lierres
Et parjurs, ou Diex est mentierres."
　　Se Salemons dist de par lui
La letre que ci vous parlui;
(See below for translation.)

This text, with its full stop, closed quotation, and new paragraph, supports the punctuation of lines 6533–42 (see n.) as a quotation from Prov. 30.8–9; it also accounts for ME *Thus* in line 6543. The texts of Méon, Ln, and Lc, however, show a comma where KA has a period (Ln 11289–92 "Enviz avient qu'il ne seit lierres / E parjurs, ou Deus est mentierres, / Se Salemons dist de par lui / La lettre que ci vous parlui" "He can hardly help being a thief and perjurer, or God is a liar, if Solomon uttered for him the very words that I spoke of to you just now"; cf. Lc 11259–62). The translator omits the last of these lines, and he misreads *Se* as "Thus" (line 6543) rather than "if"; the ME reflects the common confusion between the OF adv. *si*, *se* ("thus," etc., from Lat. *sic*) and the conj. *se*, *si* ("if," from Lat. *si*); even the spellings were confused in French (Raynaud de Lage 1962:133, 146).

6541–42　BE reads these lines as being in the voice of Fals-Semblant, who, according to BE, "says that the poor man has as many temptations to envy and fraud, as the rich has to forgetfulness of God." The misreading of the latter clause is due to the omission of a line from the Fr.; cf. 6541–43n.

6541　**Unnethe that he nys:** "it is hard if he is not; i.e. he probably is" (SK).
　　mycher: "thief" (TRg et al., except MOg "niggard, miser"), "a petty thief, a purloiner" (SK). TRg SK RB note the Fr. *lierres* (Lc 11259, above).

6542　**God is:** The suggestion of KA and of Lounsbury (1892:2.14), presumably on the basis of the Fr. *Dex est* (Lc 11260, above). SK adduces Prov. 30.9 "or being compelled by poverty, I should steal, and forswear the name of my God." GL compares line 6541. See also 6533–42n., 6541–43n.

6543　**Thus:** See 6541–43n.
　　Salamones: KA's suggestion, anticipated by UR.

6544–7692　The balance of the *Romaunt*, in the voice of Fals-Semblant, follows the original in reflecting at many points the direct influence of the writings of Guillaume de Saint-Amour, named at lines 6763, 6781. Ln (notes to 11293 and ff., especially 11513n.), Lc (notes to 11263 and ff.), RB (6552n.), FI (6553n.), and RI (6547–50n.) all refer to Guillaume's *Tractatus brevis de periculis novissimorum temporum* "Short treatise on the perils of the most recent times" (1632:17–72), to which our text refers at line 6785. Ln (11513n.) Lc (11263n.) RI all note that the 1632 ed. of Guillaume's *Opera* (Constance: Alithophilos) was actually published in Paris; Ln attributes this ed. to "Valérien de Flavigny (Jean Alethophilos)." In individual notes, Ln Lc quote the relevant parallels; in summary, these are to *De periculis*, chapters 2, 4, 5, 12, 14 (1632:21, 25, 30, 32, 48–53, 67–69); *Responsiones*, nos. 7, 11, 35 (ed. Faral 1951:341, 343, 352); *Collectiones catholicae et canonicae scripturae* (1632:218); Sermon of May 1, 1256 (1632:496).

6544–6796　This section in the Fr. (Lc 11263–494) develops an inverse attack on the institutions of communal poverty and mendicancy (Dahlberg 1971:396 n.11293–524). See 6544–7692n. for sources in Guillaume de Saint-Amour. RI (6447–50n.) states: "The mendicant orders claimed that their poverty and begging were modeled upon the example of Christ and the apostles, thereby causing a bitter theological dispute over how Jesus and his followers made their living."

6546　**yhe:** See 4659–60n.

6547–50　RB (6552n.) RI, following Ln Lc, cite Guillaume de Saint-Amour, *De periculis* 12 (1632:50–51).

Were never seen [her bred] beggyng,
For they nolden beggen for nothing.　　6550
And right thus was men wont to teche,
And in this wise wolde [it] preche
The maistres of divinite
Somtyme in Parys the citee.
　　"And if men wolde ther-geyn appose　6555
The nakid text, and lete the glose,
It myght soone assoiled be;
For men may wel the sothe see,
That, parde, they myght aske a thing
Pleynly forth, without begging.　　6560
For they weren Goddis herdis deere,
And cure of soules hadden heere.
They nolde nothing begge her fode;
For aftir Crist was done on rode,　　6564
With ther propre hondis they wrought,　131r

And with travel, and ellis nought,
They wonnen all her sustenaunce,
And lyveden forth in her penaunce,
And the remenaunt yaf awey
To other pore folkis alwey.　　6570
They neither bilden tour ne halle,
But [ley] in houses smale withalle.
　　"A myghty man, that can and may,
Shulde with his honde and body alway
Wynne hym his fode in laboring,　　6575
If he ne have rent or sich a thing,
Although he be religious,
And God to serven curious.
Thus mote he done, or do trespas,
But if it be in certeyn cas,　　6580
That I can reherce, if myster be,
Right wel, whanne the tyme I se.

6549　**her bred]** herbred MS-ST SP²-UR KA FU　　6551　**was]** were TH¹-BE SK FU-FI　　6552　**it]** *om.* MS (MS₁　*corr.*)　　6570　**folkis]** folk SK　　6572　**ley]** they MS-KA FU　　6581　**reherce]** telle UR　6582　**whanne]** w. that UR　　**the tyme I]** I the tyme MO

6549　**her bred:** KA notes the BE MO division of MS *herbred* into two words.
6551　**men:** "one" (GL).
6552　**it:** "written above the line" (KA) by MS₁.
6553–54　BE states that "the University of Paris was always hostile to the Mendicants." The statement is somewhat general; in the 1250s and later, the secular masters of the University (*maistres of divinite*), led by Guillaume de Saint-Amour, opposed the friars' privileges; see Dufeil (1972) and the notes to lines 6364–65, 6544–7692.
6555–57　"That is, 'If men would oppose the text of Scripture against these propositions, and leave the gloss, or comment, the question might soon be settled'" (BE).
6556　**nakid text . . . glose:** "simple (bare, literal) text . . . commentary (interpretation)" (SK FI RI).
6557　**assoiled:** "answere(d)" (SPg-TRg), "resolve(d)" (URg RBg), "settled" (BE), "explained" (BEg SKg₂ RBg FI), "disproven" (RIf).
6563–70　BE cites Eph. 4.28 and objects that "here St. Paul is not speaking of clergymen, but of laymen, who, before their conversion, had been thieves." Guillaume de Saint-Amour offers a better parallel: "Postquam vero Dominus . . . ab ipsis Apostolis corporaliter recessit per mortem & resurrectionem, ipsi non ad mendicandū se conuerterunt" "After the Lord, through his death and resurrection, withdrew bodily from the apostles, they did not turn to begging" (*De periculis* 12 [1632:50]). On the right of "all ministers of Christ to maintenance from the alms of the faithful," BE cites 2 Cor. 11.7ff.
6565　**ther:** KA records MO's form *her* as Skeat's suggestion; SK has *hir*, RB *her*. RBt notes that *the(i)r* is a Northern form, and RI notes that while *ther* may be a scribal error for *her*, "the C Fragment contains scattered Northern forms."
6568　**her penaunce:** KA suggests *pacience*, and GL in support notes the basis in Fr. *en pacience* (Lc 11282).
6570　**folkis:** KA endorses SK's *folk*.
6571　BE SK RB FI RI note the "allusion to the splendid houses built by the friars" (SK). RI compares *SumT* D 2099–2106. Jephson (BE), referring "to the beautiful *abbeys* built by the friars," may be thinking of the monasteries of monks as well as the houses of friars. He questions whether "these structures . . . were as conducive to personal self-indulgence as the ugly, but snug, parsonage-houses of the modern [1855] clergy."
　　bilden: "here used as a pt. tense; 'built'" (SK).
6572　**ley:** KA's suggestion. SK glosses as "lodged" and cites Fr. *gisoient* (Lc 11286).
6573–79　Ln Lc (11287–92n.) quote Guillaume de Saint-Amour, *De periculis* 12 (1632:48); RB RI so cite.
6581　**That:** "Perhaps omit *That*" (SKt GL); no ed. does so.
　　myster: "need" (URg SKg₂ FI). At line 1426, GL adduces this line.

"[S]eke the book of Seynt Austyne,
Be it in papir or perchemyne,
There as he writ of these worchynges,　6585
Thou shalt seen that noon excusynges
A parfit man ne shulde seke
Bi wordis ne bi dedis eke,
Although he be religious,　131v
And God to serven curious,　6590
That he ne shal, so mote I go,
With propre hondis and body also,
Gete his fode in laboryng,

If he ne have proprete of thing.
Yit shulde he selle all his substaunce,　6595
And with his swynk have sustenaunce,
If he be parfit in bounte.
Thus han tho bookes tolde me.
For he that wole gone ydilly,
And usith it ay desily　6600
[To] haunten other mennes table,
He is a trechour, ful of fable;
Ne he ne may, by gode resoun,
Excuse hym by his orisoun.

6583　**Seke]** Eke MS (*initial* S *cut out*) KA　6598　**tho]** the TH¹-UR FU SU FI　6599　**For]** Fro RB²
6600　**desily]** besyly TH¹-MO SK-RI　6601　**To]** Go MS MO KA　**mennes]** mennens MS KA

6583–94　Not in Ln Lc. Brink (1870:26–27) notes that the passage appears only in some French MSS and is undoubtedly interpolated. SK notes that line 6584 is "not in the F. text," and RB RI take only the first six lines, 6583–88, as corresponding to a "spurious passage" (RI) in the Fr. They cite Ln (11316–17n.), who gives only the first six of the lines (from MSS Be Bâ) and who regards them as an interpolation. KA gives the Fr. text of all 12 lines from Eg (κω), SU from Bu; Ln does not collate these MSS. In the parallels below, I quote from SU's Fr. text (11326.B¹⁻¹²).

6583　**Seke:** As KA RIt note, the initial *S* has been cut out of the MS. Cf. Fr. *cerchiez* (SU Fr. 11326.B1).
　　the book of Seynt Austyne: *De opere monachorum* (BE SK RB FI RI). BE FI cite *GP* 186–87. Augustine's name appears again at lines 6691, 6700. § Jean de Meun (if he is the author of the "interpolation") may depend on Guillaume de Saint-Amour; cf. notes to lines 6691, 6705–66. SK (6585n.) observes that Saint Augustine's arguments on manual labour for monks "are here made to suit the friars." BE notes that the prescription of manual labor accords with the rule of St. Benedict; but states that "St. Augustine's arguments do not apply to friars, who were priests actually employed in the duties of the ministry, and therefore entitled to maintenance according to St. Paul, 1 Cor. ix." Although the friars were granted the privileges of priests, they were not automatically priests unless ordained, and one of Guillaume de Saint-Amour's main points was that they were *not* in the apostolic tradition. See *Responsiones* 14 (ed. Faral 1951:345); Dahlberg (1971:393–94 n.11134); cf. 6270n.
6589–90　"Identical with 6577–78" (RI).
6592　**hondis:** KA suggests *honde* and cites line 6574; but GL compares line 6565; no ed. emends.
6595–6602　Ln Lc (11297–302n.) quote Guillaume de Saint-Amour, *De periculis* 12 (1632:49).
6595–97　"That is, 'Even though he have property, yet if he wishes to follow the counsels of perfection, he ought to sell it, and labour for his maintenance.'— Matt. xix. 2l" (BE). RB also compares Matt. 19.20–21; RI compares Luke 18.22 and notes that it is the text cited in *De periculis* 12 (1632:49); cf. 6595–6602n. above. Both RB RI adduce lines 6653–58.
6598　**tolde:** KA suggests *told it*, but no ed. so emends.
6599　**For:** RIt notes RB's misprint *Fro*.
6600　**usith it:** "*useth*, is accustomed" (FI). Since there is no antecedent for *it*, we may perhaps understand "uses [his time]." There is no parallel in the Fr.
　　desily: "foolishly" (*MED dusīliche* adv.). KA notes *besily* in UR BE MO. There is no parallel in the Fr.
6601　**To:** KA notes *to* in TH¹ UR BE.
　　mennes: KA notes *mennes* in TH¹ BE MO.
6602　BE quotes the original (Lc 11302 "lobierres est et sert de fable") and translates: "He is a deceiver, and serves as a laughing stock." In the ME, eds. gloss *fable* as "(idle) discourse" (URg-BEg), "deceitfulness" (SKg₂), "falsehood, deceit" (RBg).
　　ful: SU Fr. (11332n.; cf. Ln 11332t) identifies the Fr. parallel as the var. *plains* in MS Be.
6603–14　Lc (11303–314) quotes Guillaume de Saint-Amour, *Responsiones* 11 (ed. Faral 1951:343).
6604　"Use his praying as a pretext for idleness" (RB).

For men bihoveth, in somme gise,	6605	Men shulde hym rather mayme or bete,	6620
[Blynne] somtyme in Goddis servise		Or done of hym aperte justice,	
To gone and purchasen her nede.		Than suffren hym in such malice.'	
Men mote eten, that is no drede,		They done not wel, so mote I go,	
And slepe, and [eke] do other thing;		That taken such almesse so,	
So longe may they leve praiyng.	6610	But if they have somme pryvelege	6625
So may they eke her praier blynne		That of the peyne hem wole allege.	
While that they werke, her mete to wynne.		But how that is can I not see,	
Seynt Austyn wole therto accorde,	132r	But if the prince disseyved be;	
In thilke book that I recorde.		Ne I ne wene not, sikerly,	
Justinian eke, that made lawes,	6615	That they may have it rightfully.	6630
Hath thus forboden, by olde dawes:		But I wole not determine	
'No man, up peyne to be dede,		Of prynces power, ne defyne,	
Mighty of body, to begge his brede,		Ne by my word comprende, iwys,	
If he may swynke it for to gete;		If it so ferre may strecche in this;	

6606 **Blynne somtyme in**] Ben s. i. MS-SP³ BE-KA FU; Ben s. out of UR; Som-tyme leven SK SU-RI
6609 **eke**] *om.* MS (MS₁ MS₂ *corr.*)   6610 **So**] And s. UR   6616 **dawes**] sawes TH¹-UR FU SU FI
6617 **to**] for t. UR   6624 **That**] whiche t. UR   6631 **But**] B. yet UR

6605–07 BE (6606n.) suggests *That ben sometyme* for *Ben somtyme* in line 6606 and paraphrases "'It behoves men who are engaged in God's service, nevertheless, sometimes to go and obtain the necessaries of life.'" This reading does not quite follow the Fr.; see 6606n.

6606 **Blynne:** GL's *Blynne*, based on the Fr. *entrelessier* (Lc 11306 "leave"), has the sense "cease, (desist [from])" (URg et al.); "come to a stand . . . ; pause" (*MED blinnen* 2. [a]). For BE's reading, see 6605–07n. KA, presumably also on the basis of the Fr. *entrelaissier*, endorses SK's *Somtyme leven* and compares lines 71, 6610.

6609 **eke:** "written in the margin by the same hand" (KA), MS₁; also written above the line in a later hand, MS₂ₐ.

6613–14 As RB notes, the standard text of the Fr. (Méon, Michel, KA Fr. Ln Lc 11313–14) has "car l'Escriture s'i acorde, / qui la verité nous recorde" "Scripture, which records truth for us, agrees on this point." SU Fr. (11343–44) has the var., from MS Bu, which corresponds to *Rom* text: "Si con Saint Augustin s'acorde / El liure que ge vous recorde" "just as Saint Augustine agrees in the book which I am explaining to you." Ln (11343–44t) finds a similar var. in MSS Be Bâ. Brink (1870:32), apparently unaware of this Fr. variant, explains the English "Seynt Austyn" as a misunderstanding that arises from the Saint-Augustine interpolation that parallels lines 6583–94 (see note above).

6614 **thilke book:** Augustine, *De opere monachorum*; BE refers back to line 6583; see note.

6615–19 Ln Lc (11315–19n.) quote Guillaume de Saint-Amour, *De periculis* 12 (1632:52).

6615 **Justinian:** MS has the word underlined (not "interlined," as KA says) in red. § BE SK RB FI RI identify Justinian as the Emperor of the Eastern Empire (at Constantinople) from 527–565 and as the one "whose celebrated code called the Pandects, forms the basis of the Civil and Canon Law" (BE). SP¹, in the Annotations (sig. 4b6v) notes the reference to the "eleuenth booke of the *Code* . . . where it is enacted, that if any shal begge hauing no cause either by need or maim, the same shalbe examined and searched: and who so shall find him to counterfet, and prooueth the same, *dominium eius consequetur* [arrest follows]: and saith Bartol[us]. He shall be punished *Ad arbitrium iudicis* [at the judge's decision]." SP²·³g have much the same note, transferred to the Glossary, whence URg reproduces it, with attribution. This eleventh chapter is entitled *De mendicantibus validis*, noted in BE GL. The section of *De mendicantibus* in which this passage appears is numbered variously as 24, 25, or 26; for a modern edition see Krueger and Mommsen (1968–1970:2.435). As RB RI note, Guillaume de Saint-Amour refers to the code in *De periculis* 12 (not 2, as in RB), 1632:52: "in Iure humano, C. *De Mendicantibus Validis*" "in the civil law, in the chapter *On Healthy Beggars*."

6616 **olde:** KA SK both read MS *olde* as *old* and thus note *olde* as a change in TH¹ BE MO (KA) and TH¹ (SKt).

6631–35 Ln Lc (11331–35n.) cite Guillaume de Saint-Amour, *De periculis* 2 (1632:25); Lc adds *De periculis* 12 (1632:52–53). As RB RI observe, "Langlois notes that Guillaume de Saint-Amour uses similar caution about discussing the power of popes and bishops" (RB); and, as RI adds, "Lecoy observes that this caution applied specifically to the privilege of confession; Guillaume rejects any authority that would license mendicancy."

I wole not entremete a dele.
But I trowe that the book seith wele,
Who that takith almessis that be
Dewe to folk that men may se
Lame, feble, wery, and bare,
Pore, or in such maner care— 6640
That konne wynne hem never mo,
For they have no power therto—
He etith his owne dampnyng,
But if he lye that made al thing.
And if ye such a truaunt fynde, 6645
Chastise hym wel, if ye be kynde.
But they wolde hate you, percas,
And, if ye fillen in her laas,
They wolde eftsoonys do you scathe,
If that they myght, late or rathe; 6650

For they be not full pacient, 6635
That han the world thus foule blent.
And witeth wel that [ther] God bad 132v
The good man selle al that he had,
And folowe hym, and to pore it yeve, 6655
He wolde not therfore that he lyve
To serven hym in mendience,
For it was nevere his sentence;
But he bad wirken whanne that neede is,
And folwe hym in goode dedis. 6660
Seynt Poule, that loved al hooly chirche, 133r
He bade th'appostles for to wirche,
And wynnen her lyflode in that wise,
And hem defended truaundise,
And seide, 'Wirketh with youre honden.' 6665
Thus shulde the thing be undirstonden.

6639 **feble**] and f. UR   6645 **ye**] *om.* BE   6648 **And if**] If TH¹-SP³ FU; If that UR   6653 **that ther**] that MS-BE KA FU; that as MO; wher that SK; that though GL; that wher SU FI

6636–44   Ln Lc (11336–44n.) quote Guillaume de Saint-Amour, *De periculis* 12 (1632:52); Ln adds *Collectiones catholicae et canonicae scripturae* (1632:218) and notes that Denifle and Chatelain (ed. 1889–97:1.459n.) question the usual attribution to Guillaume. BE notes that "the book" (line 6636) appears to be Matt. 23.14, and RB RI, while they agree that the reference is "probably" (RB) or "perhaps" (RI) to that text, note that Guillaume de Saint-Amour expresses the same idea.

6643   "i.e., the able-bodied person who eats solicited food eats his own damnation" (FI).

6644   RI quotes the Fr. (Lc 11344 "se cil qui fist Adan ne ment" "if He who made Adam does not lie") and, following Lc (11344n.), notes that it is a "variation of the Pauline formula (Titus 1.2), 'Qui non mentitur deus' [God, who does not lie]."

6645–52   SK notes that this passage is not in the Fr. of Méon's ed. It is in none of the standard eds., but, as SK observes, appears in some MSS: κω λο (KA Fr. 11515–22); Be Bâ (Ln 11374t); Bu (SU Fr. 11374.B¹⁻⁸). § The content, as Ln Lc (11297–302n.) note, follows Guillaume de Saint-Amour, *De periculis* 12 (1632:49); cf. 6595–6602n.

6653–58   RI compares lines 6595–96 and the note. BE SK RB compare Matt. 19.21, and RB also compares *De periculis* 12 (1632:49); see 6595–6602n., 6595–97n.

6653   **that ther:** RB's emendation, suggested earlier by GL (see below). The various emendations all attempt to follow the subordinate structure of the Fr. (Lc 11345 "Et sachiez, la *ou* Dieu conmande . . ." "And know [that] there where God commands . . ."). KA recommends inserting "*though* before *god*"; GL so emends but notes that "*ther* (= where) would come closer to Fr. 'la au [*sic* for *ou*] Diex comande,'" and RB RI so emend. SKt RBt RIt also note the Fr. *la ou*. SK has *wher that* and SU FI have *that wher*; but, next to the word *that*, a scribe might more easily have omitted *ther* than *wher*.

6654   **good . . . that:** KA attributes to SK the suggestion "read *gode* and omit *that*," but no ed. so emends. GL RB cite the Fr. *preudon* (Lc 11346) as support for the hyphenated *good-man* (so printed in MO GL RB¹,² RI).

6655–56   **yeve : lyve:** See 2759–60n.

6661–66   Ln Lc (11353–58) quote Guillaume de Saint-Amour, *De periculis* 12 (1632:48–49). RB RI note that Guillaume quotes St. Paul, 1 Thess. 4.11–12.

6665–66   **honden : undirstonden:** KA suggests *honde : understonde*; although no ed. so emends, RB states that "*honden* is a strange archaism for the period and dialect; perhaps to be emended to *honde.*" Cf. 6592n.

6665   **Wirketh with youre honden:** See 6661–66n. BE states "It would not be easy to find any passage in which St. Paul commands the Apostles to work with their hands." Although the epistles are directed to the churches, not specifically the apostles, the churches contain members in the apostolic tradition, and 1 Thess. 4.11 (quoted by Guillaume de Saint-Amour), "work with your own hands, as we commanded you," seems a relevant source. SK suggests Eph. 4.28; but there, as BE notes elsewhere (see 6563–70n.), the recommendation of manual labor is for former thieves.

He nolde, iwys, have bidde hem begging,
Ne sellen gospel, ne prechyng,
Lest they berafte, with her askyng,
Folk of her catel or of her thing.   6670
For in this world is many a man
That yeveth his good, for he ne can
Werne it for shame, or ellis he
Wolde of the asker delyvered be.
And, for he hym encombrith so,   6675
He yeveth hym good to late hym go.
But it can hym nothyng profit;
They lese the yift and the meryt.
The good folk that Poule to preched
Profred hym ofte, whan he hem teched,   6680

Somme of her good in charite.
But therfore right nothing toke he;
But of his hondwerk wolde he gete
Clothes to wryne hym, and his mete."   6684
  "Telle me thanne how a man
          may lyven   133v
That al his good to pore hath yiven,
And wole but oonly bidde his bedis
[And never with hondes labour
          his nedes].   TH¹:163b
May he do so?"   MS:133v
  "Yhe, sir."
  "And how?"
  "Sir, I wole gladly telle yow: 6690

6667 **have**] *om.* SK   6679 **Poule**] St. P. UR   6682 **therfore**] therof TH³-BE SK RB¹-RI 6683 **hondwerk**] honde TH³ ST SP²·³; hondis UR   6688 **And never with hondes labour his nedes**] And wole but Only done that this MS₂; And wole but only done that . . . KA; A. n. w. honde l. h. nedis SK; A. n. w. h. l. h. nede is GL   *Out:* MS RI

6667   **have:** KA endorses SK's omission of this word.

6668   BE quotes 1 Cor. 9.14: "So also the Lord ordained that they who preach the gospel, should live by the gospel."

6671–78   Ln Lc (11364–70) quote Guillaume de Saint-Amour, *De periculis* 14 (1632:67); RB RI cite the same passage, but RI's page number 64 is probably an error for 67.

6677   **hym:** As RIt notes, GL RB have *bem*. GL adduces the Fr. plural pronoun *leur* (Lc 11369). See 1922n. for examples of *b(y,i)m* as pron. pl.

6679–84   Lc (11371–76) quotes Guillaume de Saint-Amour, *De periculis* 12 (1632:51). RI notes this citation, and SK RB RI compare Acts 20.33–35.

6682   **therfore:** TH³'s *therof* has been adopted by most subsequent eds., but the Fr. (Lc 11374 "n'i vosist il ja la main tendre" "he never would stretch out his hand [for, to] it") might favor the unemended form. See *OED Therefore* adv. 1. "for that (thing, act, etc.); for that, for it"; *MED ther-for(e* adv. 3. (a). SKt erroneously attributes *therof* to TH¹.

6684   BE notes that "in some instances St. Paul refused alms, but in others he asks his converts for contributions towards his necessities.—2 Cor. xi."

wryne: KA endorses SK's normalized *wryen*. *OED Wry* v.¹ gives *wr(y,i)ne* as 15th-century forms. Eds. gloss as "cover" (SPg et al.), "clothe" (RBg SK). Cf. 6795n., 6819n.

6685–92   Ln Lc (11377–86) quote Guillaume de Saint-Amour, *De periculis* 12 (1632:49–51); RB RI cite the same passage.

6685   BE SK supply speech-heading *Amour.*

6688   The text is based on TH¹, which follows ("nearly enough," says GL) the Fr. (Lc 11382 "sanz ja mes de mains laborer" "without ever working with his hands"). RI rejects the line as spurious, shows the lacuna by a line of dots, and supplies TH¹'s line in a footnote; see 892n. In MS, as KA notes, the line was "originally left blank" and filled in "by a later hand," but the words supplied are a partial repetition of the previous line. KA called the "last word illegible," but the letters *this* are fairly clear, if sprawling. The hand (MS₂c) is of the 16th century, perhaps later than the time of TH¹ (1532); it may be the same hand as that of lines 6786 and 7092, and different from those of line 5624 (MS₂b) or of lines 1892, 1984, 2036, 3490 (MS₂a). See above, "The Manuscript Hands: The Corrections."

hondes: SKt mistakenly represents TH¹ as spelling *hondis.*

nedes: In support of *nede is*, GL notes that "*labour* in sense of 'to labour for' is not otherwise known in M. E." *MED labouren* v. 6 "achieve (sth.) by work" quotes this passage along with one from Gower and four from the 15th century.

6689   **Yhe, sir:** BE SK supply speech-heading *F. Sem.*

Yhe: See 4659–60n.

And how: BE SK supply speech-heading *Amour.*

6690   BE SK supply speech-heading *F. Sem.*

Seynt Austyn seith a man may be
In houses that han proprete,
As Templers and Hospitelers,
And as these chanouns regulers,
Or white monkes or these blake—   6695
I wole no mo ensamplis make—
And take therof his sustenyng,
For therynne lyth no begging;
But other weys not, ywys,
[Yif] Austyn gabbith not of this.   6700
And yit full many a monke laboreth,

That God in hooly chirche honoureth;
For whanne her swynkyng is agone,
They rede and synge in chirche anone.
   "And for ther hat[h] ben gret discorde,   6705
As many a wight may bere recorde,
Upon the estate of mendiciens,
I wole shortly, in youre presence,
Telle how a man may begge at nede,   134r
That hath not wherwith hym to fede,   6710
Maugre his felones jangelyngis,
For sothfastnesse wole none hidyngis;

6695 **Or**] O. these UR   6697 **therof**] the t. TH³ ST   6700 **Yif**] Yit MS-KA FU   6705 **hath**] hat MS (MS₁ *corr.*)   6707 **mendiciens**] mendience SK GL RB¹·² RI   6711 **his**] this GL   **felones**] felowes TH¹-BE FU   6712 **sothfastnesse**] sothfastnesses TH³

6691–95 Ln (11414–15n.) SK RB RI note that the material on monastic life comes from Saint Augustine by way of Guillaume de Saint-Amour, *De periculis* 12 (1632:48) and *Responsiones* 7 (ed. Faral 1951:341). However, as SK RB note, the specific examples in lines 6693–95 are Jean de Meun's. Cf. 6705–66n.

6691 **Seynt Austyn:** As RB RI note, the standard Fr. has *de l'escriture* (Lc 11384–85 "of Scripture" or "of the text," i.e. Saint Augustine's *De opere monachorum*). SK adduces *De opere monachorum*, which "does not mention the Templars, &c.; these are only noticed by way of example." But some MSS read *Saint Augustin*: Za (Méon, Michel, KA Fr.); Be Bâ (Ln 11415t); Bu (SU Fr. 11415n.). Cf. 6699–6700n.

6692 RI notes, "communal property is permitted to those who have surrendered personal property to enter an order" like those in lines 6693–95. The friars, unlike the monks, had the theoretical ideal of communal as well as personal poverty.

6693 **Templers . . . Hospitelers:** "military religious orders formed in connection with the Crusades" (FI). URg, s.v. *Hospitaliers*, refers to this line but seems to conflate the two orders: "Knights Templars, or Knights of the Order of St. *John* of *Jerusalem*." The Knights Templars were founded 1119 (BE SK RB RI) by Hugh de Paganis (BE SK, quoting "Fuller, Holy Warre, 2.16, 5.2"). The Knights Hospitallers were founded ca. 1087 (RB RI; BE, quoting Fuller, says about 1099). TRg cites Du Cange, s.v. *Hospitalarius*. BE quotes passages from Fuller on both orders.

6694 **chanouns regulers:** BE SK RB FI RI identify the canons regular as canons living under a monastic rule; a canon was a member of the (usually secular) clergy attached to a cathedral. BE SK FI compare Chaucer's Canon, an Augustinian (*CYP* G 557; see Reidy's note, RI). BE, *CYP* G 557n., states that "the idea of making the cathedral clergy live together in common under a certain rule . . . appears to have originated with St. Augustin (*Aug. Serm.*, 49, *de Diversis*)."

6695 **white monkes:** Cistercians (BE SK RB FI RIf), "a reformed order of Benedictines" (BE SK RB).

blake: the original Benedictines (BE SK RB FI RIf).

6699–6700 Not in the Fr. (Méon, Michel, Ln, Lc). Ln (11422t) finds the two lines in MS Be ("Lors le porroit non autrement / Se sains Augustins ne me ment" "Otherwise one could not, if Augustine doesn't lie"), KA Fr. in MS κω (11571–72 "Quar l'en ne porroit autrement . . ."), SU Fr. in MS Bu. Cf. 6691n.

6700 **Yif:** KA's suggestion, for MS *Yit*, is based, presumably, on the Fr. *se* (Ln 11422t [see 6699–6700n.]; noted by GL).

6705–66 On the special cases in which a man may beg, Ln (11428–91n.) Lc (11407–61n.) quote Guillaume de Saint-Amour, *Responsiones* 7 (ed. Faral 1951:341–42). Guillaume cites these cases from Augustine, *De opere monachorum*.

6705 **hath:** second *h* written above the line by MS₁. KA does not note this correction.

6707 **mendiciens:** KA suggests *mendience* and, with SKt, compares line 6657. As a variant of *mendience*, this form is perhaps influenced by *mendicite*. *MED* does not list the form but (s.v. *mendience* n.) quotes this passage with the emended form.

6711 **maugre:** "*prep.* in spite of" (SKg₂).

his felones: TH¹'s *felowes* is probably a change made without reference to the Fr. (Lc 11403 "maugré les felonesses jangles" "in spite of any wicked cackle"), which supports MS. GL cites the Fr. also for the emendation of MS *his* to *this* (= these), perhaps closer, as RBt notes, to the Fr. *les*. *MED felonous* adj. shows neither the form *felones* nor this passage.

felones jangelyngis: "evil quarrelings" (FI). See *MED felonous* adj. (b).

6712 Proverbial; RB cites Haeckel (1890: no. 119), and RI cites Whiting (1968: S490).

And yit, percas, I may abey
That I to yow sothly thus sey.
  "Lo, heere the caas especial: 6715
If a man be so bestial
That he of no craft hath science,
And nought desireth ignorence,
Thanne may he go a-begging yerne,
Til he somme maner crafte kan lerne,   6720
Thurgh which without truaundyng,
He may in trouthe have his lyving.
  "Or if he may done no labour,
For elde, or sykenesse, or langour,
Or for his tendre age also,   6725
Thanne may he yit a-begging go.
  "Or if he have, peraventure,
Thurgh usage of his [noriture],
Lyved over delicously,
Thanne oughten good folk comunly   6730
Han of his myscheef somme pitee,
And suffren hym also that he
May gone aboute and begge his breed,   134v
That he be not for hungur deed.
  "Or if he have of craft kunnyng,   6735

And strengthe also, and desiryng
To wirken, as he had what,
But he fynde neithir this ne that,
Thanne may he begge til that he
Have geten his necessite.   6740
  "Or if his wynnyng be so lite
That his labour wole not acquyte
Sufficiantly al his lyvyng,
Yit may he go his breed begging;
Fro dore to dore he may go trace,   6745
Til he the remenaunt may purchace.
  "Or if a man wolde undirtake
Ony emprise for to make
In the rescous of our lay,
And it defenden as he may,   6750
Be it with armes or lettrure,
Or other covenable cure,
If it be so he pore be,
Thanne may he begge til that he
May fynde in trouthe for to swynke,   6755
And gete hym clothe[s], mete, and drynke,
Swynke he with his hondis corporell   135r
And not with hondis espirituell.

6713 **abey]** obey TH³-SP¹ UR   6720 **maner]** other TH³-UR   6728 **noriture]** norture MS BE-KA
6737 **To]** For to UR   6753 **so]** s. that UR   6756 **clothes]** clothe MS-SP³ BE-KA GL FU   6757 **his]** *om.*
KA-GL RB¹-FI   6758 **hondis]** his h. BE

6713–14 **I may abey / That . . . :** *I may abey,* 'I may suffer for it'; see Cant. Ta. C 100." (SK). "*abey,* suffer for" (FI; cf. URg TRg); "*abeye*: suffer" (RIf). The reading of SK RIf seems to take *abey* as intransitive, with *That* as a conj. FI's would take *abey* as transitive, with *That* as a relative pronoun (= "that which, what," *OED That* relative pron. 3); although FI's punctuation—a comma after *abey*—might seem to contradict the reading, the texts of RB RI, without the comma, seem to support it.
  6713 **abey:** *MED abeien* v., from Old Anglian *ābēgan* (WS *ābȳgan*), notes that the verb is "partly confused with *obeien*," from OF *obeïr.* The variant *obey* confirms this confusion.
  6718 **nought desireth ignorence:** FI paraphrases, "i.e., is not to blame"; the literal sense, "does not want ignorance," remains closer to the context, that of the cases in which one may beg.
  6728 **noriture:** KA notes TH¹'s emendation; although the MS form is normal for ME and not a substantive var., the emendation follows the Fr. *norreture* (Lc 11420) and improves rhyme and meter.
  6748 **Ony:** See 212n.
  6749 **rescous of our lay:** "defence of our law (faith, religion)" (SPg URg GL); "'rescue of our law (of faith)'; i.e. of Christianity" (SK); *rescous,* "service, endeavour to support" (SKg₂).
  6755 **May fynde:** "i.e., may find a way" (FI).
  6756 **clothes:** KA endorses (as SK's suggestion) UR's plural *clothis*; SKt compares line 6684. The Fr. has a different noun, *estovoirs* (Lc 11448 "needs").
  6757–58 **hondis corporell . . . hondis espirituell:** The word *corporell* does not appear in the Fr. (Lc 11449–50 "mes qu'il euvre des mains itex, / non pas des mains esperitex" "provided that he work with such hands, not with spiritual hands"). Following Ln (11479–80n.) and Lc (11449–50n.), RI notes that in some MSS there are two drawings, "a hand labeled 'manus corporalis' and a rectangular design containing the opening text of Genesis, labeled 'manus spiritualis.'" The drawings are reproduced by Langlois, who argues (11479–80n.) that they "must have been represented in the original manuscript; otherwise the word *iteus* ["of this sort"] would make no sense."
  6757 **Swynke he:** Perhaps subjunctive in inverted order to show condition, "If he work . . . ," rather than the imperative-equivalent (jussive subjunctive), "Let him work." GL RB RI, with commas at the end of the preceding line, favor the former, subordinate construction; BE MO SK SU FI, with periods, imply the latter, principal-clause

284

"In al [thise] caas, and in semblables,
If that ther ben mo resonables, 6760
He may begge, as I telle you heere,
And ellis nought, in no manere—
As William Seynt Amour wolde preche,
And ofte wolde dispute and teche
Of this mater all openly 6765
At Parys full solemply.
And, also God my soule blesse,
As he had in this stedfastnesse
The accorde of the universite
And of the puple, as semeth me. 6770
 "No good man oughte it to refuse,
Ne ought hym therof to excuse,

Be wrothe or blithe whoso be;
For I wole speke and telle it thee,
Al shulde I dye and be putt doun, 6775
As was Seynt Poule, in derke prisoun,
Or be exiled in this caas
With wrong, as Maister William was,
That my moder Ypocrysie
Banysshed for hir gret envye. 6780
 "Mi modir flemed hym, Seynt Amour; 135v
The noble dide such labour
To susteyne evere the loyalte,
That he to moche agilt me.
He made a book, and lete it write, 6785
[Wherin his lyfe he dyd al write], TH¹:164a

6759 **thise]** this MS-KA GL FU SU FI 6766 **full]** fully and UR 6773 **be]** thou b. UR 6782 **The noble]** This n. TH¹-SP³ SK FU SU FI; This n. man UR he beste myghte MS₂ KA; W. h. l. h. d. a. dite SP¹ UR 6786 **Wherin his lyfe he dyd al write]** Of thyngis that *Out:* MS RI

---

reading. In the Fr., Ln, with a period at the end of the preceding line, favors the principal-clause reading (Ln 11479 "Mais qu'il euvre" "But he should work"), while Lc, with comma, favors subordination (Lc 11449 "mes qu'il euvre" "provided that he work"). See Mossé (1968, secs. 126 [c], 158); Raynaud de Lage (1962:143).

 his: RIt notes that KA and SU mistakenly omit this word.

 6759 **thise:** KA's suggestion for MS *this*. GL notes that *this* is also a plural, and SU FI retain the form. As at lines 5301, 5791, the two forms are spelling variants in this line; see 5301n.

 6763 **William Seynt Amour:** Guillaume de Saint-Amour. Eds. note that he was a doctor of the Sorbonne in the middle of the 13th century, that his principal treatise against the mendicant orders, *De periculis novissimorum temporum*, evoked responses from Saint Thomas Aquinas and Saint Bonaventura and was condemned in 1256 by Pope Alexander IV (who asked King Louis IX to banish Guillaume from France). RB notes that "the statement in ll. 6769 ff. as to the sympathies of the university and community of Paris seems to be substantially true." For documentation, SK cites Méon's note (ed. 1814:2.355), which stems from Lantin de Damerey (1737, 1799); RB RI cite Ln's notes (11506n., 11513n.); see also Lc 11476n. In the autumn of 1256, at Anagni, Guillaume pleaded his answers to the charges of the friars in the *Responsiones* (the "Articuli" of Dufeil 1972:287–91); although he was acquitted of the specific charges, the previous condemnation of the *De periculis* stood, as well as the king's banishment, and Guillaume apparently spent the rest of his life in Saint-Amour, at that time outside the borders of France. For the fullest analysis of the controversy, see Dufeil (1972). Szittya (1986) explores the influence of Guillaume de Saint-Amour's antifraternalism on English ecclesiology and poetry. On Jean's indebtedness to Guillaume de Saint-Amour, see 6544–7692n. and the notes thereafter.

 6778 **Maister William:** Guillaume de Saint-Amour. See 6763n.

 6782 **The noble:** KA notes TH¹'s *This*, but SK RB RI note the Fr. *le vaillant home* (Lc 11480 "the brave man"), which might favor the definite article over the demonstrative adj.

 6784 **agilt me:** RI quotes the Fr. (Lc 11482 "Vers ma mere [var. A moi] trop mesprenoit" "He committed too great an offense against my mother [me]"). KA Fr. does not have the var., which accounts for the ME; Ln 11512t records it in MS Be; SU Fr. 11512n. takes the var. *Vers moi* from MS Bu. RI notes further, "Since Fals-Semblant often directly expresses the views of Jean de Meun, one must recall from time to time that he is in fact a villain on the side of hypocrisy." One might note also the ironic use of the confessional mode (Dahlberg 1988:120–21).

 6785 **a book:** "*De periculis*, by William of Seynt Amour" (RIf).

 6786 The text is based on TH¹, which follows the Fr. (Lc 11484 "ou sa vie fist toute escrivre" "in which he had his entire life written"). In MS, as KA notes, the line was "originally left blank" and filled in "by a later hand," but the text does not follow the Fr (*MS₂c*) is perhaps later than TH¹ (1532); see 6688n. Kaluza argues elsewhere (1893*b*:110) that, as at lines 6205 and 6318, Thynne restored the line "with the help of the French original." BE states that "in the MS. this line is erased" and the existing words "written over it"; and notes that "Speght's reading [from TH¹] agrees with the original." David (RI) omits the line as spurious in both TH¹ and the MS₂c version; he suggests (RIt) that "a better line would be *Wher he his lyf did al endite*."

  al write: KA suggests *endite* for *al write*, and RBt says that "perhaps *endite* should be substituted for *write*."

And wolde ich reneyed begging,   MS:135v
And lyved by my traveylyng,
If I ne had rent ne other goode.
What? Wened he that I were woode?   6790
For labour myght me never plese.
I have more wille to bene at ese,
And have wel lever, soth to sey,
Bifore the puple patre and prey,
And wrie me in my foxerie   6795
Under a cope of papelardie."
   Quod Love, "What devel is this that I heere?
What wordis tellest thou me heere?"
  "What, sir?"
  "Falsnesse, that apert is;
Thanne dredist thou not God?"
  "No, certis;   6800

For selde in grete thing shal he spede
In this world, that God wole drede.
For folk that hem to vertu yeven,
And truly on her owne lyven,   6804
And hem in goodnesse ay contene,   136r
On hem is lytel thrift sene.
Such folk drinken gret mysese;
That lyf may me never plese.
But se what gold han usurers,
And silver eke in [her] garners,   6810
Taylagiers, and these monyours,
Bailifs, bedels, provost, countours;
These lyven wel nygh by ravyne.
The smale puple hem mote enclyne,
And they as wolves wole hem eten.   6815
Upon the pore folk they geten

6787 **ich]** eche TH³-SP³; that eche UR   6788 **lyved]** lyue TH³-SP³; livin UR   6790 **Wened]** weneth TH¹-UR FU SU FI   6796 **papelardie]** paperlardie MS KA   6797 **this that]** that SP¹; this UR SK   6799 **Falsnesse]** Why Falsenesse UR   6805 **contene]** contente TH³-UR   6806 **sene]** isente ST-UR   6808 **may]** ne m. UR MO SK   6810 **her]** *om.* MS-SP³ BE KA FU RI   6812 **provost]** Provostes UR

6787 **ich reneyed:** "that I should renounce" (SK).
6790–96 BE notes the resemblance to "the account given of himself by the Pardonere" (*PardP* C 439–53).
6794 **patre:** to pray in the sense of repeating the Pater Noster, the Lord's Prayer (URg et al.). Cf. 7241n.
6795 **wrie:** "hide" (URg), "cover" (TRg), "disguise" (SKg₂). See also 6684n., 6819n.
    foxerie: RB FI note the Fr. *renardie* (Lc 11493 "foxiness").
6796 **papelardie:** SK recalls the earlier figure of Poope Holy (Lc 407 "Papelardie" "hypocrisy") on the wall of the garden; see 415n.
6797 **What devel:** "What the devil" (RB).
    this that: KA endorses SK's omission of *that*; UR had so emended earlier.
6799 **What, sir:** BE SK supply speech-heading *F. Sem.*
    Falsnesse: SK supplies speech-heading *Amour.*
6800 **Thanne dredist:** BE supplies speech-heading *Amour.*
    No, certis: BE SK supply speech-heading *F. Sem.*
6802 **world:** "as in v. 6843 the metre requires two syllables" (GL). Disyllabic pronunciation of MS *world* is possible, but TH¹⁻³ MO GL FU SU FI have *worlde.*
6803–04 **yeven : lyven:** See 2759–60n.
6804 **on her owne:** RB¹ RI cite Fr. *dou leur* (Ln = Lc 11502 "du leur" "of their own possessions" [RI]); RB² misprints *dou leur* as *douleur.*
6808 **may:** KA endorses SK's *ne may*, an emendation that first appears in UR.
6810 "i.e. their garners contain things of value" (SK).
    her: KA notes *her* in MO, but UR earlier had inserted *ther*, perhaps on the basis of the Fr. *leur* (Lc 11508; noted by GL RBt SU FI).
6811 **Taylagiers:** tax or toll gatherers or collectors (URg et al.). SK points out that the Fr. has no parallel (Lc 11509 "faussonier et termaieür" "counterfeiters and usurers") and compares *taillage* "tax, tribute" in *Piers Plowman* C 22.37 [21.37].
    monyours: "coyners" (SPg et al.), "money changers" (GLg); "bankers" (FI RIf), "money dealers" (RIf). Although the loose semantic parallel in the Fr. is *termaieür* (above), the form parallels the Fr. var. of *faussonier, Faus monnoier* "counterfeiters," which Ln notes in MSS C He (11539t) and which TRg adduces for the sense "coiners."
6812 **provost:** "prefect" (SKg₂ RBg), "praetor" (RBg), "magistrate" (RBg RIf), "overseer" (FI). The form, influenced probably by the Fr. pl. *prevost* (Lc 11510), may be plural as well as singular (*MED provost* n.).
6814 "The poor people must bow down to them" (SK).

Full moche of that they spende or kepe.
Nis none of hem that he nyl strepe
And wrine hemsilf wel at full;
Without scaldyng they hem pull.   6820
The stronge the feble overgoth;
But I, that were my symple cloth,
Robbe both robb[ed] and robbours,
And gile gil[ed] and gilours.
   "By my treget I gadre and threste   6825
The gret tresour into my cheste,

That lyth with me so fast bounde.
Myn high paleys do I founde,
And my delites I fulfille   136v
With wyne at feestes at my wille,   6830
And tables full of entremees;
I wole no lyf but ese and pees,
And wynne gold to spende also.
For whanne the gret bagge is go,
It cometh right with my japes.   6835
Make I not wel tumble myn apes?

6818 **he]** thei UR   6819 **hemsilf]** him-self SK RB¹-FI   **at]** atte SK GL RB¹,² RI   6823 **robbed]** robbyng MS-SP¹ MO KA FU   6824 **giled]** giling MS-SP³ MO KA FU; the g. UR   6828 **Myn]** Thus myn UR   6834 **go]** ago UR   6835 **right]** full r. UR

6818 The phrase "none of hem" is a confusing translation that combines the two referents, the spoilers and the poor, from the Fr. *nus . . . nes* (Lc 11515 "n'est nus qui despoillier nes voille" "There is no one [*nus*] who will not despoil them [*nes* = *ne les*]"). For *he* and *strepe*, see below. *Nyl* (*ne wyl*) may be either sing. or pl. (*OED Will* v.¹ A. 2, 4). The difficulties in the ME stem from the shift in the Fr. from plural subjects (Lc 11508–14) to singular (11515) and back to plural (11516).

    he: Probably this is an erroneous singular without antecedent (= one of the spoilers, the *they* of the preceding lines); as such, it was probably influenced by the preceding phrase, "none of hem," where, however, the referent of *hem* is "the poor" (FI). The form *he* may be plural (*MED he* pron.[3]), but the form *they* is used for the same referent (the spoilers) in the preceding lines and is the normal plural throughout. See above and 6819n.

    strepe: "rob" (SPg), "strip" (SPg et al.), "fleece" (SKg₂).

6819 **wrine:** "cover himself, clothe himself" (SK; SKg₂ cites the Fr. "s'afublent" = Lc 11516). SK RB RI respell as *wr(i,y)en* (OE *wreon*); GL suggests "(?) *wreen*" and notes that "the scribe frequently confuses *i* and *e*." See 6684n., 6795n.

    hemsilf: KA endorses SK's *him-self.* While *hem* may be a singular form (see 2854n., 4267n.), SK RB¹-FI take it as plural and emend to *him-s(i,e)lf(e)*, to show concord with *he* of the preceding line. SU notes the Fr. (Lc 11516 "tuit s'affublent de leur despoille" "all clothe themselves in their spoil"), which explains the shift from sing. to pl. See 6818n.

    at: KA suggests *atte.*

6820 "False-Semblant says that these usurers, tax-gatherers, and the rest, fleece the people no less effectually than if they scalded them as a butcher does a hog" (BE). BE SK note the "allusion to the common practice of scalding a hog to make the hair come off easily" (BE); FI notes that "it is customary to scald a fowl before plucking it." In reading the line as "they do not scald them before skinning, as a butcher does a hog," RB RIf suggest that the scalding is for skinning, rather than for plucking the hair (bristles) of the hog, a step preliminary to skinning. They may have been misled by SK's gloss, "*pulle,* strip them, skin them."

6823–24 **robbed . . . giled:** The emendations, noted by KA in UR BE, follow the Fr. (Lc 11521–22 "lobant lobez et lobeürs, / robe robez et robeeurs" "deceiving deceived and deceivers, [I] rob the robbed and the robbers"; noted in SU-RIt); the ME inverts the two lines and modifies the syntax slightly. The MS forms in *-ing* may stem from Fr. *lobant.* RB notes that Ln (11551–52n.) "compares Rustebuef, Estat du Monde, lines 43–46"; see Rutebeuf (ed. Faral and Bastin 1959–60:1.384).

6824 "'And beguile both deceived men and deceivers'" (SK). RI compares line 5759.

    giled: See 6823–24n.

6831 **entremees:** "dainty dishes" (URg, noting Fr. origin); "choice dishes served in between the courses at a feast" (TRg et al.; TRg SK cite Cotgrave 1611); "delicacies" (RIf).

6834–35 "For, when the great bag (of treasure) is empty, it comes right again (i.e. is filled again) by my tricks" (SK; BE FI have similar notes).

6834 **is go:** "is empty" (RIf); RI quotes the Fr. *soit vuiz* (Lc 11532 "be empty").

6835 **It cometh right:** "i.e, it is replenished" (RB RIf). RB compares *GP* 705.

    right: KA attributes to Skeat the suggestion *right yet,* but no ed. so emends.

6836 "i.e., don't I make my apes obey (tumble) well?" (FI).

To wynnen is alwey myn entent;
My purchace is bettir than my rent.
For though I shulde beten be,
Overal I entremete me;   6840
Without me may no wight dure;
I walke soules for to cure.
Of al the world cure have I
In brede and lengthe; boldly
I wole bothe preche and eke counceilen.   6845
With hondis wille I not traveilen,
For of the Pope I have the bull;

I ne holde not my wittes dull.
I wole not stynten in my lyve
These emperours for to shryve,   6850
[Or] kyngis, dukis, lordis grete.
But pore folk al quyte I lete;
I love no such shryvyng, parde,   137r
But it for other cause be.
I rekke not of pore men;   6855
Her astate is not worth an hen.
Where fyndest thou a swynker of labour
Have me unto his confessour?

6839 **I]** that I UR   6843 **cure]** the c. UR RB[1,2]   6844 **lengthe]** eke in l. UR   6851 **Or]** Of MS-UR
FU   **lordis]** and l. TH[1]-BE SK FU-FI; or l. MO   6855 **pore]** these p. UR   6858 **unto]** to TH[3]-SP[3]; to be UR

6837   RB FI RI compare *PardP* C 403.

6838   BE quotes the Fr. (Lc 11536 "mieuz vaut mes porchaz que ma rente" "my acquisitions are worth more than my regular income") and, with SK GL, notes the version in *FrT* D 1451 "My purchas is th'effect of al my rente." RB FI RI compare the closer parallel at *GP* 256 "His purchas was wel bettre than his rente." FI takes *My purchace* as "what I buy," but RIf glosses *purchace* as "total income," as opposed to *rente* "proper income."

6841–48   RI notes that these lines are not in the Fr. Ln (11568t, 11568–69n.) shows a ten-line variant text from MSS B, subsequently added in the margin of MS La: "[1] Tu sembles šainz on.—Certes voire. / [2] Ordener me fis a prouvoire, / [3] S'oi la suite de tout le monde, / [4] Tant come il dure la reonde; / [5] Par tout vois les ames curer, / [6] Nus ne peut mais sanz moi durer / [7] Et preeschier et conseillier. / [8] Senz jamais des mains traveillier. / [9] De l'apostole en ai la bule, / [10] Qui ne me tient pas pour entule." ("[1] You seem a holy man. True indeed. [2] I have fixed myself up as a priest [3] and I am followed by everyone in the world [4] as long as it stays round; [5] I go everywhere in my cure of souls [6]—no one can endure without me—[7] and I preach and counsel [8] without ever working with my hands. [9] I have the bull from the apostle [pope], [10] who doesn't consider me stupid.")

Of these ten lines, our text omits the first two, while lines 6841–44 correspond to 6, 5, 3, (4?) of the Fr. var., and lines 6845–48 to 7–10. KA Fr. follows the Michel text, roughly the same as above but without the first two lines; where Michel has "Sui le curé" for "S'oi la suite" in line 3, KA Fr. reads "S'ai la cure" from MS κω. SU Fr. (note to 11568 B[1–8]) states that MSS B κω have the ten lines, that the ME omits the first two, and that the order is different in the ME. This difference, says SU, suggests that the ME equivalents of the Fr. lines "were inserted by the reviser, who was uncertain what to do at this point. Had the original translator been following one of the MSS with the ten extra lines, then the whole ten would probably be in their proper order in the *Romaunt*."

6843–45   RI punctuates with a semicolon after line 6843 and thus takes the phrase *In brede and lengthe* as a modifier in the following clause.

6843   **world:** See 6802n.

          cure: KA notes UR's *the cure* and compares line 7680.

6845–46   RB FI RI compare *PardP* C 443–44.

6847   BE identifies the bull as the one "by which the Pope granted extraordinary jurisdiction to the friars, or mendicants, who thus became a sort of home-missionaries, independent of the bishops and parish-priests." The bull envisaged may be Alexander IV's *Quasi lignum vitae* (1255; ed. Denifle and Chatelain 1889–97:1.279–85; see Dufeil 1972:152–56); if, however, the interpolation is to be associated with the one at Ln 11222–23n., it may reflect Martin IV's bull *Ad fructus uberes* (1281; ed. Denifle and Chatelain 1889–97:1.592); see 6361–6472n.

6849   **in my lyve:** "That is, 'as long as I live'" (BE).

6851   **Or:** BE's emendation of MS *Of* follows Fr. *ou* (Lc 11541 "or"). KA inadvertently substitutes this emendation for the MS form. SU FI note misleadingly that TH[1] omits *Or*, and RIt reports only that TH[1] has the variant *Of*.

6852   **quyte:** FI suggests "quiet (i.e., unabsolved of their sins)"; but the form is not that of the adj. *quiet*. *MED quit(e* cites this form as the adv. "completely."

6856   **hen:** See 4830n.; and cf. *GP* 177, cited in 6191n.

6857   **a:** KA suggests omitting this word, but no ed. so emends.

288

"But emperesses and duchesses,
Thise queenes and eke countesses,   6860
Thise abbessis and eke bygyns,
These gret ladyes palasyns,
These joly knyghtis and baillyves,
Thise nonnes, and thise burgeis wyves
That riche ben and eke plesyng,   6865
And thise maidens welfaryng,
Wherso they clad or naked be,
Uncounceiled goth ther noon fro me.

And, for her soules savete,
At lord and lady and her meyne,   6870
I axe, whanne thei hem to me shryve,
The proprete of al her lyve,
And make hem trowe, bothe meest and leest,
[Hir] paroch prest nys but a beest
Ayens me and my companye,   6875
That shrewis ben as gret as I,
Fro whiche I wole not hide in holde   137v
No pryvete that me is tolde,

6860   **countesses**] thise c. SK   6862   **These**] And t. UR   6871   **hem**] han SU FI   6874   **Hir**] His
MS   **nys**] is TH³-UR   6877   **Fro**] For TH¹-SP³ BE MO SK FU SU FI

6859–72   On the friars' tendency to hear the confessions of females and the rich, Ln (11588–90n.) Lc (11547n., 11557–60n.) quote Guillaume de Saint-Amour, *De periculis* 5 (1632:32). BE quotes *The Testament of Love* (2.2, ed. Skeat 1897:51) and *Jack Upland* (25, ed. Skeat 1897:194); of these, only the latter refers to abuses by the friars.
6860–66   On the form *thise*, see 5301n.
6861   **bygyns:** Beguines. Francis Thynne (1599;1875:37–38), objecting to SP¹'s gloss of *bigin* as "superstitious hypocrite," writes that they are "supersticious or hipocriticall wemenne"; he adduces this passage as well as line 7366; and he quotes Matthew of Westminster's account of the Beguines. SP²·³g partly concede Thynne's point by adding "or hypocriticall woman" to the earlier gloss. BE, citing Du Cange, says that the name is derived from the "founder, St. Begga, or Begghe, Duchess of Brabant"; but see below. SK RB FI identify the Beguines as members of a lay sisterhood. RI, citing McDonnell (1954), describes the Beguines as follows: "laywomen who led religious lives but took no vows except that of chastity and followed no fixed rule. Some lived in small groups, others in larger communities, still others alone. The movement sprang up in the latter half of the twelfth century, perhaps first at Liège, but almost simultaneously elsewhere in the low countries and the Rhine valley where it was concentrated. The name, probably given to it by its detractors, had previous associations of heresy. By the mid-thirteenth century the Beguines had acquired an unsavory reputation. Cf. 7254 below."
6862   **ladyes palasyns:** "ladies connected with the court" (SK; GL RB FI RI annotate similarly). SK RB RI note the Fr. (Lc 11549 "dames palatines") and SK FI note the connection to the words *palace* (Fr. *palais*), *palatine.*
6867   **Wherso:** In MS, above and below the space between the *r* and the *s*, appear two short vertical ticks. If these are printer's marks to show space, they would strengthen Blodgett's argument that MS was printer's copy for TH¹, which separates the two elements, *Where so.* KA prints the two elements separately, *Wher so*, but they are separated in MS only by the two vertical ticks.
          clad or naked: "i.e., under all circumstances" (RB); RB RI adduce the notes to *GP* 534 on other formulations for this general sense.
6871–72   RB notes that "on the prying inquisitiveness of the friars Langlois [Ln 11588–90n.] cites De periculis," 5 (1632:32); RI compares the same passage.
6871   **hem:** While *han* (SU FI) makes sense, it seems to have arisen from Sutherland's misreading of his base text, TH¹, which, like MS, reads *hem.*
6872   FI paraphrases, "their whole lives as recompense," and quotes the Fr. (Lc 11560 "les proprietez et les vies" "properties and lives"); perhaps the ME has rather the sense, "their lifelong accumulations, their life savings."
6874–75   BE compares *SumT*; see D 1923–47. RB RI compare *De periculis* 4 (1632:30 [not 12, as in RB RI]).
6874   **Hir:** TH¹'s emendation (*Her*) may reflect the Fr. *leur* (Lc 11562 "their"). KA, however, misreads MS *His* as *Hir*, MS *his* probably anticipates *nys* in the same line.
          paroch: See 6384n.
6875–76   **companye : I:** See 6111–12n.
6875   **Ayens:** "In comparison with" (BE SK RB RIf), "compared to" (FI); see 5536n.
6877–78   On the revelation of secrets from the confession, BE notes that Jean de Meun "lays to [the friars'] charge one of the most heinous offences against the law of the church"; and further that "the obligation to secrecy . . . appears to be recognized by the law of England."

That I by word or signe, ywis,
Wole make hem knowe what it is.　　6880
And they wolen also tellen me;
They hele fro me no pryvyte.
　　"And for to make yow hem perceyven,
That usen folk thus to disceyven,
I wole you seyn, withouten drede,　　6885
What men may in the gospel rede
Of Seynt Mathew, the gospelere,
That seith as I shal you sey heere:
　　"'Uppon the chaire of Moyses'—
Thus is it glosed, doutles,　　6890
That is the Olde Testament,
For therby is the chaire ment—
'Sitte Scr[i]bes and Pharisen'—
That is to seyn, the cursid men
Whiche that we ypocritis calle.　　6895
'Doth that they preche, I rede you alle,
But doth not as they don a dele,

That ben not wery to seye wele,
But to do wel no will have they.
And they wolde bynde on folk alwey,　　6900
That ben to be giled able,　　138r
Burdons that ben importable;
On folkes shuldris thinges they couchen
That they nyl with her fyngris touchen.'"
　　"And why wole they not touche it?"
　　"Why?　　6905
For hem ne lyst not, sikirly;
For sadde burdons that men taken
Make folkes shuldris aken.
And if they do ought that good be,
That is for folk it shulde se.　　6910
Her [bordurs] larger maken they,
And make her hemmes wide alwey,
And loven setes at the table,
The firste and most honourable;
And for to han the first chaieris　　6915

6880 **Wole**] Ne wol TH¹-UR SK-RI　　6890 **is it**] it is TH¹-UR FU SU FI　　6893 **Scribes**] Scrbes MS
6900 **on**] no TH³-SP¹　　6901 **giled**] beguiled SP²-UR SK RB¹·² RI　　6907 **sadde**] the s. UR　　6911 **bordurs**]
burdons MS-SK FU　　6914 **most**] the m. UR

6879–80 **That . . . Wole:** If we read *That* as a conj. ("so that," *OED That* conj. 4. b) rather than as a relative
pron. with the antecedent *pryvete*, it is unnecessary to emend *Wole* to *Ne wol* or *Nil*. See 6880n. The ME does not
follow the construction of the Fr. Ln (11596t) notes the added lines in MSS Ba Be ("Ou par paroles bien ouvertes /
Ou par autres signes couvertes" "Either by quite open speech or by other, hidden signs"). KA (Fr. 11755–56) takes
the same lines from MS κω, SU (Fr. 11596 B¹·²) from Ba, Bu.

6880 **Wole:** TH¹, taking *That* in the previous line as a relative pron., emends to *Ne wol*; KA endorses SK's
recommendation, "Read *Nel* or *Nil*" and notes the TH¹ form; SK GL RB have *Nil* or *Nyl*. As SU notes, GL "errs in
noting" that TH¹ "reads *Wol*."

6887 Eds. note the source in Matt. 23.1–8 (BE SK GL Lc [11572–606n.]); or 1–8, 13–15 (Ln [11601–36n.,
11609–10n.] RB FI RI). RI notes that this was "a favorite text against hypocrites." Lc notes that John of Salisbury had
already cited this passage in *Policraticus* 7.21 (ed. Webb 1909:2.194, 5–6; trans. Dickinson 1927:314); cf.
6135–7334n.

6888 **you sey:** KA suggests *seye you*, but no ed. so emends.

6893 **Scribes:** MS omits the *i* but has a diagonal hairline "dot" over the *r*, all eds., including KA, print the *i*.
　　Pharisen: KA suggests *pharisien*, but no ed. so emends.

6900 **wolde:** KA suggests *wole*, but no ed. so emends.

6901 **be giled:** KA notes *be begilid* in UR, an emendation appearing first in SP².

6902 **burdons:** KA suggests *Burthens* or *Burdens* here and also for lines 6907, 6911; SK adopts the latter
form.

6905 **And why . . . it:** BE SK supply speech-heading *Amour*.
　　Why: BE SK supply speech-heading *F. Sem.*

6911 **bordurs:** KA suggests retention of MS *burdons*, respelled *burthens* or *burdens*, as at lines 6902, 6907.
Skeat (SK) prints *burdens* but notes that it is "repeated from ll. 6902, 6907" and that it "is clearly wrong. Perhaps," he
suggests, "read *borders*; F. 'philateres'"; GL RB¹-RI adopt SK's suggestion (as *bordurs*) and also cite the Fr. (Lc 11595).
Like SK, SU notes that *burdons* is "repeated erroneously from 6906 [*sic* for 6907]." FI explains as "borders of their
garments, on which were phylacteries (charms)" (so, in substance, RIf).

6912 **hemmes:** "hems of their garments, or phylacteries, upon which, in accordance with the law of Moses
(Num. xv. 38) were written texts from the Old Testament.—See Matt. xxiii. 6 [*sic* for 5?]. They were also called
Tephilli" (BE). SK takes the phylacteries as being *on* the hems, or borders. Cf. 6911n.

In synagogis, to hem full deere is;
And willen that folk hem loute and grete,
Whanne that they passen thurgh the strete,
And wolen be cleped 'maister' also.
But they ne shulde not willen so; 6920
The gospel is ther-ageyns, I gesse,
That shewith wel her wikkidnesse.
"Another custome use we:
Of hem that wole ayens us be, 6924
We hate hym deedly everichone, 138v
And we wole werrey hym as oon.
Hym that oon hatith, hate we alle,
And congecte hou to done hym falle.
And if we seen hym wynne honour,
Richesse, or preis, thurgh his valour, 6930
Provende, rent, or dignyte,
Full fast, iwys, compassen we
Bi what ladder he is clomben so;
And for to maken hym doun to go,
With traisoun we wole hym defame, 6935
And done hym leese his good name.
Thus from his ladder we hym take,
And thus his freendis foes we make;
But word ne wite shal he noon,

Till all hise freendis ben his foon. 6940
For if we dide it openly,
We myght have blame redily;
For hadde he wist of oure malice,
He hadde hym kept, but he were nyce.
"Another is this, that if so falle 6945
That ther be oon amonge us alle
That doth a good turne, out of drede,
We seyn it is oure alder deede.
Yhe, sikerly, though he it feyned, 139r
Or that hym list, or that hym deyned 6950
A man thurgh hym avaunced be;
Therof all parseners be we,
And tellen folk, whereso we go,
That man thurgh us is sprongen so.
And for to have of men preysyng, 6955
We purchace, thurgh oure flateryng,
Of riche men of gret pouste
Lettres to witnesse oure bounte,
So that man weneth, that may us see,
That all vertu in us be. 6960
And alwey pore we us feyne;
But how so that we begge or pleyne,
We ben the folk, without lesyng,

6927 **hatith]** heteth SP¹ 6931 **rent]** or r. UR 6942 **myght]** wight SP¹ 6952 **parseners]** parteners
SP¹-UR 6957 **pouste]** posteritie SP¹ 6959 **weneth]** wenneth TH³ ST

6917 **willen:** KA suggests *wille,* but no ed. so emends.
6919 **wolen:** KA suggests *wole,* but no ed. so emends.
     maister: Cf. Matt. 23.7–10; Guillaume de Saint-Amour, *Collectiones* (1632:396–408). BE adduces *SumT*
D 2186–87.
6923–36   Following Ln (11637–49n.), RB RI compare *De periculis* 14 (1632:69).
6925–26   **hym . . . hym:** "them . . . them." Some eds. respell as *hem,* the usual form of the 3 pl. object
personal pron. (line 6925: SP²,³ SK RB¹-RI; line 6926: SK RB¹-RI); KA also suggests *hem.* See 1922n.
6926   **werrey:** See 3251n.
       as oon: GL RB note the Fr. *par acort* (Lc 11610 "by agreement"), and GL suggests "? *at oon.*"
6948   **oure alder:** "of us all" (SK RB RIf). RB RI compare *GP* 586, and RB explains in the note to that line that
"*aller* (*alder*) is the old genitive plural (AS. 'ealra')." FI also notes the archaic genitive.
6949   **Yhe:** See 4659–60n.
6950   **hym deyned:** "he vouchsafed" (GL, cf. URg, s.v. *deine*); "It appeared good to him" (SKg₂). On the
impersonal construction, see *MED deinen* v.(1), sense 1. (b).
6952   **parseners:** "partners" (SK FI RIf). The variant *parteners,* with the same meaning, arose as a blend of
parcener and *part* n. (*OED Partner* sb., *MED partener(e* n.). Jephson (BE) observes that "Speght reads *parteners;* but
perseners is the old form," and he quotes the Fr. *parçonier* (Lc 11636 "participants"); his supposition that "*persener*
also means a parson" is corrected by *MED parcener* n. (a), which glosses BE's citation from Usk, *Testament of Love,*
2.2.49, as "partaker, sharer." SU errs slightly in noting that "G. [MS] has *perseners* for *parceners*"; rather than *per-,* MS
has the crossed-p abbreviation, which stands, as usual, for *p-vowel-r.*
6963–64   BE notes that "*False-Semblant* appears to forget that he is applying to the friars what St. Paul said of
himself and the other apostles.— 2 Cor. vi. 10." SK also identifies the Scriptural source. The apparent forgetting is
probably part of the ironic stance; Guillaume de Saint-Amour's argument was that the friars, in claiming apostolic
status, were pseudo-apostles; see *De periculis* 14 (1632:57–72), portions of which are translated by Miller (1977:246–50).

That all thing have without havyng.
Thus be we dred of the puple, iwis.　6965
And gladly my purpos is this:
I dele with no wight, but he
Have gold and tresour gret plente.
Her acqueyntaunce wel love I;
This is moche my desire, shortly.　6970
I entremete me of brokages,
I make pees and mariages,
I am gladly executour,　139v
And many tymes a procuratour;
I am somtyme messager—　6975
That fallith not to my myster;
And many tymes I make enquestes—
For me that office not honest is.
To dele with other mennes thing,
That is to me a gret lykyng.　6980
And if that ye have ought to do

In place that I repeire to,
I shal it speden, thurgh my witt,
As soone as ye have told me it.
So that ye serve me to pay,　6985
My servyse shal be youre alway.
But whoso wole chastise me,
Anoon my love lost hath he;
For I love no man, in no gise,
That wole me repreve or chastise.　6990
But I wolde al folk undirtake,
And of no wight no teching take;
For I, that other folk chastie,
Wole not be taught fro my folie.
　"I love noon hermitage more;　6995
All desertes and holtes hore,
And gret wodes everichon,　140r
I lete hem to the Baptist John.
I quethe hym quyte and hym relese

6965 **we**] *om.* ST-UR　6970 **is moche**] m. TH³-SP³; m. i. UR　6974 **a**] *om.* SK GL RB¹·² RI
6975 **messager**] a m. UR　6976 **fallith**] falseth TH²　6977 **enquestes**] enqueste TH¹-UR FU SU FI
6978 **not honest is**] i. n. h. TH¹-UR FU SU FI　6986 **youre**] yours TH¹-UR FU SU FI　6991 **wolde**] wol
TH³-UR　6995 **I**] I Ne UR　6999 **and hym**] a. hem FU

6965–70　Not in the Fr. texts of Méon, Michel, Ln Lc. Ln (11678t) gives a six-line var. text from MSS B (added later in La). KA Fr. supplies from κω, SU Fr. from Bu.

6970　GL quotes the Fr. (KA Fr. 11844 "Ce sont auques tuit mi desir" "They are all my desires").

　This is: KA suggests omitting *is* and compares line 6452 (see note), where *This* = *This is.*

6971–86　Lc (11649–62n.) quotes Guillaume de Saint-Amour, *De periculis* 12 (1632:48).

6971　**brokages:** In the general sense, "meanes (spokesmen)" (SPg SP²·³g), "Broker's, Factor's or any Agent's Business, or Profit" (URg), "treaty by a broker or agent" (TRg), "contracts" (SKg₂), "making deals" (FI RIf), "use of go-betweens" (RIf); more specifically, "pimping" (URg), "match-making" (SK RB). Skeat (SK) adduces his note (1886*b*:2.34) to *Piers Plowman* C 3.92 (B 2.87) [C 2.92; B 2.88] and compares *GP* 212, as has BE for the next line, on making marriages.

6973　**executour:** "executor (of wills)" (SKg₂ RB RIf), Fr. *execucions* (Lc 11651). As RB RI note, Ln (11681n.) cites Rutebeuf, *Vie dou monde* 103–04 [131–32] (ed. Faral and Bastin 1959–60:1.398 [405]).

6974　**a:** KA suggests omitting this word. GL notes that "the scribe frequently inserts *a* in such cases."

6976　"I.e., 'yet it is no real business of mine'" (SK); "is not suitable occupation (skill)" (FI).

　myster: "occupation" (SPg et al.), "profession or trade" (URg TRg SKg₂).

6978　**honest:** "honourable, (creditable)" (URg-BEg); "becoming a person of rank" (BEg; cf. RBg, *MED honest(e* adj. 2. [c]). FI's gloss, "profitable," is a connotation.

6986　**youre:** "yours." See Mossé (1968:59, sec. 68, Remark V).

6987–94　Ln Lc (11663–70n.) quote Guillaume de Saint-Amour, *De periculis* 2 [not 1, as Ln says] (1632:21). RB RI (6993–94n.) compare the same passage and, like Ln, mistake the chapter number as 1 rather than 2.

6995–7008　BE notes the distinction between the monks, who "usually built their monasteries in wild solitudes," and the friars, who "fixed their habitations in the busiest thoroughfares." BE adduces the examples of "the Dominicans . . . in the Rue St. Jacques, in Paris," and of the mendicant houses of "the Minories, Blackfriars, and Whitefriars, in the very heart of the City" of London. SK (7000n.) also notes that "the friars did not seek retirement, like the monks."

6998　BE GL RB FI RI note that "John the Baptist, because of his austere life in the wilderness, was regarded as the founder of asceticism" (RI). BE cites Luke 1.80.

　John: See 7167n.

6999　**quethe hym quyte:** TRg (s.v. *Quethe*) sees the phrase as "a translation of an old technical term in the law; 'Clamo illi quietum.'" FI reads as "declare acquitted to him (i.e., legally transferred)," RIf as "declare him free."

　hym: FU has *hem*, an error of transcription from TH¹'s *him.*

Of Egipt all the wildirnesse.	7000	And lyven in such wikkednesse.	140r:16
To ferre were alle my mansiouns		Outward, lambren semen we,	141r:19
Fro citees and goode tounes.		Full of goodnesse and of pitee,	
My paleis and myn hous make I		And inward we, withouten fable,	7015
There men may renne ynne openly,		Ben gredy wolves ravysable.	
And sey that I the world forsake,	7005	We enviroune bothe londe and [se];	
But al amydde I bilde and mak		With all the world werrien we;	
My hous, and sw[i]mme and pley therynne		We wole ordeyne of al thing,	141v
Bet than a fish doth with his fynne.		Of folkis good and her lyvyng.	7020
"Of Antecristes men am I,		"If ther be castel or citee	
Of whiche that Crist seith openly,	7010	Wherynne that ony [bouger] be,	
They have abit of hoolynesse,		Although that they of Milayne were	

7002 **citees**] al c. TH¹-UR SK-FI   7007 **swimme**] swmme MS KA   7012 *Lines* 7109-58 *appear following* 7012 *in* MS-UR FU   7013 **Outward**] All o. UR   7017 **se**] fe MS KA   7022 **Wherynne**] Within ST SP²-UR   **bouger**] begger MS MO KA; bougerons TH¹-BE SK FU SU FI; bourgerons GL

7000 **Egipt:** As FI notes, "Christian monasticism began in the 4th century in the Egyptian desert." But Kaluza (1893a:35) and RI point out that *Egipt* results from a misreading of the Fr. *e giste* (Lc 11674 "menoir et giste" "abode and lodging"). RI states that "the translation follows a variant 'degipte'"; but, although such a case is likely, KA SU Ln Lc record no such variant in the Fr.

7002 **Fro:** KA suggests "*For in* for *Fro*," probably on the basis of the Fr. (Lc 11676 "es bours, es chateaus, es citez" "in towns, in castles, in cities"). But later eds. (except FU) take lines 7001–02 as a syntactic unit ("To ferre . . . Fro" "too far . . . from") and thus do not accept KA's emendation, which would make lines 7002–03 the syntactic unit, as in the Fr.

    citees: There is no parallel in the Fr. (see above) for TH¹'s insertion of *al* before *citees*.

7007 **swimme:** GL compares *SumT* D 1926 "swymmen in possessioun."

7010–16 SK Ln (11717–18n.) RB adduce Matt. 7.15. RI adduces the same text in the note to line 7017, where the more appropriate reference is Matt. 23.15.

7012–13 **Marginal folio numbers:** I supply both folio and line numbers where passages were transposed in MS's exemplar or where other anomalies exist. See 7013–7302n.

7013–7302 In various ways, BE KA SKt RBt SU FI RIt all note that, in MS and TH¹, lines 7109–58 are misplaced before lines 7013–7108, and lines 7159–7206 after lines 7207–7302. But it was Tyrwhitt (TR 3.314) who first discovered the reason for the misplacement; see above, "The Misplaced Leaves." Line 7109 does not appear in MS but may correspond to the blank line following line 7110; cf. RBt RIt, who, perhaps correctly, read *7110* instead of *7109*; and see 7109–10n. RBt RIt also have *7304* for *7302*; the error arises from RB's use of SK's text, where, after line 7172, SK adds two lines of his own composition and thus increases the line count by 2; see 7172–73n. For further details, see notes to lines 7013–7108, 7109–7158, 7159–7206, 7207–7302.

7013–7108 "In the MS. ll. 7109–7158 (= leaf 140, l. 17-leaf 141, l. 18) are misplaced before ll. 7013–7108 (= leaf 141, l. 19-leaf 143, l. 16)" (KA 7013–7302n.).

7013 **lambren:** "lambs" (GLg SKg₂ RIf). TH¹-UR FI have *lamben*. RB RI note the MS form from AS. *lombru*, compare *children* from *cildru*, and note that "Chaucer's plural was apparently *lambes*."

7017 BE SK RB adduce Matt. 23.15. BE notes that "throughout this passage the denunciations pronounced by our Saviour on the Scribes and Pharisees are applied to the friars."

7018 **werrien:** "make war" (SKg₂), "war upon" (FI; cf. TRg); SK quotes the Fr. (Lc 11690 "avons pris guerre" "we have waged war"). See 3251n.

7021–58 SK (7022n.) notes, "this long sentence goes on to l. 7058; *if* (7021) is answered by *He shal* (7050)." GL notes that "the conclusion to these conditions [lines 7021–48] is found in v. 7049 ff."

7022 **ony:** See 212n.

    bouger: KA's suggestion for MS *begger* is slightly closer than TH¹'s *bougerons* to the Fr. *bogres* (Lc 11694 "heretics [buggers]"; noted by SK RB RI. Eds. gloss as "Buggerers" (URg, s.v. *Bougerons*); "Sodomites" (URg et al.); "heretic" (RIf).

7023 **Milayne:** For references associating heresy with Milan, RB RI cite Ln (11724–25n.), who quotes Huon de Méri, *Tournoiement Antecrist* 2772–74 (ed. Wimmer 1888:91), and Guillaume Guiart, *Chronique Métrique* 256–57 (ed. Buchon 1824–28:7.35).

(For therof ben they blamed there);
Or if a wight, out of mesure,　　　　　　7025
Wolde lene his gold and take usure,
For that he is so coveitous;
Or if he be to leccherous,
Or [thefe, or] haunte symonye,
Or provost full of trecherie,　　　　　　7030
Or prelat lyvyng jolily,
Or prest that halt his quene hym by,
Or olde horis hostilers,
Or other bawdes or bordillers,
[Or elles blamed of ony vice]　　　　　　7035
Of whiche men shulden done justice:

Bi all the seyntes that me pray,
But they defende them with lamprey,
With luce, with elys, with samons,
With tendre gees and with capons,　　　　7040
With tartes, or with [chesis] fat,
With deynte flawns, brode and flat,
With caleweis or with pullaylle,
With conynges or with fyne vitaille,　　　7044
That we, undir oure clothes wide,　　　　142r
Maken thurgh oure golet glide;
Or but [he] wole do come in haste
Roo-venysoun, bake in paste;
Whether so that he loure or groyne,

7025　**if]** of TH¹ TH³-UR FU　　7026　**his]** her TH¹-SP³ FU; there UR　　7029　**thefe or]** these that MS-KA GL FU　　7035　*Out:* MS (MS₁ *corr.*)　　7037　**me]** we TH¹-BE SK FU SU FI　　7041　**or]** and SP¹　　**chesis]** cheffis MS-BE KA FU　　7042　**deynte]** deitie SP¹　　7044　**with fyne]** f. TH²　　7047　**he]** we MS KA 7049　**he]** *om.* TH³-SP³

7029　**thefe, or:** SK's emendation, endorsed by KA, is likely on paleographical grounds (*f*/long *s*) and on the basis of the Fr. (Lc 11701 "ou lierres, ou symoniaus" "or thief, or symoniac"; noted by SK RBt SU FI RIt). GL retains MS *these that* and argues that Fr. *lerres ou* "may have been misread (?) 'lesses au,' etc."

7033　**horis hostilers:** "innkeepers for whores" (RIf). *Horis* is a noun, rather than an adjective "hoary" (FI).

7035　"Written in the margin by the same hand" (KA), MS₁; see 6190n.

elles: KA notes this expansion, in BE MO, of the MS abbreviation *ell*. SK GL RB RI have the same form (UR *ellis*), while TH¹-SP³ FU SU FI have *els*. See above, "The Manuscript Hands: The Scribe (MS₁)."

ony: See 212n.

7037　**me pray:** KA notes TH¹'s *we* and suggests spelling *praye*. RB RI support MS *me* by quoting the Fr. *que l'en proie!* (Lc 11709 "to whom one may pray!"); thus RIf reads *me pray* as "one may pray to (impersonal)."

7038　**But they defende them:** "Unless the sinners bribe the friars" (SK).

7041　**chesis:** URg defines the variant phrase *cheffis fat* as "Calves fat, or *Chevins* fat, i.e. the fat of a Mullet," citing Skinner (1671). TRg (s.v. *Cheffis*) suggests *Cheses*, on the basis of Fr. *fromages*. Jephson (BE) mistakenly reports that "Speght reads *cheses* [in fact, SP¹⁻³ all read *cheffes*], which appears to be right"; he quotes the Fr. (Lc 11714 "et de formages en glaons" "and with cheeses in wicker baskets") but does not emend his text. KA notes MO's *chessis*; SKt notes Fr. *fromages*.

7042　**flawns:** SKg₂, citing *Liber Cure Cocorum*, p.39, describes this as "a dish composed of new cheese, eggs, powdered sugar, coloured with saffron and baked in small tins called 'coffins.'" FI RIf define more simply as "flans," tarts or puddings of custard.

7043　**caleweis:** Early eds. gloss: "calure, as Salmon or other (red) fish" (SP¹g SP²g-URg). TRg comments "R7093 [line 7043] is probably miswritten. The *Orig.* has *La poire du Caillouel* and goes on to cite Cotgrave (1611). Later eds. have glossed the word only as a sort of pear. SK RB FI explain as (sweet) pears of Cailloux in Burgundy. Skeat's note (1886*b*:2.237) to *Piers Plowman* B 16.69 questions early etymologies in which the word *cailloux* (stones, flints) suggests a hard-skinned pear. He quotes Cotgrave (1611), "*Caillouet*, the name of a very sweet pear," and Lacroix (1874:116), "the *caillou* or *chaillou*, a hard pear, which came from Cailloux in Burgundy"; "to me," writes Skeat, "it is clear that the hardness resided, not in the *pear*, but in the *soil* of Cailloux." RB cites Ln (11746n.), who also quotes Cotgrave and, among others, the note in Barbazan and Méon (1808:2.279) which describes the pears as from Cailloux in Burgundy, as having a hard (*pierreuse*) brown skin, and as being good for cooking. Ln concludes that the pear may draw its name from its hardness.

·　7044　**conynges:** "conies" (BE SK), "rabbits" (BE SK FI RIf); BE SK note the Fr. *connins* (Lc 11720).

7046　**thurgh:** KA transcribes as *thourgh*, a spelling that persists through GL RB RI.

7047　**he:** TH¹'s emendation follows the Fr. *il* (Lc 11719 "he"); KA notes *he* in TH¹ UR BE MO.

7049　**groyne:** "grumble" (URg, citing Fr. *grogner*, SKg₂ RBg), "hang the lip, in discontent" (TRg), "pout, mutter" (MOg), "murmur" (SK), "complain" (RBg RIf), "groan" (FI). Skeat (SK) adduces his note to *KnT* A 2460, where he refers to *TC* 1.349.

He shal have of a corde a loigne,   7050
With whiche men shal hym bynde and lede,
To brenne hym for his synful deede,
That men shull here hym crie and rore
A myle-wey aboute and more;
Or ellis he shal in prisoun dye,   7055
But if he wole [our] frendship bye,
Or smerten that that he hath do,
More than his gilt amounteth to.
    "But, and he couthe thurgh his sleght,
Do maken up a tour of hight,   7060
Nought rought I whethir of stone or tree,

Or erthe or turves though it be,
Though it were of no vounde stone,
Wrought with squyre and scantilone,
So that the tour were stuffed well   7065
With all richesse temporell,
And thanne that he wolde updresse
Engyns, bothe more and lesse,
To cast at us by every side,   142v
To bere his good name wide,   7070
Such sleghtes [as] I shal yow nevene,   142v:4
Barelles of wyne, by sixe or sevene,   142v:3
Or gold in sakkis gret plente,

7053 **shull]** shulde TH²   7054 **myle-wey]** myle away FU   7056 **our]** his MS-UR KA GL FU
7067 **wolde]** w. him UR   7071 **sleghtes]** flightes GL   **as]** *om.* MS-KA FU   **nevene]** yeuen TH³-UR

7050 **loigne:** "a line" (URg), "tether" (BEg et al.), "length" (SK FI), "long piece" (SK), "leash" (RIf); SK adduces line 3882. Cf. 3882n.

7056 **our:** BE's emendation, noted in BE MO by KA, follows the Fr. *nos* (Lc 11728 "us"; noted by RBt RIt). GL takes *his frendship bye* as "pay for his relief." RBt, taking *his* as an objective genitive, notes that "possibly *his* is right, *his frendship* meaning 'friendship or favor for him'"; and RIt also suggests that *his* may be right, but with a different reading, "made his friendship (or peace) with us."

7057 **smerten:** "smart for" (SK RB RIf); SK RB RI quote the Fr. (Lc 11729 "ou sera puniz du meffet" "Or he will be punished for the offense").

that that: "(?) for that" (GL).

7059–74 SK (7063n.) notes that "the general sense clearly is, that the friars oppress the weak, but not the strong. If a man is master of a castle, they let him off easily, even if the castle be not built of freestone of the first quality, wrought by first-rate workmen"; on "freestone" (*vounde stone*), see 7063n. RB paraphrases: "But if a man owns a castle, even of inferior construction, and gives the friars acceptable gifts, they will quickly release him." As RI notes, "the defenses of the castle depend not on the quality of the construction but on the bribes with which it is stocked."

7063 **vounde stone:** RBt notes that the meaning of *vounde* is uncertain. SP UR gloss it as "freestone"; URg cites Skinner (1671) for this sense, and GL finds the same sense (but "with query 'found or foundation'") in Coles (1676). But TRg lists the phrase among those "not understood." KA attributes to Skeat the suggestion *bounde* for *vounde*, but SK does not so emend; "if a genuine word," writes SK, *vounde* "can only be another form of *founde*," the pa. part. of *finden*. Skeat (SK) supposes "'found stone' to mean good building-stone, *found* in sufficient quantities in the neighbourhood of a site for a castle"; he also suggests the possible sense "founded." RB RI offer much the same explanation, and GL RB FI RI note the Fr. (Lc 11733 "ne li chausist ja de quel pierre" "it matters not what sort of stone"). FI suggests that *vounde* is the southern form of *found* and glosses it as "known."

7064 "wrought with the *squire* (mason's square) and to any required *scantilone* (scantling, pattern)" (SK 7063n.); RB FI RIf gloss similarly.

squyre: "a carpenters rule" (SP²·³g); "square" (URg MOg), "(carpenter's, measuring) square" (SKg₂ et al.).

scantilone: "a measure" (SPg URg, citing "Fr. *Eschantillon*, A pattern"), "A pattern" (TRg et al.). GLg's gloss, "a mason's rule," seems closer to *squire.*

7071–72 *Marginalia:* As KA notes, "ll. 7071 and 7072 are transposed in the MS.; but the right order is marked in the [left] margin by *b, a.*"

7071 **sleghtes:** "contrivance[s]" (TRg et al.), "the missiles slung by the engines" (BE [quoting the Fr.; see below] SKg₂), "device[s]" (MOg RBg). SK notes that "the context is jocular" and that "the translator could think of no better word" than *sleghtes* for Fr. *chaillous* "stones" (Lc 11743; noted by TRg). FI explains the sense as "tricks (i.e., missiles with which the friar is pelted)."

as: KA's suggestion. SU, noting that *as* "seems necessary," cites the Fr. *que* (Lc 11743 "tex chaillous *con* m'oez nomer" "such stones as you hear me name"; Ln 11773t lists var. *qu'* from MS He).

295

He shulde soone delyvered be.
And if [he have] noon sich pitaunces,   7075
Late hym study in equipolences,
And late lyes and fallaces,
If that he wolde deserve oure graces;
Or we shal bere hym such witnesse
Of synne and of his wrecchidnesse,   7080
And done his loos so wide renne,
That al quyk we shulden hym brenne,
Or ellis yeve hym suche penaunce,
That is wel wors than the pitaunce.

"For thou shalt never, for nothing,   7085
Kon knowen aright by her clothing
The traitours full of trecherie,
But thou her werkis can aspie.
And ne hadde the good kepyng be
Whilom of the universite,   7090
That kepith the key of Cristendome,
[We had ben turmented al
     and some].   TH¹:165d:32
Suche ben the stynkyng prophetis;   MS:143r
Nys none of hem that good prophete is,

7074 **soone]** tho s. UR   7075 **he have]** *om.* MS KA   7077 **late]** lerin UR   7092 **We had ben turmented al and some]** Of all that here axe juste the ju dome. . . MS₂; Of al that here axe juste their dome KA; W. h. t. a. a. s. BE MO; They h. b. t. a. a. s. SK   *Out:* MS RI   7093 **prophetis]** fals p. SK

7075–76 **pitaunces : equipolences:** For apparent rhyme, TH¹-UR FU SU FI respell *p(i,y)tences*; RBt suggests "*equipolaunces?*" On such rhymes, cf. 6429–30n.

7075 **he have:** TH¹'s emendation, noted by KA in UR BE MO, follows the Fr. (Lc 11749 "Et s'il ne treuve tex pitances" "And if he find no such pittances").

7076 **study in equipolences:** UR TR gloss *equipolences* as "equivalents"; BE SK interpret as "subtle distinctions" (BE) or "equivocations" (SK), but, as RB RI note, Ln (11780–81n.) takes it as "des arguments équivalents"—equivalent arguments. RI explains: "in place of material bribes the friars might be bought off with flattering arguments instead of the usual attacks (*lyes and fallaces*)." The phrase comes directly from the Fr. (Lc 11750 "estudit en equipollences"; noted by BE RB RI).

7077 "The . . . line suggests that he should refrain from coarse and downright lies (*lete* = let alone)" (SK 7076n.).

late: KA suggests *late be*, but no ed. so emends.

7081 "that is, 'And cause his ill-fame [loos, praise, ironically] to spread far and wide'" (BE).

done . . . loos: "make, reputation" (FI).

7089–90 "And if it had not been for the good keeping (or watchfulness) of the University of Paris" (SK). SK FI note the allusion to Guillaume de Saint-Amour and his friends; SK compares lines 6554 (FI 6553ff.), 6766. Ln (11791n.) quotes Guillaume de Saint-Amour, *De periculis* 8 (1632:38).

7089 **ne hadde:** KA suggests *nadde*, but no ed. so emends.

7092 As BE KA SKt GL RBt SU FI RIt note, the line was left blank in MS and was filled in by a later hand ("of the time of Queen Elizabeth," says BE). The hand, MS₂, may be the same as that of lines 6688 and 6786 (see 6688n.). Thorp (1989) believes that the last word (dome . . .) is in still another hand. My transcription—"Of all that here axe juste the ju dome . . ."—differs from earlier ones: "All that here else just their dome" (BE); "Of al that here axe juste their dome" (KA text; SKt GL RBt SU RIt notes). My version treats the letter forms after *the* as an interrupted but uncanceled recopying of the word *juste*. The line is of course garbled and spurious, like lines 6688 and 6786. TH¹'s version is based on the Fr. (Lc 11764 "tout eüst esté tourmenté" "everything would have been overturned"; noted in SKt RIt); this version provides the conjectural basis for the text. RI rejects TH¹'s line as spurious (supplying it in a footnote) and shows the lacuna as a line of dots; cf. 892n.

We: "we must either read *They had been turmented* (as I give it) or else *We had turmented* (as in Bell). I prefer *They*, because it is a closer translation, and suits better with *Such* in the next line" (SK).

7093–7212 On the controversy over the "book" called *The Eternal Gospel* ("gospel perdurable," line 7102), see the notes of BE (7099n.) SK (7102n.) RB (7096n.) FI (7099n.) RI (7093–7103n.), as well as those of Ln (11802–05n.) and Lc (11761–11866n.); see also Paré (1947:180–86), Dufeil (1972:124–26), Szittya (1986:15, 27–31).

The book is now lost, but it appears to have been prepared by a Franciscan, Gerard de Borgo San Donnino, and to have embraced three works of Joachim of Flora—the *Concordia novi et veteris testamenti*, the *Apocalypsis nova*, and the *Psalterium decem chordarum*—and an introductory section by Gerard, the *Introductorius in evangelium aeternum*. According to Paré, Joachim did not think of his works as replacing the Bible, but apparently Gérard so presented them in his *Introductorius*, which "created a sensation by claiming that this 'Gospel of the Holy Ghost' would supersede that of the Son (the New Testament) as the latter had superseded the Gospel of the Father

For they, thurgh wikked entencioun,   7095
The yeer of the Incarnacioun
A thousand and two hundred yeer,
Fyve and fifty, ferther [ne neer],
Broughten a book, with sory grace,
To yeven ensample in comune place,   7100
That seide thus, though it were fable:
'This is the gospel perdurable,

That fro the Holy Goost is sent.'
Wel were it worth to bene brent!   7104
Entitled was in such manere
This book, of which I telle heere.
Ther nas no wight in all Parys,   7107
Biforne Oure Lady, at parvys,   MS:143r:16
[That (he) ne myght(e bye
    the book)]   TH¹:166a:2

7098 **ne neer]** neuer MS KA   **7104** **worth]** wrothe TH³ ST; worthi GL   **7109** **That he ne myghte bye the book]** T. they n. m. t. b. by / The sentence pleased hem wel trewly TH¹-UR FU; T. they n. m. t. b. buy BE; T. they n. m. buye t. b. MO   *Out:* MS (*blank line*) KA RI; *lines* 7109-58 *appear following* 7012 *in* MS-UR FU

(the Old Testament)" (RI). The book appeared in 1254 (not 1255, as in the Fr. and ME texts and in the notes of BE SK). In late 1254, the masters of the University of Paris, probably under Guillaume de Saint-Amour, prepared a list of 31 errors in the *Introductorius* (ed. Denifle and Chatelain 1889–97:1.272–76; cf. Ln 11796–97n.), and the ensuing controversy resulted in the condemnation of the book by Pope Alexander IV in October 1255 (ed. Denifle and Chatelain 1889–97:1.297–98). As Jephson (BE) points out, Alexander was otherwise "generally favourable to the Mendicants," but Jephson is not strictly accurate in writing that Alexander "had already condemned the book of William of St. Amour," since the *De periculis* did not appear until early in 1256 and was not specifically condemned until October 1256 (Dufeil 1972:212–39; ed. Denifle and Chatelain 1889–97:1.331–33).

SK notes that Gerard's book "emanated from the friars, but was too audacious to succeed, and hence Fals-Semblant, for decency's sake, is made to denounce it. We may note how the keen satire of Jean de Meun contrives to bring in a mention of this work, under the guise of a violent yet half-hearted condemnation of it by a representative of the friars." As Ln Lc RB RI note, most of the material in this passage comes from Guillaume de Saint-Amour, *De periculis* 8, 14 (1632:38, 68–69); thus Fals-Semblant uses the words of the friars' opponent in his self-condemnation.

7093   **prophetis:** SK inserts *fals* and argues that "it is countenanced by *traitours* in l. 7087." § "The reference," says SK, "is to the supporters of the book mentioned below," i.e., to the friars.

7098   **ferther ne neer:** TH¹'s emendation, *ne nere* for MS *neuer*, is reasonable on paleographical grounds. KA suggests "*fer ne ner* for *ferther neuer.*" Liddell (GL) would explain "ferther ne ner" by the Fr. (Lc 11768 "n'est hom vivanz qui m'en desmante" "there is no man alive who may contradict me") which suggests, he says, "neither earlier or later."

7102–05   On the title, "gospel perdurable," Ln (11802–05n.) quotes Guillaume de Saint-Amour, *De periculis* 8 (1632:38).

7104   **worth:** GL adopts KA's suggestion, "read *worthy.*"

7108   **parvys:** porch before the cathedral of Notre-Dame (URg TRg BE SK RB FI RIf), where books were sold (TRg BE SK); see further Andrew (1993:290). URg notes the form as a contraction of *paradis*; cf. 1369n.

7109–58   On the transposition, see 7013–7302n., 7013–7108n.

7109–10   BE KA SKt GL RBt SU FI RIt note MS's one-line and TH¹'s four-line versions. Several factors complicate this passage: the transpositions noted at lines 7013–7302, the omission of line 7109 in MS, the displacement of line 7110 in MS, and TH¹'s struggles to make sense of MS. SKt GL RBt SU FI note correctly that MS omits line 7109. SKt and Brusendorff (1925:299) mention the blank line that follows line 7110 (Brusendorff says line 7109), and Brusendorff writes that "Thynne . . . referred to the French original and reconstructed the passage in a somewhat clumsy way." RBt FI (and to a slight extent, SU) may suggest, unintentionally, that TH¹'s "four garbled lines" (FI) appear consecutively; they do not. David (RIt) has an explanation which recognizes that MS was printer's copy for TH¹ and which treats the passage as "a good example of Thynne's efforts to reconstruct G [MS]." This note draws heavily upon David's account.

The Fr. context clarifies the problems (Lc 11777–80 = ME 7107–10): "A Paris n'ot home ne fame, / ou parvis devant Nostre Dame, / qui lors avoir ne l'i peüst / a transcrivre, s'il li pleüst" ("There was not a man or woman in Paris who, in the parvis in front of Notre Dame, could not then have had it to transcribe if he had pleased"). The opening of the corresponding lines in MS appears on fol. 143r at the end of a transposed block: "Ther nas no wight in all parys [7107] / Biforne oure lady at paruys [7108] / But I wole stynt of this matere [7207]". To find the lines following line 7108, we turn back to fol. 140r, where they appear at the beginning of a transposed block: "And lyuen in such wikkednesse [7012] / To copy if hym talent toke [7110] / [blank line = 7109?] / There myght he se by gret tresoun [7111]."

To copy if hym talent toke.   MS:140r:17
There myght he se, by gret tresoun, MS:140r:19
Full many fals comparisoun: 7112
'As moche as, thurgh his gret myght,
Be it of hete or of lyght,
The [sonne] sourmounteth the mone, 7115
That troublere is, and chaungith soone,
And the note-kernell the shell   140v
(I scorne not that I yow tell),
Right so, withouten ony gile,

Sourmounteth this noble evangile   7120
The word of ony evangelist.'
And to her title they token Crist;
And many a such comparisoun,
Of which I make no mencioun,
Might men in that book fynde,   7125
Whoso coude of hem have mynde.
   "The universite, that tho was aslepe,
Gan for to braide and taken kepe,
And at the noys the heed upcast,

7110 **To copy if hym talent toke**] T. the c. i. h. t. t. / Of the Euangelystes booke TH¹-UR FU; T. c. i. hem t. t. BE MO   7112 **fals**] a f. TH³-UR   7113 **thurgh**] though TH²   7114 **or**] be it UR   7115 **sonne**] same MS KA   7116 **troublere**] trouble GL   7117 **the shell**] dothe t. s. UR   7118 **tell**] it t. UR   7123 **a**] *om.* TH¹-UR SK-FU SU FI   7127 **tho**] *om.* UR

Line 7109, however, is missing; it may correspond to the blank line, but the lacuna follows line 7110 rather than precedes it. In the exemplar with the quire of misplaced leaves (see above, "The Misplaced Leaves"), line 7109 must have been present with line 7110 on leaf 4r rather than 3v, since (a) all transposed blocks occur in even-numbered groups (50, 96, 96, 48) and, except in the case of leaf 4, in multiples of 24; (b) couplets are not split; (c) line 7108 clearly ends a block and, therefore, a page; (d) MS provides two lines for 7109–10. In the case of the block 7109–58, 50 lines long, we have to assume that leaf 4 in the exemplar had, exceptionally, 25 lines on each page.

TH¹, working from the Fr., patched this missing line into the first passage (which appeared later in MS, his copy) and added a line to complete the ME couplet (TH¹ fol. 165d–166a): "There nas no wight in al Parys [7107] / Beforne our Lady at paruys [7108] / That they ne myght the booke by [7109?] / The sentence pleased hem wel trewly. [?] / But I wol stynte of this matere [7207]." Of these last three lines, "the first . . . obviously renders the first half of the French couplet; the second, constructed to rhyme with it, is more obviously spurious. Editors reject the latter and print the former after Skeat's revision" (RIt). See 7109n.

As a result of this treatment, line 7110, corresponding to the second half of the Fr. couplet, remains isolated in the other passage, where TH¹ (presumably already, since the passage occurred at an earlier point in his copy) had composed another line to rhyme with it (fol. 165a): "And lyuen in suche wickednesse [7012] / To the copye / if him talent toke [7110] / Of the Euangelystes booke [?] / There myght he se by great traysoun [7111]." As David observes, TH¹'s "next-to-last line, rejected by all editors as spurious, is an effort to patch the sense in this context. The verb *copy* (transcribe) becomes *the copye* of the Gospel, where, if one wished (*if him talent took*) one might see examples of hypocrisy and treason" like those in "Matt. 7[23?].15." TH²-UR FU reprint versions substantially like TH¹'s.

7109 This is SK's emendation of TH¹, which is based on the Fr. (above). David (RIt) notes correctly that "Skeat's reconstruction, . . . though it is better Middle English and a good translation of the French, has no more textual authority than Thynne's." David omits this line from the text, represents the lacuna by a line of dots, and supplies the line in a footnote; cf. 892n. Brusendorff's statement (1925:299)—that "the true reading" is "that *be ne myghte ban* the book"—has even less foundation.

    he: SK's emendation follows the Fr. (see above).

    bye the book: BE (7110n.) suggests this emendation on the bases of the Fr. and of rhyme.

7110 **copy:** On TH¹'s *the copye*, see 7109–10n.

    hym: The variant *hem*, in BE MO, is clearly intended as a plural, to agree with *they* in line 7109.

7111 **There:** On TH¹'s interpretation, see 7109–10n.

7113–21 "a quotation from the Eternal Gospel. L. 7118 means: 'I am not mocking you in saying this; the quotation is a true one'" (SK).

7115 **sonne:** KA notes *sonne* in TH¹ MO, and *sunne* in UR BE.

7116 **troublere:** "dark[er], gloom[ier]" (TRg), "dimmer" (SK). SK GL RBt RIt cite the Fr. (Lc 11786 "qui trop est plus trouble" "which is much darker"), where the word *trouble* may account for GL's version.

7118 "That is, 'What I tell you is not said for the purpose of making a fool of you'" (BE). For SK's paraphrase, see 7113–21n. RB quotes the Fr. (Lc 11788 "ne cuidiez pas que je me moque" "don't think that I'm joking").

7119, 7121 **ony:** See 212n.

7127 **that:** "Perhaps omit *That*" (SKt).

Ne never sithen slept it fast;   7130
But up it stert, and armes toke
Ayens this fals horrible boke,
Al redy bateil [for] to make,
And to the juge the book to take.
But they that broughten the boke there   7135
Hent it anoon awey for fere;
They nolde shewe more a dele,
But thenne it kept, and kepen will,
Til such a tyme that they may see
That they so stronge woxen be   7140
That no wyght may hem wel withstonde,   141r
For by that book [they] durst not stonde.
[Away] they gonne it for to bere,
For they ne durst not answere

By exposicioun [ne] glose   7145
To that that clerkis wole appose
Ayens the cursednesse, iwys,
That in that book writen is.
Now wote I not, ne I can not see
What maner eende that there shal be   7150
Of al this [bok] that they hyde;
But yit algate they shal abide
Til that they may it bet defende.
This, trowe I best, wole be her ende.
    "Thus Antecrist abiden we,   7155
For we ben alle of his meyne;
And what man that wole not be so,
Right soone he shal his lyf forgo.   141r:18
We wole a puple upon hym areyse,   145r:17

7133 **for]** *om.* MS BE KA   7134 **to take]** they t. TH¹-UR FU SU FI   7137 **more]** it no m. TH¹-UR FU
SU FI; it m. SK; it nevere RB¹ˌ²   7138 **will]** wele TH¹-UR FU SU FI   7142 **they]** *om.* MS KA   7143 **Away]**
Alway MS KA   7145 **ne]** no MS-ST SP²ˌ³ KA FU   7146 **that that]** that the FI   7147 **the]** that
BE   7149 **I can]** can UR   7151 **bok]** whiche UR; bokes GL; *om.* MS-SP³ BE-KA FU   **hyde]** may h.
MO   7159 **a]** *om.* TH²   **upon]** on UR SK   *Lines 7159-7206 appear after* 7302 *in* MS-UR FU

7133 **for to:** KA notes (in UR MO) the insertion of *for* before *to.* MS normally has *forto* in such situations.
7134 **take:** Probably simply "take," rather than "undertake" (FI).
7135-55 RB (7134n.) RI (7135n.) explain Fals-Semblant's meaning: "The friars suppress the book until a more
propitious time, presumably the advent of their leader, Anti-Christ" (RI). RB RI (following Ln 11802–05n.) note that
the *Introductorius* was lost "and known only through attacks upon it such as the De periculis" (RI). Cf. SK (see
7152–53n.).
7137-38 **dele : will:** TH¹'s *wele* adjusts rhyme, but the auxiliary *will* is necessary to the translation of Fr.
garderont "will keep" (KA Fr. 12005, from MS κω; SU Fr. 11834.B³, from MS Bu). Feng (1990:57) accepts "the
imperfect rime [as] an exception to 'Chaucer's usage' for the sake of literal translation."
7137 Not in Lc Ln. KA gives the Fr. text from MS κω (KA Fr. 12003 "Ne moustrer neÿs ne le voldrent" "They
didn't even want to show it"), and SU from Bu (SU Fr. 11834.B¹ "Mès mostrer me mies nel vodrent" "But they didn't
want to show it to me at all"). KA suggests *it neuer* for MS *more,* presumably on the basis of the Fr.
7138 **will:** I collate TH¹'s *wele* as the possible adv. *well;* KA suggests *wel.* The Fr. future, *garderont,* supports
the verb form (above, 7137–38n.).
7142 There is no Fr. parallel, but the emendation *they,* omitted in MS, seems reasonable; KA notes the form in
UR BE MO.
7143 **Away:** KA notes TH¹'s emendation in UR BE MO. BE (n.) KA (text) SKt RIt mistranscribe MS *Alway* as
Alwey, and the -*e*- persists in GL RB RI *Awey.* There is no precise parallel in the Fr. (Lc 11805 "et se hasterent du
repondre" "and made haste to conceal it").
7145 **ne:** KA endorses UR's emendation in BE. RBt RIt note that MS *no* (= "nor") is possibly correct.
7146 **that that:** "that which"; a somewhat literal translation of Fr. *ce qu'* (Lc 11808 "what").
    wole: KA's suggestion, "read *wolde,*" follows the Fr. *volait,* but it has not been adopted.
7151 **bok:** KA's suggestion (*booke*) follows the Fr. *cil livres* (Lc 11812; noted by GL RIt).
7152-53 "This shews that Fals-Semblaunt does not *really* condemn the book; he only says it is best to suppress
it *for the present,* till Antichrist comes to strengthen the friars' cause. The satire is of the keenest. Note that, in l. 7164,
Fals-Semblaunt shamelessly calls the Eternal Gospel 'our book.' See also ll. 7211–12" (SK). Cf. 7135–55n., 7155n.
7155 **we:** "Fals-Semblant often speaks of the friars as *they,* but he is, of course, one of their party, and the *fals
horrible book* (7132) is *oure book* (7164)" (RI).
7159-7206 "In the MS. . . . ll. 7159-7206 (= leaf 145, l. 17-leaf 146, l. 16 [are misplaced] after ll. 7207–7302
(=leaf 143, l. 17-leaf 145, l. 16)" (KA, 7013–7302n.).
7159 **areyse:** KA suggests *reyse,* but no ed. so emends.

And thurgh oure gile done hym seise,　　7160
And hym on sharpe speris ryve,
Or other weyes brynge hym fro lyve,
But if that he wole folowe, iwis,
That in oure book writen is.
　"Thus mych wole oure book signifie,　7165
That while Petre hath maistrie,
May never John shewe well his myght.　145v
Now have I you declared right
The menyng of the bark and rynde,
That makith the entenciouns blynde.　　7170

But now at erst I wole bigynne
To expowne you the pith withynne:
　.　.　.　.　.　.　.　.　.
And the seculers comprehende,
That Cristes lawe wole defende,
And shulde it kepen and mayntenen　　7175
Ayens hem that all sustenen,
And falsly to the puple techen.
[And] John bitokeneth hem [that] prechen
That ther nys lawe covenable
But thilk gospel perdurable,　　7180

7166　**while]** w. that SK　　**hath]** had ST-UR　　7172　**To expowne you the pith withynne]** To e. y. t. p. w.:-- / And first, by Peter, as I wene, / The Pope himself we wolden mene SK　　7173　**the]** eek t. SK　7178　**And]** That MS-KA GL FU; For SU FI　　**bitokeneth]** betoketh TH¹·² FU SU FI　　**that]** to MS-KA FU SU FI

7160　**seise:** SU FI err in reporting TH¹'s reading as *reise*. It is *ceise*, a var. sp. (cf. *MED seisen* v.) that appears in TH¹-UR FU; TRg (TR 5.256) glosses *ceise* as a misprint for *seise*.

7165　*Marginalium:* Opposite this line, in the right margin of MS, there is a heavy "T." On the same page (145r), there is another marginal mark opposite line 7302, a line that, because of the misplaced leaves, appears a few lines higher on this same page; see 7302n. The "T" here is similar to one on 146r; see 7306n.

7166–70　RI notes: "The literal sense, 'the bark and rynde' (7169), contains the fruit or the true sense, which states that the strength of John shall not be revealed while Peter is in power." In the note to lines 7172–82, RI explains that "'Peter' stands for the present hierarchy, the secular clergy; 'John' stands for the friars, the preachers of the eternal gospel, who would replace them." FI glosses *Peter* as "the pope," *John* as "the friars," as does the Fr.; see 7172–73n.

7166　**while:** KA endorses SK's *while that*.

7167　**John:** MS shows abbreviation, *John* with a macron crossing the ascender of the *h* and extending over the *n*. The same abbreviation occurs at lines 6998, 7178, 7183, 7204; cf. Capelli (1967:185). In the ME, the abbreviation is meaningless, since a disyllable (Johan) is not metrically necessary.

7169　**rynde:** "skin (i.e., outer covering)" (FI); "literal sense" (RIf). See 7166–70n.

7172–73　BE (7173n.) first notes that "there is . . . something omitted here" and that the Fr. "enables us to supply the sense" (Lc 11830–32 = ME 7172–73): "or en veill la moële espondre. / Par Pierre veust la pape entendre / et les clers seculiers comprendre" ("I want to explain its marrow. By Peter it would signify the Pope and include the secular clergy"). The middle line is missing in the ME, which requires a couplet; Brink (1870:29) SKt GL RBt RIt note the omission and cite the Fr. KA notes in his text that there is "no gap in the MS." and records SK's suggestion, "And first by Peter, as I wene, / The Pope, as witen alle, I mene." SK includes these lines in his ed. but changes the second to read "The Pope himself we wolden mene." Since SK numbers these lines 7173–74, his count for the rest of the poem, as RBt SU RIt note, is plus two. SK explains his addition: "By Peter I wish you to understand the pope, and to include also the secular clerks, &c. John represents the friars (l. 7185 [= 7183])."

7173　**seculers:** GL suggests "(?) read *clerkes seculers*" on the basis of the Fr. *clers seculiers* (Lc 11832). FI explains them as "the secular clergy, who were locked in conflict with the friars."

7176–82　SK (7178n.) paraphrases and comments: "I.e. 'against those friars who maintain all (this book), and falsly teach the people; and John betokens those (the friars) who preach, to the effect that there is no law so suitable as that Eternal Gospel, sent by the Holy Ghost to convert such as have gone astray.' The notion is, that the teaching of John (the type of the law of love, as expounded by the friars) is to supersede the teaching of Peter (the type of the pope and other obsolete secular teachers). Such was the 'Eternal Gospel'; no wonder that the Pope condemned it as being too advanced." Earlier, Jephson (BE) had written: "it appears to have been asserted that there was a distinction between the teaching of St. Peter and that of St. John, as if the former stood most upon the principle of law and order, and the latter upon that of love. . . . From this it appears that [the friars] were by no means obsequious servants of the Sovereign Pontiff."

7178　KA's suggestion, adopted here, corresponds to the elliptical Fr. line (Lc 11836–37 "Par Jehan, les preecheürs, / qui diront . . ." "By John [it would signify] the preachers / who say . . ."; noted by RIt). § Lc (11836n.) identifies the "preecheürs" as the Dominicans and notes that the masters of the University of Paris attributed the *Introductorius* to a Dominican.

300

That fro the Holy Gost was sent
To turne folk that ben myswent.
  "The strengthe of John they undirstonde
The grace, in whiche they seie they stonde,
That doth the synfull folk converte,   7185
And hem to Jesus Crist reverte.
Full many another orribilite
May men in that book se,
That ben comaunded, douteles,
Ayens the lawe of Rome expres;   7190
And all with Antecrist they holden,   146r
As men may in the book biholden.
And thanne comaunden they to sleen
Alle tho that with Petre been;
But they shal nevere have that myght,   7195
And, God toforne, for strif to fight,
That they ne shal ynough fynde
That Petres lawe shal have in mynde,
And evere holde, and so mayntene,
That at the last it shal be sene   7200
That they shal all come therto,
For ought that they can speke or do.
And thilk lawe shal not stonde,
That they by John have undirstonde,

But, maugre hem, it shal adowne,   7205
And bene brought to confusioun.   146r:16
But I wole stynt of this matere,   143r:17
For it is wonder longe to here.
But hadde that ilke book endured,
Of better estate I were ensured;   7210
And freendis have I yit, pardee,
That han me sett in gret degre.
  "Of all this world is emperour
Gyle my fadir, the trechour,   7214
And emperis my moder is,   143v
Maugre the Holy Gost, iwis.
Oure myghty lynage and oure rowte
Regneth in every regne aboute;
And well is worthy we [maystres] be,
For all this world governe we,   7220
And can the folk so wel disceyve
That noon oure gile can perceyve.
And though they done, they dar not sey;
The sothe dar no wight bywrey.
But he in Cristis wrath hym ledith,   7225
That more than Crist my britheren dredith.
He nys no full good champioun,
That dredith such similacioun,

7187   **orribilite**] horriblee SP²,³   7197   **ynough**] y. men SK   7199   **holde**] beholde TH²   7203   **shal**] ne s. UR   7205   **adowne**] doun TH²   7206   **bene**] hem TH²   7212   **han**] had SP¹   7214   **trechour**] false t. UR   7219   **worthy**] worth SK   **maystres**] mynystres MS-KA FU   7222   **gile**] gilis UR

7186   **Jesus:** MS uses the Greek monogram ihc̄.

7195–202   "Obscure; and not fully in the F. text," notes SK (7197–204n.). The uncertain correspondence to the Fr. extends to line 7206; cf. Lc 11853–60: "mes ja n'avront poair d'abatre, / ne por occierre ne por batre, / la loi Pierre, ce vos plevis, / qu'il n'en demeurt assez de vis / qui torjorz si la maintendront / que tuit en la fin i vendront; / et sera la loi confondue / qui par Jehan est entendue" ("but they will never have the power to overcome the law of Peter, either to kill or to punish, I guarantee you this, since there will not be enough of them remaining alive to maintain it forever so that in the end everybody will come to it; and the law that is signified by John will be overthrown").

7196   **to fight:** KA suggests *ne fight*, to follow the Fr., but no ed. so emends.

7197   **ne shal ynough:** FI paraphrases: "i.e., that enough people will not remain."

   ynough: KA endorses SK's *ynough men*; to gain the extra syllable, others have *enowe* (GL) or *ynowe* (RB RI); RBt notes that the MS form is "metrically suspicious."

7201   "i.e., everyone will accept Peter's law (papal authority)" (FI).

7202   **they can speke:** "i.e., the friars can say" (FI).

7204   **John:** See 7167n.

7205   **maugre:** "in spite of." Cf. 6711n.

7207–7302   See 7159–7206n.

7215   **my moder:** "Hypocrisy" (SK RB FI RIf).

7216   **Maugre:** "in spite of." Cf. 6711n.

7219   **worthy:** KA endorses SK's *worth*. SKt adduces line 7104.

   maystres: KA's suggestion for MS *mynystres* follows the sense of the Fr. (Lc 11873 "et bien est droiz que noz resnons" "and it is quite right that we rule"; noted by RBt SU FI RIt).

7225–26   "But he who dreads my brethren more than Christ subjects himself to Christ's wrath" (SK FI).

7227   On Guillaume de Saint-Amour's sense of intellectual combat, Lc (11881n.) quotes his *Responsiones* 35 (ed. Faral 1951:352).

Nor that for peyne wole refusen
Us to correcte and accusen.   7230
He wole not entremete by right,
Ne have God in his iye-sight,
And therfore God shal hym punyshe.
But me ne rekke[th] of no vice,
Sithen men us loven comunably,   7235
And holden us for so worthy
That we may folk repreve echoon,
And we nyl have repref of noon.
Whom shulden folk worshipen so   144r
But us, that stynten never mo   7240
To patren while that folk may us see,
Though it not so bihynde be?
  "And where is more wode folye

Than to enhaunce chyvalrie,
And love noble men and gay,   7245
That joly clothis weren alway?
If they be sich folk as they semen,
So clene, as men her clothis demen,
And that her wordis folowe her dede,
It is gret pite, out of drede,   7250
For they wole be noon ypocritis!
Of hym, me thynketh, gret spite is;
I can not love hym on no side.
But beggers with these hodes wide,
With [sleighe] and pale faces lene,   7255
And grey clothis not full clene,
But fretted full of tatarwagges,
And high shoos, knopped with dagges,

7232 **iye-sight]** eyen sit UR   7233 **God shal]** s. g. TH²   7234 **rekketh]** Rekke MS BE-KA
7241 **may]** *om.* SK   7242 **bihynde]** b. hem TH¹-UR SK-FI   7243 **is]** i. there UR   7252 **thynketh]** t. it
SK GL   7253 **on]** in SP¹   7255 **sleighe]** steight MS KA; sleight BE; streight MO   7256 **And]** A. with UR

7234 **rekketh:** KA notes recketh in TH¹.
7235 **comunably:** KA suggests *comunly,* but no ed. so emends.
7241 **patren:** "repeat (say, recite) Pater-nosters" (TRg URg SKg₂ FI); SK adduces "Plowm. Crede, 6." BE notes
the derivation "from *Pater,* the initial word of the Lord's Prayer in Latin." Cf. 6794n.
  may: KA endorses SK's omission of this word.
7242 **bihynde:** RIt notes TH¹'s emendation *behynde hem* and quotes the Fr. (Lc 11896 "tout soit il darriers
autrement" "Though it be otherwise behind [their backs]").
7252 **spite:** "perhaps read *despit,*" suggests KA.
7253 **hym:** KA suggests *hem* here and notes the form in UR at line 7252. See 1922n.
7254 **beggers:** As BE SK RB RI note, the Fr. is *beguins* (Lc 11908), "members of (certain) lay brotherhoods
which arose in the Low Countries" (SK RB) in the 12th (RI) or early-13th centuries (SK). SK RB state that the names
come from Lambert Bègue, and SK RI explain the further etymology. As David (RI) puts it, *beguins* is a masc. form
derived from *beguines* (cf. 6861n.); "for the translator," he writes, "'beguins' was evidently synonymous with
'begards' or 'beguards' (New Eng. Beghards), a lay brotherhood, the male counterparts of the Beguines. The
Beghards . . . were repeatedly condemned, and in French *begard* became a general term for 'heretic.' The use here
in *Rom* is evidence for the etymological connection of *beggar* with OF *begard.*" On the condemnations, BE SK
specify those at the council of Cologne in 1260 and at the general council of Vienne in 1311.
  Skeat (SK), as RB FI note, sees the word *beggers* here as referring to the Franciscans, and he adduces line 7258
(= 7256 "grey clothis"). As David (RI) observes, *MED begger(e* n. cites this passage for sense 2, "a member of one of
the mendicant orders"; but he notes that sense 4, "rascal, knave," also applies.
7255 **sleighe:** KA notes *sleight* in BE.
7257 TRg (s.v. *Tatarwagges*) SK cite the Fr. (Lc 11911 "toutes frestelees de crotes"), which they translate as
"all bedaubed (TRg bedagled) with dirt." SK cites Godefroy (1881–1902, s.v. *frestelee*); as he notes, "the translation
freely varies from the original, in a score of places. See next line."
  fretted full of: "set thickly with" (RIf). SK glosses *fretted* as "ornamented, decked," compares line 4705
and *LGW* 1117, and notes that the use here is ironic. On SK's derivation of *fretted* "from A. S. *frætwian,* to adorn,"
see 4705n. See also 3204n.
  tatarwagges: "ragges, iagges" (SP²·³ URg), "tatter'd rags" (URg), "ragged shreds, i.e. patches coarsely
sewn on" (SK), "fluttering tatters" (SKg₂), "ragged patches" (FI), "tatters" (RIf). "The ending *-wagges,*" states SK, "is
allied to *wag.*"
7258–60 "This is a description of the habit of the Franciscans, or friars minor. They wore shoes, which are
here described as all clouted, and creaking like a quail-pipe from the coarseness of the leather of which they were
made; or else boots fitting so badly as to be wrinkled like a loose frock or *gype*" (BE). But cf. 7258–59n. for a picture,
not of poverty but of the "raffish effect" (RI, below) of false poverty.

That frouncen lyke a quaile pipe,
Or botis revelyng as a gype;
To such folk as I you dyvyse   7260
Shulde princes, and these lordis wise,
Take all her londis and her thingis,   144v
Bothe werre and pees, in governyngis;
To such folk shulde a prince hym yive,   7265
That wolde his lyf in honour lyve.
    "And if they be not as they seme,
That serven thus the world to queme,
There wolde I dwelle, to disceyve
[The] folk, for they shal not perceyve.   7270
But I ne speke in no such wise,
That men shulde humble abit dispise,

So that no pride ther-undir be.
No man shulde hate, as thynkith me,
The pore man in sich clothyng.   7275
But God ne preisith hym nothing,
That seith he hath the world forsake,
And hath to worldly glorie hym take,
And wole of siche delices use.
Who may that begger wel excuse,   7280
That papelard, that hym yeldith so,
And wole to worldly ese go,
And seith that he the world hath lefte,
And gredily it grypeth efte?
He is the hounde, shame is to seyn,   7285
That to his castyng goth ageyn.

7268 **That**] They SP²³   7270 **The**] To MS KA   7275 **clothyng**] a c. SU FI   7285 **hounde**] honde TH³ ST

7258–59   RI quotes the Fr. (Lc 11912–13 "houseaus fronciez et larges botes / qui resemblent borse a caillier" "pleated tights and big boots that look like a game bag for quail"). SK (7261n.), also noting the Fr., states that "the comparison to a quail-pipe seems like a guess" and that "the translation is sufficiently inaccurate." RI, however, comments as follows: "The sound of a pipe imitating the call of the female quail to lure the male acquired the figurative sense (see OED, s.v. *quail-pipe*) of something enticing, likened here to the raffish effect of beggars' boots. The translator has heightened the already vivid picture of the Fr. in a manner reminiscent of Langland's Prologue: 'Grete lobies and longe that lothe were to swynke Clothed hem in copes to ben knowen from othere' ([B] 55–56)." See 7259n.

7258 **knopped**: "knobbed" (SK GLg FI), "ornamented" (RIf), "furnish[ed] . . . with tufts or bunches of cloth" (*MED knoppen* v. [b]); on the senses "tyed, laced" (SP²³g URg), "buttoned, fastened" (TRg), "fastened (with a button)" (SKg, RBg), see *dagges* below.

    dagges: "(*fracturae*) latchets cut of leather" (SP²³g); "slips" (URg TRg MOg), "shreds" (TRg BEg MOg), "patches" (BEg SK FI), "clouts" (SK), "loose tags" (SKg₂); "ornamental cut-outs" (RIf). Skeat says (SK) that "a more usual sense of *dagge* is a strip of cloth"; elsewhere (SKg₂) he writes: "I can find no exact account of the fastening. . . . I suppose that the . . . tape-like strips had button-holes, through which the *knoppes* or buttons passed." Cf. *MED dagge* n.(1), 2. "a shred, tag, or strip (as of cloth or leather)."

7259 **frouncen**: "make a noise" (SP¹g), "creak" (BE), "squeak (literally, creased, wrinkled)" (RIf; cf. *MED frouncen* v. 2). These readings make sense of the comparison to a quail-pipe; see 7258–59n. The usual sense (*MED* 1. [a]) is "wrinckl[e]" (SPg FI); "shew wrinkles" (SK, comparing lines 155, 3137, RBg).

    quaile pipe: "a pipe used to call quails" (TRg et al.), "by imitating their call" (RIf). FI suggests "quail net" and states that "the term is not found elsewhere"; but *MED quaile-pipe* n. gives two other quotations, from the 15th century, for the sense "a pipe or whistle used to attract quail." SK RB note the inaccurate translation of the Fr. *borse a caillier* (above, 7258–59n.).

7260   "fitting so badly as to be wrinkled like a loose frock or *gype*" (BE).

    revelyng: "turning in and out" (SPg); "wrinkled, wrinkling" (URg et al.), "shewing wrinkles" (SK), "puckering" (SKg₂, RBg), "i.e., with elaborate folds, pleats" (RIf).

    gype: "coate full of pleits" (SP²³; cf. SKg₂), "frock" (TRg SKg₂), "cassock" (TRg SK FI), "smock" (RIf; cf. SKg₂). SK compares *gipoun* in *GP* 75.

7263–64 **thingis : governyngis**: KA attributes to Skeat the suggestion *thing : governing*, but neither SK nor any other ed. so emends.

7268 **serven**: GL suggests "(?) *semen*" but notes the Fr. *emblent* (Lc 11920 "qu'ainsint la grace du monde emblent" "and by that means they steal the world's favor"); again the translation is loose.

7270 **The**: KA notes *the* in TH¹ MO.

7280 **begger**: "Here again, *Beggar* answers to F. *Beguin*; see l. 7256 [= 7254]" (SK).

7281 **papelard**: SK adduces line 6796 and his note to line 415. See 415n.

7285–86 Eds. adduce Prov. 26.11 (RB FI RI; cf. Ln 11967–68n.) and 2 Pet. 2.22 (BE SK RB FI RI; cf. Lc 11937–38n.).

"But unto you dar I not lye.   145r
But myght I felen or aspie
That ye perceyved it nothyng,
Ye shulde have a stark lesyng   7290
Right in youre honde thus, to bigynne;
I nolde it lette for no synne."
    The god lough at the wondir tho,
And every wight gan laugh also,
And seide, "Lo, heere a man aright   7295
For to be trusty to every wight!"
    "Fals-Semblant," quod Love, "sey to me,
Sith I thus have avaunced thee,
That in my court is thi dwellyng,
And of ribawdis shalt be my kyng,   7300
Wolt thou wel holden my forw[a]rdis?"
    "Yhe, sir, from hens forewardis;   145r:16
Hadde never youre fadir heere-biforne   146r:17

Servaunt so trewe, sith he was borne."
    "That is ayens all nature."   7305
    "Sir, putte you in that aventure.
For though ye borowes take of me,
The sikerer shal ye never be
For ostages, ne sikirnesse,
Or chartres, for to bere witnesse.   7310
I take youresilf to recorde heere,   146v
That men ne may in no manere
Teren the wolf out of his hide,
Til he be [flayn], bak and side,
Though men hym bete and al defile.   7315
What! Wene ye that I [nil] bigile
For I am clothed mekely?
Ther-undir is all my trechery;
Myn herte chaungith never the mo
For noon abit in which I go.   7320

7287 **not]** to MO   7295 **aright]** ryght TH²-UR   7301 **forwardis]** forwordis MS BE-KA   7302 **sir]** sir, qð he UR   *Lines 7159-7206 appear after* 7302 *in* MS-UR FU   7306 **in that]** t. i. TH²   7314 **flayn]** slayn MS-ST UR-KA FU   **bak]** bothe b. UR   7315 **al defile]** alto d. MS KA; al to-defile BE MO   7316 **nil]** wole MS-FU

7287   RB compares the Pardoner's remark, *PardT* C 918 "I wol yòw nat deceyve."
7289   **perceyved it nothyng:** "were not at all aware of it" (FI).
7292   **lette:** FI's gloss, "hesitate," applies more to the phrase *it lette* than to *lette* alone, which has the sense "prevent, delay." See 6169n.
7300   BE SK RB FI RI refer to their notes to line 6068; see 6068n. Here the phrase has the quasi-military sense, "leader of troops," rather than "the court bouncer" (FI).
7301   **forwardis:** TH¹'s emendation (*forwardes*); KA makes the same suggestion.
7302   BE MO SK supply speech-heading *F. Sem.*
         Yhe: See 4659-60n. Here, exceptionally, GL retains *Yhe.*
         Marginalium: In MS, in the right margin opposite this and the next two lines (i.e. lines 7302, 7159-60 of the usual numbering) are ink marks consisting of a vertical and four horizontals, like a large capital E with an extra horizontal arm. These marks correspond to the position of the sequence-break caused by the misplaced leaf; see above, "The Misplaced Leaves." Five lines lower there is a large T opposite line 7165. See 7165n.
7303   Normal line-sequence resumes in MS and all eds. See 7013-7302n.
7305-06   BE MO SK supply speech-headings *Amour* and *F. Sem.*
7306   **putte . . . aventure:** "take the chance" (FI).
         Marginalium: In MS, opposite this line, there is a large T, similar to one on fol. 145r; see 7165n.
7311   FI's paraphrase, "I leave it to you," somewhat obscures the legal tone, so clear in the Fr. (Lc 11965 "a tesmoign vos en apel" "I call on you as witness"). The same ME words, followed by an additional "Explice," reappear in a 16th-century engrossing hand as a legal statement on a blank page at the end of the text (150v); see above, "Provenance" and Young and Aitken (1908:330).
7312-15   Proverbial (RB RI). RB compares "'Le loup mourra en sa peau, qui ne l'escorchera vif' (cited with other parallels by Langlois [Ln 11996-98])." RI cites Whiting (1968: W447). Lc (11966-67n.) cites Morawski (1925: no. 685).
7314   **flayn:** In support of emendation, SK cites Kaluza and the Fr. *escorchiez* (Lc 11967 "skinned"; also noted by GL SU FI); T. Thomas (URg) suggests the same emendation for UR's *slain.*
         bak: KA notes UR's *bothe bak.*
7315   **al defile:** KA attributes to Skeat the suggestion *al tofyle* for MS *alto defile*; no ed. so emends, but RBt notes the suggestion as KA's.
7316   **nil:** KA's suggestion; the negative form follows the Fr. (Lc 11969 "ne triche e lobe" "do not trick and deceive"; noted in RBt RIt).
7317-18   **mekely : trechery:** See 6111-12n.

Though I have chere of symplenesse,
I am not wery of shrewidnesse.
Myn lemman, Streyne[d]-Abstinence,
Hath myster of my purveaunce;
She hadde ful longe ago be deede,   7325
Nere my councel and my rede.
Lete hir allone, and you and me."
    And Love answerde, "I trust thee
Without borowe, for I wole noon."
And Fals-Semblant, the theef, anoon,   7330
Ryght in that ilke same place,
That hadde of tresoun al his face
Ryght blak withynne and white withoute,
Thankith hym, gan on his knees loute.   7334
    Thanne was ther nought but,
        "Every man   147r
Now to assaut, that sailen can,"
Quod Love, "and that full hardyly!"
Thanne armed they hem communly
Of sich armour as to hem felle.
Whanne [they] were armed, fers
        and felle,   7340
They wente hem forth, all in a route,
And set the castel al aboute.

They will nought away, for no drede,
Till it so be that they ben dede,
Or till they have the castel take.   7345
And foure batels they gan make,
And parted hem in foure anoon,
And toke her way, and forth they gonè,
The foure gates for to assaile,
Of whiche the kepers wole not faile;   7350
For they ben neithir sike ne dede,
But hardy folk, and stronge in dede.
    Now wole I seyn the countynaunce
Of Fals-Semblant and Abstynaunce,
That ben to Wikkid-Tonge went.   7355
But first they heelde her parlement,
Whether it to done were
To maken hem be knowen there,
Or elles walken forth disgised.   147v
But at the last they devysed   7360
That they wolde gone in tapinage,
As it were in a pilgrimage,
Lyke good and hooly folk unfeyned.
And Dame Abstinence-Streyned
Toke on a robe of kamelyne,   7365
And gan hir [graithe] as a Bygyne.

7323 **Streyned-Abstinence]** streyneth a. MS MO KA GL   7326 **my]** for m. UR   7334 **Thankith]**
Thankyng TH¹-UR FU-FI   7340 **they]** the MS KA   7346 **they gan]** g. t. UR   7357 **done]** be doin
UR   7358 **be]** om. TH²   7364 **And]** A. anon UR   7366 **graithe]** gracche MS-BE KA FU   **Bygyne]**
bygynne MS BE-KA GL

7321 **chere of symplenesse:** RI notes that the Fr. *simple et coie* (Lc 11973) is "the formula applied to the
Prioress's smile," *GP* 119.
7323 **Streyned:** KA notes TH¹'s emendation (*strayned*) and compares lines 7364, 7481. It follows the Fr.
Contrainte Atenance (Lc 11975; noted by SK RB). RI adduces line 6341; see 6341n.
    Abstinence: KA suggests *Abstinaunce* and compares lines 7354, 7481. Cf. 6429–30n.
7324 **myster:** Besides the usual sense "need," (FI RIf), RIf suggests the possibility of "benefited from?" At line
1426, GL adduces this line.
7327 **you and me:** RI notes the Fr. *moi e lui* (Lc 11979 "me and her").
7334 **Thankith:** KA GL RI transcribe as *Thankyth*.
    gan on his knees loute: KA suggests *and on his knees gan loute*, RBt RIt note the suggestion, but no
ed. so emends.
7340 **they:** KA notes *they* in BE MO.
7342 **set:** KA suggests *sette*, but no ed. so emends.
7346 **batels:** The context supports the sense "battalions" (SK RB FI RIf), rather than "attacks" (BE).
7361 **tapinage:** In "secresie" (SPg URg SK FI), in "hiding" (SKg₂ GLg RB). For the phrase, URg TRg cite the Fr.
En tapinois and provide "secretly, cunningly" (URg) and "lurking, sculking about" (TRg). SK cites Cotgrave (1611)
and SKg₂ offers "sneakingly." GLg gives "incognito," a connotation picked up in RIf's "disguise."
7365 **kamelyne:** "a (stuff, cloth) made of camel's hair" (TRg, s.v. *Cameline*, et al.), "or resembling it" (SK); but
RIf *MED* (*camelīn* n.) have only "a fabric of wool mixed with silk or other fibers." Earlier glosses identify it with
camlet (SPg URg); *OED* notes that the word *camlet* was early associated with *camel* but that it may spring from Arabic
Khaml, Khamlat "nap or pile on cloth." Smith (1982:91) notes that the context suggests a coarse rather than costly
fabric, and she finds a parallel for this sense in Rutebeuf's *Dit d'hypocrisie* 227 (ed. Faral and Bastin 1959–60:1.295).
7366 **graithe:** SP¹g and URg define *gra(t)ch* as "behave"; SP²⋅³g define *gratch* as a dialectal word meaning
"apparell"; URg (followed closely by TRg) goes on to suggest "*Gratche* is perhaps the same with *Graithe*, if not

305

A large coverechief of threde
She wrapped all aboute hir heede,
But she forgate not hir sawter;
A peire of bedis eke she bere   7370
Upon a lace, all of white threde,
On which that she hir bedes bede.
But she ne bought hem never a dele,
For they were geven her, I wote wele,
God wote, of a full hooly frere,   7375
That seide he was hir fadir dere,
To whom she hadde ofter went
Than ony frere of his covent.
And he visited hir also,
And many a sermoun seide hir to;   7380

He nolde lette, for man on lyve,
That he ne wolde hir ofte shryve.
[And with so great devocion   TH¹:167a
They made her confession,
That they had ofte, for the nones,   7385
Two heedes in one hoode at ones.
     Of fayre shappe I devyse her the,
But pale of face somtyme was she;
That false traytouresse untrewe   TH¹:167b
Was lyke that salowe horse of hewe,   7390
That in the Apocalips is shewed,
That signifyeth [tho] folke beshrewed
That ben al ful of trecherye,
And pale, through hypocrisye;

7377   **ofter**] after TH³ ST SP²·³   7381   **man**] men SP³; no m. UR   7383   *Lines* 7383-7574   *Out:* MS (*four leaves missing*); *supplied from* TH¹   7387   **devyse**] deuysed TH¹-UR MO KA FU-RB²   7390   **of**] or BE
7392   **tho**] to TH¹·² SP¹ KA FU

---

mistaken for it" and defines *greithe* as "fit, prepare, or make ready." The change, adopted first by MO, is reasonable paleographically (*c/t* confusion) and, as TRg RBt note, follows the Fr. *atourne* (Lc 12016 "et s'atourne conme beguine" "and dresses herself up as a Beguine"). Whichever word is used, eds. tend to agree that it means "clothe" (BEg et al.) or "dress" (SKg₂ et al.).

    Bygyne: See 6861n. I do not count the spelling variation recorded in the Collations as a substantive variant.

    7369   **sawter:** "The psalter, which has always formed the basis of the worship of the Church" (BE).

    7370   **peire of bedis:** BE notes that the Fr. has *paternostres* (Lc 12020), so called "because the number of pater nosters which the religious were bound to repeat were counted by them." SK FI gloss as a set or string of beads, a rosary, and BE SK FI note the same phrase in the description of the Prioress, *GP* 159.

        peire: "set, series (not necessarily two in number)" (RBg, s.v. *Paire*)

    7372   **bede:** SK FI read as past subjunctive: "might bid" (SK), "might pray" (FI); RIf, however, takes it as indicative in the phrase *hir bedes bede* "said her prayers."

    7378   **ony:** See 212n.

    7383–7574   Four leaves (BE says two) are missing from MS, and these lines are supplied from TH¹ (KA SKt GL RBt SU FI RIt) or "Speght" (BE). See above, "The Missing Leaves."

    7385–86   SK paraphrases, "They often kissed each other," and FI notes that the image is "slang for sexual intimacy." RI notes that the image is proverbial, cites Whiting (1968: H242), and notes that among Ln's examples (12063–64n.) is one in which the same image is applied to the union of Philip the Fair and Pope Clement V: "Rex, Papa, facti sunt una capa" "The King and the Pope have become a single hood." RB adduces three other examples from Ln, one of which is especially close to *RR* in time, spirit, and wording: Rutebeuf, *Dit des Règles* 172–73 (ed. Faral and Bastin 1959–60:1.276) "Je voi si l'un vers l'autre tendre / Qu'en un chaperon a deus testes" "I see one stretch out toward the other until one headdress contains two heads." Faral and Bastin note the parallel to *RR* (Lc 12033–34 "que .ii. testes avoit ensemble / en un chaperon, ce me semble" "it seems to me that there were two heads together under a single headdress").

    7387   **devyse:** BE's emendation, suggested also by KA, follows the Fr. present tense *la devis* (Lc 12035 "I *describe* her"; noted by RBt).

    7390–94   SK Ln (12066–72n.) RB FI RI adduce Rev. 6.8. Lc (12038–40n.) notes that the interpretation of the pale horse of the Apocalypse as representing hypocrites follows Guillaume de Saint-Amour's sermon of May 1, 1256 (1632:496).

    7392   **tho:** TH³'s emendation (noted by KA in BE MO) follows the Fr. definite article *la* (Lc 12039 "la gent male" "the wicked people"). GL compares line 7270; see note. Sutherland (SU) compares the Fr., but his note reads [*the*] where his text has *t(h)o*.

    7394   BE notes: "John of Meun and Chaucer disliked the parochial clergy and monks for being fat and rosy, and the friars for being pale and thin. There is an example of the same inconsistency in Matt. xi. 16, *et seq.*" But see the description of the Parson in *GP* as well as *ParsP* and *ParsT*.

For on that horse no colour is, 7395
But onely deed and pale, ywis.
Of suche a colour enlangoured
Was Abstynence, iwys, coloured;
Of her estate she her repented,
As her visage represented. 7400

She had a burdowne al of Thefte,
That Gyle had yeve her of his yefte;
And a skryppe of Faynte-Distresse,
That ful was of elengenesse;
And forthe she walked sobrely. 7405
And False-Semblant saynt, *je vous die*,
[Had], as it were for suche mistere,
Done on the cope of a frere,
With chere symple and ful pytous.
His lokyng was not disdeynous, 7410
Ne proude, but meke and ful pesyble.

About his necke he bare a Byble,
And squierly forthe gan he gon,

And, for to rest his lymmes upon,
He had of Treason a potent; 7415
As he were feble, his way he went.
But in his sleve he gan to thring
A rasour sharpe and wel bytyng,
That was forged in a forge
Whiche that men clepen Coupe-Gorge. 7420
So longe forthe her waye they nomen,
Tyl they to Wicked-Tonge comen,
That at his gate was syttyng,
And sawe folke in the way passyng.
The pilgrymes sawe he faste by, 7425
That beren hem ful mekely,
And humbly they with him mette.
Dame Abstynence first him grette,
And sythe him False-Semblant salued,
And he hem; but he not remued 7430
For he ne dredde hem not a dele.
For whan he sawe her faces wele,

7400 **As]** Right a. UR   7407 **Had]** And TH¹-KA FU   7413 **forthe]** for SP³   7423 **at]** al RB²
7430 **remued]** remeued TH¹-UR KA GL FU SU FI

7397 **enlangoured:** "languishing" (SPg), "languid, faint" (URg), "faded with languour" (TRg BEg SKg₂), "made weak or pale (with langour, by illness)" (RBg RIf).

7401 **burdowne:** (pilgrim's) staff (SPg et al.); SK RB cite the Fr. *bordon* (Lc 12047) and SK adduces lines 3401, 4092. In the latter part of *RR*, the staff and sack (line 7403 "skryppe") take on sexual significance. Cf. 3401n., 4092n.

7404 **elengenesse:** "strangeness, oddness" (URg); "care, trouble" (TRg BEg), "sadness" (MOg et al.), "cheerlessness" (SK FI), "wretchedness" (GLg). TRg SK FI cite Fr. *soussi* (Lc 12050), "i.e. *souci*, care, anxiety" (SK), and SK adduces *WBT*D 1199 "alenge."

7406–08 "False-Semblant, girt, I assure you, like a cordelier, and, as was fitting for such a necessity, clad in a friar's cope" (BE). This reading follows the TH¹ tradition; the emended version, instead of "and . . . clad," would read "had . . . put on." See 7407n.

7406 **saynt:** "girded, girt" (BE SK); so RB RIf, with a query; SK RI suggest that it is a var. sp. for *ceint*. But, as SK GL note, "no such Eng. adj. is known" (GL). SK GL RB RI note the Fr. (Lc 12052 "qui bien se ratorne" "who attires himself well"), which is not parallel. SPg URg TRg FI take it as the noun, "girdle (cin[c]ture)." SK notes the parallel in *GP* 329 "ceint," with MS variants *se(y,i)nt*. GL RB suggest the possibility that it should be emended to *faynt* "pale." As SK notes, "the epithet 'saint' is weak."

je vous die: "I tell you" (SK RIf); SK adduces *SumT*D 1832.

7407 **Had:** KA's suggestion, as SU FI note, follows the Fr. *ot* (Lc 12053 "had"). TH¹'s error results from repetition of *And* in the previous line.

mistere: "need" (SPg et al.).

7410 **His:** KA's mistranscription, *Hys*, persists in GL RB RI.

7413 **squierly:** "like a squire?" (RB FI RIf). All three eds. quote the Fr. (Lc 12059 "Emprés s'en va sanz esquier" "Then he goes without a squire"), and RB RI note the var., *son* for *sanz*, which would give the reading "His squire goes after him" (RI). Only KA Fr. 12263 has the var. *son* (from MS Fo), with the note, "the translator has perhaps read: *con*"; Ln Lc SU Fr. do not record the var. "Perhaps," notes RI, "the Fr. copy-text read 'con escuier.' Or possibly change to 'squierles.'"

7420 **Coupe-Gorge:** SK notes the Fr. *Coupe Gorge* (Lc 12066 "Cut-Throat").

7430 **remued:** BE's emendation (endorsed by KA in SK) follows suggestions of T. Thomas (URg, s.v. *Salved*: "*remeved . . .* should be *remeued*, or *remewed*") and Tyrwhitt (TRg "*remued*"); it does not change the sense. See *MED remēven* v., *remūen* v.

Alway in herte him thought so,
He shulde knowe hem bothe two,
For wel he knewe Dame Abstynaunce,　7435
But he ne knewe not Constreynaunce.
He knewe nat that she was constrayned,　TH¹:
Ne of her theves lyfe fayned,　167c
But wende she come of wyl al free;
But she come in another degree,　7440
And if of good wyl she beganne,
That wyl was fayled her thanne.
　And False-Semblant had he sayne also,
But he knewe nat that he was false.
Yet false was he, but his falsnesse　7445
Ne coude he nat espye nor gesse;

For Semblant was so slye wrought
That Falsenesse he ne espyed nought.
　But haddest thou knowen hym beforne,
Thou woldest on a boke have sworne,　7450
Whan thou him saugh in thylke araye,
That he, that whilome was so gaye,
And of the daunce joly Robyn,
Was tho become a Jacobyn.
But sothely, what so menne hym cal,　7455
Frere Prechours bene good menne al;
Her order wickedly they beren,
Suche mynstrelles if they weren.
So bene Augustyns and Cordylers,
And Carmes, and eke Sacked Freers,　7460

7437 **knewe**] ne k. TH² MO　7438 **Ne**] Nee BE　7440 **another**] othir UR　7442 **was fayled**] i-fayled w. MO　**thanne**] as t. SK GL　7444 **that**] *om.* BE　7455 **hym**] hem UR SU FI　7456 **Frere**] Freres SK GL RB¹·² RI　7458 **if**] i. that UR SK

7441–42 "The meaning is, that, even though the friars in the beginning willingly adopted the rules of abstinence enjoined by their founder, these rules had now become irksome" (BE).

7442 **thanne:** KA endorses SK's *as than*; SK GL so emend, "perhaps correctly," notes RBt.

7443 **sayne:** "seen" (TRg FI). TRg (s.v. *Saine*) notes that UR's *saine* is used for *seine* the pa. part. of *see*. KA endorses SK's spelling *seyn*.

7451 **thylke araye:** the clothing of a Dominican, hiding falsity beneath seeming (Ln 12126n.).

7453 **joly Robyn:** BE SK RB RI adduce *TC* 5.1174 and their notes. "Jolly Robin and Maid Marian were the principal characters in an interlude popular in the middle ages" (BE). TRg takes the Fr. (Lc 12099 "de la dance le biaus Robins" "the handsome Robin of the dance") to mean that Jolly Robin was the name of the dance, rather than of "a character in a rustic dance" (SK). But Ln (12129n.) identifies the names Robin and Marion as those of a literary shepherd and shepherdess, leaders of village dances. Barney (RI *TC* 5.1174n.) suggests that the reference in *TC* may be to Robin Hood, and he cites Mann (1973:222), who identifies these passages, along with *Piers Plowman* B 6.75 [6.73], as "contexts of idle amusement and self-indulgence." See also 6337n.

7454 **Jacobyn:** Dominican friar (SK RB FI RIf); Dominicans are "also called Black Friars" (SK) or Friars Preachers, as at line 7456 (SK RB); cf. 6338n.

7455 **hym:** probably singular, with the antecedent *Fals-Semblant*; UR SU FI, with the plural form *hem*, assume reference to the *Frere Prechours* of the next line. For *hym* as a possible plural, see 1922n.

7456 **Frere Prechours:** "Dominicans" (BE RIf); cf. 7454n., 6338n. KA endorses *Freres* in SK, but the evidence in *MED frēr(e* n., sense 4, indicates that the first element of such a construction was often not inflected for plural number.

　Prechours: KA mistranscribed as *preachours*, a spelling that persists in RB RI.

7457–58 "They would but wickedly sustain (the fame of) their order, if they became jolly minstrels" (SK). RB FI also take *beren* as pa. subjunctive—"would sustain" (RB) or "would represent" (FI)—and RB quotes the Fr., where the conditional-imperfect sequence is clear (Lc 12103–04 "mauvesement l'ordre tendroient / se tel menesterel estoient" "they would uphold their order badly if they were such minstrels").

7459–60 Of the four orders named here, the Fr. has only two (Lc 12105 "Cordelier et Barré," Franciscans and Carmelites; see Ln 12135–37n.); on the individual orders, see below. The orders of friars were usually counted as four (SK): Dominicans, Franciscans (the two major orders), Carmelites, and Augustinians (RB RI). The reason for the survival of these four and not of others, like the "Croutched" (SK; i.e., Crutched or Cross) Friars and the Sacked Friars, is that the Second Council of Lyons, in 1274, prohibited further recruiting in all but these four (Knowles and Hadcock 1972:247; Knowles 1948–59:1.186). They are the four orders that Chaucer speaks of in *GP* 210 (SK RI).

7459 **Augustyns:** Augustinian or Austin friars (SK GL FI RI); BE identifies them as "black friars," but that color is usually associated with the Dominicans.

　Cordylers: Franciscan friars, Friars Minor, Cordeliers (SK RB FI RI), so called because girt with a cord (URg TRg BE FI). They were also known in England as the Gray Friars (URg).

7460 **Carmes:** Carmelite friars (TRg BE SK RB FI RI) or White friars (SK); "discalced [unshod, barefoot] friars" (BE; cf. line 7461). BE notes that the Fr. (see 7459–60n.) has the word *barré* "barred," the name given to the

308

And al freres, shodde and bare
(Though some of hem ben great and square),
Ful hooly men, as I hem deme;
Everyche of hem wolde good man seme.
But shalte thou never of apparence   7465
Sene conclude good consequence

In none argument, ywis,
If existens al fayled is.
For menne maye fynde alwaye soph[y]me
The consequence to even[y]me,   7470
Whoso that hath the subtelte
The double sentence for to se.

7461 **al**] a. the UR   7467 **none**] any UR   7471 **that hath**] t. h. hadde TH¹-SP³ BE-KA GL FU; h. had UR

Carmelites from their habits of "black, yellow, and white"; later they adopted a simpler habit, "consisting of a white cloak over a black habit."

    Sacked Freers: Friars of the Sack (SK) or Friars de Penitentia (RB FI RI). TRg BE quote Matthew of Paris, for the year 1257, to the effect that the Sack Friars first appeared in London in that year. "Their formal name was Brothers of Penance of Jesus Christ, but they were generally known as Friars of the Sack from their dress, which consisted of a mantle of sackcloth over a tunic of better material" (Knowles 1948–59:1.203; cf. URg RB FI RI). Along with other minor groups, the Sack Friars were "officially condemned to extinction by the Council of Lyons in 1274" (Knowles, p. 202), but this ban referred only to recruiting, and some houses lingered on until the early 14th century (p. 203). SK, citing "Godwin, Archæologist's Handbook," lists houses at nine locations in England, and Knowles and Hadcock (1972:247–49) list seventeen.

    Lecoy (1968) cites the Council of Lyons and suggests that mention of the Sack Friars in the Fr. (Lc 12107) puts an upper limit of 1274 on the date of Jean's draft; but Emery (1960) shows that the Paris house of the order existed until at least 1289.

    7462 **great:** SKt incorrectly reports TH¹'s spelling as *greet*; SK's *grete*, found also in UR, is endorsed by KA.

    7463 "ironical" (BE).

    7465–72 Paré (1947:32–34) analyzes Jean de Meun's scholastic vocabulary in the Fr. (Lc 12109–16): "Mes ja ne verrez d'apparance / conclurre bone consequence / en nul argument que l'en face, / se deffaut existance efface; / tourjorz i troverez soffime / qui la consequance envenime, / se vos avez soutillité / d'entendre la duplicité" ("You will never see a good consequence result from appearance in any argument that one may make, if a defect annuls any existence. You will always find a sophism that poisons the consequence, as long as you have the subtlety to understand the double meaning").

    BE quotes part of the Fr. (Lc 12109–12) and paraphrases the ME: "You will never see good arise from retaining outward forms after the substance which they represent has ceased to exist." SK's reading is closer: "But you will never, in any argument, see that a good result can be concluded from the mere outward appearance, when the inward substance has wholly failed." SK RB RI compare *HF* 265–66 "Allas! what harm doth apparence, / Whan hit is fals in existence!" RI notes the proverbial aspect of the passage; cf. Whiting (1968: A152).

    Paré shows that *argument* is a synonym of "syllogism," in which the *consequence* is the logical link that attaches the conclusion to the two premises, major and minor. An argument based on *appearance* (thus defective in terms of *existence*) is not a good syllogism but a *sophism*, in which a good consequence cannot result, often because the same term is taken in two different senses in the two premises; when the two senses are shown, the sophism is revealed.

    Huppé (1948) reviews the work of Paré and finds that the C translator follows the Fr. "with considerable faithfulness" (p. 335), but that the translation "double sentence" for "duplicité" is "somewhat careless," since "the duplicity lies in appearance passing for existence. . . . Sentence itself is not double" (p. 336). Cf. 4456–69n.

    7468 **existens:** "reality" (URg et al.); "substance" (BE SK) "vs. appearance" (FI). See 7465–72n.

    7469–70 **sophyme : envenyme:** SK's respellings, endorsed by KA, of TH¹'s *sopheme : enveneme*; SK adduces the Fr. (Lc 12113–14 "soffime . . . envenime"). TH¹ may have selected the β-form *sopheme* (see *OED Sophism*; cf. *MED sophim(e* n.) and then altered *envenyme* to *enveneme*, for visual rhyme (*MED envenimen* v. shows no infin. forms in *-nem-*).

    7469 **sophyme:** "subtilt[y]" (SP²³g RBg), "(subtle) fallacy" (URg TRg), "sophistry" (URg), "stratagem" (BEg), "fallacious reasoning" (FI); "subtle argument" (RIf). Cf. 7465–72n.

    7470 **consequence:** "result" (SKg₂), "conclusion" (RIf); cf. 7465–72n.

    7471 **hath:** KA's suggestion follows the Fr. (Lc 12115 "se vos avez soutillité" "if you have the subtlety"; noted by SU).

    7472 **sentence:** "(sense), meaning" (URg et al.); cf. 7465–72n.

Whan the pylgrymes commen were
To Wicked-Tonge, that dwelled there,
Her harneys nygh hem was algate;   7475
By Wicked-Tonge adowne they sate,
That badde hem nere him for to come,
And of tidynges telle him some,
And sayd hem, "What case maketh you
To come into this place nowe?"   7480
     "Sir," sayd Strayned-Abstynaunce,
"We, for to drye our penaunce,
With hertes pytous and devoute   TH¹:167d
Are commen, as pylgrimes gon aboute.
Wel nygh on fote alway we go;   7485
Ful [dusty] ben our heeles two;
And thus bothe we ben sent
Throughout this worlde, that is miswent,
To yeve ensample, and preche also.
To fysshen synful menne we go,   7490
For other fysshynge ne fysshe we.
And, sir, for that charyte,
As we be wonte, herberowe we crave,
Your lyfe to amende, Christ it save!

And, so it shulde you nat displease,   7495
We wolden, if it were your ease,
A shorte sermon unto you sayne."
     And Wicked-Tonge answered agayne:
"The house," quod he, "such as ye se,
Shal nat be warned you for me.   7500
Say what you lyst, and I wol here."
     "Graunt mercy, swete sir dere!"
Quod alderfirst Dame Abstynence,
And thus began she her sentence:
"Sir, the firste vertue, certayne,   7505
The greatest and moste soverayne
That may be founde in any man,
For havynge, or for wytte he can,
That is his tonge to refrayne;
Therto ought every wight him payne.   7510
For it is better styll be
Than for to speken harme, parde!
And he that herkeneth it gladly,
He is no good man, sykerly.
And, sir, aboven al other synne,   7515
In that arte thou moste gilty inne.

7474 **dwelled]** dwelleth BE   7480 **into]** to TH² MO   7483 **and]** *om.* TH²   7485 **nygh]** nyght
TH¹⁻³ KA FU   7486 **dusty]** doughty TH¹-KA FU   7488 **this]** the TH³-BE   7492 **sir]** leve s. UR
7502 **mercy swete]** m. tho s. UR   7505 **certayne]** for c. UR   7509 **to]** for t. UR   7511 **be]** to b. UR

7477 **nere:** either the positive ("near") or the comparative degree ("nearer"); BE's *nerre*, may similarly be
either degree. See *MED nẹr* adv.(2) and prep., *ner(re* adv. 3. The Fr. has no exact parallel (Lc 12121 "qui leur ot dit:
'Or ça venez'" "who [i.e., Male Bouche] said to them, 'Now then, come on'").

7485 BE quotes "the Spanish proverb, 'To ride on St. Francis's mule,' meaning to go on foot."
     nygh: ST's emendation (*nigh*), noted by KA in BE MO.

7486 **dusty:** Jephson's suggestion (BE note, reported by KA), follows the Fr. *poudreus* (Lc 12130 "dusty";
noted by BE SKt RBt SU FI RIt). Jephson notes further, without citing a source, that "the court held for deciding
disputes at fairs, to which travellers of the lower orders resorted, was called the Court of *Piepoudre*."

7490–91 BE SK RB FI RI adduce Matt. 4.19; RB RI add Luke 5.10; and, for the friars' use of the text, SK RB RI
compare *SumT* D 1820.

7492 **sir:** KA suggests *sire*, but no ed. so emends. Cf. 7502n.

7493 **herberowe:** There are various spellings, but only UR's *erbo'rowe*, indicates elision; the line remains
hypermetrical without reducing the word to a disyllable.

7500 **warned:** refused, denied. See 1485n.

7502 **sir:** KA suggests *sire*, and SK RB RI so emend; but no ed. follows the same suggestion at line 7492.

7505–09 RB RI compare *ManT* H 332–33, where Scattergood's note (RI) cites Cato's *Distichs* 1.3; Albertanus
of Brescia's *De arte loquendi et tacendi*, 96; *RR* 12179–83 (= Lc 12149–53); *Rom* 1705–9 (*sic* for 7505–09).
Scattergood also compares *TC* 3.294n. and cites Hazelton's discussion (1960).

7505 BE MO SK supply speech-heading *Const. Abstinence.*

7508 **havynge:** "experience" (FI); literally, "possession" (SKg RBg), from the Fr. *avoir* (Lc 12152).

7511–12 Proverbial (RB RI); RB cites Haeckel (1890: no. 51), and RI cites Whiting (1968: H133).

7511 KA notes that UR inserts *to* before *be*.

7516 **gilty:** KA mistranscribes as *gylty*, a spelling that persists in GL RB RI.

Thou spake a jape not longe ago
(And, sir, that was right yvel do)
Of a yonge man that here repayred,
And never yet this place apayred.   7520
Thou saydest he awayted nothyng
But to disceyve Fayre-Welcomyng.
Ye sayd nothyng sothe of that;
But, sir, ye lye, I tel you plat.
He ne cometh no more, ne gothe, parde!   7525
I trowe ye shal him never se.
Fayre-Welcomyng in prison is,
That ofte hath played with you, er this,
The fayrest games that he coude,   7529
Without fylthe, styl or loude.   TH¹:168a
Nowe dare [he] nat [himselfe] solace.
Ye han also the manne do chace,

That he dare neyther come ne go.
What meveth you to hate him so
But properly your wicked thought,   7535
That many a false leasyng hath thought?
That meveth your foole eloquence,
That jangleth ever in audyence,
And on the folke areyseth blame,
And dothe hem dishonour and shame,   7540
For thynge that maye have no prevyng,
But lykelynesse and contryvyng.
    "For I dare sayne that reason demeth
It is nat al sothe thynge that semeth,
And it is synne to controve   7545
Thynge that is to reprove.
This wote ye wele, and sir, therfore
Ye arne to blame the more.

7520 **apayred]** repaired SP²,³   7525 **ne cometh]** c. UR   7530 **styl]** or s. UR   7531 **he nat himselfe]** she n. her selfe   TH¹-SP³ KA FU   7532 **do]** to TH²   7537 **foole]** foule TH³-BE   7539 **areyseth]** aryseth TH³ ST SP²-BE   7545 **to]** for t. UR   7546 **Thynge]** Any t. UR   **to]** for t. MO SK   7548 **the]** mochil t. UR; wel t. SK GL

7517   **spake:** On the var. spelling *speake* in ST-SP³, see 3041n.

    not longe ago: SK RB RI compare lines 3815–18, "where Wicked-Tongue reports evil about the author (here called the 'young man') and Bialacoil (here called Fair-Welcoming)" (SK).

7524   **you:** SP²,³ BE read *ye*, which is probably to be taken as a var. sp. (the unstressed object form) rather than as the subject form.

7531   **he nat himselfe:** UR's emendation, noted by KA in UR BE MO. The Fr. has no mark of gender in this line (Lc 12175 "or n'i s'ose mes soulacier" "now [he] does not dare solace himself there").

7532   "That is, 'You have (also) caused the man to be chased'" (BE SK).

    manne: "i.e., the Lover" (FI).

7534–42   Eds. have punctuated this passage in two principal ways: (1) with question mark after line 7536 and period after line 7542 (BE MO SK RB¹ SU FI); (2) as a single syntactic unit, with question mark after line 7542 (UR GL RB² RI). The first pattern, adopted here, follows Méon, Michel, Ln, and Lc (Lc 12178–86): "Qui vos esmut a tant li nuire, / fors que vostre male pensee / qui mainte mençonge a pensee? / Ce mut vostre fole loquence, / qui bret et crie et noise et tence, / et les blasmes aus genz eslieve / et les deshoneure et les grieve / por chose qui n'a point de preuve, / fors d'apparence ou de contreuve." ("Who incited you to harm him so much, outside of your evil mind, that has thought up many a lie? It was your foolish talk that provoked this situation; it howls and cries and chatters and quarrels; it foists blame on people and dishonors and makes trouble for them because of something that has no proof whatever outside of appearance or trickery."). While the Fr. punctuation is not probative, it reflects the textual reality of the demonstrative *Ce* (= this situation, 12181; Ln shows no var.), a word that begins a new, independent clause. It is parallel to ME *That* (line 7537), which remains a demonstrative in the first punctuation pattern but becomes a relative pronoun in the second.

7535–36   **thought : thought:** SK notes that the identical rhyme "is correct" and that it follows the Fr. *pensee : pensee* (Lc 12179–80, above).

7537   **That:** See 7534–42n.

7539   **areyseth:** "raise[s] (up)" (URg et al.); "stirs up" (SKg, *MED araisen* v. 8. [a]). TH³'s *aryseth*—the intransitive verb—does not follow the Fr. *eslieve* (Lc 12183 "et les blasmes aus genz eslieve" "and raises up scandals about people") as does TH¹'s transitive form.

7542   **contryvyng:** KA attributes to Skeat the suggestion "*controvyng* or *contrevyng*," but no ed. so emends.

7544   Proverbial (RB RI); RB compares Haeckel (1890: no. 132), RI Whiting (1968: T96).

7546   **to:** KA notes *for to* in MO; RBt notes that the change is perhaps correct.

7548   **the:** KA suggests *wel the.*

And nathelesse, he recketh lyte;
He yeveth nat nowe therof a myte.　　7550
For if he thought harme, parfaye,
He wolde come and gone al daye;
He coude himselfe nat abstene.
Nowe cometh he nat, and that is sene,
For he ne taketh of it no cure,　　7555
But if it be through aventure,
And lasse than other folke, algate.
And thou her watchest at the gate,
With speare in thyne arest alwaye;
There muse, musarde, al the daye.　　7560
Thou wakest night and day for thought;
Iwis, thy traveyle is for nought;
And Jelousye, withouten fayle,
Shal never quyte the thy traveyle.
And skathe is that Fayre-Welcomyng,　　7565
Without any trespassyng,
Shal wrongfully in prison be,
There wepeth and languyssheth he.
And though thou never yet, ywis,
Agyltest manne no more but this　　7570
(Take nat a-grefe), it were worthy

To putte the out of this bayly,
And afterwarde in prison lye,
And fettre the tyl that thou dye;]　　7574
For thou shalt for this synne dwelle　MS:148r
Right in the devels ers of helle,
But if that thou repente thee."
"Ma fay, thou liest falsly!" quod he.
"What? Welcome with myschaunce nowe!
Have I therfore herberd yowe,　　7580
To seye me shame, and eke reprove?
With sory happe, to youre bihove,
Am I today youre herbegere!
Go herber yow elleswhere than heere,
That han a lyer called me!　　7585
Two tregetours art thou and he,
That in myn hous do me this shame,
And for my sothe-saugh ye me blame.
Is this the sermoun that ye make?
To all the develles I me take,　　7590
Or elles, God, thou me confounde,
[But, er men diden this castel founde],
It passith not ten daies or twelve,
But it was tolde right to myselve,

　　7553　**coude himselfe nat]** ne c. n. h. UR; c. n. h. MO　　7560　**the]** t. longe UR　　7574　**fettre the]** fettred t. TH³-UR; fettred ther BE　　*Lines* 7383-7574　*Out:* MS　　7575　**for this]** fro t. BE　　7592　*Out:* MS (MS₁ *corr.*)　　7593　**passith]** passid RB¹·²　　**or]** of BE　　7594　**was]** is SU FI

　　7550　**myte:** "small bit" (SKg₂), "smallest coin" (FI). See 4830n.
　　7558　**her:** KA attributes to Skeat the suggestion *heer*, but SK, like UR BE, has *here*.
　　7560　"Meditate there, you sluggard, all day" (SK).
　　7571–72　**worthy : bayly:** See 6111–12n. Kaluza (1893*a*:106) includes this as an *-y: -yĕ* rhyme, apparently taking *bayly[e]* as "jurisdiction." Feng (1990:59n.) takes *bayly* as "castle," from OF *baille*.
　　7571　BE paraphrases: "That is, 'Take it not amiss that I tell you that it would be a good deed to put you out of the town.'" SK reads: "Take it not amiss; it were a good deed."
　　7575–76　Jephson (BE), quoting the Fr., thinks that "Chaucer is responsible for this coarseness," and Lounsbury (1892:2.119) argues for Chaucer's authorship by adducing this passage, which, he writes, "has nothing whatever to support it or suggest it in the French poem"; cf. Kittredge (1892:21) and Brusendorff (1925:410–11). But Jephson and Lounsbury had the Méon (or Michel) text (12452 "Vous en irez où puis d'enfer" "You will go to the pit of hell"). Kaluza (1893*a*:60–61) and SK, countering Lounsbury, note the var. *cul* "pit, backside," for *puis*, and *cul* appears in the texts of Ln Lc (Lc 12218); BE SK RB RI, as well as Lounsbury, all note the Fr. and compare *SumP* D 1665–1708.
　　7575　SKt notes that MS resumes.
　　7579　"An exclamation signifying that he wished them the very opposite of welcome" (BE); SK also notes the irony, "What? you are anything but welcome"; and RB notes that *with myschaunce* is "here, as frequently, a curse."
　　7582　**bihove:** "(behoof), advantage" (URg et al.), "profit" (GLg et al.), rather than "need" (FI).
　　7584　**herber:** KA suggests *herberwe*, but no ed. so emends.
　　7586　**tregetours:** "cheats" (URg, noting derivation from medieval Latin; cf. TR 4.299–302), "deceivers" (MOg SK FI), "tricksters" (SKg₂); SK compares line 6267 *treget* "deceit."
　　7588　KA records "Omit *ye* [SK]"; but no editor so emends.
　　7592　"Written in the margin by the same hand" (KA), MS₁; see 6190n.
　　7593　**passith:** RB's *passid* follows KA's suggestion. The Fr. has the simple past *passerent* (Lc 12235 "passed").
　　7594　**myselve:** SU notes that TH¹ omits *-e* in *myselu*; FU also does so.

And as they seide, right so tolde I, 7595
He kyst the rose pryvyly!
Thus seide I now, and have seid yore;
I not where he dide ony more.
Why shulde men sey me such a thyng,
If it hadde bene gabbyng? 7600
Ryght so seide I, and wole seye yit; 148v
I trowe, I lied not of it.
And with my bemes I wole blowe
To alle neighboris a-rowe,
How he hath bothe comen and gone." 7605
 Tho spake Fals-Semblant right anone:
"All is not gospel, oute of doute,
That men seyn in the towne aboute.
Ley no deef ere to my spekyng;
I swere yow, sir, it is gabbyng! 7610
I trowe ye wote wel, certeynly,
That no man loveth hym tenderly
That seith hym harme, if he wote it,
All be he never so pore of wit.
And soth is also, sikerly 7615

(This knowe ye, sir, as wel as I),
That lovers gladly wole visiten
The places there her loves habiten.
This man yow loveth and eke honoureth;
This man to serve you laboureth, 7620
And clepith you his freend so deere;
And this man makith you good chere,
And everywhere that [he] you meteth,
He yow saloweth, and he you greteth. 7624
He preseth not so ofte that ye 149r
Ought of his come encombred be;
Ther presen other folk on yow
Full ofter than he doth now.
And if his herte hym streyned so
Unto the rose for to go, 7630
Ye shulde hym sene so ofte nede,
That ye shulde take hym with the dede.
He cowde his comyng not forbere,
Though [me] hym thrilled with a spere;
[It nere] not thanne as it is now. 7635
But trustith wel, I swere it yow,

7600 **it hadde]** that i. h. UR; i. ne h. MO 7614 **be he]** h. b. RB¹·² RI 7615 **is]** it is MO
7623 **everywhere]** euerie man SP²·³ **he]** *om.* MS-SP³ BE-KA FU 7625 **that]** as TH² 7626 **come]**
comyng TH¹-UR FU SU FI 7628 **than]** t. that SK 7630 **Unto]** Vnder TH² 7634 **me]** he MS-SP¹ KA GL
FU; ye SP²-MO SK; men SU FI 7635 **It nere]** I neŕ MS (I nerer KA); I n'ere UR

7598 **where:** "whether."
   ony: See 212n.
7603 **bemes:** "trumpettes" (SPg et al.; URg et al. note derivation from OE). GL notes the Fr. *boisines* (Lc 12243
"trumpets"), and SK adduces *HF* 1240.
7604 **a-rowe:** KA notes MO's hyphenation of MS *a rowe.*
7607–08 RB notes that "this sounds proverbial" and cites Ln (12277n.), who adduces Gautier de Coincy, *Les
Miracles de la Sainte Vierge* 594–95 (ed. Poquet 1857: col. 662). RB compares Haeckel (1890: no. 134), and RI cites
Whiting (1968: G401).
7612 **hym:** "indefinite pronoun" (GL).
7619 **This man:** "i.e., the Lover" (FI).
7623 **he:** KA notes *he* in UR. In not expressing the subject in the subordinate clause, MS follows the Fr. (Lc
12261 "cist par tout la ou vos encontre" "this [man], everywhere [he] meets you").
7626 **come:** SKt reports the reading of "Th." as *comynge*, but, of TH¹⁻³, only TH³ has *-e*; TH¹ has *comyng.* On
the sense "coming, arrival," SK cites Stratmann's dictionary of ME, s.v. *cume*; see *MED come* n.(1) 1. (a).
7631 "You must (would SK) necessarily see him so often" (BE SK).
7634 "'Though one pierced him with a spear' (reading *me* for Thynne's [*sic for* MS's] *he*)" (RB).
   me: RB's emendation (= "one," impersonal [RIf]) follows the Fr. *en* (Lc 12272 "s'en le deüst tout vif
larder" "if one were to spit him alive"; noted by RB RI). SU FI's *men* has the same sense; see *MED me* pron.(1), *men*
pron. indef. KA notes *ye* in UR MO. ·
   thrilled: "pierced" (SPg et al., s.v. *thirle(d)*, SKg, FI RI; URg et al. note derivation from OE). This sense
of OF *larder* derives from the culinary practice of piercing meat to insert strips of fat (*lard*) in preparation for
grilling. Lcg, s.v. *larder*, corrects Lng, who, following Godefroy (1881–1902), gives only "brûler, griller"; cf. Tobler-
Lommatzsch (1925– :5.169) "spiessen, durchboren," with quotations from the Fr. *Roman* (Ln = Lc 3253, 3722, 9298,
12272).
7635 **It nere:** TH¹'s emendation corresponds roughly to the Fr. (Lc 12273 "il ne fust pas ore en ce point" "he
would not now be in this situation"). KA notes the change in TH¹ BE MO.

That it is clene out of his thought.
Sir, certis, he ne thenkith it nought;
No more ne doth Faire-Welcomyng,
That sore abieth al this thing. 7640
And if they were of oon assent,
Full soone were the rose hent;
The maugre youres wolde be.
And sir, of o thing herkeneth me,
Sith ye this man that loveth yow 7645
Han seid such harme and shame now,
Witeth wel, if he gessed it,
Ye may wel demen in youre wit
He nolde nothyng love you so, 149v
Ne callen you his freende also, 7650
But nyght and day he wol[d]e wake
The castell to distroie and take,
If it were soth as ye devise;
Or some man in some maner wise
Might it warne hym everydele, 7655
Or by hymsilf perceyven wele.
For sith he myght not come and gone,
As he was whilom wont to done,

He myght it sone wite and see;
But now all otherwise [doth] he. 7660
Thanne have [ye], sir, al outerly
Deserved helle, and jolyly
The deth of helle, douteles,
That thrallen folk so giltles."
　　Fals-Semblant proveth so this thing 7665
That he can noon answeryng,
And seth alwey such apparaunce
That nygh he fel in repentaunce,
And seide hym, "Sir, it may wel be.
Semblant, a good man semen ye, 7670
And, Abstinence, full wise ye seme.
Of o talent you bothe I deme.
What counceil wole ye to me yeven?" 150r
　　"Ryght heere anoon thou shalt be shryven,
And sey thy synne withoute more; 7675
Of this shalt thou repent sore.
For I am prest and have pouste
To shryve folk of most dignyte
That ben, as wide as world may dure.
Of all this world I have the cure, 7680

7642 **were]** *om.* BE　　**hent]** ybent UR　　7643 **The]** Tho t. UR　　7651 **wolde]** wole MS-KA FU SU
FI　　7660 **doth]** wote MS-KA FU　　7661 **ye]** we TH¹-UR FU; *om.* MS KA　　7665 **proveth so]** s. p. TH¹-UR
FU SU FI　　7666 **can]** ne c. UR　　7669 **be]** bo FU　　7676 **repent]** r. The UR

7643　"'The blame (lit. the ill will) would be yours.'" (SK).
　　The maugre youres: "'In spite of you'" (BE SKg₂).
　　maugre: "blame" (SK RB); "blame (fault)" (FI); "ill will" (RIf). SK compares line 4399 "for the use of
maugre as a sb." See 3144n., 4399n.
　　youres: "agrees with *gre* in maugre" (BE); "stands for *your*, gen. pl. of *you*" (Skeat 1878c:4.258). Cf.
2386n.
　　7651　**wolde:** KA endorses SK's emendation and notes that Skeat compares line 7649 *nolde.* It is the
conditional construction, however (line 7653 *If it were . . .*), that principally supports the pa. t. here.
　　7659　**wite and see:** FI cites the Fr. (SU Fr. 12322 "s'en fust aperceü" "would guess"; =Lc 12292 "l'eüst
aperceü" "would have noticed it").
　　7660　**doth:** KA's suggestion follows the Fr. *fet* (Lc 12293 "acts"; noted by SKt RBt-RIt).
　　7661　**ye:** BE's emendation, noted in BE MO by KA, follows the Fr. *vos* (Lc 12294 "you"; noted by SU FI). TH²'s
we may have arisen from misreading a Fr. *uos* as *nos.*
　　7662　**jolyly:** "richly, deservedly" (SKg₂); "especially; a curious use" (SK); "?fully" (GL); "completely" (FI);
"very much, decidedly" (*MED jolīlī* adv. [f], where this is the sole quotation). SK RB FI see *jolyly* as an intensifying
adv. that corresponds to Fr. *bien* (Lc 12295 "la mort d'enfer bien deservie" "well deserved the death of hell"); but GL
holds that *bien* "is translated by *douteles*" and that the intensifying use of *jolyly* "is difficult to explain." The Fr. has
two adverbs, *outreement* and *bien*, while the ME has three, *outerly, jolyly,* and *douteles*; of these three, *douteles* is a
sentence adv., while the other two correspond to the two Fr. advs. in modifying the verb.
　　7666　**he:** "i.e., Wicked-Tongue" (FI).
　　7673–74　**yeven : shryven:** KA suggests *yiven*, and RB RI so spell. Cf. 2759–60n.
　　7674　BE SK supply speech-heading *F. Sem.*
　　7677–82　On the friars' power to hear confessions anywhere, BE RI compare lines 6364–65 (see note above),
and RB compares *GP* 218 ff. BE SK note that friars' license was not, like the parish priest's, confined to any single
parish.
　　7678–79　"'To shrive folk that are of the highest dignity, as long as the world lasts.' So in the F. text" (SK).

And that hadde never yit persoun,
Ne vicarie of no maner toun.
And, God wote, I have of thee
A thosand tyme more pitee
Than hath thi preest parochial,　　　　　　7685
Though he thy freend be special.
I have avauntage, in o wise,

That youre prelatis ben not so wise
Ne half so lettred as am I.
I am licenced boldely　　　　　　7690
To reden in divinite
And longe have red . . .
Explicit

7681 **never yit**] y. n. SP³　7682 **Ne**] No SK　7683 **wote**] it w. UR　7684 **tyme**] tymes TH¹-UR SK
FU-FI　7685 **thi**] the SP¹　7686 **he**] *om.* TH²　7688 **prelatis**] Priests SP²·³　7691 **To reden in
divinite**] I. d. for t. r. TH¹-MO FU-FI; I. d. t. r. SK　7692 **And longe have red**] And to confessen out of drede /
If [I. that UR] ye wol you nowe confesse / And leaue your synnes more and lesse / Without abode, knele downe
anon / And you [ye MO] shal haue absolucion. TH¹-MO SK-FI　*Colophon:* **Explicit**] ¶. Finis. / Here endeth the
Romaunt of the / Rose: And here foloweth / the boke of Troy- / lous and Cre- / seyde. TH¹·³ FU; ¶ Here endeth the
Romaunt / of the Rose. / ¶ Here after foloweth the Booke / of Troilus and Cre- / seide. ST SP¹; ¶ Here after
followeth the Booke of / Troilus and Creseide. SP²; ¶ Here after followeth the Booke of Troilus and Creseide SP³;
Here endeth the Romaunt of the Rose. UR FI; Finis SU　*Out:* BE GL

7683–89　Ln (12345–51n.) quotes Guillaume de Saint-Amour, *De periculis* 4 (1632:12 [*sic for* 30]).

7688　*Marginalium:* "7690. Urry. p.268" in Thomas Martin's hand (Young and Aitken 1908:330). Cf. above,
"Provenance" and "Other Marginalia."

7689　BE adduces *SumT* D 2008, where the friar speaks of vicars as "lewed," unlearned.

7691–92　TH¹'s six-line conclusion (noted in KA RIf) appears with few variants (see collation) in the text of all
eds. except RI (and, of course, KA, which is based on MS). All these versions accept TH¹ as independent textual
authority. David (RI), however, follows Blodgett (see above, "The Glasgow MS and the Thynne Print") in seeing MS
as printer's copy for TH¹ and therefore as the sole textual authority; he cites Kaluza's earlier arguments in that
direction. To follow those arguments, we compare the Fr., which has eight lines (Lc 12323–30) where TH¹ has six:
"voire, par Dieu, pieça leü. / Por confessor m'ont esleü / li meilleur qu'en puisse savoir / par mon sens et par mon
savoir. / Se vos volez ci confessier / et ce pechié sanz plus lessier, / sanz fere en ja mes mencion, / vos avrez
m'asolucion" ("In fact, by God, I have lectured [= read] for a long time. The best people that one may know have
chosen me as confessor on account of my sense and my knowledge. If you will confess here and abandon this sin
without further ado, without making any further mention of it, you will have my absolution"). As Kaluza
(1893*b*:109) points out, Skeat argues that the last four lines show that MS was copied from "O" (the hypothetical
original of both MS and TH¹) at a later period than the manuscript used by TH¹, "viz., at a period when O. was
somewhat damaged or torn at the end of its last page" (SK 1.14). The assumption here is that TH¹'s lines are
authentic, and SK clarifies this assumption in his note to line 7694 (= 7692): "The fact that Thynne gives the last six
lines correctly shews that his print was *not* made from the Glasgow MS." But Kaluza (p. 110) compares the Fr. and
the ME and concludes that the last lines in TH¹ are Thynne's addition; that the translator of Fragment C would not
have used the colorless "And to confessen out of drede" as a translation for the three lines of the Fr. (Lc 12324–26)
about how the best people had chosen him as confessor; that the continuation is wrongly translated, in that the
phrase *ce pechié* concerns a quite specific sin of Malebouche, the defamation of Bel-Acueil; that the false rhyme
anoon : absolucioun suffices to indicate Thynne's hand; and that TH¹'s readings "have the value only of the editor's
conjectures, not the authority to claim a more correct manuscript." Supported by Blodgett's conclusion that MS was
TH¹'s copy-text, David (RI) accepts Kaluza's arguments that the conclusion is spurious, "tacked on by Thynne to
prevent ending in mid-sentence." It is "very loosely related to the Fr. . . . [It] omits the MS's 'And longe have red,'
which corresponds to 'pieç'a leü'; it skips over the lines that Fals-Semblant has confessed the very best people; 'senz
plus laissier' is transformed into 'more and lesse'; the particular sin of slander becomes generally *synnes*. Finally,
'anon : absolucion' is a highly suspicious rhyme."

7691　BE regards the MS version as "transposed so as to spoil the rhyme." See 7691–92n.

To reden: BE SK point out that to read was to give lectures; SK adds that to do so in divinity was a
"privilege reserved for doctors of divinity."

7692　**longe have red:** KA, following the Fr. (above), suggests adding *parde* after *red*. SK regards this MS
reading as wrong and the TH¹ reading as authentic; see 7691–92n. In fact, as RI notes, this phrase more closely
follows the Fr. *pieça leü* (Lc 12323, above) than does TH¹'s version, "And to confessen out of drede," which relates
very vaguely to the next three lines of the Fr. (above).

BE RI note that "the episode concludes with Fals-Semblant using his razor to slit the throat and cut out the tongue of Male Bouche" (RI). SK GL note that the Fr. continues for nearly another 9,500 lines (Lc ends at 21750). "Thus," says SK, "the three fragments of the translation make up less than a third of the original."

After the last line of MS and before the Explicit, there is a smudged area of about five lines, where something has been scraped away. Blodgett (1975:62; 1984:40) notes that "even ultra-violet light reveals nothing more than that there was once writing there, perhaps in sixteenth-century secretary hand."

Colophon: SK SU FI note that MS closes after line 7692 with the word *Explicit*, for TH¹'s colophon, partially noted by SK SU, see collation.

Bibliographical Index

Aimon de Varennes. *See* Alfons Hilka, ed. 1932.

Alanus de Insulis   1855. *Opera. PL* 210.

Alderson, William L., and Arnold C. Henderson   1970. *Chaucer and Augustan Scholarship.* University of California Publications, English ser., 35. Berkeley, Los Angeles, and London: University of California Press. Abridged version of the chapter on John Urry in Ruggiers, ed. 1984, pp. 93–115, 269–73.

Aldine Edition   1845. *The Poetical Works of Geoffrey Chaucer, with Memoir by Sir Harris Nicolas.* 6 vols. London: William Pickering. *Rom* is in vol. 4. For the 1866 revision, *see* Richard Morris, ed. 1866*b*.

———— 1846. *Chaucer's* Romaunt of the Rose, Troilus and Creseide, *and the Minor Poems, with Life of the Poet by Sir Harris Nicolas.* 3 vols. London: William Pickering. Reprint of vols. 4–6 of Aldine Edition 1845, with Nicolas's Life. *Rom* is in vol.1.

Anderson, Robert, ed.   1793. *The Works of the British Poets.* Vol. 1, Chaucer, Surrey, Wyatt, and Sackville. Edinburgh: Mundell.

Ando, Shinsuke   1970. The Language of *The Romaunt of the Rose* (Fragment A) with Particular Reference to Chaucer's Relationship to Middle English Provincial Poetry. *Studies in English Literature,* English Number 1970. Tokyo: English Literary Society of Japan, 63–74.

———— 1986. The English Tradition in Chaucer's Diction. In Julian N. Wasserman and Robert J. Blanch, eds., *Chaucer in the Eighties,* pp. 163–174. Syracuse, NY: Syracuse University Press.

Andreas Capellanus. *See* E. Trojel, ed. 1892; P.G. Walsh, ed. and trans. 1982.

Andrew, Malcolm   1993. Explanatory Notes. *The General Prologue. A Variorum Edition of the Works of Geoffrey Chaucer,* vol. 2, part 1B. Norman: University of Oklahoma Press. *See also* Daniel J. Ransom 1993.

Anonymous. *See* Unidentified reviewer.

Arden, Heather M.   1987. *The Romance of the Rose.* Boston: Twayne.

Arnold, T.   1878*a.* The Date of the "Court of Love." *Academy,* June 1, p. 489.

———— 1878*b.* The Date of the "Court of Love" and the "Romaunt of the Rose." *Academy,* July 20, pp. 66–67.

Auerbach, Erich   1965. *Literary Language and Its Public in Late Latin Antiquity and in the Middle Ages,* trans. Ralph Manheim. New York: Pantheon. Originally published as *Literatursprache und Publikum in der lateinischen Spätantike und im Mittelalter.* Bern: A. Franke Verlag, 1958.

Badel, Pierre-Yves   1970. Raison "fille de Dieu" et le rationalisme de Jean de Meun. In *Mélanges de Langue et de Littérature du Moyen Âge et de la Renaissance offerts à Jean Frappier,* vol. 1, pp. 41–52. Publications Romanes et Françaises, 112. Geneva: Droz.

———— 1980. *Le* Roman de la Rose *au XIVe siècle: Etude de la Réception de l'œuvre.* Publications Romanes et Françaises, 153. Geneva: Droz.

Baird, Joseph L., and John R. Kane, trans.   1978. *La Querelle de la Rose: Letters and Documents.* North Carolina Studies in the Romance Languages and Literatures, 199. Chapel Hill, NC: University of North Carolina, Department of Romance Languages.

Baird, Lorrayne Y.   1977. *A Bibliography of Chaucer, 1964–1973.* Reference Guides in Literature ser. Boston: G. K. Hall; London: George Prior.

————, and Hildegard Schnuttgen   1988. *A Bibliography of Chaucer 1974–1985.* Hamden, CT: Archon

Baisier, Leon   1936. *The Lapidaire Chrétien: Its Composition, Its Influence, Its Sources.* Washington, D.C.: Catholic University of America.

Baker, Donald, ed.   1984. *The Manciple's Tale. A Variorum Edition of the Works of Geoffrey Chaucer,* vol. 2, part 10. Norman: University of Oklahoma Press.

Baldwin, Charles Sears   1928. *Medieval Rhetoric and Poetic (to 1400).* New York: Macmillan. Reprint. Gloucester, MA: Peter Smith, 1959.

Bale, John 1557–59. *Scriptorum illustrium Maioris Brytannie catalogus.* 2 vols. in 1. Basle. Originally published as *Illustrium majoris Britanniae scriptorum summarium.* Ipswich: John Overton, 1548. Reprint. Farnsworth, England: Gregg International Publishers, 1971.

Barbazan, Etienne, and D. M. Méon, eds. 1808. *Fabliaux et contes des poètes françois.* 4 vols. Paris: B. Warée oncle.

Barney, Stephen A. 1979. *Allegories of History, Allegories of Love.* Hamden, CT: Archon.

Barron, W. R. J. 1965. "Luf-Daungere." In F. Whitehead et al., eds., *Medieval Miscellany Presented to Eugène Vinaver,* pp. 1–18. Manchester: Manchester University Press.

Bell, John, ed. 1782. *The Poets of Great Britain Complete from Chaucer to Churchill.* Edinburgh: Apollo Press, by the Martins. Vols. 1–14, Chaucer's works. *Rom* is in vols. 7–8.

Bell, Robert, ed. 1854–56. *Poetical Works of Geoffrey Chaucer,* 8 vols. Annotated Edition of the English Poets. London: John W. Parker and Son. Vol. 7, *The Romaunt of the Rose,* published in 1855. [Notes by John Mountenay Jephson.]

———, ed. 1878. *Poetical Works of Geoffrey Chaucer.* Rev. ed., 4 vols., "with a preliminary essay by W. W. Skeat." London: George Bell. Vol. 4, *The Romaunt of the Rose.* [Skeat has additional notes.]

Bennett, J. A. W. 1982. *Nosce te ipsum:* Some Medieval and Modern Interpretations. In Piero Boitani, ed., *The Humane Medievalist: Essays in English Literature and Learning from Chaucer to Eliot,* pp. 135–72. Rome: Edizioni di Storia e Letteratura.

Benson, Larry D., gen. ed. 1987. *The Riverside Chaucer.* 3d ed. Boston: Houghton Mifflin. Alfred David, ed., *Rom.*

Benson, Robert G. 1980. *Medieval Body-Language: A Study of the Use of Gesture in Chaucer's Poetry.* Anglistica, 21. Copenhagen: Rosenkilde and Bagger.

Benton, John F. 1968. Clio and Venus: An Historical View of Medieval Love. In F.X. Newman, ed., *The Meaning of Courtly Love,* pp. 19–42. Albany, NY: State University of New York Press.

Besant, Walter 1871. *Le Roman de la Rose. Athenaeum,* Jan. 21, p. 90.

Bieler, Ludovicus, ed. 1957. *Boethius: Philosophiae consolatio.* Corpus Christianorum, Series Latina 94. Turnholti (Belgium): Typographi Brepols.

Bloch, Oscar, and Walther von Wartburg 1968. *Dictionnaire étymologique de la langue française.* 5th ed. Paris: Presses universitaires de France.

Blodgett, James E. 1975. *William Thynne and His 1532 Edition of Chaucer.* Ph.D. diss., Indiana University.

——— 1979. Some Printer's Copy for William Thynne's 1532 Edition of Chaucer. *The Library,* 6th ser., 1:97–113.

——— 1984. William Thynne (d. 1546). In Ruggiers, ed. 1984, pp. 35–52.

Bloomfield, Morton W. 1963. A Grammatical Approach to Personification Allegory. *MP* 60:161–71. Reprinted in Morton W. Bloomfield, *Essays and Explorations,* pp. 243–60. Cambridge, MA: Harvard University Press, 1970.

Blount, Thomas 1656. *Glossographia: Or a Dictionary Interpreting all such Hard Words. . . as are now used in our refined English Tongue.* London. Reprint. Menston, England: Scolar Press, 1969.

Boethius, Anicius Manlius Severinus. *See* Ludovicus Bieler, ed. 1957.

Bonnell, Thomas F. 1987. John Bell's *Poets of Great Britain.* The "Little Trifling Edition" Revisited. *MP* 85:128–52.

Bosworth, Joseph, and T. Northcote Toller, eds. 1882–98. *An Anglo-Saxon Dictionary.* Oxford: Clarendon Press. *An Anglo-Saxon Dictionary Supplement,* edited by T. Northcote Toller. Oxford: Clarendon Press, 1921.

Bourdillon, F. W. 1906. *The Early Editions of the* Roman de la Rose. The Bibliography Society Illustrated Monographs, 14. London: Chiswick Press.

Bowden, Muriel 1948. *A Commentary on the General Prologue to the Canterbury Tales.* New York: Macmillan.

Boyd, Beverly 1973. *Chaucer and the Medieval Book.* San Marino: Huntington Library.

Braddy, Haldeen 1979. The French Influence on Chaucer. In Rowland, ed. 1979, pp. 143–59.

Bradshaw, Henry 1889. *Collected Papers of Henry Bradshaw.* Cambridge: Cambridge University Press.

Brewer, Derek [D. S.] 1955. The Ideal of Feminine Beauty in Medieval Literature, Especially "Harley Lyrics," Chaucer, and Some Elizabethans. *MLR* 50:257–69.

―――― 1966. The Relationship of Chaucer to the English and European Traditions. In *Chaucer and Chaucerians: Critical Studies in Middle English Literature*, pp. 1–38. London: Nelson; University: University of Alabama Press.

―――― 1969. Introduction. In *Geoffrey Chaucer: The Works 1532, With Supplementary Material from the Editions of 1542, 1561, 1598 and 1602*. Menston, England: Scolar Press.

――――, ed. 1978. *Chaucer: The Critical Heritage*. 2 vols. London, Henley, and Boston: Routledge and Kegan Paul.

Brink, Bernhard ten 1867. Zum Romaunt of the Rose. *Jahrbuch für romanische und englische Literatur* 8:306–14.

―――― 1870. *Chaucer. Studien zur Geschichte seiner Entwicklung und zur Chronologie seiner Schriften*. Münster: Adolph Russell.

―――― 1877–93. *See* Bernhard ten Brink 1883–96.

―――― 1878. Beiträge zur englischen Lautlehre. *Anglia* 1:512–53.

―――― 1883–96. *History of English Literature*, trans. Horace M. Kennedy, William Clarke Robinson, and L. Dora Schmitz. 2 vols. in 3. London: G. Bell and Sons; New York: Henry Holt. Originally published as *Geschichte der englischen Literatur*. 2 vols. Berlin: Robert Oppenheim, 1893.

―――― 1884. Chaucers Sprache und Verskunst. Leipzig: Weigel.

―――― 1892. Zur Chronologie von Chaucers Schriften. *EStn* 17:1–23.

―――― 1901. *The Language and Metre of Chaucer*, trans. M. Bentinck Smith from the 2d ed., rev. Friedrich Kluge (Leipzig: C.H. Tauchnitz, 1899) of *Chaucers Sprache und Verskunst*. London and New York: Macmillan.

Bronson, Bertrand H. 1940. Chaucer's Art in Relation to His Audience. In *Five Studies in Literature*, pp. 1–53. University of California Publications in English, vol. 8, no. 1. Berkeley: University of California Press.

―――― 1947. Personification Reconsidered. *ELH* 14:163–77.

―――― 1960. *In Search of Chaucer*. Toronto: University of Toronto Press.

Brunner, Karl 1963. *An Outline of Middle English Grammar*, trans. Grahame Johnston. Oxford: Blackwell.

Brusendorff, Aage 1925. *The Chaucer Tradition*. Copenhagen: Branner; London, Oxford University Press. Reprint. Gloucester, MA: Peter Smith, 1965.

Bryan, W. F., and Germaine Dempster, eds. 1941. *Sources and Analogues of Chaucer's Canterbury Tales*. Chicago: University of Chicago Press. Reprint. New York: Humanities Press, 1958.

Buchon, Jean Alexandre, ed. 1824–28. *Collection des chroniques nationales françaises*. 47 vols. Paris: Verdière.

Burchfield, R. W. See *Oxford English Dictionary* 1972–86.

Burke, John, and John Bernard Burke 1844. *A Genealogical and Heraldic History of the Extinct and Dormant Baronetcies of England, Ireland, and Scotland*. 2d ed. London: J.R. Smith. Reprint. Beccles: Clowes, 1964.

Buss, Robert Woodward 1920. *Fleetwood Family Records*. London: privately printed.

Butler, Alban 1963. *Butler's Lives of the Saints*, eds. Herbert Thurston and Donald Attwater. 4 vols. New York: P. J. Kenedy.

Caie, Graham D. 1974. An Iconographic Detail in the *Roman de la Rose* and the Middle English *Romaunt. ChauR* 8:320–23.

Campbell, Alistair 1959. *Old English Grammar*. Oxford: Clarendon Press.

Campbell, Lily B., ed. 1938. *The Mirror for Magistrates*. Cambridge: Cambridge University Press.

Cappelli, Adriano 1967. *Lexicon Abbreviaturarum: Dizionario di Abbreviature Latine et Italiane*. 6th ed. Milan: Hoepli.

Carlson, David 1989. The Writings and Manuscript Collections of the Elizabethan Alchemist, Antiquary, and Herald Francis Thynne. *Huntington Library Quarterly* 52:203–72.

Catholicon Anglicum. *See* Sidney J. H. Herrtage and H. B. Wheatley, eds. 1881.

Chalcidius. *See* J. H. Waszink, ed. 1962.

Chalmers, Alexander, ed. 1810. *The Works of the English Poets from Chaucer to Cowper*. Vol. 1, Chaucer. London: J. Johnson.

Chance, Jane. *See* Jane Chance Nitzsche 1975.

Chartularium universitatis parisiensis. *See* Henri Denifle and Emile Chatelain, eds. 1889–97.

Cheney, C. R.   1945. *Handbook of Dates for Students of English History.* London: Royal Historical Society. Reprint, 1970.

Cherniss, Michael D.   1975. Irony and Authority: The Ending of the *Roman de la Rose. Modern Language Quarterly* 36:227–38.

Chesterton, G. K.   1932. *Chaucer.* London: Faber and Faber; New York: Ferrar and Rinehart. 2d ed. London: Faber and Faber, 1948. Reprint. New York: Pellegrini & Cudahy, 1949.

Child, F. J.   1870. The "Roman de la Rose." *Athenaeum,* Dec. 3, p. 721.

Chiswick Edition   1822. *The British Poets, Including Translations.* Vols. 1–5, *The Poems of Geoffrey Chaucer.* Chiswick: C. Wittingham. *Rom* is in Vol. 3.

Chrétien de Troyes.   *See* Alexandre Micha, ed. 1965; William Roach, ed. 1959; Mario Roques, ed. 1963, 1965, 1966.

Cicero.   *See* William Falconer, ed. and trans. 1923; G.L. Hendrickson and H. M. Hubbell, eds. and trans. 1939.

Cipriani, Lisi   1907. Studies in the Influence of the *Romance of the Rose* upon Chaucer. *PMLA* 22:552–95.

Claudian, Claudius.   *See* Maurice Platnauer, ed. and trans. 1922.

Clemen, Wolfgang   1963. *Chaucer's Early Poetry,* trans. C. A. M. Sym. London: Methuen. Originally published as *Der junge Chaucer.* Kölner anglistische Arbeiten, 33. Bochum-Langendreer: H. Poppinghaus, 1938.

Cline, Ruth H.   1972. Heart and Eyes. *RPh* 25:263–97.

Colby, Alice M.   1965. *The Portrait in Twelfth-Century French Literature.* Geneva: Droz.

Coles, Elisha   1676. *An English Dictionary.* London: Printed for Samuel Crouch. Facsimile ed. Menston, England: Scolar Press, 1971.

Cook, Albert S.   1887. *The Romaunt of the Rose* and Professor Skeat's Vocabulary Test. *MLN* 2:143–46.

———   1916a. Two Notes on Chaucer. *MLN* 31:441–42.

———   1916b. The Historical Background of Chaucer's Knight. *Transactions of the Connecticut Academy of Arts and Sciences* 20:116–240.

———   1919. Chaucerian Papers—I. *Transactions of the Connecticut Academy of Arts and Sciences* 23:1–63.

———   1924. Chaucer and Venantius Fortunatus. *MLN* 39:376–78.

Corpus Juris Civilis.   *See* Paul Krueger and Theodor Mommsen, eds. 1968–70.

Cotgrave, Randle   1611. *A Dictionarie of the French and English Tongues.* London: Adam Islip. Reprint. Hildesheim: Georg Olms, 1970.

Craik, George Lillie   1844–45. *Sketches of the History of Literature and Learning in England.* 6 vols. London: Charles Knight.

Crawford, William R.   1967. *Bibliography of Chaucer 1954–63.* Seattle and London: University of Washington Press.

Crow, Martin M., and Clair C. Olson, eds.   1966. *Chaucer Life-Records.* Oxford: Clarendon Press; Austin: University of Texas Press.

Cunningham, James V.   1952. The Literary Form of the Prologue to the *Canterbury Tales. MP* 49:172–81.

Cursor Mundi.   *See* Richard Morris, ed. 1874–93.

Curtius, Ernst Robert   1953. *European Literature and the Latin Middle Ages,* trans. Willard R. Trask. London: Routledge; New York: Pantheon Books. Originally published as *Europäische Literatur und lateinisches Mittelalter.* Bern: A. Francke Verlag, 1948.

Dahlberg, Charles   1961. Macrobius and the Unity of the *Roman de la Rose. SP* 58:573–82.

———   1969. Love and the *Roman de la Rose. Speculum* 44:568–84.

———, trans.   1971. *The Romance of the Rose by Guillaume de Lorris and Jean de Meun.* Princeton: Princeton University Press. Reprint. Hanover and London: University Press of New England, 1983.

———   1977. First Person and Personification in the *Roman de la Rose*: Amant and Dangier. *Mediaevalia* 3:37–58.

———   1981. [Review of Badel 1980]. *Speculum* 56:844–47.

———   1988. *The Literature of Unlikeness.* Hanover, NH: University Press of New England.

David, Alfred   1969. [Review of Sutherland ed. 1968]. *Speculum* 44:666–70.

———   1976. *The Strumpet Muse: Art and Morals in Chaucer's Poetry.* Bloomington and London: Indiana University Press.

―――― 1985. An Iconography of Noses: Directions in the History of a Physical Stereotype. In Jane Chance and R. O. Wells, Jr., eds., *Mapping the Cosmos*, pp. 76–97, 162–63. Houston: Rice University Press.

―――― 1987. *See* Larry D. Benson, gen. ed. 1987.

Davis, Norman, et al. 1979. *A Chaucer Glossary.* Oxford: Clarendon Press.

Day, Mabel, and Robert Steele, eds. 1936. *Mum and the Soothsegger.* EETS, o.s. 199. London: Oxford University Press.

Dedeck-Héry, V. L. 1952. Boethius' *De Consolatione* by Jean de Meun. *MS* 14:165–275.

Dempster, Germaine 1932. *Dramatic Irony in Chaucer.* Stanford University Publications in Language and Literature, vol. 4, no. 3. Stanford: Stanford University Press. Reprint. New York: Humanities Press, 1959.

―――― 1941. The Pardoner's Prologue. In Bryan and Dempster, eds. 1941, pp. 409–14.

Denifle, Henri, and Emile Chatelain, eds. 1889–97. *Chartularium universitatis parisiensis.* 4 vols. Paris: Delalain.

Dickinson, John, trans. 1927. *The Statesman's Book of John of Salisbury.* New York: A. A. Knopf. Reprint. New York: Russell and Russell, 1963.

Diekstra, F. N. M. 1981. Chaucer's Way with his Sources: Accident into Substance and Substance into Accident. *ES* 62:215–36.

―――― 1988. Chaucer and the Romance of the Rose. *ES* 69:12–26.

Dillon, Bert 1974. *A Chaucer Dictionary: Proper Names and Allusions, excluding Place Names.* Boston: G. K. Hall.

Dobson, E. J. 1968. *English Pronunciation 1500–1700.* 2d ed. 2 vols. (pages numbered continuously). Oxford: Clarendon Press.

Donaldson, E. Talbot 1954. Chaucer the Pilgrim. *PMLA* 69:928–36. Reprinted in Donaldson 1970c, pp. 1–12.

―――― 1970a. Criseide and Her Narrator. In Donaldson 1970c, pp. 65–83.

―――― 1970b. The Psychology of Editors of Middle English Texts. In Donaldson 1970c, pp. 102–18.

―――― 1970c. *Speaking of Chaucer.* London: Athlone Press; New York: Norton.

Donaldson-Evans, Lance K. 1978. Love's Fatal Glance: Eye Imagery and Maurice Scève's Délie. *Neophilologus* 69:202–11.

Du Cange, Charles du Fresne 1937–38. *Glossarium Mediae et Infimae Latinitatis,* rev. D. P. Carpenter, G. A. L. Henschel, Léopold Favre. 10 vols. Paris: Librairie des sciences et des arts. Orig. ed. 1678.

Du Pré, Jean, ed. 1493. *Le Roman de la Rose par Guillaume de Lorris et Jean de Meung.* Paris: Jean Du Pré. Facsimile ed. Paris: Delarue, 1878.

Dufeil, M.-M. 1972. *Guillaume de Saint-Amour et la polémique universitaire parisienne 1250–1259.* Paris: Picard.

Ebert, Adolf 1862. [Review of Sandras 1859]. *Jahrbuch für romanische und englische Literatur* 4:85–106.

Eckhardt, Caroline D. 1984. The Art of Translation in *The Romaunt of the Rose.* *SAC* 6:41–63.

Economou, George 1975. Chaucer's Use of the Bird in Cage Image in the *Canterbury Tales.* *PQ* 54:679–83.

Ellis, Alexander J. 1869–89. *On Early English Pronunciation.* 5 vols. (pages numbered continuously) EETS, e.s. 2, 7, 14, 23, 56. London: Trübner.

Emerson, Ralph Waldo. *See* Alfred R. Ferguson et al., eds. 1971– .

Emery, Richard W. 1960. A Note on the Friars of the Sack. *Speculum* 35:591–95.

Emmerson, Richard Kenneth, and Ronald B. Herzman 1987. The Apocalyptic Age of Hypocrisy: Faus Semblant and Amant in the *Roman de la Rose.* *Speculum* 62:612–34.

Evans, Joan, and Mary S. Serjeantson 1933. *English Medieval Lapidaries.* EETS, o.s. 190. London: Oxford University Press. Reprint, 1960.

Ewert, A., ed. 1944. *Marie de France: Lais.* Blackwell's French Texts. Oxford: Blackwell.

Falconer, William A., ed. and trans. 1923. *Cicero: De senectute, De amicitia, De divinatione.* Loeb Classical Library. Vol. 154. London: Heinemann; New York: Putnam's. Reprint Cambridge, MA: Harvard University Press, 1979.

Fallows, David 1980. Lai. In Stanley Sadie, ed., *The New Grove Dictionary of Music and Musicians* 10:364–76. London: Macmillan.

Fansler, Dean Spruill   1914. *Chaucer and the Roman de la Rose*. Columbia University Studies in English and Comparative Literature. New York: Columbia University Press. Reprint. Gloucester, MA: Peter Smith, 1965.

Faral, Edmond   1912*a*. Une chanson française inédite. *Romania* 41:265–69.

———   1912*b*. Une chanson française du XIIIe siècle. *Romania* 41:412–14.

———   1924. *Les Arts Poétiques du XIIe et du XIIIe siècle: recherches et documents sur la technique littéraire du Moyen Âge*. Bibliothèque de l'Ecole des hautes études, fasc. 238. Paris: Champion. Reprint, 1962.

———, ed.   1951. Les "Responsiones" de Guillaume de Saint-Amour. *Archives d'histoire doctrinale et littéraire du moyen-âge* 18 (25e et 26e années):337–94.

———, and Julia Bastin, eds.   1959–60. *Rutebeuf: œuvres complètes*. 2 vols. Paris: Picard.

Feng, Xiang   1990. *Chaucer and the "Romaunt of the Rose": A New Study in Authorship*. Ph.D. diss., Harvard University.

Ferguson, Alfred R., et al., eds.   1971– . Ralph Waldo Emerson, *The Collected Works*. Cambridge, MA: Belknap Press.

Fick, W.   1886*a*. Zur Frage von der Authenticität der mittelenglischen Überzetzung des Romans von der Rose. *EStn* 9:161–67.

———   1886*b*. [Reply to Skeat 1886*a*]. *EStn* 9:506.

Finlayson, John   1988. Chaucer's Prioress and *Amor Vincit Omnia. Studia Neophilologica* 60:171–74.

———   1990. The *Roman de la Rose* and Chaucer's Narrators. *ChauR* 24:187–210.

Fisher, John H., ed.   1977. *The Complete Poetry and Prose of Geoffrey Chaucer*. New York: Holt. 2d ed., with text and notes unchanged, 1989.

Fleming, John V.   1965. The Moral Reputation of the *Roman de la Rose* Before 1400. *RPh* 18:430–35.

———   1967. Chaucer's Squire, the *Roman de la Rose,* and the *Romaunt. N&Q* n.s.14 [212]:48–49.

———   1969. *The* Roman de la Rose: *A Study in Allegory and Iconography*. Princeton: Princeton University Press.

———   1984. *Reason and the Lover*. Princeton: Princeton University Press.

———   1986*a*. The Garden of the *Roman de la Rose*: Vision of Landscape or Landscape of Vision? In Elizabeth B. MacDougall, ed., *Medieval Gardens*, pp. 201–34. Washington, D.C.: Dumbarton Oaks.

———   1986*b*. Smoky Reyn: From Jean de Meun to Geoffrey Chaucer. In Leigh A. Arrathoon, ed., *Chaucer and the Craft of Fiction*, pp. 1–21. Rochester, MI: Solaris Press.

Floire et Blancheflor.   See Margaret Pelan, ed. 1937; Jean-Luc Leclanche, ed. 1980.

Frank, Robert W.   1953. The Art of Reading Medieval Personification-Allegory. *ELH* 20:237–50.

———   1972. *Chaucer and* The Legend of Good Women. Cambridge, MA: Harvard University Press.

Frappier, Jean   1959. Variations sur le thème du miroir, de Bernard de Ventadour à Maurice Scève. *Cahiers de l'Association internationale des études françaises* 11: 134–158.

French, Robert Dudley   1947. *A Chaucer Handbook*. 2d ed. New York: Crofts. 1st ed., 1927.

Friedman, Lionel J.   1959. "Jean de Meung," Antifeminism, and "Bourgeois Realism." *MP* 57:13–23.

———   1962. Jean de Meun and Ethelred of Rievaulx. *L'Esprit Créateur* 2:135–41.

———   1965. Gradus Amoris. *RPh* 19:167–77.

Furnivall, Frederick J.   1868. *A Temporary Preface to the Six-Text Edition of Chaucer's Canterbury Tales: Part I*. Chaucer Society, 2d ser., 3. London: Trübner. Pages 107–11 of this essay appear in Richard Morris, ed. 1870.

———   1871. *Trial Forewords to my "Parallel-Text Edition of Chaucer's Minor Poems" for the Chaucer Society, (with a try to set Chaucer's Works in their right order of time)*. Chaucer Society, 2d ser., 6. London: Trübner.

———   1878. Skeat and Bell's Chaucer. *Academy*, April 27, p. 365.

———   1890. Notes and News. *Academy*, July 5, pp. 11–12.

———, ed.   1911. *The Romaunt of the Rose. A Reprint of the First Printed Edition by William Thynne, A. D. 1532*. Chaucer Society, 1st ser., 82. London: Kegan Paul. Reprint New York: Johnson, 1967. [Introduction by W. W. Skeat].

Gallacher, Stuart A.   1963. Castles in Spain. *Journal of American Folklore* 76:324–29.

Garbáty, Thomas Jay   1967. *Pamphilus, De amore*: An Introduction and Translation. *ChauR* 2:108–34.

Gautier de Coincy.   *See* Alexandre Poquet, ed. 1857.

Geissman, Erwin W. 1952. *The Style and Technique of Chaucer's Translations from French*. Ph.D. diss., Yale University.

Geoffrey of Vinsauf. In Faral 1924, pp. 194–262.

Giamatti, A. Bartlett 1966. *The Earthly Paradise and the Renaissance Epic*. Princeton: Princeton University Press. Reprint. New York: Norton, 1989.

Gilman, Arthur, ed. 1880. *The Poetical Works of Geoffrey Chaucer*. 3 vols. Boston: Houghton, Mifflin. *Rom* is in vol. 3.

Glare, P. G. W. See *Oxford Latin Dictionary* 1982.

Glasgow University, Hunterian Museum. *See* John Young and P. Henderson Aitken 1908.

Globe Edition. *See* Alfred W. Pollard, ed. 1898.

Godefroy, Frédéric 1881–1902. *Dictionnaire de l'ancienne langue française*. 10 vols. Paris: F. Vieweg.

Golden Legend. *See* Th. Graesse, ed. 1890; Granger Ryan and Helmut Ripperger, trans. 1941.

Goldin, Frederick 1967. *The Mirror of Narcissus in the Courtly Love Lyric*. Ithaca: Cornell University Press.

Gower, John. *See* G. C. Macaulay, ed. 1899–1902.

Graesse, [Johann Georg] Th[eodor], ed. 1890. *Jacobi a Voragine Legenda Aurea*. 3d ed. Koebner: Breslau. Reprint. Osnabrück: Otto Zeller, 1969.

Greg, W. W. 1927. *The Calculus of Variants: An Essay on Textual Criticism*. Oxford: Clarendon Press.

Griffith, Dudley David 1955. *Bibliography of Chaucer 1908–1953*. University of Washington Publications in Language and Literature, 13. Seattle: University of Washington Press.

Guiart, Guillaume. *See* Jean A. Buchon, ed. 1824–28.

Guillaume de Saint-Amour 1632. *Opera omnia*. Constance: Alithophilos.

———. *See* Edmond Faral, ed. 1951.

Guillaume de Lorris and Jean de Meun. *See* Charles Dahlberg, trans. 1971; Jean Du Pré, ed. 1493; Ernest Langlois, ed. 1914–24; Félix Lecoy, ed. 1965–70; Clément Marot, ed. 1529; Pierre Marteau, ed. 1878–80; M. Méon, ed. 1814; Francisque Michel, ed. 1864.

Guiot de Provins. *See* John Orr, ed. 1915.

Gunn, Alan M. F. 1951. *The Mirror of Love: A Reinterpretation of "The Romance of the Rose."* Lubbock, Texas: Texas Tech Press; 2d printing, 1952.

Haeckel, Willibald 1890. *Das Sprichwort bei Chaucer*. Erlangen and Leipzig: Georg Böhme. Reprint. Amsterdam: Rodopi, 1970.

Halliwell-Phillipps, James O. 1847. *A Dictionary of Archaic and Provincial Words*. London: J. R. Smith.

Hammond, Eleanor P. 1908. *Chaucer: A Bibliographical Manual*. New York: Macmillan. Reprint. New York: Peter Smith, 1933.

Harley, Marta Powell 1986. Narcissus, Hermaphroditus, and Attis: Ovidian Lovers at the Fontaine d'Amors in Guillaume de Lorris's *Roman de la Rose*. PMLA 101:324–37.

Hassell, James Woodrow 1982. *Middle French Proverbs, Sentences, and Proverbial Phrases*. Toronto: Pontifical Institute of Mediaeval Studies.

Hazelton, Richard M. 1960. Chaucer and Cato. *Speculum* 35:357–80.

Hendrickson, G. L., and H. M. Hubbell, eds. and trans. 1939. *Cicero: Brutus and Orator*. Loeb Classical Library. Vol. 342. London: Heinemann; Cambridge, MA: Harvard University Press. Rev. ed., 1962.

Herben, Stephen J. 1937. Arms and Armor in Chaucer. *Speculum* 12:475–87.

Herrtage, Sidney J. H., and H. B. Wheatley, eds. 1881. *Catholicon Anglicum*. EETS, o.s. 75. London: Trübner. Reprint. New York: Kraus, 1973.

Hetherington, John R. 1964. *Chaucer 1532–1602: Notes and Facsimile Texts*. Birmingham: Vernon House.

Hicks, Eric, ed. and trans. 1977. *Le débat sur "Le Roman de la Rose": Christine de Pisan, Jean Gerson, Jean de Montreuil, Gontier et Pierre Col*. Paris: Champion.

Hilka, Alfons, ed. 1932. *Aimon de Varennes: Florimont*. Göttingen: Gesellschaft für romanische Literatur.

Hill, Thomas D. 1974. Narcissus, Pygmalion, and the Castration of Saturn: Two Mythographical Themes in the *Roman de la Rose*. *SP* 71:404–26.

Hillman, Larry H.   1980. Another Look into the Mirror Perilous: The Role of the Crystals in the *Roman de la Rose. Romania* 101:225–38.

Hinckley, Henry B.   1906. Chaucer and *Ywaine and Gawin. Academy*, Dec. 22, pp. 640–41.

———   1907*a*. Chaucer Again [Reply to Skeat 1906]. *Academy*, Jan.26, p. 99.

———   1907*b. Notes on Chaucer: A Commentary on the Prolog and Six Canterbury Tales.* Northampton, MA: Nonotuck Press. Reprint. New York: Haskell, 1970.

Hopwood, Charles Henry, ed.   1904–05. *Middle Temple Records.* 4 vols. London: Butterworth.

Hult, David F.   1981. The Allegorical Fountain: Narcissus in the *Roman de la Rose. RR* 72:125–48.

———   1984. Closed Quotations: The Speaking Voice in the *Roman de la Rose. YFS* 67:248–69.

———   1986. *Self-Fulfilling Prophecies: Readership and Authority in the First* Roman de la Rose. Cambridge: Cambridge University Press.

Huon de Méri.   *See* Georg Wimmer, ed. 1888.

Huppé, Bernard F.   1948. The Translation of Technical Terms in the Middle English *Romaunt of the Rose. JEGP* 47:334–42.

Isidore of Seville.   *See* W. M. Lindsay, ed. 1911.

Jacobus de Voragine.   *See* Th. Graesse, ed. 1890; Granger Ryan and Helmut Ripperger, trans. 1941.

Jauss, Hans Robert   1964. La transformation de la forme allégorique entre 1180 et 1240: d'Alain de Lille à Guillaume de Lorris. In Anthime Fourrier, ed., *L'humanisme médiéval dans les littératures romanes du XII*ᵉ *au XIV*ᵉ *siècle*, pp. 107–42. Paris: Klincksieck.

———   1968–70. Entstehung und Strukturwandel der allegorischen Dichtung. In *La littérature didactique, allégorique, et satirique*, vol. 6, tomes 1 and 2 of *Grundriss der romanischen Literaturen des Mittelalters*, 1.146–244, 2.203–80 (bibliography). Heidelberg: Carl Winter.

Jean de Meun.   *See* V. L. Dedeck-Héry, ed. 1952 and Guillaume de Lorris.

Jephson, John M.   *See* Robert Bell, ed. 1854–56.

John of Salisbury.   *See* John Dickinson, trans. 1927; Clement C. J. Webb, ed. 1909.

Johnston, Oliver M.   1908. The Description of the Emir's Orchard in *Floire et Blancheflor. ZRPh* 32:705–10.

Jones, Charles   1972. *An Introduction to Middle English*. New York: Holt, Rinehart, and Winston.

Justinian.   *See* Paul Krueger and Theodor Mommsen, eds. 1968–70.

Kaluza, Max   1888. [Announcement of ed. of Kaluza 1891]. *Academy*, Sept. 1, p. 134.

———   1889. Zur Texterklärung des "Romaunt of the Rose." *EStn* 13:528–29.

———   1890. [Letter to F. J. Furnivall on the three fragments of the *Rom*]. *Academy*, July 5, pp. 11–12.

———, ed.   1891. *The Romaunt of the Rose, from the unique Glasgow MS, Parallel with its Original, Le Roman de la Rose.* Chaucer Society, 1st ser., 83. London: Kegan Paul, Trench, Trübner. Reprint. New York: Johnson, 1967.

———   1893*a. Chaucer und der Rosenroman: Eine litterargeschichtliche Studie.* Berlin: Emil Felber.

———   1893*b*. [Review of Kaluza, ed. 1891]. *EStn* 18:106–11.

———   1895. Zur Verfasserfrage des Romaunt of the Rose. *EStn* 20:338–40.

———   1896. [Review of Skeat, ed. 1894 *The Complete Works of Geoffrey Chaucer*, and 1895, *The Student's Chaucer*]. *EStn* 22:271–88.

———   1897. Der Reim *Love : Behove*, Rom. of the Rose v. 1091f. *EStn* 23:336–38.

———   1898. Erwiderung [zu Luick 1898]. *EStn* 24:343.

———   1901. [Review of] Walter W. Skeat [1900] *The Chaucer Canon. Deutsche Litteraturzeitung*, Apr. 6, cols. 863–66.

Kane, George, ed.   1960. *Piers Plowman: The A Version.* London: Athlone Press.

———   1965. Piers Plowman: *The Evidence for Authorship.* London: Athlone Press.

———, and E. Talbot Donaldson, eds.   1975. *Piers Plowman: The B Version.* London: Athlone Press.

Kelly, Douglas   1978*a. Medieval Imagination. Rhetoric and the Poetry of Courtly Love.* Madison: University of Wisconsin Press.

———   1978*b. Translatio studii*: Translation, Adaptation, and Allegory in Medieval French Literature. *PQ* 57:287–310.

Khinoy, Stephan A.   1972. Inside Chaucer's Pardoner? *ChauR* 6:255–67.

Kissner, Alfons   1867. *Chaucer in seinen Beziehungen zur italienischen Literatur.* Marburg: no publisher.

Kittredge, George Lyman 1892. The Authorship of the English *Romaunt of the Rose. Harvard Studies and Notes in Philology and Literature* 1:1–65.

———— 1915. *Chaucer and His Poetry.* Cambridge, MA: Harvard University Press.

Knowles, Dom David 1948–59. *The Religious Orders in England.* 3 vols. Cambridge: Cambridge University Press.

————, and R. Neville Hadcock 1972. *Medieval Religious Houses: England and Wales.* New York: St. Martin's.

Knowlton, Edgar C. 1920. The Allegorical Figure Genius. *Classical Philology* 15:380–84.

———— 1924. Genius as an Allegorical Figure. *MLN* 39:89–95.

Koch, John 1890. *The Chronology of Chaucer's Writings.* Chaucer Society, 2d ser., 27. London: Kegan Paul, Trench, Trübner.

———— 1900*a.* Werden Abschnitte des me. Rosenromans mit Recht Chaucer zugeschrieben? *EStn* 27:61–73.

———— 1900*b.* Nochmals der Mittelengl. Rosenroman. *EStn* 27:227–34.

———— 1902. [Review of] Walter W. Skeat, *The Chaucer Canon. EStn* 30:450–56.

———— 1912. Neuere Chaucer-Literatur. *EStn* 46:98–114.

———— 1921. Alte Chaucerprobleme und Neue Lösungsversuche. I. *Romaunt of the Rose. EStn* 55:161–74.

———— 1925. Der Gegenwärtige Stand der Chaucerforschung. *Anglia* 49:193–243.

Koeppel, Emil 1892. Chauceriana. *Anglia* 14:227–67.

———— 1898. Chaucers "Romaunt of the Rose" und Sackvilles "Induction." *Archiv* 101:145–46.

———— 1914. [Review of] Dean Spruill Fansler, Chaucer and the Roman de la Rose. *Anglia Beiblatt* 25:203–05.

Köhler, Erich 1963. Narcisse, la fontaine d'amour et Guillaume de Lorris. *Journal des Savants,* pp. 86–103. Reprinted in Anthime Fourrier, ed., *L'humanisme médiéval dans les littératures romanes du XIIe au XIVe siècle,* pp. 147–66. Paris: Klincksieck, 1964.

Kölbing, E. 1888. Zu Chaucer's Sir Thopas. *EStn* 11:495–511.

Krueger, Paul, and Theodor Mommsen, eds. 1968–70. *Corpus Juris Civilis.* 3 vols. Berlin: Weidmann. Originally published, 2 vols., 1872–77.

Kruger, Steven F. 1992. *Dreaming in the Middle Ages.* Cambridge: Cambridge University Press.

Kuhl, E. P. 1945. Chaucer and the Red Rose. *PQ* 24:33–38.

Kunstmann, John G. 1940. Chaucer's "Archangel." *MLN* 55:259–62.

Kurath, Hans. See *Middle English Dictionary* 1952– .

Lacroix, Paul 1874. *Manners, Customs, and Dress During the Middle Ages and During the Renaissance Period.* London: Chapman and Hall.

Lange, Hugo [Julius Hugo, J. H.] 1901. Lydgate und Fragment B des *Romaunt of the Rose. EStn* 29:397–405.

———— 1903. Zu Fragment B des ME Rosenromans. *EStn* 31:159–62.

———— 1910. [Notice of work on *Rom* 505–06 and 1091–92]. *Anglia Beiblatt* 21:316–17.

———— 1911. Rettungen Chaucers. Neue Beiträge zur Echtheitsfrage von Fragment A des mittelenglischen Rosenromans. I. *Anglia* 35:338–46.

———— 1912. ———— II. *Anglia* 36:479–91.

———— 1913. ———— III. *Anglia* 37:146–62.

———— 1914. Zur Datierung des mittelenglischen Rosenromanfragments A. *Anglia* 38:477–90.

Langhans, Viktor 1918. *Untersuchungen zu Chaucer.* Halle: Niemeyer.

Langland, William. See George Kane, ed. 1960; George Kane and E. T. Donaldson, eds. 1975; Derek Pearsall, ed. 1979; W. W. Skeat, ed. 1886.

Langlois, Ernest 1904. Anc. franç. *vizele. Romania* 33:405–07.

———— 1910. *Les manuscrits du Roman de la Rose, description et classement.* Travaux et mémoires de l'Université de Lille. n. s. 1. Droit et lettres, vol. 7. Lille: Tallandier.

————, ed. 1914–24. *Le Roman de la Rose par Guillaume de Lorris et Jean de Meun.* 5 vols. SATF, 63. Paris: Librairie de Firmin-Didot (vols. 1–2); de Honoré Champion (vol. 3); de Édouard Champion (vols. 4–5).

Lantin de Damerey, J. B. 1799. Supplément au glossaire du Roman de la Rose. In *Le Roman de la Rose par Guillaume de Lorris et Jean de Meung,* vol. 5, pp. 123–328. Paris: J. B. Fournier. Originally published separately in 1737 as supplement to Lenglet du Fresnoy's 1735 ed. of the *Roman de la Rose*.

Lawton, David   1985. *Chaucer's Narrators*. Chaucer Studies 13. Cambridge: D. S. Brewer.

Leclanche, Jean-Luc, ed.   1980. *Le conte de Floire et Blancheflor*. Paris: Champion.

Lecoy, Félix, ed.   1965–70. *Guillaume de Lorris et Jean de Meun, Le Roman de la Rose*. 3 vols. Les classiques français du moyen âge, 92, 95, 98. Paris: Champion.

———   1968. Sur la date du *Roman de la Rose*. *Romania* 89:554–55.

Legenda aurea.   *See* Th. Graesse, ed. 1890; Granger Ryan and Helmut Ripperger, trans. 1941.

Legouis, Emile   1913. *Geoffrey Chaucer*, trans. L. Lailavoix. London: Dent; New York: Dutton. Originally published as *Geoffrey Chaucer*. Les Grands Écrivains Étrangers. Paris: Bloud, 1910.

Lenglet du Fresnoy.   *See* J. B. Lantin de Damerey 1799.

Lewis, C. S.   1936. *The Allegory of Love: A Study in Medieval Tradition*. Oxford: Clarendon Press.

Liddell, Mark H.   1898. *See* Alfred Pollard, ed. 1898.

Lindner, F.   1887. Die englische Übersetzung des Romans von der Rose. *EStn* 11:163–73.

———   1893. [Review of] Max Kaluza. Chaucer und der Rosenroman. . . . *EStn* 18:104–05.

Lindsay, W. M., ed.   1911. *Isidori Hispalensis Episcopi Etymologiarum sive originum libri XX*. 2 vols. Oxford: Clarendon Press.

Longo, John Duane   1982. *Literary Appropriation as* Translatio *in Chaucer and the* Roman de la Rose. Ph.D. diss., Princeton University.

Lorris, Guillaume.   *See* Guillaume de Lorris.

Louis, René   1974. *Le Roman de la Rose: Essai d'interprétation de l'allégorisme érotique*. Paris: Champion.

Lounsbury, Thomas R.   1892. *Studies in Chaucer: His Life and Writings*. 3 vols. New York: Harper; London: James R. Osgood, Mc Ilvaine. Reprint. New York: Russell and Russell, 1962.

———   1894*a*. The "Romaunt of the Rose." *Manchester Guardian*, Apr. 18, p. 8.

———   1894*b*. The Romance of the Rose: Discussion of the Chaucerian Authorship. *New York Daily Tribune*, May 6, p. 23.

———   1895. [Review of Skeat, ed. 1894]. *New York Daily Tribune*, Feb. 24, p. 20; Mar. 3, p. 22.

Lowes, John Livingston   1934. *Geoffrey Chaucer and the Development of his Genius*. Boston: Houghton Mifflin; London: Oxford University Press.

Luick, Karl   1896. *Untersuchungen zur englischen Lautgeschichte*. Strassburg: Trübner.

———   1898. Der Reim *Love : Behove* im *Rom. of the Rose*. *EStn* 24:342–43.

Luria, Maxwell   1982. *A Reader's Guide to the* Roman de la Rose. Hamden, CT: Archon.

Lynch, Kathryn L.   1988. *The High Medieval Dream Vision: Poetry, Philosophy, and Literary Form*. Stanford, CA: Stanford University Press.

Macaulay, G. C., ed.   1899–1902. *The Complete Works of John Gower*. 4 vols. Oxford: Clarendon Press.

McDonnell, Ernest W.   1954. *The Beguines and Beghards in Medieval Culture*. New Brunswick, NJ: Rutgers University Press.

McIntosh, Angus, M. L. Samuels, and Michael Benskin   1986. *A Linguistic Atlas of Late Mediaeval English*. 4 vols. Aberdeen: Aberdeen University Press.

McKerrow, Ronald B.   1928. *An Introduction to Bibliography for Literary Students*. 2d impression, with corrections. Oxford: Clarendon Press. 1st ed., 1927.

Magoun, Francis P., Jr.   1955. Chaucer's Mediaeval World Outside of Great Britain. *MS* 17:117–42. Incorporated into Magoun 1961.

———   1961. *A Chaucer Gazetteer*. Chicago: University of Chicago Press; Uppsala: Almqvist & Wiksell.

———   1977. Two Chaucer Items. *NM* 78:46.

Manly, John Matthews   1926. Chaucer and the Rhetoricians. Warton Lecture on English Poetry, 17. *PBA* 12:95–113. Also published separately. Reprinted in Richard Schoeck and Jerome Taylor, eds., *Chaucer Criticism*, vol. 1, *The Canterbury Tales*, pp. 268–90. Notre Dame, IN: University of Notre Dame Press.

Mann, Jill   1973. *Chaucer and Medieval Estates Satire: The Literature of Social Classes and the "General Prologue" to the "Canterbury Tales"*. Cambridge: Cambridge University Press.

Mannyng, Robert, of Brunne.   *See* Idelle Sullens, ed. 1983.

Marie de France, *Lais*.   *See* A. Ewert, ed. 1944.

Marot, Clément, ed.   1529. *Le Rommant de la Rose*. Paris: Galliot du Pré.

———— 1954–57. *Le roman de la rose, dans la version attribuée à Clément Marot*, eds. Silvio F. Baridon and Antonio Viscardi. 2 vols. Testi e Documenti di Letteratura Moderna. Milan: Istituto Editoriale Cisalpino.

Marsh, George P. 1860. *Lectures on the English Language.* New York: Scribner.

Marteau, Pierre [Jules Croissandeau, pseud.], ed. and trans. 1878–80. *Le Roman de la Rose par Guillaume de Lorris et Jean de Meung.* 5 vols. Paris: P. Daffis (vols. 2–5); Orleans: H. Herluison. Reprint. Nendeln: Kraus Reprints, 1970.

Mary, André, ed. and trans. 1951. *La fleur de la poésie française depuis les origines jusqu'a la fin du XVe siècle.* Paris: Garnier.

Matthew of Vendôme. In Faral 1924, pp. 106–93.

Mayhew, Anthony L., ed. 1908. *Promptorium Parvulorum.* EETS, e.s. 102. London: Kegan Paul, Trench, Trübner.

Mead, William E. 1901. The Prologue of the Wife of Bath's Tale. *PMLA* 16:388–404.

Méon, M., ed. 1814. *Le Roman de la Rose, par Guillaume de Lorris and Jean de Meung.* Nouvelle éd. rev. et corr. 4 vols. Paris: P. Didot l'aîné.

Merlo, Carolyn 1981. Chaucer's "Broun" and Medieval Color Symbolism. *College Language Association Journal* 25:225–26.

Mersand, Joseph 1939. *Chaucer's Romance Vocabulary.* 2d ed. New York, Comet Press. Reprint. Port Washington, N. Y.: Kennikat Press, 1968. 1st ed., 1937.

Micha, Alexandre, ed. 1965. *Chrétien de Troyes: Cligés.* Les classiques français du moyen âge, 84. Paris: Champion.

Michel, Francisque, ed. 1864. *Le Roman de la Rose, par Guillaume de Lorris and Jean de Meung.* 2 vols. Paris: Firmin Didot.

Middle English Dictionary 1952– . Ed. Hans Kurath et al. Ann Arbor: University of Michigan Press.

Miller, Frank Justus, ed. 1916–21. *Ovid: Metamorphoses.* Loeb Classical Library. Vols. 42–43. London: Heinemann. Reprint. Cambridge, MA: Harvard University Press, 1984.

Miller, Robert P. 1955. Chaucer's Pardoner, the Scriptural Eunuch, and the Pardoner's Tale. *Speculum* 30:180–99.

————, ed. 1977. *Chaucer: Sources and Backgrounds.* New York: Oxford University Press.

Morawski, Joseph 1925. *Proverbes français antérieurs au XVe siècle.* Paris: Champion.

Morel-Fatio, A. 1913. Châteaux en Espagne. In *Mélanges offerts à M. Emile Picot*, 1.335–42. Paris: E. Rahir.

Morris, Lynn King 1985. *Chaucer Source and Analogue Criticism: A Cross-Referenced Guide.* Garland Reference Library of the Humanities, 454. New York and London: Garland.

Morris, Richard, ed. 1866a. *Dan Michel's Ayenbite of Inwyt.* EETS, o.s. 23. London: Trübner. 2d ed., 1965. Reprint. Millwood, NY: Kraus, 1975.

————, ed. 1866b. *The Poetical Works of Geoffrey Chaucer.* The Aldine Edition. 6 vols. London: Bell and Daldy; rev. ed. 1870, reprinted London: George Bell & Sons, 1902. *Rom* is in Vol. 6, glossary in Vol. 1.

————, ed. 1870. On the Genuineness of the Romaunt of the Rose and the Poems attributed to Chaucer. Reprint of Furnivall 1868:107–11; in rev. ed. (1.265–71) of Morris, ed. 1866b.

————, ed. 1874–93. *Cursor Mundi.* 7 vols. (pages numbered continuously). EETS, o.s. 57, 59, 62, 66, 68, 99, 101. London: Kegan Paul, Trench, Trübner.

Morrison, Paul G. 1955. *Index of Printers, Publishers, and Booksellers in Donald Wing's Short-title Catalogue.* Charlottesville: University of Virginia Press for Bibliographical Society of the University of Virginia.

Mossé, Fernand 1968. *A Handbook of Middle English*, trans. James A. Walker. 5th printing, corrected. Baltimore: Johns Hopkins Press.

Moxon, Edward, ed. 1843. *The Poetical Works of Geoffrey Chaucer . . . By Thomas Tyrwhitt.* London: Edward Moxon.

Mum and the Soothsegger. *See* Mabel Day and Robert Steele, eds. 1936.

Murphy, James J. 1971. *Medieval Rhetoric: A Select Bibliography.* Toronto: University of Toronto Press. 2d ed. Toronto Medieval Bibliographies, 3, 1989.

———— 1974. *Rhetoric in the Middle Ages.* Berkeley: University of California Press.

Murray, James A. H. See *Oxford English Dictionary* 1884–1928.

Muscatine, Charles   1953. The Emergence of Psychological Allegory in Old French Romance. *PMLA* 68:1160–82.

———   1957. *Chaucer and the French Tradition: A Study in Style and Meaning.* Berkeley and Los Angeles: University of California Press.

———   1963. *The Book of Geoffrey Chaucer: An Account of the Publication of Geoffrey Chaucer's Works from the Fifteenth Century to Modern Times.* San Francisco: Book Club of California.

Mustanoja, Tauno F.   1960. *A Middle English Syntax,* part 1, *Parts of Speech.* Mémoires de la Société Néophilologique de Helsinki, 23. Helsinki: Société Néophilologique.

Nabokov, Vladimir   1959. The Servile Path. In Reuben A. Brower, ed., *On Translation,* pp. 97–110. Cambridge, MA: Harvard University Press. Reprint. New York: Oxford University Press, 1966.

Naunin, Traugott   1929. *Der Einfluss der mittelalterlichen Rhetorik auf Chaucers Dichtung.* Bonn: Friedrich Wilhelms-Universität.

Nichols, Stephen G.   1983. *Romanesque Signs: Early Medieval Narrative and Iconography.* New Haven: Yale University Press.

Nicolas, Sir Harris.   *See* Aldine Edition 1845, 1846.

Nitzsche, Jane Chance   1975. *The Genius Figure in Antiquity and the Middle Ages.* New York: Columbia University Press.

Nolan, Barbara   1977. *The Gothic Visionary Perspective.* Princeton: Princeton University Press.

Nordahl, Helge   1978. *Ars fidi interpretis:* Un aspect rhétorique de l'art de Chaucer dans sa traduction du *Roman de la Rose. Archivum Linguisticum* 9:24–31.

Norgate, Fr.   1894. The Romaunt of the Rose. *N&Q,* 5th ser., 5:446–47.

Nykrog, Per   1986. *L'Amour et la Rose: Le grand dessein de Jean de Meun.* Harvard Studies in Romance Languages, 41. Lexington, KY: French Forum.

Onions, C. T., et al.   1966. *The Oxford Dictionary of English Etymology.* Oxford: Clarendon Press.

Orr, John, ed.   1915. *Les œuvres de Guiot de Provins.* Manchester: Manchester University Press.

Ovid, *Metamorphoses. See* Frank J. Miller, ed. 1916–21.

Oxford English Dictionary   1884–1928. Ed. James A. H. Murray et al. 10 vols. Oxford: Clarendon Press.

———   1933. Reprint with *Supplement.* 13 vols. Oxford: Clarendon Press.

———   1971. Compact ed. 2 vols. New York: Oxford University Press.

———   1972–86. *Supplement,* ed. R. W. Burchfield. 4 vols. Oxford: Clarendon Press. Supersedes the *Supplement* of 1933.

Oxford Latin Dictionary   1982. Ed. P. G. W. Glare. Oxford: Clarendon Press; New York: Oxford University Press.

Palsgrave, John   1530. *Lesclarcissement de la langue francoyse.* London: Pynson, Haukyns. Reprint. Paris: Imprimerie nationale, 1852.

Pannier, Léopold   1882. *Les lapidaires français du moyen âge.* Bibliothèque de l'école des hautes études, 52. Paris: F. Vieweg. Reprint. Geneva: Slatkin Reprints, 1973.

Paré, Gérard   1947. *Les idées et les lettres au XIIIe siècle: Le Roman de la Rose.* Bibliothèque de Philosophie, 1. Montréal: Université de Montréal, le centre de psychologie et de pédagogie.

Paris, Gaston   1881. Jakemon Sakesep, auteur du Roman du Chastelain de Couci. *Histoire Littéraire de la France* 28:352–90.

Parkes, M. B.   1969. *English Cursive Book Hands 1250–1500.* Oxford: Clarendon Press. Reprint. Berkeley: University of California Press, 1980.

Patrologiae cursus completus. Series Latina   1844–58. Ed. J.-P. Migne. 221 vols. Reprint. Paris: Garnier; Turnholti (Belgium): Typographi Brepols, various dates.

Pauli, Reinhold   1860. *Bilder aus Alt-England.* Gotha: F. A. Perthes.

Payen, Jean-Charles   1976. *La Rose et l'Utopie: révolution sexuelle et communisme nostalgique chez Jean de Meung.* Paris: Editions Sociales.

Payne, Robert O.   1963. *The Key of Remembrance: A Study of Chaucer's Poetics.* New Haven: Yale University Press. Reprint. New York: Greenwood Press, 1973.

———   1978. Chaucer's Realization of Himself as Rhetor. In James J. Murphy, ed., *Medieval Eloquence,* pp. 270–87. Berkeley: University of California Press.

Pearsall, Derek, ed.   1979. *Piers Plowman by William Langland: An Edition of the C-text.* Berkeley: University of California Press.

————, ed. 1984a. *The Nun's Priest's Tale. A Variorum Edition of the Works of Geoffrey Chaucer*, vol. 2, part 9. Norman: University of Oklahoma Press.

———— 1984b. Thomas Speght (ca. 1550–?). In Ruggiers, ed. 1984, pp. 71–92.

————, ed. 1987. *Manuscripts and Texts: Editorial Problems in Later Middle English Literature.* Cambridge, England; Wolfeboro, NH: D.S. Brewer.

Peck, Russell A. 1988. *Chaucer's* Romaunt of the Rose *and* Boece, Treatise on the Astrolabe, Equatorie of the Planetis, *Lost Works, and Chaucerian Apocrypha: An Annotated Bibliography, 1900 to 1985.* Toronto: University of Toronto Press.

Peden, Alison M. 1985. Macrobius and Mediaeval Dream Literature. *Medium Ævum* 54:59–63.

Pelan, Margaret, ed. 1937. *Floire et Blancheflor.* Paris: Société d'édition: Les belles lettres.

Piers Plowman. See George Kane, ed. 1960; George Kane and E. T. Donaldson, eds. 1975; Derek Pearsall, ed. 1979; W. W. Skeat, ed. 1886.

Platnauer, Maurice, ed. and trans. 1922. *Claudian.* Loeb Classical Library. Vols. 135–36. London: Heinemann; New York: Putnam's. Reprint. Cambridge, MA: Harvard University Press, 1972.

Plato. *See* J. H. Waszink, ed. 1962.

Plummer, John F., III 1995. *The Summoner's Tale. A Variorum Edition of the Works of Geoffrey Chaucer*, vol. 2, part 7. Norman: University of Oklahoma Press.

Pollard, Alfred W. 1892. [Review of Lounsbury 1892]. *Academy*, Feb. 20, pp. 173–74.

———— 1893. *Chaucer.* London: Macmillan. 2d ed., London: Macmillan, 1931.

————, et al., eds. 1898. *The Works of Geoffrey Chaucer.* The Globe Edition. London: Macmillan. Reprint. 1965. Mark H. Liddell, ed., *Rom.*

————, and G. R. Redgrave 1926. *A Short-title Catalogue of Books Printed in England, Scotland, & Ireland, and of English Books Printed Abroad, 1475–1640.* London: Oxford University Press for the Bibliographical Society.

————, and ———— 1976–86. *A Short-title Catalogue of Books Printed in England, Scotland, & Ireland, and of English Books Printed Abroad, 1475–1640.* 2d ed., ed. W. A. Jackson, F. S. Ferguson, and Katharine F. Pantzer. 2 vols. London: The Bibliographical Society.

Pope, Mildred K. 1934. *From Latin to Modern French.* Manchester: Manchester University Press.

Poquet, Alexandre Eusèbe, ed. 1857. *Les miracles de la Sainte Vierge . . . par Gautier de Coincy.* Paris: Parmantier and Didron.

Postgate, J. P., ed. and trans. 1962. *Tibullus* [poems of]. In *Catullus, Tibullus, and Pervigilium Veneris.* Loeb Classical Library. Vol. 6. Rev. ed. Cambridge, MA: Harvard University Press. 1st ed. London: Heinemann, 1913.

Potansky, Peter 1972. *Der Streit um den Rosenroman.* Munich: Fink.

Pound, Louise 1896. *The Romaunt of the Rose*: Additional Evidence that it is Chaucer's. *MLN* 11:97–102.

Preston, Raymond 1952. *Chaucer.* London and New York: Sheed and Ward. Reprint. New York: Greenwood Press, 1969.

Prins, Anton Adriaan 1952. *French Influence on English Phrasing.* Leiden: Universitaire Pers Leiden.

Promptorium Parvulorum. See Anthony L. Mayhew, ed. 1908.

Prothero, G. W. 1888. *A Memoir of Henry Bradshaw.* London: Kegan Paul, Trench, & Co.

Puttenham, George [Richard?] 1589. *The Arte of English Poesie.* London: Richard Field. Facsimile reprint. Menston, England: Scolar Press, 1968.

Quilligan, Maureen 1977. Words and Sex: The Language of Allegory in the *De planctu naturae*, the *Roman de la Rose*, and Book III of *The Faerie Queene. Allegorica* 2:195–216.

———— 1979. *The Language of Allegory: Defining the Genre.* Ithaca: Cornell University Press.

———— 1981. Allegory, Allegoresis, and the Deallegorization of Language: The *Roman de la Rose*, the *De planctu naturae*, and the *Parlement of Foules.* In Morton W. Bloomfield, ed., *Allegory, Myth, Symbol*, pp. 163–86. Cambridge, MA: Harvard University Press.

Raby, F. J. E. 1953. *A History of Christian-Latin Poetry from the Beginnings to the Close of the Middle Ages.* 2d ed. Oxford: Clarendon Press. 1st ed., 1927.

Ransom, Daniel J. 1993. Textual Notes. *The General Prologue. A Variorum Edition of the Works of Geoffrey Chaucer*, vol. 2, part 1A. Norman: University of Oklahoma Press. *See also* Malcolm Andrew 1993.

Raynaud de Lage, Guy 1962. *Introduction à l'ancien Français.* 3d ed. Paris: Société d'Edition d'Enseignement Supérieur.

————, ed. 1966. *Le Roman de Thèbes.* 2 vols. Paris: Champion

Reese, Gustave 1940. *Music in the Middle Ages.* New York: Norton.

Reeves, W. P. 1923. *Romance of the Rose,* 1705. *MLN* 38:124.

Riverside Chaucer. See Larry D. Benson, gen. ed. 1987.

Roach, William, ed. 1959. *Chrétien de Troyes: Le Roman de Perceval ou Le Conte du Graal.* Geneva: Droz.

Robertson, D. W., Jr. 1951. The Doctrine of Charity in Mediaeval Literary Gardens: A Topical Approach through Symbolism and Allegory. *Speculum* 26:24–49.

———— 1962. *A Preface to Chaucer: Studies in Medieval Perspectives.* Princeton: Princeton University Press.

———— 1974. Chaucer's Franklin and His Tale. *Costerus,* n.s. 1:1–26.

Robinson, F. N., ed. 1933. *The Poetical Works of Chaucer.* Boston: Houghton Mifflin.

————, ed. 1957. *The Works of Geoffrey Chaucer.* 2d ed. Boston: Houghton Mifflin; London: Oxford University Press.

Root, Robert Kilburn 1922. *The Poetry of Chaucer: A Guide to its Study and Appreciation.* 2d, rev., ed. Boston and New York: Houghton Mifflin. Reprint. Gloucester, MA: Peter Smith, 1957. 1st ed., 1906.

————, ed. 1926. *The Book of Troilus and Criseyde by Geoffrey Chaucer.* Princeton: Princeton University Press. Reprint. 1945.

———— 1941. The Monk's Tale. In Bryan and Dempster, eds. 1941, pp. 615–44.

Roques, Mario, ed. 1963. *Le Chevalier de la charrete [Lancelot].* Vol. 3 of *Les Romans de Chrétien de Troyes.* Paris: Champion.

————, ed. 1965. *Le Chevalier au lion (Yvain).* Vol. 4 of *Les Romans de Chrétien de Troyes.* Paris: Champion.

————, ed. 1966. *Erec et Enide.* Vol. 1 of *Les Romans de Chrétien de Troyes.* Paris: Champion.

Roscow, Gregory H. 1981. *Syntax and Style in Chaucer's Poetry.* Cambridge: D. S. Brewer.

Rowland, Beryl, ed. 1979. *Companion to Chaucer Studies.* Rev. ed. New York: Oxford University Press. 1st ed., 1968.

Ruggiers, Paul G., ed. 1979. *The Canterbury Tales: A Facsimile and Transcription of the Hengwrt Manuscript, with Variants from the Ellesmere Manuscript.* [*A Variorum Edition of the Works of Geoffrey Chaucer,* vol.1.] Norman: University of Oklahoma Press.

————, ed. 1984. *Editing Chaucer: The Great Tradition.* Norman, OK: Pilgrim Books.

Russell, J. Stephen 1988. *The English Dream Vision: Anatomy of a Form.* Columbus: Ohio State University Press.

Rutebeuf. *See* Edmond Faral and Julia Bastin, eds. 1959–60.

Ryan, Granger, and Helmut Ripperger, trans. 1941. *The Golden Legend of Jacobus de Voragine.* New York, London, Toronto: Longmans, Green.

Saintsbury, George 1906. *A History of English Prosody from the Twelfth Century to the Present Day.* Vol. 1. London and New York: Macmillan. 2d ed. London: Macmillan, 1923.

Sandras, Etienne-Gustave 1859. *Etude sur G. Chaucer considéré comme imitateur des trouvères.* Paris: Auguste Durand.

Schaar, Claes 1955. *The Golden Mirror: Studies in Chaucer's Descriptive Technique and its Literary Background.* Lund: Gleerup. Reprint with index, 1967.

Schick, Josef, ed. 1891. *Lydgate's Temple of Glas.* EETS, e.s. 60. London: Kegan Paul, Trench, Trübner.

———— 1893. [Review of] Max Kaluza, *Chaucer und der Rosenroman. Deutsche Litteraturzeitung,* June 3, cols. 680–84.

Schoch, A. D. 1906. The Differences in the Middle English "Romaunt of the Rose" and their Bearing upon Chaucer's Authorship. *MP* 3:339–58.

Schöffler, Herbert 1918. Graynes de Paris. *Anglia Beiblatt* 29:46–48.

Shannon, E. F. 1913. Notes on Chaucer. *MP* 11:227–36.

———— 1941. The Physician's Tale. In Bryan and Dempster, eds. 1941, pp. 398–408.

Shoaf, R. A. 1979. Notes toward Chaucer's Poetics of Translation. *SAC* 1:55–66.

Short Title Catalogue. See Alfred W. Pollard and G. R. Redgrave 1926, 1976–86; Donald Wing 1945–51.

Sieper, Ernst 1898. Les Echecs Amoureux. *Eine altfranzösische Nachahmung des Rosenromans und ihre englische Übertragung.* Weimar: Emil Felber.

————, ed. 1901–03. *Lydgate's Reson and Sensuallyte*. EETS, e.s. 84, 89. London: Kegan Paul, Trench, Trübner. Reprint. London: Oxford University Press, 1965.

Simpson, Percy 1935. *Proof-Reading in the Sixteenth, Seventeenth, and Eighteenth Centuries*. London: Oxford University Press. Reprint. 1970.

Skeat, Walter W. 1874. A Test for the Genuineness of Some of Chaucer's Poems. *N&Q*, 5th ser., 1:185–86.

———— 1878a. The "Court of Love." *Academy*, June 8, p. 512.

———— 1878b. The "Romaunt of the Rose." *Academy*, Aug. 10, pp. 143–44.

———— 1878c. *See* Robert Bell, ed. 1878.

———— 1880. Note on "The Romaunt of the Rose." In Chaucer, *The Prioresses Tale* . . . . 3d ed. Oxford: Clarendon Press, 1880:lxxxiii–xciv. Reprinted as Skeat 1884; Skeat 1888c (with revision in final paragraph).

———— 1884. Why "The Romaunt of the Rose" is Not Chaucer's. In *Essays on Chaucer . . . Part V.* Chaucer Society, 2d ser., 19: 437–51. London: Kegan Paul. Reprint of Skeat 1880.

———— 1886a. Zu: Englische Studien IX, p. 161 ff. [On Fick 1886a]. *EStn* 9:506.

————, ed. 1886b. *The Vision of William concerning Piers the Plowman in three parallel texts together with Richard the Redeless*. 2 vols. London: Oxford University Press.

———— 1887. Postscript on "The Romaunt of the Rose." In Isabel Marshall and Lela Porter, eds., *Ryme-Index to the Manuscript Texts of Chaucer's Minor Poems*. Chaucer Society, 1st ser., 78:vi–viii. London: Kegan Paul. Reprint. Chaucer Society, 1st ser., 80:x–xvi, 1889.

———— 1888a. A Further Note on the "Romaunt of the Rose." *Academy*, Sept. 8, pp. 153–54.

————, ed. 1888b. Chaucer, *The Minor Poems*. Oxford: Clarendon Press. 2d ed., 1896.

———— 1888c. Note on "The Romaunt of the Rose." In Chaucer, *The Prioresses Tale* . . . . 4th ed. Oxford: Clarendon Press, 1888:lxxxiii–xciv. Rev. reprint of Skeat 1880, 1884.

———— 1890. The Romaunt of the Rose. *Academy*, July 19, pp. 51–52.

———— 1891. The Three Fragments of "The Romaunt of the Rose." *Academy*, Aug. 15, p. 137.

———— 1892a. A Few Words on Chaucer's Rimes. *Academy*, Feb. 27, pp. 206–07.

———— 1892b. Some Rimes in Gower. *Academy*, Mar. 5, pp. 230–31.

————, ed. 1894a. *The Complete Works of Geoffrey Chaucer*. 6 vols. Oxford: Clarendon Press. 2d ed., 1899. Reprint. London: Oxford University Press, 1963. *Rom* is in vol. 1.

———— 1894b. [letter in response to the unidentified reviewer (1894a) of Skeat's ed. 1894]. *Manchester Guardian*, Mar. 5, p. 8.

———— 1894c. The Romaunt of the Rose: Fragment B. In *Essays on Chaucer, . . . Part VI.* Chaucer Society, 2d ser., 29: 673–83. London: Trübner.

———— 1896. Lydgate's Testimony to "The Romaunt of the Rose." *Athenaeum*, June 6, p. 747.

————, ed. 1897. *Chaucerian and Other Pieces Being a Supplement to the Complete Works of Geoffrey Chaucer*. Oxford: Clarendon Press. Reprint. London: Oxford University Press, 1963. Vol. 7 of the *Complete Works*, 2d ed., 1899.

———— 1899. "The King's Quair" and "The Romaunt of the Rose." *Athenaeum*, July 8, pp. 66–67; July 22, pp. 129–30.

———— 1900. *The Chaucer Canon*. Oxford: Clarendon Press.

———— 1905. Introduction. In *The Works of Geoffrey Chaucer and Others, Being a Reproduction in Facsimile of the First Collected Edition 1532 from the Copy in the British Museum*. London: Alexander Moring/De La More Press; Henry Frowde/Oxford University Press.

———— 1906. [Reply to Hinckley 1906]. *Academy*, Dec. 29, p. 647.

———— 1911. Introduction to Furnivall, ed. 1911, pp. v–ix.

Skinner, Stephen 1671. *Etymologicon Linguae Anglicanae*. London: Roycroft.

Smith, Jeremy J. 1991. Private communication.

Smith, Merete 1982. Literary Loanwords from Old French in *The Romaunt of the Rose*: A Note. *ChauR* 17:89–93.

Snyder, Edward D. 1920. The Wild Irish: A Study of Some English Satires against the Irish, Scots, and Welsh. *MP* 17:687–725.

Spearing, A. C. 1976. *Medieval Dream-Poetry*. Cambridge: Cambridge University Press.

Speght, Thomas, ed. 1598. *The Workes of our Antient and Learned English Poet, Geffrey Chaucer, newly Printed*. London: Adam Islip for Bonham Norton. 2d, rev., ed., 1602. 3d ed., with minor revisions, 1687.

Speirs, John   1951. *Chaucer the Maker.* London: Faber and Faber. 2d, rev., ed. 1960. Reprint. 1967.

Spelman, Sir Henry   1687. *Glossarium Archaiologicum.* 3d ed. London: Tho. Braddyll. 1st ed. London: Alice Warren, 1664.

Spurgeon, Caroline F. E.   1925. *Five Hundred Years of Chaucer Criticism and Allusion 1357–1900.* 3 vols. Cambridge: Cambridge University Press. Reprint. New York: Russell and Russell, 1960. Originally published as Chaucer Society, 2d ser., 48–50, 52–56. London: Trübner, 1908–17.

Stahl, William H., trans.   1952. *Macrobius: Commentary on the Dream of Scipio.* New York and London: Columbia University Press.

Starnes, De Witt T., and Gertrude E. Noyes   1946. *The English Dictionary from Cawdrey to Johnson 1604–1755.* Chapel Hill: University of North Carolina Press.

Steiner, George   1975. *After Babel: Aspects of Language and Translation.* London and New York: Oxford University Press. 2d ed., 1992.

Stow, John, ed.   1561. *The workes of Geffrey Chaucer, newlie printed, with diuers addicions, whiche were neuer in print before.* London: Jhon Kyngston for Jhon Wight.

Studer, Paul, and Joan Evans, eds.   1924. *Anglo-Norman Lapidaries.* Paris: Champion. Reprint. Geneva: Slatkin Reprints, 1976.

Sullens, Idelle, ed.   1983. *Robert Mannyng of Brunne: Handlyng Synne.* Medieval and Renaissance Texts and Studies, 14. Binghamton, NY: Medieval and Renaissance Texts and Studies.

Sutherland, Ronald   1959. The *Romaunt of the Rose* and Source Manuscripts. *PMLA* 74:178–83.

———, ed.   1968. *"The Romaunt of the Rose" and "Le Roman de la Rose": A Parallel-Text Edition.* Berkeley: University of California Press. 1st published, Oxford: Blackwell, 1967.

Sykes, Frederick H.   1899. *French Elements in Middle English.* Oxford: H. Hart.

Szittya, Penn R.   1986. *The Antifraternal Tradition in Medieval Literature.* Princeton: Princeton University Press.

Tanner, Thomas   1748. *Bibliotheca Britannico-Hibernica.* London: William Bowyer.

Tatlock, John S. P.   1907. *The Development and Chronology of Chaucer's Works.* Chaucer Society, 2d ser., 37. London: Kegan Paul, Trench, Trübner. Reprint. Gloucester, MA: Peter Smith, 1963.

———, and Arthur G. Kennedy   1927. *A Concordance to the Complete Works of Geoffrey Chaucer and to the* Romaunt of the Rose. Washington, D.C.: Carnegie Institution. Reprint. Gloucester, MA: Peter Smith, 1963.

Thévet, André   1584. *Les vrais pourtraits et vies des hommes illustres.* Paris: Keruert and Chaudiere. Reprint. 2 vols. Delmar, NY: Scholars' Facsimiles & Reprints, 1973.

Thompson, D'Arcy W.   1938. "Archangel" as a Bird-Name in Chaucer. *N&Q* 175:332.

Thompson, Nesta Mary   1926. A Further Study of Chaucer and "The Romance of the Rose." Ph.D. diss., Stanford University.

Thorp, Nigel   1989. Private communication.

Thoss, Dagmar   1972. *Studien zum Locus Amoenus im Mittelalter.* Vienna: W. Braumüller.

Thynne, Francis   1599. *Animadversions vppon the Annotacions and Corrections . . . of Chaucers workes . . . 1598,* ed. G. H. Kingsley, 1865. EETS, o.s. 9. London: Oxford University Press. Rev. F. J. Furnivall, 1875. Reprint. 1965. Also published by Chaucer Society, 2d ser., 13. London: Trübner.

Thynne, William, ed.   1532. *The Workes of Geffray Chaucer newly printed with dyuers workes whiche were neuer in print before.* London: Thomas Godfray. 2d ed. London: William Bonham, 1542. 3d ed. London: Thomas Petit, ? 1550. *See also* Skeat 1905 *and* Brewer 1969.

Tibullus.   *See* J. P. Postgate, ed. and trans. 1962.

Tobler, Adolf   1892. Nochmals zum *Beaudous* Roberts von Blois. *Archiv* 88:375–76.

———, and Erhard Lommatzsch   1925– . *Altfranzösisches Wörterbuch.* 10+ vols. Berlin: Weidmann. Reprint. Wiesbaden: F. Steiner, 1956– .

Todd, Henry J.   1810. *Illustrations of the Lives and Writings of Gower and Chaucer: Collected from Authentick Documents.* London: F. C. and J. Rivington.

Trojel, E., ed.   1892. *Andreae Capellani regii Francorum De amore libri tres.* Copenhagen: G.E.C. Gad. Reprints. Munich: Wilhelm Fink, 1964 and 1972.

Tuve, Rosemond   1933. *Seasons and Months: Studies in a Tradition of Middle English Poetry.* Paris: Librarie Universitaire. Reprint. Cambridge: D. S. Brewer, 1974.

———   1966. *Allegorical Imagery: Some Mediaeval Books and their Posterity.* Princeton: Princeton University Press. Reprints. 1974 and 1977.

Tyrwhitt, Thomas, ed.   1775. *The Canterbury Tales of Chaucer.* 4 vols. Additional 5th vol., containing glossary, 1778. London: T. Payne. Reprint. New York: AMS Press, 1972. 2d ed. 2 vols. Oxford: Clarendon Press, 1798.

Unidentified reviewer   1892*a*. [Review of Lounsbury 1892]. *Nation*, Mar. 17, pp. 214–26; Mar. 24, pp. 231–33.

———   1892*b*. [Review of Lounsbury 1892]. *Atlantic Monthly* 69:554–59.

———   1894*a*. [Review of Skeat, ed. 1894*a*]. *Manchester Guardian*, Feb. 27, p. 4.

———   1894*b*. [Rejoinder to Skeat 1894*b*]. *Manchester Guardian*, Mar. 7, p. 7.

Urry, John, ed.   1721. *The Works of Geoffrey Chaucer.* London: Bernard Lintot. [Glossary by Timothy Thomas, with the assistance of William Thomas.]

Van Dyke, Carolynn   1985. *The Fiction of Truth: Structures of Meaning in Narrative and Dramatic Allegory.* Ithaca: Cornell University Press.

Vance, Eugene   1981. Chaucer, Spenser, and the Ideology of Translation. *Canadian Review of Comparative Literature* 8:217–38.

Vitz, Evelyn B.   1973. The *I* of the *Roman de la Rose*, trans. Barbara DiStefano. *Genre* 6:49–75.

Wallace, David   1985. Chaucer and the European *Rose*. In Paul Strohm and Thomas J. Heffernan, eds., *Studies in the Age of Chaucer: Proceedings, No. 1, 1984: Reconstructing Chaucer*, pp. 61–67. Knoxville, TN: New Chaucer Society.

———   1986. Chaucer's Continental Inheritance: The Early Poems and *Troilus and Criseyde*. In Piero Boitani and Jill Mann, eds., *The Cambridge Chaucer Companion*, pp. 19–37. Cambridge: Cambridge University Press.

Walsh, P. G., ed. and trans.   1982. *Andreas Capellanus On Love.* London: Duckworth.

Walther, Hans   1963–69. *Proverbia sententiaeque Latinitas medii aevi.* 6 vols. Göttingen: Vandenhoek & Ruprecht.

Wartburg, Walther von   1922–65. *Französisches Etymologisches Wörterbuch.* 21 vols. Bonn, Leipzig, Tübingen, Basel: various.

Warton, Thomas   1774–81. *History of English Poetry.* 3 vols. London: J. Dodsley.

———   1871. *History of English Poetry*, ed. W. Carew Hazlitt. 4 vols. London: Reeves and Turner. Reprint. Hildesheim: Georg Olms, 1968.

Waszink, Jan H., ed.   1962. *Plato: Timaeus a Calcidio translatus commentarioque instructus.* London: Warburg Institute; Leiden: Brill.

Webb, Clement C. J., ed.   1909. *Ioannis Saresberiensis episcopi Carnotensis Policratici sive De nugis curialium et vestigiis philosophorum libri VIII.* 2 vols. Oxford: Clarendon Press. Reprint. New York: Arno Press, 1979.

Webster, C. M.   1932. Chaucer's Turkish Bows. *MLN* 47:260.

Weiss, Alexander   1985. *Chaucer's Native Heritage.* American University Studies, ser. 4: English Language and Literature, 11. New York: Peter Lang.

Wetherbee, Winthrop   1971. The Literal and the Allegorical: Jean de Meun and the *De Planctu Naturae. MS* 33:264–91.

———   1972. *Platonism and Poetry in the Twelfth Century.* Princeton: Princeton University Press.

Werner, Jakob   1966. *Lateinische Sprichwörte und Sinnsprüche des Mittelalters aus Handschriften gesammelt.* 2d ed., rev. Peter Flury. Heidelberg: C. Winter. 1st ed., 1912.

Whatley, Gordon   1989. Private communication.

Whiting, Bartlett Jere   1934. *Chaucer's Use of Proverbs.* Harvard Studies in Comparative Literature, 11. Cambridge, MA: Harvard University Press. Reprint. New York: AMS Press, 1973.

———   1941. The Wife of Bath's Prologue, The Wife of Bath's Tale. In Bryan and Dempster, eds. 1941, pp. 207–68.

———, and Helen Wescott Whiting   1968. *Proverbs, Sentences, and Proverbial Phrases from English Writings Mainly Before 1500.* Cambridge, MA: Belknap Press/Harvard University Press; London: Oxford University Press.

Whitteridge, Gweneth   1950. The Word *archaungel* in Chaucer's *Romaunt of the Rose. English and Germanic Studies* 3:34–36.

Wilson, John [Christopher North, pseud.]   1845. North's Specimens of the British Critics. No. IV. Dryden on Chaucer. *Blackwood's Edinburgh Magazine* 57: 617–46. Reprint. Delmar, NY: Scholars' Facsimiles & Reprints, 1978, pp. 157–240.

Wimmer, Georg, ed. 1888. *Li Tornoiemenz Antecrit von Huon de Mery.* Marburg: N. G. Elwert.

Wimsatt, James I. 1968. *Chaucer and the French Love Poets.* Chapel Hill: University of North Carolina Press. Reprint. New York: Johnson Reprints, 1972.

——— 1970. *Allegory and Mirror: Tradition and Structure in Middle English Literature.* New York: Pegasus.

——— 1975. Chaucer and French Poetry. In Derek Brewer, ed., *Geoffrey Chaucer,* pp. 109–36. Athens: Ohio University Press.

Wing, Donald Goddard 1945–51. *Short-Title Catalogue of Books Printed in England, Scotland, Ireland, Wales, and British America, and of English Books Printed in Other Countries, 1641–1700.* 3 vols. New York: Columbia University Press. 2d ed. New York: Modern Language Association, 1972– .

Work, James A. 1941. The Manciple's Tale. In Bryan and Dempster, eds. 1941, pp. 699–722.

Wright, Cyril E. 1960. *English Vernacular Hands from the Twelfth to the Fifteenth Centuries.* Oxford: Clarendon Press.

Wright, Constance S. 1990. The Printed Editions of Chaucer's *Legend of Good Women:* 1532–1889. *ChauR* 24:313–19.

Wright, Steven Alan 1986. *Literary Influence in Medieval Literature: Chaucer and the* Roman de la Rose. Ph.D. diss., Indiana University.

Wright, Thomas, ed. 1847–51. *The Canterbury Tales of Geoffrey Chaucer.* 3 vols. Vols. 24–26 of *Early English Poetry, Ballads, and Popular Poetry of the Middle Ages.* London: Percy Society.

Wülker, Richard 1893*a.* [Review of] Max Kaluza, Chaucer und der Rosenroman. *Anglia Beiblatt* 14:337–38.

——— 1893*b.* [Review of] The Romaunt of the Rose from the Unique Glasgow Ms. Parallel with its Original Le Roman de la Rose, ed. by Max Kaluza. *Anglia Beiblatt* 14:338–39.

Young, John, and P. Henderson Aitken 1908. *A Catalogue of the Manuscripts in the Library of the Hunterian Museum in the University of Glasgow.* Glasgow: J. Maclehose.

Zink, Michael 1986. The Allegorical Poem as Interior Memoir, trans. Margaret Miner and Kevin Brownlee. *YFS* 70:100–26.

Zumthor, Paul 1972. *Essai de poétique médiévale.* Paris: Editions du Seuil. Trans. by Philip Bennett, under the title *Toward a Medieval Poetics.* Minneapolis and Oxford: University of Minnesota Press, 1992.

——— 1974. Narrative and Anti-Narrative: *Le Roman de la Rose,* trans. Frank Youmans. *YFS* 51:185–204. Originally published as Récit et anti-récit: *Le Roman de la Rose. Medioevo Romanzo* 1:5–24, 1973.

General Index